PRESIDENTIAL SCANDALS

PRESIDENTIAL SCANDALS

JEFFREY D. SCHULTZ

CQ PRESS

Washington, D.C.

CQ Press

A Division of Congressional Quarterly Inc.

1414 22nd St., N.W.

Washington, DC 20037

(202) 822-1475; (800) 638-1710

www.cqpress.com

Printed in the United States of America

03 02 01 00 99   5 4 3 2 1

Library of Congress Cataloging-in-Publication Data

Schultz, Jeffrey D.

   Presidential scandals/Jeffrey D. Schultz

     p. cm.

   Includes bibliographical references and index.

   ISBN 1-56802-414-2 (alk. paper)

     1. Presidents—United States—History. 2. Political corruption—United States—History.

   3. United States—Politics and government. I. Title.

   E176.1.S353 2000

   973'.09'9 21—dc21

                                    99-043953

CONTENTS

PREFACE

M y earliest political memories are of running around our three-bedroom ranch house in Middle America chanting "Nixon, Nixon is our man; McGovern belongs in the garbage can!" I'm sure I did that mostly to annoy my babysitter and her leftist boyfriend. Not much later, I saw Nixon, the first president to resign from office, wave goodbye as he boarded the presidential helicopter. I did not understand what had happened—it was a bit much for an eight year old to get—but I knew it was important.

Twenty-five years later, as I write the preface to *Presidential Scandals,* I understand more but realize that I was naïve, as I think most Americans (and most political scientists, for that matter) are, about the history of presidential scandal in America. There was no single work—until this one—that chronicled the many charges of political scandal against the chief executive. I was surprised to find more than 150 instances of presidential scandal that had to be included in this book.

To decide what to put in and what to leave out, I first had to establish a working definition of scandal. The one I settled on, with the aid of my editors at CQ Press, was the following: a scandal is any action that was considered dishonest or a violation of propriety at the time of the presidency or that would have been considered as such had it come to light at the time. Making a rudimentary distinction between scandal and corruption, we agreed that all occurrences of corruption were scandalous, but not all scandals involved corruption. Therefore, private events like sexual infidelity would be included, even though they may have had no official bearing on the performance of the officeholder. Events that involved high-ranking officials (cabinet level, in most cases) also were included, as were events that took place either before or after a president's term. Admittedly, this definition is not exacting, but the purpose of this volume is not to examine the nature of scandal. Rather, it is to provide a single source for information on the many scandals in U.S. presidential history so that readers can see them in context when they are discussed today.

Among the chief motivators for me to compile this book were the charges against President Bill Clinton, only the second president in the nation's history to be impeached. I watched with interest as political commentators and journalists (sometimes one and the same) compared the charges against Clinton with earlier presidential scandals and other historic eras. These comparisons were often made with an eye either to defending Clinton's actions or condemning them. It seemed to me that frequently apples were being compared to oranges and it was difficult to see when scandalous acts were truly similar.

CHANGING MORES OF SOCIETY

One of the questions that must be asked when looking at presidential scandals is whether the changing mores of society have affected our conception of scandal. Surprisingly, the answer is no, but a qualified no. Let me start with the no and then address the qualifications. Most of the situations we consider scandalous today were considered scandalous in their day, too. For example, marital infidelity has always been a source of concern. Financial misconduct such as taking kickbacks or bribes has always been taboo. In addition, some activities by members of the executive branch, while legal, have raised eyebrows because they seem to skirt the law. During Woodrow Wilson's administration, for example, Secretary of State William Jennings Bryan accepted outside speaking fees; and during James Monroe's administration, Secretary of War John C. Calhoun awarded military contracts to a friend. Federal laws have tightened some of the legal loopholes that members of the executive branch slipped through in the past. The result is that many of the actions that were perceived as improper or a potential conflict of interest have now been codified into illegalities.

To a large extent, the events described in this book also show that voters have usually distinguished between private and public acts when it counted most—on election day. For example, there is not a single case of a candidate losing an election as a result of marital infidelity. Some readers may argue that Gary Hart was bounced out of the 1988 presidential race because of his indiscretions, but one could also argue that what happened to Hart was not about his girlfriend Donna Rice, but the way Hart challenged the press to prove a rumor. In any event, the effect of his indiscretion will never be known because he chose to drop out before testing the electoral waters. It appears that a candidate could father a child out of wedlock and win the presidency. Voters certainly knew of Grover Cleveland's illegitimate child, and still they elected him. So, although the study is not scientific, it seems that the mores of society, while not exactly the same as in the past, have remained relatively constant.

What has changed over time is the speed with which scandals are made public. Many of the scandals discussed in this volume were unknown when the president involved was in office. For that reason, it is impossible to judge how the public would have reacted had news of the scandals broken.

We do know that later generations can be more critical of scandalous behavior than the generation that lived through the events. A prime example is the legacy of Warren G. Harding, who presided over one of the country's most scandal-ridden administrations. Harding died in the midst of the Teapot Dome oil leasing debacle, but he was still an extremely popular president. His reputation survived the investigation conducted in subsequent administrations. Today, however, historians and the general public have a low opinion of Harding as a president.

Perhaps what is missing in the evaluation by subsequent generations is the affection (deserved or otherwise) that many people naturally feel for their president. Other factors may come into play, but the tendency of the public to forgive people they believe they know cannot be discounted. An example of this phenomenon is the legacy of Ronald Reagan, whose administration had its share of scandal. Reagan's charisma and his unparalleled communication skills made him one of the most popular presidents of all time, and he remains so today.

THE REAL COST OF SCANDAL

The real cost of political scandal may be its effect on an administration's ability to function. An administration defending itself from charges of corruption may have to spend much of its political capital trying to make friends rather than using it to enact a legislative agenda. In addition to their political costs, scandals also divert the energies of an administration from other activities. While a crisis is being addressed, little else can be accomplished because so many hands are needed to deal with the political fallout. The impeachment trial of Andrew Johnson, although it did not remove him from office, so weakened him that he lost the struggle with Congress over Reconstruction of the South following the Civil War. Ulysses S. Grant's administration was unable to accomplish even its modest legislative goals because of the constant barrage of scandals.

In calculating the amount of political capital necessary to withstand a charge, a president at times must decide whether to defend or sacrifice individual members of his cabinet or inner circle. The danger in this situation is in underestimating what is necessary to defend one person and risk losing a great deal more. This was nearly the case during Andrew Jackson's administration. Jackson's decision to stick by Secretary of War John Eaton, whose wife had a bad reputation and was shunned by Washington society, led his cabinet to resign. Jackson's determination was based more on personal loyalty than political calculation, as he and Eaton had been friends for many years. In addition, Jackson was inclined to defend a woman's honor, no matter how undeserving she might be.

It is also dangerous for a president to be too quick to cut off support.

The Clinton administration spent too much political capital defending Zoë Baird's nomination to be attorney general. When Kimba Wood, the second nominee, faltered, the administration gave up without a fight, even though many thought she could have been confirmed.

ROLE OF THE MEDIA

One of the most important elements of any scandal and its effect on politics is the role played by the media. If the press decides to ignore a questionable situation, it may never develop into a scandal. The press can also give a scandal "legs." However, it is too simplistic to assess the importance of the media simply in terms of coverage; it is equally important to look at how the media cover an event.

In the past, newspapers aligned themselves with one political party or another, and their biases were well known. In the late twentieth century, the mainstream media—newspapers, news magazines, and television—are not partisan in their overall reporting, unless picking and choosing what to cover can be considered partisan. The growth of all-news programming, with its need to fill hours of air time with talk, and of unfiltered sources such as the Internet has changed the picture. Rumors, claims, and charges surface more easily today than in the past when the mainstream press was the primary source for news. Those accused may feel compelled to rebut the charges and thereby prolong the life of the stories. The competition among traditional and nontraditional media for readers/viewers/surfers puts more stories out there, some of which are quickly forgotten.

REPUBLICAN SCANDALS VERSUS DEMOCRATIC SCANDALS

People have asked me whether there is any difference between the types of scandals that occur in Republican and Democratic administrations. I have not used a spreadsheet to analyze them, but it is apparent to me that there is no party division of scandals. Democrats are no more likely to be involved in sex scandals than Republicans. Republicans are no more likely to be seen as favoring big business than Democrats. In fact, what comes of looking at scandals is that they may have more to do with the fact that politicians want to wield political power and reward friends and supporters than with their party.

Take Lord Acton's dictum about the corrupting nature of power, add to it the fact that most politicians have enough *hubris* to make them ripe for a fall, and the climate for scandal is created. Must we then accept a certain degree of scandalous behavior from our elected officials? It seems that the answer to that question is yes. As Publius wrote in *The Federalist* more than 200 years ago, "If men were angels, then no government would be necessary." As long as we need government and as long as ambitious men and women seek office, we are likely to have scandals.

This conclusion is not as bleak as it may seem. In fact, there is a silver lining. The system of government established by the Framers has survived many tests, including the times when less than honorable men steered the ship of state. One can look at the number of scandals and still come away with a deep respect for America's constitutional government. In many other countries, scandals of the nature described in this book might have led to the collapse of the government or worse.

ACKNOWLEDGMENTS

A blank screen may have replaced the traditional blank piece of paper, but one fact about writing has not changed—it is a solitary activity. Still, there are always many who must be thanked for the successful publication of a book, and this book is no different. I thank David Tarr at CQ Press. Dave helped me take an idea and shape it into a coherent book. He is a splendid editor. CQ Press is blessed with many fine editors, and Carolyn Goldinger is another. She took my rough prose and turned it into a very readable book.

Mike Perry and Mark Bearce deserve special mention for their help with various sections of the book. I could not have finished it in a timely manner without their assistance. Others, including Bill Baron, Linda Baron, and my sister Nancy Schultz, helped by researching scandals, finding documents, and performing many other tasks.

My agent-mentor-friend, George T. Kurian, and his equally wonderful other half, Annie, have always been among my biggest supporters. George's wise counsel and Annie's smiling voice lifted the spirits of an author on many a gray Monday morning.

My wife, Elena, and my son, Sasha, are my constant sources of inspiration. My son, especially, because he reminds me that the books that I am working on are not as important as reading to him before he (and I) take a nap.

If praise is to be had for this work, the aforementioned should share in it. However, any remaining errors are mine alone, and all rotten tomatoes should be thrown my way.

PRESIDENTIAL SCANDALS

GEORGE WASHINGTON

First President
1789–1797

George Washington was born February 22, 1732, on his family's estate in Westmoreland County, Virginia. He was the eldest of five children born to Augustine and Mary Ball Washington, Augustine's second wife. Washington also had two half brothers, Lawrence, who acted as George's guardian after the death of his father in 1733, and Augustine, known as "Austin."

Unlike his half brothers, Washington was not sent to England for a formal education. Instead, he had tutors and attended school on an irregular basis, but received an education that was common to colonial Virginia. By age eleven, he had learned to read, write, and do basic mathematics. Discouraged from pursuing a naval career, Washington joined a surveying party sent out to the Shenandoah Valley by Lord Fairfax in 1748. Washington lived with Lawrence at his estate, Mount Vernon, where he learned farming and improved his surveying skills. In 1751 he accompanied Lawrence, who was ill with tuberculosis, to Barbados.

Washington began his long military career in 1752, when he was appointed a major in the militia. His first assignment was to deliver an ultimatum to the French, who were building fortifications in English territory at Fort Le Boeuf, Pennsylvania. Washington was promoted to lieutenant colonel in 1754 and oversaw the construction of Fort Necessity in southwestern Pennsylvania. After suffering a humiliating defeat and the insubordination of British officers under his command, Washington resigned his commission. However, he returned to military service as aide-de-camp to Edward Braddock, a British general fighting in the French and Indian Wars. Braddock was mortally wounded in 1755 in a battle at the Monongahela River, and Washington was forced to retreat. Promoted to colonel and regimental commander, Washington resigned from the militia in December 1758 after being elected in July to the Virginia House of Burgesses.

Washington married Martha Dandridge Custis, a wealthy twenty-seven-year-old widow with two children, on January 6, 1759. Her property added 15,000 acres to Washington's estate. While serving in the house (1759–1774), Washington became one of the leaders of the opposition to British colonial policy. Although he condemned the Boston Tea Party of December 1773, he also realized that reconciliation with England was not possible. Washington was selected as a delegate to both the First and Second Continental Congresses, where he served on various committees concerned with the military.

In June 1775 the congress named him commander of the Continental army. Although his troops were poorly trained and undisciplined, Washington managed to outlast British efforts and win the war for independence. The British surrendered October 19, 1781. With the Treaty of Paris (1783) signed, Washington resigned his commission and returned home to Mount Vernon, which he had inherited from Lawrence's widow. His long absence from home had left his finances in a state of disrepair.

The young nation's finances were also in bad shape. It was clear that the Articles of Confederation were inadequate to solve the problems and needed to be revised. Washington went to Philadelphia as a delegate to the Constitutional Convention of 1787 and presided over it as its president. In 1789 he received the unanimous vote of the electoral college and began the first of two terms as president of the United States.

Washington faced many critical issues that would shape the new nation. He supported the Bank of the United States and maintained U.S. neutrality in the war between France and Britain. He also established the precedent of forming a cabinet of executive officers to perform the many functions of government. Ordering the governors of several states to send their militia into western Pennsylvania, Washington brought an end to the Whiskey Rebellion, which had threatened the internal security of the nation. Washington was anxious to return to private life and refused to seek a third term. In his farewell address, he warned against the dangers of political parties, which he had seen create conflict in his administration.

Retiring to Mount Vernon in 1797, he spent the last two years of his life as a gentleman farmer, overseeing much needed repairs to his estate and entertaining friends. In 1799, when war with France seemed a strong possibility, President John Adams appointed him commander in chief of the army. War was averted, and Washington's retirement continued undisturbed. He died December 14, 1799. In his will, he provided for the emancipation of his slaves.

SHENANDOAH VALLEY LAND THEFT

While Washington was away fighting the British during the Revolutionary War, squatters took control of land he owned in the Shenandoah Valley. After the war, Washington evicted the squatters and had to defend his right to the land in the courts and the press.

Washington had purchased a bond that entitled him to 3,000 acres in the Shenandoah Valley in 1770 from Capt. Thomas Posey, a neighbor who had been awarded the claim by the King's Proclamation of 1763. In 1771 Washington had the land surveyed by Colonel William Crawford, the regular surveyor for the College of William and Mary. Washington wrote the following account of the events in a letter to John Havie dated March 19, 1785: "Colo. Crawford, a liver on Yohioghaney, an old and intimate acquaintance of mine, undertook to procure for me a tract of land in that Country; and accordingly made choice of the one, now in dispute, on the waters of Racoon and Millers runs, branches of Shurtees Creek, surveyed the same, amounting to 2813 acres, and purchased in my behalf the claim of some person to a part of the land, who pretended to have a right thereto."

However, in 1773 new squatters moved onto the land. These individuals were told that Washington owned the property and would exercise his title to it. In 1774 Washington was recognized as the rightful owner, but he did not have the squatters immediately removed. During the Revolutionary War, the squatters stayed put while Washington was off leading the Continental army against the British. After the war, Washington attempted to have them removed, which resulted in a heated dispute over the squatters' rights to part of the property. Washington was forced to take out space in several newspapers explaining how he had come to own the tract of land. In his advertisement, Washington challenged anyone to prove that his account of the facts was not true and that he was not the rightful owner of the land. No one came forward to challenge him, and the matter quickly disappeared.

EXTRAMARITAL AFFAIRS AND ILLEGITIMATE CHILDREN

Washington was accused of having several extramarital affairs and fathering at least two illegitimate children, including Secretary of the Treasury Alexander Hamilton.

Sarah "Sally" Cary Fairfax

Sally Fairfax was the wife of George Washington's best friend and neighbor, Col. George William Fairfax. A few years her junior, Washington met Sally when he was sixteen. Sally's company was a source of great joy to him, but it seems their relationship was innocent. In September 1758, after he was engaged to be married to Martha Custis, Washington sent a letter to Sally admitting his love and asking if it was returned. It appears that Sally did not—or, rather, could not—return young Washington's love. Wilson Miles Cary, Sally's descendent and biographer, wrote that the two had consummated their love, but there is no proof that the feelings between Washington and Fairfax were ever expressed in a sexual relationship.

Lawrence Posey

Capt. Thomas Posey, a neighbor of Washington's, often visited Mount Vernon to drink and to borrow money. Over the years, Washington had signed several notes for Posey and had given him cash as well. While Washington was known as a generous man to those down on their luck, the continued beneficence to Captain Posey—a man few believed would or could ever repay his debts—raised questions. Some suggested that Lawrence Posey, Thomas's son, looked strikingly like Washington. Rumors circulated that Lawrence was Washington's illegitimate son from a liaison in Barbados some years earlier and that Posey had agreed to raise the boy as his own if Washington would provide the necessary financial support.

Alexander Hamilton

Alexander Hamilton was also included in the gossip concerning Washington. Some speculated that Hamilton was Washington's illegitimate son from an affair in Barbados.

Mary Gibbons

Pro-British sympathizers, who sought to undermine General Washington's public standing, manufactured a story that he had an affair with a woman named Mary Gibbons. The group published a phony trial account in which Gibbons admitted having intimate relations with Washington and stealing military secrets.

PADDED EXPENSE ACCOUNT

Instead of drawing a salary for his services as commander of the Continental army, Washington was allowed to submit his expenses. The nearly $450,000 Washington claimed was ten times the salary he would have drawn and included questionable items.

One Washington biographer credits the general with establishing the padded expense account. During the Revolutionary War, Washington agreed to forgo a salary as long as his expenses were reimbursed. His expense account included travel for his wife, Martha, and others to visit him at various outposts, charges incurred in the keeping of his slaves, and the keep of several people such as his secretary and aide-de-camp. His expenses totaled $449,261. This figure included 6 percent interest on the personal funds he loaned to the military. Martha Washington's travel bill alone exceeded $27,000. This sum of money is staggering in comparison to the $49,000 he would have received in salary.

ALEXANDER HAMILTON, SECRETARY OF THE TREASURY

Alexander Hamilton was a lightning rod of controversy for the Washington administration. It seemed Hamilton's political enemies would stop at nothing to remove him from his position as a principal adviser to the president. The Democratic-Republicans' desire to undo Hamilton often had the impact of dividing Washington's government. While some of the "scandals" discussed below were in reality policy disputes between the Federalists led by Hamilton and the Democratic-Republicans led by Thomas Jefferson, the latter did his best to represent Hamilton's policies as scandalous doings. That being said, several events in Hamilton's life clearly would have been seen as scandals had they been fully understood at the time.

National Bank and the Newspaper War

Secretary of the Treasury Alexander Hamilton and Secretary of State Thomas Jefferson engaged in an ongoing battle of words in the nation's newspapers. Each charged the other with trying to undermine the newly created government. Jefferson accused Hamilton of wanting to subvert the government to the interests of wealthy bank owners and to establish a monarchy. Hamilton retorted that Jefferson was using government employees to attack the administration's policies and called on Jefferson to resign if he could not support them.

Alexander Hamilton's most controversial policy was his advocacy of a national bank. He saw the bank as the cornerstone of a nation with a sound fiscal system. His plan faced obstacles not only in Congress but also within the administration. Hamilton had convinced the president that the Constitution had authorized Congress to create a national bank and that the congressional opposition—led by James Madison—and the administration opposition—led by Thomas Jefferson—were merely mistaken.

Jefferson encouraged a part-time translator at the State Department, Philip Freneau, to edit a newspaper opposing Hamilton. The *National Gazette* began publication with the specific purpose of scuttling Hamilton's plan for the bank. The Democratic-Republicans played on the hatred that many Americans felt for the British banking system. Critics writing in the *National Gazette* argued that the British bank was a corrupt, privileged institution that hurt agricultural interests. The paper developed a conspiracy theory in which Hamilton and the bank's wealthy stockholders sought to control Congress in order to make the legislature a pawn of the executive.

Alexander Hamilton

The newspaper attacks on Hamilton continued for months. Jefferson repeated the criticism to President Washington directly. The president rejected the notion that the financial program outlined by Hamilton had any monarchical purposes, but he questioned Hamilton extensively about the criticisms. Although Washington was irritated by the growing attacks in the newspapers, he refrained from commenting, perhaps hoping that the controversy would subside.

In the summer of 1792, however, Hamilton struck back against the Democratic-Republican press, especially the *National Gazette.* In the *Gazette of the United States,* a newspaper under his influence, Hamilton used a pseudonym to write, "The editor of the *National Gazette* receives a salary from the government . . . the design of [the editor] is to vilify those to whom the voice of the people has committed the administration of public affairs." The war of words continued throughout the summer with Hamilton calling on Jefferson to resign if he could not support the decisions of the administration, and Jefferson's allies in the press shooting back.

The growing hostilities worried the president, who appealed to both Hamilton and Jefferson to refrain from further public attacks on each other. Although chastened, neither withdrew from the onslaught. Hamilton argued that his criticisms were against a political party in Congress that jeopardized the stability of the young nation by attacking its fiscal system. Jefferson denied having control over Freneau and asserted that Hamilton's system "was calculated to undermine and demolish the republic."

The newspaper war persisted for the rest of the year and would likely have continued if Hamilton had not called it off. Hamilton backed down when he found out that the Democratic-Republicans knew about his affair with Maria Reynolds.

Maria Reynolds Affair

Alexander Hamilton was blackmailed by James Reynolds, the husband of a woman with whom he had an adulterous affair. When Reynolds asked Hamilton for a government job, Hamilton refused, and Reynolds took proof of the affair and alleged misdeeds to Hamilton's political opponents.

In 1791 Hamilton began an adulterous relationship with Maria Reynolds, a beautiful, sensuous woman who came from Dutchess County gentry. Her husband, James Reynolds, blackmailed Hamilton, not only for money but also to secure a post in the Treasury Department. Hamilton paid James several hundred dollars to keep him from making the affair public, but refused to give him a job on the federal payroll. The affair ended in the summer of 1792.

However, that was not the end of the episode. In December 1792 James Reynolds and his partner, Jacob Clingman, who were awaiting trial in a Philadelphia jail for defrauding the government, contacted Rep. Frederick Muhlenburg of Pennsylvania. The two men claimed they had proof that

Hamilton had been speculating with government funds. They offered the information to Muhlenburg in exchange for their freedom. Sen. James Monroe of Virginia, Rep. Abraham Venable of Virginia, and Muhlenburg met with James and Maria Reynolds, who produced letters that seemed to support their claim.

On the morning of December 15, the three members of Congress confronted Hamilton with the charges. At his home that evening, Hamilton produced a number of letters that convinced the Congress members that, although Hamilton had been the victim of a blackmail scheme, he had not engaged in speculation with government funds. Because the events involved wholly private activity on Hamilton's part, the issue was dropped. The story would have remained secret had it not been leaked to James Thomson Callender, a publisher who printed it in his *History of the United States for the Year 1796.*

William Duer

A friend and political appointee of Alexander Hamilton, William Duer embezzled more than $200,000 from the Treasury. Hamilton did not attempt to recover the money. Hamilton also helped secure a low-interest loan for a business of Duer's in which Hamilton was a primary partner.

Hamilton appointed his friend William Duer to the post of assistant secretary of the Treasury. Duer was a financier with large holdings in New York State. Using his position of power, Duer speculated with public money, and Hamilton asked him to resign. However, Hamilton did not attempt to recover the money—more than $200,000—that Duer had stolen from the Treasury. The comptroller of the Treasury brought suit against Duer, and his downfall was one of the chief causes of the financial panic that struck the nation in 1792. Duer died in prison.

How involved Hamilton had been with Duer's speculations is unclear. Hamilton made no attempt to protect his friend from prosecution by the comptroller. However, it is known that in 1791, Hamilton, Duer, and others established the Society for Useful Manufactures, a gigantic industrial corporation that had a privileged New Jersey charter. Hamilton had arranged for the corporation to receive low-interest loans from the Bank of New York, a federal depository, with the explicit assurance that the Treasury of the United States would continue to use the bank.

Giles Resolutions

Hamilton had violated the clear intentions of Congress by mixing funds that were to be kept separate. This revelation led to a wider probe of the Treasury Department and to Rep. William B. Giles of Virginia sending the House nine resolutions charging various crimes.

Hamilton had devised a creative plan to help retire the national debt without an increase in taxes. He intended to borrow funds from abroad at

5 percent interest and pay off loans to the government that were at 6 percent. Hamilton sought to use the international funds to first pay off the national bank stock subscription. Although this plan was innovative and legal, it led to a congressional investigation on how earlier foreign loans had been used. Hamilton's report to the investigating committee showed that he had violated Congress's intentions by mixing two separate loans into one pool. The accounting showed that funds intended for domestic operations had been used to pay foreign debt and funds earmarked for foreign debt repayment had been used for domestic expenditures. The funds totaled about $14 million, and Hamilton had disbursed money with the authorization of the president and others, including the sinking-fund committee.

Hamilton's Democratic-Republican foes used this revelation to charge that he had illegally used public monies. Rep. William B. Giles of Virginia, working under the close supervision of Thomas Jefferson, introduced five resolutions that called for further investigation of how the money was handled and of Hamilton for ignoring the clear intention of Congress. Among the charges Giles leveled was that Hamilton had concealed shortages in accounts, unlawfully favored the Bank of the United States, and had drawn upon European funds for the specific benefit of speculators. Even Hamilton's supporters had to vote in favor of an investigation or be accused of covering up his wrongdoing.

The Democratic-Republicans had planned that the resolutions would stand without rebuttal until after their March 3, 1793, recess. However, Hamilton submitted seven reports containing 60,000 words that covered the entire financial history of the U.S. government to date. Meanwhile, Giles had been appointed to head a special committee to investigate the Treasury Department and Hamilton's personal finances. Hoping to find misdeeds, the committee was disappointed—there was no evidence of wrongdoing.

Working from a draft provided by Jefferson that charged Hamilton with all kinds of crimes and calling for his removal from office, Giles rejected the more extreme resolutions and instead submitted nine for consideration by the House of Representatives on February 28, 1793. On March 1, the House voted. The resolutions were defeated by large majorities, with only five members, including James Madison, voting in favor of all nine.

While most considered the House vote a full exoneration of Hamilton, Sen. James Monroe published a long vitriolic pamphlet, *An Examination of the Late Proceedings in Congress Respecting the Official Conduct of the Secretary of the Treasury,* in which he attacked Hamilton and repeated the charges that had already been voted upon. Philip Freneau, publisher of the *National Gazette,* claimed that a fair hearing was not possible because of the speed with which Hamilton had responded to the charges. Congress members from Virginia who had not supported the resolutions were also harassed by the Democratic-Republican–controlled press. Hamilton countered with the wide distribution of the House proceedings, which were corrected at his request. Pro-Hamilton newspaper editors throughout the country made clear that the House had exonerated Hamilton of any misdeeds.

JAY TREATY

John Jay, the first chief justice of the United States, was sent to Britain to negotiate a treaty. The Treaty of Amity, Commerce, and Navigation, popularly known as the Jay Treaty, was signed in London on November 19, 1794. Jay managed to secure the major goals of his mission: the British promised to evacuate their northwest posts by 1796 and to allow a limited right of American vessels to trade with the British West Indies. The treaty left to mixed commissions of British and American members other issues such as the boundary between Maine and New Brunswick, the payment of prewar debt by the United States, and payment by the British for illegally capturing American ships.

All in all, the treaty appeared to be a successful conclusion to the diplomatic mission. However, when its details were made public on November 2, 1795, many Americans were outraged and branded Jay a traitor. The anger over the treaty was orchestrated by Democratic-Republican forces who wanted to sour relations between the United States and England in favor of France. Party newspapers rallied against the agreement, which had been ratified by a scant two-thirds majority and signed by President Washington on June 25, 1795. Democratic-Republicans in the House of Representatives threatened to withhold funding for the mixed commissions. This dilemma was staved off by a powerful speech by Fisher Ames of Massachusetts.

Edmund Randolph, Secretary of State

Edmund Randolph was charged with accepting bribes from the French government to spark the Whiskey Rebellion in western Pennsylvania.

Washington selected Edmund Randolph of Virginia to replace Thomas Jefferson as secretary of state in his second administration. During the discussions of whether the president should sign the Jay Treaty, Randolph—a close friend and political ally of Jefferson—was actively lobbying against the measure. The Federalists believed that Randolph's influence on the president was interfering with the adoption of the treaty and sought to discredit him.

The British minister delivered to Timothy Pickering, the secretary of war, and Oliver Wolcott, Hamilton's successor at the Treasury Department, a captured French report written by Joseph Fauchet, the French envoy, that implicated Randolph as having sought money from Fauchet at the time of the Whiskey Rebellion. The document said in part, "A few thousand dollars would have decided between war and peace! So the con-

**Edmund
Randolph**

sciences of the so-called American patriots already have their price!" The language was damning considering the generally known fact that Randolph was in dire financial conditions.

Pickering and Wolcott showed the dispatch to Washington and persuaded him not to seek further explanation from the French. Some scholars have speculated that Randolph had sought money from the French in order to obtain evidence that implicated the British in the Whiskey Rebellion. Randolph had planned to uncover British complicity by protecting some flour merchants from their British creditors by advancing them money on their contracts. Heeding the advice of Pickering and Wolcott, Washington took the documents on face value and signed the treaty. He and the two secretaries confronted Randolph with the evidence against him. Randolph was vague about the events described in the dispatch. When it became apparent he would be asked to resign, Randolph did so, but under protest.

His public attempts to clear his name only further convinced the Federalists of Randolph's duplicity. In fact, his public statements were often more attacks on Washington's handling of the events than a plausible explanation of Fauchet's dispatch. Although he was never charged with a crime, Randolph's reputation was destroyed. When Wolcott and Pickering, who succeeded Randolph as secretary of state, discovered shortfalls in State Department accounts, Randolph attempted to make good with his own money, which ruined him. It also brought to an end Washington's attempt to include Federalists and Democratic-Republicans in his cabinet.

George Washington

With the adoption of the Jay Treaty, Democratic-Republicans began to attack the president directly. They said he was too closely allied with British interests and suspected him of plans to establish a monarchy.

The Jay Treaty was the last straw for many Democratic-Republicans who thought the government of the new nation was too close to British interests. This sentiment and their criticism of President Washington began when he issued the Neutrality Proclamation of 1793, which stated that the United States would remain neutral in the war between France and Britain. The Democratic-Republicans believed the United States should have sided with France, in part as payment for French support in the American Revolution. Nevertheless, Democratic-Republican critics were becoming more focused on the president and his role in what they saw as a growing British favoritism.

Thomas Jefferson, who had resigned as secretary of state, was one of the most vocal critics. He wrote in the wake of Washington's support for the Jay Treaty, "An Anglican monarchical, and aristocratical party has sprung up, whose avowed object is to draw over us the substance, as they have already done the forms, of the British government. . . . It would give you a fever were I to name to you the apostates who have gone over to these heresies, men who were Samsons in the field and Solomons in the council, but who have had their heads shorn by the harlot England."

With Jefferson entering the fray directly, Democratic-Republican editors like Philip Freneau of the *National Gazette* were emboldened in their attacks on Washington and his administration. Freneau had been criticizing official dinners and formal receptions as courtly levees as early as 1792. The Philadelphia *Aurora,* one of the president's harshest critics, published a piece that stated: "If ever a nation was debauched by a man, the American nation has been debauched by Washington. If ever a nation was deceived by a man, the American nation has been deceived by Washington. Let his conduct, then, be an example to future ages; let it serve to be a warning that no man may be an idol." The *Aurora* even advocated Washington's impeachment for monarchical tendencies.

The attacks continued for the remainder of Washington's presidency. Democratic-Republicans hurled charges that his entire administration, which was responsible for the establishment of a national bank, a standing army, and other evils, had subverted the republican nature of the Revolution. In his farewell message, Washington addressed the growing partisanship that he saw dividing the country. He cautioned against the evils of faction and the undue influence of foreign states. With this, his only public pronouncement on the vicious attacks, he retired from public office.

BIBLIOGRAPHY

Anderson, Dice Robins. *William Branch Giles: A Study in the Politics of Virginia and the Nation from 1790 to 1830.* Gloucester, Mass.: P. Smith, 1965 (c1914).

Banning, Lance. *After the Constitution: Party Conflict in the New Republic.* Belmont, Calif.: Wadsworth, 1989.

Booth, David A. *The Constitutional and Political Aspects of the Jay Treaty, 1794–1796.* Ann Arbor, Mich.: University Microfilms, 1957.

Boyd, Steven R., ed. *The Whiskey Rebellion.* Westport, Conn.: Greenwood Press, 1985.

Cary, Wilson Miles. *Sally Cary: A Long Hidden Romance of Washington's Life.* New York: De Vinne Press, 1916.

Cobbett, William. *A New Year's Gift to the Democrats; or, Observations on a pamphlet, entitled, "A Vindication of Mr. Randolph's Resignation."* Philadelphia: T. Bradford, 1796.

Cooke, Jacob E., ed. *The Reports of Alexander Hamilton*. New York: Harper and Row, 1964.

Forman, Samuel Eagle. *The Political Activities of Philip Freneau*. Baltimore: Johns Hopkins University Press, 1970.

Freeman, Douglas S. *George Washington: A Biography*. New York: Scribner's, 1954.

Hagood, Wesley O. *Presidential Sex: From the Founding Fathers to Bill Clinton*. Secaucus, N.J.: Carol Publishing Group, 1998.

Hamilton, Alexander. *The Works of Alexander Hamilton*. New York: G. P. Putnam's Sons, 1904.

Jones, Robert Francis. *The King of the Alley: William Duer—Politician, Entrepreneur, and Speculator, 1768–1799*. Philadelphia: American Philosophical Society, 1992.

Kitman, Marvin. *George Washington's Expense Account*. New York: Simon and Schuster, 1970.

McDonald, Forrest. *The Presidency of George Washington*. Lawrence: University Press of Kansas, 1974.

———. *Alexander Hamilton: A Biography*. New York: Norton, 1979.

Miller, John C. *Alexander Hamilton: Portrait in Paradox*. New York: Harper, 1959.

Mitchell, Jack. *Executive Privilege: Two Centuries of White House Scandals*. New York: Hippocrene Books, 1992.

Nordham, George W. *George Washington's Women: Mary, Martha, Sally, and 146 Others*. Philadelphia: Dorrance, 1977.

Reardon, John J. *Edmund Randolph: A Biography*. New York: Macmillan, 1975.

Ross, Shelley. *Fall from Grace: Sex, Scandal and Corruption in American Politics from 1702 to the Present*. New York: Ballantine Books, 1988.

Woodward, C. Vann. *Responses of the Presidents to Charges of Misconduct*. New York: Dell Publishing, 1974.

Woodward, W. E. *George Washington: The Image and the Man*. New York: Boni and Liveright, 1926.

JOHN ADAMS

Second President
1797–1801

John Adams was born in Braintree (now Quincy), Massachusetts, on October 30, 1735. Little is known of his childhood except that he was a carefree boy who initially resisted the formal education his father sought for him. As a young student, Adams attended a number of schools, including Joseph Cleverly's Latin school, which he disliked immensely, and one run by John Marsh, which he enjoyed. In 1751 Adams entered Harvard College, where he received a classical education. His years at Harvard inflamed "a love of Books and a fondness for study" that would remain with him throughout his life. Graduating in 1755, he studied law under James Putnam of Worcester and was admitted to the bar in 1758.

Adams practiced law in Boston and established himself as a capable young lawyer. In 1770 he defended the British soldiers charged with killing colonists on March 5, 1770 (the Boston Massacre). Adams successfully won the acquittals of six of the defendants. The remaining two were convicted of manslaughter, which carried a penalty of branding on the thumbs. Although he was harassed by many for taking the cases—some suggested he did it only for the large fee (almost twenty guineas)—Adams believed that the soldiers deserved a fair trial and a vigorous defense.

Adams was elected to the General Court (lower house) of Massachusetts in 1770, where he represented Boston. Three years later, he was elected by his colleagues to serve in the Governor's Council (upper house), but his election was vetoed by the royal governor because of his favorable comments on the Boston Tea Party. Elected as a delegate to the Continental Congress in 1774, Adams tried to convince southern colonists that a break from England was the only sound policy. He served in the congress until 1777.

In 1778 he was sent to France as part of the mission headed by Benjamin Franklin. However, Adams left France after only a year because of the mutual dislike between him and the French and his disgust with Franklin's romantic liaisons. In 1779 he drafted the Massachusetts constitution as part of the state's convention in 1779 and 1780. Also in 1780 he served as ambassador to the Netherlands, where he secured both Dutch recognition of the United States and a substantial loan to fund the war effort. From the Netherlands, he went back to Paris to be part of the team negotiating the settlement of the Revolutionary War. John Jay, Franklin, and Adams ignored the instructions that congress had given them, namely that any treaty must be acceptable to the French foreign ministry. Instead the three successfully negotiated a treaty—the Treaty of Paris (1783)—that established the Mississippi River as the western boundary of the United States. (France had been willing to settle for the Appalachian Mountains.) In 1785 he went to England as the new nation's first ambassador to Great Britain, but he asked to be recalled in 1788, citing the inability to carry on diplomatic relations with the British so soon after the war.

From 1789 to 1797 Adams served as vice president in George Washington's administration. Adams had few formal duties as vice president and was immediately bogged down in minute details of protocol, form, and precedent. When the issue of how to address the president arose, Adams, as president of the Senate, proposed "His Highness, the President of the United States and Protector of their Liberties." This suggestion was met with derision, and Adams was referred to as His Rotundity, the Duke of Braintree, and His Superfluous Excellency.

In 1796 Adams was the obvious candidate to replace the retiring Washington. He faced a strong opponent in Thomas Jefferson, who had left Washington's administration in order to more openly criticize its Federalist policies. Jefferson's Democratic-Republicans viciously attacked Adams, his alleged monarchical tendencies, and his support of Federalist policies. While Washington openly endorsed Adams as his successor, Alexander Hamilton was working behind the scenes to have Thomas Pinckney—the vice-presidential candidate on the Federalist ticket—elected president. When New England electors discovered the plan, Hamilton's intrigue led to the election of Adams as president and Jefferson as vice president—perhaps, at least from Hamilton's view, the worst of all possible outcomes.

During Adams's single term, the administration's central problem was the deteriorating relationship with France and the possibility of war. This crisis led to several political scandals in the Adams administration, including the XYZ Affair and the passage of the Alien and Sedition Acts (both discussed in more detail below). Although he avoided a war with the French, Adams was unable to defeat Jefferson in the election of 1800.

With Federalist control of the executive branch coming to an end, Adams spent his last night in office signing appointments to the federal bench. Because federal judges serve for life, Adams could control the judiciary and extend the influence of the Federalists many years into the future. His dislike of Jefferson was so great that he left town early on the morning of Jefferson's inauguration so that he did not have to see the new president take office.

Adams returned to Quincy, where he thought he would have a few years with his wife, Abigail Smith Adams, whom he had married in 1764. However, Adams lived more than twenty-five years after leaving the White House. During his retirement, he read voraciously and corresponded with colleagues, even those with whom relations were strained because of political differences. He rekindled his friendship with Thomas Jefferson such as they had not enjoyed since the Revolution. In 1820 he served as a presidential elector and voted for James Monroe. That same year, he also served as a delegate to the state constitutional convention. In 1824, Adams saw his son, John Quincy Adams, elected the sixth president of the United States. He died on July 4, 1826, on the nation's fiftieth birthday.

THE XYZ AFFAIR

The government of France was engaged in an undeclared naval war against American shipping, and U.S. diplomats were sent to Paris to negotiate a settlement. French agents known simply as X, Y, and Z sought bribes from the Americans in return for a meeting with the French Directory. Even though dispatches from France revealed the duplicity of the French, the Democratic-Republicans charged that Adams was trying to create a standing army as a way to destroy the Republic and establish a monarchy.

John Adams had inherited from the Washington administration the growing deterioration of relations with France. The worsening relationship had two causes. First, the French and their Democratic-Republican supporters in the United States were outraged by both the Proclamation of Neutrality of 1783 and the Jay Treaty, which they took as signs of America's preference for the English. Second, the French Directory had engaged in undeclared warfare against American shipping, including the issuance of false letters of marque and forged letters of commission for ships operating in the western Atlantic. In fact, French activities were far worse than British attempts to control American shipping. By June 1797 more than 300 American ships, their crews, and cargo had been preyed upon by ships operating under French colors.

When the Directory refused to receive the American ambassador to France, Adams sought to solve the growing crisis by sending a delegation. The president appointed Elbridge Gerry, a Jeffersonian, along with John Marshall and Charles Cotesworth Pinckney, two staunch Federalists. The three diplomats arrived in Paris in October 1797, at the height of the Directory's power; Napoleon had just defeated the Austrians. Talleyrand, the French minister of foreign affairs, sent word through messengers that the three diplomats would have to pay a bribe of $250,000 to Talleyrand directly and secure a $10 million loan as compensation for Adams's anti-French comments just to enter into negotiations to end French pirating. When Talleyrand's representative was pushed for an alternative, he

(Monsieur Y) warned the diplomats of the power of the French party in America and the fate of minor European nations that refused the Directory. After several months of such meetings, Marshall and Pinckney left France. Gerry remained, believing that his presence might help prevent war.

As dispatches from the three diplomats began to reach the desk of Secretary of State Timothy Pickering, the seriousness of the situation became clear. Pickering quickly shared the dispatches with the president, who held a cabinet meeting to discuss options. Adams addressed a joint session of Congress on March 19, 1798. In a strongly worded message, Adams said he was bringing the diplomats home, and he called for the increased defense of the seas as the only way to avoid conflict with France. Jefferson, who privately referred to Adams's address as insane, encouraged the Democratic-Republicans to seek the full disclosure of the dispatches the president had cited. Adams complied. In the documents sent to Congress, Talleyrand's representatives were simply referred to as "X, Y, and Z."

When the congressional Democratic-Republicans saw the dispatches, they realized that they had made a political blunder in requesting their release. However, rather than join the Federalists in anger over French actions, they attacked the president for putting the Directory in a position that left it no choice but to refuse negotiations. Some Democratic-

The "Paris monster" here cries, "I must have money," while diplomat Charles Pinckney, on the left, retorts, "We will not give you six pence." The French government refused to officially receive the American diplomats without a substantial payment.

Republican–controlled newspapers printed an outrageous story claiming that the agents did not represent the French government but were confidence men who tried to fleece the newly arrived diplomats.

The false stories and the attacks on Adams could not hide the truth of France's intrigues. A tide of anti-French sentiment swept over the country. One result was the adoption of a policy of armed neutrality, which led to the establishment of a standing army under the command of former president George Washington and Alexander Hamilton as Washington's chief general. A further result was the founding of a school for gunners and sappers at West Point, New York, today the U.S. Military Academy.

In the end, France backed down from its position. A large part of its navy was corralled in Egypt by the British, and Talleyrand did not want to provoke the Americans into a war. The embargo on American ships was lifted, and all letters of marque and commission were rescinded. These actions renewed Democratic-Republican claims that the Directory had not been party to the events and that the whole XYZ Affair had been a hoax propagated by Federalist warmongers.

Although the United States avoided war with the French and signed a commercial treaty with them in 1800, many Democratic-Republicans clung to the belief that the whole episode was an attempt by the Federalists to destroy the Republic and establish a monarchy. This charge had been leveled many times against Washington, Adams, and Hamilton during Washington's administration.

ALIEN AND SEDITION ACTS

The XYZ Affair had raised concerns about the growing influence of the French faction in America. Congress enacted four measures, collectively known as the Alien and Sedition Acts, to empower the president to control antigovernment activities. Adams was accused of using these measures against his political opponents.

The XYZ Affair left a legacy of suspicion. Although President Adams did not share the belief held by many Federalists that there was a Democratic-Republican conspiracy supported by the French, he was concerned. In an attempt to curb French intrigue that threatened America's neutrality and, some argued, her survival, Congress passed four laws that collectively became known as the Alien and Sedition Acts.

The first piece of legislation was the Naturalization Act, which extended to fourteen the number of years an immigrant must wait until he could become a citizen and vote. The second law, the Alien Friends Act, authorized the president to deport any alien he considered dangerous. The third, the Alien Enemy Act, vested the president with the power to deport any alien from a country with which the United States was at war. Finally, the Sedition Act established punishments—fines and/or imprisonment—for individuals who attempted to thwart federal law or who made false, scandalous, and malicious statements about federal officials.

It was the Sedition Act that had the most direct and immediate impact. Many Democratic-Republican editors moderated their attacks of the administration in fear that they would be found guilty of sedition. Enforcement of the act fell to Secretary of State Timothy Pickering. His zeal in prosecuting earned him the title "the Scourge of Jacobinism." The administration indicted fourteen editors under the act and harassed many others, including Ben Bache and William Duane of the Philadelphia *Aurora,* John Daly Burk of the New York *Time Price* and Matthew Lyon of the *Vermont Journal.* Lyon was jailed for his offenses shortly after winning reelection to the House of Representatives in 1798.

The two alien acts went unenforced because Adams resisted Pickering's pleas to begin mass deportations. Nevertheless, many French aliens left the United States after 1798 because the climate had become inhospitable. In the end, the alien acts had the intended effects without any prosecutions.

Adams had not requested the passage of the acts, but he neither opposed them nor attempted to veto them as unconstitutional. Rather, he believed they were necessary (although he had tried to make Hamilton look responsible for their passage) to restrain those who opposed his call for a more vigorous national defense.

CABINET INSUBORDINATION

Several members of the cabinet were more loyal to Alexander Hamilton than to the president. Adams finally had to relieve them of their posts when they backed the revolutionary activities of Francisco de Miranda and opposed a peaceful settlement of differences with France.

When Adams took office in 1797, he retained most of his predecessor's cabinet. He did so in part because the theory behind the cabinet was not a settled issue: Did the cabinet officers serve at the president's pleasure or because of merit that deserved a degree of independence? Adams had retained them, but it became clear that three of the most important— Secretary of State Timothy Pickering, Secretary of the Treasury Oliver Wolcott, and Secretary of War James McHenry—were more loyal to Hamilton than to Adams or his administration. This situation had become abundantly clear when McHenry orchestrated Washington's insistence that Hamilton be second-in-command of the army. Additionally, the men would often consult with Hamilton on matters of policy and present his position to the president.

Pickering and McHenry were involved in outright insubordination: under Hamilton's leadership, they attempted to support, through covert operations, the activities of Francisco de Miranda, a Venezuelan revolutionary who wanted to oust Spain from the Western Hemisphere. The plan was that under the cover of war with France, the American army under Hamilton and the British navy would attack the relatively weak Spanish empire. The plot had drawn into its conspiracy Rufus King, the ambassador to Great Britain.

Timothy Pickering

In August 1798, when most of the plan was final, Pickering and McHenry presented it to Adams for approval. Adams dismissed the scheme as a foolish plot that would suck America into the perpetual wars of Europe.

On February 18, 1799, Adams appointed William Vans Murray—without consulting his cabinet or Congress—as an envoy to settle the disputes with France. The Hamilton wing of the party—who wanted war with the French—managed to postpone the envoy's departure. It soon became clear to Adams that people in his own cabinet were responsible for his inability to send Vans Murray on the mission. On May 6, 1800, Adams berated McHenry for his insubordination and subservience to Hamilton. The following day McHenry resigned his post. Four days later, when Pickering refused to submit his resignation, Adams dismissed him. As a final move, Adams began to demobilize the army as no longer necessary, thus cutting further into Hamilton's power.

FEDERALIST CRITICISM OF ADAMS

The wing of the Federalist Party controlled by Alexander Hamilton was highly critical of Federalist president John Adams. In a letter to fellow Federalists, Hamilton stated that Adams was not fit to serve as president because of his character defects.

The split between Hamilton and Adams over France and Adams's sending of William Vans Murray to settle claims divided the Federalist Party beyond repair. After February 1799 the Democratic-Republicans could restrain their attacks on the Adams administration because the Hamilton faction was doing the job for them. Most of the criticism was behind the scenes in private correspondence, but some became public. The Democratic-Republicans intercepted and published a letter Hamilton sent to Federalists throughout the country. Hamilton's letter said that Adams had a particular character defect that prevented him from being an effective leader. The letter claimed that Adams was "eccentric, propitious neither to the regular display of sound judgment nor to steady perseverance in a systematic plan of conduct." To these charges were added vanity and "jealousy capable of discoloring every object." The Democratic-Republicans sat back and watched the Federalists destroy each other with charges of intrigues, disloyalty, and other offenses. In the end, the Democratic-Republicans could take heart that Adams would be the last Federalist president.

BIBLIOGRAPHY

Adams, John. *Autobiography.* Boston: Little, Brown, 1850.

Brown, Ralph A. *The Presidency of John Adams.* Lawrence: University Press of Kansas, 1975.

DeConde, Alexander. *The Quasi-War: The Politics and Diplomacy of the Undeclared Naval War with France, 1797–1801.* New York: Scribner's, 1966.

Ellis, Joseph J. *Passionate Sage: The Character and Legacy of John Adams.* New York: Norton, 1993.

Ferling, John E. *John Adams: A Life.* New York: Henry Holt, 1996.

Kurtz, Stephen G. *The Presidency of John Adams: The Collapse of Federalism, 1795–1800.* Philadelphia: University of Pennsylvania Press, 1957.

Mitchell, Jack. *Executive Privilege: Two Centuries of White House Scandals.* New York: Hippocrene Books, 1992.

Smith, James Morton. *Freedom's Fetters: The Alien and Sedition Laws and American Civil Liberties.* Ithaca, N.Y.: Cornell University Press, 1956.

Smith, Page. John Adams. Garden City, N.Y.: Doubleday, 1962.

Thompson, C. Bradley. *John Adams and the Spirit of Liberty.* Lawrence: University Press of Kansas, 1998.

Woodward, C. Vann. *Responses of the Presidents to Charges of Misconduct.* New York: Dell Publishing, 1974.

THOMAS JEFFERSON

Third President

1801–1809

orn April 13, 1743, in what is now Albemarle County, Virginia, Thomas Jefferson was the eldest son and third child of Peter and Jane Jefferson. A bookish child, he studied under a number of tutors from age nine to sixteen. In 1760 Jefferson enrolled at the College of William and Mary and spent two years studying science, math, philosophy, and literature. In 1762 he began a five-year apprenticeship under George Wythe to study law. Jefferson was admitted to the bar in April 1767.

Jefferson practiced law for two years before his election to the Virginia House of Burgesses. During his five years in the legislature, he strengthened his conviction that reconciliation with Britain was impossible. In 1774 he made the case against Parliament in "Summary View of the Rights of British America." Appointed to the Continental Congress in 1775, Jefferson served on the committee charged with drafting the Declaration of Independence. The committee, which included John Adams, Benjamin Franklin, Roger Sherman, and Robert R. Livingston, selected Jefferson to write the text because of his reputation for powerful prose. The document, slightly modified by the congress, is an eloquent statement of fundamental political principles.

From 1776 to 1779 Jefferson served in the House of Delegates before becoming governor of Virginia. His two-year term as governor during the Revolutionary War was unsuccessful from his perspective. In 1781 he was forced to abandon his capital, Richmond, to advancing British troops. A year later, on September 6, 1782, his wife, Martha, died. They had been married only ten years. He served as a member of the Continental Congress (1783–1784), which helped organize the Northwest Territory. In 1784 he replaced the ailing Benjamin Franklin as the U.S. ambassador to France.

Returning to the United States in 1790, Jefferson served as secretary of state during President George Washington's first term. He tried to strengthen U.S. ties with France and was disappointed by Washington's Proclamation of Neutrality in 1793. He was also the leading opponent of

Alexander Hamilton's fiscal plans, and the two often clashed over policy. Jefferson resigned from the cabinet when it became clear that Washington supported Hamilton on the most crucial policy issues.

In 1797 Jefferson came in second in the presidential election and became John Adams's vice president, a position that bored him. In 1800 the congressional Democratic-Republicans met and nominated Jefferson for president. Running against Adams, Jefferson received seventy-three electoral votes, the same number as Aaron Burr, who had been running as Jefferson's vice-presidential candidate. Burr refused to concede, and the election was thrown into the House of Representatives, which took thirty-six ballots to decide in favor of Jefferson. Ironically, Jefferson was aided by Hamilton, who saw Jefferson as the lesser of two evils and encouraged the Federalists to support him. Burr became vice president. The election led to the adoption of the Twelfth Amendment, which provides for presidential and vice-presidential candidates running on the same ticket.

Jefferson was easily reelected in 1804 with George Clinton of New York as his vice president. During his two terms, Jefferson oversaw the territorial expansion of the country with the Louisiana Purchase in 1803 and the funding of the Lewis and Clark Expedition (1804–1806). He also waged an ongoing war against the pirates of the Barbary states that finally ended in 1805. In March 1807 Jefferson signed the law that would end the importation of slaves beginning January 1, 1808.

When Jefferson retired in 1809, he was severely in debt and sold his personal library of more than 6,500 volumes to the government. His books became the foundation of the Library of Congress. Throughout his retirement, he maintained a prodigious correspondence and renewed his friendship with John Adams. Jefferson also worked tirelessly to found the University of Virginia at Charlottesville, which opened in 1825. He designed the buildings, developed the curriculum, hired the faculty, and served as the university's first rector. Jefferson died the following year on July 4 at his home, Monticello.

SEXUAL LIAISONS AND ILLEGITIMATE CHILDREN

After his wife died, Thomas Jefferson was rumored to have had a number of sexual relationships. The women included Sally Hemings, one of his slaves, and Dolley Madison, among others. The level of detail concerning the liaisons varies greatly. This section discusses each of the alleged affairs in chronological order, starting with a relationship that began before his marriage.

Betsey Moore Walker

Betsey Walker was the wife of Thomas Jefferson's neighbor and friend, John Walker. While the exact nature of the affair is lost in the conflicting stories of the people involved, all acknowledge that there was at least one encounter between Jefferson and Betsey Walker. In the summer of 1768, when her husband was at an Indian conference in Albany, New York, Jefferson made advances to Betsey Walker that seem to have been reciprocated. John Walker did not learn of the affair until 1784 because Betsey waited for Jefferson, who had been appointed ambassador to France, to leave the country before telling her husband. When Jefferson returned, Walker challenged him to a duel. Pistols were avoided, and the matter was settled at James Madison's home. Walker later wrote to Gen. Light-Horse Harry Lee about the events. Walker claimed that Jefferson had tried to seduce Betsey for a period of eleven years (1768 to 1779) including eight years after his marriage to Martha Wayles Skelton in 1872. Walker's letter also claims that Betsey never gave into any of Jefferson's advances. Thomas Paine—the eternal skeptic—wrote of the affair, "We have heard of a ten year siege of Troy, but who ever heard of a ten year siege to seduce." It would appear that either Walker's letter is exaggerated in its time frame, as Jefferson claimed, or that his wife was less innocent than he maintained.

Maria Cosway

A forty-one-year-old widower, Jefferson was appointed ambassador to France in 1784. When he arrived the following year, Jefferson at first found sexual ethics in Paris distasteful. Aristocrats, diplomats, and other well-placed men all seemed to have young mistresses. Jefferson's initial objections faded once he met Maria Louisa Catherine Cecilia Hadfield Cosway, a twenty-seven-year-old, Italian-born artist who was married to English miniaturist painter Richard Cosway. Jefferson was introduced to Maria by Col. John Trumbull, an American veteran and painter. Maria and Jefferson seem to have fallen in love on first sight. Richard Cosway did not object to their liaison, as he was also having affairs. Maria and Jefferson had a brief affair that ended in October, when she returned to London with her husband. However, it is clear from the twelve-page letter Jefferson wrote to her on October 12 that he was smitten. The letter, known as the "My Head and My Heart" letter, is a symbolic dialogue between his heart (emotion) and his head (reason). His head warns him against becoming too close, while his heart speaks of the joy Maria has brought him. Maria returned to Paris in August 1787 for a four-month rekindling of the affair. However, by the time she returned to London, the flames of passion had died. The two never saw each other again, although they corresponded throughout their lives.

Angelica Schuyler Church

After Jefferson's affair with Maria Cosway ended, Col. John Trumbull introduced him to Angelica Schuyler Church. Ironically, Mrs. Church was the sister-in-law of Jefferson's political rival, Alexander Hamilton. During the winter of 1787, Jefferson and Church had a brief affair that ended when she left for England.

Sally Hemings

Sally Hemings became the property of Thomas Jefferson as part of the inheritance his wife, Martha, received from her father's estate. Martha's father, John Wayles, had a long-term relationship with Elizabeth Hemings, Sally's mother, that resulted in six children, and Sally was Martha's half sister. Sally was only nine when Martha Jefferson died in 1782. On her deathbed, Jefferson promised never to remarry, an oath he kept. Still mourning his wife, Jefferson left for France as the U.S. ambassador.

In 1787, when he learned of a whooping-cough epidemic in Virginia, he sent for his younger daughter, Polly, and a suitable slave who could care for her. Sally was chosen. She was almost sixteen at the time and, because she was one-quarter black, could easily have passed for white, by most accounts. Abigail Adams, in Paris at the time, thought that nothing good would come of Sally's presence there and suggested that she be returned to Virginia.

The affair between Jefferson and Sally Hemings most likely began in the summer of 1788 or early the following year. Some have suggested that the relationship with Sally is what eventually soured Jefferson's affair with Maria Cosway. While in Paris, Jefferson purchased fine clothes for Sally and was often in her company.

Jefferson returned to the United States in early 1789, but Sally and Polly remained in Paris. Then a strange event took place: Sally, who was legally free if she remained in France, decided to return to Virginia, but not before receiving a promise from Jefferson that he would free her children when each reached age twenty-one. When she arrived back at Monticello, she was visibly pregnant and gave birth either in late 1789 or early 1790. In all, Sally had seven children, and she claimed they were Jefferson's. Of the five children who lived to maturity, three were freed at twenty-one; the other two were listed as runaway slaves whom Jefferson made no attempt to recover. After Jefferson's death in 1826, Sally went to live with her sons Eston and Madison near Monticello. She died in 1835.

Rumors about Jefferson's affair with a slave were widespread. Jefferson never commented on them, but his daughter Martha insisted that he could not have been the father of Sally's children. On September 1, 1802, a pamphleteer named James Thomson Callender, who had once earned Jefferson's praise for criticizing President John Adams, published the following story in the *Richmond Recorder:*

> It is well known that the man, whom it delighteth the people to honor, keeps and for many years has kept, as his concubine, one of his slaves. Her name is Sally. The name of her eldest son is Tom. His features are said to bear a striking resemblance to those of the president himself. . . .

By this wench Sally, our president has had several children. There is not an individual in the neighborhood of Charlottesville who does not believe the story, and not a few who know it. . . .

Mute! Mute! Mute! yes very Mute! will all those republican printers of biographical information be upon this point.

Other newspapers corroborated the story that Callender had printed.

In recent years, the story has again been raised by those seeking to prove that Jefferson was in fact the father of Hemings's children, a charge on which most Jefferson biographers have either been silent or have denied. Some have suggested that Jefferson's nephew, Peter Carr, was the more likely father. Eugene A. Foster, a retired University of Virginia pathologist, conducted DNA studies on descendants of Hemings and Carr. DNA was collected from a descendant of Jefferson's paternal uncle Field because Jefferson had no male children by Martha.

The conclusions of the study, which were published in *Nature* magazine, were that Eston Hemings was Thomas Jefferson's son. The study also found that Peter Carr could not have been the father because the DNA on the Y chromosome did not match and disproved the claim by the descendants of Thomas Woodson that he was fathered by Jefferson. The results, however, do not rule out that Jefferson's younger brother Randolph was the true father, as suggested by some biographers, because he and Jefferson shared the same Y chromosome pattern.

Dolley Madison

Of all of Jefferson's alleged sexual adventures, perhaps the least likely to be true was an affair with Dolley Madison. A report first printed in a Federalist newspaper in 1808 claimed that Dolley Madison had sex with the former president in return for his support of her husband's candidacy for president. While there was never any proof of the events, neither Jefferson nor Dolley ever bothered to deny the story.

AARON BURR, VICE PRESIDENT

Aaron Burr was a controversial figure throughout his single term as vice president. He was not a close political ally of Jefferson's and had tried to win the presidency himself when the election of 1800 was thrown into the House of Representatives. Three events that shaped Burr's legacy are discussed below.

Burr-Hamilton Duel

Aaron Burr was charged with murder for killing Alexander Hamilton in a duel.

Aaron Burr

On July 11, 1804, Aaron Burr, vice president of the United States, shot and killed Alexander Hamilton on a secluded dueling ground in Weehawken, New Jersey. The two men had been bitter political enemies for years. The final straw for Burr was Hamilton's activity in the New York gubernatorial race of 1804. Burr had hoped to win this office, as his prospects for remaining Jefferson's vice president were slim. In the end he lost to his rival whom Hamilton had helped. Burr found out about some disparaging remarks Hamilton had made and immediately challenged him to a duel. By most accounts, Hamilton fired his pistol into the air rather than at Burr, but Burr fired directly at Hamilton and fatally wounded him.

A New York City coroner's jury, which had no jurisdiction over the case because the killing had occurred in New Jersey, concluded that Burr and his associates "did kill and Murder" Hamilton. A grand jury in the state changed the charge to a misdemeanor. However, in Bergen County, New Jersey, a grand jury with jurisdiction indicted Burr for murder, and the governor refused to quash the indictment. Burr, indicted in two jurisdictions, returned to Washington, D.C., which had no extradition agreement with the states, to serve as president of the Senate during the impeachment trial of Justice Samuel Chase. Burr was never tried.

Conspiracy of 1804

Disgruntled New England Federalists sought the support of Aaron Burr, who was a candidate for governor of New York, for a plan to separate New England from the rest of the United States.

During his campaign for governor of New York in 1804, Burr was approached by a number of Federalists who were tired of Jefferson's administration and the overwhelming influence of Virginia in the national government. These conspirators hoped to make New England into a separate country, but believed their plan would not succeed without the support of New York. Hoping to increase his political power, Burr considered the scheme, but, in the end, remained noncommittal. His loss in the election and the subsequent duel with Hamilton made Burr no longer useful to the plotters. In any case, the conspiracy proved to be all idle talk and no action, and it quickly disappeared.

The Burr Conspiracy

Burr developed a treasonous scheme to form a new country out of the western parts of the United States from south of the Ohio River to Louisiana and tried to interest Britain and Spain in the idea.

Even before he left the vice presidency in 1805, Burr was planning to incite a rebellion in the West. In response to the rumors spreading about the plot, on October 22, 1806, President Jefferson convened a cabinet meeting to discuss what action the government should take. John Graham, a special agent, was sent to investigate and to put military leaders on their guard. The evidence the administration had was fragmentary, but it seemed that James Wilkinson, commanding officer of the army and governor of the Louisiana territory, was involved.

To accomplish his plan, Burr would need money and supplies. While he was still vice president, Burr proposed to the British ambassador, Anthony Merry, that the British government provide the financial support. Merry passed this information on to the foreign office in London. Burr also joined forces with Wilkinson, who wanted to invade Mexico. Burr decided to merge the two plots to secure Wilkinson's participation and a stronghold in New Orleans.

The British were interested in helping Burr, but could not because of the war they were fighting with the French. Burr next approached the Spanish with the idea. The Spanish ambassador, Don Carlos Martinez de Yrujo, was not interested at first. However, Burr's agent, former New Jersey senator Jonathan Dayton, convinced Martinez de Yrujo that the Jefferson administration had aided Venezuelan revolutionary Francisco de Miranda in his activities against Spain (see page 31). With the possibility of Spanish support, the plot was changed to exclude invasions of Mexico and the Floridas. According to the new plan, the whole affair would begin with a coup d'état in Washington. Spain decided not to participate. Undeterred, Burr tried to pull together the necessary forces and supplies.

Jefferson continued to receive information about the growing conspiracy from people like Joseph H. Daveiss, the U.S. attorney for Kentucky. Daveiss's information was corroborated by letters to Jefferson from Col. George Morgan, whom Burr had visited, and a New York congressman, who informed the president that Comfort Tyler was raising men for an expedition in the West. In the end, however, it was a letter from Wilkinson to Jefferson that led to action. The letter, dated October 21, 1806, was received November 25, and it outlined the details of the plot.

On June 24 and 25, 1807, a grand jury returned indictments for treason and misdemeanor against Burr, Tyler, Dayton, Sen. John Smith of Ohio, Harman Blennerhasset, an Englishman of Irish descent, and two other men. The chief witness in the case was Wilkinson, who barely avoided indictment himself. The trial began August 3. Despite the testimony of Wilkinson and others, the government failed to prove that Burr was on Blennerhasset's Island in the Ohio River on December 10, 1806, when hostilities broke out. The jury returned a verdict that said Burr "is not proved to be guilty by any evidence submitted to us." The jury seemed to believe that Burr was the principal conspirator, but that the government had failed to put him at the scene of the crime.

Burr and his co-conspirators were not out of the fire yet. They still faced charges of treason and misdemeanor in Ohio and Kentucky. The federal court, however, only remanded the prisoners for trial on the lesser charge. Burr posted bail and fled to England. Wilkinson, who had been removed as governor of Louisiana, returned to his military command and continued to be a source of scandal in the Jefferson and Madison administrations.

JAMES WILKINSON, GOVERNOR OF LOUISIANA TERRITORY

James Wilkinson, Jefferson's appointee to be governor of Louisiana, was in the pay of the Spanish. He passed sensitive documents to Spanish agents about border policy and diplomatic negotiations, and Jefferson was slow to react to the overwhelming proof of his duplicity.

James Wilkinson over the years had developed a reputation as "the most skillful and unscrupulous plotter this country has ever produced." During the Washington and Adams administrations, Wilkinson served as the ranking general of the army. At the time, it was rumored that he was in the pay of the Spanish. However, nothing came of those rumors.

During the Jefferson administration, Wilkinson was commanding general of the army and was paid 12,000 pesos by the Spanish in 1804 in return for information about American boundary policies, military readiness, and diplomatic plans. At the same time, Wilkinson was also drawing questionable advances on his salary and payments of claims submitted under the authorization of Secretary of War Henry Dearborn.

The president learned of Wilkinson's duplicity in a letter from Joseph H. Daveiss, the U.S. attorney for Kentucky. Daveiss, a Federalist and a relative of Chief Justice John Marshall, told the president that Wilkinson—then governor of the Louisiana Territory, a post to which Jefferson had appointed him—was not only taking money from Spain, but also was participating in a large-scale plot to take over the West. Jefferson took the advice of Treasury Secretary Albert Gallatin and ignored the information.

Jefferson finally removed Wilkinson from office in March 1807, but Wilkinson kept his military command. Still, Jefferson continued to hear about Wilkinson's subversive activities. In a letter dated July 6, 1807, Sen. John Smith of Ohio alerted Jefferson of the truth of the allegations and warned him that it would be used against him if he was not careful.

Although I am a friend of Gen. Wilkinson, I think it my duty to inform you, that it had been confidently asserted to me by one of your friends and mine, since I arrived in this city [New Orleans] and only two or three days ago, that Gen. Wilkinson had been in Spanish pay for many years, and that the most unequivocal proofs of it are in the hands of a few designing Federalists, who are waiting with anxious hope for the time when you may have committed your reputation with the General's and then publish the evidence of his guilt.

In late December 1807, John Randolph, one of the administration's severest critics, called for an investigation of Wilkinson. Randolph had received information about him from a former Wilkinson associate, Daniel Clark. The House met in January and February 1808 to consider the charges against Wilkinson, but could not come to a final resolution as the hard evidence it needed had been sent to Spain by the Spanish governor of West Florida. Modern scholars with access to Spanish archives, however, have confirmed that Wilkinson was in the pay of Spain while he was also part of the Burr conspiracy.

The administration ordered Secretary of War Dearborn to convene a military court of inquiry. The court, made up of three lower-ranking officers who were unlikely to convict Wilkinson, believed his story that the money he had received was for a debt that was due him on an old tobacco contract. With the military court exonerating him, the House did not continue its investigation; rather it left the matter for Jefferson to handle. The only action Jefferson took was to reassign Wilkinson to a New Orleans command.

THE TWO MILLION ACT

Jefferson sought to bypass normal funding procedures to gain the money necessary to acquire the Floridas from Spain. His methods brought condemnation from members of his own party as well as from Federalists, who feared that the money would be wasted on ineffective bribes of French officials.

Jefferson's secretary of state, James Madison, had been pressuring the Spanish to give up the Floridas, but without success. On December 3, 1805, Jefferson submitted his annual message to Congress, in which he outlined his anger and growing frustration with Spanish depredations on the borders of the Floridas. Three days later, Jefferson sent a second message and various diplomatic reports to Congress. This message was secret and requested an undisclosed sum of money for an unspecified purpose:

The present crisis in Europe is favorable for pressing such a settlement, and not a moment should be lost in availing ourselves of it. Should it pass unimproved, our situation would become much more difficult. Formal war is not necessary. It is not probable it will follow. But the protection of our citizens, the spirit and honor of our country, require that force should be interposed to a certain degree. It will probably contribute to advance the cause of peace. But the

course to be pursued will require the command of the means which
it belongs to Congress exclusively to yield or to deny.

Treasury Secretary Gallatin hoped to use the funds as an earnest of American intentions once possession of the Floridas had been secured and as a way of skirting the Senate, which might oppose a treaty.

When informed that Jefferson had requested $2 million to purchase the Floridas, John Randolph of Virginia, chairman of the House Ways and Means Committee and Jefferson's staunch opponent, protested. Randolph objected to both the tactic and the goal. He also feared that the money would be used to bribe the French into pressuring the Spanish because Madison had told him privately the funds would be used for that purpose. Jefferson's bypassing the Federalist members of Congress had inadvertently created strong opposition to his plan in his own party.

Nevertheless, Jefferson got the Two Million Act through Congress. He accomplished it by having Barnabas Bidwell of Massachusetts replace Randolph as chairman of Ways and Means. Jefferson's activities were widely condemned as executive influence—a form of political corruption in which the executive (usually a monarch) interferes with the democratic nature of the parliament. Jefferson signed the bill in February 1806, and it was made public in April. In the end, the plan did not accomplish the goal of Spain surrendering the Floridas. In fact, as feared, the money did little except line the pockets of French agents.

POST OFFICE INVESTIGATIONS

Gideon Granger, Jefferson's second postmaster general, was accused of using postal contracts as bribes to gain a favorable result for a New England land company. Jefferson did not remove Granger because the president hoped the patronage would strengthen his party in the Federalist stronghold of New England.

John Randolph, a growing thorn in the side of the Jefferson administration, initiated another charge against a Jefferson appointee in 1805. He charged that Gideon Granger of Connecticut was using the patronage of the Post Office in behalf of himself and other shareholders of the New England Mississippi Land Company. The company, which had business before Congress that grew out of the Yazoo land grants in Georgia, had tried to get William Duane, the influential editor of the *Philadelphia Aurora,* to back the Yazoo claim. According to Randolph's account, Granger had employed a secret agent to lobby Congress and to bribe members by awarding them lucrative mail contracts in exchange for their support.

Granger maintained his innocence and on February 1, 1805, requested that the House investigate the matter. Congress appointed a special committee in March 1806, but this committee requested a postponement of its report until the next session of Congress. The report was never released, and the matter died.

Jefferson seems to have paid little attention to the serious charges that were leveled against Granger. The president saw Granger as a much needed ally in the heavily Federalist New England states and hoped to use the post office to strengthen his party's supporters in Massachusetts and Connecticut.

MIRANDA EXPEDITION

Jefferson's administration was embroiled in the international controversy of Gen. Francisco de Miranda, who sought to free Venezuela from Spanish control. While in Washington, D.C., Miranda was led to believe that the administration supported his venture. However, a number of individuals were prosecuted for aiding Miranda, including Samuel Ogden and William Smith, John Adams's son-in-law. They claimed that the administration had been involved in the activities for which they were being prosecuted.

Early in February 1806, Gen. Francisco de Miranda, a Venezuelan revolutionary, sailed from New York aboard the ship *Leander,* on which he carried military supplies and a complement of 180 to 200 men. Miranda, who hoped to liberate his country from Spanish control, had been—he believed—assured that the Jefferson administration would not try to prevent his mission. Miranda had met with Jefferson and Secretary of State Madison a number of times the previous fall and had been given a sympathetic hearing, but no formal endorsement. The arms and the troops, however, were in violation of a law that prevented the fitting of an American ship for an assault against a country with which the United States was not at war.

The French government protested the U.S. participation in the Miranda expedition. At the time, Spain was in the control of France: Joseph Bonaparte sat on the Spanish throne, and French troops occupied the country. Bowing to French diplomatic pressure, Jefferson ordered a full investigation. A federal grand jury indicted Samuel G. Ogden, the owner of the ship, and William S. Smith, surveyor of the Port of New York and son-in-law of John Adams.

The two men appealed their indictments to the Senate and House through memorials (statements of fact addressed to a government), arguing that if they had committed any crimes, they had done so with the full knowledge and support of the Jefferson administration. The Senate expunged its record of the memorials and debates surrounding the cases on its last day in session. The House voted out a four-part resolution that supported the administration's claim that it had not been involved in authorizing in any way the Miranda expedition.

But Ogden and Smith faced trial for arming a ship in violation of U.S. law. The defense attorneys subpoenaed Secretary of State James Madison, Secretary of War Henry Dearborn, and Secretary of the Navy Robert

Smith. The cabinet officers did not wish to testify in open court and offered to submit affidavits instead. The administration worried that the scandal might grow into something bigger if the men were forced to testify. The judge ruled that any testimony that they might offer would be moot, so they did not have to testify.

Smith and Ogden were acquitted of the charges in July 1807. Jefferson had already removed Smith from his post as surveyor. Jefferson also removed the marshal for the federal court in New York, John Swartwout, a loyal supporter of Burr and friend of Smith. Jefferson believed that Swartwout had packed the jury with Federalists who would be sympathetic to Ogden and Smith's claim that the administration had been involved.

JOSIAH QUINCY'S ATTEMPT TO IMPEACH JEFFERSON

Rep. Josiah Quincy attempted to impeach Jefferson on charges that he had refused to accept the resignation of a port collector because he wanted to save the post for a colleague.

Rep. Josiah Quincy of Massachusetts was perhaps the most vocal critic of Jefferson and his administration. He took great pleasure at embarrassing the president at every opportunity. On January 25, 1809, less than two months before Jefferson would leave office anyway, Quincy tried to impeach him. The House resolutions charged that for two years the president had repeatedly refused to accept the resignation of Benjamin Lincoln, the collector of the Port of Boston, because he wanted to hold the post open for Henry Dearborn, his secretary of war. According to Quincy, Jefferson wanted to wait until the end of his administration when Dearborn was no longer needed in the cabinet and then reward him with the lucrative post in Boston.

The House voted 93–24 to consider the allegations and requested all relevant correspondence between the parties. After an intense debate in which it was argued that Lincoln could have resigned whenever he wanted, that Jefferson had not committed any specific crime by wanting to hold the post for Dearborn, and that the House lacked jurisdiction in the case, the House voted 117–1 to reject the resolutions. Dearborn eventually became the collector for Boston.

Josiah Quincy

NEW ORLEANS BATTURE CASE

Jefferson was sued after he left office for a decision he made regarding a batture (the alluvial land between a river and a levee) on the Mississippi

River while he was president. He evicted the claimants to the property for squatting on public lands. The case raised the important issue of whether a president could be sued for his official decisions.

The New Orleans Batture case involved Edward Livingston and the government of the United States. The Batture St. Marie was a long shoal or beach formed by silt. For half a year the batture was covered with water and used as free anchorage, and for the other half it was a landing place and source of sand and dirt for the city. In 1803 Edward Livingston, a New York lawyer who was in default to the U.S. Treasury to the tune of $100,000, moved to New Orleans. He acquired a financial stake in the batture, which was considered public property, by taking up the legal case of the landholder fronting it. Estimates placed the value of the batture at more than $500,000. To the surprise of many, the territorial court, in 1807, ruled in Livingston's favor that the batture was an alluvium and as such the rightful property of the owner of the land bordering the river. The public outcry was intense, and, when Livingston proposed making improvements to the property that would alter the channel of the river and possibly put parts of New Orleans under water at times, the city was on the verge of a riot. Gov. William C. Claiborne of the Louisiana Territory—a Jefferson appointee—appealed to Washington to intervene because the batture, if it was public property, belonged to the U.S. government. In November 1807 Jefferson ordered Livingston's eviction, by force if necessary, as an intruder on the public lands. The administration took the position that the territorial court's decision was null because it did not have the jurisdiction to hear the case and the federal government had not been a party to the court's decision. Jefferson used the Squatters' Act of 1807 to remove Livingston.

Livingston went to Washington to plead his case and lobby members of Congress, but the president had already obtained the support of Congress on the matter. In May 1810, after Jefferson was out of office, Livingston filed suit against him in Richmond, Virginia, for trespass and claimed personal damages of $100,000. The case raised many questions, including whether a former president could be sued for actions he had taken in behalf of the public interest. Jefferson knew that the government would come to his rescue if necessary, but that he had to put on a defense to prevent the case from becoming a partisan scandal.

Jefferson engaged three prestigious Virginia attorneys—George Hay, William Wirt, and Littleton W. Tazewell—to argue the case for him. The defense became a study in the history of sovereign and riparian rights to navigable waters starting with Herodotus. In the end, the attorneys, with Jefferson's constant guidance, had developed three approaches: first, the land was public; second, executive officers must be given discretion when acting, even if in error, in the public interest; and, third, the Richmond court had no jurisdiction over an offense that had taken place in New Orleans. The third argument proved successful. Livingston had chosen the

Richmond federal circuit because Chief Justice John Marshall would be one of the judges to hear the case, and Livingston hoped to capitalize on the ill will between Jefferson and Marshall. However, Marshall and another judge ruled that they did not have jurisdiction.

Once the case was dismissed, Jefferson went on the offensive in shaping public opinion. He arranged for the printing and distribution of 250 copies of his side of the story, *The Proceedings of the Government of the United States in Maintaining the Public Right to the Beach of the Mississippi.* Jefferson argued that even if the batture was an alluvium it belonged to the United States. Further, he attacked the notion that any individual had the right to threaten the safety of the people of New Orleans by constructing so-called improvements on his land. Finally, Jefferson rejected the notion that he was personally liable for the decisions he had made as president, even if in error. Jefferson wrote, "If a functionary of the highest trust, acting under every sanction which the Constitution had provided for his aid and guide, and with the approbation, expressed or implied, of its highest councils, still acts on his own peril, the honors of his country would be but snares to ruin him."

Livingston, for his part, was unrelenting, and he too published a defense of his actions and a condemnation of the government's taking of his property. He eventually gained title to the batture and was able to settle his debt with the federal government in 1830. Beginning in 1831, Livingston served as secretary of state in the reorganized cabinet of Andrew Jackson, replacing Martin Van Buren who had resigned over the Eaton Affair (see page 59).

BIBLIOGRAPHY

Abernathy, Thomas P. *The Burr Conspiracy.* New York: Oxford University Press, 1954.

Brodie, Fawn M. *Thomas Jefferson: An Intimate History.* New York: Bantam Books, 1974.

Chase-Riboud, Barbara. *Sally Hemings.* New York: Avon, 1992.

Cox, Isaac J. "General Wilkinson and His Later Intrigues with the Spaniards." *American Historical Review* 19 (July 1914): 794–812.

Cunningham, Noble E., Jr. *In Pursuit of Reason: The Life of Thomas Jefferson.* Baton Rouge: Louisiana State University Press, 1987.

Dabney, Virginius. *The Jefferson Scandals: A Rebuttal.* New York: Dodd, Mead, 1981.

Gordon-Reed, Annette. *Thomas Jefferson and Sally Hemings: An American Controversy.* Charlottesville: University Press of Virginia, 1997.

Hagood, Wesley O. *Presidential Sex: From Founding Fathers to Bill Clinton.* Secaucus, N.J.: Carol Publishing Group, 1998.

Hatcher, William B. *Edward Livingston: Jeffersonian Republican and Jacksonian Democrat.* University, La.: Louisiana State University Press, 1940.

Hunt, Irma. *Dearest Madame: The President's Mistresses.* New York: McGraw-Hill, 1978.

Jacobs, James R. *Tarnished Warrior: Major General James Wilkinson.* New York: Macmillan, 1938.

Malone, Dumas. *Jefferson and His Time.* 6 volumes. Boston: Little, Brown, 1948–1981.

——. *Jefferson the President.* 2 volumes. Boston: Little, Brown, 1970–1974.

Mitchell, Jack. *Executive Privilege: Two Centuries of White House Scandals.* New York: Hippocrene Books, 1992.

Pancake, John S. "Aaron Burr: Would-be Usurper." *William and Mary Quarterly* 8 (April 1951): 204–213.

Peterson, Merrill D. *Thomas Jefferson & The New Nation.* New York: Oxford University Press, 1970.

Ross, Shelley. *Fall from Grace: Sex, Scandal and Corruption in American Politics from 1702 to the Present.* New York: Ballantine Books, 1988.

Schachner, Nathan. *Aaron Burr: A Biography.* New York: A. S. Barnes, 1937.

Woodward, C. Vann. *Responses of the Presidents to Charges of Misconduct.* New York: Dell Publishing, 1974.

JAMES MADISON

Fourth President
1809–1817

Born at the home of his grandparents at Port Conway, King George County, Virginia, on March 16, 1751, James Madison grew up in Orange County on a plantation that came to be known as Montpelier. From the age of eleven he studied under Donald Robertson, whom Madison credited with much of his later success. In 1769 he enrolled as a sophomore at the College of New Jersey (Princeton). After graduating, Madison stayed in Princeton to study theology and Hebrew under John Witherspoon until the spring of 1772.

Returning home, Madison began a study of law, but interrupted it when he was elected to the Committee of Safety for Orange County in 1774. In October 1775 he was commissioned a colonel in the county militia, but his poor health prevented him from seeing any action in the war. A delegate to the Virginia Convention in 1776, he served on the Privileges and Elections Committee. Once the new Virginia constitution was adopted, he served in the House of Delegates until 1777, when he was defeated for reelection.

He served on the council of state from 1778 to 1779, and became the youngest member of the Continental Congress in 1780. An advocate of a strong national government, Madison took on many leadership roles in his years of service. Once again elected to the House of Delegates in 1784, Madison led the fight against the establishment of the Episcopal church as the state church in Virginia.

As a delegate to the Annapolis Convention of 1786, which issued the call for the Philadelphia Constitutional Convention the following year, Madison played a major role in creating a new structure for the government. The Virginia Plan, the basis of the U.S. Constitution, was largely his work. In addition, his essays in the *Federalist Papers* explaining how the government would function helped to get the document ratified. He also led the successful fight for ratification in Virginia. His accomplishments earned him the title of Father of the Constitution.

In 1789 he was elected to the House of Representatives, defeating James Monroe. Originally one of George Washington's chief supporters in Congress, Madison soon began to side with Thomas Jefferson and his allies against the president and Alexander Hamilton. Madison served in the House until 1797. He married Dorothea Payne Todd, known as "Dolley," a widow with one son, on September 15, 1794.

Madison drafted the Virginia Resolutions that sought to void the Alien and Sedition Acts. In 1799 he was elected to the Virginia House of Delegates for the third time and served until Jefferson appointed him secretary of state, a position he held during both of Jefferson's terms (1801–1809). During this time, he oversaw the purchase of the Louisiana Territory from France and dealt with the British and French, whose navies routinely harassed American ships.

Jefferson openly favored Madison as his successor, but the nomination was in doubt as two other candidates, James Monroe and George Clinton, were also interested. In the end, Madison was the overwhelming choice to face the Federalist candidate, Charles Cotesworth Pinckney of South Carolina, who had run against Jefferson in 1804. Madison easily defeated Pinckney, winning twelve of seventeen states.

During his first term, Madison struggled to deal with deteriorating relations with Great Britain that would eventually lead to the War of 1812. He was reelected to a second term, defeating De Witt Clinton, the nephew of his vice president, George Clinton. Like Madison, De Witt Clinton was a Democratic-Republican. He was nominated by an anti-Madison wing of the party and supported by the Federalists, who did not field a candidate in 1812.

On June 1, 1812, President Madison formally asked Congress to declare war against Great Britain, and the hostilities lasted until 1814. The United States prevailed, but not before the British occupied Washington and burned many government buildings, including the Capitol and the White House. The Treaty of Ghent, signed December 24, 1814, ended the fighting but settled little else; Britain gave no guarantee that she would allow the safe passage of U.S. ships.

Madison also oversaw the chartering of the Second Bank of the United States in 1816. The bank remained in operation until President Andrew Jackson vetoed its reauthorization.

Madison retired to Montpelier in March 1817 where successive bad tobacco and wheat crops threatened his livelihood. In 1819 he was one of the organizers of the American Colonization Society that founded Liberia in West Africa as a colony for former American slaves. In addition, Madison worked closely with Jefferson to establish the University of Virginia and in 1826 succeeded Jefferson as rector. In 1829 he represented Orange County at the Virginia Constitutional Convention, where he tried to mediate the growing tensions between large slaveholders in the east and the frontiersmen of the west. He died June 28, 1836, after a six-month illness.

JAMES WILKINSON

During the Madison administration, James Wilkinson was once again investigated for being in the pay of the Spanish. He was also investigated for incompetence as a military officer both prior to and during the War of 1812.

James Wilkinson, who had been investigated several times during the Jefferson administration on suspicion that he was in the pay of the Spanish government, was again investigated by the U.S. House of Representatives in 1810. Wilkinson was cleared of any wrongdoing in the earlier probes, but still had a cloud of suspicion hanging over him. President Jefferson, rather than relieving Wilkinson of his command, simply transferred him to a new command in New Orleans. Thus, Madison inherited the problem.

The House examination continued to focus on whether Wilkinson had accepted money from the government of Spain. But rather than conducting a full investigation with a formal report, the House simply passed its preliminary findings on to President Madison for his review. Wilkinson took the unusual step of requesting a military court of inquiry. When Madison refused, Wilkinson asked that Madison order fourteen army officers to go to Washington to testify in his behalf. Madison also refused this request.

Late in 1810 the House debated Wilkinson's record and the charges that his inept or corrupt command was responsible for the unusually high mortality rate among his troops. The House debate did not result in any actions taken against the general. In 1811, however, Madison—based on the evidence provided to him by the House—authorized a court-martial on the same charges. When the military court cleared Wilkinson of any wrongdoing in December 1811, Madison restored Wilkinson to active duty.

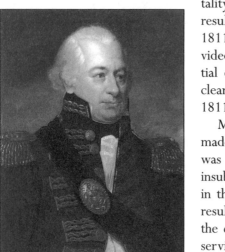

James Wilkinson

Madison made the same mistake that Jefferson had made in keeping Wilkinson. Despite his acquittals, it was clear that Wilkinson was an incompetent and insubordinate soldier. His inadequacies proved costly in the War of 1812. Again facing court-martial as a result of his disastrous command, he was acquitted on the charges of incompetence, but not reinstated for service. Madison had finally had enough of Wilkinson.

BIBLIOGRAPHY

Brant, Irving. *James Madison.* Indianapolis: Bobbs-Merrill, 1941–1961.

Jacobs, James R. *Tarnished Warrior: Major-General James Wilkinson.* New York: Macmillan, 1938.

Ketcham, Ralph. *James Madison: A Biography.* New York: Macmillan, 1971.

Rutland, Robert A. *James Madison: The Founding Father.* New York: Macmillan, 1987.

Woodward, C. Vann. *Responses of the Presidents to Charges of Misconduct.* New York: Dell Publishing, 1974.

JAMES MONROE

Fifth President
1817–1825

James Monroe was born April 28, 1758, in Westmoreland County, Virginia. He was the eldest son of Elizabeth and Spence Monroe, a planter of modest means. Little is known about James Monroe's childhood. He received a formal education at the Campbelltown Academy, which he attended from age eleven. At sixteen he entered the College of William and Mary at Williamsburg, Virginia. When his father died, James inherited his estate.

His studies at William and Mary were interrupted by the prospects of war. In 1775 Monroe was among a number of men who raided the governor's palace and stole more than 200 muskets and 300 swords with which the Williamsburg militia was armed. In March 1776 Monroe entered the Continental army as a lieutenant. He saw action in some of the most important and memorable battles of the Revolutionary War and was among the soldiers who crossed the Delaware with Washington on Christmas night. His service at Brandywine and Germantown in 1777 led to his promotion to major. He survived the brutal winter at Valley Forge in 1777 and 1778. Dissatisfied with his post as aide-de-camp to Gen. William Alexander (also known as Lord Stirling), Monroe resigned his commission and attempted to raise a company of Virginia volunteers. In 1780 Gov. Thomas Jefferson commissioned Monroe as a lieutenant colonel and appointed him military commissioner of Virginia.

Monroe began his political career in the Virginia Assembly in 1782. A year later he was elected to the Continental Congress, a post he held until 1786. During this time, Monroe also studied law under Jefferson's guidance. Admitted to the bar in 1786, Monroe practiced law until 1790. During the Virginia ratifying convention in 1788, he voted against the adoption of the Constitution, but sought a seat in the House of Representatives, which he lost to James Madison by 300 votes. In 1790 he was appointed to the U.S. Senate where he sided with Jefferson's Democratic-Republicans.

Appointed ambassador to France in 1794, Monroe found himself in a difficult position because he, like Jefferson, wanted to support France in her war with Britain, but Washington was neutral. As ambassador, Monroe secured the release of Thomas Paine, who had been imprisoned for his criticism of the execution of Louis XVI. Monroe also opposed the Jay Treaty, but did not say so in public. When he did not defend the treaty to French officials, however, he was recalled in 1796.

Monroe was elected governor of Virginia and served from 1799 to 1802. In 1803 President Jefferson appointed him special envoy to help negotiate the Louisiana Purchase, which added 828,000 square miles to the United States. Later that year, he became ambassador to Great Britain. With U.S.-British relations deteriorating, Monroe's tenure in London was rocky, but he served until 1807.

Monroe unsuccessfully sought the 1808 Democratic-Republican presidential nomination with the support of John Randolph and other southerners who disliked James Madison. He was elected governor of Virginia once again, but resigned in April 1811 to become Madison's secretary of state. As relations with Great Britain deteriorated, Monroe knew that war was on the horizon, but thought it was no worse than the current situation. During the War of 1812, in which the British burned Washington, D.C., Monroe served as secretary of war and as military commander of the district.

In 1816 Monroe handily defeated Sen. Rufus King of New York for the presidency. His election killed off the ailing Federalist Party, and for a brief period there was only one political party. The absence of an organized opposition meant that partisan politics was at a minimum, and a Boston newspaper described Monroe's first term as the "era of good feelings." During his administration, the Missouri Compromise, marking the boundary between slave and free states, was adopted. He also declared the Monroe Doctrine, which advised European powers that any attempts to establish new colonies or to interfere with independent nations in the Western Hemisphere would be regarded as unfriendly acts.

Monroe retired to an estate, Oak Hill in Loudoun County, Virginia, which Jefferson had designed for him. Badly in debt, Monroe pressed the federal government for money that he was owed for past service. In 1826 he was appointed to the board of regents of the University of Virginia. He served as president of the Virginia Constitutional Convention in 1829. After the death of his wife Elizabeth (married February 16, 1786) in 1830, he moved to New York City, where he lived with his daughter, Maria, and son-in-law, Samuel Gouverneurs. He died July 4, 1831.

FURNITURE FUND

After the White House and its furnishings were burned by the British in 1814, Congress established a fund to refurnish it. Because it would take months—perhaps as long as a year—to obtain quality furniture from Europe, President Monroe offered to lend his own furniture. However, soon after the agreement was made, Monroe began to use the furniture fund as a discretionary account.

The destruction of the White House in 1814 set off a train of events that would culminate in accusations of financial irregularity that troubled the final days of James Monroe's presidency. The White House not only needed to be rebuilt, but also it needed to be restocked with furniture of sufficient quality for a head of state. With that in mind, on March 3, 1817, the day before Monroe's inauguration, Congress established a furniture fund of $20,000 to be spent as the new president wished.

Monroe appointed two men to oversee the fund: William Lee, second auditor of the Treasury, was to make the plans and purchase the furniture, and Samuel Lane, commissioner of public buildings, was to control the fund and disburse the money. The choice of Lane was to prove unfortunate, but Monroe may have had little choice. Congress had not voted money for staff to oversee the refurbishing, so neither Lee nor Lane would be paid for their work.

Lee quickly determined that the proper furniture could not be found in the United States and that they would have to turn to France. The items would have to be ordered from abroad, built, and then shipped across the Atlantic on slow sailing vessels. There was no way that anything would arrive in time for the diplomatic receptions of the next fall. Monroe then suggested that his own furniture be used. He had purchased much of it in Europe and had planned to sell the pieces eventually. The new purchases

British troops in front of a burning White House in 1814. The ruin of the interior and all of the furnishings led to the first major scandal of the Monroe administration.

were proving more expensive than Congress had thought, so the entire fund and more was going to be needed.

In the meantime, the White House would have some furniture to meet the immediate needs, and, if Congress voted additional money, Monroe's furniture could be purchased in addition to the pieces already ordered from Europe. If not, he promised to take the things back, absorbing the loss in wear and tear. In May 1817 Monroe's furniture was assessed at just over $9,000. At that point the problems began: even though Monroe had said that payment could be delayed, Lane immediately gave him $6,000 from the furniture fund. Later, the fact that only a few knew about this deal would create the impression that all was not as it should be.

Monroe needed the money to finance a domestic tour that was partly political and partly tied to his presidential responsibilities. He had to meet the expenses himself because Congress did not yet fund such travels. Monroe paid for his trip with the furniture money and in the fall returned the $6,000 to the fund. With his furniture as collateral, he had, in effect, used government money as an interest-free loan. In his defense, Monroe could point out that he was also loaning his furniture without charging for damages.

The problem then deepened. With the furniture fund in debt by almost $11,000, Monroe was forced to appeal to Congress for more money. Unfortunately, while Lee was quick to tell Congress how generous Monroe had been to lend his furniture, he did not tell the members how the president had been using the money. Congress appropriated $30,000 on April 20, 1818. Four days later, Monroe wrote Lane altering his original offer. He claimed that he no longer wanted to sell his furniture. He would let the government use it in exchange for an interest-free loan to be repaid when enough new furniture had arrived. Monroe later explained that he had not really intended to take back his now well-worn furniture. Instead, he was thinking of the possibility of his death. He would get money now for necessary expenses, but, if he died before it was paid back, he felt certain that Congress would write off the debt.

Monroe spent the money for additional travel, and in 1821 he quietly altered what had been the loan into a payment to himself. Monroe did cover his actions with one additional provision. When he left office, he promised to ask Congress to approve the sale. If it did not, he would return the money and take his furniture. He even set aside funds to be used for repayment if he died.

Although Monroe was being less than candid with Congress, he was not engaging in any wrongdoing. But another furniture fund transaction was more dubious. Both the furniture and 1,200 bottles of champagne and other wine needed for White House entertaining were ordered from the same French merchant and billed together. Because Congress did not fund presidential entertainment, Monroe should have paid for the wine out of his own pocket. Instead, apparently without informing Monroe, Lane used

the furniture fund to pay for it. The problem might not have been discovered—at least while Monroe was still in office—if Lane had not died in
1822. When his estate was settled, that error was discovered along with
the fact that some $20,000 of other public money was unaccounted for. In
addition, it appeared that over the years Lane had covered thousands of
dollars of Monroe's expenses out of his own funds.

Twice, Congress appointed a committee to investigate Lane's finances.
Neither resolved the problem, and throughout Monroe insisted that when
Congress had appropriated the money for the furniture fund, the money
became his to spend as he chose. He may have been right, but his behavior
left an impression that he had something to hide.

Finally in January 1825, just before he left office, Monroe called on
Congress to do a full investigation of all his finances since he had entered
public service in 1794. The investigation proved nothing: the records were
so erratically kept that nothing *could* be proved from them. But in the end
both Congress and the general public were satisfied that Monroe had simply been too focused on public affairs to notice what Lane was doing.

YELLOWSTONE EXPEDITION

*The War Department under John C. Calhoun awarded a contract to James
Johnson to provision an expedition to the West and establish a post where the
Missouri and Yellowstone Rivers meet. Johnson was a brother of Rep. Richard
M. Johnson, Calhoun's friend and a future vice president. The original expedition was to cost $12,000. However, Johnson kept coming back for more
money, and Calhoun continued to authorize the expenditures ($71,000). As
the popularity of the expedition grew, President Monroe asked Calhoun to
authorize an additional $142,500. Even with funding at this level, the
whole adventure was abandoned as too expensive.*

When a vigorous young John Calhoun took over the War Department
in 1818, he threw his support behind a brilliant plan to build a system of
coastal and frontier forts supplied by enough waterways and roads for the
rapid transport of troops from one region to another. If successful, the
project would provide the nation with the sort of defense it had so sadly
lacked during the War of 1812.

The frontier posts had additional purposes. The plan's supporters
accepted the fact that white settlers would be moving westward as the century advanced. Whether their movement would be peaceful or not
depended on whether good relations with the Indians could be maintained. The posts, placed far in advance of white settlement, were not to
be heavily garrisoned. Instead, they were to keep peace with the Indians by
carrying out three policies. First, they would prevent British traders from
coming down from Canada and stirring up trouble among the Indians. Second, they would allow the government to regulate trade with the Indians,
preventing their exploitation by fur traders all too eager to use liquor and

all too willing to see the tribes exterminated. Third, it was hoped that with the assistance of the posts, the Indians would have thirty years to prepare for the settlements. However, fur trading interests, from the wealthy John Jacob Astor down to the lowly wilderness trapper, strongly objected to proposed government regulation of their business.

One part of the plan called for the establishment of a post where the Yellowstone River joins the Missouri River (near the Montana-North Dakota border). For that purpose, an expedition was to be mounted and its provisions were to be supplied by a government contractor. By modern standards, the contract would not pass muster. The contractor, James Johnson, was a brother of Kentucky congressman Richard M. Johnson, who was, in turn, chairman of the House Committee on Military Affairs and a friend of Calhoun's. In

John Calhoun

the early nineteenth century, however, such arrangements were not unusual. Calhoun later justified his failure to put the contract out for bid by claiming that the government could not publicize the movement of troops.

Indeed, there was no reason to believe that James Johnson would not do a good job. He had a reputation as a dependable and experienced contractor. During the War of 1812, he had done an excellent job feeding Andrew Jackson's army in New Orleans, and in 1818 he had supply contracts with government posts that totaled almost $200,000.

Some of Johnson's difficulties stemmed from the uncertainties of trying to transport large quantities of supplies on poorly mapped rivers. Other problems arose when the normal difficulty of financing any large-scale enterprise on the frontier, where banks were few and unreliable, was compounded by a financial crisis in the West in 1819. In fact, the first indication the expedition was in trouble came when, after getting the usual War Department advance, Johnson asked for another $12,000 to cover money lost when one of his subcontractors defaulted. Finally, while the expedition was very popular on the fringes of civilization, the further inland it moved, the more hostility it met from those who quite rightly suspected the new posts would stop their exploitation of the Indians.

When Johnson demanded an additional $50,000, Calhoun became worried. He became even more upset when Monroe, who was traveling in more settled parts of the West, found that the expedition was politically popular and told Calhoun to give it another $142,500. In the end, the rising expenses and difficulties with the four steamboats hired to transport supplies forced the expedition to a halt. No one involved benefited, least of all Johnson, who was forced to sell off properties to cover debts he had acquired. The task had simply been beyond his abilities. Perhaps unfairly, its failure discredited both the president and his secretary of war.

Along with the controversy surrounding the Elijah Mix contract (see below), the failure of the Yellowstone expedition would play into the hands of Calhoun's foe, the ambitious William Crawford, secretary of the Treasury. Crawford had two reasons for wanting to discredit Calhoun and his plan. First, Calhoun, young and popular, posed a serious threat to the aging Crawford's hopes for winning the presidency in 1824. Second, Crawford and his followers believed that the nation was spending too much money on defense. Adopting the same tactic he would later use against Sen. Ninian Edwards in the A. B. papers controversy (see page 47), Crawford went on the attack. Through friends in Congress, the War Department was repeatedly called upon to investigate or explain some detail or another. Discovering actual fraud was less important to Crawford and his allies than convincing the public that something was wrong with the defense budget. Aiding Crawford was the fact that, with the nation in recession, people were in no mood to see money spent on distant military posts, where the benefits, if any, would be realized decades in the future.

Aided by the failure of the Yellowstone expedition, the attacks by Crawford and his congressional allies had their desired effect. Calhoun's plan for gradually and peacefully bringing Indians into the expanding nation was abandoned. Calhoun's biographer, Charles Wiltse, had this to say about the result: "It was a far-sighted policy which might have saved a vast deal of bloodshed had it been adopted; but it was more than fifty years before any part of it became law, and well over a century before it was finally put into practice." Frontier posts would not advance ahead of settlements, protecting the Indians from white exploitation. Instead, they would follow settlers to crush the resistance of Indians who had learned through bitter experience to distrust the white man.

ELIJAH MIX CONTRACT

The War Department's chief clerk, Maj. Christopher Van Deventer, authorized a contract, with Secretary of War John Calhoun's knowledge, for his brother-in-law, Elijah Mix, to build fortifications in Virginia. Although the practice was not illegal, Congress investigated the actions because Van Deventer had a personal financial stake in the operation.

Calhoun's War Department continued to be a source of controversial practices. In July 1818 the department's chief clerk, Maj. Christopher Van Deventer, signed a contract with his brother-in-law, Elijah Mix, for the provision of stone for the construction of fortifications near Old Point Comfort, Virginia. There was nothing illegal in Van Deventer's awarding the contract to his brother-in-law, but Mix's bid was so low that he could not secure a bond for the project. Van Deventer helped to secure the contract and its bond by putting up one-fourth of the money.

Secretary Calhoun warned Van Deventer that he would be held responsible if Mix failed to live up to the contract's demands. In April 1819 Van Deventer increased his holding of the contract by another quarter. In the fall, he sold his entire interest in the project.

President Monroe had received an anonymous letter charging that Van Deventer had a personal stake in the contract, a clear conflict of interest. Monroe turned the letter over to Calhoun, who once again warned Van Deventer of the dire consequences of Mix's failure. A witness overheard Calhoun warn Van Deventer.

Congress got wind of the situation and began an official investigation. The House requested all documents pertaining to the contract and in 1822, after a lengthy investigation, censured Van Deventer for his actions and publicly criticized the War Department's procurement practices. The issue resurfaced after Calhoun had become vice president, when letters published in December 1826 in the *Alexandria Gazette* charged him with a conflict of interest.

THE A. B. PLOT

In a series of anonymous letters, Monroe's secretary of the Treasury, William Crawford, was charged with mismanagement and corruption in dealing with deposits of the federal government. Three congressional investigations never fully confirmed nor dismissed the allegations, which implicated other members of the cabinet, including John C. Calhoun and John Quincy Adams as well as President Monroe himself.

On January 20, 1823, a letter signed "A. B." was printed in the *Washington Republican*. It was addressed to Joseph Gales and William Seaton, printers to Congress, but its purpose was to attack William Crawford, Monroe's secretary of the Treasury and the man considered most likely to win the 1824 presidential election.

From the beginning, politics would play a major role in the ensuing scandal. The *Washington Republican* represented Democratic-Republicans who backed John Calhoun's presidential candidacy. For many of those who backed Calhoun or John Quincy Adams, the letter and those that followed proved that Crawford was morally unfit for public office. For those who supported Crawford, the attacks were unjustified and were part of a plot to discredit him.

The allegations against Crawford fit into two categories. The first to come to public attention was of a partial cover up, and there the evidence was undeniable. A year earlier Secretary Crawford had submitted to Congress a report detailing how the Treasury had handled money received from the sale of public land. "Yet it is a fact," A. B. claimed, "that parts of those documents implicating Mr. Crawford the most strongly, were suppressed." Examination proved the charge to be correct. The printed version did not follow the originals: five major portions had been omitted. A Treasury Department clerk, Asbury Dickens, took responsibility for four deletions, claiming (wrongly) that the passages were not relevant to the investigation. He had no explanation for the fifth deletion.

Examination of the fifth led to the second category of charges, that Crawford had violated the law by displaying favoritism toward some western banks. The evidence was found in an April 1819 letter from the Bank of Steubenville to Crawford. The bank had been in financial trouble, which worsened when two United States banks demanded that it pay the notes they were holding. The letter thanked Crawford for doing more than they had asked, when, rather than redeeming the bank notes, he had them transferred to the Steubenville bank, allowing it to hold its own bad notes.

Even worse was an earlier letter to that same bank in which he said that he was looking into ways to use western bank funds that had depreciated in value to pay for road construction contracts. That meant the bad bank notes would be unloaded by converting them into more expensive contracts whose cost would be borne by the War Department.

Congress responded by appointing a committee to investigate. In the House, the debate was dominated by Rep. Daniel P. Cook of Illinois, a supporter of John Quincy Adams. Cook publicly denied being the author of the controversial letters. He stated, however, that the author was known to him and was a member of Congress. We now know that A. B. was Cook's father-in-law, Sen. Ninian Edwards, also of Illinois. Although the committee report was weak, it uncovered favoritism in the way public money had been deposited in state banks. Even with Crawford's supporters trying to blame the controversy on a conspiracy, enough evidence reached the public to damage Crawford's popularity. In an April letter, Calhoun happily noted that Crawford's supporters were "much broken" and their chief "much depressed."

In February 1824 Senator Edwards was nominated ambassador to Mexico. By then his participation in the plot was suspected, and Crawford's congressional supporters threatened to block his appointment. Then something odd happened: the opposition vanished, and Edwards was approved with a large majority.

What happened next looks suspiciously like a conspiracy. On the eve of Edwards's departure for Mexico, Crawford provided Congress with the report and correspondence it had requested more than a year earlier. The timing was not accidental. It allowed Crawford's defenders to claim (as they did) that Edwards had left the country rather than deal with the evidence. The report contained what one historian termed "the lie direct," but about something Edwards could easily refute.

William Crawford

Unfortunately for Crawford, their timing was slightly off. Edwards found out about the report and delayed his departure for a day to collect material for a response, which he wrote as he traveled westward by stage. In an April 6 letter he admitted to writing the A. B. letters, claimed that the congressional investigations had been superficial, and leveled six charges against Crawford.

At this point, Congress should have conducted a full-scale investigation. Unfortunately, Henry Clay was appointed to head the investigating committee. Suspecting that Crawford's ill health would force him from the presidential race, Clay began to court Crawford's supporters in the hope that they would turn to him as their candidate. Instead of investigating Crawford, the committee demanded that Edwards return to the capital. Adams was furious, charging that the fuss about Edwards was intended "to excite odium against him as an accuser, and to prepare for a whitewashing of Crawford."

When Edwards returned, the debate turned ugly. Sen. James Noble of Indiana claimed that Edwards had told him that he did not write the A. B. papers and that he actually admired the way Crawford had handled the western banks. Noble claimed that Edwards had intended the remark to ensure his confirmation. The testimony of others was confused, but the most likely explanation is that Edwards never made the remarks that Noble claimed. (He was ill and kept to his room the day he was said to have made them.) Those who thought Edwards made similar remarks were probably confusing two things, denying authorship of the A. B. papers and denying any plot. The confusion was an easy one to make. Crawford's critics had always denied that a plot existed, and his defenders had always tried to connect the papers to an alleged plot.

As Adams suspected, Crawford's defenders were able to use Edwards to divert attention away from their man. Monroe's own weakness and the zeal of some to please Crawford meant that Edwards was discredited and forced to resign. But Edwards's efforts did not go unappreciated. When he was not invited to the Capitol dinner on July 4, 1824, Adams, Calhoun, and Postmaster General John McLean made public their refusal to attend. In the next election the citizens of Illinois chose Edwards as their governor.

BIBLIOGRAPHY

Ammon, Harry. *James Monroe: The Quest for National Identity*. New York: McGraw-Hill, 1971.

Cunningham, Noble E. *The Presidency of James Monroe*. Lawrence: University Press of Kansas, 1996.

Cutler, Wayne. "The A. B. Controversy." *Mid-America* (January 1960).

Meyer, Leland W. *The Life and Times of Colonel Richard M. Johnson of Kentucky*. New York: Columbia University Press, 1932.

Mitchell, Jack. *Executive Privilege: Two Centuries of White House Scandals.* New York: Hippocrene Books, 1992.

Mooney, Chase C. *William H. Crawford, 1772–1834.* Lexington: University Press of Kentucky, 1974.

Wilmerding, Lucius, Jr. "James Monroe and the Furniture Fund." *New York Historical Society Quarterly* (April 1960).

———-. *James Monroe: Public Claimant.* New Brunswick, N.J.: Rutgers University Press, 1960.

Wiltse, Charles M. *John C. Calhoun, Nationalist, 1782–1828.* Indianapolis: Bobbs-Merrill, 1944.

———-. "John C. Calhoun and the A. B. Plot." *The Journal of Southern History 13* (February 1947): 46–61.

Woodward, C. Vann. *Responses of the Presidents to Charges of Misconduct.* New York: Dell Publishing, 1974.

JOHN QUINCY ADAMS

Sixth President
1825–1829

orn July 11, 1767, John Quincy Adams was the eldest son of John
Adams, the second president of the United States. From age ten to
seventeen, he lived in various cities in Europe, where his father
served as a diplomat. He continued the excellent education he had
received at home from his parents and his father's law clerks at schools in
Paris and Amsterdam. Returning to the United States in 1785, Adams,
who had mastered Latin, Greek, French, Dutch, and Spanish, studied
under his uncle John Shaw before being admitted to Harvard as a junior.
Graduating in 1787, Adams placed second in his class. For the next two
years he studied law under Theophilus Parsons at Newburyport, Massachusetts, and was admitted to the bar in July 1790.

Adams practiced law, but had few clients. In 1794 President George
Washington appointed him ambassador to the Netherlands. His chief duty
was to see that the repayment of Dutch debt went smoothly. In 1797
Washington appointed him ambassador to Portugal, but when John Adams
became president, the appointment was changed to minister to Prussia.
Also that year, Adams married Louisa Catherine Johnson, the daughter of
an American merchant and English mother who had grown up in England
and France. In Berlin, he negotiated the Prussian-American Treaty of 1799
and continued to report on events in Europe.

Returning to the United States in 1801 after Thomas Jefferson became
president, Adams began his legislative career as a Federalist. He was elected to the Massachusetts Senate in 1802. Winning over Timothy Pickering
in a race for the U.S. Senate in 1803, Adams was supportive of the Democratic-Republican president and was the only member of the Federalist
Party in Congress to favor the Louisiana Purchase. Because he backed Jefferson, Adams was not reelected in 1808 and resigned in June.

President James Madison appointed Adams ambassador to Russia in
1809. In St. Petersburg, Adams succeeded in securing the release of American ships being held in Denmark as well as a promise of neutrality for

American ships entering Russian ports. Preferring to remain in the foreign service, Adams declined a seat on the U.S. Supreme Court. Adams headed the delegation that negotiated the Treaty of Ghent in 1814, which brought a formal end to the War of 1812. He then served as ambassador to Great Britain from 1815 to 1817.

The gifted American diplomat again returned to the United States in 1817 to assume responsibilities as secretary of state during James Monroe's administration. During this time, he was instrumental in settling the northern border of the United States with Canada. He conducted successful negotiations with Spain on the transfer of the Floridas to the United States. He helped the president formulate the Monroe Doctrine, a warning to European nations of the consequences of interfering with nations in the Western Hemisphere. Adams served as secretary of state from 1817 to 1825 with great distinction.

With the Federalist Party almost out of existence, the Democratic-Republicans were the only significant political party. However, the party's nominating caucus in Congress no longer had the power it once enjoyed. It picked William H. Crawford of Georgia as the party's nominee, but the caucus was attended by fewer than one-third of those eligible. Indeed, several state caucuses refused to go along with the congressional caucus's choice. Adams's supporters rallied at Faneuil Hall in Boston in February 1824 to secure his nomination. The Massachusetts legislature formally endorsed Adams on June 10, and the rest of New England followed shortly thereafter. Henry Clay of Kentucky and Andrew Jackson of Tennessee had also received their home states' nominations as well as the support of other western states.

The election had no clear issues and turned instead on sectional loyalties and personalities. Jackson won a plurality of both the popular vote and electoral votes, but he did not have enough electoral votes to win. The election was thrown into the House of Representatives, which selected Adams after Clay—who was in fourth place and dropped from contention—threw his support to Adams. John C. Calhoun, Crawford's running mate, easily won the post of vice president.

During his administration, Adams sought to make internal improvements through an ambitious program of road and canal construction. He also proposed higher tariffs on imported manufactured goods that came to be known to its critics as the Tariff of Abominations (1828). Adams was soundly defeated for reelection by Andrew Jackson in 1828.

In 1830, after a year in retirement, Adams was elected to the House of Representatives on the Anti-Masonic Party ticket, becoming the only former president ever to serve in the House. Adams switched his party affiliation to the newly formed Whig Party and spent the next seventeen years in the House.

Although he was not an abolitionist, in 1844 he succeeded in having the so-called gag rule (1836) repealed. The rule had prevented debate on slavery from being brought to the floor of the House. He had also argued the case of black mutineers aboard the ship *Amistad* before the Supreme Court in 1841 and succeeded in securing their release from prison.

Often in the minority, he supported the rechartering of the Bank of the United States, which Jackson killed with a veto. Adams voted against war with Mexico in 1846 and opposed the annexation of Texas. He also led the fight for the acceptance of the gift of James Smithson of England for the establishment of the Smithsonian Institution. The bill was signed into law by President James K. Polk in 1846. The former president earned the respect of his political friends and enemies alike in his second career as a member of Congress. He was given the nickname "Old Man Eloquent" in the process.

On February 21, 1848, Adams suffered a severe stroke after vigorously opposing the awarding of medals to certain generals for their service in the Mexican War. He was paralyzed on his right side and is reported to have said, "This is the end of earth," followed by either, "but I am composed," or "I am content." He then slipped into a coma from which he did not recover. He died two days later.

ELECTION OF 1824

The election of 1824 was the first in which a candidate who did not win a plurality of the popular vote was elected president. In a three-way race, John Quincy Adams was selected by the House of Representatives to serve as president. Adams's chief opponent, Andrew Jackson, accused Adams of stealing the election by engaging in a "corrupt bargain" with Henry Clay, another of the candidates. According to Jackson, Clay threw his support behind Adams in return for a high-ranking post in the administration.

The election results for 1824 did not produce a winning candidate; none of the four reached the necessary 131 electoral college votes. Andrew Jackson of Tennessee had mustered 41 percent of the popular vote and 99 electoral votes, John Quincy Adams had won 31 percent of the popular vote and 84 electoral votes. Henry Clay of Kentucky had garnered 13 percent of the popular vote, and William Crawford of Georgia won 11 percent, but Crawford had collected 41 electoral votes and Clay 37. With no candidate having a majority of the electoral college, the election was sent to the House of Representatives, as provided by the Constitution, where each state would be allowed one vote. Clay was dropped from the balloting, as only the top three finishers were sent to the House.

Both Jackson and Adams began the process of lobbying for support. Adams knew that even if he won in the House, the election would be divisive. There was even some talk of civil war. On January 1, 1825, Rep. Robert P. Letcher of Kentucky told Adams that he had the support of the Kentucky delegation. On January 9, Clay informed Adams that he supported him over Jackson and promised to work for Adams's election in the

House. Clay saw Adams as the least of three potential evils and could agree with him on some future plans, including higher tariffs and improvements to the nation's infrastructure.

Adams was not enthusiastic about the prospects of winning. He wrote, "To me the alternatives are both distressing in prospect, and the most formidable is that of success. All the danger is on the pinnacle. The humiliation of failure will be so much more compensated by the safety in which it will leave me that I ought to regard it as a consummation devoutly to be wished, and hope to find consolation in it."

Adams was caught in the middle. On the one hand, Clay and his supporters expected to be rewarded for their support. On the other hand, Jackson and Crawford made it clear that if Clay were rewarded with a high post in an Adams administration, there would be widespread public anger over a corrupt bargain. Jackson and Crawford even considered uniting forces to secure the presidency for Jackson. However, their efforts failed. On the day of the House vote on February 9, Adams had the support of thirteen state delegations to Jackson's seven and Crawford's four. Carrying the six New England states and New York, Adams also was delivered Kentucky, Missouri, and Ohio from Clay and managed to take Louisiana, Illinois, and Maryland from Jackson.

Jackson and his supporters immediately complained that a corrupt bargain had been made between Adams and Clay in which Clay was rewarded with the post of secretary of state in exchange for Clay's states. The Jacksonians were successful in convincing most of the country that a corrupt swap had taken place and that the popular will of the people had been ignored. Both Clay and Adams denied that there had ever been any talk of a quid pro quo. Clay even challenged to a duel the anonymous author of a letter in a Philadelphia newspaper to protect his honor. The author of the offending letter, which did not stay anonymous long, was Rep. George Kremer of Pennsylvania, who said he was willing to substantiate his charges, but failed to do so during a House investigation.

Andrew Jackson did not let go of the issue. In 1827 he charged that Rep. James Buchanan of Pennsylvania had tried to make a similar deal with Jackson on Clay's behalf. However, Buchanan denied that he was an agent of Clay's, claiming he had approached the general only as a friend of Jackson.

In the end, there was little, if any, proof of a corrupt bargain or even a gentlemen's agreement about the election. However, the charges were damaging enough to cripple the Adams administration from the very beginning.

ELECTION OF 1828

The campaign of 1828 was particularly unpleasant. Both Adams and Jackson were subjected to attacks on their personal lives as well as their records of service.

The campaign of 1828 was one of the nastiest on record in American history, with both sides leveling accusations (some true) at each other at a furious pace. Because Jackson had lost in 1824 because of what many believed to be a corrupt bargain, his supporters in the press constantly reminded the public of the stolen election. They accused Adams of being a monarchist who had engaged in premarital sex with his wife, whom they claimed was illegitimate. The Jacksonian press even accused Adams of having secured sexual partners for the Russian czar, Alexander I, because Adams had recommended a young American woman to work as a nursemaid in the czar's household. This charge resulted from a number of letters the nursemaid wrote to her family in which she described the czar's sexual adventures. Adams was also accused of having low morals because he had installed a billiard table in the White House and swam nude in the Potomac River. Adams had, indeed, installed a billiard table in the White House and did swim nude in the Potomac—a practice he continued well into his late seventies when he was a member of Congress.

Adams's supporters were not above the mudslinging. They claimed that Jackson's mother had been a prostitute and that he was the illegitimate son of a mixed race man named Jack. The more irresponsible elements of Adams's press even said that Jackson had a brother who was a slave. His military career was portrayed in the worst possible manner, making him appear a butcher. The charge that struck hardest was that Jackson was a home wrecker and a seducer who persuaded his wife, Rachel, to desert her first husband. Rachel was charged with being an adulterer and bigamist, charges that were technically true as she had not received a valid divorce before marrying Jackson in the Natchez Territory in 1791. The couple remarried in 1794 to correct the invalidation of their first marriage (see page 58).

The campaign was a bitter one with both sides walking away battered and bruised.

BIBLIOGRAPHY

Bemis, Samuel F. *John Quincy Adams: Foundations of American Foreign Policy.* New York: Knopf, 1949.

Falkner, Leonard. *The President Who Wouldn't Retire: John Quincy Adams, Congressman from Massachusetts.* New York: Coward-McCann, 1967.

Mitchell, Jack. *Executive Privilege: Two Centuries of White House Scandals.* New York: Hippocrene Books, 1992.

Morgan, William G. "John Quincy Adams versus Andrew Jackson: Their Biographers and the 'Corrupt Bargain' Charge." *Tennessee Historical Quarterly* (Spring 1967).

Nagel, Paul C. *John Quincy Adams: A Public Life, A Private Life.* New York: Knopf, 1997.

Stenberg, Richard R. "Jackson, Buchanan and the 'Corrupt Bargain' Calumny."
    Pennsylvania Magazine of History and Biography (1934).

Wiltse, Charles M. *John C. Calhoun, Nationalist, 1782–1828*. Indianapolis: Bobbs-
    Merrill, 1944.

Woodward, C. Vann. *Responses of the Presidents to Charges of Misconduct*. New York:
    Dell Publishing, 1974.

ANDREW JACKSON

Seventh President
1829–1837

Andrew Jackson was born March 16, 1767, on his family's farm at Waxhaw, South Carolina. He was the youngest of three boys born to Andrew and Elizabeth Jackson, who had emigrated from Ireland. Several days before young Andrew's birth, his father died from an injury sustained on the farm. The boy was raised by his mother, with the help of an uncle and older brother.

Andrew had learned to read by the time he was five, but received only a rudimentary education at a country school. At age thirteen Andrew and his brother Robert joined the militia and fought in the Revolutionary War. They were wounded and made prisoners of war by the British in 1781. Andrew was abused by a British officer and scarred on the hand from a saber blow.

At the age of seventeen, Andrew moved to Salisbury, North Carolina, where he read law for two years. In 1788 he went to Nashville, Tennessee, to serve as public prosecutor. An outstanding young lawyer, he was also fiercely jealous of his honor; he engaged in brawls and killed several men in duels for insulting his wife, Rachel.

In 1796, when Tennessee became a state, Jackson was elected its first representative to the House of Representatives, where he served a single term. He was appointed to fill a vacancy in the U.S. Senate from November 1797 to April 1798. He returned to Tennessee and served on the state superior court until 1804.

Nicknamed "Old Hickory" for his toughness in battle, Jackson saw active combat during the War of 1812 as a major general in the Tennessee militia. By March 1814 he was promoted to major general in the regular army. He became a national hero when his troops defeated the British at New Orleans in 1815.

Jackson returned to politics in 1823, when he was once again appointed a U.S. senator. In 1824 he became the front-runner for the Democratic Party's presidential nomination. He was unsuccessful in that election; even though he received more of the popular vote than any other candidate, he did not have a majority of electoral votes. In the House of Representatives the second place finisher, John Quincy Adams, was elected president when Henry Clay threw his support behind him.

In 1828, however, Jackson won the presidency and served two terms. In his first annual message to Congress, Jackson recommended eliminating the electoral college, which had cost him the 1824 election. He also objected to officeholders who seemed to enjoy life tenure; he believed instead that offices should rotate among deserving applicants. Jackson was a polarizing figure, often portrayed as "King Andrew I" in cartoons. The volatile political climate fostered the rise of two cohesive political parties—the Democrats, who supported Jackson and his policies, and the Whigs, who opposed him.

Unlike previous presidents, Jackson did not defer to Congress in policy making. In fact, he used his powers of party leadership and the veto to shape policy to his agenda. The greatest political battle of his administration centered on the Second Bank of the United States. The two leading Whigs, Henry Clay and Daniel Webster, led the fight for its recharter in Congress. "The bank," Jackson told Martin Van Buren, "is trying to kill me, but I will kill it!" Jackson vetoed the rechartering.

In 1832 he was reelected with more than 56 percent of the popular vote and almost five times as many electoral votes as his opponent, Clay. During his second term, Jackson continued to fight Congress and powerful leaders including his own vice president, John C. Calhoun, who headed a faction trying to get a reduction in a high protective tariff. When South Carolina undertook to nullify the tariff, Jackson ordered armed forces to Charleston and privately threatened to hang Calhoun. Violence seemed imminent until Clay negotiated a compromise: tariffs were lowered, and South Carolina dropped nullification.

Jackson exercised the veto twelve times; his six predecessors combined had used it only ten times. But Jackson and his populist sentiments had great impact on American politics. With his support, Martin Van Buren was elected president in 1836. However, Van Buren also inherited the economic impact of Jackson's veto of the bank. The depression that struck in 1837 was due in part to the lack of a sound banking system. After he left office, Jackson returned to Nashville and his home, the Hermitage. He died there in June 1845.

RACHEL JACKSON

Jackson's original marriage to Rachel Donelson Robards was invalid, making Rachel a bigamist—a charge leveled during the election of 1828. Rachel Robards thought she was divorced from her first husband at the time, but she was wrong.

In August 1791 Andrew Jackson married Rachel Donelson Robards in Natchez, Mississippi. Their marriage was on shaky ground from the beginning. First, as Protestants marrying in Spanish territory, they had failed to request and to receive permission from the Roman Catholic church to marry. However, more disastrous was the fact that Rachel was still married to Capt. Lewis Robards at the time.

Rachel Jackson

Rachel had married Robards in 1785, and the union was anything but happy. Robards was an insanely jealous man, who often accused his wife of marital infidelity. After several separations and reconciliations, Rachel left her Kentucky home to live with relatives. In her company was a young boarder in her household, Andrew Jackson.

Robards challenged Jackson to a fistfight and, when Jackson countered with the offer of a duel, Robards backed down. Robards wrote to Rachel in the fall of 1790 that the Virginia courts had agreed to an annulment. In fact, his divorce petition had been denied. In late 1793, a friend, John Overton, informed Jackson that Robards had only recently (September 27 of that year) been granted a divorce on the grounds that his wife was living in adultery with Jackson.

Rachel and Andrew renewed their marriage vows on January 18, 1794, in Nashville, but the damage was done. Jackson would spend years defending his wife's honor in duels. Killing several men, Jackson himself was shot by an opponent named Charles Dickason in 1806. The bullet remained in Jackson's body the rest of his life. Dickason was shot dead.

Jackson's marriage was used against him in his bid for the White House. His opponents were merciless in their attacks, labeling him an adulterer and his wife a bigamist. Political cartoons, campaign slogans, and pamphlets all drew attention to the details (and exaggerations) of the events. His campaign printed numerous pamphlets defending her honor. The gossip took its toll on Rachel, who was ill, and she died of a heart attack in December 1828, three months before Jackson's inauguration. At her funeral, Jackson said, "In the presence of this dear saint, I can and do forgive my enemies. But those vile wretches who have slandered her must look to God for mercy."

PEGGY EATON

Peggy Eaton was the wife of John Eaton, a friend of Jackson's from Tennessee. Eaton was appointed secretary of war in Jackson's administration, but his wife became such a controversial figure that the entire cabinet resigned except for one member. Peggy Eaton had a reputation for promiscuity, which caused Washington society to shun her. President Jackson held a special meeting to resolve the "petticoat war," but he was unsuccessful.

Peggy O'Neale Eaton was the daughter of a Washington, D.C., tavern owner and keeper of the Franklin House inn. Early in her life she had earned a reputation as the kind of girl that boys like and of whom women disapprove. Rumors swirled that by the time she was sixteen, one boy had committed suicide over her, two others had fought a duel, and another would have eloped with her had she not kicked over a flower pot on the way down from her second story window.

Peggy married navy lieutenant John Timberlake, a hard-drinking man who was away at sea for long stretches of time. Peggy remained with her father in Washington. One of the regular boarders at the Franklin House was Sen. John H. Eaton of Tennessee. A wealthy widower, Eaton had been generous to the O'Neale family in times of financial hardship.

Andrew Jackson met Peggy when he stayed at the Franklin House at Eaton's invitation, and he called her "the smartest little woman in America." But not everyone—especially the wives of politically powerful men— saw her the same way. Former president James Monroe and his wife, Elizabeth, barred Peggy from events they hosted. Matters worsened when Eaton began to escort Peggy to social functions all over the city.

In April 1828 Peggy received news that her husband had died at sea. Jackson told Eaton that if he loved Peggy he should marry her and end the gossip. Eaton did marry her, but the gossip did not end.

When Jackson was elected president, he appointed Eaton to the post of secretary of war. The result was to thrust the "Eaton malaria," as Martin Van Buren called it, into the cabinet itself. Jackson, for his part, was inclined to defend women in distress, as he had with Rachel. Two clergymen, J. M. Campbell and Ezra Stiles Ely, tried to warn the president about Peggy's reputation and about what they had uncovered in their investigations of the situation. Both men were treated to the president's temper.

In an unprecedented move, Jackson called a special meeting to discuss whether Eaton had engaged in "criminal intercourse with Mrs. Timberlake." Jackson hoped the meeting, which was attended by most of the cabinet as well as the two clergymen, would bring to an end the "petticoat war." Jackson finished the meeting, and he thought the controversy, by declaring that Peggy had been "chaste as a virgin" when she married Eaton. No one dared remind Old Hickory that she had borne two children by her first husband before marrying Eaton.

With the matter resolved—or so he thought—Jackson held his first official cabinet dinner and had Peggy seated next to him. When she arrived in a low-cut, one-shouldered gown, many of the cabinet members' wives were shocked. She walked onto the dance floor with a partner, and the other wives left for their seats. The beginning of the social season in Washington was a disaster. Van Buren was next to give a formal dinner. He invited Mr. and Mrs. John Branch—Mrs. Branch was the sole surviving daughter of Thomas Jefferson. Branch accepted for himself, but declined for his wife, citing "circumstances unnecessary to detail." In the end many of the wives simply did not come to the event. A second dinner by Van Buren and Sir Charles Vaughan, the British ambassador to the United States, was condemned by the press as an attempt to foist an unworthy person on Washington society.

The social feud had developed into a power struggle within the Jackson cabinet. On one side was Vice President John C. Calhoun and his wife, Floride, who refused to associate with the Eatons. On the other was Secretary of State Van Buren, who was loyal to Jackson's wishes that Peggy be accepted into polite society. Members of the cabinet and foreign diplomats were forced to take sides in the growing controversy. The dispute even extended to Jackson's family. His niece, Emily Donelson, who had been acting as hostess of the White House, also refused to invite Peggy to dinner. Jackson asked Emily to leave.

After two years of infighting over Peggy Eaton, Van Buren offered a solution to the stalemate that was crippling Jackson's administration. He, along with Eaton, would resign from the cabinet, and the other secretaries would be asked to submit their resignations. With that, the cabinet was dissolved and a new group selected that did not include any of the previous incumbents except Postmaster General William T. Barry. The American public sided with Jackson and in 1832 rewarded him with reelection and Van Buren with the vice presidency. John C. Calhoun was, as Jackson told Van Buren, "politically dead."

Peggy Eaton's life ended on a tragic note. At the age of sixty she married Antonio Buchignani, a nineteen-year-old dance instructor whom she had hired to teach her granddaughter Emily how to dance for her debut. However, after five years of marriage, Buchignani stole all of her money and left with Emily for Italy. Peggy died alone and penniless in 1879.

SPOILS SYSTEM

Andrew Jackson is blamed for introducing the spoils system into American politics. Critics claimed the system, by which the party that wins the election doles out federal jobs, undermined the idea that people held their posts because of their expertise and talent.

When Andrew Jackson became president in 1829, it was only the second time in American history that the reins of power were transferred from one political party to another. The first instance was the election of Thomas Jefferson in 1800, when the Democratic-Republicans took over from the Federalists. Jefferson did not fire large numbers of Federalist officeholders and replace them with his own party members. He, like most politicians of his time, refused to use the institutions of government to further party politics. When Jackson was elected, however, he signaled that he had a different theory.

Jackson called his theory "rotation in office." It was Sen. William L. Marcy of New York, a close political ally of Martin Van Buren, who coined the phrase *spoils system* from the old adage, "To the victor belong the spoils of the enemy." Jackson claimed that he was trying to reform the government's habit of passing offices from one generation to the next like property, but his detractors argued that with the spoils system he had introduced the worst political practice imaginable.

Despite the criticism, Jackson did not fire large numbers of officeholders. The federal government employed about 10,000 workers, exclusive of the post office. In his first eighteen months in office, Jackson dismissed less than 10 percent of them. In fact, during his two terms, he replaced only about 15 percent of the total number. Even though he did not fully implement the rotation of office system he described, Jackson sought to make the distribution of federal jobs more democratic. He argued that the offices existed for the benefit of the people, that no person had an intrinsic right to them, and, therefore, the removal of an officeholder was not in and of itself a political wrong.

Jackson's approach was quite controversial at the time, but subsequent administrations accepted it and used it. Before the formation of a professional civil service, starting with the passage of the Pendleton Act under President Chester A. Arthur, Jackson's argument for rotation was used by his successors to justify wholesale replacements. Today, a new president is expected to appoint his own people to the top administrative positions in the executive branch, but most of the other jobs are protected by civil service regulations.

Jackson had initially believed that the rotation would end the widespread corruption in the federal government. He claimed that the "era of good feelings" was in fact an "era of corruption." His opponents feared that the spoils system gave too much power to the executive. They dubbed Jackson "King Andrew I" and called themselves "Whigs" to show their opposition to his monarchical authority.

SENATE CENSURE OF JACKSON

The failed effort to recharter the Second Bank of the United States led to the Senate censuring President Jackson for usurping power. Jackson protested the censure, calling it unconstitutional. He had it expunged from the Senate records when his party gained control of that body.

When Jackson vetoed the rechartering of the Second Bank of the United States in July 1832, Henry Clay, his Whig opponent in the presidential election of that year, made it the leading issue of the campaign. However,

Jackson was reelected in a decisive manner, and he took the election results to mean that the American people wanted an end to the Second Bank. To accomplish this, Jackson needed to remove the funds from the bank and redistribute them to state banks. The problem was that Jackson had no authority to remove the funds, as Congress had specifically delegated that power to the secretary of the Treasury.

The Whigs argued that the money should remain in the bank because the funds were safe and the administration of the bank efficient. Secretary of the Treasury Louis McLane agreed with the Whigs and tried to persuade Jackson not to remove the funds. McLane resigned to become secretary of state, and Jackson appointed William J. Duane of Pennsylvania to replace him. Much to Jackson's chagrin, Duane also agreed with the Whigs. Duane thought the removal of funds was not only unwise, but quite possibly illegal. Through letters and discussions, Jackson tried to convince Duane of his point of view, but Duane would not budge.

At a cabinet meeting on September 8, 1833, Jackson spelled out the reasons he wanted the funds removed from the bank. Attorney General Roger B. Taney had drafted the remarks. When Duane still refused to change his mind, Jackson fired him and appointed Taney as acting secretary of the Treasury. Taney began the process of withdrawing funds from the Second Bank and depositing them in state banks.

In his annual message to Congress on December 3, Jackson took full responsibility for the action. Eight days later the Senate asked Jackson for

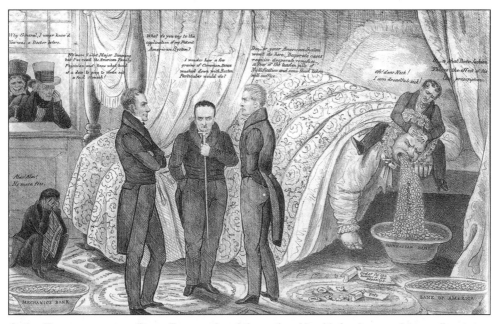

Acting Treasury secretary Roger Taney ordered the national bank's funds moved to smaller state banks. This cartoon depicts the bank as a huge woman vomiting coins into basins marked with the names of state banks.

the text of his remarks to the September 8 cabinet meeting. Jackson refused. "The executive is a coordinate and independent branch of the Government equally with the Senate," he said, "and I have yet to learn under what constitutional authority that branch of the Legislature has a right to require of me an account of any communications, either verbally or in writing, made to the Heads of the Departments acting as a Cabinet council."

The Senate shot back immediately. Under the Constitution, it said, it was Congress that had control of public funds and that the Act of 1789 creating the Treasury Department made it responsible to Congress rather than to the president. On March 28, 1834, Henry Clay introduced a resolution censuring Andrew Jackson:

> Resolved, that the President, in the late Executive proceedings in relation to the public revenue, had assumed upon himself authority and power not conferred by the Constitution and laws, but in derogation of both.

The resolution was adopted by a vote of 26 to 20. In a further reprimand of the president, the Senate refused to confirm Taney's appointment as secretary of the Treasury.

Jackson's response on April 15 argued that the censure was unconstitutional. He believed that if his actions deserved a resolution of censure then he must have committed a high crime or misdemeanor and that the Constitution provides only one remedy—impeachment. The Senate ignored the president's protest, and the House made no move to impeach him. Instead, when forces close to Jackson regained control of the Senate in 1837, they expunged the censure resolution from the *Senate Journal.*

THE TRAIL OF TEARS

Many of Jackson's critics say that his policy of states' rights led to the forced removal of the Cherokee Nation from Georgia.

During the early 1830s the question of the removal of Indian tribes became a crisis for the Jackson administration. The Supreme Court ruled in two separate cases (*Cherokee Nation v. Georgia,* 1831; *Worcester v. Georgia,* 1832) that the federal government, not the states, had ultimate jurisdiction over the tribes. Jackson was concerned about these rulings because he did not want to interfere with states' rights.

With the Court ruling that Georgia could not pass laws regulating activity on Indian lands, questions arose about whether Jackson would enforce the verdict. More than thirty years after the controversy, Horace Greeley recalled being told that Jackson had said of the chief justice, "Well, John Marshall has made his decision, now let him enforce it." It is unlike-

A 1942 painting depicting the Trail of Tears, Jackson's forced expulsion of Cherokee Indians from Georgia.

ly that Jackson ever made that statement, but it accurately reflects his attitude.

Jackson wanted to respect states' rights without giving in to a claim of nullification by Georgia. He also favored the removal of the Indians as a way to maintain peace. He kept pressuring the Cherokees to move and did nothing to help them retain their land from the unconstitutional assaults by the state of Georgia.

The Cherokees were divided on the question of relocating. Those who wanted to stay were often threatened, and their leader, John Ross, was imprisoned. Under the Treaty of New Echota, the Cherokees agreed to move west. The terms gave the Indians until 1838 to leave, but white settlers began to push the issue in 1836. The Cherokees were forced out on the so-called Trail of Tears; more than 4,000 of the 16,000 who began the journey died.

Jackson's critics accused him of "genocide" for his refusal to intercede and enforce the decisions of the Supreme Court and the terms of the treaty. His defenders claimed that Jackson believed both whites and Indians were better off separated from each other. Jackson, according to these apologists, feared that if the Indians remained in the East they would become extinct.

WILLIAM T. BARRY, POSTMASTER GENERAL

William Barry, Jackson's selection to run the burgeoning Post Office Department, was incompetent. He failed to draw up proper contracts, collect funds due the Treasury, or deal with the deterioration of service.

The size of the Post Office had grown considerably and by 1829 had about 11,000 employees, more than tripling its size in fifteen years. By 1834 the Post Office budget constituted nearly one-eighth of the total federal budget, and its jobs provided ample opportunity for political patronage.

Jackson selected William Barry, a former U.S. representative and U.S. senator from Kentucky, as his second postmaster general. Barry, however, was not up to the task. A sloppy record keeper, he often made contracts on scraps of paper without dating them and was slow to collect revenues. Service deteriorated, and, as the delivery of the mails grew worse, criticism mounted. At the same time, Post Office expenditures were rising. In fact, the department ran deficits of more than $300,000 in 1833 and more than $500,000 in 1834. Barry and his chief clerk, Obadiah Brown, took gifts from postal contractors who submitted low bids on projects only to come back later and renegotiate the contracts, offering improved but unnecessary services. In this way, a bid such as the one made by James Reeside in 1831 to deliver mail on two routes in Pennsylvania for $275 a year was converted into a $7,500-a-year contract.

In 1834 Abraham Bradley, an assistant postmaster who had been removed in 1829, wrote a letter to the *Daily National Intelligencer* accusing Barry of incompetence. When Jackson ordered Barry to economize, he could find only $75,000 worth of savings, mostly in southern routes. The growing outcry led to two separate congressional investigations, one in the Senate under Whig control and one in the House under Democratic control. Reports of widespread corruption poured into the committees. In early 1835 Brown resigned, and Barry followed suit on April 8. Barry was appointed ambassador to Spain, but died en route in Liverpool, England. Jackson then selected Amos Kendall, who proved to be an able administrator. Kendall cleaned up the Post Office Department and had it back in the black by October.

BIBLIOGRAPHY

Cole, Donald B. *The Presidency of Andrew Jackson.* Lawrence: University Press of Kansas, 1993.

Erickson, Erik M. "The Federal Civil Service under President Jackson." *Mississippi Valley Historical Review* 13 (March 1927): 517–540.

Gerson, Noel Bertram. *That Eaton Woman: In Defense of Peggy O'Neale Eaton.* New York: Crown Publishers, 1974.

Hagood, Wesley O. *Presidential Sex: From the Founding Fathers to Bill Clinton.* Secaucus, N.J.: Carol Publishing Group, 1998.

Mitchell, Jack. *Executive Privilege: Two Centuries of White House Scandals.* New York: Hippocrene Books, 1992.

Perdue, Theda, and Michael D. Green, eds. *The Cherokee Removal.* Boston: Bedford Books, 1995.

Remini, Robert V. *Andrew Jackson and the Bank War.* New York: Norton, 1967.

——. *The Life of Andrew Jackson.* New York: Harper and Row, 1988.

Ross, Shelley. *Fall from Grace: Sex, Scandal, and Corruption in American Politics from 1702 to the Present.* New York: Ballantine Books, 1988.

Somit, Albert. "Andrew Jackson as Administrative Reformer." *Tennessee Historical Quarterly* (September 1954).

Schlesinger, Arthur M., Jr. *The Age of Jackson.* Boston: Little, Brown, 1945.

Stickney, William, ed. *Autobiography of Amos Kendall.* Boston: Lee and Shepard, 1872.

Taylor, George R. *Jackson vs. Biddle's Bank.* Lexington, Mass.: Heath, 1972.

Ward, John W. *Andrew Jackson: Symbol of an Age.* New York: Oxford University Press, 1953.

Woodward, C. Vann. *Responses of the Presidents to Charges of Misconduct.* New York: Dell Publishing, 1974.

MARTIN VAN BUREN

Eighth President
1837–1841

Born December 5, 1782, in Kinderhook, New York, Martin Van Buren was the first president not of British descent and the first born a U.S. citizen. The seven who preceded him, although native born as required by the Constitution, came into the world before the United States was free of British rule. He was the third child of Maria and Abraham Van Buren, who was a tavernkeeper and farmer. Martin attended school until age fourteen, when he began to study law under Francis Sylvester, a successful Federalist attorney in Kinderhook. After six years with Sylvester, Van Buren worked in the New York City offices of William P. Van Ness for a year before being admitted to the bar in 1803. One of his earliest cases was the successful defense of Van Ness on charges that he was an accessory to murder for his involvement in the duel between Aaron Burr and Alexander Hamilton in 1804. Van Ness had acted as Burr's second. Van Buren practiced law with his half brother, James Van Alen, in Kinderhook and in 1808 succeeded him in the post of surrogate of Columbia County.

Van Buren won election to the state senate in 1812. He was appointed state attorney general in 1815 and served from 1816 to 1819, while retaining his senate seat. The "Little Magician" or the "Fox of Kinderhook," as he was often called, was a shrewd politician and leader of the so-called Albany Regency, a political machine that controlled New York politics through patronage, party newspapers, and a coherent Democratic caucus in the state legislature. In 1821 that legislature appointed him to the U.S. Senate and reappointed him in 1827.

Van Buren made an unsuccessful bid for the vice presidency as William H. Crawford's running mate in 1824. Running for governor in New York in 1828, Van Buren used his influence in the Northeast to help Andrew Jackson get elected president. Van Buren won the governorship but resigned when Jackson named him secretary of state. He became Jackson's most trusted adviser. Van Buren, along with others, left the cabinet when he and Jackson attempted to end the controversies between those loyal to Jackson and those loyal to Vice President John C. Calhoun (see Peggy Eaton, page 59). Presiding over the Senate, Calhoun blocked Van Buren's appointment to be ambassador to England when he cast the deciding vote to break a tie.

At their first nominating convention in 1832, the Democrats adopted a rule requiring a two-thirds majority for nomination. Despite opposition to Van Buren as the party's nominee for vice president in 1832, Jackson was able, through the two-thirds rule, to secure the nomination for his loyal supporter. Van Buren was elected vice president that year and won the presidency in 1836. His term was marked by a severe economic depression caused by a number of factors, including uncontrolled western expansion. Ironically, the principal cause was the lack of a sound banking system, a result of Jackson's veto of the Second Bank's charter. The economic crisis doomed his reelection chances, and he was defeated by the Whig Party candidate in the election of 1840.

Van Buren did not retire from politics, but actively sought the Democratic presidential nomination in 1844. Although he was the front-runner going into the convention, his opposition to the annexation of Texas cost him the nomination when Andrew Jackson and other southerners withdrew their support. The nomination eventually went to James K. Polk of Tennessee.

In 1848 Van Buren made one last run for the White House on the Free Soil ticket. The Free Soil Party was an alliance of former members of the Liberty Party, antislavery Whigs, and New York Democrats known as Barnburners. The party opposed the extension of slavery into the newly acquired territories in the southwest. Van Buren did not win a single state, and his candidacy cost the Democrats New York and the election, which Whig Zachary Taylor won. Retiring from politics, Van Buren died at Kinderhook July 24, 1862.

ILLEGITIMATE SON OF AARON BURR

Martin Van Buren was rumored to have been the illegitimate son of Aaron Burr, vice president during Thomas Jefferson's first administration.

Rumors spread that Martin Van Buren was the illegitimate son of Vice President Aaron Burr, even though there was not a single piece of evidence to support the story. The likely origin of the rumor is probably the fact that as a young attorney in New York Van Buren had defended William Van Ness of New York. Van Ness had acted as Aaron Burr's second in his duel with Alexander Hamilton. With Hamilton shot dead, Van Ness was charged as an accessory to murder. Van Buren vigorously defended him and won his acquittal. However, because Burr was an unsavory character and the killer of one of America's founders, Van Buren's reward was to be linked with Burr as the offspring of an illicit affair.

RICHARD JOHNSON, VICE PRESIDENT

War Hero

When Johnson became Van Buren's running mate, the press began to question the hero status Johnson had gained as the supposed slayer of Tecumseh.

Johnson's claim to fame was that he allegedly killed the Indian leader Tecumseh while serving under the military command of William Henry Harrison, a future president. No one knew for certain who fired the fatal shot, but, as leader of the troops that engaged Tecumseh, Johnson was credited with the deed. He became a national hero and the inspiration for

a five-act play, *The Warrior Sage*. Johnson went on to serve in both the House of Representatives and the U.S. Senate before being selected as Van Buren's running mate in 1836. However, by that time, the events surrounding his war record had been exaggerated in a book, *Authentic Biography of Colonel Richard M. Johnson,* by William Emmons. In Emmons's account, Johnson, although wounded several times, pursued Tecumseh in the battle and was about to be struck dead by the Indian warrior's tomahawk when he shot Tecumseh dead. The events mattered little until the election campaign and the press began to wonder if Johnson's claim concerning Tecumseh's slaying was true and, if so, whether a lucky shot qualified a man to be vice president.

Richard Johnson

Black Mistresses and Illegitimate Children

Vice President Johnson shocked Washington society by maintaining black mistresses whom he brought to social events.

More embarrassing to the campaign of 1836 were the reports of Johnson's longtime affair with a slave named Julia Chinn, whom he had inherited and with whom he had several children. It seems that Johnson took up with Julia to spite his mother, who had meddled in a relationship he was having with a seamstress. Newspapers across the country entered the controversy on one side or the other, but Van Buren supported his vice-presidential candidate. On election day, Van Buren was easily elected, but Johnson fell one vote short. The vice-presidential election was sent to the Senate (for the first time in U.S. history), and, by a 33 to 16 vote, Johnson was elected vice president.

However, the controversy did not end there. Johnson took a second black mistress, who later ran off with an Indian. Unfazed, Johnson took up with a third black woman and escorted her to Washington social events. In 1840 the Democrats dropped Johnson from the ticket for reelection.

SAMUEL SWARTWOUT AND JESSE D. HOYT

Samuel Swartwout and Jesse D. Hoyt, appointed by Andrew Jackson and Martin Van Buren, respectively, stole millions of dollars from the government while serving as collectors for the Port of New York.

Samuel Swartwout had been appointed to the post of collector for the Port of New York by Andrew Jackson in 1829. When Swartwout's second term expired in 1838, Martin Van Buren—who had opposed his original appointment—did not retain him. Out of a job, Swartwout sailed to Europe, taking with him the proceeds from two terms of corruption. An audit revealed that Swartwout had defrauded the government of nearly $2.25 million. Outraged that so much money could be stolen from the government, Van Buren appointed a longtime political friend, Jesse D.

CALLED TO ACCOUNT.

Speaker of the House James K. Polk, perceived as a friend to the administration, was prevented from appointing the committee to investigate the Swartwout embezzlement scandal. In this 1839 cartoon, a kneeling Polk is berated for this failure by Van Buren, represented as Satan.

Hoyt, to the post and empowered him to fix the problem. Instead, Hoyt followed Swartwout's lead and helped himself to his own share of government funds. However, Van Buren did not know of Hoyt's theft until it was unearthed by the Poindexter Commission during the Tyler administration.

EXTRAVAGANT EXPENSES

Van Buren was accused of having an extravagant lifestyle as president while the nation struggled with economic hardship.

When Van Buren became president in 1837, the nation was on the verge of economic collapse. The depression that began that year and lasted throughout his term was the result of uncontrolled western expansion and the lack of a solid banking system. The latter could be traced to Andrew Jackson's veto of the Second Bank of the United States. Critics accused Van Buren, who was always fastidiously dressed and maintained an impeccable appearance, of spending exorbitant sums of money to redecorate and entertain at the White House. The fact that Van Buren spent far less than any of his predecessors did not matter to his critics.

BIBLIOGRAPHY

Curtis, James C. *The Fox at Bay: Martin Van Buren and the Presidency, 1837–1841.* Lexington: University Press of Kentucky, 1970.

Alexander, Holmes Moss. *The American Talleyrand.* New York: Harper, 1935.

Mitchell, Jack. *Executive Privilege: Two Centuries of White House Scandals.* New York: Hippocrene Books, 1992.

Meyer, Leland W. *The Life and Times of Colonel Richard M. Johnson of Kentucky.* New York: Columbia University Press, 1967.

Niven, John. *Martin Van Buren: The Romantic Age of American Politics.* New York: Oxford University Press, 1983.

Ross, Shelley. *Fall from Grace: Sex, Scandal, and Corruption in American Politics from 1702 to the Present.* New York: Ballantine Books, 1988.

Wilson, Major J. *The Presidency of Martin Van Buren.* Lawrence: University Press of Kansas, 1984.

Woodward, C. Vann. *Responses of the Presidents to Charges of Misconduct.* New York: Dell Publishing, 1974.

WILLIAM HENRY HARRISON

Ninth President
1841

William Henry Harrison is the only president who does not have a scandal associated with his administration. His presidential term was too short for any maladministration to take place on his watch. Also, his life before he became president offered no instances that would have been considered scandalous. What follows, then, is a brief biography.

The last president to be born a British subject, William Henry Harrison was born February 9, 1773, on Berkeley plantation in Charles City County, Virginia. His father, Benjamin Harrison, was a prominent patriot, who signed the Declaration of Independence, served in the Virginia House of Delegates, and was governor of Virginia from 1781 to 1784. Tutored at home, William Harrison entered Hampden-Sydney College at the age of fourteen to pursue a career in medicine. He was an enthusiastic student. While at school, he underwent a religious conversion and became a Methodist. He next attended an academy in Southampton County, Virginia. In 1790 he became an apprentice to Dr. Andrew Leiper of Richmond, Virginia, and the following year enrolled at the University of Pennsylvania Medical School. He studied in Philadelphia under Dr. Benjamin Rush, but the untimely death of his father and lack of funds required him to end his studies in 1791.

Harrison joined the army and within a year had risen from the rank of ensign to lieutenant. In 1793 he began service under Maj. Gen. "Mad" Anthony Wayne. At the Battle of Fallen Timbers in August 1794, Harrison distinguished himself and was cited for his bravery. He was present at the signing of the Treaty of Greenville in 1795 that ended the Indian wars in the Northwest Territory. On November 25 that year he married Anna Tuthill Symmes. By 1797 he had achieved the rank of captain, but the following year he resigned his commission to serve as secretary of the Northwest Territory. In 1799 he was elected by the territorial legislature as its delegate to the House of Representatives. A year later he was appointed governor of the Indiana Territory by President John Adams.

Remaining neutral in the election of 1800, Harrison continued to serve as Indian Territory governor until the outbreak of the War of 1812. Commissioned a major general of the Kentucky militia in 1812, he was ultimately promoted to major general in command of the Northwest frontier. Harrison became a national hero when his troops successfully recaptured Detroit from the British. He resigned from the army in May 1814 because of differences with the secretary of war, John Armstrong.

Harrison settled in Cincinnati, Ohio, and was elected to the U.S. House of Representatives in 1816. He served on a number of military committees. In 1819 he was elected an Ohio state senator, a post he held until 1821. In 1822 he lost a bitter contest for another term in the House to James William Gazlay. However, in 1825 Harrison was elected to the United States Senate where he served for three years before being named ambassador to Colombia. Appointed by President John Quincy Adams, Harrison was recalled by President Andrew Jackson.

He returned to his farm at North Bend, Ohio. In 1834 he was appointed clerk of the Court of Common Pleas for Hamilton County, the post from which he would win the presidency in 1840. In 1836 he stood as the Whig nominee for president, but was defeated by Martin Van Buren. In 1840, however, the economic recession of the Van Buren administration improved Whig chances of electoral success. Harrison defeated Henry Clay to capture the nomination, largely because of the anti-Masonic sentiment at the convention that worked against Clay, who was a Mason. John Tyler of Virginia, a Clay supporter, was chosen as vice president. In the general election, Harrison soundly defeated the weakened Democrat Van Buren.

At his inauguration, March 4, 1841, Harrison gave a one-hour, forty-minute speech on a blustery, cold day without wearing a hat, gloves, or an overcoat. Caught in a downpour as he walked back to the White House, he came down with a cold (diagnosed as "bilious pleurisy"). He died of pneumonia April 4, 1841. His brief administration had consisted mostly of fending off opportunistic job seekers who hoped Harrison would purge the government of Jacksonians and replace them with Whigs.

BIBLIOGRAPHY

Cleaves, Freeman. *Old Tippecanoe: William Henry Harrison and His Times.* New York: Scribner's Sons, 1939.

Goebel, Dorothy B. *William Henry Harrison: A Political Biography.* Indianapolis: Historical Bureau of the Indiana Library, 1926.

JOHN TYLER

Tenth President
1841–1845

John Tyler was born March 29, 1790, at Greenway, on the James River in Charles City County, Virginia. He was the sixth of eight children born to Mary and John Tyler, a prominent planter and governor of Virginia (1808–1811). At age twelve Tyler attended the preparatory school associated with the College of William and Mary; he graduated from the college in 1807. He studied law under his father and Edmund Randolph in Richmond and was admitted to the bar in 1809.

In 1811 Tyler was elected to the Virginia House of Delegates. He led the successful effort to admonish Virginia's two U.S. senators for their votes in favor of the Bank of the United States, against the instructions from the state legislature. A Jeffersonian Republican, Tyler served in the house until 1816. During the War of 1812, he joined the Charles City Rifles as a captain, but saw no action. In 1813 he married Letitia Christian. Seven of their eight children lived to maturity. Letitia Tyler died in 1842.

Running on a states' rights platform, Tyler was elected to the U.S. House of Representatives in 1816. In Congress he attempted to censure Gen. Andrew Jackson for his invasion of Florida and opposed the Missouri Compromise as an unconstitutional restriction on slavery. In poor health, he resigned his seat in 1821. He was once again elected to the Virginia House of Delegates in 1823 and supported first William H. Crawford and then John Quincy Adams in the election of 1824. The following year he was elected governor of Virginia.

In 1827 Tyler resigned as governor of Virginia to accept a seat in the U.S. Senate. He was elected over incumbent John Randolph. Even though Tyler had supported Adams in the election of 1824, he became one of the president's harshest critics in the Senate. In 1828 Tyler supported Andrew Jackson for president. However, once again, Tyler showed his independence when he criticized the Jackson administration for its handling of South Carolina's threat to nullify a tariff bill. Although he doubted states could legally nullify federal laws, he opposed Jackson's threat to use force to collect the tariffs. Tyler continued to be a vocal critic of Jackson and was soon aligning himself with Whigs like Henry Clay. When the Virginia legislature sent instructions to its senators to vote to expunge the censure of Jackson from the record, Tyler resigned his seat rather than comply.

In the election of 1836, Tyler was the vice-presidential candidate for the Whigs, receiving forty-seven electoral votes. In 1838 he was once again elected to the Virginia House of Delegates, where he served as speaker from 1839 to 1840.

At the Whig national convention in December 1839, Tyler supported Henry Clay. However, the nomination went to William Henry Harrison, and Tyler was selected as the vice-presidential nominee. Tyler's presence on the ticket made it more appealing to the southern states. He was not active in the formation of Harrison's cabinet; indeed, he was surprised to learn of the president's death, because no one had told him of Harrison's illness. On April 6, 1841, he was sworn in as the tenth president of the United States, becoming the first vice president to succeed to the office on the death of the incumbent.

Tyler believed that taking the oath of office was unnecessary and said so, even though he did it. The next month Congress adopted a resolution recognizing Tyler as president, not acting president. Tyler's succession to the office set two precedents. First, the oath of office must be administered to the vice president before he becomes president. Second, the duly sworn vice president becomes the president with all the powers and responsibilities of the office.

Tyler soon found himself a president without a party when all the members of the cabinet except Secretary of State Daniel Webster resigned because of Tyler's two vetoes of bills to reestablish a national bank. Despite this mass exodus, Tyler was successful in settling the boundary between Maine and New Brunswick with the 1842 Webster-Ashburton Treaty, and he approved the annexation of Texas in 1845. Declining to make a third-party run for a second term, Tyler retired from office. In the 1844 election he supported James K. Polk over his former political ally Henry Clay because Polk shared his views on the annexation of Texas.

Returning to Sherwood Forest, his 1,200 acre plantation near Richmond, with his twenty-four-year-old bride, Julia Gardiner, whom he had married on June 26, 1844, Tyler raised a second family of seven children. Active at the College of William and Mary, he served as chancellor late in his life. He also became a Democrat again but was not active in politics. In February 1861, however, he served as part of a peace convention in Washington, D.C., to settle the growing crisis between North and South and prevent war. When the convention failed to find a compromise, Tyler urged Virginia to secede from the Union. Serving as a member of the Provisional Congress of the Confederacy, he was elected to the Confederate House of Representatives in November 1861, but died on January 18, 1862, before taking office.

THE POINDEXTER COMMISSION

Tyler appointed a three-man commission to investigate charges of fraud in the New York Custom House without congressional approval. The House tabled a resolution condemning the president's actions, and instead added a slap on the wrist to an appropriations bill.

In May 1841 President John Tyler, without the approval of Congress, appointed a three-man commission headed by former governor and senator George Poindexter of Mississippi. The purpose of the commission was to investigate rumors of fraud in the New York Custom House that had occurred during the Van Buren administration. The commission discovered that Jesse D. Hoyt had embezzled funds.

The Whig-controlled House took little comfort in the findings of fraud by the Democrats. Instead, it demanded that Tyler explain his authority to appoint such a commission, how much the commissioners were paid, and where the funds had come from. Tyler responded that his authority to appoint the commission stemmed from his constitutional duty to execute the laws. He did not answer the other questions.

The House was faced with two issues. The first was the president's refusal to give information to a committee. The second was the unauthorized payment of private citizens with federal funds. Not satisfied with Tyler's response, the House Committee on Public Expenditures subpoenaed information from Poindexter directly. On April 29, 1842, when the Poindexter Commission released its report to the president, the House demanded a copy. The president complied the following day. In May, by a vote of 86 to 83, the House passed a resolution that read in part:

> The President has no rightful authority to appoint and commission officers to investigate abuses, or to provide information for the President to act upon, and to compensate such officers at public expense, without authority by law.

Although the resolution was tabled at the urging of John Quincy Adams, the House added a provision to an appropriations bill, which passed August 26, forbidding the practice of paying agents or commissioners with public funds without the prior approval of Congress.

IMPEACHABLE OFFENSES REPORT

A select committee of Congress issued a report condemning certain actions of the president. The report stated that Tyler deserved to be impeached, but it did not recommend articles of impeachment because the committee believed he would not be convicted. Nevertheless, Rep. John Minor Botts of Virginia presented formal articles of impeachment in the House, an indication of the hostility between the House and the president. For his part, Tyler asserted that the information sought by Congress was protected by executive privilege.

John Minor Botts

When President Tyler vetoed a fourth economic measure the Whig Congress sent to him for his signature, the House did not place his veto message on the record. Instead, the House appointed a select committee, chaired by former president John Quincy Adams of Massachusetts and John Minor Botts of Virginia, a political enemy of Tyler's, to report on the veto. The majority report was highly critical, claiming that Tyler had upset the constitutional balance in which the president was to be "dependent upon and responsible to" Congress. It stated that Tyler's repeated vetoes had nullified "the whole action of the Legislative authority of this Union." As an example of Tyler's duplicity, the report cited the fact that he had promised a certain congressman that he would support the bill he had just vetoed. It concluded that Tyler deserved to be impeached for his actions, but that articles of impeachment were not recommended because they would fail if brought to the floor at this time. Instead, by a vote of 100 to 80, the House adopted the report of the committee along with its statements that Tyler had committed impeachable offenses.

Tyler formally protested the committee's report and its adoption by the House on August 30, 1842. He demonstrated his anger by charging that the House had gone out of its way to present his motives in the worst possible light. He railed that the House must impeach him and give him the chance to defend himself against the charges in a Senate trial. Tyler argued that if the charges in the report were true—and he believed they were not—that he deserved to be impeached and removed from office:

> I am charged with offenses against the country so grave and heinous as to deserve public disgrace and disenfranchisement. I am charged with violating pledges which I never gave, with usurping powers not conferred by law, and above all, with using powers conferred upon the President by the Constitution from corrupt motives and for unwarrantable ends.

The House refused to accept his protest or place it on the record. Instead, it criticized the president for violating the House's privileges in preparing such a report. And the matter did not end there. In January 1843 Representative Botts presented nine formal articles of impeachment. Six of the charges, which were called abuses of power, were in reality presidential prerogatives such as appointments and removals and the exercise of the veto. The other three charges, however, were legitimate in light of Tyler's actions:

I charge him with gross official misconduct, in having been guilty of shameless duplicity, equivocation, and falsehood, with his late Cabinet and Congress . . . by which he has brought such dishonor on himself as to disqualify him from administering the Government with advantage, honor, or virtue, and for which alone he would deserve to be removed from office.

I charge him with an illegal and unconstitutional exercise of power, in instituting a commission to investigate past transactions under a former administration of the custom house of New York, under the pretense of seeing the laws faithfully executed . . . with having directed or sanctioned the appropriation of large sums of the public revenue to the compensation of officers of his own creation, without the authority of law; which, if sanctioned, would place the entire revenues of the country at his disposal.

I charge him with the high misdemeanor of having withheld from the Representatives of the people information called for, and declared to be necessary to the investigation of stupendous frauds and abuses alleged to have been committed by him against the Government, both upon individuals and the Government itself, whereby he becomes accessory to those frauds.

On January 18, 1843, the House, 127–83, defeated a motion to appoint a committee to investigate these charges. Again, most members refused to support the motion because they did not think they had the votes necessary to force the issue.

Tyler did not have to respond because no formal charges were brought against him, but he sent a message on January 31, in which he responded indirectly to Botts's charges. Tyler argued that at times the executive had to deny requests for information because such disclosures would be detrimental to his constitutional obligation to enforce the laws. He stated that Congress had earlier acknowledged executive privilege as a legitimate and necessary power derived from the very nature of the presidency. He denied that all information in the control of the executive "must necessarily be subject to the call of the House of Representatives merely because they related to a subject of the deliberations of the House." "Certain communications [were] privileged," and "the general authority to compel testimony must give way in certain cases to the paramount rights of individuals or of the Government."

WEBSTER-ASHBURTON TREATY

To help secure Maine's support in the boundary negotiations between the United States and Canada, President Tyler authorized Secretary of State Daniel Webster to use funds that were intended for secret activities abroad to hire agents to lobby Maine politicians and newspaper editors. Some of the money may have gone to fix a murder trial of a Canadian citizen in New York with the intention of smoothing U.S.-Canadian relations.

By the 1840s disputes about the exact location of the border between Maine and the Canadian province of New Brunswick threatened to erupt into another war between the United States and Great Britain. Both nations hoped to avoid armed combat, but Maine—a party to whatever deal was to be made—refused to cooperate in negotiations. Maine was unyielding in its claim to the entire territory under dispute, approximately 12,000 square miles. The state insisted that it had a constitutional right to be protected by the federal government against foreign invasion.

To encourage Maine's participation in negotiations, President Tyler authorized Secretary of State Daniel Webster to hire private agents to persuade local newspaper editors and state legislators to support the talks scheduled to take place between Webster and Lord Ashburton. These agents, who were employed secretly, were paid from a presidential contingency fund, known as the secret service fund, which had been authorized yearly since 1810 for covert activities abroad. Francis O. Smith, a politician, attorney, and newspaper publisher, was one of the leaders behind the propaganda idea. He had suggested engaging locals to mingle with Maine politicians, pressing the idea that it would be to the state's benefit to be more flexible on the land claims. Smith had also tried in the 1830s to convince Martin Van Buren of a similar approach to the problem.

Daniel Webster

Some have charged that the Tyler administration used improper influence in a trial in New York to smooth relations with Canada. Alexander McLeod, a Canadian citizen, was charged with murder in state court. When his case came to trial, the two main witnesses against him did not show up to testify. Without them, the prosecution's case was weak, and McLeod was acquitted. Webster's record books show a payment of $1,000 to the attorney general of the United States for services performed in New York at the same time as the trial. There is no proof that the money was used to obstruct justice, but a full accounting of the funds has never been made.

Democrats did not learn of these events until after Tyler had left office. And in 1846, they used the revelations to attack Webster, who by then was a U.S. senator from Massachusetts. In February a New York Democratic senator charged that Webster had interfered with the McLeod trial in "an attempt on the part of the authorities at Washington to arrest the ordinary course of justice, and prevent a trial on the merits." In April Rep. Charles J. Ingersoll of Pennsylvania, the Democratic chairman of the Committee on Foreign Affairs, accused Webster of unlawfully spending the contingency fund without Tyler's knowledge, of keeping the money for long periods of time, and for owing the government more than $2,000 when he left the State Department in 1843. Webster was also charged with hiring agents with government funds to corrupt party presses in Maine. A special committee was established to investigate Ingersoll's charges.

The House investigation drew the new president, James K. Polk, into the fray as he defended executive privilege. On April 9 the committee asked Polk to send it Tyler's record of all payments made from the contingency fund during Webster's term. Polk refused. He reminded the committee that the 1810 law creating the fund had specifically differentiated between public and secret expenditures. For secret funds, the president merely had to show certificates that proved he had authorized the expenditure; he did not have to disclose the purpose. Polk did, however, note that there was an exception to this rule, namely national security. Polk also stated that if the House was in the process of impeaching the parties involved, that too might create an exception to the rule.

Former president Tyler was summoned to testify before the committee. He refused to name any of the agents who had been employed in Maine. Tyler further testified that he had authorized Webster to make payments, but insisted that the money was not used to bribe officials or editors, but merely to engage others in the debate surrounding the peace negotiations. Francis Smith, the primary agent in Maine, confirmed this distinction in later testimony. Smith had lobbied the Portland *Christian Mirror* and the Portland *East Argus* to run editorials in favor of a settlement that did not drag the process out for years. The papers argued that the only alternative to a reasonable settlement was a protracted war that would be costly to both sides. To the charge that Webster had left the State Department owing it $2,000, Tyler answered that Webster had returned the money out of his own pocket and was due reimbursement once vouchers were presented that confirmed his expenditures.

Splitting 4–1, the Committee on Official Misconduct of the Late Secretary of State not only cleared Webster of all charges against him, but also it refused to pass judgment on the issue of funds appropriated for secret activities abroad being used to influence internal political events.

BIBLIOGRAPHY

Cumming, Hiram. *Secret History of the Perfidies, Intrigues, and Corruptions of the Tyler Dynasty.* Washington, D.C.: Self-published, 1845.

Merk, Frederick. *Fruits of Propaganda in the Tyler Administration.* Cambridge: Harvard University Press, 1971.

Mitchell, Jack. *Executive Privilege: Two Centuries of White House Scandals.* New York: Hippocrene Books, 1992.

Morgan, Robert J. *A Whig Embattled: The Presidency Under John Tyler.* Lincoln: University of Nebraska Press, 1954.

Peterson, Norma Lois. *The Presidencies of William Henry Harrison and John Tyler.* Lawrence: University Press of Kansas, 1989.

Woodward, C. Vann. *Responses of the Presidents to Charges of Misconduct.* New York: Dell Publishing, 1974.

JAMES K. POLK

Eleventh President
1845–1849

James K. Polk, the first "dark horse" president, was the last of the Jacksonian Democrats to occupy the White House. Born in Mecklenburg County, North Carolina, on November 2, 1795, Polk was the first of ten children born to a prosperous farmer. The family moved to a frontier settlement in Tennessee when Polk was ten years old, and his parents taught him reading and mathematics. An industrious student, he graduated with honors from the University of North Carolina in 1818. He then moved to Nashville, and, after practicing law, served in the Tennessee legislature from 1823 to 1825. There he became a friend of Andrew Jackson, then a U.S. senator. On January 1, 1824, Polk married Sarah Childress, the daughter of a prominent planter.

Elected to the House of Representatives in 1824, Polk acted as floor manager for President Jackson in the "bank war" (see page 62). He served seven consecutive terms in the House and was Speaker of the House from 1835 to 1839. He left the House to become governor of Tennessee. After one term he was defeated for reelection in a tide of sentiment against President Martin Van Buren.

In the presidential election of 1844 Van Buren was expected to win the Democratic nomination; Polk was the leading vice-presidential candidate. The balloting became deadlocked, however, and the convention turned to Polk as a compromise candidate. On the ninth ballot, Polk secured the nomination and became the first dark-horse candidate of a major party. The Whigs, encouraged by the Democrats' selection, jeered, "Who is James K. Polk?"

Both Van Buren and Henry Clay, the Whig standard bearer, had tried to take the western expansionist issue out of the campaign by opposing the annexation of Texas to the United States. With the support of Andrew Jackson, "Young Hickory," as Polk was dubbed, supported an expansionist policy. He advocated the annexation of Texas, a settlement with Britain over the disputed boundary of Oregon, and the acquisition of California.

The annexation of Texas was popular in the slave-holding South, while Oregon appealed to northerners.

On the Oregon question, Polk campaigned for a settlement with Britain that would set the northern boundary of Oregon at 54°40'. "Fifty-four forty or fight" became one of the rallying cries of the 1844 election. On election day, Polk defeated Clay by a comfortable margin in the electoral college, although the popular vote was close.

Congress acted quickly on the expansionist mood of the nation. Even before Polk took office, it passed a joint resolution calling for the annexation of Texas. Annexation ultimately would be determined by war with Mexico (1846–1848). The dispute with Britain over the Oregon Territory was resolved in 1846 in a compromise. The acquisition of California was more difficult than Texas and Oregon. Polk sent John Slidell as an envoy to offer Mexico as much as $20 million, plus settlement of damage claims owed to Americans, in return for California and the New Mexico territory. When Slidell was not even received, Polk ordered Gen. Zachary Taylor to cross the Rio Grande into Mexico. As hostilities broke out, Congress declared war. In 1848 Mexico and the United States signed the Treaty of Guadalupe Hidalgo, which ceded New Mexico and California to the United States in return for $15 million and U.S. assumption of the damage claims.

Polk did not seek a second term. He had accomplished his major goals, including expanding the borders of the United States. On June 15, 1849, he died in Nashville, three months after leaving the White House.

THE ROORBACK FORGERY

During the presidential campaign of 1844, an abolitionist newspaper reprinted an extract from a book that described Polk's inhumane treatment of his slaves. The account turned out to be a campaign trick.

Henry Clay

Political campaigns in the nineteenth century were often marked by ad hominem attacks on the candidates rather than on the issues. Polk was the victim of such an attack in 1844, but his campaign may have struck the first blow when it charged that Henry Clay, his opponent, had broken all ten of the Ten Commandments and was living in a brothel in Washington, D.C. The Whigs countered by focusing on Polk's expansionist tendencies and portraying him as a cruel slave owner. The Whigs hoped that abolitionist Democrats would be so offended by these stories that they would vote for Clay.

On August 21, 1844, the abolitionist *Chronicle* of Ithaca, New York, published extracts from *Roorback's Tour through the Southern and Western States in the Year*

1836, supposedly written by a German tourist, Baron von Roorback. The newspaper editors reproduced an excerpt from the book that described a slave trader's encampment in Tennessee. That portion read in part, "Forty of these unfortunate beings had been purchased, I was told, by the Hon. J. K. Polk, the present speaker of the house of representatives; the mark of the branding iron, with the initials of his name on their shoulders distinguishing them from the rest." The story was reprinted in other abolitionist papers.

As soon as the Democrats discovered that the passage cited was a fake, they published the truth. In fact, Polk's name never even appeared in the book. The plot seems to have backfired on Clay, himself a slaveholder, and he was attacked as a hypocrite. The incident was the source of a new political term, *roorback,* which refers to a falsehood spread for political effect.

JAMES BUCHANAN, SECRETARY OF STATE

When Polk heard rumors that his secretary of state, James Buchanan, was passing information to the press, Polk called on Congress to investigate the rumors. Congress found no basis for the charges.

Polk—a good Jacksonian—was sensitive to charges of corruption or even its appearance within his administration. He sought to remove Gen. Winfield Scott from his command of American forces in Mexico after hearing rumors that Scott had bribed Mexican officials to obtain a peace settlement. When charges were raised against Secretary of State James Buchanan of leaking to the press secret documents concerning the delicate negotiations with Great Britain on the Oregon Territory, Polk called for an investigation by Congress, even though no real evidence existed. The Senate investigated the allegations and cleared Buchanan of any wrongdoing.

WASHINGTON GLOBE

Polk helped Thomas Ritchie, a newspaper editor from Richmond, Virginia, and a political supporter, to purchase the Washington Globe. *Half the funds needed were advanced from the U.S. Treasury against future printing contracts that would be awarded to the paper.*

When Polk became president in 1845, he attempted to replace Francis P. Blair, the editor of the *Washington Globe,* with an editor who would be more favorable to Polk and his administration. Polk's choice, Thomas Ritchie, an editor from Richmond, did not have enough money to buy the Democratic paper from Blair. Half of the $35,000 needed for the purchase was advanced by the Treasurer of the United States against future printing contracts that would be awarded to the *Globe.* (Until the investigation by the Covode Committee in 1860, it was common practice to award government printing contracts to a newspaper favorable to the administration.

See page 105.) The other half of the funds were drawn from government deposits from a Pennsylvania bank owned by Democratic senator Simon Cameron. It was not until 1847 that Polk's secretary of the Treasury, Robert J. Walker, recalled the loan. By that time, the *Globe* had served its political purpose and had reaped the benefits of many lucrative government printing contracts.

BIBLIOGRAPHY

Bergeron, Paul H. *The Presidency of James K. Polk.* Lawrence: University Press of Kansas, 1987.

Hoyt, Edwin Palmer. *James Knox Polk.* Chicago: Reilly and Lee, 1965.

McCoy, Charles A. *Polk and the Presidency.* Austin: University of Texas Press, 1960.

Mitchell, Jack. *Executive Privilege: Two Centuries of White House Scandals.* New York: Hippocrene Books, 1992.

Morrel, Martha McBride. *Young Hickory: The Life and Times of President James K. Polk.* New York: E. P. Dutton, 1949.

Schroeder, John H. *Mr. Polk's War: American Opposition and Dissent, 1846–1848.* Madison: University of Wisconsin Press, 1973.

Sellers, Charles G. *James K. Polk, Continentalist, 1843–1846.* Norwalk, Conn.: Easton Press, 1966.

Woodward, C. Vann. *Responses of the Presidents to Charges of Misconduct.* New York: Dell Publishing, 1974.

ZACHARY TAYLOR

Twelfth President
1849–1850

Zachary Taylor was born November 24, 1784, while his family was traveling from Virginia to their new home near Louisville, Kentucky. He received only the most basic education in Kentucky. In 1808 he entered the army, where he spent most of his adult life. Commissioned a first lieutenant, Taylor saw service in New Orleans under Gen. James Wilkinson and served as commandant of Fort Knox, at Vincennes in the Indiana Territory. By 1810 he had risen to the rank of captain and had won the admiration of William Henry Harrison, governor of the territory. In June of that year, Taylor married Margaret Mackall Smith, the daughter of a wealthy Maryland planter.

During the War of 1812, Taylor was breveted to the rank of major for his efforts in defending Fort Harrison on the Wabash River. He oversaw the construction of Fort Johnson at Des Moines, rising to the rank of major in January 1815. At the end of the war, his rank was reduced to captain, and he resigned his commission.

Taylor returned to the army after a one-year hiatus. In 1816 he was commissioned a major and assigned to various posts; by 1832 he had been promoted to colonel. Taylor saw military action in the Black Hawk War (1832) and the second Seminole War (1837–1840). During the latter, he was breveted from colonel to brigadier general and put in charge of all U.S. forces in Florida. In 1841 Taylor was given command of the southern division of the army and reassigned to Baton Rouge, where he bought a plantation.

When the United States annexed Texas in 1845, President Polk ordered Taylor to position troops along the Rio Grande to defend it against Mexico. During the Mexican War, Taylor distinguished himself in battle and was promoted to major general. When his forces were outnumbered at Buena Vista, in February 1847, the Mexican general Santa Ana called for him to surrender or be slaughtered. Taylor refused and defeated Santa Ana's army in a pitched battle. He earned the nickname "Old Rough and Ready" and became a national hero.

Seeking to capitalize on Taylor's popularity, the Whig Party looked to him as its presidential candidate in the 1848 election. At the Whig convention in Philadelphia in June, Taylor won the nomination on the fourth ballot over Gen. Winfield Scott, Sen. Daniel Webster of Massachusetts, and the seventy-year-old Henry Clay of Kentucky. Millard Fillmore of New York was his running mate. Taylor's opponent in the election was Democrat Lewis Cass of Michigan. In a competitive race in which both candidates won fifteen states, Taylor took the electoral college vote, 163–127.

The most important issue of his administration was slavery and whether it should be allowed to exist in western territories that would be applying for statehood. Although a slave owner himself, Taylor opposed the extension of slavery into new territories. He opposed the Compromise of 1850, a series of congressional acts led by Senator Clay intended to satisfy both the North and the South on the question of slavery in the newly acquired territories. Taylor made it clear that he intended to veto the compromise. He believed the Union must be preserved, and he was prepared to use the army to defend it. Had he not died, the Civil War might have taken place a decade earlier than it did. But Taylor succumbed to a gastrointestinal illness caused by poor sanitary conditions in the sweltering heat of Washington, D.C., on July 9, 1850. Fillmore, who succeeded Taylor as president, supported the compromise, which kept the Union together temporarily.

THE GALPHIN CLAIM

Newspapers questioned whether George W. Crawford, Taylor's secretary of war, had used his influence in the payment of a pre–Revolutionary War debt in which he held a financial stake. The federal government settled the debt by paying its face value plus interest for seventy-three years.

As a military officer who won fame fighting in the Indian and Mexican wars, President Taylor attached high value to his reputation for integrity. In April 1850, however, his administration came under intense fire from foes in the Democratic Party. The issue was whether Secretary of War George W. Crawford had used his office to ensure a large settlement in a claim against the government that was more than three-quarters of a century old.

The story began in 1773 before the Revolution against Britain. To acquire land from the Creek and Cherokee Indians for their Georgia colony, the British had agreed to pay the debts the Indians owed to fur traders. One of the traders, George Galphin, received a certificate from the Crown promising more than $43,000. Before Galphin could collect, however, the Revolutionary War began, and Galphin joined the rebel cause. When the British paid other traders after the war, they refused his claim.

With Georgia's acquisition of the Indian lands, it seemed reasonable to conclude that the state had taken on the debts tied to those lands. For some forty years Galphin and his heirs tried to claim their money from the state.

President Zachary Taylor and his cabinet, left to right, Reverdy Johnson, William Meredith, William Preston, Taylor, George Crawford, Jacob Collamer, Thomas Ewing, and John Clayton.

From time to time, the Georgia legislature would recognize the validity of their claim, but it was never able to come up with the funds. Later, when the land was transferred to federal control, the state came to regard payment as a federal responsibility. In 1837 Georgia's governor, William Schley, told President Andrew Jackson that Georgia recognized the claim as just, but that "it arose under a treaty stipulation the fulfillment of which devolved…not on Georgia, but on the government of the United States," which succeeded that of Britain.

In 1846, during President Polk's administration, Congress began to act on the matter. In August 1848 the Galphin bill coasted through both houses of Congress without debate and became law. (Some who later criticized the Taylor administration for its handling of the claim voted for the bill.) Robert Walker, the secretary of the Treasury, paid the $43,518.97 principal, but, because the legislation was unclear, he left a decision about the interest to his Whig successor.

In May 1849, the Galphin family filed a legal brief demanding their interest from the Taylor administration. Initially, the comptroller, Elisha Whittlesey, recommended that no interest be paid, but changed his mind and recommended that interest be paid from 1838, when the family began to pursue payment at the federal level. Because of the large sum involved, Secretary of the Treasury William Meredith passed the case to Attorney General Reverdy Johnson, who concluded that the government must pay more than seventy-three years of interest on the debt. On the basis of Johnson's opinion, Meredith paid the family an additional $191,352.89, a considerable sum in that day.

If all the money had gone to Galphin's descendants, there would have been no controversy. But in April 1850, Democratic newspapers began to question a disturbing fact. Before he took office, George Crawford had been the Galphin family's attorney and had acquired a right to half of any settlement. It was not possible to argue that he had unduly influenced the previous (Democratic) administration. But when the actions of two Whig cabinet members, Meredith and Johnson, enriched a fellow member by almost $100,000, there was at least the appearance of wrongdoing.

Meredith and Johnson denied any collusion with Crawford for the best of reasons: they said they had not known of his connection to the Galphin case. Crawford later claimed he had taken the case to President Taylor and explained that it had nothing to do with the War Department. Taylor is said to have replied that taking an office in the government did not curtail any "preexisting individual rights."

Some question whether Crawford really made the circumstances clear to the president. Although he was a capable military leader, Taylor was inexperienced in politics. If Crawford had pointed out the potential political fallout and perhaps involved the rest of the cabinet in any decision, the Taylor administration might have moved more carefully than it did. It could have taken steps to involve congressional Democrats, whose Georgia delegates were strong supporters of the Galphin family. It might also have pressured Crawford to accept a payment that more accurately reflected his work on the case.

To his credit, Crawford requested an investigation by the House of Representatives. Five Democrats and four Whigs were appointed to the committee. All nine agreed that Galphin's original claim should be paid. On other matters, they split along party lines. Two Democrats argued that interest should not be paid at all; three, that it should have been paid only with congressional approval. All four Whigs asserted that "law and precedent" argued that principal and interest should be paid. On that matter, the Whigs undoubtedly were right. However, some Democrats had good reasons for sponsoring a resolution that called for "a law prohibiting any member of the Cabinet from deciding on any claim or demand...in which any other member of the same Cabinet shall be interested."

No evidence was found that Crawford had used his office wrongly. The payment the Galphin family received clearly was justice long delayed. Crawford's payment for his role may have been overly large, but that was a decision the family had made when success was uncertain. The family's judgment may have exposed Crawford's greed, but it did not make him a criminal.

THOMAS EWING, SECRETARY OF INTERIOR

Thomas Ewing, a Whig Party loyalist, became the source of controversy for his role in firing Democratic federal employees and replacing them with Whig supporters. Recognized as the administration's hatchet man, Ewing resigned after Taylor died.

One of the first jobs facing Taylor when he was elected president was replacing the large number of entrenched Democrats with members of his own party. Because he had spent his career as a military officer, not as an active politician, he knew few politicians personally. He left it to experienced members of his cabinet to dispense the spoils of his electoral victory. The newly created Department of the Interior went to Sen. Thomas Ewing of Ohio.

Ewing was a large, powerful man who soon gained the reputation as the administration's hatchet man. He firmly believed that wherever possible Democrats should be thrown out of office and replaced with Whig loyalists. With a whole new department to staff and his active role in other appointments, Ewing was widely criticized by Democrats in Congress. The Democratic press, which had benefited from twenty years of Democratic control of patronage, also took issue with the wholesale firings and hirings.

Battered by the Galphin affair, Taylor's administration was an easy target for the press and for Congress. A resolution was passed authorizing the investigation of Ewing and his handling of patronage jobs. Taylor had already decided to purge his cabinet of several members—including the controversial Ewing—when he fell ill and died in July 1850. His successor, Millard Fillmore, accepted the resignations of Ewing and other officials and replaced them with men who were loyal to him and untouched by the patronage investigation.

BIBLIOGRAPHY

Bauer, K. Jack. *Zachary Taylor: Soldier, Planter, Statesman of the Old Southwest.* Newtown, Conn.: American Political Biography Press, 1994.

Ewing, Thomas. *The Autobiography of Thomas Ewing.* Columbus: Heer Printing, 1912.

Hamilton, Holman. *Zachary Taylor: Soldier in the White House.* Indianapolis: Bobbs-Merrill, 1951.

McKinley, Silas B. *Old Rough and Ready: The Life and Times of Zachary Taylor.* New York: Vanguard Press, 1946.

Mitchell, Jack. *Executive Privilege: Two Centuries of White House Scandals.* New York: Hippocrene Books, 1992.

Smith, Elbert B. *The Presidencies of Zachary Taylor and Millard Fillmore.* Lawrence: University Press of Kansas, 1988.

Woodward, C. Vann. *Responses of the Presidents to Charges of Misconduct.* New York: Dell Publishing, 1974.

MILLARD FILLMORE

Thirteenth President
1850–1853

orn in a log cabin in Cayuga County, New York, on January 7, 1800, Millard Fillmore was the son of a struggling tenant farmer. His education was limited to the basics of reading, writing, and mathematics until he was nineteen, when he was sent to an academy at New Hope. There he flourished under the guidance of Abigail Powers, whom he married in 1826. In 1819 his father arranged for him to study law under Judge Walter Wood in Montville. Two years later he left Judge Wood after an argument about Fillmore's performance of legal work outside the office. Moving to Aurora, near Buffalo, to join his parents, he taught school and continued to study law. In 1823 he was admitted to the bar.

Active in the Anti-Masonic Party, which opposed secret societies, Fillmore was elected to the New York state assembly in 1829. He served three one-year terms before being elected to the U.S. House of Representatives. After his first two terms, Fillmore became active in building the Whig Party in New York, and he was reelected to Congress in 1836, serving until 1843. The following year he became the party's vice-presidential nominee on the ticket headed by Theodore Frelinghuysen of New Jersey. He also stood as the Whig nominee for governor of New York in 1844, losing to the Democratic candidate, Silas Wright, by slightly more than 10,000 votes. Fillmore reentered elected public service three years later, when he was elected comptroller of New York State.

At the Whig national convention in 1848, Fillmore was nominated on the second ballot to run with presidential candidate Zachary Taylor. He was chosen in part to balance the ticket as an opponent of slavery. Fillmore played virtually no role in the Taylor administration. He was not part of the decision to fill the cabinet with party loyalists or to dispense patronage jobs (see page 90). After Taylor's death on July 9, 1850, Fillmore succeeded to the presidency.

Fillmore inherited the problems of a nation struggling over the slavery issue. One of the major issues was the debate over the Compromise of

1850, devised by Henry Clay, to make concessions to both northern and southern interests. President Taylor had opposed the compromise and sought the admission of California as a free state. Fillmore, however, believed the compromise was in the best interests of the nation. By trying to appease all elements except hard-core abolitionists, the compromise managed to postpone the Civil War for a decade. Fillmore's support of it and the Fugitive Slave Act, which made federal officials responsible for capturing and returning runaway slaves, cost him the presidential nomination in 1852.

Fillmore returned to Buffalo, where his wife and daughter died within sixteen months of their return. He traveled within the United States and then toured Europe. While in Europe, he was nominated for the presidency by the American (Know Nothing) Party, a nativist group that opposed immigration and Roman Catholics and sought to lengthen the time necessary for individuals to become citizens. Accepting the nomination, Fillmore returned to the United States in June 1856. He was endorsed by the dying Whig Party, whose northern members had formed the Republican Party and nominated John C. Fremont as their candidate. Carrying just one state (Maryland), Fillmore finished third in a three-man race that saw Democrat James Buchanan victorious.

Retired from politics, Fillmore married Caroline McIntosh, the widow of a prominent Albany businessman, in 1858. The Fillmores lived in Buffalo, and he administered Caroline's vast fortune. When the Civil War broke out in 1861, Fillmore supported the Union's cause, but he came under attack for his earlier endorsement of the Fugitive Slave Act, and a mob vandalized his home after Lincoln was assassinated. Fillmore died on March 8, 1874, after suffering two strokes the previous month.

THOMAS CORWIN, SECRETARY OF TREASURY

When James Guthrie became secretary of the Treasury in Franklin Pierce's administration, he discovered that his predecessor, Thomas Corwin, had violated the specifics of the Independent Treasury Act of 1846 by depositing money in banks rather than in federal depositories.

In the weeks before President Taylor's death, the controversy surrounding the Galphin family's claim (see page 88) had led Taylor to consider creating a new cabinet untainted by scandal. Succeeding him as president, Fillmore had an opportunity to do just that. Existing tensions between the new president and Taylor's old cabinet led the cabinet members to resign. Fillmore accepted their resignations but asked for a month to find replacements. They gave him a week.

With the nation in crisis over the spread of slavery to the territories, Fillmore needed officials who would not exacerbate the tensions. He wanted Thomas Corwin, Ohio's most respected Whig politician, as postmaster general. Corwin declined but agreed to become secretary of the

James Guthrie

Treasury. Fillmore, more politically experienced than Taylor and aware that the Whigs were already tainted by scandal, was careful to avoid any charges of misbehavior by his administration. The trouble came later, in 1853, when the Whig administration was replaced by a Democratic one under Franklin Pierce.

Pierce appointed James Guthrie of Kentucky as secretary of the Treasury. When Guthrie, during the course of his duties, looked at Corwin's management of the Treasury, he discovered that his Whig predecessors had been lax about following the requirements of the Independent Treasury Act of 1846. According to that law, all federal money was supposed to be held in federal depositories. Without informing the public, Corwin had allowed some of the money to be deposited in banks. No money had been lost or stolen, so there was little political fallout. Guthrie simply moved the money back where it legally should have been.

Corwin's behavior was more a matter of politics than of crime. Until the debate over slavery overshadowed other concerns, one of the chief points of contention between Whigs and Democrats had centered on how the government should handle money raised as taxes before it was paid out in expenses.

Before Andrew Jackson's presidency, the United States had followed the example of European countries in having a national bank that handled government money, depositing or withholding deposits in other banks in an effort to ensure its safety and to regulate the money supply. In 1832 Jackson, reflecting a frontiersman's distrust of banks, had vetoed the renewal of the national bank's charter. A strong advocate of states' rights, he believed that federal money should be deposited in banks run by the states. In the spring of 1837 that policy had disastrous consequences when a depression left many banks unable to repay their government deposits. Jackson had used mistakes made by the national bank to destroy it, but the state banks were shown to be capable of even more costly mistakes than the national bank.

In 1840 the Democrats came up with a solution, the Independent Treasury Act. Rather than risk its money in banks, the government would simply hold all revenues in depositories placed around the country, paying out money only to cover expenses. Because it made the government independent of the nation's banking system, the scheme was called an independent treasury. In addition to the fact that the government would earn no interest on its assets, the idea had another major economic drawback. Created during a depression when banks were failing, an independent treasury was useless during a time of rapid expansion. A booming economy would increase tax revenue and fill government coffers. The money would then lie fallow at the very time when the country needed capital to build new factories, railroads, and canals.

In 1841 the Whigs tried to reestablish a national bank. Failing that, they consoled themselves by abolishing the independent treasury, which meant funds once more had to be moved to state banks. In 1846 the Democrats again passed the Independent Treasury Act, which Corwin felt duty-bound to violate. Secretary Guthrie's behavior after replacing Corwin illustrates one problem created by the law. With the economy booming, money— much needed elsewhere—was beginning to pile up in government depositories. To get rid of this surplus, Guthrie had to pay off government debts earlier than scheduled to get it back into circulation. Through brokers, he began to buy U.S. bonds on the open market and announced that bonds due for payment in July could be redeemed any time after March 10. It was an awkward way to deal with a problem that could have been dealt with better by giving the federal government a role in the nation's banking system. In the long run, history would vindicate Corwin's flexible approach.

BIBLIOGRAPHY

Carroll, Stephen G. *Thomas Corwin and the Agonies of the Whig Party.* Boulder: University Press of Colorado, 1970.

Mitchell, Jack. *Executive Privilege: Two Centuries of White House Scandals.* New York, Hippocrene Books, 1992.

Nichols, Roy F. *Franklin Pierce, Young Hickory of the Granite Hills.* Philadelphia: University of Pennsylvania Press, 1958.

Rayback, Robert J. *Millard Fillmore: A Biography of a President.* Newtown, Conn.: American Political Biography Press, 1959.

Smith, Elbert B. *The Presidencies of Zachary Taylor and Millard Fillmore.* Lawrence: University Press of Kansas, 1988.

Timberlake, Richard H., Jr. "The Independent Treasury and Monetary Policy before the Civil War." *Southern Economic Journal* 27 (October 1960): 92–103. Available on microfilm.

Woodward, C. Vann. *Responses of the Presidents to Charges of Misconduct.* New York: Dell Publishing, 1974.

FRANKLIN PIERCE

Fourteenth President
1853–1857

Franklin Pierce was born in Hillsborough, New Hampshire, November 23, 1804, the sixth of eight children of Benjamin and Anna Pierce. Franklin attended private schools and enrolled at Bowdoin College in Maine at age fifteen. Graduating third in his class, he returned to New Hampshire, where he studied law and was admitted to the bar in 1827, the year his father, Gen. Benjamin Pierce, became governor of the state. In 1829 Franklin Pierce was elected to the state legislature, and two years later he became its Speaker. Elected to the U.S. House of Representatives in 1833, he became a political ally of President Andrew Jackson. In 1837 the New Hampshire legislature elected Pierce to the U.S. Senate, but he served only five years.

Pierce returned to New Hampshire, believing he would be better able to support his family as an attorney. In 1844 President James K. Polk appointed him U.S. district attorney for New Hampshire. Over the next two years Pierce refused several offers of political positions, including another Senate term, because he wished to remain at home.

However, in 1846 war broke out with Mexico, and Pierce volunteered. Commissioned a brigadier general in the regular army, he led the Ninth Regiment. He returned to New Hampshire as a hero despite his undistinguished service. In 1852 he was nominated for president by the Democratic Party on the forty-ninth ballot. The party sought and found in Pierce a candidate who could unequivocally support the Compromise of 1850. Pierce, a true dark horse, won decisively in the electoral college (254–42), but achieved only a marginal popular vote victory over the Whig candidate, Gen. Winfield Scott.

In his inaugural address Pierce proclaimed an era of peace and prosperity at home and vigor in relations with other nations. Pierce, who wished to expand the territory of the United States, was often deterred from action because he did not wish to excite the wrath of northerners, who accused him of acting in behalf of southerners eager to extend slavery.

However, the most violent confrontation over slavery involved the Kansas-Nebraska Act, which repealed the Missouri Compromise and reopened the question of slavery in the West. This measure, sponsored by Sen. Stephen A. Douglas of Illinois, led to a rush of settlers to the Kansas Territory in the hopes of settling the slavery issue in their favor. Shooting broke out, and "bleeding Kansas" became a prelude to the Civil War.

By the end of his administration, Pierce could claim "a peaceful condition of things in Kansas." But, to his disappointment, the Democrats refused to renominate him, turning to the less-controversial James Buchanan of Pennsylvania. Pierce returned to New Hampshire to nurse his ailing wife who had never fully recovered from the death of their son. After two years of travel in Europe, Pierce and his wife returned to Hillsborough in 1859. Pierce believed that his presidency had been successful in protecting private property, but failed to understand the growing moral outrage over slavery. He was concerned when Abraham Lincoln was elected, fearing sectional difference. He lived to see the end of the Civil War and some of the consequences of Reconstruction. He died October 8, 1869.

DRUNKENNESS

Several personal tragedies, including the death of his son, led Pierce to begin drinking heavily while he was president. Some contemporaries questioned whether he was sober enough to perform his duties.

A few weeks before the newly elected president Franklin Pierce was scheduled to move to Washington and assume his duties, his eleven-year-old son, Bennie, was killed in a train wreck in Andover, Massachusetts. The boy was caught under the train and crushed to death while his parents watched helplessly. This event had a profound influence on Pierce's administration because his wife, Jane, remained in mourning for two years and did not serve as hostess at the White House. She blamed Franklin for the death of their son and the fact that they had to leave New Hampshire for Washington.

Pierce's grief was compounded by the deaths of Vice President William R. King and a close friend, New Hampshire senator Charles G. Atherton. Both men died shortly after Pierce took office. Jane Pierce took these events as further signs that they were being punished by God.

Critics and supporters alike worried that the emotionally shaken president was drinking to deaden the pain of losing his son and his friends and to deal with his wife's bitterness. His critics, however, went on to argue that Pierce was an unstable alcoholic unable to perform his duties as president.

Jane Pierce

Although it is clear that he was prone to bouts of drinking, there is no evidence he was unable, even under these stressful circumstances, to perform the duties of the office.

ANDREW REEDER, GOVERNOR OF KANSAS

Andrew Reeder was involved in widespread land speculations in Kansas while serving as governor. These deals included purchasing a tract directly from the Indians, an action prohibited by federal law. He also tried to establish the territory's seat of government on land he owned. Finally, Reeder participated in election frauds that delayed the admission of Kansas as a state because of competing slave and antislavery forces.

Both sides in the slavery debate knew that the future of the institution might hinge on whether the Kansas Territory would permit or prohibit slavery. If slavery could establish itself in the fertile grasslands of the Midwest, it would be far more difficult to uproot. If it could not, then Missouri's border with Kansas would provide yet another outlet for fugitive slaves. The moment the territory was opened for settlement on May 30, 1854, the bitter struggle began. Both sides soon turned to intimidation and violence in an effort to drive out their foes.

The problem was made worse by confused and unsettled land titles. Originally Kansas had been reserved for the Indians, and the federal government was still in the process of evicting them when white settlers began to arrive and squat on land they wanted. With so many occupying land for which they held no clear title, often the only way to settle disputes was by force.

In such circumstances, even the best of territorial governments would have faced trouble. Kansas did not get that kind of government. Pierce, a loyal Democrat, appointed pro-slavery administrators to every important position. In turn, those territorial officials permitted election fraud on a massive scale. Thousands of Missouri slave owners crossed the border to vote illegally in Kansas, which made it impossible for the debate over a free or slave Kansas to be settled democratically.

From his party's perspective, Pierce also made a disastrous choice for territorial governor. In an effort to appear even-handed, he selected a southerner to govern the Nebraska territory and a northerner for Kansas. Superficially, Andrew H. Reeder appeared to be fine for Kansas: he had a reputation as a loyal party member and a southern sympathizer. But Reeder had never held political office, and his willingness to put party interests foremost had never been tested. What he was good at was land speculation, and the unsettled land titles in Kansas proved to be a temptation he could not resist. Appointed in June 1854, Reeder did not arrive in Kansas until the fall. When he arrived, his opponents would later allege, he spent much of his time looking for good land to buy.

In January 1855 Reeder and two federal judges in the territory bought four large tracts of land from Indians. When claims were later made that the Indians had been cheated, Reeder pointed out that the price he and his partners had paid was more than four times what the government was paying the Shawnee for similar land. A more serious charge concerned how the land had been obtained. Indian Bureau policy required purchases to be made through Indian agents rather than directly. For that reason, the Indian commissioner in Washington disallowed the purchase and informed President Pierce about the matter.

To his credit, Reeder was now doing more than speculating in land. He was taking his job as governor seriously, so much so that pro-slavery groups began to regard him as a foe. He investigated the contested elections and easily came to the conclusion that they were frauds. In spring 1855 he traveled to Washington to inform the president of that fact. Loyal to his party, Pierce instead asked for evidence of *anti*-slavery fraud, something Reeder had not uncovered. Pierce also asked Reeder to explain his land purchase and, at the time, publicly claimed to be satisfied with the explanation. Later Reeder said that Pierce had asked him to resign, promising to make arrangements to "promote [Reeder's] private interests." If that was true, and Pierce never denied Reeder's claims, then Reeder may be more respectable than many historians have portrayed him. Given a choice between personal profit and fair elections, Reeder chose the latter.

Refusing to resign, Reeder returned to Kansas and clashed with the new, illegally elected legislature. Although he seems to have had no objections to slavery, Reeder was outraged at the voter fraud and how slavery opponents were treated. In his remaining months as governor, he vetoed laws so outrageous they made it illegal even to read a Free Soil newspaper. Pro-slavery leaders, now convinced that Reeder was supporting the abolitionists, began to use the land speculation charges against him.

The Kansas legislature was in an excellent position to observe the governor. When Reeder issued his call for the legislature to meet on July 2, 1855, he brought them to Pawnee City. The large stone meeting hall and plentiful lodging made it an excellent place to meet, but Reeder had another purpose in mind. His four tracts of land were in Pawnee City, and, if the location became the state capital, his investment would bring lucrative returns. The legislators were in no mood to help him. Pawnee City was 100 miles from the Missouri border, a long distance to travel by horse and wagon. The legislature immediately adjourned and moved to the more conveniently located Shawnee Mission, just across the border from Missouri. From their new location, the state legislature called on Pierce to remove Reeder from office and threatened to hold their own election to choose someone in his place.

Even a blameless Reeder would have had trouble surviving such attacks. Tainted by charges of land speculations, he was doomed. On July 28, 1855, Pierce dismissed him from office. Reeder did not go quietly. He began to speak publicly about what was happening in Kansas and, in the 1856 elections, he supported the new Republican Party and its presidential candidate, John C. Fremont.

Pierce was equally angry. In his 1856 State of the Union address he attacked Reeder and tried to shift blame for the troubles in Kansas to antislavery societies. Events in Kansas were hurting the Democrats in the North, and the situation was made worse by the fact that the party had placed in office someone who was now a vocal critic of their territorial policies. At the presidential nominating convention, delegates withheld enough votes from Pierce to award the nomination to James Buchanan.

BIBLIOGRAPHY

Gara, Larry. *The Presidency of Franklin Pierce.* Lawrence: University Press of Kansas, 1991.

Hawthorne, Nathaniel. *The Life of Franklin Pierce.* Reprint of the 1852 edition. New York: Garrett Press, 1970.

Mitchell, Jack. *Executive Privilege: Two Centuries of White House Scandals.* New York: Hippocrene Books, 1992.

Nevins, Allan. *Ordeal of the Union.* New York: Scribner's Sons, 1947.

Nichols, Roy F. *Franklin Pierce, Young Hickory of the Granite Hills.* Philadelphia: University of Pennsylvania Press, 1958.

Woodward, C. Vann. *Responses of the Presidents to Charges of Misconduct.* New York: Dell Publishing, 1974.

JAMES BUCHANAN

Fifteenth President
1857–1861

James Buchanan was born April 23, 1791, near Mercersburg, Pennsylvania, where his well-to-do family had a frontier trading post. At the age of sixteen, he left Mercersburg to attend Dickinson College, graduating with honors in 1809. He studied law under James Hopkins in Lancaster, Pennsylvania, and was admitted to the bar in 1812. Although he originally opposed the War of 1812, in 1814 Buchanan enlisted in a special company of dragoons. He served under Maj. Charles Ridgely in the defense of Baltimore.

Buchanan began his political career as a Federalist and was elected to the state assembly in 1814. First elected to the U.S. House of Representatives in 1820, where he served for five terms, he became a Jacksonian Democrat after the demise of the Federalist Party in 1824.

A staunch ally of President Andrew Jackson, Buchanan was appointed ambassador to Russia in 1831 and negotiated the first U.S. commercial treaty with that nation. Returning to the United States, he was elected to the Senate where he served from 1834 to 1845. He was President James K. Polk's secretary of state from 1845 to 1849 and helped negotiate a settlement of the Oregon Territory border with Great Britain. President Franklin Pierce selected him as ambassador to Great Britain, and, therefore, Buchanan was out of the country during the most intense political conflicts over slavery in the Kansas Territory.

Because Buchanan was immune from the Kansas controversy, the Democrats turned to him as their standard-bearer in 1856, and he won the election largely because of his appeal in the South. As president-elect, Buchanan thought the growing crisis over slavery would dissipate if he maintained a diplomatic sectional balance in his appointments. He also tried to convince people of the wisdom of accepting constitutional law as the Supreme Court interpreted it in cases such as the upcoming *Scott v. Sandford*. The public was following the so-called *Dred Scott* case with great interest.

In his inaugural address, March 4, 1857, the president referred to the territorial question as "happily, a matter of but little practical importance" because the Supreme Court was about to settle it "speedily and finally." Two days later, the Court announced in *Dred Scott* that Congress had no constitutional power to deprive persons of their property rights in slaves in the territories. Buchanan then urged that Kansas be admitted to the Union as a slave state. This call angered many in both parties, and Kansas would remain a territory until the Civil War.

The newly formed Republican Party won a plurality of seats in the House of Representatives in 1858. However, the evenly balanced Senate and Buchanan's use of the veto prevented the new party from pursuing its antislavery agenda. The government stalemate had dramatic effects on the Democratic Party. It split into northern and southern wings, and each nominated its own candidate for the presidency in 1860, neither of them Buchanan. The result was the election of Republican Party candidate Abraham Lincoln.

South Carolina had vowed to secede from the Union if Lincoln were elected, and on December 20 the state voted to carry out its threat. Buchanan denied the legal right of states to secede but held that constitutionally he could do nothing about it. Instead, he sought a compromise that would keep the secession movement from growing. He supported a plan introduced in the Senate by John Crittenden of Kentucky that proposed extending to the Pacific the Missouri Compromise line prohibiting slavery and protecting slavery where it already existed. Buchanan even called for a constitutional convention to put the slavery issue to a vote. In the end, all his peacemaking efforts failed. Taking a more militant tack, Buchanan sent an unarmed merchant ship, *Star of the West,* to carry reinforcements to Fort Sumter, South Carolina. On January 9, 1861, the vessel was fired upon and driven away. On February 8, other southern states joined South Carolina to form the Confederate States of America.

Leaving office in March 1861, Buchanan retired to Wheatland, his home in Lancaster, Pennsylvania. He rarely commented in public on issues of national interest, but carried on voluminous correspondence and wrote in his own defense *Mr. Buchanan's Administration on the Eve of the Rebellion,* which was published in 1866. He was a loyal supporter of Lincoln's administration and of Andrew Johnson's Reconstruction policy. Buchanan died June 1, 1867.

ANNE CAROLINE COLEMAN

It is believed that Buchanan's former fiancée committed suicide shortly after breaking off their engagement. Buchanan had deposited letters in a bank vault, which he said would explain the circumstances, but after his death the letters were destroyed.

In the summer of 1819 James Buchanan, a successful lawyer of twenty-eight, proposed to the wealthy twenty-three-year-old Anne Caroline Coleman. Buchanan had met Anne the previous year through a mutual friend, Molton Rogers. The couple seemed destined for a life of happiness. However, rumors began to circulate that Buchanan was interested in Anne only for her father's money; Robert Coleman was one of the richest men in Pennsylvania. There was also talk that Buchanan was seeing another young woman. To add to the difficulty, Buchanan was involved in a time-consuming lawsuit regarding the Columbia Bridge Company, in which many leading citizens of Lancaster owned shares, that required him to be in Philadelphia.

Whatever the cause, Anne broke off the engagement at the end of the summer. Buchanan hoped that time would resolve the problem. However, Anne continued to refuse to see him, and his letters were returned unopened. On December 9 Anne died from what appeared to be a drug overdose. She had gone to Philadelphia to visit her sister, Margaret Hemphill, in an attempt to end her depression. Neither the exact cause of her death or of the broken engagement was ever determined. Buchanan had deposited in a New York bank vault papers to be opened upon his death. He said the documents would explain the events in more detail, but the mystery remains unsolved. The papers were destroyed unopened because his executors found a note in Buchanan's handwriting instructing them to do so.

HOMOSEXUALITY

There is circumstantial evidence that Buchanan may have been carrying on a homosexual relationship with William R. King, a fellow member of Congress.

James Buchanan, the only bachelor to become president, may have decided never to marry after Anne Coleman's death. However, some historians believe that Buchanan did not marry because he was homosexual. It is thought that he and William Rufus King, a fellow member of Congress, had a homosexual relationship. King, the only bachelor to be elected vice president, died of tuberculosis just one month after taking the oath of office as Franklin Pierce's vice president. For nearly twenty-three years, Buchanan and King were roommates in Washington, D.C. Some evidence indicates that people were aware of a relationship between the two men. In a letter to Sarah Polk, Aaron Brown, a representative from Tennessee, refers to King as "Mrs. B" and "Buchanan's wife."

William R. King

ELECTIONS OF 1856 AND 1858

Buchanan used lucrative government contracts as a way to raise money, which improved the chances of the Democratic Party in the elections of 1856 and 1858.

There is clear evidence that the Democratic Party took improper, if not illegal, actions to win elections in 1856 and 1858. Buchanan's role in these dealings, direct and indirect, became part of the subject matter investigated by the Covode Committee in 1860. (See page 105.)

During the elections of 1856, Buchanan's close friend, George Plitt of Philadelphia, promised lucrative naval contracts to businessmen for their support of Buchanan's candidacy. These contracts were in fact authorized after Buchanan's election. Isaac Fowler, the postmaster of New York City, funneled large sums of post office money into Buchanan's election efforts there. He eventually fled the country when a congressional investigation showed he had stolen $160,000.

Cornelius Wendell, the government's largest recipient of printing contracts, charged the government inflated prices and used the money to pay for the support of various pro-Democratic newspapers and as a kickback fund that went into the election coffers of Buchanan and other prominent Democrats. Although most of this money was used for legitimate purposes, such as printing and distributing campaign documents, some of it went to buy votes in Indiana and Pennsylvania. The party even transplanted immigrants to vote in crucial states, even though they were not eligible to vote. John Forney, who led this operation, wrote to Buchanan that "we have naturalized a vast mass of men and assessed many of the native-born citizens."

During the 1858 election the administration engaged in bribery and influence peddling of the grossest sort to win support for the LeCompton Compromise, which favored slavery in Kansas. Buchanan fired anti-LeCompton Democrats from their government posts and filled these jobs with men who supported the measure. He dispensed cash to solidify the votes of individual congressmen. Buchanan even moved to oust unsupportive members of the House and Senate who were up for reelection in 1858.

The most notorious example involved Sen. Stephen A. Douglas of Illinois. Buchanan fired the Douglas supporter who was serving as postmaster for Chicago and replaced him with arch rival Isaac Cook. Cook had once been removed from government office because he had defaulted on a debt he owed the government. When Buchanan nominated him for postmaster, Secretary of the Treasury Howell Cobb was instructed to accept a plot of land in Chicago from Cook as full repayment of the debt. Cobb had earlier refused to accept the land because it was unclear that Cook held title to it. Even though Buchanan knew that Cook was stealing funds from the post office, he kept him on because he was an effective local opponent to Douglas and Douglas's supporters.

PUBLIC PRINTING SCANDALS

In a scandal that ultimately became part of the Covode Committee investigation, Buchanan's administration was examined for using government printing contracts for party purposes.

In the summer of 1858 Congress decided to end some of the most egregious abuses connected with the awarding of government printing contracts. This kind of abuse had been common since Andrew Jackson's administration (1829–1837). The unearthing of graft and overpayments persuaded Congress to pass laws forbidding double payment for printing the same document for both the House and the Senate and prohibiting the subcontracting of printing, which had resulted in unreasonable prices. The law forbade the individuals who won congressional contracts from selling them to jobbers like Cornelius Wendell, who had made millions from the printing contracts from 1853 to 1860. The committee behind the legislation also discovered that the superintendent of public printing had consistently extorted bribes and kickbacks from contractors. The superintendent was indicted and convicted on the charges and sent to federal prison.

Buchanan appointed George Bowman, a Pennsylvania editor, to the post of superintendent, and Bowman put a stop to the illegal practices. Cornelius Wendell announced that he would no longer support the *Washington Union,* the administration paper, because the changes in the laws had cut into his profits. Buchanan tried to get Bowman to take the position as editor of the *Union,* but Bowman refused, citing financial considerations. Buchanan solved this problem by having Attorney General Jeremiah S. Black arrange a contract that violated the spirit if not the letter of the 1858 law. The scheme involved Bowman taking over the editorship of the *Union* and Wendell paying him a salary of $10,000 for his services. In return, Wendell would be given the Senate printing. Wendell would use some of the proceeds to support two additional newspapers in Pennsylvania that backed Buchanan.

The establishment of the Government Printing Office in 1860 ended this particular form of corruption once and for all. No longer could a government printing contract become the source of political funds.

THE COVODE COMMITTEE

The House of Representatives began an in-depth investigation of Buchanan's activities to see if the president had used money, patronage, or other improper means to influence decisions of Congress. The committee, headed by John Covode of Pennsylvania, was particularly interested in the LeCompton Compromise and government printing contracts.

On March 5, 1860, the House of Representatives adopted a resolution to investigate whether President Buchanan had tried to influence the votes of members of Congress by improper means. Speaker of the House William Pennington appointed John Covode of Pennsylvania, who originated the resolution, to chair the committee. Buchanan incorrectly assumed that the idea for the committee came from John Forney, a Pennsylvania political operative who had broken ranks with Buchanan when he did not reward him with a high-ranking post in the administration. Buchanan also believed that the investigation might have been the work of those who supported Stephen Douglas for the party's nomination at Charleston.

The real forces behind the committee's creation had other axes to grind. First, the Senate was busy investigating whether the Republican Party had backed the raid on Harper's Ferry by John Brown's men. In retaliation, the Republican-controlled House wanted to use the Covode investigation as a means of exposing Democratic Party corruption. Second, John Covode had a grudge against Buchanan because the president had vetoed a land grant bill Covode sponsored. The bill, which would have established land grant colleges, also called for large tracts to be available to the railroad company in which Covode was involved. Third, the Douglas Democrats hoped that the investigation would embarrass the president by reexamining his role in the Kansas constitution and the handling of patronage in Illinois. Thus, the Republicans and Douglas Democrats formed an alliance to attack the president on many fronts.

Buchanan protested the formation of the committee. "The House has made my accuser [John Covode] one of my judges. . . . Since the time of the Star Chamber and of general warrants there has been no such proceeding. . . . I defy all investigations. Nothing but the basest perjury can sully my good name." Despite Buchanan's protests, the committee went about its work enthusiastically.

The committee heard from many witnesses, most of whom were political enemies of the president or disgruntled former officeholders. During the three months of testimony, the committee uncovered a number of scandals and improper practices. Included in its discoveries was a practice common to every administration since Andrew Jackson—the use of public offices and certain types of public funds for political purposes. Partisan editors would receive lucrative printing contracts in exchange for editorial support. The investigation uncovered the events surrounding the appointment of Isaac Cook of Chicago as postmaster and showed that the brother of the collector of Philadelphia customs was on the government's payroll while editing a Democratic newspaper.

John Floyd, secretary of war, was investigated for naval contracts that had been awarded for political reasons and for his authorization to sell government land at low prices to political friends. Buchanan was aware of Floyd's activities and had voided one of the contracts.

However, the most damaging testimony and the real focus of the investigation were Buchanan's connection with the printing contracts and his efforts to push the LeCompton Compromise through the House. Cornelius Wendell, once the driving force behind the *Washington Union,* the administration's paper, became one of the star witnesses against Buchanan. Wendell detailed how the lucrative printing contracts were divided among Democratic Party candidates and editors. Wendell revealed that between $30,000 and $40,000 had been spent to bribe members of Congress to support the LeCompton Compromise.

The other star witness was John Forney, who had once been Buchanan's lieutenant in Pennsylvania. Forney claimed that he had been awarded $80,000 worth of post office printing in return for endorsing the LeCompton Compromise in his editorial columns. In May the committee was given additional ammunition against the administration when Postmaster General Joseph Holt discovered that New York City postmaster Isaac Fowler had embezzled more than $160,000 and fled to Europe.

The hearings were supposed to be secret, but the charges against Buchanan were regularly leaked to the press; Buchanan's defense was not reported until the final report was issued. When the committee concluded its work in June, it had the hearings printed and bound and sent all over the country. The huge tome seemed to convict the president by its size alone. The majority report, a thirty-page document, was mailed to hundreds of thousands of locales. The lone Democrat on the committee, Warren Winslow of North Carolina, prepared a minority report with the aid of the White House.

Buchanan responded June 22. First, he attacked the committee's procedures, steering clear of the substance of the charges, as many were true. "It was a secret committee in regard to the testimony which could by possibility reflect on my character," he wrote. "The poison was left to produce its effect upon the public mind, whilst the antidote was carefully withheld." Second, he attacked the motives of those investigating him. Buchanan argued that his accusers were "interested parasites and informers." He further believed that the American people would never believe such men because the people "detest delators and informers." Finally, he said he was not trying to save his own skin, but the executive branch from encroachment by the legislature. The Covode Committee had "acted as though they possessed unlimited power . . . to degrade the Presidential office itself to such a degree as to render it unworthy of the acceptance of any man of honor or principle." The founding fathers, he continued, had most feared "the aggrandizement of the legislative at the expense of the executive and judicial departments."

Buchanan trumpeted that the partisan investigation had not resulted in a resolution of impeachment or even a censure. "I have passed triumphantly through this ordeal. My vindication is complete," he said. However, his administration, already considered a lame duck, suffered throughout the country from the investigation and its negative reports.

JOHN B. FLOYD, SECRETARY OF WAR

Even after Congress restricted Secretary of War John Floyd's authority to sign contracts, he continued to sign inflated contracts, which he funded by floating bogus bonds.

The Covode Committee was particularly critical of the activities of Secretary of War John Floyd. Even though Floyd was clearly incompetent, Buchanan did not ask for his resignation. Instead, he told Floyd to refrain from writing any further contract acceptances for New York weapons brokers Russell, Majors, and Waddell. The government still owed the gun brokers for their services during the Mormon crisis, an armed conflict between the Mormon settlers of the Utah Territory and federal authorities. Throughout Buchanan's administration, Congress had been cutting defense expenditures. As a result, many contracts were left unpaid for long periods of time. Without authorization, Floyd would sign the bills, thereby indicating that the government intended to pay them. Russell, Majors, and Waddell used the signed bills as collateral in obtaining loans. Congress reprimanded Floyd and ordered him to stop committing the government's money, but he continued.

As if his carrying on this practice was not bad enough, Floyd managed to make matters worse. A relation named Godard Bailey, who was a clerk in the Department of Interior, had been helping Floyd by giving Russell, Majors, and Waddell negotiable bonds that were held in trust for the Indians. No proof ever surfaced that either Bailey or Floyd profited from the transactions, but the New York firm exchanged Floyd's contract acceptances for $870,000 worth of bonds. Interior Secretary Jacob Thompson was ignorant of the transaction, and Floyd claimed he himself knew nothing of the exchange. The story broke on December 22, 1860, when several newspapers reported that some of the bonds had made their way to market.

Buchanan again failed to act decisively, even though he had decided it was time for Floyd to go. Buchanan first asked Attorney General Jeremiah S. Black to suggest to Floyd that he should resign, but Black refused to do so. Buchanan then sent Vice President John Breckinridge to ask Floyd for his resignation, which Floyd did not offer. Not wanting to fire

John B. Floyd

Floyd on Christmas Day, Buchanan held a cabinet meeting the next day. Interior Secretary Thompson denounced Floyd and threatened to prosecute everyone including him. Black mentioned that Pittsburgh citizens were complaining about an impending shipment of cannons to forts in Texas. They believed the shipment of U.S. arms to Texas, where there were growing sectional differences, was treason. Floyd had ordered the guns to Texas on December 20. Buchanan canceled the order, and Floyd, looking for a reason other than the threat of prosecution to resign, took Buchanan's cancellation as a personal insult and resigned.

BIBLIOGRAPHY

Curtis, George T. *Life of James Buchanan: Fifteenth President of the United States.* Freeport, N.Y.: Books for Libraries Press, 1969.

Hagood, Wesley O. *Presidential Sex: From Founding Fathers to Bill Clinton.* Secaucus, N.J.: Carol Publishing Group, 1998.

Klein, Philip Shriver. *President James Buchanan: A Biography.* Norwalk, Conn.: Easton Press, 1962.

Meerse, David E. "James Buchanan, Patronage, and the Northern Democratic Party, 1857–58." Ph.D. dissertation, University of Illinois, 1969.

Mitchell, Jack. *Executive Privilege: Two Centuries of White House Scandals.* New York: Hippocrene Books, 1992.

Nevins, Allan. *The Emergence of Lincoln.* New York: Scribners, 1950.

Nichols, Roy F. *The Disruption of American Democracy.* New York: Macmillan, 1948.

Ross, Shelley. *Fall from Grace: Sex, Scandal, and Corruption in American Politics from 1702 to the Present.* New York: Ballantine Books, 1988.

Smith, Elbert B. *The Presidency of James Buchanan.* Lawrence: University Press of Kansas, 1975.

Woodward, C. Vann. *Responses of the Presidents to Charges of Misconduct.* New York: Dell Publishing, 1974.

ABRAHAM LINCOLN

Sixteenth President
1861–1865

Abraham Lincoln was born February 12, 1809, in a one-room log cabin in Hardin (now Larue) County, Kentucky. He was the second of the three children of Nancy and Thomas Lincoln, a poor farmer and carpenter. When Abe was seven years old, the family moved to Spencer County, Indiana. His mother died in 1818, and his father married a widow, Sarah Bush Johnston, who had three children of her own. His stepmother was a loving woman who encouraged Abe to read, and, although he had only a year or two of formal education, he became an avid reader.

In 1831 Lincoln settled in New Salem, Illinois, and worked in a general store. He joined the militia during the Black Hawk War (1832), serving as captain of a company of volunteers. He reenlisted several times during the conflict without seeing any action. Returning to Illinois, he ran for the state legislature as a Whig in 1832, but was defeated. Later that year he bought an interest in a general store. When the store failed, Lincoln was left with debts that would take him seventeen years to repay. He worked as a surveyor and was appointed postmaster of New Salem by President Andrew Jackson in 1833, even though he had supported Henry Clay in the election of 1832. He held the post until 1836.

In 1834 Lincoln was elected to the Illinois legislature as a Whig. He began studying law by reading borrowed law books and was licensed to practice shortly after winning his second term. He served four terms and campaigned for Whig candidates in general elections as well as practicing law.

In 1846 Lincoln was elected to the U.S. House of Representatives, where he served on the Post Office and Post Roads Committee. He was a loyal Whig and opposed the Mexican War, blaming President James K. Polk for starting the conflict. Lincoln had promised his party in Illinois that he would serve only one term in the House. Declining an appointment in the Oregon Territory, he resumed his law practice. Elected once again to the state legislature in 1854, he resigned to run for the U.S. Senate. He lost to Lyman Trumbull in a close race that turned on Lincoln's opposition to the spread of slavery to the territories.

No longer comfortable in the Whig Party, which was divided over the expansion of slavery, Lincoln joined the newly formed Republican Party and campaigned for John C. Fremont in 1856. In 1858 he was nominated to run for the U.S. Senate. His well-known acceptance speech, in which he said "A house divided against itself cannot stand," paraphrased the Bible. Lincoln went on to say he did not believe the Union would be dissolved, that in time the nation would be either all slave or all free. Campaigning around Illinois, Lincoln and his opponent, Democratic senator Stephen A. Douglas, the author of the Kansas-Nebraska Act, engaged in a series of seven debates that drew large crowds. In a close election in the legislature, Douglas retained his seat, 54–46, but the debates made Lincoln famous all over the country.

When the Republican National Convention opened in Chicago in May 1860, William H. Seward of New York was the leading candidate for the presidential nomination. On the third ballot, however, the nod went to Lincoln. Hannibal Hamlin of Maine was selected as his running mate. Lincoln faced three opponents in the fall, two of them Democrats. Northern Democrats nominated Senator Douglas, and southern Democrats nominated Vice President John C. Breckinridge of Kentucky, who had served one term with President James Buchanan. The third opponent was John Bell of Tennessee, nominated by the Constitutional Union Party—a coalition of the old-line Whig Party and the American (Know Nothing) Party. With the votes splintered, Lincoln won the presidency with only 40 percent of the popular vote and 180 electoral votes—all from the North and the West.

Lincoln did not expect to be renominated in 1864 because of the poor progress of the war. But when his party gathered in Baltimore in June, he was nominated without opposition. However, Vice President Hamlin, who wanted to remain on the ticket, was replaced at Lincoln's request by Andrew Johnson, a southern Democrat who had stayed loyal to the Union. In the general election, Lincoln faced Gen. George B. McClellan of New Jersey, the former commander in chief of the army. In the early going, it seemed that McClellan might win on his platform of peace, but Union victories turned the tide, and Lincoln won twenty-two of the twenty-five states of the Union. The eleven states of the Confederacy did not participate.

Beginning in 1861, the war effort consumed the Lincoln administration. At first it went poorly for the Union, which suffered a number of defeats. McClellan was an overly cautious leader, and Lincoln replaced him with Gen. Ambrose E. Burnside. Initially, Lincoln had maintained that the war was about the sanctity of the Union, but in time slavery came to the forefront. In September 1862 Lincoln issued the Emancipation Proclamation, which, on January 1, 1863, would free the slaves in those states still at war with the Union. A largely symbolic act, the proclamation was a clear sign that the war would end slavery if the Union won. In 1864 Lincoln appointed Gen. Ulysses S. Grant as commander of all Union armies. Grant was an effective military commander and forced the surrender of the Confederacy. On April 9, 1865, Gen. Robert E. Lee surrendered his army to Grant at Appomattox Court House.

Lincoln hoped to pursue a lenient course of Reconstruction in the South, believing that was the best way to heal the wounds of war. However, on April 14, 1865, Lincoln was shot by John Wilkes Booth while attending the play *Our American Cousin* at Ford's Theatre and died the next day.

MARY TODD LINCOLN

Mary Todd Lincoln was a controversial first lady. She was scorned by southerners who believed she had turned her back on her family's heritage. Northern critics questioned her loyalty to the Union and accused her of being unpatriotic because of her extravagant spending.

White House Renovations

Every presidential administration since William Henry Harrison had been allotted $20,000 for refurbishing and redecorating the White House, along with a stipend for repairs. Most of the administrations used the funds very poorly with little to show for it. Lincoln's predecessor had spent the money on a glass-domed conservatory, some crystal, and gold teaspoons. In other administrations, most of the money lined the pockets of dishonest dealers. The administration of these and other funds for public buildings was the responsibility of a commissioner, who was appointed by the president to this plum patronage post.

Mary Lincoln used her influence to have William S. Wood of New York appointed commissioner. Unknown to the Lincolns before 1861, he had impressed Mary Lincoln with the arrangements he made for the first family to travel from Springfield, Illinois, to Washington, D.C. Wood and Mary Lincoln had become friends and, as at least one person suggested, perhaps more than friends. Lincoln received an anonymous letter in June 1861 that warned him about "the scandal of your wife and Wood. If he continues as commissioner, he will stab you in your most vital part." According to White House secretaries, the Lincolns fought over Wood, but in the end Mary prevailed, as she often did.

Mary took to the task of refurbishing and repairing the dreary White House with her characteristic energy. She sought to make the long-neglected mansion into a place more fitting for the president of the United States. Exactly what her efforts cost is still a question, although it is clear that she overspent the $20,000 four-year allowance by more than $6,700 in just the first year. Newspapers began to report her extravagances, but she remained undaunted. Finally, her husband, who was slow to catch on, interceded.

Lincoln refused to sign the vouchers and told Mary that she must take responsibility for what she spent. She pleaded with aides and friends to convince the president to sign the vouchers and to ask Congress for a special appropriation to cover the charges. In past administrations Congress had often buried such excesses in other spending bills with little, if any, discussion.

In the fall of 1861 the Senate failed to confirm Wood, who had been serving as acting commissioner. Mary quickly sought another commissioner who might solve her problems. She persuaded the president to appoint Benjamin French, who had served in the same capacity during Franklin Pierce's administration. French tried to intercede in Mary's behalf

Mary Todd Lincoln

with the president, who responded, "I'll pay it out of my pocket first—it would stink in the nostrils of the American people to have it said the President of the United States had approved a bill overrunning an appropriation of $20,000 for 'flub dubs,' for this damned old house, when the soldiers cannot have blankets."

French, who admired Mary Lincoln and her efforts, was nothing if not resourceful. He found other ways to finance her cost overruns. As commissioner of public buildings, French had at his control funds for projects on other federal buildings. He would simply reassign money from another project to cover the White House expenses. He convinced others, including Interior Secretary Caleb Smith, that this practice was common and not illegal. In the next session of Congress, French persuaded a member to include a $4,500 appropriation.

Mary Lincoln, for her part, looked for ways to pay the expenses without using the president's $25,000 annual salary. First, she sold the White House furniture she was replacing and ordered the sale of manure from the stables at an inflated price of ten cents a wagonload. Next, she cut the White House staff to the bare bones, even dismissing those who were on the federal payroll. She performed many of the duties herself and collected the salary for the expenses. Finally, John Wart, the gardener, padded his expense account and kicked back money to her, while keeping some for himself for good measure. With the efforts of French, Wart, and Mary, the cost overruns were financed with funds other than the president's salary.

A Confederate Spy

During the Civil War, Mary Todd Lincoln's family became a center of some controversy and a brief investigation by a joint committee of Congress. Mary came from a prominent slaveholding family in Kentucky. When the war erupted, some of her siblings and half siblings supported the Confederacy and some supported the Union. Although divided families were not uncommon, her family's situation was a source of suspicion.

Several of the Todd brothers were killed while serving in the Confederate Army. Mary's half sister Emilie Todd Helm lost her husband, Confederate general Benjamin Hardin Helm, at Chattanooga. Lincoln had offered Helm a high-ranking post in the Union Army, but he turned it down.

Rumors circulated that Mary Lincoln remained in close contact with her Confederate family members and may have passed information. Eventually, a congressional committee met in secret to draw up charges. While the committee was in session, President Lincoln surprised the members by making an appearance. He had not been asked to testify; nor had he been informed of the exact context of their investigation. The president read the following statement:

> I, Abraham Lincoln, President of the United States, appear of my own volition before this Committee of the Senate to say that I, of my own knowledge, know that it is untrue that any of my family hold treasonable communication with the enemy.

He then rose and left the room. By tacit agreement, the committee dropped its investigation.

JOHN C. FREMONT, COMMANDER OF THE WESTERN DEPARTMENT

John C. Fremont's administration of the Western Department drew criticism for political cronyism and for his defiance of Lincoln's orders.

In July 1861 Lincoln appointed Maj. Gen. John C. Fremont, the Republican Party nominee for president in 1856, as commander of the Western Department with headquarters in St. Louis. Fremont became involved in a political feud with Frank Blair Jr., whose brother was in Lincoln's cabinet and whose father was one of Lincoln's closest advisers. As Blair and Fremont struggled for control of Missouri politics, Blair and other officials reported to Washington that Fremont was "extravagant" and that his command was brimming with a "horde of pirates" who were defrauding the army. Alarmed, Lincoln dispatched Adj. Gen. Lorenzo Thomas to investigate. Thomas reported that Fremont was incompetent and that dubious army purchases had been made.

Meanwhile, a congressional subcommittee headed by Elihu B. Washburne of Illinois conducted an investigation of the Western Department, which was followed later by a war claims commission. Washburne found that much of what Blair had charged was true. Fremont, for example, had established his headquarters in a mansion that cost the government $6,000 a year in rent. The general had surrounded himself with California cronies who made huge profits by securing army contracts without competitive bidding, a violation of the law. One contract, for example, was awarded to a Californian for the construction of thirty-eight mortar-equipped boats at $8,250 apiece—about twice what they were worth. Another Fremont friend, who had no experience in fort construction, nevertheless received a $191,000 contract to build a series of forts that should have cost about one-third that much. In addition, Fremont had given favorite vendors "the most stupendous contracts" for railroad cars, horses, mules, tents, and other equipment, much of it inferior in quality.

Of greater concern was that Fremont issued a military decree abolishing slavery in Missouri—a move that violated Lincoln's policy in 1861 of fighting to save the Union, not to free the slaves. Fremont proved himself to be not only a poor administrator but also an insubordinate officer, and Lincoln relieved him of his command in October 1861. Still, Lincoln did not think Fremont personally dishonest. "His cardinal mistake," the president remarked, "is that he isolates himself, and allows nobody to see him; and by which he does not know what is going on in the very matter he is dealing with."

SIMON CAMERON, SECRETARY OF WAR

Simon Cameron's solution to the problem of equipping Union soldiers proved costly and wasteful, but President Lincoln defended him.

Secretary of War Simon Cameron was responsible for spending enormous sums of money to supply and equip Union armies. But the War Department was so understaffed that the secretary turned to state governors and private citizens for help. The result was widespread chaos, as agents representing state governors, as well as the Ordnance, Quartermaster, and Commissary Bureaus of the War Department, competed with one another in spending federal funds for war materiel.

Informed of certain irregularities in War Department spending, Congress in July 1861 twice demanded that Cameron provide specific information on all government contracts awarded since March 4. But both times Cameron refused to comply, and the House established a special committee on contracts to investigate. After hearing testimony and examining war expenditures, the committee produced a 1,109-page indictment of maladministration in Cameron's office. The committee's principal complaint was the secretary and his maze of agents—some unscrupulous, others inept—had thrown competitive bidding to the winds and had bought exclusively from favorite middlemen and suppliers, many of them "unprincipled and dishonest." Thanks to a combination of inefficiency and fraud, the War Department had purchased huge quantities of rotted blankets, tainted pork, knapsacks that came unglued in the rain, uniforms that fell apart, discarded Austrian muskets, and hundreds of diseased and dying

Simon Cameron

horses—all at exorbitant prices. In one instance, the War Department had sold a lot of condemned Hall carbines for a nominal sum, bought them back at $15 apiece, sold them at $3.50 apiece, and bought them back again at $22 apiece.

The list of abuses seemed endless. One Boston agent, charging the government a percentage of the contracts he arranged, made $20,000 in one week. Another agent acquired two boats for the War Department at a price of $100,000 each after the navy had rejected them as unsafe; one of the vessels sank on its first voyage. Then there were the activities of Alexander Cummings, one of Cameron's political lieutenants. Cameron had appointed Cummings to be the supervisor of army purchases in New York City. By Cummings's authority, the government spent $21,000 for straw hats and linen pantaloons and bought "army supplies" such as Scotch ale, herring, and barreled pickles. In addition, Cummings had contracted for 75,000 pairs of overpriced shoes from a company that occasionally loaned him money.

The House committee criticized such "prostitution of public confidence to purposes of individual aggrandizement" and castigated Cameron's office for treating congressional law as "almost a dead letter," for awarding contracts "universally injurious to the government," and for promoting favoritism and "colossal graft."

By January 1862 Lincoln had decided that Cameron was not the man to run the War Department. Although Cameron had not realized financial gains from the contracts scandals, he was plainly an incompetent administrator. In addition, he too had violated Lincoln's policy regarding slaves and Negroes. Without the president's approval, Cameron had released a War Department report in which he called for the enlistment of black soldiers, a move the president at this time officially opposed. In mid-January, when the Russian ministry became vacant, Lincoln appointed Cameron to fill it and named Edwin Stanton to head the War Department. In a letter to Cameron, however, Lincoln extolled him for his "ability, patriotism, and fidelity to public trust."

Before leaving office, Cameron tried to defend himself. On January 15 he told the Senate that he had never made "a single contract for any purpose whatever." At that, Rep. Henry L. Dawes of Massachusetts produced documents proving that all but 64,000 of 1,903,000 arms contracted for between August 1861 and January 1862 had been ordered under Cameron's direction. On April 30 the House censured him for entrusting men like Alexander Cummings with public money.

In a May 26 message to Congress, Lincoln responded to Cameron's censure, insisting that the president and all other department heads were "equally responsible with him for whatever error, wrong, or fault was committed in the premises." When war broke out, Lincoln explained, Congress was not in session, the capital was threatened with occupation, and the nation was on the brink of disaster. Lincoln and his cabinet officers together had decided that they must assume broad emergency powers or let the government fall. Accordingly, the president had directed that Secretary of the Navy Gideon Welles empower several individuals—including Welles's brother-in-law—to move troops and supplies to protect the capital. The president had allowed Cameron to authorize Alexander Cummings and the governor of New York to transport troops and acquire supplies for the public defense. Because Lincoln believed that southern sympathizers were employed in government departments, he had chosen private citizens known for "their ability, loyalty, and patriotism" to spend public money without security, but without compensation either. Thus, Lincoln had directed that Secretary of the Treasury Salmon P. Chase advance $2 million to John A. Dix, George Opdyke, and Richard M. Blatchford of New York to buy arms and make military preparations. All these emergency actions, the president stated, had received the unanimous approval of his cabinet.

Lincoln conceded that these measures were "without authority of law," but he argued that they were absolutely necessary to save the government in the crisis that followed the attack on Fort Sumter. He did not deny that misdeeds had occurred in War Department operations, nor did he claim that the House censure was unjustified. But he was not willing, he said, to let that censure fall on Cameron alone.

Meanwhile, at Lincoln's urging, Stanton set about reorganizing the War Department, centralizing its activities, and conducting an official audit of its contracts. By canceling many contracts and adjusting others, Stanton's auditors saved the government almost $17 million. At the same time, with the administration's full support, Congress enacted laws that required open and competitive bidding in government purchasing and subjected contractors to court-martial for fraud.

SALMON CHASE, SECRETARY OF THE TREASURY

Salmon Chase was forced to turn a blind eye to the corruption of his Treasury agents by the ongoing trade between the North and the South.

Most of the charges of misconduct in the Treasury Department focused on trade in the southern states. Although commerce with the Confederacy was illegal, the government adopted an intricate system of licenses and permits to regulate business in occupied areas. Much of it was done under the supervision of the Treasury Department, with Chase himself issuing permits, drawing up regulations, and appointing Treasury agents to enforce them. The trouble was that huge profits could be made in the exchange of vital supplies for southern cotton, which was in short supply in the North and commanded an extraordinary price. As a result, the system of trade "became an open invitation to corruption," as speculators swarmed into occupied territories and set about bribing army officers and Treasury agents.

Chase was appalled at the amount of corruption and fraud going on, but knew that he could not possibly "look after all the agents of the department." His political opponents, however, claimed that he was blind to the misdeeds of his own appointees. In 1864 Rep. Frank Blair Jr. proclaimed "that a more profligate administration of the Treasury Department never existed, that the whole Mississippi Valley is rank and fetid with the frauds and corruptions of its agents." Indeed, fraud and corruption were rampant among the agents, but Chase's honesty and integrity were beyond reproach. Additionally, Chase's department was one of the best managed during the war despite the misdeeds of the field agents.

SUSPENSION OF HABEAS CORPUS

During the Civil War President Lincoln had many anti-Union newspaper editors jailed and subjected civilians to trial by military courts. Lincoln's suspension of civil liberties is considered one of the most serious attacks on the Constitution in U.S. history.

Lincoln believed that the Union had to deal harshly with "the enemy in the rear." The Confederacy had "a most efficient corps of spies, informers, suppliers, and aiders and abettors" of the rebellion who took advantage of "Liberty of speech, Liberty of the press and Habeas corpus" to disrupt the Union war effort. Consequently, he suspended the writ of habeas corpus and authorized army commanders to declare martial law in various areas behind the lines and to try civilians in military courts. Lincoln defended his check on civil liberties, contending that strict measures were imperative if the laws of the Union—and freedom itself—were to survive the war.

At first, responsibility for suppressing disloyal activities was divided among the State, War, and Navy Departments, with William H. Seward's State Department playing the largest role. Seward not only censored the telegraphs and the mails, but used government agents, U.S. marshals, city police, and some private informers to maintain surveillance of "suspicious" persons and to help arrest them. By May 1861 many of Seward's techniques troubled Lincoln, and he issued an executive memorandum saying that "unless the necessity for these arbitrary arrests is manifest, and urgent, I prefer they should cease."

In 1862 Lincoln centralized internal security matters in Stanton's War Department. Stanton created a corps of civilian provost marshals, but he allowed them too much independence in policing and jailing people suspected of disloyalty. The marshals' zealous, far-ranging operations led to

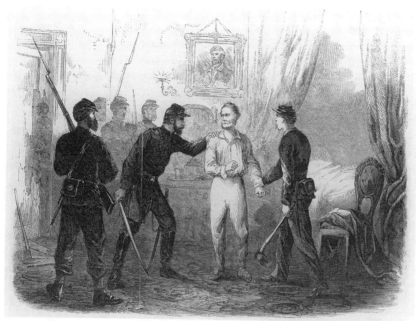

The arrest of Clement Vallandigham, a southern sympathizer, for disloyalty. He was tried and convicted in a military court in Ohio, even though civilian courts were open.

widespread criticism of the Lincoln administration. At the same time, Stanton empowered army officers to apprehend anybody who discouraged volunteering or otherwise helped the enemy. All told, some 13,000 persons—most of them antiwar Democrats—were seized and imprisoned under Stanton's authority. The outcry against arbitrary arrests was so strident that Lincoln and Stanton both tried to restrain excessive use of power whenever they could. Both speedily ordered the release of people arrested without sufficient cause, especially political prisoners. Also, when Gen. Ambrose Burnside suspended the publication of the *Chicago Times*—a paper highly critical of Lincoln and the war effort—the president promptly revoked the order.

The most controversial military arrest was that of Clement L. Vallandigham, a leading antiwar Democrat from Ohio. In 1863 he toured his state denouncing the war, the draft, and the despotism of the Lincoln government, and calling for a negotiated peace with the Confederacy. During one of his orations, an officer in civilian dress, detailed from General Burnside's headquarters, stood near the platform taking notes. Three days later the army arrested Vallandigham, and a military commission sentenced him to imprisonment for the duration of the war. When Ohio Democrats cried out in protest, Lincoln replied, "Must I shoot a simple-minded soldier boy who deserts, while I must not touch a hair of a wily agitator who induces him to desert?" Lincoln refused to pardon Vallandigham, instead ordering him banished to the Confederacy.

GIDEON WELLES, SECRETARY OF THE NAVY

By employing private individuals to secure ships for the Union navy, Gideon Welles enabled a close relative to amass a fortune.

Although the House committee on contracts found no outright corruption in navy purchasing, it discovered that George D. Morgan—Gideon Welles's brother-in-law—had amassed a personal fortune as Welles's New York agent. Charging a commission of 2.5 percent on all contracts he arranged, Morgan had made $95,000 in four and a half months in 1861. The commissions came from the vendors, but several shipowners testified that the government actually paid them. It was standard practice, they said, to add commissions to the sale price for ships.

John P. Hale, chairman of the Senate Committee on Naval Affairs and a political foe of Welles, called for an investigation. On January 11, 1862, the Senate demanded a full report on Morgan's purchases, and Welles responded with a thorough accounting. In his defense, Welles insisted that in the crisis of 1861 there had been neither the time nor opportunity to use competitive bids in buying privately owned vessels. To enforce the southern blockade, the navy needed a fleet in a hurry, and the best way to acquire one, Welles argued, was to centralize purchases in the hands of a businessman like Morgan, whose loyalty and integrity Welles could guarantee. Welles argued that Morgan was entitled to his commission, which was the usual rate charged by New York shipbrokers. And Welles gave evidence that Morgan had driven hard bargains and that the boats he had purchased were excellent.

Unimpressed with Welles's arguments, Senator Hale charged him with nepotism and corruption and went on to imply that the entire Lincoln administration was infested with graft. When newspapers joined Hale in demanding Welles's resignation, the president stood by his secretary and refused to dismiss him. For one thing, with the public in an uproar over Union military procrastination and ineptitude, Lincoln could ill afford another admission of weakness in his official family. For another, Welles was a capable man, and on the whole he ran an honest and reliable department. In the Senate, meanwhile, Hale insisted that Welles be censured. On February 14 the Senate rejected the motion by a vote of 31 to 5.

BIBLIOGRAPHY

Baxter, Jean H. *Mary Todd Lincoln: A Biography.* New York: Norton, 1987.

Bradley, Erwin S. *Simon Cameron, Lincoln's Secretary of War: A Political Biography.* Philadelphia: University of Pennsylvania Press, 1966.

Charnwood, Lord. *Abraham Lincoln.* Lanham, Md.: Madison Books, 1998.

Hendrick, Burton J. *Lincoln's War Cabinet.* Boston: Little, Brown, 1946.

Hertz, Emanual. *Lincoln Talks: A Biography in Anecdote.* New York: Viking Press, 1939.

Mitchell, Jack. *Executive Privilege: Two Centuries of White House Scandals.* New York: Hippocrene Books, 1992.

Niven, John. *Gideon Welles: Lincoln's Secretary of the Navy.* New York: Oxford University Press, 1973.

Paludan, Phillip S. *The Presidency of Abraham Lincoln.* Lawrence: University Press of Kansas, 1984.

Sandburg, Carl. *Abraham Lincoln.* 6 volumes. New York: Harcourt, Brace, 1926–1939.

Thomas, Benjamin P. *Abraham Lincoln.* New York: Knopf, 1952.

Woodward, C. Vann. *Responses of the Presidents to Charges of Misconduct.* New York: Dell Publishing, 1974.

ANDREW JOHNSON

Seventeenth President
1865–1869

Born December 29, 1808, in Raleigh, North Carolina, Andrew Johnson grew up in poverty. His father, a porter in a local inn, died when Andrew was only three years old, leaving his mother the sole breadwinner of the Johnson household. Neither of his parents could read or write, and Andrew received no formal education.

He was apprenticed to a tailor in Raleigh at the age of fourteen, and his fellow workers taught him to read. The strong-willed Johnson soon became disenchanted with working as an unpaid laborer. When he was sixteen he ran away and worked as a journeyman tailor in South Carolina. Returning to Raleigh in 1826, he convinced his mother and stepfather to move west with him. They settled in Greeneville, Tennessee, where he opened a tailor shop. Later he married Eliza McCardle, a native Tennessean.

With his wife's help he improved his reading and writing and learned mathematics. As Johnson's business prospered, his workshop became a center for local political discussion, and he began to develop his political ideas, hone his speaking skills, and gather a following among the local tradesmen.

Johnson's struggle out of poverty played an important role in shaping his political ideas. An early Democrat of the Andrew Jackson school, Johnson helped to found the Democratic Party in his region of the state, where he consistently emphasized his belief in the working class and the sanctity of states' rights. Johnson was elected an alderman of the Greeneville Town Council in 1828 and mayor in 1831. From that point his political career advanced meteorically. He won a seat in the Tennessee state legislature in 1835 and was reelected in 1839 and in 1841. Two years later he gained his first national office with election to the U.S. House of Representatives on the Democratic ticket. Johnson held the office for the next four elections before a Whig redistricting plan made his reelection impossible. He was elected governor of Tennessee in 1853 and 1855 and a U.S. senator in 1857.

Johnson's political ideas were also influenced by geography and the people he represented. Located in the mountainous eastern part of Tennessee, Greeneville was a region of small, independent landowners. Unlike western Tennessee, the east lacked the large plantations and passionate proslavery sentiments. Johnson was firmly proslavery, but uninterested in the issue; instead, he decried the privilege of the southern aristocracy and focused his energies on defending the common man and the independent farmer from what he believed were the evils of a centralized federal government. Representative Johnson took particular pride in his sponsorship of the Homestead Act, which proposed granting 160 acres of federal land to anyone who would live on it and work it for five years. Slave owners opposed the Homestead Act because it dispersed the vast frontier lands among small farmers, prohibiting the concentration of land into large plantations that could support the South's "peculiar institution." Johnson's sponsorship of the act was the first of many principled stances that finally estranged him from the proslavery elements of the Democratic Party.

Johnson's tenure in the Senate coincided with growing regional strife over slavery, which led finally to the secession of the southern states. Johnson supported the states' right to maintain slavery, but opposed the attempts to introduce it in the West. Johnson also opposed the idea of secession and spoke harshly against the "traitors" who would divide the nation. He was convinced that secession would ultimately lead to numerous independent nation-states that would benefit only the entrenched aristocrats of the old South. Johnson's fame as one of the Union's strongest defenders from the South earned him enmity at home, even as it made him a more visible hero in the North.

When the southern states formally seceded from the Union, Tennessee joined the Confederacy. Johnson was the only southern legislator who remained in the Senate, marking him a pariah among Democrats and southerners and necessitating his family's flight from their home in Tennessee.

When the war turned decisively in the Union's favor, President Abraham Lincoln rewarded Johnson's loyalty by making him military governor of the defeated regions of Tennessee. Johnson took to the task with relish. He proclaimed himself the Moses of the newly freed slaves, pronounced harsh punishments on Confederate leaders and loyalists, and instituted reforms that would later give shape to his national Reconstruction policies.

With the end of the war in sight, Lincoln set out to secure reelection. He made Andrew Johnson his running mate on the 1864 National Union ticket, which combined the Republican Party with Democrats who had stayed loyal to the Union. Lincoln believed that a broad national coalition was necessary to take on the enormous task of reconciling and rebuilding a nation suffering the wounds of civil war. Lincoln's Unionists were reelected in a landslide. At the inauguration, a visibly inebriated Vice President Johnson had to be removed from the podium, giving rise to one of the charges against his character that would follow him throughout his term.

Johnson had been vice president only a few weeks when John Wilkes Booth assassinated President Lincoln at Ford's Theatre in Washington, D.C. Lincoln died April 15, 1865, and Johnson was catapulted into the presidency. Secretary of State William Seward was also severely wounded. Johnson escaped Lincoln's fate only by chance when his would-be assassin suffered second thoughts and ended up drunk at the hotel where the vice president was lodged.

Less than a week had passed since Gen. Robert E. Lee had surrendered the Confederate army, marking the official end of the Civil War. Although Lincoln had already begun to develop a plan for the enormous task of reconstructing the South and settling more than 4 million freed slaves, no coherent policy was in place when he died. In a great historic irony, the task of reshaping and rebuilding the rebellious South fell to an accidental president who was both a southerner and a Democrat. His entire administration was consumed with the battle over Reconstruction, an ordeal that led to his eventual impeachment.

Denied renomination, Johnson retired to his home in Greeneville. Eight years earlier the town's leaders had hung a banner reading "Andrew Johnson, Traitor" across the main street because of his decision to side with the Union. In contrast, the former president was welcomed home with a sign that read "Andrew Johnson, Patriot."

He remained active in Democratic Party politics throughout his retirement, running unsuccessfully for the U.S. Senate in 1871 and the House of Representatives in 1872. Campaigning against President Ulysses S. Grant, Johnson worked for the election of Horace Greeley in 1872. In 1875 Johnson made a successful bid for the U.S. Senate, becoming the only former president to serve in that body. In his only speech on the Senate floor, Johnson condemned the Grant administration's Reconstruction policy. He died July 31, 1875.

DRUNKENNESS

Critics of President Johnson claimed he was a drunkard, unable to perform the duties of his office.

Ironically, in his early days, Johnson seems to have shunned the excessive consumption of alcohol when most around him were imbibing great quantities. But on the day of President Lincoln's second inauguration, Johnson was drunk and had to be helped from the podium. The event caused concern among members of the president's cabinet. Treasury Secretary Hugh McCulloch raised the issue with the president. Lincoln reportedly said, "Don't you bother about Andy Johnson's drinking. He made a bad slip the other day, but I have known Andy a great many years, and he ain't no drunkard." Serving four years in Johnson's administration and seeing him daily convinced McCulloch that his initial impression was wrong.

Despite Lincoln's statements, McCulloch's first-hand experiences, and those of people who knew him well in Tennessee, Johnson was unable to shake the charge that he was a drunk. In part, the allegation stuck because the press and others were hostile to him for his stance on Reconstruction. Historians also have been loose with the facts concerning Johnson's drinking. A number have written that Johnson was in the midst of a "drunken orgy" when he addressed a crowd in Cleveland, Ohio, during a tour to promote his Reconstruction plan in 1866. The charge was repeated by the respected historian James Ford Rhodes in his seven-volume *History of the United States from the Compromise of 1850,* which began publication in 1893. However, the charges seem to be false, as newspaper reporters who were on the trip testified that there was no drinking.

IMPEACHMENT

Johnson was impeached for violating the Tenure in Office Act, which prevented the president from firing a member of his cabinet without the approval of the Senate. However, the real cause was his battle with Congress over Reconstruction policy. In the end, Johnson avoided removal from office by a single vote.

Johnson was a determined, stubborn man, preferring conflict to compromise and given to unrestrained verbal abuse when provoked by his enemies. These same traits that had brought Johnson from obscurity to the nation's highest office would cost him dearly. From the beginning the Johnson administration seemed determined to clash with a Congress dominated by Republicans who aimed to punish the southern states that had betrayed the nation and caused untold bloodshed. Many Union loyalists saw the rebellious states as conquered provinces. They believed they had the right to dictate the terms by which the southern states would be readmitted to the Union.

Johnson, with his strong bias toward states' rights, argued that, as soon as they had demonstrated loyalty, the states should be readmitted without unreasonable interference from the North. He also believed that the federal government could not legitimately make decisions affecting the southern states without first restoring their representation in Congress. Johnson's goal was to use Reconstruction to destroy the southern aristocracy and put political power into the hands of the common (white) man, but he was distressed that the government might try to intervene in sensitive internal issues, such as the fate of the freedmen or the shape of local governments.

In late spring 1865 the House and Senate adjourned and were not to resume deliberations until autumn. Many believed that the legislative branch should handle Reconstruction and that the president should call a

The backers of President Johnson's Reconstruction program are depicted here as muzzled dogs. The press and the public were hostile to Johnson because they considered his policies too soft on the defeated South.

special session of Congress for that purpose. Ignoring criticism, the president took action himself. He immediately signed two proclamations that formed the cornerstone of his very moderate plan of Reconstruction.

The first proclamation restored all rights of citizenship to those southerners who would swear allegiance to the United States. The second instructed the conquered states to hold constitutional conventions to appoint new governments. It barred the participation of Confederate leaders and other disloyal elements in an attempt to dilute their political influence. In addition, Johnson's plan obligated the states to repeal all legal provisions related to secession, repay all accrued war debts, and ratify the Thirteenth Amendment eliminating slavery.

Johnson's plan was greeted with a sigh of relief in the South, where its conditions for reintegration into the Union were perceived as both swift and mild. But the reaction in the northern states, particularly among the radical element of the Republican Party that controlled Congress, was decidedly different. Discontent turned to fury as evidence mounted that Reconstruction was not achieving the results the Republicans wanted. Letters to congressional offices reported a return to the ante bellum status quo. White plantation owners were abusing newly freed blacks, in many cases restoring the spirit, if not the letter, of slavery. Many states implemented "black codes," laws that prohibited ownership of land by the freedmen, banned them from testifying against white men in court, and, in some cases, even allowed plantation owners to force former slaves to work. Equally troubling were reports that some of the same men who had agitated for secession were now controlling important government patronage and rebuilding their political base.

For most Republicans, it seemed grossly unjust to deliver people from slavery only to shirk all responsibility for them, letting their old masters dominate them with new forms of repression. And it seemed equally ludicrous that the leaders of the rebellion should be pardoned and allowed to rebuild their political power without paying for their treachery, in many cases without even renouncing the principles that had caused the war. In short, Johnson's critics blamed him for surrendering the Union's hard-won gains.

An irate Congress reconvened in December with the Republican majority determined to take control of the Reconstruction process. The first step was to refuse to seat the newly elected southern members. Congress then created a special committee of fifteen to evaluate the administration's progress and recommend new legislation based on its findings. This move was the opening salvo in a bitter struggle between the executive and legislative branches that would define Johnson's presidency and ultimately lead to his impeachment. But first, the Republican majority attempted to relieve the president of his duty to oversee Reconstruction.

One by one, Congress nullified Johnson's Reconstruction proclamations, restoring military rule to the secessionist states and embarking on an ambitious legislative program. The House then moved to extend the life of the Freedmen's Bureau, an agency that provided schools, medical assistance, and resettlement programs for southern blacks. Abraham Lincoln had created the bureau to provide the freedmen with basic necessities as a necessary step for integrating them into society.

It was taken for granted that Johnson would approve the bureau's extension. Instead, on February 18, 1866, the president vetoed it, deriding the bureau as a corrupt system of "immense patronage" and a naked attempt to extend federal authority beyond its constitutional mandate. This veto was the first of twenty-nine, significantly more than any president before him. To many, Johnson's southern racist colors were now exposed. He criticized Congress for attempting to extend benefits to the blacks that the government did not give to "our own people," as he characterized white Americans. Johnson also criticized Congress for unconstitutionally making laws while eleven states remained unrepresented. The president, Johnson claimed, is chosen by all the people of the United States, and thus has a broader view of the national interest than the members of Congress, who are elected in single districts.

If the Republicans were surprised by Johnson's veto, they were enraged by the arrogant language of his veto message. But their attempt to override the veto failed by two votes, and the renewal of the Freedmen's Bureau was effectively blocked. Although the Republicans had the necessary majority, a few senators refused to overturn the president's decision. Moderate Republicans recognized that many northern business interests supported Johnson's decision, as did the majority of the cabinet, and they hesitated to openly break with the president on such a controversial measure.

Johnson sincerely believed that the bureau was an unconstitutional infringement on the right of states to manage their internal affairs. His veto, however, was part of a broader political strategy. He hoped to provoke the Radical Republicans into opposing him, allowing him to divide them from the more moderate members of the party. He then planned to form a new coalition of northern Republican moderates and southern Democratic loyalists who would support his election in 1868.

In March Congress approved legislation that guaranteed equal protection under the law to all citizens, regardless of their race, creed, or color. For many Republicans, the Civil Rights Act was an expression of the principles for which the country had gone to war in the first place, and its passage was a major element in the Reconstruction of the South. Johnson was expected to sign the bill, for to do otherwise would be political suicide. As one senator wrote, "We all feel that the most important interests are at stake...If the president vetoes the Civil Rights Bill, I believe that we shall be obliged to draw our swords for a fight and throw away the scabbards."

Against the advice of many of his closest supporters, Johnson vetoed the bill, ending all possibility of future compromise between himself and Congress. The Radicals declared war. In an expression of their anger, the Senate ruled to expel Democrat John Stockton of New Jersey on a questionable technicality. The next step was to override Johnson's veto of the civil rights bill.

Later that year Congress underscored its defiance of the president by approving the text of the Fourteenth Amendment, which would make the main provisions of the vetoed Civil Rights Act part of the Constitution. The amendment was sent to the states for ratification where, ironically, it was rejected by every state except Tennessee, Johnson's adopted home. The president criticized the amendment as a hypocritical attempt by Republicans to force the South to accept rules that had yet to be enforced even in the North. Unratified, the amendment became an issue during the 1866 midterm congressional elections.

With the executive and legislative branches bitterly divided, the midterm elections were an important referendum on the course of Reconstruction. The Republican victory was sweeping: the party increased its majority in both houses of Congress, making symbolically important gains in the South and West. On their return to the Capitol, they wasted no time in attempting to wrest control of Reconstruction from Johnson.

With the Military Reconstruction Act of 1867, the Republicans divided the South into military zones, denied the states representation in Congress, and once again imposed martial rule. Congress demanded that the states hold new conventions, reform their governments, ratify the Fourteenth Amendment, and extend the franchise to all black males before they would be allowed reentry into the Union. With the exception of Secretary of War Edwin M. Stanton, the members of the cabinet saw the legislation as an unconstitutional congressional usurpation of executive powers. Johnson's newly appointed attorney general, Henry Stanbery, encouraged the president's veto, which was subsequently overridden in the Senate. Johnson was furious. He began a systematic resistance to the Reconstruction effort in a bald attempt to subvert congressional objectives, publicly criticizing the Republicans and unabashedly using his constitutional authority as commander in chief to remand orders and replace officers who were loyal to the Republicans.

The Radical majority responded by targeting the executive powers that made Johnson's resistance possible. They passed the Army Appropriations Act, requiring that Johnson send all orders to the military through Gen. Ulysses S. Grant, the commander of the army. In so doing, Congress instructed the military to carry out a policy that was opposed by its constitutional commander in chief. An institutional crisis was building.

In February 1867 Congress fired a second salvo at Johnson—the Tenure in Office Act. The act denied the president the ability to remove or replace without Senate consent any appointee who had been approved by the Senate. This act was a direct challenge to presidential authority, robbing Johnson of the ability to exercise his influence through patronage and denying him even the right to make changes in his own cabinet without congressional consent. Three members of Johnson's cabinet had already resigned because they disagreed with his policies, and the Republicans in Congress feared that he might eliminate other loyal Republicans, such as Secretary of War Stanton. A Lincoln appointee, Stanton was Johnson's harshest critic in the cabinet. The Tenure in Office Act would block Johnson from replacing Stanton with a politically loyal ally. Stanton and the Tenure in Office Act added the last bit of fuel to the smoldering hostility between Congress and the president, which resulted in his impeachment.

Johnson waited for Congress's summer recess before challenging the Tenure in Office Act. Taking advantage of a provision that allowed the president to suspend officials pending congressional hearings, he fired Stanton and appointed Grant, a moderate Republican, as acting secretary of war, a post Grant reluctantly filled. Johnson wanted to force a showdown: if Congress refused to approve Stanton's dismissal, Johnson would challenge the constitutionality of the act before the courts; if Congress backed away from a head-on confrontation with the president, Johnson would have won a major political battle and succeeded in removing a terrible nuisance from his administration.

What Johnson failed to appreciate was the degree of Republican contempt for him and the response it would trigger. The Radicals had considered impeaching the president ever since the 1866 election when they gained the necessary majorities in the House and Senate. The Republicans

believed the Democrat they had inadvertently placed in the White House
had betrayed them and that the national wound would never heal as long as
Johnson was there to thwart their Reconstruction policies. Even so, all but
the most radical Republicans hesitated to step into the impeachment abyss,
believing that it was better to maneuver around the difficult president.

An avowed Johnson enemy, Ohio representative James M. Ashley had
repeatedly attempted to bring a motion of impeachment since March
1867. Ashley accused the president of abusing the appointment power,
abusing the pardoning power, corruptly disposing of property of the United States, and conspiring to commit high crimes with others. Ashley even
asserted that the president was an agent of the South, going so far as to suggest that Lincoln was murdered so that Johnson would become president
and subvert Republican plans for Reconstruction. No evidence was ever
presented to lend credence to such an incendiary charge, but some Radicals believed it.

Ashley's impeachment motion came to a vote in December. It was
approved 5–4 in the House Judiciary Committee and debated intensely on
the floor of the House for two days before being rejected by a vote of
108–57. Proving his political ineptness yet again, Johnson interpreted the
defeat as a signal of his growing strength and an indication that many members of Congress were beginning to accept the wisdom of his policies. Thus
encouraged, he set out on his most aggressive campaign yet to derail the
Radical Republican plan for Reconstruction. In a flurry of activity, Johnson ousted Radical military officers, countermanded orders, and began to
actively and vocally encourage southern opposition.

Meanwhile, the Senate began deliberating Stanton's removal, finally
invoking the Tenure in Office Act and restoring the secretary of war in
utter disregard of Johnson's protests. Grant stepped aside, happy to leave
the center of the storm, and a victorious Stanton returned to the cabinet,
whereupon Johnson removed him again. The president had now violated
the letter of the law for the first time in his administration. It was as if he
was daring Congress to step over the carefully drawn line and impeach
him. Stanton barricaded himself in his office and refused to budge, citing
the president's illegal defiance of the law. Smelling blood, Johnson's critics
moved quickly. Rep. John Covode of Pennsylvania introduced a resolution
to impeach the president on February 24, 1868, for firing Stanton. Even
before the formal articles were submitted, the full House voted 126–47 to
impeach the seventeenth president of the United States.

The Constitution states that in cases of impeachment, the House shall
indict and the Senate try, with the chief justice of the United States presiding. Impeachable acts are defined as "Treason, Bribery, or other high
Crimes and Misdemeanors," a vague definition that gave the Republicans
ample room to maneuver. In many ways, the eleven articles of impeachment that the House brought against Johnson were questionable at best
and grossly partisan at worst. In addition to the charge of illegally firing

Stanton, the House charged Johnson with attempting to induce a Union general to accept orders in violation of the Army Appropriations Act. Other articles accused the president of denying the authority of Congress, of attempting to bring its members "into disgrace," and of speaking disrespectfully of Congress "in a loud voice."

To make the case for impeachment before the Senate, the House appointed seven managers, all Radical Republicans, including Thaddeus Stevens. Stevens was ill during the trial, but he hated Johnson with such a passion that he insisted on being carried into the Senate chamber so that he would not miss the president's anticipated defeat.

The chief justice was Salmon P. Chase, a northerner with great political ambition, who had served as secretary of the Treasury during much of the Lincoln administration. He resigned from the cabinet in 1864, whereupon Lincoln appointed him chief justice. Chase, who planned to run for president, was determined to prevent the impeachment proceedings from becoming a political witch trial led by the angry mob of Republicans who controlled the Congress.

The Radicals, for their part, did their best to limit Chase's role in the trial, but were rebuffed by the wily chief justice. Chase realized that because this was the first presidential impeachment trial in American history, his actions would establish the precedent for future trials. He rose to the importance of the occasion, steering the proceedings in a narrowly legalistic direction and ensuring that it was conducted with a spirit of judicial impartiality that guaranteed the president a fair trial at the hands of his political enemies.

Critics later accused Chase of helping the president's defense by ruling in his favor on questions of procedure and the admissibility of evidence. It is not known if Chase harbored strong prejudices regarding the wisdom or propriety of the impeachment of the president, or if he let those prejudices influence his rulings. What is known is that Chase did not like Sen. Benjamin Wade of Ohio, who, as president pro tempore of the Senate, was next in the line of presidential succession if Johnson were convicted. Nevertheless, Chase's performance as a trial judge was generally regarded as remarkably artful and upright, considering the extreme delicacy of the situation.

Chase interpreted impeachment as a legal, not political, tool. He attempted to prevent the trial from turning into a referendum on the president's politics and his ability to govern by forcing the House managers to concentrate on strict legal arguments based on the eleven articles of impeachment and accepting what would become the main premise of the Johnson defense—that a clear violation of the law was the only "high crime or misdemeanor" that warrants the removal of a sitting president. This distinction forced the managers to concentrate almost entirely on the articles that concerned the president's removal of Stanton, the only charge that stood up under scrutiny. Chase had succeeded in suppressing incendi-

Salmon Portland Chase

ary partisan attacks, a move that had a decisive effect on the outcome of the trial.

Attorney General Stanbery resigned to head the president's defense team. Stanbery had encouraged the president not to remove Stanton, but now he assumed his new role with relish. Johnson had unsuccessfully nominated Stanbery to the Supreme Court before naming him attorney general, and Stanbery was loyal to the president and a harsh critic of Congress's Reconstruction policy.

William Maxwell Evarts, recommended to Johnson by Evarts's friend and fellow New Yorker, Secretary of State Seward, joined Stanbery in the defense. Evarts was an eloquent lawyer with high standing and impeccable Republican credentials. During the war he had served as a trusted emissary for President Lincoln, making numerous trips to England to convince the British that they should neither recognize the Confederate states nor supply them with weapons and ships.

The first and possibly most important move by the defense was to rein in the president. They persuaded Johnson to refrain from making incendiary public comments, as well as avoid appearing in the Senate chamber during the trial. Stanbery and Evarts pursued two defense strategies that at times appeared to contradict one another. They first argued that the Tenure in Office Act did not apply to Stanton's dismissal because Johnson had not appointed him. The prosecution responded that this defense was spurious and that Johnson did appoint Stanton de facto by allowing him to continue as secretary of war for most of his administration. The second defense took the stance that the president had violated the Tenure in Office Act to force the issue before the courts to test its constitutionality. The defense also attempted to show the Senate that Stanton's dismissal was based on the recommendation of high-ranking army officers who thought it necessary for the good of the service and the country.

The Republican prosecutors countered by pointing out that the Constitution granted the president veto power if he disagreed with proposed legislation and gave Congress the means to overturn a veto. The Republicans insisted that the president was obligated to enforce the laws—even those he disliked. Johnson, they said, had violated his constitutional duty and threatened the balance of powers. The president, they claimed, like any citizen, must be prepared to face the legal results of his actions. In Johnson's case, that meant impeachment.

The Republican dominance in Congress was absolute, and many believed that the president's conviction was a certainty. Public opinion had swung decidedly against him. Johnson was in shock: his plan to build a coalition of Republican and Democrat moderates that would win him election in November dissolved before his eyes, and he was abandoned even by those southerners who had praised his attempts to block the Republican Reconstruction policy. The president was politically dead. Before the first vote was taken, Johnson's counsel quietly suggested to moderate members of the Senate that, if acquitted, the president would serve out the remainder of his term without making further attempts to obstruct Congress.

On May 16 the Senate voted 35–19 on the first article, falling one vote short of the necessary two-thirds majority. Seven moderate Republicans crossed party lines and voted for Johnson's acquittal, saving the president by the slimmest of margins. Ten days later the Senate voted on two more of the charges, in each case again falling short by just one vote.

Lyman Trumbull, one of the seven Republican senators who voted for acquittal, explained his vote by stating, "No future president will be safe who happens to differ with the majority of the House and two-thirds of the Senate on any measure deemed by them as important." He viewed it as a dangerous breakdown of the separation of powers so carefully designed by the Framers.

Other Republicans voted to acquit in the belief that a Benjamin Wade presidency would be even worse than Johnson's. After all, Congress had now effectively neutered Johnson by demonstrating that his presidency dangled by a thread. Whatever the case, the Senate adjourned the proceedings after the failure of the third vote. A few diehard Radicals insisted on continuing the effort to oust him, but their shouts now fell on deaf ears.

Confronted with a formidable Republican majority in both chambers, the president received no cooperation from the Congress he had constantly obstructed and insulted. The Reconstruction of the South proceeded on indisputably Republican terms. Johnson served his remaining ten months in office quietly, signing the legislation the Republican-controlled Congress put before him, the lamest of lame duck presidents.

BIBLIOGRAPHY

Benedict, Michael L. *The Impeachment and Trial of Andrew Johnson.* New York: Norton, 1973.

Berger, Raoul. *Executive Privilege: A Constitutional Privilege—A Myth.* Cambridge: Harvard University Press, 1974.

Dewitt, David M. *The Impeachment and Trial of Andrew Johnson, Seventeenth President of the United States.* New York: Macmillan, 1903.

Lomask, Milton. *Andrew Johnson: President on Trial.* New York: Farrar, Straus, 1960.

McKitrick, Eric L. *Andrew Johnson and Reconstruction.* Chicago: University of Chicago Press, 1960.

Mitchell, Jack. *Executive Privilege: Two Centuries of White House Scandals.* New York: Hippocrene Books, 1992.

Sefton, James E. *Andrew Johnson and the Use of Constitutional Power.* Boston: Little, Brown, 1980.

Smith, Gene. *High Crimes and Misdemeanors: The Impeachment and Trial of Andrew Johnson*. New York: Morrow, 1977.

Stryker, Lloyd P. *Andrew Johnson: A Study in Courage*. New York: Macmillan, 1929.

Winston, Robert E. *Andrew Johnson: Plebeian and Patriot*. New York: Holt, 1928.

Woodward, C. Vann. *Responses of the Presidents to Charges of Misconduct*. New York: Dell Publishing, 1974.

ULYSSES S. GRANT

Eighteenth President
1869–1877

Hiram Ulysses Grant was born April 27, 1822, in Point Pleasant, Ohio, near Cincinnati. He was the eldest of the six children born to Hanna and Jesse Grant, a tanner. Through his father's efforts, Grant received an appointment to West Point in 1838, but he was an unwilling student there. Grant—whose name was improperly recorded as Ulysses Simpson Grant—graduated in the middle of his class. From 1843 to 1854 he was in the infantry, serving under Gen. Zachary Taylor during the Mexican War. On August 22, 1848, Grant married Julia Boggs Dent, the sister of his West Point roommate, in St. Louis, Missouri. When he returned to civilian life, Grant went to work for his father in Galena, Illinois.

At the outbreak of the Civil War, Grant sought to be recommissioned in the army; instead, he received a gubernatorial appointment to command an unruly volunteer regiment in June 1861. Grant whipped the volunteers into shape and by September he had risen to the rank of brigadier general of volunteers. In February 1862 he defeated Confederate forces at Fort Henry, Tennessee. Ten days later he achieved the first major Union victory of the war by capturing Fort Donelson on the Cumberland River in Tennessee. When the Confederate commander asked for terms of surrender, Grant replied, "No terms except an unconditional and immediate surrender can be accepted." The victory netted the Union 15,000 Confederate prisoners, and Grant received not only promotion to major general but also a national reputation.

Grant's efforts at Shiloh Church were less successful, and the Union forces suffered heavy losses. But President Lincoln defend him by saying, "I can't spare this man—he fights." At Vicksburg, Mississippi, Grant captured 20,000 Confederate soldiers, but, more important, his victory there gained control of the Mississippi River for the Union and effectively split the South in two. In March 1864 he was appointed general in chief of the army. He ordered Gen. William T. Sherman to drive through the South, while he and the Army of the Potomac pinned down Gen. Robert E. Lee's Army of Northern Virginia. On April 9, 1865, Lee surrendered his army at Appomattox Court House, bringing the war to a close.

Grant was the logical choice as the Republican presidential candidate in 1868. Many Americans hoped that his election would mean the end to the growing turmoil of Reconstruction, but the Grant administration did not live up to that expectation. Although Grant was a man of scrupulous honesty, his administration was marred by numerous scandals, some of which involved his close friends and family. In fact, political corruption—labeled "Grantism"—became synonymous with his administration.

During his reelection campaign in 1872, Grant was attacked by Liberal Republicans who sought dramatic reforms of the government. Mocking the Liberal Republicans as "narrow-headed men" with their eyes so close together that "they can look out of the same gimlet hole without winking," Grant's wing of the party came to be known proudly as "the Old Guard," but in fact it was not very adept at guarding anything. Not a strong legislative leader and lacking the skill to drive policy, Grant let Congress shape Reconstruction during his two terms. His weakness allowed the Radical Republicans to develop a harsh plan to deal with the defeated South. Grant occasionally aided the plan by adding the threat and the use of military force.

After retiring from the presidency, Grant invested all of his money in his son's brokerage partnership. The firm went bankrupt, taking Grant with it. In a further blow, he learned that he had throat and mouth cancer. Grant began writing his memoirs, hoping to pay off his debts and provide for his family. The two-volume work, *Personal Memoirs of U. S. Grant,* sold 300,000 copies and ultimately earned nearly $450,000. He died July 23, 1885, just four days after finishing the book.

BLACK FRIDAY: THE GOLD PANIC OF 1869

President Grant's brother-in-law Abel Corbin was implicated in a gold speculation scheme that caused a panic in the market in 1869. At the center of the scheme were two financiers, Jay Gould and James Fisk, who tried to corner the gold market. Their success depended on persuading Grant to stop selling the government's gold, which was where Corbin came in.

The events of the Gold Panic of 1869 involved two of America's most notorious speculators, Jay Gould and James Fisk Jr. These two hoped to use personal contact with President Grant to influence the nation's monetary policy and in the process make themselves rich. The scheme started June 15, when, on his way to Boston, Grant dined with Gould and Fisk aboard one of Fisk's steamers. Gould tried to convince the president to discontinue his practice of selling $2 million in gold each month. Abel Corbin, who was married to Grant's sister, pointed out that the sale of gold would adversely affect the sale of U.S. agricultural products overseas.

Thinking he had prevailed with the president, Gould convinced investors that the government was halting sales of gold reserves. In the meantime, Gould and Fisk continued to buy contracts for the delivery of gold. However, it seems that Grant never actually said anything that should have led the two to believe he planned to withhold gold from sale. In fact, several times during the late summer, Grant wrote to Treasury Secretary George S. Boutwell that his administration was committed to neutrality between the speculators in the gold market and to continue with normal sales.

On September 17 Corbin—persuaded by Gould—wrote to Grant encouraging him not to keep down the price of gold by selling more of the government's supply. By this time, gold stood at $132 an ounce, and the two speculators had contracts for at least twice the available supply. Gould was in for at least $50 million. When Corbin's letter reached Grant in Pennsylvania, Grant instructed his secretary to wire Corbin "letters delivered all right." Grant then destroyed Corbin's letter. The confusion over the words "all right" led to further increases in the prices of gold; some took it to mean that Grant had agreed not to sell additional reserves, but apparently he had meant only that the letters had arrived "all right."

Grant was concerned about his brother-in-law's speculation in the gold market and wrote a letter to his sister, Virginia Grant Corbin, telling her that her husband should back out. Because the letter to "Sis" no longer exists, it is impossible to gauge its tone. What is known is that Corbin read the letter to Gould on September 22. He also asked Gould to take all his gold contracts off his hands so that he could tell the president he had complied with his wishes. Gould understood the letter to mean that a large gold sale was on the horizon. He began to sell his contracts in secret so as not to create a panic that would cost him millions.

On September 24 Grant returned to Washington and met with Secretary Boutwell to discuss the price of gold, which by then had surpassed $160 an ounce. Boutwell ordered the immediate sale of $4 million of gold, and, within an hour, the price fell more than $20 an ounce. Many speculators lost millions, including Fisk. The large-scale sell-off had a dramatic effect on the economy, and a congressional committee decided to investigate the matter, especially when rumors that both the president's wife, Julia, and Gen. Horace Porter, Grant's secretary, had been involved as speculators. Corbin had told Gould that Julia needed $25,000 on account. Gould forwarded the money to Corbin who used it to pay off a loan he had at his own bank.

James Garfield, a Republican of New York and a future president, chaired the congressional commit-

Julia Grant

tee. Corbin admitted that he had speculated with an account in excess of $1.5 million. Fisk claimed that Corbin's account was actually set up for Julia Grant, Horace Porter, and Corbin, all of whom were to share equally. However, records show that neither Julia Grant nor General Porter had ever received any money from the sale of the gold. In fact, Fisk's assertion was all that implicated them. The committee did discover that Gen. Daniel Butterfield, assistant treasurer of the United States, had borrowed from the testimonial fund given to Grant in 1866 and had made a $25,000 profit speculating in gold. Grant fired Butterfield.

Several minority members of the committee wanted to hear testimony from Julia and Virginia, especially about the "Sis letter." The White House refused the invitations, as well as a request that the president testify. Secretary Boutwell and General Porter appeared before the committee. Boutwell came in for criticism because he had been indecisive on gold prices. In the end, however, the committee could find no criminal wrongdoing on the part of Grant, Julia Grant, General Porter, or Secretary Boutwell.

GEORGE M. ROBESON, SECRETARY OF THE NAVY

Secretary Robeson accepted kickbacks from A. G. Cattell & Company, a food contractor. Congress's investigation did not result in impeachment or criminal prosecutions because of its inability to follow the money trail.

The case of George M. Robeson, appointed secretary of the navy in 1869, may be one of the clearest unprosecuted cases of bribery and kickbacks in U.S. history. At the time of his appointment, Robeson, a lawyer, had a net worth of about $20,000. In the eight years he served as navy secretary, his net worth grew to more than $300,000, a remarkable sum considering his government salary was only $8,000 per year.

It seems that just as Robeson joined the Grant administration, A. G. Cattell & Company, a Philadelphia grain firm, began receiving large government contracts to supply foodstuffs. When allegations surfaced in 1876 that Robeson had been accepting bribes and kickbacks from Cattell, he released his bank statements, which showed more than $320,000 in deposits. The congressional investigating committee combed through Cattell's books. Although it uncovered circumstantial evidence, including a house on Long Branch that the Cattell family had given to Robeson, the committee could not prove that Cattell had paid money to Robeson because the

George Robeson

company's books were in such a mess.

In July 1876 the committee released a report in which it accused the secretary of gross misconduct and stated, "A system of corruption has grown up . . . likely to be known hereafter as 'Cattellism.' " The House briefly toyed with the idea of impeaching Robeson, but it refrained in large part because it was in the midst of impeaching President Grant's former secretary of war, William W. Belknap. In the end, no formal charges were brought against Robeson, who resigned as secretary. Two years later he was elected to the House of Representatives from New Jersey, serving from 1879 to 1883.

WILLIAM W. BELKNAP, SECRETARY OF WAR

Grant appointed Gen. William W. Belknap secretary of war on October 25, 1869. Belknap was involved in two separate scandals, one of which led to his impeachment.

Franco-Prussian War

Belknap was investigated for violating the neutrality laws by selling weapons to known French agents during the Franco-Prussian War.

Two of the president's most persistent critics in the Senate, Carl Schurz of Missouri and Charles Sumner of Massachusetts, charged that in 1870 Secretary of War William Belknap violated the neutrality laws by selling government arms to agents of the French government during the Franco-Prussian War. Belknap had purchased a large number of obsolete rifles from the Remington Company. Soon after, he learned that Remington was acting as an agent for the French government. Belknap sold the weapons to a neighbor of the Remington family who could then send them to France. Belknap also had the army sell to the French more than 54 million cartridges for the obsolete guns.

A congressional committee investigated the senators' charges. Despite the substantial evidence that Belknap had knowingly sold the weapons to agents of the French government, the committee could not cite a violation of a specific law and dropped the matter.

Fort Sill Trading Post

Secretary Belknap was investigated and impeached for accepting a kickback on the award of a trading post at Fort Sill.

In 1870 Belknap's wife, Carrie Tomlinson Belknap, made an agreement with a friend, Caleb P. Marsh, a New York contractor, that her husband would give Marsh the trading post at Fort Sill in the Indian Territory (now southwestern Oklahoma) in exchange for an annual payment of $6,000. John S. Evans, the incumbent in the trading post, traveled to Washington

William W. Belknap

to prevent his business being taken from him. Rather than fight for the post, Marsh struck a deal with Evans that allowed him to continue doing business there in return for an annual payment of $15,000 (later reduced to $12,000). With a contract drawn up by Marsh's attorney, the deal was signed: Marsh would take his proceeds and pass half of them on to Carrie Belknap in quarterly payments. However, in December 1870 Carrie died of tuberculosis, after receiving only one payment.

The payments continued to be made to Carrie's widowed sister, Amanda Tomlinson Bower, who was caring for the Belknaps' infant child. The child died in June 1871. While Amanda traveled in Europe and spent large sums of money, Belknap collected the payments. He and Amanda married December 11, 1874. The payments from Marsh continued until they were discovered by the congressional investigating committee. By that time, Belknap had received more than $20,000 from Marsh.

Belknap denied any knowledge of the money, but Marsh told the investigating committee that payments were "sent according to the instructions of the Secretary of War; sometimes in bank-notes . . . I think on one or more occasions by certificate of deposit on the National Bank of America in New York. Sometimes I paid him in New York in person." Marsh testified February 29, 1876. On March 1 Belknap briefly appeared before the committee.

The next morning, as it became clear that the House Committee on Expenditures in the War Department would impeach Belknap, he resigned. Even so, the impeachment went forward. The Senate trial ended in a vote of 37 to 24, failing to reach the two-thirds needed to convict. However, all but one of those voting not guilty did so because they believed that because Belknap had resigned the Senate had no jurisdiction in the case.

Belknap's illegal activities clearly were grounds for impeachment, but similar violations on the part of Grant's brother, Orvil, brought no such consequences. Information came to light in March 1876 that Orvil Grant was sharing ownership of four trading posts in much the same manner as Belknap. Grant took no action, and Orvil continued to benefit from his relationship with the president.

SANTO DOMINGO ANNEXATION

Grant's personal secretary, Orville E. Babcock, was sent to negotiate with the president of Santo Domingo concerning U.S. annexation of the island. Before defeating the proposed treaty, the Senate held hearings to discover if anyone in the administration had benefited personally from the transaction.

In his memoirs, written in 1885, President Grant pointed to the proposed annexation of Santo Domingo as a critical event and lost opportunity. He wrote, "It is possible that the question of a conflict between the races may come up in the future. . . . It was looking to the settlement of this question that led me to urge the annexation of Santo Domingo during the time I was President of the United States." If these were his true sentiments, they were not raised in January 1870 when he sent the treaty to the U. S. Senate for approval. The treaty called for the annexation of the Caribbean nation of Santo Domingo (Dominican Republic today) in exchange for $1 million. Grant's idea was that blacks could be moved there if good relations between the races could not be maintained.

Whatever motive Grant cited, the idea of annexation and the treaty resulted from some backroom deals by land speculators and corrupt Dominican politicians. Col. J. W. Fabens was the co-owner with Gen. W. L. Cazneau of several New York companies that were speculating in land and resources in Santo Domingo. The president of Santo Domingo, Buenaventura Báez, encouraged Fabens and Cazneau to pursue an annexation deal with the Grant administration. The corrupt Báez hoped to profit by selling his nation to the United States.

Fabens suggested to Grant that the United States should pursue annexation because Santo Domingo was rich in resources. In July 1869 Grant sent his secretary, Col. Orville Babcock, to meet with Báez in Santo Domingo, and, with the aid of Fabens and Cazneau, the parties agreed to a draft treaty. Babcock presented his findings to Grant's cabinet. Despite his ore samples, stories of the wealth of Santo Domingo, and the president's insistence that the unsatisfactory portions of the treaty could be renegotiated, the cabinet showed no support for annexation. Grant and Secretary of State Hamilton Fish decided to pursue annexation without the further assistance of the cabinet.

In November Babcock returned to Santo Domingo with official instructions from Secretary Fish on the terms for annexation. Babcock carried a bank draft of $100,000 and more than $50,000 in arms and ammunition to be used as a down payment on the final purchase price. He negotiated a treaty that called for a $1 million payment. U.S. naval forces were left in the region to protect Báez from political unrest. There was growing intelligence that Haiti planned to invade Santo Domingo.

Grant sought the support of influential senators, including Charles Sumner, Republican of Massachusetts, the chairman of the Foreign Relations Committee. Visiting Sumner at his home one evening in January 1870, Grant believed he had convinced the senator to support the annexation. Newspaper editor John W. Forney, who was at Sumner's home that night, confirmed that Sumner had agreed to annexation. However, when the treaty came to the Senate for ratification, Sumner opposed it.

On March 10 Babcock testified before the Senate committee. The hearings were brief because there was little support for annexation. When Sumner sent the treaty to the floor for a vote, only two committee members supported it. With the chances of ratification waning, Secretary Fish began to lobby senators. However, in mid-May, Sen. Carl Schurz reported to Fish that thirty-two of the seventy-two senators opposed annexation; the treaty seemed doomed.

With information provided by an assistant secretary of state, the Senate began to investigate allegations of misconduct and corruption in relation to the treaty. Senator Schurz, among others, charged that Babcock had a personal stake in the annexation of Santo Domingo. In fact, President Báez had offered Babcock valuable land to secure his commitment to the treaty, but Babcock refused it, saying it would kill the treaty if discovered.

Schurz's accusations did not end there. In the minority report on annexation, he derided Grant's handling of the annexation and specifically the activities of Babcock and the U.S. ambassador to Santo Domingo concerning Davis Hatch. Hatch was an American citizen who had been condemned to death for leading uprisings against Báez in favor of another Dominican. Before Babcock's initial visit to Santo Domingo, Hatch's death sentence had been commuted to banishment, but he was still in jail. Báez decided to keep Hatch in jail—with Babcock's knowledge—to prevent Hatch from speaking out against the treaty. Schurz used this revelation and others to publicly humiliate the president. However, the Senate's majority report found no wrongdoing by Babcock or any others.

The fight over annexation continued. Grant took the conflict with Sumner personally and struck back. Because there was little he could do to Sumner, Grant decided to remove John Lothrop Motley, a political ally of Sumner, from his post as ambassador to England. The vacancy gave the administration a plum appointment to offer a senator in return for support for the treaty. However, on June 30, 1870, the Senate officially rejected the treaty of annexation, ending months of feuding between Grant and Sumner. The conflict left both the cabinet and Grant's party sharply divided.

THE ADMINISTRATION OF WASHINGTON, D.C.

Three separate charges of corruption in the administration of the District of Columbia were raised during Grant's presidency.

Boss Shepherd

Executive administrators of the District of Columbia were investigated for fraud and cronyism in the awarding of contracts to improve the infrastructure of the nation's capital.

The rapidly growing city of Washington, D.C., was not providing the necessary public services to its residents. Among other complaints, the city had open sewers and poorly paved roads. In 1871 Congress responded by making the city into a territory under the jurisdiction of the executive branch. Henry D. Cooke of the First National Bank of Washington and brother of Jay Cooke, the country's leading banker, was named the territory's first governor. Alexander Shepherd, who was highly successful in the plumbing supply business, was named vice president of the Board of Public Works and became the active manager of the District's government.

Shepherd's foresight and planning dramatically improved the city's services, but they came at great cost. As the city's debt increased, charges were made of corruption and favoritism in the selection of developers and road builders. In 1874 Congress created a joint select committee to investigate. The committee criticized both Shepherd and Cooke for their administration of the city and its contracts. Shepherd refused to resign, even though Cooke had already done so in the wake of the Freedman's Ring (see below). Rep. Robert B. Roosevelt, a Democrat of New York, likened Shepherd to Boss William Tweed, the notorious leader of Tammany Hall, New York City's Democratic machine. Despite the criticism on Capitol Hill, Grant named Shepherd the new governor. In 1876, when the government of the District was changed to a commission form, Grant named Shepherd a commissioner, but the Senate rejected his nomination.

Freedman's Ring

Congress investigated the failure of the Freedman's Savings Bank and the administration of the Freedmen's Bureau to see if fraud had been involved in either.

During a severe economic panic in 1873, many financial institutions failed, including Freedman's Savings Bank, where most of the depositors were former slaves. The bank's failure sparked a congressional investigation in 1876 that was highly critical of the chief investment officer, Henry Cooke. Under growing criticism for his part in Boss Shepherd's contracting scandals and the Freedman's Ring, Cooke resigned as territorial governor in 1873.

In addition to Freedman's Savings Bank, the defunct Freedman's Bureau came under scrutiny. Its commissioner, Gen. Oliver O. Howard, was charged with poor administration, specifically, that his disbursement officer had skimmed off money intended to pay bonuses to blacks who had served in the Civil War. Rather than deal with the charges directly, Grant allowed Howard to appoint a military court of inquiry to investigate. The 1874 court cleared Howard of any wrongdoing, but he remained a controversial individual. Grant took the advice of Gen. William T. Sherman and transferred Howard to duty in the Northwest to avoid further criticism.

The Safe Burglary Conspiracy

A staged break-in at the offices of the governor of the District of Columbia led to a congressional investigation and criminal prosecutions of several members of the administration.

Boss Shepherd and his associates remained the targets of criticism by a group of citizens known as the Memorialists and their leader, Columbus Alexander. The case of the safe burglary conspiracy involved U.S. attorney for the District of Columbia Richard Harrington, who was charged with committing fraud.

The events surrounding the burglary were reported in the *New York Times.* According to that account, Harrington, in conjunction with Secret Service chief H. C. Whitley, hired William Benton and George E. Miles to break into Harrington's office safe. On April 23, 1874, Harrington notified Washington chief of police, Maj. A. C. Richards, that he had received a tip that his office safe would be burglarized that evening. Richards sent a detachment of police to cover several of the doors. Governor Shepherd's brother, Thomas M. Shepherd, was passing by and was given a post across the street.

Miles, a professional safe cracker, and Benton were instructed to open the safe and remove some documents that the Memorialists wanted for their investigations of Harrington. As Miles blew open the safe, the police moved in. Miles escaped out the back door. Shepherd pursued, but Miles eluded him. Meanwhile Benton, who had the documents in question, also fled the building. Richards wanted to nab him, but Harrington convinced Richards to let Benton lead them to the mastermind of the safe burglary. Benton went straight to Columbus Alexander's home.

The plot to implicate Alexander in ordering the burglary would have worked except that when Benton arrived at Alexander's home, he could not wake anyone to answer the door. Despite Benton's repeated attempts, Alexander slept through the events. Richards became suspicious and began an investigation, ultimately leading to a House committee inquiry, which cleared Alexander. The report was sent to both Secretary of Treasury Benjamin H. Bristow and Attorney General George H. Williams for further action.

In September, Harrington, Whitley, and three other men, including a Secret Service agent, were indicted for conspiracy. However, the case was withdrawn on a technicality in December. Harrington was re-indicted on April 9, 1876, after Attorney General Edwards Pierrepont granted Whitley immunity in exchange for his testimony. Whitley not only testified against Harrington, but also implicated Orville Babcock, the president's former secretary and commissioner of public buildings. According to Whitley, Babcock had brought Whitley into the conspiracy because Babcock feared Alexander's inquiry would unveil misdeeds on his part. Babcock had used Whitley to maintain surveillance on reporters investigating him in relation to the Whiskey Ring (see page 149).

Babcock admitted that he told Whitley to report to Harrington, but denied he knew the reason for Harrington's request of Secret Service aid. Interestingly, Babcock took offense at Whitley's claim that Harrington and Babcock had bungled the safe burglary. Babcock was indicted on April 15 for conspiracy to "injure and oppress Columbus Alexander." The main case against Babcock was that he was the only official of high enough rank that could have brought the Secret Service into the conspiracy. Babcock was acquitted September 29.

CUSTOM HOUSES INVESTIGATIONS

Congress investigated the custom houses of New York and New Orleans to see if there had been any official mismanagement or corruption.

On July 1, 1870, President Grant, at the insistence of Sen. Roscoe Conkling of New York, appointed Thomas Murphy as the collector of the Port of New York. Murphy hired George K. Leet, a member of Grant's wartime staff, and turned over to him the general business, which included collecting storage charges on imported goods not picked up by merchants within two days.

Soon merchants were complaining to the Grant administration about the storage charges in New York that were being imposed by a monopoly controlled by Leet, Stocking & Company. In October 1871 Grant wrote to Murphy, "There is so much noise, and talk, and scandal, about this young man Leet . . . on account of his being with me during the war, that I think I had better stop that, and I think that the young man had better leave." Grant's secretary, Gen. Horace Porter, echoed similar sentiments on behalf of the president when he wrote to Murphy on October 31. Murphy, however, convinced Grant that it was not necessary to fire Leet.

On January 3, 1872, the Senate Committee on Investigation and Retrenchment held hearings to examine charges against the New York Custom House of fraud, bribery, and excessively high rates. The committee released its findings on June 4. Although the report did not specifically implicate Grant in any of the scandals, it found that all but one of the custom house inspectors admitted to taking bribes and that two witnesses had perjured themselves before the committee. Grant removed Leet from his post. Murphy had resigned months earlier in November 1871 and had been replaced by Chester A. Arthur, another Conkling man (and a future president).

The New Orleans Custom House was another source of consternation for Grant. The collector of the port was James F. Casey, a brother-in-law of Grant's wife, Julia Dent Grant. The chief complaint against Casey was that he had not fired all the Democrats and replaced them with Republicans. On July 12, 1870, Treasury Secretary George Boutwell complied with a Senate request to turn over letters from these disgruntled Republicans calling for Casey's dismissal.

However, the investigation that followed leveled more serious charges against Casey. His political rivals accused him of using custom house money to pay bribes. The committee report was held back in the hopes that Casey would resign, but he did not. In March 1873 Grant reappointed him to a three-year term. The report was largely discounted as a political attack, and the Senate confirmed Casey to the post.

CRÉDIT MOBILIER

Even though President Grant was not personally involved with Crédit Mobilier, the scandal was popularly regarded as an incident typical of Grantism. The scandal began before he became president, but the investigation took place on his watch.

For Americans of the 1870s, the name *Crédit Mobilier* denoted the most notorious political scandal and lowest form of corporate thievery and fraudulent practice. Created to facilitate construction of the transcontinental railroad, Crédit Mobilier was a corporate funnel through which huge amounts of public money flowed for the building of the Union Pacific Railroad. Rep. Oakes Ames, a Republican of Massachusetts, and his cohorts earned profits of nearly $20 million.

In 1864 Thomas C. Durant, vice president of the Union Pacific Railroad, acquired a moribund railroad construction syndicate, the Pennsylvania Fiscal Agency. Durant renamed it Crédit Mobilier of America, emulating a similar French organization. Investments from Massachusetts shovel manufacturers Oakes Ames, Oliver Ames, and others bolstered the syndicate's capital, and in 1865 it received a contract to build the Union Pacific as far as the 100th Meridian (today, Kearney, Nebraska). By the time the track reached this goal in 1867, however, the directorate of Crédit Mobilier had split into factions: Durant was ousted, and Oliver Ames became the president of the Union Pacific. A group of trustees, headed by Rep. Oakes Ames, secured additional contracts to complete construction, to be paid for by Crédit Mobilier. As the line was built and turned over to the Union Pacific, Crédit Mobilier presented the railroad with inflated bills, which were paid with a combination of cash and Union Pacific stock. These payments drained the railroad's cash reserves and loaded it with debt. What would happen in the end was that Crédit Mobilier would own all of Union Pacific and the government and other shareholders would lose out.

To forestall a congressional investigation of cost overruns and construction delays, in late 1867 Oakes Ames distributed shares of Crédit Mobilier stock among senators and representatives. The recipients included House Speaker Schuyler Colfax of Indiana (a future vice president), federal railroad director and New York representative James Brooks, Sen. James Blaine of Maine, and future president James A. Garfield. The stock was sold at par but below market value, and purchasers were allowed the pay out of future dividends. Oakes Ames wrote, "I don't fear any investigation here . . . I have used [the stock] where it will do the most good for us, I think."

During 1868 and 1869, charges that the Union Pacific's directors had diverted company assets and made themselves rich through Crédit Mobilier sporadically circulated in the press and Congress, but no investigation ensued. By May 1869, when the railroad was at last opened, Union Pacific had paid Crédit Mobilier more than $50.8 million in cash and another $23 million in stocks, income bonds, and land-grant bonds. The cash amount sufficed to meet construction costs; the remainder represented the managers of Union Pacific stripping the railroad of Congress's intended endowment.

The story became known in 1872 when a disgruntled former associate of Oakes Ames filed affidavits alleging misuse of Crédit Mobilier stock. At the height of the 1872 presidential campaign, the *New York Sun* published these charges, supported by damaging letters from Ames. Those members of Congress who had accepted Crédit Mobilier stock and the associated profits, including Colfax and Garfield, distanced themselves from Ames. Driven by public pressure, two congressional investigations convened in December 1872: the Poland Committee investigated whether any member of Congress had been bribed, while the Wilson Committee probed the possible defrauding of the government by Crédit Mobilier. The Poland Committee report called for expelling Oakes Ames and James Brooks from the House of Representatives. Ames declared that his motive had been patriotism, that he had never intended bribery, and that, financially, he would have been better off had he never heard of Union Pacific. To the Wilson Committee's charges of fraud, Ames responded that the company had made less than $10 million on construction contracts worth more than $70 million.

The House had also considered impeaching Colfax, who was vice president at the time. However, the report concluded that the acts he committed were not impeachable. Instead, Grant denied Colfax renomination in 1872. His new vice president, Henry Wilson, admitted that his wife had purchased stock in the company, but, when he learned that legislative favors might be expected, he had asked that the money be refunded and refused the profit of $814 due to his wife.

On February 25, 1873, Ames and Brooks were censured by the House of Representatives for their activities on behalf of the syndicate. Both men died within months of the conclusion of the investigations. Federal attempts to recover fraudulent construction overcharges proved unsuccessful because Union Pacific's directors refused to sue Crédit Mobilier.

ROBERT C. SCHENCK,
AMBASSADOR TO GREAT BRITAIN

Ambassador Schenck allowed his name to be used by a silver mining compa-
ny, in which he was a stockholder, to encourage investment. When advised to
withdraw from the company by the secretary of state, Schenck delayed his
announcement so that he and his friends could liquidate their holdings
before the stock collapsed.

Rep. Robert C. Schenck of Ohio, a close associate of businessman Jay
Cooke, lost his reelection bid in 1870 and was looking for a new position.
Never shy about his ambitions for wealth, Schenck had written to his
daughter on July 27, while he was still serving as chairman of the House
Ways and Means Committee, "Yesterday I got down town to meet Mr. Jay
Cooke. I am gradually willowing the ground and personally putting in the
seed for profitable enterprises." He had considered taking an appointment
with the Northern Pacific Railroad as a congressional lobbyist, but instead
took Grant's offer to be ambassador to England.

While serving in London, Schenck used his position to encourage
British investors to buy shares of the Emma Silver Mining Company, a
Utah enterprise in which he and Cooke were invested. On November 27,
1871, Secretary of State Hamilton Fish sent Schenck a letter saying that he
and the president advised him "to withdraw your name from the management of the company." On December 6 Schenck took the advice and
resigned from the company, but he kept it quiet until January 12, 1872, so
that he and his friends could sell their shares before his announcement
depressed the stock's price.

The following year, the Emma Silver Mining Company failed. Three
years later, Rep. Abram Hewitt, a Democrat of New York, conducted an
investigation of the corporation. His report concluded that Schenck "was
not guilty of a fraud or any fraudulent intention," but that he had shown
very poor judgment. In May 1876 Schenck resigned his post and left England under the threat of legal action.

SANBORN CONTRACT

William A. Richardson, acting Treasury secretary, awarded John D. Sanborn
a contract to collect delinquent tax revenues at a commission of 50 percent.
The enterprising Sanborn went after money that even the government had
not tried to collect. He also engaged in unethical and illegal activities to
increase his take. The House Ways and Means Committee called for Richard-
son's resignation. Instead, Grant appointed him to the federal bench.

From its earliest times the United States had employed a moiety system—the payment to the informer of a portion of delinquent taxes collected. The system was coming under severe criticism, and in 1872, with

President Grant's support, Congress enacted a bill that that ended it. However, Rep. Benjamin F. Butler, Republican of Massachusetts, attached a rider to an appropriations bill that authorized the Department of Treasury to appoint up to three private third-party contractors to collect delinquent taxes.

In August Treasury Secretary George Boutwell authorized John D. Sanborn, a friend of Butler's, to collect delinquent taxes for a commission of 50 percent of the take. The authorization was signed by William A. Richardson, another friend of Butler's, who was serving as acting secretary of the Treasury.

The following year, the House Ways and Means Committee began an investigation into Sanborn's contract because many of his practices and the sums of money he was making were causing alarm. In less than a year, Sanborn had earned $213,500. The way he came by these sums raised serious concerns about the activities of Treasury Secretary Richardson, who had taken over the job in March 1873.

According to the committee, the Treasury Department had encouraged its own collectors to ignore some accounts so that Sanborn would have additional targets. On at least one occasion, Sanborn burst into the Internal Revenue Bureau's Boston office demanding lists of delinquent taxpayers. In another scheme, Sanborn sent false statements to the 592 railroads listed in *Appleton's Railway Guide* demanding payment of delinquent taxes that were not owed. The committee concluded that a number of factors had converged to give Sanborn unprecedented government power, but it could not find any specific violations of the law with which to charge Richardson. Instead, members called upon Grant to fire him. When Grant refused, the House moved to censure Richardson. At that point, Richardson resigned to take an appointment by Grant to the U.S. Court of Claims, and the Senate, in the hands of the Stalwarts, confirmed him. In June 1874 Grant appointed former solicitor general Benjamin Bristow as Treasury secretary. Bristow had a reputation as a shrewd, conscientious, and persistent watchdog.

WHISKEY RING

An investigation into the failure of the government to collect taxes on nearly 15 million gallons of alcohol annually uncovered widespread corruption in the revenue department and led to accusations against Grant's son and brother. The scandal also brought down many of the president's close associates, including his personal secretary, Orville Babcock.

If not the administration's worst scandal, perhaps the most devastating to President Grant was the Whiskey Ring, which led to accusations of wrongdoing by his eldest son, Frederick Dent Grant, and by Orvil Grant, the president's brother. The federal government had experienced problems collecting the taxes due on the distribution of distilled spirits since the administration of Andrew Johnson. Estimates placed the lost revenue at between $10 million and $14 million annually. Various methods were used to defraud the Treasury Department and the Internal Revenue Bureau, including falsely reporting the amount of alcohol produced and forging Internal Revenue stamps. What stood in the way of solving this problem was the willingness of Internal Revenue officials to accept bribes.

Secretary of the Treasury Benjamin Bristow was determined to put an end to the frauds. Bristow had decided to send investigators to collectors' offices in December 1874 to review records. However, Col. Orville Babcock, Grant's secretary, blocked the inspection and sent a message to his co-conspirators that it was okay to continue the operations. Babcock's wire was signed "Sylph," a code for recent illicit pleasures. When Bristow tried to change collection districts so that he might ascertain which were honest and which were corrupt, the St. Louis collector, Gen. John McDonald, persuaded Grant to revoke the order.

Bristow's early efforts failed because he had underestimated the level of corruption in his own department. He received authorization and $125,000 in funding to try again. Confiding in only one other member of the Treasury Department, Solicitor Bluford Wilson, Bristow organized a secret force of incorruptible agents and sent them to distilleries in St. Louis, Milwaukee, and Chicago. Bristow and Wilson also hired Myron Colony, an investigative reporter for the *St. Louis Democrat*. Colony had been recommended by the paper's editor, George Fishback, who wrote to Bristow, "If the Secretary wants to break up the powerful ring which exists here, I can give him the name of a man who, if he receives the necessary authority and is assured of absolute secrecy about the matter, will undertake to do it, and I will guarantee success."

In April 1875 McDonald once again attempted to prevent Bristow from discovering the truth by pleading with Grant to make certain records off-limits to the zealous Treasury secretary. McDonald claimed that the contents would be damaging not only to distillers, but also to many loyal party members. However, this time Grant refused to intervene, and McDonald resigned his post. His colleagues began to destroy records to keep Bristow from piecing together the rings. But on May 10, sixteen distilleries were raided, and documents from the offices of collectors of Internal Revenue were seized. The records were put under seal until they could be examined by Bristow and Attorney General Edwards Pierrepont.

The investigation would touch many friends of the president as well as prominent politicians of the day. As the result of a raid in Milwaukee, E. W. Keyes, the state patronage boss, was indicted. In another case, former senator Matthew Carpenter of Wisconsin was convicted for aiding a ring.

However, the most important raid involved St. Louis distilleries and the central collection office where John McDonald had once been in charge. McDonald was not only an appointee of President Grant, but also a friend and frequent guest at the White House. Grant had accepted several gifts from McDonald, including a team of horses—Grant later purchased the team—that the president used on a visit to St. Louis. McDonald even fixed the outcome of a horse race at the St. Louis fair so that Grant's colt would win the blue ribbon.

McDonald had formed a ring of officers and distillers, using blackmail to force distillers into partnership with him. He or his agents would find some violations of the complicated liquor laws and then approach the distillers with the choice of either participating in the ring or facing prosecution and continued harassment. Many relatively honest distillers found it easier to go along with McDonald than to fight him.

A shrewd businessman, McDonald brought in outside financial managers to handle the vast sums of money he was stealing. With more than $2.5 million in ill-gotten gains, McDonald spent the money for both political and personal purposes. He strengthened the Republican Party organization in St. Louis by purchasing a newspaper that was favorable to the party's causes. He also spent to bolster the Grant wing of the party against a growing Liberal Republican-Democratic coalition. Money had been funneled into Grant's 1872 reelection campaign by the campaign's manager, William E. Chandler. Additionally, William Avery, chief clerk of the Treasury, and Orville Babcock received money.

By May 13 nearly 350 men from Boston to Galveston, Texas, had been arrested. Bristow told Hamilton Fish, "Babcock is as deep as any in the Whiskey Ring, [and] that he has most positive evidence." When Bristow and Fish met with the president, Grant maintained, "There is at least one honest man in St. Louis on whom we can rely—John McDonald. I know that because he is an intimate acquaintance and confidential friend of Babcock's." At that point, Bristow replied, "McDonald is the head and center of all the frauds." In July Bristow and Pierrepont told Grant that Babcock was also involved in the ring. Grant did not comment specifically on Babcock's case, but wrote, "Let no guilty man escape if it can be avoided. Be specially vigilant . . . against all those who insinuate that they have high influence to protect, or to protect them."

In August Bristow confronted Babcock with the telegram signed "Sylph." Babcock maintained that the telegram had nothing to do with the Whiskey Ring. Grant sided with Babcock, perhaps because he distrusted Bristow's assistant, Bluford Wilson. Friends of Babcock's had told Grant that he too was a victim of Wilson's spying and that Babcock was being made a scapegoat to embarrass the president. On December 2 Babcock asked Grant to appoint a military court of inquiry to investigate him. Grant and his cabinet agreed and appointed a panel of three generals who were believed to be sympathetic to Babcock. When U.S. Attorney David P. Dyer was asked to turn over all relevant documents, Dyer's response was to ask the grand jury for an indictment against Babcock, which he secured on December 9. The military court of inquiry was disbanded.

Grant's distaste for the manner in which Bristow and Wilson were obtaining convictions was growing. He told Wilson he did not like the fact that so many were going to prison on the word of "confessed perjurers and felons." On January 26, 1876, Attorney General Pierrepont ordered that no further grants of immunity were to be given in exchange for testimony. This order made the prosecution of the principal figures difficult and most assuredly would protect Babcock from conviction.

As if Babcock's indictment was not bad enough, in January newspapers began to print stories that implicated not only Grant's eldest son, Frederick, but also the president's brother, Orvil. The president wanted the matter of his family resolved quickly and ordered Pierrepont to bring the reporters before a grand jury so that they could produce any hard evidence they had, and, if they had none, to have their names published as slanderers.

Grant considered going to St. Louis and testifying in Babcock's behalf. He was persuaded instead to give a deposition, which was read at the trial on February 17. Babcock was acquitted eleven days later, but could not return to Washington. His position as Grant's secretary had been given to Grant's second son, Ulysses S. Grant Jr. With no savings, Babcock became a lighthouse inspector and drowned at Mosquito Inlet, Florida, in 1884.

Congress, which was looking into the matter for itself, called Bristow before the investigating committee in July 1876. He had left the cabinet and was estranged from the president, but refused to testify about "what occurred between the President and myself . . . [which] I think is a matter of the highest privilege, of which I have no right to speak at all." When pressed, Bristow still refused to divulge anything.

McDonald went to prison and wrote a book in which he tried to prove that others, especially Babcock, also belonged in jail for their part in the Whiskey Ring. Many of the documents McDonald cites are part of the Bristow Papers in the Library of Congress and suggest that Babcock was guilty. McDonald also tried to implicate Grant in criminal activities, but had no evidence of that.

COLUMBUS DELANO, SECRETARY OF THE INTERIOR

Interior Secretary Columbus Delano was charged with corruption, bribery, and fraud in connection with land deals in the West that benefited associates, including his son, John Delano, a surveyor. The controversy led to a congressional investigation in 1876.

The charges of corruption that ultimately led to the resignation of Columbus Delano came from Treasury Secretary Benjamin Bristow, who saw Delano as a threat to his presidential aspirations. Prior to his appointment as interior secretary, Delano had served as a U.S. representative from Ohio and as head of the Internal Revenue Bureau.

In 1875 Secretary Bristow received a letter dated March 24 from L. C. Stevens, chief clerk of the Surveyor's Office in Cheyenne, Wyoming. Stevens also sent several canceled checks, an endorsed bank draft, and other documents showing that John Delano, Secretary Delano's son, had received surveying contracts for land that did not need surveying at the time. The documents also showed that John Delano was blackmailing clerks in the land office. Stevens's letter claimed that the secretary had personally written a thank-you note to Surveyor General Silas Reed for John Delano's contracts.

Bristow showed Grant the documents and suggested that he ask Delano to resign. On April 29 Surveyor General Reed, in a meeting with the president, asked Grant to return the documents to him, as it was clear that Stevens had stolen them from the office and from John Delano. Although Grant refused to turn over the documents, he also did not pursue the matter. At the conclusion of the meeting, Reed telegraphed Stevens that he was fired. Reed replaced Stevens with his son, Charles J. Reed.

With anti-administration newspapers making hay of the story, Secretary of State Hamilton Fish also suggested getting rid of Delano. Grant saw that move as "retreating under fire," and he continued to support Delano. Grant gave the documents back to Secretary Bristow, who had requested their return once it became clear that Grant was not planning on acting on the information. From Grant's perspective, there was a clear conflict of interest in John Delano's receiving special contracts, but nothing illegal had occurred. On July 2 Bristow returned the documents to Stevens. Bristow told Stevens there was nothing more he could do because the matter did not involve his department.

The affair would have ended there, but opposition newspapers continued to pound away at Grant, Delano, and Reed. It seems that the information Stevens was supplying the papers also implicated Grant's brother Orvil in a similar scheme. In fact, when asked by a member of Congress during the 1876 investigation whether the president's brother did surveying work in the territory, Stevens stated that he doubted Orvil had ever been to the territory. On August 7, 1875, Grant wrote to Reed accepting his resignation. He also accepted Delano's resignation, but did not make it public until the fall when Bristow threatened to resign if Delano did not. In October Grant appointed Zachariah Chandler as interior secretary.

DRUNKENNESS

Throughout his administration, Grant was rumored to be alcoholic.

During his military career Grant had been known to drink when there were lulls in military action. This habit, many assumed, carried over to Grant's presidency. Despite the rumors that he drank, there is no solid evidence that he did so to the point of inebriation. More important, no reputable claim was ever made that Grant performed any of his duties under the influence of alcohol. It seems that the boredom of being in a military camp and his loneliness at being separated from his wife and children played roles in his consumption of alcohol.

BIBLIOGRAPHY

Boynton, H. V. "The Washington 'Safe Burglary' Conspiracy." *American Law Review* 11 (1877): 401ff.

———. "The Whisky Ring." *North American Review* 123 (October 1876): 280ff.

Bridges, Roger D. *The Impeachment and Trial of William Worth Belknap, Secretary of War.* Master's thesis, State College of Iowa, 1963.

Carpenter, John Alcott. *Ulysses S. Grant.* New York: Twayne Publishers, 1970.

Gillette, William. *Retreat from Reconstruction.* Baton Rouge: Louisiana State University Press, 1979.

Goldhurst, Richard. *Many Are the Hearts: The Agony and the Triumph of Ulysses S. Grant.* New York: Reader's Digest Press, 1975.

Grant, Ulysses S. *Memoirs and Selected Letters.* New York: Library of America, 1990.

Hesseltine, William B. *Ulysses S. Grant: Politician.* New York: Dodd, Mead, 1935.

Klein, Maury. *Union Pacific: The Birth of A Railroad, 1862–1893.* Garden City, N.Y.: Doubleday, 1987.

McCabe, James Dabney. *Behind the Scenes in Washington.* New York: Arno Press, 1974.

McDonald, John. *Secrets of the Great Whiskey Ring; and Eighteen Months in the Penitentiary.* St. Louis: W. S. Bryan, 1880.

McFeely, William S. *Grant: A Biography.* New York: Norton, 1981.

Mitchell, Jack. *Executive Privilege: Two Centuries of White House Scandals.* New York: Hippocrene Books, 1992.

Therry, James R. *The Life of General Robert Cumming Schenck.* Ph.D. dissertation, Georgetown University, 1968.

United States House Committee on Banking and Currency. *Investigation into the Causes of the Gold Panic.* Washington, D.C.: Government Printing Office, 1870.

Woodward, C. Vann. *Responses of the Presidents to Charges of Misconduct.* New York: Dell Publishing, 1974.

RUTHERFORD B. HAYES

Nineteenth President
1877–1881

Rutherford B. Hayes was born October 4, 1822, in Delaware, Ohio, eleven weeks after his father died. Raised by his mother, who was left a substantial estate, and an uncle, young Hayes attended private schools and was admitted to Kenyon College in Gambier, Ohio, at age sixteen. He graduated in 1842 as class valedictorian and studied law at a firm in Columbus before enrolling in Harvard Law School. Hayes graduated in January 1845 and was admitted to the Ohio bar May 10.

From 1845 until the outbreak of the Civil War, Hayes practiced law in Fremont, Ohio, and in Cincinnati. During this period he also became active in politics, campaigning for Whig candidates Zachary Taylor in 1848 and Winfield Scott in 1852 and Republican candidate John C. Fremont in 1856. On December 30, 1852, Hayes married Lucy Ware Webb, a graduate of Wesleyan Female College in Cincinnati. From 1858 to 1860 he served as solicitor for the city of Cincinnati.

In June 1861 Hayes was commissioned a major in the Twenty-third Ohio Volunteer Infantry Regiment. In his four years of service, he was involved in more than fifty battles, was wounded several times, and attained the rank of major general. Elected to the U.S. House of Representatives, he resigned from the army in June 1865.

Hayes had won in the 1864 election without campaigning because, as he put it, "An officer fit for duty who at this crisis would abandon his post to electioneer for a seat in Congress ought to be scalped." Hayes was easily reelected in 1866 and voted in favor of the impeachment of Andrew Johnson. In 1867 he ran for governor of Ohio. He defeated Democrat Allen G. Thurman and was reelected in 1869. As governor, Hayes trimmed state debt by 20 percent while focusing on education, prison reform, and the civil rights of blacks. Unwilling to break the two-term precedent for governor, Hayes returned to the practice of law. He was defeated for election to Congress in 1872 by the Liberal Republican candidate, Henry B. Banning. However, in 1875 Hayes was again elected governor of Ohio.

The Republican convention of 1876 began with Rep. James G. Blaine of Maine the clear front-runner for the nomination. By the sixth ballot, however, Hayes was in second place, and a surging anti-Blaine movement put him over the top on the seventh ballot. Rep. William A. Wheeler of New York was nominated to run for vice president. In the general election Hayes faced Democrat Samuel J. Tilden of New York. Tilden was a strong challenger for a number of reasons: first, voters were disgusted by the scandals that had plagued the Grant administration; second, as governor of New York, Tilden had earned a reputation as an effective reformer; and, third, the Democrats had regained control of several southern states. The election ended in a dispute over electoral votes. Hayes became president, even though Tilden had won the popular vote by more than 250,000 votes. (See below.)

As part of the Compromise of 1877, Hayes ended Reconstruction by removing federal troops from the South. He fought against the monetary policy that favored the use of silver to back currency instead of the gold standard. This policy was eventually adopted over his veto in the Bland-Allison Act, which authorized the Treasury to purchase between $2 million and $4 million in silver each month. Hayes sought to reform the civil service by barring political activity by federal employees. He also tried to create a system in which civil servants were professionals who gained employment by merit, not political patronage. He opposed the Burlingame Treaty of 1868, which allowed for the unrestricted importation of Chinese labor. He favored limits on Chinese immigration and pursued an 1880 treaty to that end.

Hayes declined to seek a second term in 1880 and returned to Fremont, Ohio. During his retirement years, he served as director of the George Peabody Educational Fund and John F. Slater Fund, which promoted black education through scholarships; the black educator and activist W. E. B. Du Bois was a recipient of a Slater Fund scholarship. Hayes served in various capacities at a number of Ohio institutions of higher learning, including Ohio State University and Western Reserve University. He also stayed active in politics, supporting Republican candidates, promoting temperance, and opposing women's suffrage. He died on January 17, 1893, several days after suffering a heart attack.

THE ELECTION OF 1876

In what many historians believe to be one of the most corrupt elections in U.S. history, Hayes attained the White House in exchange for ending Reconstruction and withdrawing federal troops from the South.

As the presidential election of 1876 approached, the Republican Party knew it was in trouble. Political corruption was widespread in both parties, but with Grant in the White House, most of the public's outrage focused on the Republicans. The Civil War was fading in the public's memory, weakening a once-useful device. "Liberty and Union" would continue to be a Republican slogan, but people were beginning to forget that the Democrats had been the party of slavery and disunion. Most important, an economic depression led those who voted their pocketbooks to blame the party in power. With Hayes as the candidate and New York representative William Wheeler as his running mate, the Republican Party had picked perhaps the best team it could for a difficult election. At the end of June the Democrats also chose a governor as their candidate, Samuel Tilden of New York.

Hayes did almost no campaigning, but depended on party regulars to get out the vote in each state. From the start, astute observers suspected that the election would be far from honest. Hayes, always the realist, predicted that if he lost it would be "by bribery & repeating" in the North and by "violence and intimidation" in the South. Events proved him right—particularly in the South. Hayes said later that, as he and his wife went to bed on election night, "both of us felt more anxiety about the South—about the colored people especially than about anything else sinister about the result."

The initial returns gave the election to the Democrats by 250,000 popular votes and 18 electoral votes. On his own, Hayes never would have contested the election, but at a critical moment a few Republican officials realized that decisive action might transform defeat into victory. Late on the night of the election, Gen. Daniel E. Sickles, a leading member of the Republican National Committee from New York, telegraphed party leaders in South Carolina, Louisiana, Florida, and Oregon: "With your state sure for Hayes, he is elected. Hold your state." Sickles was right: with the electoral votes of those four states, Hayes would win by the narrowest of margins.

The three southern states held the key. All across the South, Democrats had used violence and intimidation on a massive scale to keep Republicans, both black and white, from voting. In most of the region, protesting the results would do no good: the political machinery was firmly in Democratic hands. But South Carolina, Louisiana, and Florida still had Republican-controlled governments. If enough Tilden votes could be declared invalid, Hayes could carry those states and, with Oregon's votes, win the election. South Carolina was the easiest, as Hayes had won there by almost 1,000 votes. Florida was a bit more difficult; unofficial tallies had him losing by a mere ninety-four votes. Hardest of all would be Louisiana, where the unofficial tallies had Tilden winning by 6,300 votes.

In South Carolina, the five members of the election board, all Republicans, wasted no time invalidating the votes from two counties to ensure not only that Hayes won, but also that the party retained the legislature and the governor's office. In Louisiana, Republicans assumed that, because the majority of the state's registered voters were black, the election should

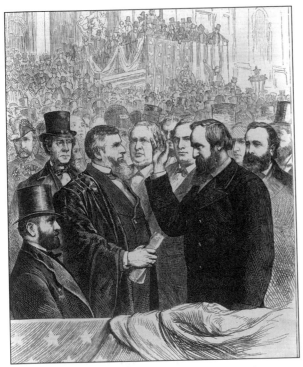

The new president, right, takes the oath of office from Chief Justice Morrison Waite.

have gone to Hayes. Meeting in early December, the all-Republican board invalidated 13,000 Democratic votes and 2,000 Republican votes, giving the election to Hayes. In Florida, both parties had engaged in so much fraud that historians have never settled who actually won. What is known is that the election board (with one Democrat) tossed out enough votes to give Hayes the victory by 900 votes. If certified by Congress, Hayes would win the presidency by a single electoral vote.

The Democrats, far from conceding, sent a rival set of electoral votes to Congress. With the Senate in Republican hands and the House Democratic, the stage was set for what could have been a serious struggle. A bipartisan committee recommended that the election be decided by a commission—also bipartisan—with fifteen members, five from the Senate, five from the House, and five from the Supreme Court. Hayes and some Republicans opposed the plan, preferring a more certain one in which Thomas Ferry, the Republican president of the Senate, would decide for himself which votes to accept. But Tilden, the Democrats, and enough Republicans supported the commission idea for it to pass both houses of Congress.

The commission was to be made up of five Democrats and five Republicans from Congress, two Democrats and two Republicans from the Court, and one independent justice, David Davis. But just before the commission was to meet, the Illinois legislature elected Davis to the Senate, and Justice Joseph Bradley, another Republican, took his place. With eight Republicans and seven Democrats on the commission, its decisions were not surprising. On all the major points, the Republicans won on a straight party vote.

In the midst of all this partisan politics, it was obvious that the Republican Senate would accept the commission's findings. But why would the Democratic House go along? The process through which enough Democratic votes were won was complex. Hayes himself seems to have been too politically squeamish to be closely involved in what his representatives did, but in the end the South received some promises from the Republicans.

The region would get money for internal improvements, subsidies for the Texas and Pacific railroad, and a larger voice in federal jobs in the South. Only as an afterthought was the most important promise made—the removal of federal troops from the former Confederacy. In return, southern Democrats promised that the South would abandon its political violence, protect the rights of blacks, and help elect a Republican as Speaker of the House.

Even then, enough Democrats filibustered to delay a decision until almost the last moment. The final stage in the long struggle came during the early hours of March 2, 1877, when the members of Congress assembled in the House chamber, which was guarded by fourteen armed men. Unable to block acceptance of Wisconsin's electoral votes, at 4:05 a.m. the president of the Senate declared Hayes the winner, 185 votes to 184. Three days later he was sworn in as the nineteenth president.

The judgment of history has not been kind to Hayes. It is quite likely that, based on votes cast, Tilden should have carried both Florida and Louisiana and thus the election. On the other hand, Hayes was probably right in his belief that, had all the southerners been free to vote as they chose, he would have won.

For southern blacks the decision probably made little difference. Hayes was sadly mistaken in his belief that if treated gently the more moderate southerners would end the violence. By the end of 1877, both southern Democrats and the Hayes administration had abandoned their promises. Without federal troops, the South became solidly Democratic and remained so for almost a century.

CUSTOM HOUSE INVESTIGATIONS

Hayes had appointed a special commission to investigate charges of corruption in custom houses, especially the New York Custom House, which had been an ongoing source of patronage for Sen. Roscoe Conkling. The investigation implicated future president Chester A. Arthur.

Corruption in U.S. custom houses had been the subject of investigation for years. Custom house practices were undoubtedly questionable and often involved outright theft of government funds. Hayes, who had run as a reformer of the civil service, decided to take on the problems of political patronage and illegalities in custom houses. Because it was the largest, the New York Custom House was also the most corrupt. Traditionally, local political bosses dispensed the posts as they saw fit and controlled the appointees. Sen. Roscoe Conkling had the patronage of the New York Custom House, and he secured the appointments of future president Chester A. Arthur as collector of customs and Alonzo B. Cornell as naval officer.

In April 1877 President Hayes ordered Treasury Secretary John Sherman to appoint a commission to investigate the practices of the custom houses. In New York, John Jay, a Conkling political enemy, was named to

Roscoe Conkling

chair the commission. On May 24 the Jay Commission issued its first report, which charged Arthur and Cornell with numerous violations of policy. Among the charges were that Arthur had made appointments for political reasons rather than for the purposes of collecting revenue, that Cornell was in violation of an executive order that barred him from holding a political position (chairman of the Republican State Committee) as well as a public post, that the custom house employed more than 200 petty bureaucrats who performed no public service, and that both Arthur and Cornell were derelict in the performance of official duties.

Rather than take on Conkling in a showdown the administration might not win, Secretary Sherman advised Arthur to cut the staffing at the custom house by 20 percent and to institute some other reforms. Arthur made some changes, but he also made official complaints about the partisan Jay Commission. Additionally, Arthur and Cornell were requested to resign quietly and offered political cover as an incentive. Hayes suggested that they say that the needed reforms could be better carried out by new personnel, but they had no intention of giving up their posts.

Hayes finally took direct action in October by sending the Senate some nominations to replace Arthur and Cornell. Senators who saw the president's move as a threat to their own power of patronage supported Conkling in defeating the nominations. Hayes sent a second slate of nominees who were also rejected. Waiting for Congress to recess, Hayes removed Arthur and Cornell and appointed Edwin A. Merritt and Silas W. Burt to the posts. Hayes did not cite any charges as reasons for the removals, preferring to let the matter die quietly. However, he included the Jay Commission report listing the charges of corruption against Arthur and Cornell when he formally submitted their replacements' names to the Senate. In the end, the Senate voted to confirm Merritt and Burt.

EXECUTIVE ORDER BANNING POLITICAL ACTIVITY

Hayes issued an executive order that banned the practice of assessing federal employees a percentage of their wages as political party contributions, but during the midterm elections of 1878 he himself violated the order.

When Rutherford Hayes gave his inaugural address on March 5, 1877, he delighted reformers by promising to lead a "return to the principles and practices of the founders of the Government" by carrying out a "thorough, radical and complete reform" of the nation's civil service system. Civil service appointments, he said, should not be dictated by politics nor should capable workers be fired because they had supported the wrong party in the last election.

Reform was certainly needed. For a half century, government jobs had been doled out according to the spoils system. Those who worked for the winning candidate during his campaign shared in the victory by being rewarded with jobs, whether they were qualified for them or not. Once hired, they were expected to devote time and money to those who had provided their jobs. Both parties depended on that money for campaigns. Each year, civil servants were assessed between 2 percent and 7 percent of their salaries for political purposes.

Hayes wasted no time. Seven weeks after taking office he described his plan: "Legislation must be prepared & Executive rules and Maxims. We must limit, and narrow the area of patronage—we must stop interference of federal officers with elections. We must be relieved of Congressional dictation as to appointments." Hayes was taking on a huge task that would be made no easier by a hostile Congress. Even Hayes's cabinet had only one man, Interior Secretary Carl Schurz, who was committed to the reforms. Still, Hayes started off well by declaring in the face of family pressure, "No person connected to me by blood or marriage will be appointed to office."

On June 22 he took his first major step. He issued an executive order to all branches of the federal government declaring, "No officer shall be required or permitted to take part in conventions or election campaigns." Although federal appointees could speak and vote as ordinary citizens, "No assessments for political purposes on officers or subordinates should be allowed." On its face, this executive order was revolutionary, and it created quite a stir within the executive branch. But Hayes was no radical. By temperament, he liked to move slowly and carefully. A practical man, he understood that fifty years of patronage could not be reversed overnight. If those who had been appointed by the spoils system were adequate for their jobs, he preferred to leave them in place. If not, he waited until their terms expired before replacing them. Even with the notoriously corrupt New York Custom House, he tried to allow those he wanted out to resign voluntarily. Hayes also preferred to allow time for the political parties to shift from patronage-inspired party workers to a voluntary system.

However, when it benefited his party, Hayes was willing to ignore his order. For the 1878 midterm elections, George Gorham, the secretary of the Republican Congressional Committee, sent letters to all federal employees making more than $1,000 a year, calling on them to "voluntarily" give the party 1 percent of their salaries. The letter claimed that the contributions would face no "official objections"—a vague reference to Hayes's order. The money did the party little good: Republican members fared poorly in the fall elections even though Hayes remained popular. In 1879 Gorham told a Senate investigation of the still-disputed 1876 election that Hayes had seen and approved the solicitation letter. Hayes remained silent in the face of the allegations that he had violated his own order. The temptation must have been difficult to resist: in 1878 his party raised $93,000 from officeholders, and in 1880 they raised more than $100,000. Hayes seems to have simply ignored the situation.

Troubles in the cabinet also continued to hinder his efforts. In his inaugural address, Hayes had promised to serve only one term. By doing so, he hoped to prevent his supporters from using patronage to ensure his reelection. That may have worked, but it created another problem. Members of his cabinet—particularly John Sherman in Treasury—were zealously using their appointment power to win friends for a run at the presidency in 1880.

Reformers grew frustrated with the slow, inconsistent pace of change. On his side, Hayes told a friend that he believed that such critics were

> without experience in practical affairs—have never been responsible for results—are without training in actual government, or law making—are soon hot and soon cold. You can't fight but one battle at a time—two at most. This they don't know.

Given his cautious approach, by 1880 Hayes was beginning to think he had done almost all he could do to reform the system. In his third annual address to Congress, he emphasized the need for legislation to ensure that the civil service did not remain politicized. The problem, he privately wrote a friend in January, was that Congress had "no champions of Civil Service Reform." Men who "would float or lean that way" were not enough. What was needed was "some earnest man to propose the bills, to make argument, and champion the cause as a hobby."

In his fourth and final address to Congress, Hayes spoke of two topics close to his heart. Upset that the agreements he had made with southern Democrats had come to nothing and that the region was dominated by a single party that championed white supremacy, he called on Congress to investigate violations of black voting rights and to appropriate money to prosecute the offenders. He also asked them to empower a commission to create a system of competitive examinations for the entire civil service and to pass laws to protect government workers from political assessments. In the end, the more pragmatic reformers recognized that, given the role that patronage had played in the nation's politics, Hayes had accomplished much in four years. He had begun the process of reforming the civil service, but it would be up to others to complete the task.

RICHARD W. THOMPSON, SECRETARY OF THE NAVY

Richard W. Thompson accepted a position with a French syndicate wishing to build a canal across the isthmus of Panama, which placed him in direct conflict with the stated policy of the Hayes administration that the United States should control such a canal.

In May 1879 Ferdinand de Lesseps, the builder of the Suez Canal, launched an ambitious plan to construct a canal across the isthmus of Central America that would be paid for by private funds. Although the de Lesseps plan had attracted little financial backing, it did attract the consternation of President Hayes. He was determined that such a canal must not be controlled by Europeans, especially the French. He sought to secure that any railroad or canal that crossed the continent would be under U.S. control. To that end, he ordered naval vessels on either side of the isthmus to establish a naval presence that would ensure U.S. control.

Hayes's hostility to the de Lesseps plan met with mixed reaction. After all, de Lesseps was not an agent of the French government, and American investors were free to buy stock in his enterprise. But Hayes did not back down. In a March 1880 message to Congress, Hayes once again asserted that any canal must be American and that no foreign control, even by private individuals, could be tolerated.

De Lesseps left New York on April 1 without securing the funding he needed from New York backers. In another effort to attract Americans, de Lesseps formed an American syndicate and invited former president Ulysses S. Grant to head it. When Grant declined, de Lesseps offered the post to Secretary of the Navy Richard W. Thompson. Hayes, who learned of the offer in August, warned Thompson not to accept because de Lesseps would use the association to create the illusion of U.S. government support. Thompson could not refuse the $25,000 a year salary (his cabinet position only paid $8,000). But Thompson did not resign his cabinet post when he accepted the presidency of the American syndicate in December. Hayes learned of Thompson's decision, and he demanded and received Thompson's immediate resignation.

Richard Thompson

PONCA INDIAN REMOVAL

The Sioux Indians were promised land that belonged to the Ponca Indians, who were ultimately moved to other lands in the Indian Territory, but not before a long and difficult struggle that wound up in a congressional investigation.

The problem that led to the Ponca removal crisis of the Hayes administration began during Grant's presidency. According to the Sioux Treaty of 1868, the Sioux Indians were promised the 96,000-acre Ponca Reserve along the Missouri River, even though this land had already been reserved for the Ponca Indians by treaties made in 1858 and 1867. The Sioux moved onto this land and began to harass the Poncas, who requested the right to move with the Omahas to land in Nebraska. When Congress failed to act, the Poncas requested new lands in the Indian Territory (Oklahoma). In 1876 Congress allocated both land and money for the Ponca Indians to settle in the Indian Territory.

In the Hayes administration, Carl Schurz was appointed interior secretary, the post that included overseeing Indian affairs. Schurz upheld the 1876 decision, and the Poncas were moved from the Ponca Reserve to the Indian Territory. The Poncas were unhappy with the new lands, and four of their chiefs—White Eagle, Standing Buffalo, Standing Bear, and Big Chief—visited Hayes at the White House asking for his assistance.

Hayes asked Schurz to resettle the Poncas. Schurz asked them to remain in the Indian Territory, but to find another plot of 96,000 acres that they preferred. The leadership settled on lands at the Salt Fork of the Arkansas River, even though Congress refused to compensate the tribe for the loss of houses and other expenses. The situation seemed to be resolved, except that one of the chiefs, Standing Bear, wanted to return to the ancestral lands in Nebraska to bury his grandchild. He and his followers were arrested on their trek north. Freed on a writ of habeas corpus by a federal judge, Standing Bear and a young Omaha named Bright Eyes went on a national tour to publicize the story of the Ponca Indians.

Despite the publicity, Schurz stuck to the decision that the Poncas should remain in Indian Territory. Hayes—embarrassed by the situation—appointed a commission made up of Interior Department representatives, military men, and members of the Ponca Relief Committee of Boston to devise a solution. The commission recommended that each Ponca be allowed to live in either the Indian Territory or the Ponca Reserve. On February 1, 1881, Hayes asked Congress to approve the commission's report. The Poncas could choose where they wanted to live and were given title to their share of the 96,000 acres and compensated for the losses caused by the original removal.

THE STAR ROUTE AFFAIR

Postal fraud that began under Hayes set off an investigation that ran through the Garfield and Arthur administrations before it was concluded. Second Assistant Postmaster Thomas J. Brady, who had provided crucial southern votes for Hayes, headed a ring that defrauded the government of vast sums of money on the so-called Star Routes.

After the Civil War, the demands on the U.S. postal system grew at a dramatic pace. To supplement its regular operations, the post office used trains, steamships, and the pony express. By the end of 1876 the government was employing more than 134 pony express and stagecoach lines to help deliver mail, especially in the West. The emblem of these private carriers was a star, hence the term Star Routes.

The second assistant postmaster general was responsible for coordinating these private deliverers. In the Hayes administration, Thomas J. Brady, a holdover from the Grant administration, continued in the job and developed a simple scheme to defraud the government. The operators of the Star Routes would petition the government for changes in their contracts, which, they said, would enable them to offer more and faster service, but at an increased cost. Brady, who was authorized to approve such changes, would simply sign off on the petitions. The providers would kick back a portion of the new funds without improving the service. The ring included a number of leading Republicans at the Post Office and the Treasury Department and Sen. Stephen W. Dorsey of Arkansas, who was the secretary of the Republican National Committee in 1880.

Knowledge of the scheme did not come to light until after President Hayes had left office. He may have suspected that something was amiss when Brady kept appealing to Congress for deficiency appropriations. In 1880 alone Brady asked Congress to approve an additional $2 million for cost overruns. However, it appears that both Congress and Hayes thought the expenses were the result of extravagance and not fraud.

If Hayes was unaware of the corruption, Vice President–elect Chester A. Arthur was keenly aware of Dorsey's participation in the use of Star Route funds in the election. In a speech delivered February 11, 1881, Arthur honored Dorsey for his activities in securing Indiana—a Democratic state—in the election of 1880. A few days later, Sen. James G. Blaine of Maine confirmed that he knew that Dorsey and Brady were using the Star Routes as a way to defraud the government of money.

Hayes left Washington still ignorant of the whole story, which would not come to light until 1881 (see page 172). Hayes denied he knew about the wrongdoing and pointed out that he had not appointed Brady. Further, he had on a number of occasions raised the issue of costs with both of his postmasters general, David M. Key and Horace Maynard. Hayes had even changed the policy that allowed Brady to approve contract changes. Without mentioning that he believed fraud to be taking place, Hayes required that all increases had to be approved by the postmaster general in consultation with the president and cabinet. But, in the end, the full exploration of the Star Routes would have to wait for a later administration.

BIBLIOGRAPHY

Barnard, Harry. *Rutherford B. Hayes and His America.* Indianapolis: Bobbs-Merrill, 1954.

Davidson, Kenneth E. *The Presidency of Rutherford B. Hayes.* Lawrence: University Press of Kansas, 1972.

Fowler, Dorothy G. *The Cabinet Politician: The Postmasters General, 1829–1909.* New York: Columbia University Press, 1943.

Hayworth, Paul L. *The Hayes-Tilden Disputed Presidential Election of 1876*. Cleveland: Burrows Bros., 1906.

Hoggenboom, Ari. *Rutherford B. Hayes:Warrior and President*. Lawrence: University Press of Kansas, 1995.

Klotsche, J. Martin. "The Star Route Cases." *Mississippi Valley Historical Review* 3 (December 1935): 407–418.

Mitchell, Jack. *Executive Privilege: Two Centuries of White House Scandals*. New York: Hippocrene Books, 1992.

Shores, Venila L. *The Hayes-Conkling Controversy*. Master's thesis, Smith College, 1919.

Woodward, C. Vann. *Reunion and Reaction*. Garden City, N.Y.: Doubleday, 1956.

———. *Responses of the Presidents to Charges of Misconduct*. New York: Dell Publishing, 1974.

JAMES GARFIELD

Twentieth President
1881

orn November 19, 1831, in Cuyahoga County, Ohio, James Garfield grew up on a farm under the care of his mother, Eliza Garfield, and an uncle. His father, who had been a famous wrestler, died when Garfield was a baby. His mother was forced to sell part of her farmland, leaving the family to survive on only thirty acres. After working on the farm during summers and attending schools during the winter months, Garfield enrolled at Williams College in Massachusetts in 1854. At Williams, he was the oldest student and was respected by his classmates. He was a champion debater and active in the literary and theological societies. He graduated with honors in 1856.

After considering the ministry, Garfield chose teaching as his profession. He returned to Hiram, Ohio, where he became an instructor at his former school, the Western Reserve Eclectic Institute. He served as president of the school from 1857 to 1861. Finding his profession lacking in intellectual challenge, Garfield studied law and was admitted to the bar in 1860. He married Lucretia Rudolph, in November 1858, after a long courtship.

In 1859 Garfield began a single two-year term in the Ohio state senate. Supporting the antislavery bloc, he praised the work of abolitionist John Brown and campaigned for Abraham Lincoln in 1860. After the Civil War broke out, he joined the Union army in August 1861. He was commissioned as a lieutenant colonel in Ohio's Forty-second Regiment; by the time he left the service in December 1863, he had risen to the rank of major general. Garfield saw action at Shiloh before falling ill and returning to Ohio. In September 1862 he was elected to the U.S. House of Representatives but remained in military service.

After the battle of Chickamauga in September 1863, in which he was cited for bravery, Garfield was promoted to major general. He resigned his commission in December to take his seat in the House, where he served from 1863 until 1880. A hawkish Republican, he criticized President Lincoln for not conducting the war more aggressively. When the war ended, he supported the harsh Reconstruction policies of the radical wing of his party, advocating the confiscation of Confederate property and the execution or exile of Confederate leaders. After Lincoln's assassination, however, Garfield tried to bridge the gap between the Radical Republicans in Congress and the Reconstruction policies of President Andrew Johnson. In the end, Garfield voted for the impeachment of Johnson in 1868.

Garfield supported, if unenthusiastically, Ulysses S. Grant's election in 1868 and reelection in 1872. During his time in Congress, Garfield became the leading expert on financial matters and chaired at various times the Appropriations Committee and the Banking and Currency Committee. He was, along with many other members of Congress, implicated in the Crédit Mobilier bribery scandal (see below), but it had little effect on his electoral success. He served on the electoral commission that settled the election of 1876 in favor of Rutherford B. Hayes. During Hayes's administration, Garfield was minority leader in the House. He was elected to the U.S. Senate in 1880, but he gave up the seat in favor of the presidency.

At the Republican National Convention in Chicago, in June 1880, the leading candidate for the nomination was former president Grant, who sought an unprecedented third term. Incumbent president Rutherford B. Hayes kept his 1876 promise not to seek the nomination in 1880. Grant had the support of the conservative Stalwart Republicans, while the less radical Half Breeds supported either James G. Blaine of Maine or John Sherman of Ohio. Garfield was head of the Ohio delegation and leader of the Sherman forces. After Roscoe Conkling had placed Grant's name in nomination, Garfield gave the nominating speech for Sherman.

After thirty-three ballots, the convention appeared to be deadlocked: Grant had 300 votes (70 shy of the nomination), while Blaine had between 270 and 285, and Sherman about 100 votes. On the thirty-fourth ballot the Wisconsin delegation cast sixteen votes for Garfield, who reaffirmed his support for Sherman. On the next ballot, Garfield received fifty votes, and the movement to draft him as a compromise candidate was on its way. On the thirty-sixth ballot, Garfield was nominated with 399 votes to Grant's 306. As a token to the Stalwarts, Chester A. Arthur of New York was selected as his running mate.

In an uneventful election, Garfield defeated Democratic nominee Winfield S. Hancock. Each candidate received slightly more than 48 percent of the vote and carried nineteen states, but Garfield's states added up to 214 electoral votes and Hancock's only 155. After his inauguration, Garfield's short administration was focused on two issues: patronage in the custom houses, which had been investigated during Hayes's administration, and the Star Route fraud.

Garfield was shot twice in the back on July 2, 1881, by Charles J. Guiteau, a Stalwart Republican, who ironically had supported his election. Guiteau had done so believing that his support could be converted into a plum political appointment. When he came to Washington seeking a diplomatic appointment, he was politely refused. Guiteau bought an expensive pistol, a .44 British Bulldog (he chose it because he thought it would look good in a museum afterward) and stalked the president for weeks before shooting him. Garfield did not die immediately—and very likely did not die from the gunshot wounds. Rather, the unsanitary operating conditions of the time led to infections and ultimately to bronchopneumonia. He died September 19. His assassin was convicted of his murder and hanged on June 30 in the following year.

EXTRAMARITAL AFFAIRS

Rumors of Garfield's infidelities circulated while he was in the White House. One rumor claimed that he visited a prostitute in New Orleans shortly after he was elected president. Although Garfield and his wife, Lucretia, denied such rumors as "nothing more nor less than an infamous lie," Garfield was not always faithful to his wife.

Rebecca Jane Selleck

Although technically not an extramarital affair because Garfield was not married at the time, he was involved with Rebecca Selleck while engaged to his future wife, Lucretia. He and Lucretia met in 1849 and became engaged in the fall of 1854. He met Rebecca Selleck on Thanksgiving Day in 1855, while visiting a mutual friend, Mrs. Maria Learned of Poestenkill, New York. Garfield was a senior at Williams College at the time and spent the short Thanksgiving break close to school instead of returning to Ohio. Mrs. Learned, who was secretly in love with Garfield herself, encouraged the relationship between him and Rebecca.

The three met often in what was at first a platonic relationship. Once Maria made clear to Rebecca that she should pursue James, a physical relationship began. Garfield found Rebecca to be everything that his future wife was not. Rebecca was engaging, sensuous, and beautiful. Lucretia was thoughtful and admired for her intellect. As his senior year progressed, Rebecca and Lucretia became friends, and Lucretia shared her secrets regarding James with Rebecca, not suspecting that the two were having an affair.

When Garfield returned to Hiram after graduating from Williams, Lucretia learned the truth of the affair. She was angered more by Rebecca's betrayal of their friendship, it seems, than James's. He married Lucretia in 1858 out of a sense of duty, not of love.

Lucia Gilbert Calhoun

In October 1862 Garfield had a brief affair with a *New York Times* reporter, Mrs. Lucia Gilbert Calhoun. He admitted the affair to his wife, and it is documented in letters to her. She eventually forgave him. In 1867 Garfield met with Lucia in New York to retrieve papers in her possession. Lucretia seemed to resign herself that she was in a loveless marriage to a man who would stray.

SCANDALS AS A MEMBER OF CONGRESS

While serving as a member of Congress from Ohio, Garfield was implicated in several scandals. None had a lasting impact on his political career, but each called his judgment into question.

Crédit Mobilier

Garfield was implicated in a bribery scandal connected with Crédit Mobilier, a construction company with ties to the building of the Union Pacific Railroad. The scandal involved several members of Congress. Conflicting stories have Garfield accepting ten shares of the company's stock and receiving a dividend payment.

In 1872, while a representative from Ohio, Garfield was caught in the Crédit Mobilier scandal that occurred during Grant's administration (see page 146). Oakes Ames, who controlled the company, provided a list of politicians to whom stock in the company had been given or sold. Garfield's name was on the list. When he heard of the charges, Garfield strenuously denied that he was a stockholder, and on September 16 he had an interview published in the *Cincinnati Commercial* to that effect.

Ames testified on December 17 that he had agreed to secure for Garfield ten shares of stock that Garfield could buy when he had the necessary funds ($1,000). When asked if Garfield had ever been paid dividends on the stock, Ames stated that Garfield had once received $300 or $400.

Garfield, who was called to testify on January 14, 1873, confirmed that he had been offered ten shares of stock, but claimed that he regarded the shares as an option that he never exercised. He said the $329 that he received from Ames was a loan. Garfield stated that he had repaid the loan and that he had not exercised the option on the stock. Garfield believed this testimony would bring an end to the investigation of his role.

On January 22, however, Ames was recalled to answer further questions about Garfield's participation in the scandal. Ames testified that on June 19, 1868, the ten shares that had been reserved for Garfield had paid a dividend of $1,329. Ames then testified that he gave Garfield $329 (a check for that amount had been cashed with the sergeant at arms on June 22) using the $1,000 to pay for the stock.

The two men differed on only two important points. First, they disagreed as to whether Garfield had become a subscriber to the company or had merely been given an option to become a stockholder. Second, they disagreed as to whether the $329 was a loan or a payment of dividends. Garfield was unable to show any proof that he had repaid the loan. Still, he never had taken ownership of the stock certificates. In the end the committee could not sort out the matter. It simply reported the facts and recommended no punishment for Garfield. His relatively minor role did no significant harm to his career.

The "Salary Grab"

Garfield was roundly criticized for his support—albeit grudging—of a bill that increased congressional salaries by 50 percent.

In 1873 Rep. Benjamin F. Butler of Massachusetts introduced an amendment that would raise congressional salaries by 50 percent. Although Garfield opposed the measure, he served on the conference committee that approved it. He voted for the conference bill after getting his fellow representatives to agree that the increase in salary would be offset by the elimination of the mileage credit, which compensated members for travel to and from their districts. When the bill came before the House, Garfield voted for the act. It became known as the Salary Grab Act of 1873.

When he returned to Ohio after casting his vote for the measure—the final bill of the session—he was met with a storm of criticism. The early effects of the great panic of 1873 were already being felt in agricultural communities, and the Crédit Mobilier scandal did not help matters. Political allies and newspapers that had supported Garfield turned against him. If 1873 had been an election year, Garfield surely would have been defeated, even according to his friends.

Recognizing the outcry as serious, Garfield returned his share of the salary increase to the Treasury and published an open letter to his constituents. Nonetheless, conventions held in three of the counties Garfield represented passed motions of censure. The state Republican convention in May condemned both Crédit Mobilier and the salary grab. Congress wasted no time repealing the unpopular measure.

De Golyer–McClelland Paving Contract

A congressional investigation into the excessive sums spent on infrastructure improvements in the District of Columbia disclosed that Garfield, while chairman of the House Ways and Means Committee, had represented a Chicago paving company that was under investigation.

In the early 1870s Washington, D.C., was in the midst of an public improvement program that included street pavings. De Golyer–McClelland Company of Chicago was bidding on a $700,000 paving contract and planned to provide its patented wood pavement. The company engaged Richard C. Parsons, a Cleveland attorney, to serve as its representative to the District's Board of Public Works. Parsons was given a fee of $6,000 and promised an additional $10,000 if he was successful in his efforts. He was drawn away on another case before he could present his case to the board, and he secured Garfield's services for $5,000.

When a congressional committee began to investigate the extravagant expenditures on the paving contracts for the District, the De Golyer contract and Garfield's participation came to light. Garfield was severely criticized in the press, especially in the *Chicago Tribune.* Garfield argued that his services were legal in nature, not political. He had prepared a brief concerning the company's patent. He never appeared before the Board of Public Works in behalf of the company and he mentioned the company only once to Alexander Shepherd, the head of the District's government. The investigating committee found no wrongdoing on Garfield's part.

Three years later, however, in 1876 a second investigation was launched. This one was under the control of Democratic representative John M. Glover of Missouri. Glover's committee discovered a number of letters and telegrams between G. R. Crittenden, the agent who originally had hired Parsons, and one of the company's partners. In a document dated May 30, 1872, Crittenden wrote that he had been able to secure the services of Garfield, chairman of the Appropriations Committee and one of the strongest men in Congress. The clear implication of Crittenden's letter was that Garfield was on the take.

On March 1, 1877, Garfield appeared before the committee and denied any wrongdoing. The committee was moved by Garfield's passionate defense of his actions and found no evidence that he knew of Crittenden's portrayal of his services to De Golyer. The matter resurfaced briefly during Garfield's campaign for president in 1880.

THE STAR ROUTE AFFAIR

Soon after Garfield took office, a scandal over fraudulent contracts erupted in the Post Office Department. The Star Route affair would not be concluded until the administration of Chester A. Arthur.

Even before he took office, Garfield knew that something was wrong in the Post Office Department. He turned to Thomas L. James to serve as postmaster general and to lead an investigation. On March 9, 1881, James formally opened an investigation into corruption in the Post Office. One month later, James and his special postal agent, P. H. Woodward, reported what they had learned about the Star Route frauds. Garfield immediately brought Wayne MacVeagh, the attorney general, into the investigation.

On April 19 Garfield insisted that the matter be dealt with swiftly. The next day, Thomas Brady, the second assistant postmaster general and one of the leaders of the fraud, resigned. The investigation brought to light many instances of gross corruption. In a period of five years, $4 million had been stolen from the postal service. One of the most corrupt individuals was Stephen W. Dorsey, secretary of the Republican National Committee and Garfield's campaign manager. Altogether, Dorsey and his associates had stolen more than $500,000.

MacVeagh warned Garfield about the political consequences of pursuing charges against people like Dorsey, but Garfield insisted that it was his responsibility to prosecute corruption wherever and against whomever it might lead. The political fallout was great, and Brady implicated the president in the scandal. Garfield had written a letter to Jay Hubbell of the Republican Congressional Committee inquiring about Brady's use of Post Office assessments to raise funds for the 1880 election. Brady said he took the letter to mean that Garfield had wanted him to use Star Route funds for campaign purposes. Comments by Chester Arthur, the vice president–elect, at a dinner in Dorsey's honor did not help matters either. Arthur had commended Dorsey's ability to deliver Indiana, a Democratic state. Although he did not use the word *bribery,* it was clear that Arthur knew that Dorsey had paid money to secure support for the Republican ticket.

Garfield, although at times reluctant to prosecute political friends like Dorsey, ultimately saw no other choice. On June 28 Dorsey and his counsel appealed to Garfield and tried to convince him that there was no case. The next day, the president complained to James that the case was moving too slowly. That was the last action taken by Garfield on the Star Routes matter; he was shot four days later.

BIBLIOGRAPHY

Bates, Richard O. *The Gentleman from Ohio.* Durham, N.C.: Moore Publishing, 1973.

Caldwell, Robert G. *James A. Garfield: Party Chieftain.* New York: Dodd, Mead, 1931.

Hagood, Wesley O. *Presidential Sex: From Founding Fathers to Bill Clinton.* Secaucus, N.J.: Carol Publishing, 1998.

Leech, Margaret, and Harry J. Brown. *The Garfield Orbit.* New York: Harper and Row, 1978.

Mitchell, Jack. *Executive Privilege: Two Centuries of White House Scandals.* New York: Hippocrene Books, 1992.

Peskin, Allan. *Garfield.* Kent, Ohio: Kent State University Press, 1978.

Ross, Shelley. *Fall from Grace: Sex, Scandal, and Corruption in American Politics from 1702 to the Present.* New York: Ballantine Books, 1988.

Smith, Theodore Clarke. *The Life and Letters of James Abram Garfield.* New Haven: Yale University Press, 1925.

Woodward, C. Vann. *Reunion and Reaction.* Garden City, N.Y.: Doubleday, 1956.

———. *Responses of the Presidents to Charges of Misconduct.* New York: Dell Publishing, 1974.

CHESTER A. ARTHUR

Twenty-First President
1881–1885

Born October 5, 1829, in Fairfield, Vermont, Chester A. Arthur was one of nine children of an Episcopal clergyman who had emigrated from Northern Ireland. The family moved frequently as his father was transferred among many parishes. Arthur studied at home with his father until he was fifteen, when he entered Union College. Graduating three years later, he taught school at the North Pownal Academy and studied law. In 1853 he joined a New York law firm and was admitted to the bar a year later. He married Ellen Lewis Herndon in 1859.

As a lawyer Arthur often defended fugitive slaves and free blacks who suffered discrimination. In a successful suit he represented Lizzie Jennings, a free black woman, who had been ejected from a whites-only streetcar. After a brief stint in Kansas, Arthur returned to New York, where he campaigned for the newly formed Republican Party's candidate, John C. Fremont, in the 1856 presidential campaign. In 1860 he supported the candidacy of Abraham Lincoln.

Arthur served in the New York State militia from February 1858 to December 1862, rising to quartermaster general. After the Civil War, he practiced law and took an active role in Republican Party politics. By the time Ulysses S. Grant was elected president in 1868, Arthur was Sen. Roscoe Conkling's principal lieutenant in the state's Republican machine. In 1871 President Grant appointed him customs collector for the port of New York, a lucrative post. He held this position until the reform-minded Rutherford B. Hayes removed him in 1878. Arthur then resumed his practice of law.

At the Republican Party convention in 1880, Arthur was a pro-Grant delegate. When the nomination when to James A. Garfield, the delegates sought to smooth party divisions by selecting a Stalwart (radical) Republican from New York as the vice-presidential candidate. Levi P. Morton declined, and Garfield chose Arthur, who was nominated on the first ballot. Garfield and Arthur narrowly defeated the Democratic ticket in the popular vote, but their win in the electoral college was a decisive 214–155.

Garfield served not quite eight months as president. On July 2, 1881, he was shot by an assassin—Charles J. Guiteau, a disgruntled patronage seeker. Garfield initially survived the wounds but died on September 19, and Arthur was sworn in as president. As president Arthur demonstrated his independence by backing the investigations of post office scandals (see below). In spite of his support for the partisan system of dispensing patronage jobs, he signed into law the Pendleton Civil Service Reform Act (1883), which created a civil service system based on merit rather than patronage.

Arthur did not win his party's nomination in 1884 because, in the eyes of the Stalwarts of the party, he had become a reformer. Instead, the nomination went to Sen. James G. Blaine of Maine. Arthur retired to New York City and briefly resumed the practice of law. On November 18, 1886, he died, after having most of his public and private papers burned.

CORRUPTION AT THE NEW YORK CUSTOM HOUSE

Arthur was investigated for fraud while serving as collector of customs at the port of New York in the 1870s.

An investigation of the New York Custom House took place during the administration of Rutherford B. Hayes (see page 159). At the time, Arthur was the collector of customs and oversaw the activities of nearly 1,000 officials. Although Arthur was cleared of any specific wrongdoing and was never prosecuted, Hayes removed him from the post as part of his fight against the spoils system.

THE STAR ROUTE FRAUDS

The investigation into postal fraud on the Star Routes began during the administration of President Hayes and continued through President Garfield's brief tenure. During Arthur's administration the investigation came to a conclusion.

One of the first tasks of the Arthur administration was to prosecute the individuals responsible for the Star Route frauds. At the center of the controversy were Stephen W. Dorsey, former Arkansas senator and secretary of the Republican National Committee, and Thomas J. Brady, second assistant postmaster and an appointee of President Grant. Dorsey and Brady were accused of heading a ring that defrauded the government by inflating the costs of mail delivery contracts in the West. Although the prosecutions began under President Garfield, they were delayed when Garfield was shot. Postmaster General Thomas James and Attorney General Wayne

MacVeagh retained Col. George C. Bliss of New York and Benjamin H. Brewster of Philadelphia to serve as the chief prosecutors.

MacVeagh resigned on November 8, 1881, fearing that the prosecutions in the case were being unduly delayed by the new president. Arthur selected Brewster as attorney general, which left more of the prosecutorial responsibility to Bliss. While these events transpired, Dorsey and his cronies claimed their innocence in the nation's newspapers. The delays gave Dorsey an advantage in the court of public opinion.

On May 20, 1882, an indictment was returned against Dorsey, Brady, and six others. On May 29 all but one of the defendants appeared in court, where they entered pleas of not guilty to the charges. It was clear from the outset that the courtroom battle would be a long one. The trial began June 1 and stretched on for months as the defense put on a parade of witnesses to justify the amounts charged by the contractors for mail delivery. Arthur's secretary of the interior, Henry Teller, was called as a defense witness. As a senator from Colorado he had encouraged an increase in mail delivery and had lobbied the Post Office for improved services. One member of the jury claimed that he had been approached by the prosecution to vote "guilty" in exchange for a bribe. The jury retired for deliberations on September 8 after a long, hot summer of testimony in Washington, D.C.

The jury convicted two defendants, acquitted two others, but was unable to come to a verdict on Dorsey, Brady, and the remaining two. The vote for these four had been eleven "guilty" votes and one "not guilty." The judge ordered a new trial for the two convicted men and the four with the hung jury. The new trial was a replay of the first, but with some new witnesses. On June 14, 1883, the jury found the defendants not guilty. Despite evidence of jury tampering by the defense, no prosecution resulted from that charge. With the primary culprits exonerated, the government also dropped a number of cases pending against minor players as the likelihood of convicting them was poor.

Congress investigated to see if Arthur had stalled or inhibited the prosecutions. Before a congressional committee, Brewster testified in 1884 that the president had always supported the prosecutions and had cooperated fully with them. Brewster testified before the Springer committee, which was established to investigate the Star Routes:

> I want this work to be done as you are doing it, in the spirit in which you are doing it; I want it to be done earnestly and thoroughly. I desire that these people shall be prosecuted with the utmost vigor of the law. I will give you all the help I can. You can come to me whenever you wish to, and I will do all I can to aid you.

In 1884 the government tried to recover the overpayments in civil court, but a circuit court ruled in *United States v. Cosgrove* that the government would have to prove fraud to recoup the overcharges. With that decision, the cases of the Star Route frauds were brought to an end after spanning four administrations and nearly twenty years.

The public's outrage over the Star Routes led to massive reform in the Post Office, including improvements that led to immediate savings of more than a half million dollars a year. Moreover, an aroused public opinion strengthened the movement for civil service reform, and Congress changed the methods for awarding Star Routes contracts.

POLITICAL ASSESSMENTS IN THE ELECTIONS OF 1882

President Arthur allowed members of his administration to solicit assessments from federal employees for campaign purposes in violation of the law.

Despite an 1876 law and an executive order issued by President Hayes in 1877 banning political assessments—contributions from federal workers to election campaigns—the practice continued during the Arthur administration. During the midterm campaign in 1882, the Republican Congressional Committee sent a letter soliciting contributions from federal employees. The typical amount requested was 2 percent of a worker's income. In July Arthur issued a statement that government employees were free to give or not to give and that their job security would not be affected either way. It is likely that Arthur came to this conclusion after Attorney General Benjamin Brewster's interpretation of the 1876 statute. Brewster said that the law as written did not apply to funds solicited for congressional campaigns.

During the campaign, members of the administration actively solicited funds. William E. Chandler, secretary of the navy, went to New York with Arthur's approval to raise funds. Charles Folger, secretary of the Treasury, made patronage jobs available across the country. These activities did not go unnoticed. In his first annual address to the national Civil Service Reform League on August 2, 1882, writer and lecturer George William Curtis criticized the president's actions, noting Arthur's failure to reappoint more than half the officers whose terms had expired. Curtis branded the failure to reappoint the same as removal.

If anything, Arthur's activities in the matter were mixed. Although defending the practice of assessments, he refused to pardon Gen. Newton M. Curtis for violating the 1876 law. Curtis was serving both as a Treasury agent and as a member of the New York Republican state committee. His conviction ultimately was upheld by the U.S. Supreme Court.

Arthur used the congressional defeat of the Republicans in 1882 as proof that the American people wanted civil service reform. (Republicans lost

William Eaton Chandler

the House but maintained control of the Senate.) The lame duck Congress passed the Pendleton Act (1883), which was an effort to replace the "spoils system" of federal employees with a merit system and establish a modern civil service. Naturally, when the Democrats regained the White House in 1885, they quickly discovered that the Pendleton Act meant that patronage jobs were limited. Many Republican officeholders had become civil service employees who could not be removed simply because of the election results.

WILLIAM W. DUDLEY, COMMISSIONER OF THE PENSIONS OFFICE

William Dudley used his office and its employees to drum up support for Republican candidates in Indiana and Ohio.

During the elections of 1884, pensions commissioner William W. Dudley, who had been appointed by Arthur and whose resignation was to take effect on November 10, took a leave of absence to campaign in Ohio and Indiana, both hotly contested states. Dudley was accompanied by Estes G. Rathbone, chief of the division of special examiners in the Pensions Office—a division that had more than 100 employees. All were charged with advising pension claimants to vote for the Republican "soldier ticket" of Sen. James G. Blaine of Maine and John A. Logan of Illinois for president and vice president, respectively. A vote for the soldier ticket, the pension applicants were told, would be advantageous to their pension claims.

The *New York Times,* on October 20, 1884, exposed the use of pension office employees for election purposes and condemned the practice. Although Arthur probably could have prevented or halted the use of federal employees for such purposes, he did not. The reason for his silence was, according to George Howe, one of his leading biographers, "to avert further disastrous dissensions in his party."

BIBLIOGRAPHY

Doenecke, Justus D. The *Presidencies of James A. Garfield and Chester A. Arthur.* Lawrence: University Press of Kansas, 1981.

Hoogenboom, Ari. *Outlawing the Spoils.* Urbana: University of Illinois Press, 1961.

Howe, George F. *Chester A. Arthur: A Quarter-Century of Machine Politics.* New York: Dodd, Mead, 1934.

Josephson, Matthew. *The Politicos, 1865–1896.* New York: Harcourt, Brace, 1938.

Mitchell, Jack. *Executive Privilege: Two Centuries of White House Scandals.* New York: Hippocrene Books, 1992.

Reeves, Thomas. *Gentleman Boss: The Life of Chester A. Arthur.* New York: Harcourt, Brace, 1975.

Woodward, C. Vann. *Responses of the Presidents to Charges of Misconduct.* New York, Dell Publishing, 1974.

GROVER CLEVELAND

Twenty-Second President
1885–1889
Twenty-Fourth President
1893–1897

Grover Cleveland was born March 18, 1837, to Ann and Richard Cleveland, a Presbyterian minister, in Caldwell, New Jersey. He was the fifth of nine children. The Cleveland family moved to upstate New York in 1841. Cleveland studied law while serving as a law clerk and was admitted to the bar in 1859. First elected to local posts in Buffalo in 1862 and 1863, he became active in Democratic Party politics and was appointed assistant district attorney. During the Civil War he was conscripted into the Union army, but, as was allowed by the draft laws, he paid a substitute to serve in his place. He lost the election for district attorney in 1865 but five years later was elected sheriff of Erie County. At the end of his term, in 1873, he practiced law in Buffalo.

After Cleveland was elected mayor of Buffalo in 1881, his political career skyrocketed. The following year he was elected governor of New York. In 1884 he won the Democratic Party's presidential nomination as the "clean government" candidate and defeated Republican James G. Blaine. With the electoral support of Republican Party reformers known as the Mugwumps, he was the first Democrat elected president since the Civil War. He also was the first president to marry while serving in the White House; in June 1886 he married Frances Folsom, who was twenty-seven years younger than he.

Two economic issues shaped much of Cleveland's first term. He opposed the majority of his party and favored the gold standard. He worked to lower tariffs but was unsuccessful in budging Congress on that issue; however, tariffs become the central issue in the next presidential election. Although Cleveland won the popular vote in 1888, he lost in the electoral college to the Republican candidate, Benjamin Harrison. After this defeat, he practiced law in New York.

In 1892 the Democratic Party nominated Cleveland again, and he defeated Harrison in a rematch. Back in office, Cleveland again supported the gold standard and orchestrated the repeal of a law that required the coinage of silver. He also sought a reduction in tariffs but reluctantly let a tariff-reduction bill become law without his signature because of its protectionist provisions. The most important political event of this term took place in 1894, when a strike at the Pullman Palace Car Company triggered a nationwide strike by the American Railway Union. Violence erupted in Chicago, and Cleveland sent in federal troops over the protest of the governor of Illinois. Although the Supreme Court eventually ruled that the president's actions were constitutional as emergency powers, his reaction to the Pullman strike and his support of the gold standard cost Cleveland his party's nomination in 1896. The Democrats turned to a pro-silver populist, William Jennings Bryan, as their candidate. Cleveland retired to Princeton, New Jersey, where he died in 1908.

FATHER OF AN ILLEGITIMATE CHILD

During Cleveland's bachelor days in Buffalo, he—or one of his friends—fathered a son by Maria Crofts Halpin. Cleveland provided for the support of both mother and child and later arranged for a wealthy family to adopt the boy.

Less than two weeks after Cleveland won the presidential nomination in 1884, allegations surfaced that he was a fornicator and the father of an illegitimate ten-year-old boy. Maria Crofts Halpin claimed that Cleveland was the father of her son, Oscar Folsom Cleveland. At the time of their relationship (1873–1874), Cleveland was finishing his tenure as sheriff in Buffalo and entering into private law practice. Halpin, a young widow, had recently moved to Buffalo, after leaving her two children in New Jersey.

The Republicans, hopeful of winning New York State and the presidency, took every advantage of the scandal. Newspapers across the country ran editorials and cartoons calling Cleveland unfit to serve as president. The party subsidized the printing and distribution of a song by the National Music Company of Chicago entitled "Ma! Ma! Where's My Pa?" Although party loyalists rallied to make the most of the events, others like Henry Ward Beecher, an influential clergyman, sided with Cleveland. Beecher went so far as to say, "If every New Yorker who had broken the Seventh Commandment were to vote for Cleveland, he would carry the state by a large majority."

Although Cleveland never denied that he was the child's father, the child's paternity was uncertain because Maria Halpin had been intimate with many of Cleveland's friends. But Cleveland took responsibility for him and allowed him to use his last name. He resisted pressure from Halpin to marry her, and she began drinking. Cleveland had her committed to an asylum and paid for the child's keep in an orphanage. After Maria was released, Cleveland gave her money to start a business in Niagara Falls, New York. When her attempt to sue for custody of the boy failed in the

Cleveland's illegitimate child was the subject of many editorials, cartoons, and the song, "Ma, Ma, Where's my Pa?"

courts, she kidnapped Oscar in 1876. Finding the boy and Maria three months later, Cleveland paid her to leave town and give up parental rights. He found a wealthy New York couple to adopt Oscar, who later became a physician. Halpin moved to New Rochelle and married.

Ironically, during the election, Cleveland's staff found evidence that the Republican candidate, James G. Blaine, had married his wife in a shotgun marriage, with the birth of their first child coming just three months later. Cleveland refused to use the information, but it was published in party newspapers. Blaine concocted a story that he and his wife had been married secretly six months before the public ceremony. In the end, the election turned not on the sexual improprieties of the candidates but on the prejudicial comments of a Blaine supporter, the Reverend S. D. Burchard, who on October 29, 1884, described the Democrats as "the party of Rum, Romanism, and Rebellion." Roman Catholic voters, especially the Irish, took offense at the comment and at Blaine's failure to distance himself from it. They turned out in greater numbers than anticipated and handed Cleveland New York by 1,150 votes. In the Democrat's 219–182 victory in the electoral college, New York's thirty-six votes were decisive.

The Democrats captured the White House and the last laugh. They finished the Republican song "Ma! Ma! Where's My Pa?" with the line, "Gone to the White House, Ha! Ha! Ha!"

AUGUSTUS H. GARLAND, ATTORNEY GENERAL

During Cleveland's first term, Augustus H. Garland was accused of using his position as attorney general to pursue a challenge to invalidate the telephone patent held by Alexander Graham Bell and the Bell Telephone Company. Garland was a major stockholder in the rival Pan-Electric Company, and he stood to become a very rich man if the Bell patent could be invalidated.

In 1883, while still a senator from Arkansas, Augustus Garland was presented with shares valued at $500,000 in a new corporation called the Pan-Electric Company and appointed the company's attorney. Pan-Electric had no capital or credit; its sole property was a telephone patent, which was worthless unless Alexander Graham Bell's patent (1876 and 1877) could be invalidated. With Bell's patent out of the picture, Pan-Electric would grow rich. As the company's attorney, Garland wrote an opinion stating that Pan-Electric's rights did not in any way infringe on those of the Bell Company.

When Garland became attorney general in Cleveland's first administration, he did not surrender his stock, although he must have been aware that holding it could become an embarrassment. The promoters of Pan-Electric had offered shares to a number of influential men, who turned them down. In 1885 the company asked Garland to institute a government suit to test the Bell patent. Garland declined. A few weeks later, when Garland was taking a vacation at his home near Little Rock, the acting solicitor general, John Goode, began a test suit of the Bell patent against which there were several claims.

The press immediately raised questions about the propriety of the case against Bell, considering Garland's holdings in the rival Pan-Electric Company. Garland held one-tenth of the total outstanding stock, with, critics pointed out, a potential worth of millions of dollars. President Cleveland asked Garland for an explanation. On October 8, 1885, Garland replied in a long letter, acknowledging his relationship with Pan-Electric. But he insisted that the solicitor general's decision to pursue the case had been reached without his knowledge or consent. He also admitted that he had failed to advise the solicitor general of his holdings and the possible perception of a conflict of interest.

Cleveland instructed Goode to revoke the steps he had taken to prosecute the case and referred the matter for investigation to Interior Secretary L. Q. C. Lamar. Early in 1886 Lamar shocked many when he decided that a suit should be brought to test the Bell patent. Lamar's decision again roused criticism from the press. The press contended that the suit

President Cleveland's cabinet officers. Augustus Garland is in the front row, second from the right.

would be prosecuted by the Justice Department, and the attorney general who headed it had a large personal financial stake in its outcome.

Congress formed a committee to investigate the matter. On April 19, 1886, Garland testified frankly and fully. He denied that the stock was a gift, saying that he had helped to organize Pan-Electric Company and had paid an assessment for that purpose with the stock being his remuneration. He claimed that he never had any idea of using his official influence on behalf of the company. The committee divided along party lines. It issued a report in which the Democratic majority concluded that Garland, Goode, and Lamar had done nothing "dishonest, dishonorable, or censurable." The Republicans, however, charged that Garland and Goode had been engaged in a speculative scheme for their own enrichment.

Cleveland took no action against Garland and did not seek his resignation. Criticism of Garland continued throughout the summer and fall of 1886, however. In November a circuit court in Cincinnati dismissed the case against the Bell patent. Garland's stockholdings—now worthless—were no longer an issue. Although Garland finished his term quietly, Goode, who had been awaiting confirmation as solicitor general, was not confirmed by the Republican-dominated U.S. Senate.

WILLIAM F. VILAS, SECRETARY OF THE INTERIOR

The Senate investigated William F. Vilas, Cleveland's second secretary of the interior, for conflict of interest. The investigation was to determine whether the Superior Lumber Company, of which Vilas was a shareholder, had been given special access to Indian lands.

In 1887 William F. Vilas of Wisconsin, a businessman and prominent Democrat who had helped Cleveland secure the party's presidential nomination, was appointed secretary of the interior, replacing L. Q. C. Lamar. Shortly after his confirmation, several Republican senators began to question whether Vilas was profiting from rulings made by his department. The department had facilitated the logging of Indian lands in Wisconsin by the Superior Lumber Company, in which Vilas was a shareholder. In March 1888 the Senate Select Committee on Indian Traders began a formal investigation. Vilas cooperated with the committee. He turned over all pertinent correspondence and at the committee's request suspended logging operations until the Senate had resolved the matter to its satisfaction.

The Senate report, issued in 1889, found that there had been neglect of duty and abuse of official power on the part of several local officials in Wisconsin. It also determined that Vilas, as head of the Interior Department, was fully responsible and censurable for his subordinates' misconduct. In the minority report, the Democrats cleared Vilas and the local officials of any wrongdoing. Both reports cleared Vilas of the charge that he personally had profited from the logging on Indian lands because the Superior Lumber Company had not been involved in the logging operations under investigation.

JAMES VAN ALEN, AMBASSADOR TO ITALY

Critics charged that James Van Alen had contributed $50,000 to Cleveland's presidential campaign fund in 1892 in exchange for an appointment as ambassador to Italy.

James Van Alen of Rhode Island was a wealthy businessman and Democratic Party donor. In 1892 he contributed nearly $50,000 to the party's campaign fund. When reports appeared that Cleveland planned to appoint Van Alen as ambassador to Italy, even Democrats protested the decision. Cleveland could not believe that the press and other critics would accuse him of striking a deal with Van Alen in exchange for the diplomatic post. In a letter to a friend, the self-righteous Cleveland wrote, "No one will accuse me of such a trade."

Instead of appointing someone else and avoiding criticism, Cleveland, in October 1893, did name Van Alen as minister to Italy. The Senate acted quickly on the nomination and confirmed him. A few weeks later, however, Van Alen resigned, citing the furor his appointment had caused. Cleveland urged Van Alen to remain: "We should not yield to the noise and clamor which have arisen from these conditions." Van Alen was unmoved by Cleveland's arguments and resigned, bringing the controversy to an end.

JOHN G. CARLISLE,
SECRETARY OF THE TREASURY

John Carlisle was involved in two congressional investigations, one concerning tariffs, and the other on the sale of gold.

The Wilson-Gorman Tariff of 1894

During Cleveland's second term, press reports forced the Senate to investigate whether John G. Carlisle, secretary of the Treasury, had brokered a deal in which Henry O. Havemeyer, president of the American Sugar Company, had donated more than $100,000 to Cleveland's campaign in exchange for a favorable sugar tariff.

On May 14, 1895, while the Senate was debating the schedules for the Wilson-Gorman Tariff, the *Philadelphia Press* and other newspapers published charges that the American Sugar Company, which controlled 80 percent of the industry, had played a direct role in writing the sugar schedules. The newspapers claimed that the company, through its president, Henry O. Havemeyer, had given more than $100,000 to Cleveland's 1892 campaign fund in return for help on the tariffs. The papers alleged that John G. Carlisle, secretary of the Treasury, had participated in the bargain and assisted in its execution.

The Senate appointed an investigating committee headed by George Gray of Delaware. The investigation was a political minefield: a thorough investigation would have revealed that several senators were involved in possible wrongdoing in relation to the sugar schedules, and a superficial one would have brought charges by the press that the committee was whitewashing the story. Havemeyer was called to testify before the committee. Arrogant and hot-tempered, he told the committee that his company's practice was to give money to political campaigns, but he claimed that these donations were not a partisan issue. For example, he said, in New York, where the Democrats usually had a majority, they received money, while in Massachusetts the Republicans were the recipients. In return, the company "got a good deal of protection." When pressed to produce the financial statements to back up this claim of bipartisan donations, Havemeyer refused and was supported by the committee's chair.

The investigation discovered that several senators had used their insider knowledge of the sugar schedules to participate in speculation. Sen. John R. McPherson, Democrat of New Jersey, testified that he had purchased 300 shares of stock and transferred them to his son. He also admitted that he had purchased 1,000 shares by accident when he sent a buy order to his broker and then, having second thoughts, tried to cancel it. He sold those shares but not before making $1,500. Sen. Matthew S. Quay, Republican of Pennsylvania, testified that he had been active in trading sugar stock for more than twenty months. Ironically, his last trade was on the day the Senate was voting on the sugar schedule. Quay testified that he did "not feel that there is anything in my connection with the Senate to interfere with my buying or selling the stock when I please."

The committee found ample evidence that senators were engaged in questionable activities, and it censured the American Sugar Company. It found no wrongdoing by Carlisle. If the investigation had dug deeper, it would have uncovered widespread speculation throughout Cleveland's administration. An official in the Interior Department told one reporter that Daniel S. Lamont, secretary of war and a close friend of the president's, had given him insider information on the sugar schedules that enabled him to turn a $5,000 investment into $34,000.

Gold Reserves

During his tenure as Treasury secretary, Carlisle was investigated for the way he handled a private sale of government bonds to New York banking interests. The sale, intended to replenish the government's shrinking gold reserves, was particularly generous to the banking houses of J. P. Morgan and August Belmont. The two houses netted more than $7 million in profits.

In 1893 the United States went into an economic depression. More than 500 banks failed, and large numbers of bankruptcies caused high unemployment rates. One of Cleveland's responses to the Panic of 1893 was to authorize the purchase of several million ounces of gold from private holders to maintain the nation's gold reserves. Between February 1894 and February 1896 the president authorized four bond issues. In February and November 1894 the administration held two sales of $50 million worth of ten-year bonds at 5 percent interest. The sales had little effect on the size of the gold reserve. Agents, including Secretary Carlisle, were asked to explore the possibility of a private sale of bonds to the banking houses of J. P. Morgan and August Belmont. A deal was struck in which Morgan and Belmont agreed to purchase $62 million in bonds with gold. Half would be drawn from overseas and the rest from the hoards of the banking establishments. In return, the syndicate was given bonds at 4 percent with a markup of 104.25 or a surcharge of 4.25 percent. The February 1895 deal raised the gold reserve to more than $105 million.

The sale failed to shore up the gold reserve, and a fourth offering of $100 million in bonds was necessary. A public offering was made in the spring of 1896. This final sale stabilized the gold reserves; in the process Cleveland had floated a federal debt of $262 million.

The third bond issue was particularly controversial because it netted its subscribers more than $7 million in profit. That sale and the resulting profits triggered a congressional investigation inquiring whether the president and Carlisle had formed a corrupt alliance with the banking interests. Congressional critics pointed out that the Morgan deal was contrary to Cleveland's professed policy of divorcing the federal government from the banking industry. The Senate investigation of 1896 found no evidence that either Cleveland or Carlisle had personally profited from the transactions. Cleveland's sale of bonds was a defense of the gold standard, which was a matter of personal conviction on his part.

BIBLIOGRAPHY

Barnes, James Anderson. *John G. Carlisle, Financial Statesman.* New York: Dodd, Mead, 1931.

Ford, Henry Jones. *The Cleveland Era.* New Haven: Yale University Press, 1919.

Hagood, Wesley O. *Presidential Sex: From Founding Fathers to Bill Clinton.* Secaucus, N.J.: Carol Publishing, 1998.

Merrill, Horace S. *William Freeman Vilas: Doctrinaire Democrat.* Madison: The State Historical Society of Wisconsin, 1954.

———. *Bourbon Leader: Grover Cleveland and the Democratic Party.* Edited by Oscar Handlin. Boston: Little, Brown, 1957.

Mitchell, Jack. *Executive Privilege: Two Centuries of White House Scandals.* New York: Hippocrene Books, 1992.

Nevins, Allan. *Grover Cleveland: A Study in Courage.* New York: Dodd, Mead, 1932.

Tugwell, Rexford G. *Grover Cleveland.* New York: Macmillan, 1968.

Welch, Richard E., Jr. *The Presidencies of Grover Cleveland.* Lawrence: University Press of Kansas, 1988.

Woodward, C. Vann. *Responses of the Presidents to Charges of Misconduct.* New York: Dell Publishing, 1974.

BENJAMIN HARRISON

Twenty-Third President
1889–1893

orn August 20, 1833, at the home of his paternal grandfather, William Henry Harrison, in North Bend, Ohio, Benjamin Harrison was seven years old when his grandfather was elected president of the United States. Harrison was educated at home and at a number of small schools where he excelled. In 1847 he began study at Farmers' College, a preparatory school in Cincinnati. In 1850 he was admitted to Miami University in Oxford, Ohio, as a junior and in 1852 graduated near the top of his class. He studied law for two years with a Cincinnati firm and was admitted to the bar in 1854. On October 20, 1853, Harrison married Caroline Lavinia Scott, the daughter of his professor of chemistry and physics at Farmers' College.

In 1854 Harrison moved to Indiana and formed a law partnership with William Wallace, an established Indianapolis lawyer. In 1856 he joined the Republican Party and campaigned for its first presidential candidate, John C. Fremont. Harrison was elected Indianapolis city attorney in 1867, and the following year he was appointed secretary of the Republican state central committee. For a short period in 1861 and 1862, he served as supreme court reporter of Indiana and then entered the army.

Serving in the Seventieth Indiana Infantry Regiment from July 1862 until June 1865, Harrison rose from the rank of second lieutenant to brigadier general. He saw action at a number of locations and was part of Gen. William T. Sherman's march to Atlanta. After the war, Harrison returned to his post as supreme court reporter as well as to the private practice of law. In 1871 President Grant appointed him defense counsel for the army personnel who were being sued by Lambdin P. Milligan for illegal arrest and court martial. The U.S. Supreme Court had already ruled in *Ex parte Milligan* (1866) that Milligan was entitled to seek damages, and Harrison's job was to limit the damages to a token amount. The court awarded Milligan $5.

In 1872 Harrison ran for the Republican gubernatorial nomination, but lost. Four years later there was a brief movement to make him the Republican Party nominee for president. Instead he ran for governor, but lost to his Democratic opponent. He supported the nominations and campaigns of Rutherford B. Hayes in 1876 and James A. Garfield in 1880. In 1881 the Indiana legislature elected Harrison to the U.S. Senate. During his term Harrison was a strong supporter of veterans' pensions and became known as the "soldier's legislator." He also supported high tariffs and the exclusion of Chinese immigrants. He lost his seat in 1888 when Democrats took control of the Indiana legislature.

Announcing his candidacy for the Republican nomination for president in February 1888 at the Michigan Club in Detroit, he acknowledged his lack of a power base in the party, but declared that he was "a rejuvenated Republican." Sen. James G. Blaine of Maine was the front-runner going into the June convention in Chicago. Blaine withdrew his name, recognizing that the Republicans would have a better chance to unseat the incumbent, Grover Cleveland, if either Harrison or John Sherman of Ohio was the candidate. On the eighth ballot, Harrison secured the nomination along with Levi P. Morton of New York as his running mate.

The leading issue in the campaign was the tariff. Harrison favored high tariffs, and Cleveland wanted to cut them. Harrison won in part because the Tammany Hall machine worked against Cleveland in New York. Harrison lost the popular vote by about 100,000 votes, but won the electoral college vote, 233–168.

During his administration, Harrison continued to champion Civil War veterans by signing into law the Dependent and Disability Pensions Act of 1890. Other major pieces of legislation that were enacted during his administration include the Sherman Antitrust Act, which was the first act to attempt to curb the power of monopolies, and the McKinley Tariff Act, which set tariffs at an average rate of 48 percent.

But the McKinley Tariff proved unpopular enough to cost Harrison a second term, and Grover Cleveland came back to the White House in 1892. Harrison retired to Indianapolis, in mourning for his wife who had died just two weeks before the election. He returned to the practice of law and in the spring of 1894 delivered a series of lectures on constitutional law at Stanford University. He married Mary Scott Lord Dimmick, twenty-five years his junior, on April 6, 1896. A movement took shape to nominate Harrison for the presidency in 1896, but he announced in February that he would not accept it. Between 1897 and 1899, Harrison served as counsel to Venezuela in its boundary dispute with British Guiana before an international arbitration panel in Paris. Despite his efforts, Britain was awarded 90 percent of the territory. President William McKinley appointed Harrison to the Permanent Court of Arbitration in 1900. However, Harrison never served on the court. On March 13, 1901, he died of pneumonia.

WILLIAM DUDLEY, TREASURER OF THE REPUBLICAN NATIONAL COMMITTEE

Democratic newspapers in Indiana reprinted a letter allegedly written by William Dudley to county Republican leaders in Indiana instructing them to use the "block of five" method—one person pays five others—to buy votes for Harrison in the state's close race.

As the presidential election of 1888 grew near, political forecasters in both parties were convinced that the popular vote would be close. The outcome might be influenced by an unexpected event that could turn projected victories in a few states into losses—a situation ripe for dirty tricks. Four states were regarded as especially critical. Cleveland had won in 1884 because the Democrats had carried Connecticut, Indiana, New Jersey, and New York by narrow margins. If Benjamin Harrison could carry those states in 1888, the Republicans would return to the White House.

By August, the Republicans were confident that they would win New York. Their support for high tariffs went over well in a manufacturing state. They were less confident about the more agricultural Indiana. A straw poll taken two months before the election showed the Democrats ahead and left Harrison worried that he might lose in his home state. State party officials feared much the same, and in mid-October the state chairman wrote to the Republican National Committee with a desperate plea, warning that the Democrats, "abundantly supplied with money are using it quite lavishly … and I feel certain that they intend perpetrating the greatest frauds." Harrison agreed with their assessment, writing to a colleague that he believed Democratic "managers are counting wholly for success upon the free use of money late in the campaign." For that purpose, he said, the Democrats were making a careful list of "floats," a term for voters who were susceptible to last-minute persuasion or outright purchase for prices ranging from $2 to $15. In response, the national committee began to pour money into Indiana.

There seems little doubt that both parties were buying votes in Indiana and had been doing so for a long time. Still, there is some truth to Republican assertions that they had been forced into a bidding war by the Democrats. Culturally and geographically, the state was tied to the South, a region that violence and corruption had, in the aftermath of the Civil War, transformed into one-party states. Indiana Democrats imitated their colleagues in the South by using violence to keep black men from voting. In an era of dirty politics, the Democrats were dirtier than the Republicans.

By October 27 Harrison was more confident. He wrote to a colleague, "If we can secure an approximately fair election, I think we are safe." Those hopes would explode four days later when a Democratic paper called the *Sentinel* published what it said was a facsimile of an October 24 letter written by William W. Dudley, treasurer of the Republican National Committee, to Indiana's Republican county leaders. (Like many of those around

Harrison, Dudley was a Civil War veteran and had lost a leg at Gettysburg.) Most of the letter was unremarkable. The writer urged the Republicans "to make the Democrats pay highly for voters to exhaust their resources ... [and to] prevent frauds in the ballot boxes. He wanted every Republican at the polls, and every suspicious voter challenged." That was no more than sensible strategy. The more the Democrats were forced to spend in the weeks leading up the campaign, the less they would have to buy voters on election day. It was the last sentence that created the furor: "Divide the floaters into blocks of five and put a trusted man with the necessary funds in charge of these five and make him responsible that none get away and that all vote our ticket."

Often in politics, what is actually happening matters less that the impression that is created by some passing event. Only the most naive citizens were unaware of their state's voter fraud. But here was a letter talking about how to do it, a tantalizing secret revealed for all to see. The fact that it was from the East also played on the legitimate fears of many that if elections could be bought, out-of-state interests could do the buying as easily as locals.

Dudley wasted no time proclaiming the letter a fraud and suing the newspapers that had printed it. Interviewed by a Republican newspaper on November 1, Dudley's son said the signature did not look like his father's. Others were convinced it was true, although no careful examination was undertaken. True or false, the Democrats wasted no time publicizing its contents in two crucial states, New York and Indiana, and the Republicans countered with denials.

Harrison, who placed a high value on his reputation for integrity, was enraged at both Dudley and the Democrats. Two years earlier, when he was running for the U.S. Senate, the *Sentinel* had carried a story accusing "the notorious Col. Dudley" of being back East, "raising a large sum of money from the beneficiaries of the high tariff and other monopoly legislation to secure the re-election of Ben Harrison by bribery, if all other means fail." That particular story was false. Although Dudley was in the East, he was not fund raising. At that time Harrison had made it clear to his friends and advisers that he wanted nothing to do with bribery.

Partisans on both sides expected Harrison to defend Dudley. He did not, even when Louis T. Michener, Indiana's attorney general, told him that he believed the letter was a forgery. The most he would do was issue a short statement denying any complicity on his part. Harrison was probably being no more than careful. He could not make a claim he did not know to be true, particularly since no one had shown him the letter. But the Democrats denounced him for his silence, and mutual friends believed Dudley had been betrayed. The result was a breach between the two that kept them from talking to one another for many years. Sad as it was, the rift may be the best indication that the letter was a forgery. On several occasions, Michener tried to reconcile the two and found Harrison more than willing to meet his former friend. Dudley, however, refused to act until Harrison vindicated him in public. Such an enormous amount of wounded pride suggests Dudley's innocence. Years later, as widowers, the two began to correspond.

JAMES R. TANNER AND THE PENSION BUREAU

James Tanner, a vigorous champion of veterans, was accused of violating reg- ulations in order to increase the number of individuals receiving pensions, including employees of the bureau, and for showing favoritism to a pension lawyer friend.

In Congress, Benjamin Harrison's zeal for providing pensions for Civil War veterans earned him the nickname "the soldier's senator." Twice in the mid-1880s he introduced legislation to liberalize pension benefits in the Republican Senate only to have the bills defeated in the Democratic House. During the 1880s war veterans, organized as the Grand Army of the Republic (GAR), had become a powerful political force. Running for president in 1888, Harrison made appeals for their roughly 1.3 million votes, promising that he would not use "an apothecary's scale to weight the rewards of the men who saved the country."

After the election, Harrison's mailbox began to fill with letters asking him to appoint James R. Tanner as his commissioner for pensions. Tanner was a GAR commander from New York who had lost both legs as a cor- poral in the second battle of Bull Run. He was well known among veter- ans for his zeal to provide them with ample benefits. In 1885 he had told the annual GAR National Encampment, "No man goes farther than I do on that point." Harrison appointed Tanner March 26, 1889, and soon found, to his regret, that Tanner meant every word of that claim. Harrison would have done better had he listened to warnings that Tanner was unqualified for the job and little more than "a loud-mouthed Grand Army stump speaker." There were also disturbing rumors that he had disreputable ties to pension claims agents.

Harrison needed someone who would administer the law quietly and fairly. He got the opposite. After taking office, Tanner summed up his phi- losophy in a much-publicized speech in Tennessee. "For twenty years I have been able only to plead," he said, "but now I am thankful that at these fin- ger-tips there rests some power ... though I may wring from the hearts of some the prayer, God help the surplus." The last phrase was a reference to a budget surplus, which was due primarily to high import duties imposed to protect domestic industry. Democratic and independent papers were soon filled with vivid descriptions of how quickly the surplus was being depleted by Tanner's generous hand. While most recipients of Tanner's bounty were happy to take the money, some protested. For example, Sen. Charles Manderson of Nebraska found that, without any effort on his part, he had been re-rated and awarded arrears of $4,300. News that the senator was questioning the generous bounty reached Tanner's superior, Interior Secretary John W. Noble, who informed Manderson that the grant was illegal. Manderson returned the certificate he had received but not cashed. Soon more people were approaching Noble and Harrison with reports of suspicious things happening in the pension office. Rep. Joseph Cheadle of Indiana discovered the infamous forty-eight-hour cases, in which requests from New York pensioners were being rushed through, especially if they came from one particular lawyer, Tanner's friend George E. Lemon.

Noble conducted his own investigation and discovered more examples of corruption, including ten cases where bureau employees had been re-rated and received first payments on their arrears totaling $16,739. When he brought this problem to Tanner, the commissioner's response was belligerent. "While the Secretary of the Interior has the power to reverse the decisions of the Commissioner of Pensions on appeal by a claimant against whom the Commissioner had decided," he said, "on the other hand, if for any reason it be held that the claimant had been *granted too much pension,* the Commissioner himself is the only person who has the power *to call a halt* and reduce the pension." Noble replied that Tanner was "laboring under a great misapprehension" as to his authority. When Tanner still refused to obey, Noble responded by telling him he was "not only disrespectful, but insubordinate to the last degree."

With the papers now full of embarrassing accounts of corruption and rebellion, Harrison and Noble both knew that Tanner had to go. The difficulty lay in finding a way to get rid of him. Tanner was extremely popular with veterans, particularly in the Midwest, and the annual encampment of the GAR was coming up at the end of August 1889 in Milwaukee. Tanner attended, but he did not, as the administration feared, try to rally support for a service pension that would pay all Civil War veterans irrespective of their condition. Perhaps sensing the trouble he was in, Tanner tried to remain uncontroversial. When one delegate offered a resolution condemning "the wicked and malignant criticism of our distinguished comrade," Tanner asked that it be withdrawn. The replacement resolution merely expressed confidence in "his integrity and our approval of his avowed purpose." Along with Tanner himself, it asked for "the fullest investigation of the management of his office."

Tanner may have been hoping for a highly publicized investigation to give him a national platform on which to advance his ideas. Harrison and Noble thought otherwise. In later interviews with the press, Tanner complained that Noble's quiet probe had resembled a Star Chamber investigation. He said:

In fact, the only information I had about the results of their operations was when the honorable secretary himself, one day when I was in his office, asked me if I knew what the commission said about the operations of the Pension Bureau. I told him that I had not been favored in that respect in the slightest degree. He replied that I had granted more pensions and paid out more money in the same time than my distinguished predecessor did. I replied that I hope to God that the charge was true on the record, for I had plastered Indiana with promises last fall that should be the fact if General Harrison came into power as President.

Efforts by friends to bring Tanner into line with the administration failed. Harrison received Noble's report and it was passed on to Tanner at a White House meeting on September 11. Late that night, Harrison sent a U.S. marshal to Tanner's home in Georgetown to ask him to resign or be suspended. Tanner agreed to resign effective the next day. Harrison had been careful not to make public statements about the controversy, which allowed both the administration and Tanner to claim that the resignation was based on differences between Noble and Tanner and meant that Noble took the bulk of the anger from veterans.

In accepting the resignation, the president noted that he did not intend to impugn Tanner's honesty. And Tanner was honest. Except for giving his daughters jobs in the bureau, Tanner had not personally profited from his generosity. In a sense, he was being punished for the rarest of political crimes—he kept his word. The Boston *Globe* wrote: "If he had been a man who could understand that the party's promises in its platforms and on the stump are not at all what the party intends to carry out, he would have been in office today." Led by Rep. Benjamin Enloe of Tennessee, the Democrats made an effort to investigate Tanner but got nowhere. The Republicans were in control and they believed that they had done all they needed to do when Tanner was removed.

The Tanner controversy was a warning that the Republican Party did not heed. Its defense of high import tariffs had won it the support of industry, and its support of generous veterans pensions could provide the critical swing vote in tight elections. The two policies worked together because the tariffs could fund the pensions. But those who did not benefit from either manufacturing or pensions had the strong impression that the party was in the grip of two powerful special interests. Two pieces of legislation that Harrison signed into law the following year, the McKinley tariff and the Disability Pension Act, strengthened that conviction. The pension act codified a generous system of payments that proved in the long run to be far more expensive than Tanner's clumsy efforts. Between 1891 and 1895, the number of pensioners rose almost 30 percent (from 676,000 to 970,000) and, by the time Harrison left the White House, yearly expenditures on pensions had grown 60 percent (from $81 million to $135 million). The growing anger of the general public would be reflected in major Republican losses in the 1890 and 1892 elections.

GREEN B. RAUM AND THE PENSION BUREAU

The House of Representatives investigated Green Raum on charges that he was accepting bribes in return for favorable and expedited rulings on cases before the Pension Bureau.

After James Tanner resigned as commissioner of the Pension Bureau, President Harrison wasted no time seeking a replacement. The president initially offered the job to Maj. George Warner of Missouri. Warner, the last commander in chief of the Grand Army of the Republic, declined. On September 13, the New York *Herald* published remarks attributed to Warner that hinted at the problems facing Harrison. Warner was quoted as saying:

Tanner's replacement must "coolly and deliberately put himself forward as a martyr. . . . Tanner knocked an end out of the Pension Bureau, and there is a Conemaugh Valley flood rushing through. I am asked to stand in front of the stream and attempt to stem it. . . . All of the elements are against me. The conservative, level-headed sentiment of the country has unfortunately arrived at the conclusion that the Pension Office as administered during the past few months was a political machine for the destruction of the surplus. . . . If I try to satisfy the people, I will offend the old soldiers, and if I try to satisfy the old soldiers, I will offend the people.

The following day, the *New York Times* printed Warner's denial, but noted that the remark was true, whether or not Warner had said it.

On October 19, 1889, Gen. Green Berry Raum accepted the job. At first the choice seemed wise; even administration critics praised it. Raum had been wounded at Missionary Ridge, Georgia, fulfilling one of the office's unwritten requirements. He had also served in a wide variety of positions—a railroad president, member of Congress, commissioner of internal revenue, and a pension lawyer. Unfortunately Raum proved to have the opposite set of vices from Tanner's. Where Tanner had been too vocal, Raum was too secretive. Where Tanner's financial irregularities had benefited others, Raum's benefited himself.

By the summer of 1890, rumors had begun to circulate about Raum. The resulting investigation by a House committee split along party lines, with the Republican majority proclaiming him innocent. In the next Congress, the Democrats took power in the House and reopened the investigation. The hearing's 2,000 pages of testimony contained more than enough evidence to prove the Democrats right, and even Republican newspapers began calling for Raum's removal.

Some of the charges focused on the Universal Refrigerator Company, which Raum headed. Citing personal privacy, he refused (until much later) to open the company's books to scrutiny, but claimed that no one at the Pension Bureau owned any stock in the company. During the investigation, however, it came out that Raum had organized a subsidiary company and that his private secretary at the Pension Bureau and an assistant secretary of the Interior were among the directors. Raum's secretiveness suggested that something illegal was happening.

A second set of charges focused on George Lemon, the same dubious pension lawyer that James Tanner had treated with special favor. Lemon had urged Raum to use a completed files system. Applications for pensions that had been certified by the applicants or their lawyers to be complete would be put into a separate file and that file would be dealt with before any others. In practice, the relatively few lawyers who knew about the system could get money for their clients more quickly than other applicants. Lemon's firm, with twice as many clients as its closest competitor, would benefit the most. Raum brought the completed files idea before his staff, but it was rejected. About that time, Raum needed some money for his investments and he asked Lemon for a loan. Lemon refused. On January 6, 1890, Raum instituted the completed files system in the Pension Bureau. The following day, Lemon endorsed $12,000 in notes for Raum. Although the system may have made claims-processing more efficient (hence the Republican defense of Raum), the benefits fell on a select few, and a large portion of the early cases placed in the completed case file belonged to Lemon.

The third set of charges was more personal. Raum had appointed his twenty-three-year-old son, Green B. Raum Jr., as head of the Appointment Division of the Pension Bureau. Evidence was presented that the younger Raum had sold offices, gambled during office hours, and was either careless or corrupt in handling department funds. After a Department of Interior investigation, Junior was forced to resign. There was also evidence that another son, John Raum, was receiving special treatment in his own cases as a pension attorney.

The last set of charges was political. Members of Congress had the privilege of calling special attention to pension cases. Raum had given the Republican opponent of a Democratic House member, George W. Cooper of Indiana, the same privilege, just as if he were an elected official (perhaps helping him to curry the favor of some voters). In that particular case, however, the Republicans had their own evidence of corruption among Democrats. Representative Cooper had apparently allowed a Washington, D.C., pension agent to use his authority to speed the processing of claims.

Taken together, the investigations of these four sets of charges offered more than enough evidence that Raum was corrupt and should be removed from office. Harrison stuck by him, however, and Raum remained in office for the rest of the Harrison administration. Perhaps Harrison was simply unwilling to get embroiled in another controversial resignation. Perhaps too, the widespread political corruption of the era simply made action unnecessary. After all, his Democratic predecessor,

Grover Cleveland, had appointed John C. Black as his pension commissioner even though Black had himself been pensioned in 1878 as a "physical wreck" and awarded a substantial $100 per month pension, which he continued to collect while serving in public office.

Harrison's handling of Civil War pensions infuriated reform-minded citizens. Harvard University president Charles W. Elliot cited the pension scandal as one of the three reasons for his leaving the Republican Party. In an October 1889 speech Elliot said that the pension scandal "is a crime against all honest soldiers and against Republican institutions; and it is a Republican administration which has brought that system into this condition, the present administration being the worst of all." In the elections of 1890 and 1892 the Republicans would pay a heavy price at the polls for attempting to buy soldiers' votes with public money.

THE CAPE MAY COTTAGE CONTROVERSY

While the White House was undergoing major renovations, President Harrison and his wife stayed in a cottage in Cape May, New Jersey, that had been built for the first family by Postmaster General John Wanamaker and several friends. Newspapers criticized the Harrisons for using the cottage as an improper gift.

Beginning in summer 1890, the White House was scheduled to undergo four months of extensive repairs, and the president and his wife needed a place to stay. To escape the heat and humidity of a Washington summer, the Harrisons moved to the same cool southern New Jersey coastline they had enjoyed the previous summer.

The initial news coverage of their impending vacation was routine. The Indianapolis *Journal,* Harrison's hometown paper, reported on May 29, "The President and his family will summer in Cape May Point, New Jersey, either with the Postmaster General, who has a cottage there, or in a cottage that is being specially constructed for that purpose." Within a few weeks, however, other newspapers were attaching a more sinister meaning to that "specially constructed" cottage. On June 11 a New York *Sun* editorial asked, "Who are those generous individuals that have bestowed upon Mrs. Benjamin Harrison a cottage at Cape May Point, clear of encumbrance." The *Sun* called for the names of those who had financed the cottage and warned, "The President who takes a bribe is a lost President." Soon the press was afire. Words like "Gift Grabber" began to be hurled about, and Cape May real estate agents began to hope for a booming business in lots near what they were already advertising as "The President's Home." Other newspapers stood up for the president; the Philadelphia *Inquirer,* in an interview with Caroline Harrison discovered that, although she was pleased that this as yet unseen cottage would be available for them, she was inclined to see it as for temporary occupancy rather than something the Harrisons would own. Her attitude changed when she actually

John Wanamaker

saw the "cottage." Its broad porches and twenty airy rooms delighted her.

At that point the most controversial event in the entire affair occurred. The lot on which the cottage was built had been purchased on March 3 by Postmaster General John Wanamaker and some Philadelphia friends who seemed to have intended to make a gift of the cottage to the president, much as the house at Long Branch had been given to President Grant.

On July 2, however, Harrison wrote to Wanamaker, enclosing $10,000, and asking him to "be good enough to see to the right disposition of the check enclosed." The amount was a fair purchase price for the house and would, in fact, be exactly what the Harrisons would receive for it six years later. Newspapers divided in their interpretation of that check. The (Democratic) *New York Times* claimed that Harrison had paid for the cottage only after his foul deed was exposed. A friendlier Washington *Star* suggested another interpretation: "So far as accepting the cottage as a gift, the moment the matter was brought to the President's attention he thanked the gentlemen for their great kindness but distinctly declined to accept it as a gift."

The most likely scenario is this: Wanamaker and his friends, knowing of the repairs on the White House and that Harrison and his wife had enjoyed Cape May the previous summer, had decided to build the cottage as a gift. Whether they expected to recoup the investment through political favors or were speculating in local real estate is not known. Harrison, busy with debates over the tariff, does not seem to have encouraged or discouraged their efforts. As his actions suggest, it is quite possible that he decided that if his wife liked the cottage, he would buy it, which would explain why he had the money readily available. If not, his friends could easily recoup their investment by selling the cottage, made all the more valuable by a presidential stay. His "see to the right disposition" remark suggests that he did not know who helped to finance the cottage.

In late summer another controversy erupted. Still needing to remain away from the White House, the president and his family arranged to stay in a mountain cottage at Cresson Springs, Pennsylvania (near Altoona). Again charges were made that the president was staying rent-free, courtesy of the Pennsylvania Railroad. The controversy died after a railroad spokesman announced that the cabin had been rented "at a fair price" through a real estate agency.

BIBLIOGRAPHY

Glasson, William H. *Federal Military Pensions in the United States.* New York: Oxford University Press, 1918.

Journal of the Twenty-Third Annual Session of the National Encampment, Grand Army of the Republic (1889).

McMurry, Donald L. "The Political Significance of the Pension Question, 1885–1897." *Mississippi Valley Historical Review* IX, No. 1 (June 1922): 19–36.

——. "The Bureau of Pensions During the Administration of President Harrison." *Mississippi Valley Historical Review* XIII, No. 3 (December 1926): 343–364.

Mitchell, Jack. *Executive Privilege: Two Centuries of White House Scandals.* New York: Hippocrene Books, 1992.

Sievers, Harry J. *Benjamin Harrison: Hoosier President.* Chicago: Henry Regnery, 1968.

Socolofsky, Homer E., and Allan B. Spetter. *The Presidency of Benjamin Harrison.* Lawrence: University Press of Kansas, 1987.

Woodward, C. Vann. *Responses of the Presidents to Charges of Misconduct.* New York: Dell Publishing, 1974.

WILLIAM MCKINLEY

Twenty-Fifth President
1897–1901

Born in Niles, Ohio, on January 29, 1843, William McKinley was the seventh of nine children. The family moved to Poland, Ohio, where William attended Union Seminary, a local private school. He entered Allegheny College in Meadville, Pennsylvania, at the age of seventeen but withdrew because of illness. When the Civil War began in 1861, McKinley enlisted as a private with the Twenty-third Ohio Volunteers. He saw action at Antietam and was appointed to the staff of Col. Rutherford B. Hayes. By the time the war ended he was a twenty-two-year-old major and had been decorated for bravery.

McKinley attended Albany Law School from 1866 to 1867. Returning to Ohio, he was admitted to the bar in 1867. He set up a law office in Canton and became active in Republican Party politics. In 1869 he was elected Stark County prosecutor but was defeated for reelection in 1871. Earlier that same year, he married Ida Saxton, the daughter of a prominent banker who had founded a newspaper, the *Canton Repository*.

McKinley practiced law until his election to the U.S. House of Representatives in 1876. Reelected to two additional terms, he was the apparent winner by eight votes in 1882, but the seat was challenged and awarded to the Democrat. After sitting out for one term, McKinley was reelected to Congress and served until 1891. McKinley earned a reputation as a staunch supporter of high tariffs as a means of protecting U.S. industries. He sponsored the McKinley Tariff of 1890, which raised tariff rates to new heights. In 1890 he, along with many other Republicans, was defeated. Back in Ohio, he was elected governor and served two two-year terms. He drew national attention when he used the national guard to put down labor unrest in Akron and elsewhere in the state.

When the Republicans met in convention in St. Louis, Missouri, in June 1896, McKinley was the front-runner for the presidential nomination and won easily on the first ballot. Garret A. Hobart of New Jersey was selected as his running mate. His opponent in the race was William Jennings

Bryan, running as a Democrat and Populist. The issue that cut across party lines was currency—the gold standard or the free coinage of silver. Bryan crisscrossed the nation giving stump speeches advocating silver, while McKinley, who supported the gold standard, conducted a "front porch" campaign from his home in Canton.

After winning the presidency, McKinley's priority was improving the nation's economy, which had been in a depression. His first term, however, was dominated by the Spanish-American War of 1898. He also oversaw the annexation of Hawaii in 1898 and authorized Secretary of State John Hay to establish an "open door" policy toward trade with China.

In 1900, when the Republicans met in Philadelphia to select their nominee, McKinley faced only token opposition. The real issue was the selection of a vice-presidential candidate because Hobart had died in November 1899. Theodore Roosevelt, the reform governor of New York, was the convention favorite. Encouraged by Sen. Henry Cabot Lodge of Massachusetts, who saw the post as a step toward the White House for Roosevelt, and New York political boss Thomas Platt (who wanted Roosevelt and his reforms out of New York), Roosevelt accepted the nomination. In the election of 1900, McKinley squared off against Bryan for a second time and roundly defeated him.

On September 5, 1901, McKinley delivered an address at the Pan-American Exposition in Buffalo, New York. At a public reception the next day he was shot a by self-proclaimed anarchist, Leon Czolgosz, an unemployed millworker from Detroit. The president underwent two surgeries, but his condition worsened. He died on September 14, the third president to die at the hands of an assassin. Six weeks later Czolgosz was executed.

RUSSELL A. ALGER, SECRETARY OF WAR

Russell Alger came under intense scrutiny in 1898 and 1899 for his management of the Spanish-American War. He was investigated by several House committees, found to be an incompetent administrator, and was asked to resign.

Americans' sympathy toward Cubans seeking independence from Spain had caused strained relations between the United States and Spain for several years. After the mysterious sinking of the battleship USS *Maine* in Havana harbor on February 15, 1898, relations worsened. The American public—informed only by sensationalistic newspaper articles—demanded vengeance. On April 25 McKinley reluctantly asked Congress for a declaration of war against Spain.

The United States was not prepared for war. Although some efforts had been made to prepare the navy to fight beyond the nation's shores, the army was small, poorly equipped, and experienced only in small-scale skirmishing with Native Americans. In different circumstances, the rush to war would have been disastrous, but the Spanish were in even worse shape than the Americans. After only a few months, on August 12, Spain signed an armistice ending the fighting and signaling to the world that the United States had become a major power.

Initially, Americans were elated that victory had been achieved at so low a cost: only 281 had died in battle. At the war's end, a darker picture began to emerge. During the war and its immediate aftermath, an estimated 3,500 men died of malaria. On the morning of August 4, the first hints of trouble appeared on the front pages of newspapers across the country. Someone had leaked to the press the text of a telegram that Gen. William Shafter, head of the Fifth Corps in Cuba, had sent to the War Department the day before. The news was grim: 75 percent of Shafter's men had malaria, making them little more than an "army of convalescents." Weakened by the disease, they were in danger of dying of yellow fever. "In my opinion, there is but one course to take," General Shafter warned, "and that is to immediately transport the Fifth Corps ... to the United States."

As soon as the telegram arrived, the secretary of war, Russell A. Alger, authorized Shafter to send all the men he could spare to a convalescent camp being prepared for them at Montauk on Long Island. The next day Alger gave Shafter full control of all vessels in Santiago harbor and ordered other vessels to sail for Cuba. To the public, however, it looked like the McKinley administration was reacting to a scandal it could not conceal.

The real story is more complex. When the war began, the U.S. Army was not only ill prepared to fight beyond its shores but also knew little about fighting in the tropics. At the time doctors understood little about the connection between typhoid fever and poor sanitation. Also unknown was that mosquitoes spread malaria and yellow fever. Army doctors followed the accepted wisdom of the day: whenever possible, they transferred infected men to higher, cooler ground. If the infection persisted, the men were transferred again in the hope that eventually they would escape the contagion, whatever its cause. Following that policy, General Shafter had concealed from Washington the seriousness of the conditions in Cuba until his August dispatch. Without accurate information, the War Department had little reason to speed preparations for receiving the sick. When the news of the epidemic broke, the convalescent camp in Montauk was not prepared to receive the soldiers who were being rushed to it. Because the camp was near New York City, the sensationalist "yellow press" found it easy to fill its pages with stories of soldiers lying sick on the ground in tents.

Needing a scapegoat, the public turned to the civilian most responsible for the conduct of the war—the secretary of war. Alger refused to resign. In part from friendship, in part from political necessity, McKinley refused to get rid of Alger. Firing his war secretary would be an admission that the appointment was a mistake, and, as long as the public's wrath was focused on Alger, McKinley could escape criticism.

Alger was not the only reason the military was so unprepared. Poorly funded by Congress for decades, the military, at the start of the war, barely had enough supplies for its peacetime strength. Rapid mobilization meant that many units were ill equipped when they shipped out. Lacking the sense of imminent danger felt by many European countries, the United States had not kept up with advances in tactics. The only thing the army was good at was generating mountains of paperwork. Fears of a procurement scandal had created a sluggish and highly centralized supply system that was not well adapted for war.

Even the most capable secretary of war caught in this situation would have had trouble turning such an army into an effective fighting force, and Alger was not up to the task. President McKinley found him to be "a little bit shifty" and driven by emotional impulse rather than careful thought. A general who knew him well would refer to him as "the most egotistical man with whom I have ever come in contact." Alger had an inflated opinion of the nation's military prowess that came from fighting thirty-three years earlier on the winning side in the Civil War and spending years giving speeches to veterans' groups. On August 24, 1892, at a veterans' banquet he declared the nation's army "the best under God's footstool." When an English friend asked how the country would respond if attacked by a great European power, he replied that "in thirty days we could put millions of fighting men in the field, and back them up with a wall of fire in the person of the veteran."

Pressure from the public forced Alger to request a congressional investigation. The result was the Dodge commission, headed by Grenville Dodge, a former Civil War general and Republican representative from Iowa. The commission began hearings in September 1898 and issued a report in February 1899. Although some believed the report whitewashed the scandal, it exposed enough of the deficiencies in the general administration of the War Department to begin a reform and modernization effort. Rather than concentrating on finding scapegoats, the committee focused on what needed to change.

McKinley hoped the report would clear Alger of the most serious charges and allow him to retire gracefully. But Alger refused to take the hint and told a reporter that he planned to stay on for the rest of the president's term. In June 1899 Alger himself provided McKinley with an excuse to get rid of him. He announced that he would run against Sen. James McMillan, a friend of McKinley's, for one of Michigan's senatorial seats. That was the last straw. Vice President Hobart was sent to inform Alger that he must resign. Given no other option, he resigned on July 19, 1899.

In retrospect, the United States was fortunate that the failings of its military were exposed in a war it was still able to win easily. Two decades later it would fight in a far larger war in Europe.

THE CUBAN POST OFFICE INVESTIGATION

The McKinley administration escaped charges of corruption until the spring of 1900, when the corruption in the Cuban Post Office was discovered. An investigation of charges of embezzlement implicated close friends of the president, including Mark Hanna, a powerful politician and businessman.

When the United States occupied Cuba after the Spanish-American War, Gen. Leonard Wood became military governor of Cuba. Wood, an army physician, was an excellent choice. Before the war he had been McKinley's personal physician. During the war he served as regimental commander of the famous Rough Riders, and at the close of the fighting he had been made military governor of Santiago. At that time 200 people a day were dying in an epidemic caused by poor sanitation and the presence of unburied bodies. Wood acted decisively, and within a month the death rate had been reduced by more than 80 percent.

During the U.S. occupation, the Cuban Post Office was placed under the authority of the U.S. Post Office. When General Wood learned that the head of the Post Office's finance department had run off with public money, he had the culprit, Charles F. Neely, arrested. From Neely, he learned that the corruption extended to the top. The director of the Cuban Post Office, Estes G. Rathbone, among others, was involved in a plot to embezzle at least $100,000. The discovery was politically explosive. With the presidential election only months away, the Democrats were eager to find charges to hurl at the Republicans.

In Washington, the postmaster general appointed his fourth assistant, Joseph L. Bristow, to investigate the charges. Known as a skilled investigator, Bristow had reason to be concerned about how much support the president would give him. Rathbone's friend Mark Hanna was a powerful Republican senator and a close friend of McKinley's. Meeting with Bristow just before he left for Cuba, McKinley assured him that he had nothing to fear. "I have been more pained by this scandal," the president said, "than by anything else that has occurred during my Administration. These people are our wards. They have great confidence in our integrity and a reverence for the American name, and to think that the trusted officials whom we have sent there should plunder their revenues and steal their money is a great humiliation to me."

Power broker Marcus Hanna, standing right, with William McKinley and members of his family.

He went on to tell Bristow: "Be thorough; do no one an injustice but shield nobody who has committed a wrong. I want every offender properly punished." McKinley would prove as good as his word.

Hanna's reaction was very different. During the McKinley administration, Hanna had exploited his friendship with the president to place his choices in civil service jobs, often in defiance of the law. He did not hesitate to threaten Bristow, at one point telling the investigator, "If you bring my friend to trial, you will never get to be more than a captain doctor in the army." But with McKinley's support, Bristow found that he had nothing to fear. He later wrote of the gratitude he felt for the president's "cordial support"—an appreciation that grew even more when he "learned that McKinley's support had been given in the face of the intense hostility of Hanna ... and all Rathbone's friends." In the end, those directly involved in the embezzlement, including Rathbone, were arrested and convicted.

Hanna did not destroy Bristow's career. In 1902 rumors surfaced that fraud and bribery had existed in the Post Office for several administrations. The next president, Theodore Roosevelt, appointed Bristow to lead an investigation that resulted in forty-four indictments. Years later, Bristow published a book describing his experience investigating corruption.

BIBLIOGRAPHY

Bristow, Joseph L. *Fraud and Politics at the Turn of the Century.* New York: Exposition Press, 1952.

Cosmas, Graham A. *An Army for Empire.* Columbia: University of Missouri Press, 1971.

Gould, Lewis L. *The Presidency of William McKinley.* Lawrence: University Press of Kansas, 1980.

Leech, Margaret. *In the Days of McKinley.* New York: Harper, 1959.

Mitchell, Jack. *Executive Privilege: Two Centuries of White House Scandals.* New York: Hippocrene Books, 1992.

Morgan, H. Wayne. *William McKinley and His America.* Syracuse: Syracuse University Press, 1963.

Olcott, Charles S. *The Life of William McKinley.* Boston and New York: Houghton Mifflin, 1916.

Speilman, William Carl. *William McKinley: Stalwart Republican.* New York: Exposition Press, 1954.

Woodward, C. Vann. *Responses of the Presidents to Charges of Misconduct.* New York: Dell Publishing, 1974.

THEODORE ROOSEVELT

Twenty-Sixth President
1901–1909

Born October 27, 1858, in New York City, Theodore Roosevelt was a sickly child who suffered from severe asthma and other maladies. Too sick to attend school regularly, Roosevelt was tutored by a maternal aunt and others. He was admitted to Harvard in 1876 as a freshman and excelled in the sciences, German, rhetoric, and philosophy. He graduated magna cum laude in 1880 and entered law school at Columbia University, but dropped out the following year to run for the New York state assembly. On October 27, 1880, he married Alice Hathaway Lee, the daughter of a prominent Boston banker. Alice Roosevelt died four years later of Bright's disease and complications of childbirth.

After his election to the state assembly, Roosevelt also joined the national guard and by 1885 rose from second lieutenant to captain. In the assembly, Roosevelt, a Republican, showed his political independence by supporting measures favored by the Democratic governor, Grover Cleveland. Roosevelt was defeated for reelection in 1883 and spent two years in the Dakota Territory working as a rancher and deputy sheriff. He ran for mayor of New York in 1886, but lost. He turned his attention to writing and, during his lifetime, published more than forty books. On December 2, 1886, he married Edith Kermit Carow.

From 1889 to 1895 Roosevelt served as a member of the U.S. Civil Service Commission. Originally appointed by President Benjamin Harrison, he was reappointed by President Grover Cleveland. In 1895 he became president of the New York City Police Board and undertook a massive cleanup of the police force. President William McKinley appointed Roosevelt assistant secretary of the navy in 1897. He resigned to command the First U.S. Volunteer Cavalry Regiment, also known as the Rough Riders, during the Spanish-American War. Roosevelt became a national hero when he led a charge up Kettle Hill, one of the San Juan Hills.

Returning as a hero, Roosevelt was elected governor of New York with the support of party boss Thomas C. Platt. However, Platt and his cronies were disappointed at the reformist/progressive nature of Roosevelt's policies. Platt wanted to get the reformist governor out of New York. With the position of vice president open because of the death of Vice President Garret Hobart, Platt began a campaign to have Roosevelt fill the number two spot on the McKinley ticket. Sen. Henry Cabot Lodge of Massachusetts supported Roosevelt, and the nomination was easily secured.

Roosevelt was sworn in as president on September 14, 1901, nine days after McKinley was shot in Buffalo, New York. Roosevelt, age forty-two, became the youngest man ever to serve as president. In 1904 the Republican Party easily renominated the popular Roosevelt, and he defeated Alton B. Parker of New York by more than 2.5 million votes and an electoral college vote of 336 to 140.

During his administration, Roosevelt oversaw the initial construction of the Panama Canal. He helped settle the Anthracite Coal Strike of 1902 by threatening to seize the mines. A lover of the outdoors, Roosevelt established the first national wildlife refuge at Pelican Island, Florida, in 1903 and continued to pursue conservation throughout his term. In his annual message to Congress in 1904, he issued the Roosevelt Corollary to the Monroe Doctrine; it stated that the United States would intervene in the Western Hemisphere to maintain stability. He won the Nobel Peace Prize in 1906 for brokering an end to the Russo-Japanese War. Also in that year, he signed into law the Meat Inspection Act and the Pure Food and Drug Act. He began the enforcement of antitrust policies and sought to strengthen regulatory agencies such as the Interstate Commerce Commission. In an effort to curb Japanese immigration to the United States, the two countries forged the so-called Gentleman's Agreement of 1907.

Roosevelt had announced four years earlier that he would not seek a second full term, and he worked for the election of his hand-picked successor, William Howard Taft. Retiring from the White House, Roosevelt went on a safari during 1909 and 1910. He was disappointed with the Taft administration's conservative policies and decided in 1912 to seek the Republican Party nomination. However, the party selected Taft. Roosevelt and his progressives bolted and formed a third party candidacy on the Progressive, or Bull Moose, ticket. On October 14, 1912, Roosevelt was shot in the chest by John N. Schrank, who claimed that the ghost of McKinley had appeared to him and told him to shoot his successor. Roosevelt continued to his destination to deliver a speech before seeking medical treatment. On election day Roosevelt's third party candidacy split the Republican vote between Taft and himself and ensured the victory of the Democratic candidate, Woodrow Wilson.

After his defeat, Roosevelt returned to adventuring with a trip through Brazil. He also resumed writing, serving as associate editor of *Outlook* from 1910 to 1914. In addition to his books, he wrote regularly for the *Kansas City Star* from 1917. When the United States entered World War I, he offered to raise a group of volunteers, but President Wilson refused the offer. He died January 6, 1919, of a coronary embolism only hours after finishing an editorial critical of Wilson's League of Nations.

INDIAN, POST OFFICE, AND OREGON LAND SCANDALS

Scandals plagued the Roosevelt administration. Midlevel government officials swindled the Creek Indians of their land, engaged in land speculation on federal property in Oregon, and accepted bribes for the execution of postal duties.

In September 1903 the *Literary Digest* made the following observation: "Few imagined when President Roosevelt took the oath of office, that one of the slogans of the next campaign might be—Turn the rascals out!" Democratic papers expressed even more outrage, claiming that if the Republicans remained in power four more years, "corruption will be entrenched in every department." Both prophecies proved wrong. The scandals may have appeared during 1902 and 1903—Roosevelt's second and third years in office—but their roots lay in previous administrations. When the president dealt with them decisively, his reputation not only remained intact but was enhanced.

The Indian land scandal was so minor that most of Roosevelt's biographers pay little attention to it. With whites eager to acquire Indian land and with a paternalistic policy placing whites in ultimate control of that land, the temptation for fraud was great. But the federal agents involved in swindling land from the Creeks and other tribes were in minor positions, and their eventual prosecution relieved the administration of any responsibility for their wrongdoing.

The Oregon land fraud, however, was a different matter. The tracts of land were much larger, and every member except one of the state's all-Republican congressional delegation was prosecuted for playing a role. Public awareness began in November 1902 when Roosevelt and Interior Secretary Ethan A. Hitchcock forced Binger Hermann, commissioner of the General Land Office, to resign. They discovered that Hermann had suppressed reports of a land fraud conspiracy involving major politicians, government officials, and large timber and mineral interests in his home state of Oregon. Evidence came to light that in one township, for example, twelve homestead claims were fraudulent. Those who claimed to be homesteaders had never seen the land and were being paid by others to acquire it in exchange for more valuable land elsewhere when the homestead area became part of a forest reserve.

A year-long investigation ensued, and on November 6, 1903, Attorney General Philander Knox, having determined that the allegations were true, appointed Francis J. Heney, a talented and aggressive California

Ethan A. Hitchcock, fourth from the left, and the other members of Theodore Roosevelt's cabinet

Democrat, as special prosecutor. Heney brought indictments against 146 people. The most important was against John H. Mitchell, a longtime U.S. senator. He was charged with accepting a $1,000 bribe to conspire with Hermann in a scheme to speed along the illegal land grants. Refusing to resign from the Senate, Mitchell was sentenced to six months in prison but served none of it. He died in December 1905 while his case was still on appeal. Hermann was charged with conspiracy to defraud the government, and Rep. John Williamson with subornation of perjury. Both men fought long and hard, and by 1913 the cases against them were dropped without a conviction. During 1908 the government had dropped the prosecutions of the remaining defendants.

Among those convicted was S. A. D. Putter, who served seventeen months of a two-year sentence for his role as "king" of the Oregon land fraud ring. The whole affair changed Putter into an ardent conservationist, and in his 1908 *The Looter of the Public Domain* he described, in sometimes flowery language, what had happened from the perspective of an insider. Putter believed that Roosevelt came out of the scandal with his reputation enhanced:

> I have no hesitancy in asserting that had not the President interfered when he did in October 1902, and put a stop to the carnival of looting then in progress by making a provisional suspension of the affected districts for forest and reserve purposes, it would have ... become merely a question of time measured by a short span of years when the Sierra Nevada and Cascade ranges of mountains would have become shorn of their magnificent heritage.

Putter, however, went wrong when he tried to place most of the blame for the land fraud on wealthy easterners, but he was not alone; many in the Pacific Northwest were sympathetic with those who were fired or indicted. The Portland Bar Association protested the appointment of the outsider, Heney, to head the investigation. Although most newspapers agreed with Mitchell's conviction, a Salem paper shrilly claimed that the government "pursued the methods of Russian spies and detectives." Hermann was forced out of office for his role in the fraud, but six months later he was elected to represent Oregon in Congress.

The third scandal was much less messy for Republicans. Near the end of September 1903, Roosevelt wrote to his friend, Henry Cabot Lodge, that he was "making a grand round-up of the people who have gone crooked." He was referring to rumors about a scandal in the Post Office Department that had first come to his attention the previous December. His delight stemmed from the fact that, as he had told Lodge in May 1903, "My course has simply been to cut out rottenness which had existed in the Department long before my term. I am inclined to be thankful that [August W.] Machen is an inheritance from Cleveland."

Roosevelt consulted his postmaster general, Henry C. Payne, and the chairman of the House Committee on Post Offices and Post Roads about the rumors, and all agreed that an investigation was needed, but they waited until March 7, 1903, when Congress was not in session, to authorize it. The investigation found little. When a Post Office cashier went to the press in May with accusations of corruption, the newspapers began to complain of a cover-up. At that point, Roosevelt set up a full-scale investigation with a special prosecutor. On September 4, Roosevelt told Postmaster General Payne, "I would far rather incur the hostility of a Congressman or a Senator than do something we ought not to do." Some politicians were apparently unhappy with the investigation.

Roosevelt had told his special prosecutor, Charles J. Bonaparte, that he wanted "exact justice in all these matters; and if possible I should like to prevent men getting the idea that I am shielding anyone." He got exactly that. By the middle of October, twenty-nine men had been charged, and the total eventually grew to forty-four. Some were quite important. John Tyner, who had been President Grant's postmaster general and who was currently an attorney for the Post Office, was charged with fraud and with receiving a bribe. He escaped conviction only because his wife and sister-in-law removed critical documents from his safe. Others proved less skilled at concealing their crimes. The head of the Division of Salary and Allowance, George W. Beavers, was sentence to two years in prison. August Machen, the Cleveland appointee Roosevelt had mentioned to Lodge, was fined $10,000 and sentenced to four years in prison. Two others were convicted of offering bribes to government employees.

In fall 1903 Lodge wrote to Roosevelt:

I am grieved to hear that the thing is getting worse. I thought the worst was known before I left, but in any event that is not an issue which I fear politically, for it is so perfectly clear that the wrong doers were not of your creation and that, on the contrary, you have been the man to probe the sores fearlessly and cut out the affected parts. My own belief is that that will help rather than hurt.

In general, Lodge's verdict has been the verdict of history. By promptly investigating and seeing that wrongdoers were punished, Roosevelt looked better to the general public after the Indian and Oregon land frauds and the Post Office scandals than he had before.

THE PANAMA CANAL PURCHASE

Charges of corruption were made against President Roosevelt and administration officials concerning the amount of money paid to buy land for the canal and the way the canal's path was decided. Roosevelt tried to sue for criminal libel the newspapers that attacked his credibility.

At the beginning of the twentieth century, there was widespread agreement that the United States should build a canal in Central America, but no agreement over whether the canal should go through Nicaragua or Panama. Over time Theodore Roosevelt came to the conclusion that the route through Panama was by far the better choice. In *Theodore Roosevelt's Caribbean,* Richard Collin credits Roosevelt with a much broader vision than his critics. The technical superiority of the Panama route—the fact that it was shorter and would accommodate vessels with a much deeper draft than the alternative—also meant that the United States needed to build it, if for no other reason than to prevent a European power from doing it first and establishing an influence in the region.

Years later, in a March 23, 1911, speech, Roosevelt hinted at the historic importance of his role in the canal debate. He said that if he had followed the "general conservative method" of his predecessors, he would have given Congress a lengthy paper on the canal, they would have debated the matter, and "the beginning of the canal would be 50 years in the future." Instead, he "started the canal and then left Congress not to debate the canal, but to debate me." Roosevelt took a Congress that was vaguely leaning toward a Nicaraguan route and bent it to his will, a step that proved extremely popular. Just before the 1904 elections Roosevelt instructed a political aide, "Tell our speakers to dwell more on the Panama Canal. . . .We have not a stronger card."

The popularity of the canal with the public also meant that those who wanted Congress to lead in foreign policy, and particularly Democrats who resented Roosevelt's success, had every motive to find or manufacture something to discredit what he had done. Roosevelt was shrewd enough to realize this. In September 1904 he wrote to Joseph Cannon, the

Republican Speaker, "Our opponents can criticize what we did at Panama only on condition of misstating what was done."

Some efforts were made to discredit Roosevelt by exaggerating the role the United States had played in the Panamanian revolution. But few Americans cared, and anyone who knew the region's history knew that Panama had been trying to break away from Colombia for most of the nineteenth century, and on numerous occasions the United States military had helped to ensure Colombian control. This time all the United States had to do to ensure Panamanian success was to end U.S. support for Colombian rule.

Far more explosive were claims that much of the $40 million paid to the French for their defunct canal project had gone into the hands of Americans with ties to Roosevelt. Accusations came from Henry Watterson, the respected owner and editor of the *Louisville Courier-Journal,* which favored the Nicaraguan route. In September 1903 Watterson claimed that of the $40 million, "twenty are for the thieves in France and twenty for the grey wolves of the American Senate." These charges were unsubstantiated, and most other newspapers ignored them.

But the story did not go away. It heated up, probably not by accident, just before the 1908 election. On October 3 an article in the (Democratic) *New York World* claimed that a syndicate that included Charles P. Taft, brother of Secretary of War William Howard Taft, and Douglas Robinson, the president's brother-in-law, had purchased the French canal stock for $3.5 million and then resold it to the United States for $40 million. No evidence was offered to back up the allegation. A search in Paris and Washington had failed to turn up a list of stockholders who had sold their stock.

Roosevelt at the site of construction of the Panama canal

What happened was this: the original French canal company had gone bankrupt at the end of 1888, leaving some $400 million in stocks unredeemed. To protect the stockholders' identities, the list of investors was sealed by court order for twenty years with the records to be destroyed after that. But because the newspaper story had named names and figures, other papers began to pick it up. The *Indianapolis News* clumsily claimed that the president's failure to produce evidence as to who received the money, "is the equivalent to something like a confession." When Roosevelt blasted the *News* for practicing "every form of mendacity known to man," its editor tried to evade responsibility by claiming that it did not originate the stories and thus was not making any claims for their truthfulness.

The president tried to reassure the public about the $40 million payment. In a public statement he said, "The United States Government did not pay a cent of the $40,000,000 to any American citizen." He explained that the money was paid to the French government and that the J. P. Morgan Company had handled the transfer. An American company, which had taken over the assets of the bankrupt French canal company, and the French bankruptcy court were responsible for paying back investors. The U.S. government had no knowledge of who received the money because it had not purchased the defunct company; rather, it had bought only the Panamanian assets.

Some of the accusations show that newspapers made little effort to understand what actually happened. On December 8, 1908, the *World* posed what it must have thought was a killer question: Why did the United States pay $40 million for a bankrupt property worth perhaps $4 million? The answer lay in the canal commission's November 1901 report. The Panamanian route was still less expensive than the Nicaraguan route, even when the costs of buying out the French and acquiring their railroad, land, buildings, and excavations were added together. The money paid to the French represented a mere tenth of what France had actually spent on the project. It was true that, with no other buyers, it might have been possible to force the French to accept a rock-bottom price, but continuing good relations with France was worth more than the money. Roosevelt also wanted to pay Colombia for its loss to retain its good will, but proponents of the Nicaraguan canal made that impossible.

Another aspect of the newspaper allegations has gone largely unnoticed. The French company had sold about $400 million in securities to tens of thousands of citizens all over France to fund the construction of a canal that Roosevelt was now seeking to buy for $40 million. For fifteen years the company that issued them had been bankrupt, and the stocks virtually worthless. Yet, if the accusations are true, a small syndicate of Americans slipped into the country and, in less than a year, bought up half or more of those stocks without the French government noticing. If true, it meant that a French bankruptcy court and a French company paid out hundreds of millions of francs, thinking the money was going to thousands of their citizens, when all the time it was going to that shadowy handful of foreigners. Four years later, when the American press was filled with stories of this scandal, the French remained blissfully unaware of what had been done to them.

Even the Democrats seemed to agree that, for all his political ambitions, Roosevelt's motives were free of greed. In 1906, when nothing more than rumors were swirling about, they had suggested that Roosevelt had been snookered by a group of greedy schemers. In 1908 the Democrats refused to make the *World* allegations an issue in the presidential election. Roosevelt seems to have suspected that some of the canal's promoters may have taken advantage of their positions to enrich themselves and said as much in a June 3, 1905, letter to Taft.

Unfortunately, Roosevelt failed to just allow his accusers' claims to self-destruct. Instead, he started criminal libel proceedings in federal court against the *New York World* and the *Indianapolis News.* The case was eventually decided by the U.S. Supreme Court, which ruled against the government January 3, 1911. Today, virtually no one defends Roosevelt's attempt to prosecute the newspapers that accused him. The papers had been irresponsible, but had Roosevelt succeeded in punishing them, the government would have acquired a dangerous new power.

CORPORATE DONATIONS
IN THE 1904 ELECTION

Charges of coercion were made against Commerce and Labor Secretary George B. Cortelyou, who also headed the Bureau of Corporations. Newspapers reported that Cortelyou used his government post to secure large corporate contributions to Roosevelt's campaign fund in the 1904 election.

On February 7, 1903, Theodore Roosevelt told a group of reporters that large corporations did not look with favor on the Department of Commerce and Labor bill then pending in Congress. The bill would create a bureau of investigations with the power to probe corporate wrongdoing. Speaking off the record, he told the reporters that six senators had just received a telegram from John D. Rockefeller Sr. that said in effect: We are opposed to any anti-trust legislation. Our counsel, Mr. ——, will see you. It must be stopped.

Politically, it was a brilliant stoke. Speaker of the House Joe Cannon might lament that "the Rockefeller telegrams originated in the brain of the President," but the public was outraged, and congressional resistance collapsed utterly. Three days later and by a lopsided vote of 251 to 10, the House passed the bill with all Roosevelt's amendments intact. The Senate rushed it through the next day.

As best anyone can tell, there never was any telegram from the widely hated Rockefeller. The following Thursday, however, the New York *American* published a February 6 telegram to Pennsylvania senator Matt Quay from Rockefeller's lawyer, John D. Archbold. It protested "vexatious interference with the industrial life of the country."

Having created his Bureau of Investigations and appointed his personal secretary, George B. Cortelyou, to be the first secretary of the new Department of Commerce and Labor, Roosevelt then did virtually nothing with his new weapon. In April 1903 he lamented to a friend about his situation. "President of the United States, I'd rather be *e-lect-ed* to that office than have anything tangible of which I know. But I shall never be elected to it. *They* don't want it ... Hanna and that crowd. . . . They've finished me ... I have no machine, no faction, no money." A president by succession rather than election, Roosevelt was exaggerating the opposition he was getting from Mark Hanna, who had been President McKinley's friend and supporter, and the Republican Party's big business faction. He was right, however, in his belief that corporate financial support for his campaign would make a 1904 win far easier. In a bid for that money, he toned down his rhetoric, and the corporate world quickly fell in line. On December 8 the *Wall Street Journal* reflected the views of big business when it noted, "The President makes clear that his policy, neither in intention nor fact, is directed against wealth." The only business that retained his ire was Standard Oil Company. During the heat of the 1904 campaign, when he heard rumors that the oil giant had given his campaign a large donation, he told Cortelyou, who had become his campaign manager, to return the money. He made no similar objections about other corporate donors.

In the 1904 elections, the Democrats also hoped to win corporate support by portraying Roosevelt as dangerous and unpredictable. In the past two elections, they had been badly hurt when William Jennings Bryan linked the party to midwestern agricultural interests. This time they chose Alton B. Parker, a judge on New York state's highest court, in an effort to appeal to the East. Nothing came of it. For more than a year Roosevelt's relatively mild behavior had been smoothing corporate feathers, and the near certainty of his coming victory had not escaped the attention of big business. Corporate donors usually prefer to give to a winner, even if their money buys nothing more than a chance to be heard. Giving to a loser, however ideologically compatible, is regarded as a waste of money.

On October 1 Joseph Pulitzer attempted to inject life into the moribund Democratic campaign by publishing a lengthy editorial in the *New York Times* and *World* as well as the *Brooklyn Eagle*. He pointed to the all too obvious fact that the Bureau of Corporations had been in existence for precisely 583 days, yet it had done nothing of importance. Did the corporations, he asked Roosevelt, "that were pouring money into your campaign assume that they are buying protection?" In an era when the law did not require the reporting of campaign donations, he called on the president to tell the country how much money his campaign had received from various corporate trusts. Rather than attack the wildly popular Roosevelt directly, Pulitzer focused on Cortelyou, Roosevelt's campaign manager, charging him with something called "Cortelyouism."

Even that was not enough to awaken the passive Democratic candidate. For three weeks Parker said nothing, sparing Roosevelt the need to offer anything in rebuttal. Then Parker learned of a New York City conference at which a group of wealthy men had agreed that Roosevelt's election was necessary and that they would supply the money for his victory. Growing desperate in the last days of his campaign, on October 31 Parker gave a speech repeating Pulitzer's charges about corporations believing they were buying protection, and the next day he called on Roosevelt to release a list of his corporate donors. The first was a charge Roosevelt could not deny, and the second was something he wanted to avoid. But on November 3 the politically inexperienced Parker went too far and accused Roosevelt of using information that the Bureau of Corporations had gathered to black- mail businesses for donations. That charge was something Roosevelt could deny, and he did so in words that sealed Parker's fate. The accusation, he said, was "unqualifiedly and atrociously false." Both parties, he noted, had received corporate donations but, if elected, he promised to go "into the Presidency unhampered by any pledge, promise, or understanding of any kind, sort, or description," excepting only the promises he had made open- ly to the American people. It worked. Roosevelt carried every state out- side the solidly Democratic South, winning 336 electoral votes to Parker's 140 and a popular majority of more than 2.5 million votes.

Unfortunately for Roosevelt, his victory did not keep troubling facts from surfacing from time to time. In testimony before a committee of the New York legislature in 1905, insurance company executives told of large donations they had made the year before to the Republican National Com- mittee. On April 2, 1907, the *New York World* announced that it had acquired a letter in which Union Pacific's Edward H. Harriman described how he had given $50,000 and collected another $200,000 to ensure a Republi- can victory in New York State. Harriman confirmed that the letter was authentic, but Roosevelt denied Harriman's interpretation of events. In his defense, Roosevelt produced an October 6, 1906, letter he had written in which he said that Harriman was so angry at the Republicans after the 1904 elections, that he was not going to give them any money in 1906.

In 1904 Roosevelt had promised not to seek another term. But when his chosen successor, William Taft, broke with the policies of the Roosevelt administration, Roosevelt was angry. In February 1912 he announced that he would challenge Taft for the Republican nomination. That provoked anger within his own party and became one reason for a Senate investiga- tion into the finances of all campaigns since 1900, which was led by pro- gressive Republican Moses E. Clapp of Minnesota. The hearings disclosed that not only had the Republicans raised far more than the Democrats in 1904 ($2,195,000 versus $700,000), but also that 72.5 percent of the Republican money came from corporate donors, particularly U.S. Steel, Standard Oil, and J. P. Morgan Company. The best news the Republicans could unearth from the committee's investigation was that the Democrats' much smaller campaign chest included three donors who gave more than $100,000 compared to the Republicans' four.

If corporate executives thought that their generosity would buy pro- tection, they soon discovered otherwise. Roosevelt was only waiting for a mandate from the people before turning on the powerful trusts. One example illustrates better than any other what happened. Testifying before the 1912 Clapp Committee, Standard Oil's John Archbold said that Cortelyou had not returned the company's $125,000 as Roosevelt had ordered. (Roosevelt, it seems, did not find that out until September 1908.) What had all that money bought? Archbold was profoundly bitter. "Deepest Abyssinia," he told the Clapp Committee, "never saw anything like the course of treatment we received at the hands of the administration following Mr. Roosevelt's election in 1904."

The rumors and allegations about the 1904 election fostered a drive for campaign reform. In his first address to Congress after the election, Roosevelt called for a law that would require political candidates and committees to release their expenditures to the public. Near the end of 1905 he recommended that corporations be banned from making political contributions. In early 1907 Congress prohibited corporations and national banks from contributing to candidates in federal elections. In 1910 Congress passed a campaign disclosure law, and in 1911 it amended that law to limit the amount that candidates for Congress could spend and to require statements of contributions.

U.S. STEEL'S MERGER WITH TENNESSEE COAL AND IRON

Congress investigated a corporate merger, which had been approved by President Roosevelt in violation of the antitrust laws he helped enact. Roosevelt was attempting to prevent the collapse of a financial institution and stem a growing panic.

The Panic of 1907 began with problems in the copper market. Unstable market conditions had driven down the price of copper, and, in an effort to bring the price back up, copper producers and the financial houses connected with them had been investing heavily in copper. Finally, one company could take the stress no longer and began dumping copper on the market, sending prices plummeting. On Monday, October 21, rumors linked the Knickerbocker Trust Company to copper, and the next day Knickerbocker experienced a run on its cash reserves. Secretary of the Treasury George Cortelyou had gone to New York City that Monday to meet with J. P. Morgan. Morgan refused to save Knickerbocker Trust, and a few days later its reserves were gone. The panic targeted another victim—the Trust Company of America. Cortelyou agreed to transfer $25 million in government funds to New York City's endangered banks. By Thursday afternoon, it seemed likely that the Trust Company of America might be saved.

Unfortunately, the crisis was not over. The next week, New York City announced that it would spread its payroll payments over a number of days to spare the already strained banks. News from other parts of the country suggested that businesses were beginning to retrench. The Santa Fe Railroad, for instance, announced that it was delaying a $7 million improve-ment in its tracks. During the panic, a national bank and three other trust houses in addition to Knickerbocker failed.

By the first weekend in November attention had turned to Moore and Schley, a large underwriting firm. If it failed, the Trust Company of Amer-ica would again be in trouble. If Moore and Schley could be saved, the panic might be halted. The plan hatched at Morgan's mansion was to save Moore and Schley by selling its Tennessee Coal and Iron Company stocks to U.S. Steel. Two representatives of U.S. Steel, Elbert H. Gary and Henry C. Frick, agreed to the purchase, but Frick insisted that no deal could be made until Roosevelt personally guaranteed that U.S. Steel would not be prosecuted for an antitrust violation.

Gary and Frick arranged for a special train—a locomotive and one car—to take them overnight from New York to Washington. They needed the president's answer before the stock exchange opened at 10 o'clock. Roosevelt saw them while at breakfast. Critics later claimed that Gary and Frick rushed the president into a hasty decision with little information to act on, but there was good reason for the haste. More appropriate was crit-icism that focused on the quality of their information. They never told him the name of the company they were attempting to save, and for political reasons Roosevelt did not ask. But the president was left with the impres-sion that he was rescuing a large brokerage house rather than an under-writer. Gary and Frick also claimed that U.S. Steel was acting in the national interest rather than self-interest, paying a "price somewhat in excess of true value." Others noted that they had gotten an excellent deal on a temporarily depressed stock. Finally, many questioned whether the crisis situation had created circumstances that enabled U.S. Steel to bypass the usual antitrust scrutiny by simply asserting that the purchase would keep their share of the steel market below 60 percent.

Forced to decide quickly, Roosevelt agreed to the sale. A few minutes later he dictated a letter that said, "While of course I could not advise them to take the action proposed, I felt it no public duty of mine to interpose any objections." Made in the space of a few minutes under intense pres-sure, the decision would haunt him the rest of his life.

In the immediate aftermath, however, the decision seemed wise. With the news that the sale had been approved, the stock market quickly turned optimistic and bullish. The next day U.S. Steel purchased majority control in Tennessee Coal and Iron Company from Moore and Schley and, by the end of the week, the market was calm.

The first to criticize the scheme was William Jennings Bryan, who attacked it two weeks later in his magazine, *The Commoner.* During the next year's elections Bryan continued to make it an issue, calling the deal monopolistic. Roosevelt replied that the merger had raised U.S. Steel's market share by only 4 percent and was necessary to end the panic.

Following the 1908 elections, Congress got involved with an investigation of its own. On January 4, 1909, the Senate asked the outgoing administration why it had not begun antitrust proceedings against U.S. Steel. Roosevelt responded that Congress could not give such orders to the executive branch. On January 22, the commissioner of corporations told the Senate Judiciary Committee that by law the confidential information that corporations had supplied his bureau could be released only with the approval of the president. With his typical flair for the dramatic, Roosevelt told the committee that they would have to impeach him to get the information, but a few days later he released all the pertinent documents. In the end, a minority on the Senate committee concluded that Roosevelt had been deceived about the situation and that the merger did indeed violate the Sherman Antitrust Act. The Republican majority concluded that, because Roosevelt had not actually authorized the purchase, he had done nothing wrong.

On March 3, 1909, William Taft was sworn in as president. In July 1910 the Taft administration began an antitrust investigation of U.S. Steel, and the following summer, a Democratic-dominated House began its own investigation. Its majority report was strongly critical of Roosevelt's actions and claimed that the panic had already begun to subside the week before the controversial merger. On October 26, 1911, the Taft administration began antitrust proceedings against U.S. Steel. That action so enraged Roosevelt that it became a motivation for his decision to run against Taft for the Republican nomination in 1912. On March 1, 1920, the final act in the drama took place: the U.S. Supreme Court issued its opinion in *United States v. U.S. Steel,* ruling that "the law does not make mere size an offense" and declaring that Roosevelt had been guilty of no wrongdoing.

Historians disagree about the wisdom of Roosevelt's decision. On one hand, the merger did not increase U.S. Steel's share of the market over the long term. On the other hand, the merger provided the company with a competitive advantage in the South and allowed the parent company to manipulate its southern affiliate in ways that prevented competition. Finally, like all historical "what ifs," the role the merger played in ending the panic can never be determined. It is possible that the market's turnaround was not caused by the rescue of a single underwriting firm, but because of what the informal agreement said about Roosevelt. By agreeing to a compromise, Roosevelt signaled to the financial community that he was not the inflexible, antibusiness ideologue some were portraying him to be.

ABUSE OF THE SECRET SERVICE

Roosevelt sought to expand the role of the Secret Service, but members of Congress objected. Roosevelt managed to create a new organization in the Department of Justice, which eventually became the Federal Bureau of Investigation.

Corruption within the postal service, the exploitation of public lands, and the growth of monopolistic trusts are not crimes that usually bring victims complaining to the nearest police station. When Theodore Roosevelt expanded the role of government into new areas and aggressively sought to punish crimes that had long been ignored, he needed an agency to look into these sorts of criminal activities and prosecute wrongdoers. Roosevelt turned to the Secret Service and pushed it to expand beyond its traditional role of prosecuting counterfeiters and guarding the president to take on added responsibilities.

Congress objected to this new and greatly expanded Secret Service. During the winter of 1908–1909, as Roosevelt was about to leave office, Congress added an amendment to an appropriations bill limiting the Secret Service to its traditional roles. The main sponsors of the bill were Speaker Joseph Cannon and Rep. James A. Tawney of Minnesota, a member of the Republican Old Guard, which had long been a thorn in Roosevelt's flesh. The members had their reasons. Some disliked seeing their colleagues prosecuted in the Oregon land fraud scheme (see page 208). Others with close ties to big business disliked antitrust prosecutions and thought that curtailing enforcement would be a clever way to weaken the law. Still others suspected that Roosevelt would use Secret Service agents to spy on the private activities of members of Congress and blackmail them into supporting his political agenda. Finally, there were those who were genuinely suspicious at any expansion in the powers of the government.

Roosevelt did not take kindly to what Congress had done. In his December 8, 1908, message to the legislature, he said, "This amendment has been of benefit only, and could be of benefit only, to the criminal classes." That would have been bad enough, but Roosevelt went on: "The chief argument in favor of the provision was that Congressmen did not themselves wish to be investigated by Secret Service men." If Congress wanted to protect its ranks, the President suggested sarcastically, "a special exception could be made in the law prohibiting the use of the Secret Service force in investigating members of Congress."

Needless to say, Roosevelt's words won him no support in Congress. On December 11, Rep. James B. Perkins of New York warned that for the sake of the dignity of Congress, the statement made by the president "cannot be lightly disregarded." In a unanimous vote, the House called for a committee to decide how they should respond. The resulting resolution demanded that Roosevelt present proof of wrongdoing on the part of any of its members. In the Senate, Nelson Aldrich of Rhode Island drafted a resolution that even Roosevelt's friend Henry Cabot Lodge supported. When Roosevelt tried to send the Senate a message on December 19, it was Lodge who rose to his feet and asked the Senate to set aside its usual deference to a message from the president by calling out, "Let the reading of the journal go on." The Senate decided to rebuke the president by taking no notice of his remarks.

Aware that he was not being heard, on January 4, 1909, Roosevelt sent the House a special message that increased their hostility. He denied that members of Congress were being followed and repeated his belief that weakening the powers of the Secret Service would only help criminals. The next day, he wrote to Sen. Eugene Hale of Maine giving as an instance of congressional crime the fact that his old foe, South Carolina senator Benjamin R. Tillman, was abusing his franking privilege. It was a most unimpressive performance.

On January 8, the House voted 211 to 36 to reject the president's January 4 message. Speaker Cannon, perhaps too obsessed with the power struggle then taking place between the legislative and executive branches, proclaimed it the greatest legislative victory over the executive since the Senate's censure of Andrew Jackson over the Bank of the United States. It was hardly that. For all his shrill rhetoric, Roosevelt was right. Congress *did* need to expand the executive branch to give it the resources necessary to prosecute crimes that Congress itself had identified.

Roosevelt had the last word. Six months earlier on July 26, 1908, he and Attorney General Charles J. Bonaparte had created a new agency within the Department of Justice. That agency eventually became the Federal Bureau of Investigation.

BIBLIOGRAPHY

Chessman, G. Wallace. *Theodore Roosevelt and the Politics of Power.* Prospect Heights, Ill.: Waveland Press, 1969.

Collin, Richard H. *Theodore Roosevelt's Caribbean.* Baton Rouge: Louisiana State University Press, 1990.

Ford, Benjamin T. "A Duty to Serve: The Governmental Career of George B. Cortelyou." Ph.D. dissertation, Columbia University, 1963.

Fowler, Dorothy G. *The Cabinet Politician, The Postmaster General, 1829–1909.* New York: Columbia University Press, 1943.

Gatewood, Willard B., Jr. *Theodore Roosevelt and the Art of Controversy.* Baton Rouge: Louisiana State University Press, 1970.

Gould, Lewis L. *The Presidency of Theodore Roosevelt.* Lawrence: University Press of Kansas, 1991.

Hagedorn, Hermann. *The Roosevelt Family of Sagamore Hill.* New York: Macmillan, 1954.

Harbaugh, William H. *Power and Responsibility: The Life and Times of Theodore Roosevelt.* New York: Farrar, Straus, and Cudahy, 1961.

Hill, Howard C. *Roosevelt and the Caribbean.* New York: Russell and Russell, 1965.

McCullough, David. *Mornings on Horseback.* New York: Simon and Schuster, 1981.

Messing, John. "Public Lands, Politics, and Progressives: The Oregon Land Fraud Trials, 1903–10." *Pacific Historical Review* 35 (February 1966): 35–66.

Mitchell, Jack. *Executive Privilege: Two Centuries of White House Scandals.* New York: Hippocrene Books, 1992.

Morris, Edmund. *The Rise of Theodore Roosevelt.* New York: Coward, McCann, and Geoghegan, 1979.

O'Callaghan, Jerry A. "Senator Mitchell and the Oregon Land Frauds, 1905." *Pacific Historical Review* 21 (August 1952): 87–103.

Overacker, Louise, and Victor J. West. *Money in Elections.* New York: Arno Press, 1932.

Peirce, Clyde. *The Roosevelt Panama Libel Cases.* New York: Greenwich Book Publishers, 1959.

Pringle, Henry F. *Theodore Roosevelt: A Biography.* New York: Harcourt, Brace, 1931.

Putter, S.A.D., and Horace Stevens. *The Looters of the Public Domain.* New York: Arno Press, 1908.

Wiebe, Robert H. "The House of Morgan and the Executive, 1905–1913." *American Historical Review* 65 (October 1959): 49–60.

Winkler, John K. *W. R. Hearst: An American Phenomenon.* New York: Simon and Schuster, 1928.

Woodward, C. Vann. *Responses of the Presidents to Charges of Misconduct.* New York: Dell Publishing, 1974.

WILLIAM HOWARD TAFT

Twenty-Seventh President
1909–1913

Born in the Mount Auburn section of Cincinnati, Ohio, on September 15, 1857, William Howard Taft was described as a fun-loving, active, well-behaved child. His father, Alphonso Taft, was a prominent Cincinnati lawyer who served as secretary of war and attorney general in the Grant administration and later as U.S. ambassador to Austria-Hungary and Russia. After graduating second in his high school class in 1874, William Taft attended Yale University where he also finished second in his class in 1878. He returned to Cincinnati to study law in his father's firm and at the University of Cincinnati. He was admitted to the bar in 1880 before his graduation.

Taft held a number of minor government posts, including assistant prosecutor of Hamilton County (1881–1882) and collector of internal revenue for Ohio's First District (1882–1883). In 1884 Taft worked for the nomination of Chester A. Arthur, but supported the Republican Party's eventual nominee, James G. Blaine. From 1885 to 1887 Taft was assistant solicitor for Hamilton County, a position that fostered his interest in a career on the judicial bench. He married Helen Herron, the eldest daughter of a Cincinnati judge, on June 19, 1886.

In 1887 Taft was appointed judge of the superior court in Cincinnati where he served until Benjamin Harrison appointed him U.S. solicitor general in 1890. Two years later, Harrison named him to the U.S. District Court for the Sixth Circuit. He also served as dean of the University of Cincinnati Law School from 1896 to 1900.

President William McKinley selected Taft to be commissioner of the Philippines. The commission was charged with establishing a civil government for the territory. After playing a major role in the creation of the government, Taft was appointed governor general of the Philippines in 1901. During his tenure, he twice turned down President Theodore Roosevelt's offers of a seat on the U.S. Supreme Court so that he could finish the work he had started in the Philippines.

In 1904 Taft returned to the United States and became Roosevelt's secretary of war, but his activities ranged beyond oversight of the military. Taft visited the construction site of the Panama Canal. He also served as acting secretary of state during the illness of John Hay in 1905 and provisional governor of Cuba in 1906. That same year, Taft again refused an offer to be nominated to the Supreme Court. He knew that he was the leading contender for the Republican nomination for president, and party leaders and his wife urged him to run.

Even though he had publicly declared his desire to be on the Court, Taft, with the enthusiastic support of Roosevelt, secured the Republican Party nomination for president on the first ballot. The party chose James S. Sherman of New York as his running mate. Taft's opponent was two-time losing nominee William Jennings Bryan. The campaign was a dull one, with Taft being portrayed as the logical extension of the Roosevelt presidency; he won with 321 electoral votes to Bryan's 162.

Taft indeed continued much of the policy agenda of the Roosevelt administration. He oversaw a reduction in tariffs, extended the regulatory reach of the Interstate Commerce Commission to include telephones, and used the power of the U.S. economy in foreign relations throughout Asia and Latin America. He also vigorously enforced antitrust legislation. In 1912 Taft was defeated for reelection because a disgruntled Theodore Roosevelt made a third party run for president, splitting the Republican vote and giving the victory to Democrat Woodrow Wilson.

Out of office, Taft became a law professor at Yale University in 1913, a post he held until his appointment as chief justice of the United States in 1921. President Warren G. Harding nominated Taft to fill the vacancy created when Chief Justice Edward D. White died. Over the next nine years, Taft wrote more than 250 opinions, nearly one-sixth of all the cases decided. He also persuaded Congress to appropriate money for the Supreme Court Building, which he did not live to see completed. In failing health, Taft retired from the Court February 3, 1930. He died March 8, the only person to serve as both president and chief justice of the United States.

RICHARD BALLINGER, SECRETARY OF THE INTERIOR

Ballinger was accused of misusing his position as secretary of the interior to profit from a land speculation deal in Alaska. The widely publicized scandal led to criticism of Taft for his handling of the situation.

In November 1909 an article titled "The Whitewashing of Ballinger" appeared in *Collier's* magazine. Its target was Interior Secretary Richard Ballinger, and the subtitle "Are the Guggenheims in Charge of the Department of the Interior?" left no doubt that the editors thought that serious misdeeds were occurring high up in the Taft administration. (The Guggenheim family's wealth came principally from mining.)

The article dealt with 100,000 acres of land rich in coal in the Alaskan interior. An 1873 law allowed individuals to purchase up to 160 acres of that land for $10 an acre. Far from being a bonanza for developers, the scheme had been a failure. The plots were not large enough to make mining feasible even in developed areas, much less in the wilds of Alaska. It was far easier to get larger plots of land fraudulently under looser laws governing agricultural land. Aware of the situation, Congress was attempting to reach a consensus about how the law should be changed. The coal would have to be mined by large corporations but without giving huge profits to a wealthy few. Some members of Congress wanted the land to be sold at market value once it could be surveyed and the value estimated. Others wanted the government to take royalties on each ton of coal mined.

Until the land could be assessed, Theodore Roosevelt had banned the sale of coal-rich land in the public domain. Outside Alaska the ban caused few problems: mines were producing ample supplies of high-quality, inexpensive coal. But in Alaska the situation was far different. Coal that cost a little over $2 a ton in Seattle could cost as much as $20 a ton in Juneau. Alaska was in a bind. It could not get cheap coal because transportation costs were high, and it could not reduce transportation costs by attracting railroads because the price of coal was so high. Secretary Ballinger understood that locally mined coal might alleviate the problem.

With most Alaskan coal land out of bounds, attention focused on the roughly 900 applications for 100,000 acres that predated Roosevelt's executive order. It was well known that many of the applications were fraudulent—the alleged buyers were simply front men for corporations. In their attempts to engulf Ballinger's department in scandal, critics such as L. R. Glavis (a former Interior Department employee and the author of the *Collier's* article) obscured some critical information: first, none of 900 claimants had yet acquired title to any land, and, second, claims were being investigated carefully so that most, if not all, of the fraudulent claims would be ferreted out. The Guggenheims were clearly not "in charge of the Department of the Interior."

To justify their cries of corruption, Ballinger's critics focused on some investors called the Cunningham group for its leader, Clarence Cunningham. One historian wrote:

> In 1905 the Cunningham group appeared to be an exception to the general run of Alaska claimants. They were businessmen of moderate means, widely known in the northwestern states of Washington, Oregon, and Idaho for their venturesome forays in such enterprises as sawmills and mines. Throughout their erratic career these claimants were never charged with being dummies.

While he was in private practice, Ballinger had given the group legal advice. Knowing them to be sincere, if somewhat naive, he attempted to

speed the processing of their claim before additional congressional legislation complicated it. That act lay at the center of the accusation against
Ballinger.

As often happens, the real situation was far different from what was
presented to the public. Both Taft and Ballinger were committed to conservation, and nothing ever came of the allegations that they were in the
pay of giant mining trusts. They simply disagreed with the way policies had
been carried out under Theodore Roosevelt. Impatient with the slow pace
of change, Roosevelt had attempted to do by executive order what should
have been done through legislation. Ballinger expressed that thought in a
letter to Taft: "The real animus against me lies in the fact that I have had to
treat so many of my predecessor's acts as unsupported by law."

He was right. Legally, there was little difference between Roosevelt's
ban on the sale of land that, under law, could be sold under certain conditions, and another president's attempt to sell the land in violation of those
conditions. Ethically, it is difficult to fault Ballinger for helping middle-
class businessmen without pointing out that Roosevelt had set aside vast
tracts of public land as game preserves, which, in that era, would be used
almost exclusively by wealthy hunters such as himself.

The ensuing controversy led Ballinger to ask Congress to hold hearings,
which began in early 1910. In retrospect, the evidence presented against
Ballinger was remarkably thin. Even Glavis, his chief accuser, admitted that
"there is nothing in any of these things upon which a criminal charge could
be predicated; still I think it was far more cowardly for him to take the
action he did than if a man actually stole money, for which he could be
convicted." University of Pennsylvania law professor George Pepper,
another of Ballinger's critics, described the secretary's wrongdoing as a
"series of successive blows dealt by Mr. Ballinger at interests which were
vital to a group of men who had dedicated their lives to a cause." Ballinger's
real crime was not that he had broken the law, but that he had enforced
existing law.

Ballinger may have been innocent of wrongdoing, but he looked bad in
the press. His foes were far better at manipulating the media, and *Collier's*
secretly paid the brilliant Louis Brandeis $25,000—a huge fee—to repre-
sent Glavis. Brandeis discovered that Taft had backdated a memorandum
and used it to smear the administration.

Even after Congress cleared him, rumors and attacks continued to
haunt Ballinger. That, along with declining health, led him to submit his
resignation on March 6, 1911. In accepting that resignation, Taft leveled
harsh words at Ballinger's foes. His secretary, he said, was the victim of one
of the "most unscrupulous conspiracies" in history, one led by people who
used the "meanest of methods" while claiming to be "actuated by the spirit of self-sacrifice for their fellow men."

The Ballinger case continues to be of interest today and for good reason. Traditionally, charges of corruption come from the other party, mak-

ing the partisan interests of each side obvious. In this case, the charges came from within the Republican Party and pitted a group that wanted to work within the democratic process against another group so dedicated to their cause that they slandered anyone who stood in their way. The Interior Department was supposed to represent the interests of all the American people in public lands; those who accused Ballinger wanted the department to represent their cause and their cause alone.

The scandal had many losers. After investing tens of thousands of dollars of their own money, Cunningham and his friends were denied their claim in court. In the next presidential election the Republicans, split between the Taft and the Roosevelt factions, lost to the Democrats. And, even though coal was mined by congressional authority, Alaska never developed an effective rail system, and even today the state's transportation costs remain high and many of its communities are isolated.

HARVEY WILEY, CHIEF CHEMIST OF THE FDA

Harvey Wiley, chief chemist of the Food and Drug Administration and early champion of pure food laws, was threatened with dismissal for violating the per diem payment law for outside scientists hired by the government.

Usually the subject of a scandal is not eager to see the story in the papers. But on July 13, 1911, the *New York Times* broke a story that had been given to it by the accused, Harvey W. Wiley, chief chemist in the FDA's Bureau of Chemistry. Wiley's campaign to end the adulteration of the nation's food had made him highly popular with the public and the press. As the story of the charges against him spread across the nation, President William Taft, Secretary of Agriculture James Wilson, and Congress were inundated with letters in his behalf.

But Wiley was not universally popular. The pure food campaign had earned him powerful enemies both within and outside the Department of Agriculture. Even the experts with whom Wiley worked could not agree on just which food additives were harmful or how products should be labeled. Some resented Wiley's habit of bypassing them and taking his views to the public, particularly when he sensationalized a subject to attract support. Outside the department, the hatred for Wiley was even greater. The possibility of bans on deceptive advertising of foods and patent medicines had led to the formation of an Advertisers' Protective Association. Among food processors, the situation was more complex. Butter distributors and the distillers of fine whiskies supported his efforts to accurately label oleomargarine and cheap whiskey. Processors who had invested in one form of food preservation were often delighted when Wiley targeted a competing method. Overall, however, the way the 1906 Pure Food and Drug Act was enforced was upsetting many people.

President Taft and his cabinet. Attorney General George Wickersham recommended firing Harvey Wiley.

Within the Department of Agriculture, Wiley clashed with George P. McCabe, the department's solicitor, and Frederick I. Dunlap, the Bureau of Chemistry's associate chemist. Eventually, the conflict focused on Dr. Henry H. Rusby of New York College of Pharmacy. In 1907 Rusby had been paid $20 a day to examine drugs entering the country through New York harbor. In May 1909, however, his pay was cut to $9 a day to comply with advice from the attorney general that $9 was the most Congress had authorized for scientific investigators. Although he did not like the cut, Rusby continued to work for the government until the end of 1910. At that time he appeared in court as an expert witness for the government and asked for $50 a day. McCabe ruled that he was still entitled only to $9. Rusby had paid more than that to a substitute to teach his classes, so now his work for the government was costing him money. In an effort to compromise, Rusby offered to both test drugs and testify in court for $20 a day. Wiley then recommended that Rusby be given the $50 for court testimony, but McCabe refused. Another solution was suggested. To resolve scientific disputes, the bureau used a Referee Board made up of scientists who were paid an annual salary rather than hired by the day. Wiley got Secretary Wilson to approve paying Rusby $1,600 a year.

In March 1911, while Wiley was out of town, Frederick Dunlap used his position as acting chief to examine the correspondence about Rusby's salary. He took the evidence he uncovered to McCabe and Wilson, who passed the information to a committee that included McCabe. The committee ruled that the annual contract had been an attempt to conceal the fact that Rusby's pay violated the law. Since the only motive had been to retain a talented expert, the punishment was unusually harsh. Rusby was to be fired. The chief of the Drug Division, who had negotiated the agreement, was to be demoted. Wiley was expected to resign. Secretary Wilson then took the case to Taft's cabinet. There Attorney General George W. Wickersham, another foe of Wiley, offered to review the case and, on May 13, he advised the president to get rid of Wiley. For two months Taft did nothing, but on July 7 he asked Wilson to inform Wiley and the others accused so they could defend themselves.

The documents arrived at Wiley's farm on a Saturday. He was elated, crying out, "Victory, victory, victory!" The charges, he said, would allow him to expose the conspiracy against him. At the office the following Monday, an assistant asked about their defense. "We need no defense." Wiley replied, "I am planning an attack." The article in the *New York Times* was part of that attack. He also sent an explanation to Taft. Soon the uproar in the press and the letters from the public were having the desired effect. Wilson no longer supported the committee's recommendations, and the attorney general apologized for his earlier stance. Realizing that the situation had serious political implications, Taft began to pay closer attention to the congressional investigation into the strife within the bureau over the pure food law.

On September 14, Taft said there was enough precedent for Wiley's decision to pay Rusby an annual salary and ample justification for doing what was necessary to retain the services of an expert. Both the public and the press praised Taft's leadership in the matter. Wiley was elated and thought Taft's remarks signaled the end of his opponents' power. In that he was disappointed. Despite his lack of ability, Wilson was too popular with rural voters to be dismissed, and in its investigation Congress had concluded that, in some of their disputes with Wiley, McCabe and Dunlap may have been right. In his zeal, Wiley had sometimes forgotten the need to be just and fair.

BIBLIOGRAPHY

Anderson, Donald F. *William Howard Taft: A Conservative's Conception of the Presidency.* Ithaca: Cornell University Press, 1973.

Anderson, Judith I. *William Howard Taft: An Intimate History.* New York: Norton, 1981.

Anderson, Oscar E. *The Health of a Nation: Harvey W. Wiley and the Fight for Pure Food.* Chicago: University of Chicago Press, 1958.

Coletta, Paolo E. *The Presidency of William Howard Taft.* Lawrence: University Press of Kansas, 1973.

Glavis, L. R. "The Whitewashing of Ballinger." *Collier's,* November 13, 1909.

Mason, Alpheus T. *Bureaucracy Convicts Itself: The Ballinger-Pinchot Controversy of 1910.* New York: Viking, 1941.

McGeary, M. Nelson. *Gifford Pinchot: Forester-Politician.* Princeton: Princeton University Press, 1960.

Mitchell, Jack. *Executive Privilege: Two Centuries of White House Scandals.* New York: Hippocrene Books, 1992.

Penick, James, Jr. *Progressive Politics and Conservation.* Chicago: University of Chicago Press, 1968.

Pringle, Henry F. *The Life and Times of William Howard Taft.* Norwalk, Conn.: Easton Press, 1939.

Richardson, Elmo R. *The Politics of Conservation.* Berkeley: University of California Press, 1962.

Woodward, C. Vann. *Responses of the Presidents to Charges of Misconduct.* New York: Dell Publishing, 1974.

WOODROW WILSON

Twenty-Eighth President
1913–1921

oodrow Wilson was born December 28, 1856, in Staunton, Virginia. When he was two, the family moved from Virginia to Augusta, Georgia, where his father, Joseph Wilson, became pastor of the First Presbyterian Church. The Civil War kept Woodrow from attending school until he was nine years old. In 1870 the Wilsons moved to Columbia, South Carolina, where Joseph Wilson took a teaching position.

Woodrow briefly attended Davidson College before entering Princeton University. He graduated in 1879 and began studies at the University of Virginia Law School, but he completed only two years because of poor health. He passed the bar in 1882. After practicing law for a year, he attended Johns Hopkins University, earning a Ph.D. in political science in 1886. While at Johns Hopkins, he met and married Ellen Louise Axson, the daughter of a Presbyterian minister.

Wilson held teaching posts at Bryn Mawr College, Wesleyan University, and Princeton. He served as Princeton's president from 1902 to 1910 and built a reputation as reform-minded educator. He was elected governor of New Jersey in 1910 as a Democrat, and in 1912 became the party's candidate for president after forty-six ballots. Luckily for Wilson, the Republicans were divided between those who had renominated President William H. Taft and those who favored former president Theodore Roosevelt, running on the Bull Moose Party ticket. With the Republican vote split, Wilson won the election with only 42 percent of the popular vote, but 435 of the 531 electoral votes.

As president, Wilson initiated a program of progressive reforms by immediately introducing several major pieces of legislation. The first to pass was the Underwood Act, which reduced tariffs to their lowest level since before the Civil War. Attached to the measure was a graduated federal income tax. The passage of the Federal Reserve Act provided the nation with the more elastic money supply it badly needed. In 1914 antitrust legislation established the Federal Trade Commission to prohibit unfair business practices. Wilson was also instrumental in the passage of a law to prohibit child labor and another that limited railroad workers to an eight-hour day.

With a narrow win over the Republican challenger, Charles Evans Hughes, Wilson was reelected in 1916. With war raging in Europe, the slogan, "He kept us out of war," would not remain true much longer. On April 2, 1917, Wilson asked Congress for a declaration of war on Germany. When the armistice was signed two years later, Wilson went to Paris to take part in the peace negotiations. He had outlined his war objectives and a plan for peace in the "Fourteen Points" speech of January 8, 1918. Returning to the United States with a punitive treaty that failed in so many respects, Wilson did succeed with the inclusion of the League of Nations. However, the Senate refused to ratify the treaty, and Wilson, trying to save it from defeat, suffered a stroke and nearly died while on a national tour to mobilize public sentiment.

Wilson's wife, Ellen, died August 6, 1914, and he married Edith Bolling Galt, the widow of a Washington businessman, on December 18, 1915. With her help, Wilson served out the remainder of his second term. Retiring from public life, he died in 1924.

EXTRAMARITAL AFFAIR

Wilson engaged in an extramarital affair with a married woman that began when he traveled to Bermuda for his health.

Woodrow Wilson was the president of Princeton University when he met Mary Peck in 1907. His doctors had ordered him to take a vacation to recover his health, and he traveled alone to Bermuda, where Mary Peck was recovering from a bout of depression. At this time, she was married to her second husband, Thomas D. Peck, a factory-owner from Pittsfield, Massachusetts. Her first husband, Thomas Hulbert, a mining engineer in the Canadian wilderness, had died in a work-related accident. The affair between Wilson and Mary Peck started either on Wilson's second visit to Bermuda in 1908 or during a visit to her in New York City in 1909 after Mary had separated from Peck. The two corresponded frequently and met whenever they could in her New York apartment. The affair ended before his election as governor of New Jersey in 1910, but rumors of it surfaced in 1912 when the Pecks filed for divorce. According to the rumors, Peck was using several of Wilson's letters to Mary as proof of infidelity.

Wilson's political opponents in the 1912 election knew about the letters but refused to exploit them. As Theodore Roosevelt stated, "You can't cast a man as a Romeo who looks and acts so much like an apothecary's clerk." Wilson had prepared a press release that admitted to "a passage of folly and gross impertinence," but did not need to make it public. In any event, Ellen Wilson discovered the affair and forgave him. In fact, over the next few years, Mary Peck either hosted the Wilsons or was hosted by them, including a solo visit by Woodrow to New York in 1912. Wilson last saw Mary after Ellen's death in 1915. Mary wrote of the events in her 1933 book, *The Story of Mrs. Peck.*

DIGGS-CAMINETTI AFFAIR

Attorney General James C. McReynolds interfered with the prosecution of a case in California because the father of one of the accused was being appointed to a sensitive post in the executive branch.

In March 1913 California newspapers carried the story of two men in their late twenties, married and with children, who had disappeared along with two young women, one nineteen and the other twenty. Both women had been living at home with respectable parents. What made the event newsworthy was that these were no ordinary men. One was Maury I. Diggs, the California state architect and the son of a wealthy landowner. The other was Farley D. Caminetti, the son of Anthony Caminetti, an influential Democrat in the California Senate. Before the affair was resolved, it would involve high officials in every branch of the federal government.

The couples were found in a cottage in Reno, Nevada, and authorities decided to charge the men under the Mann Act, which made it a federal offense to take a woman over state lines for immoral purposes. (The Mann Act was intended to curb prostitution.) Pursuing the case under federal law also shifted the trial from Sacramento, the state capital, to San Francisco, where the political connections of the men's families were less strong. The district attorney who took on the case later explained, "I was assured by scores of the best men in Sacramento that the money of the Diggs family would corrupt any local jury that could be secured, and numerous instances were brought to my attention where this was true."

Then something intervened to give the Caminetti family a strong influence in the nation's capital and thus over federal cases. District Attorney Gavin McNab had hints of what was to come when Senator Caminetti persuaded him to postpone the cases—the men were being tried separately—for two weeks until May 19 when he would be back from Washington, D.C. But on May 16 McNab received a telegram from his boss, Attorney General James McReynolds. The message was blunt and to the point: "Please write me fully concerning charges against Caminetti and Diggs and take no further affirmative action in respect of same until you receive advice from me."

McNab agreed to the two-week postponement, but noted in his May 17 reply to McReynolds that the case was an "aggravated one." In a May 20 telegram he pointed out that, in addition to the Mann Act charges, Diggs and his lawyer were charged with trying to persuade one of the two women to commit perjury. That same day it became clear why the administration was taking an interest in the case: Secretary of Labor William B. Wilson announced that Senator Caminetti was to be appointed commissioner general of immigration, a powerful and politically sensitive position.

McReynolds later claimed that he had intended to delay the case only long enough for the elder Caminetti to take care of pressing business in immigration. But his explanation did not say why the Diggs case also had to be delayed or why the elder Caminetti's presence was necessary for his son's trial to go forward. Rep. James Robert Mann, Republican of Illinois, author of the Mann Act, observed sarcastically that the son was a mere "youthful boy of 27 years" whose "guileless innocence" required his father's protection since he had "only seven lawyers" assisting him. Clearly, it was not the father's legal advice that was needed, but his political connections.

Complying with McReynolds's request for a full report on the case, McNab sent him twelve pages. Although respectful, the report warned McReynolds that neither the public nor the press would tolerate even the appearance of favoritism in the case. McNab noted, "No case in this part of the State has brought forth more universal condemnation; no case has so roused the sense of public decency or called forth such bitter strictures from the press of California."

McReynolds, perhaps having second thoughts, wired McNab to "proceed with [the cases] as you have planned." Thanking him, McNab wrote: "Owing … to the peculiarly aggravated character of the offense, public opinion throughout the State has been burning at white heat, and the press watches with a scrutinizing eye every action that is taken in court in regard to the cases." At this point, Senator Caminetti asked McNab to delay the cases until "after July or August." Instead, McNab, believing that he had McReynolds's support, set a court date for July 26.

In a June 18 telegram McReynolds bluntly ordered McNab "to postpone trial of these cases until the autumn." Two days later McNab responded with two strongly worded telegrams, one to McReynolds and one to President Wilson. To McReynolds, he wrote, "I am profoundly convinced the action taken will destroy the prestige and ruin the usefulness of this office and result in the ultimate escape from punishment of certain of these defendants." The telegram to Wilson said, "Neither my private honor nor sense of public duty can permit me thus to destroy the prestige of this office." To both McNab also sent his resignation.

McReynolds's only comment about McNab's resignation was, "A Republican District Attorney has resigned and I am shedding no tears." A San Francisco newspaper reported that Wilson showed more wisdom, retiring "into seclusion at the White House." His secretary later announced that Wilson had neither known about nor authorized the order to delay the prosecutions. The pressure to delay appears to have come from Caminetti through the secretary of labor to the attorney general.

Republicans had no difficulty being outraged, but Democratic response varied widely. On June 28 the staunchly Democratic *New York World* condemned McReynolds's action and called for his resignation. Wilson publicly defended his attorney general, but privately admitted that a mistake had been made. Secretary of State William Jennings Bryan, although conceding that Caminetti's son was "guilty of gross and criminal conduct," still proclaimed the father a "progressive Democrat" concerned with "the advancement of human welfare." Perhaps the most tasteless response came from Texas representative Martin Dies, who attacked the muckraking press and claimed the fuss was about no more than "a little fornication case."

Democratic control of Congress kept any serious investigation from occurring, and McReynolds was able to shield some of the more critical evidence from the Republicans. But it was obvious that what one Republican termed "insidious political pull" had been used. He compared the Diggs-Caminetti case with another in which the accused—an ordinary man without political connections—had been indicted under the Mann Act on May 1 and, after a quick trial, was sentenced to two years in prison on June 21.

For Diggs and Caminetti, however, even conviction in court did not bring immediate imprisonment. At great expense, their appeals went all the way to the Supreme Court, and, even after the Court ruled almost four years later, on January 15, 1917, that the Mann Act did apply to their case, another delay ensued while an appeal for a presidential pardon was mounted and hundreds of signatures collected. Wilson refused to grant a pardon, telling Caminetti's mother that he needed to consider "the public point of view" as well as his sympathy for her.

However, when Diggs complained that it would be too traumatic for him to be locked up in San Quentin, a prison he had helped to design, both he and Caminetti were allowed to go to McNeil prison, a minimum security facility in Washington State. Few, if any, of the almost 400 others in prison for Mann Act violations were treated as leniently.

WILLIAM JENNINGS BRYAN, SECRETARY OF STATE

Bryan's critics claimed that the summer lectures he gave on the chautauqua circuit were not only unprofessional but also violated ethics rules forbidding outside compensation.

Some scandals say as much about the accusers as they do about the accused. In no case is that more true than with the furor that arose in 1913, when Secretary of State William Jennings Bryan announced that during the summer he would speak on the Chautauqua circuit just as he had for the previous eighteen years. The waves of criticism heaped upon him would not have been much worse had he announced that he was abandoning his wife to run off with a chorus girl.

Bryan had a practical reason for continuing on the lecture circuit. He had earned a good deal of money over the years as one of the nation's most popular speakers and donated much of it to many churches and charities. Although his $12,000 a year salary as a cabinet secretary was ample, it was not adequate for those responsibilities. In May he had written his brother Charles, "I find that my salary will not meet my expenses, while my official duties reduce to a minimum my time for lecturing." He was forced to cut his contributions in half and lecture from mid-July to mid-September to maintain the rest. Ever the team player, before doing so he sought and got Wilson's permission.

As often happened when Bryan clashed with his critics, the chasm between his culture and theirs opened still wider when he tried to explain himself. Many of his foes lived a world where financial difficulties were not discussed in polite company and where trying too hard to make money was frowned upon. The liberal *Nation* reflected this attitude when it professed to be "deeply outraged by the spectacle of the Secretary of State appearing nightly under canvas for pay." If Bryan had journeyed to Harvard to give a virtually identical speech to a more prestigious audience, with his honorarium provided by a wealthy donor, there would have been no fuss. But a secretary of state was supposed to be above making money and appearing "in company with acrobats and vaudeville performers of every kind." For his detractors, the Great Commoner's behavior was all too common. Worse still, he actually enjoyed what he was doing. One of his biographers noted that he "returned to his department refreshed and stimulated by his contact with the masses."

Hints at his critics' real motivation appeared when the *Nation* assured "Mr. Bryan that *in this part of the country* our feeling is shared by *all those*

William Jennings Bryan

who reverence our institutions and believe in their being dignified by those entrusted with the duty of governing" (italics added). The "this part of the country" remark should not be taken too literally. Although Bryan was most popular in the agricultural Midwest, millions of easterners liked him, and it was to them that he was giving his controversial speeches. He deliberately chose to lecture in locations near Washington, so that he would not be away too long. The *Nation* was referring to a certain class of people, wherever they lived, who valued dignity over Bryan's homespun virtues.

Bryan also had his defenders. One noted, "The very fact that the papers which are hostile to the administration, and the Republican Senators make so much of it, shows how hard-pressed they are for a real issue." The Senate debate over the matter was partisan. The vote on a snide resolution asking Bryan "to advise the Senate what would be a proper salary to enable the present Secretary of State to live with comfort" divided along party lines. All the Democrats and two Republicans voted against it. One senator said, "Before Mr. Bryan became Secretary of State Republicans predicted that he would ruin the country if he ever got into office; but now that he is in office they insist that the country will go to ruin if he leaves Washington for a few days."

JAMES M. SULLIVAN, AMBASSADOR TO THE DOMINICAN REPUBLIC

James Sullivan was accused of misdirecting federal deposits of customs money to a bank owned by a political friend. Sullivan also used his influence with the Dominican government to secure lucrative contracts for his brother.

On June 22, 1914, Secretary of State William Jennings Bryan wrote the president a letter in which he described his appointment policy:

> My own disposition, as you know, is to use our prominent Democrats, not only as a reward for what they have been, but because distinction puts them in a position to do something in the future. We have been quite short of prefixes. While Republicans have been able to introduce Secretary so-and-so, Ambassador so-and-so, and Minister so-and-so, not to speak of the smaller officials, we have usually had to confine ourselves to Mister or Honorable.

One of the prominent Democrats upon whom Bryan wanted to bestow the title *ambassador* was James M. Sullivan, a New York lawyer, prize fight promoter, and a Democratic activist in the election of 1912. Bryan did not know Sullivan personally, but at the request of New York senator James A. O'Gorman, Sullivan was appointed ambassador to the Dominican Republic on August 12, 1913. On August 20 Bryan wrote a letter to Walter W. Vick, receiver general of customs in the Dominican Republic (and the party's New York headquarters manager in 1912). The letter begins by asking "what positions you have at your disposal with which to reward deserving Democrats?" Bryan's seeming indifference to whether an ambassador he had recommended had the necessary skills is evident in his remark that he did "not know to what extent a knowledge of Spanish is necessary." The letter closed with Bryan's claim that Sullivan was "a strong, courageous, reliable fellow" who would fit in well. Events proved otherwise.

Apparently unknown to Bryan, Sullivan had the covert political support of well-connected New York financiers who were officials in the Banco Nacional de Santo Domingo. In addition, one of his cousins was an official in the bank and in the Dominican Department of Public Works. American influence over the republic's finances and the number of high-level jobs held by U.S. citizens contributed to the difficulties the Wilson administration faced. Americans might complain about the corruption in Latin American politics, but a great deal of that corruption was coming from the United States.

During this period, Dominican politics were in a state of confusion. José Bordas Valdés had been elected provisional president in April 1913 but was intent on staying in power by whatever means necessary when his one-year term expired. Opposing him was a popular revolution led by Gen. Desiderio Arias, a talented demagogue and smuggler. Over the next two years, the Wilson administration teetered from idealistic rhetoric about democracy to threats of armed intervention and managed to alienate virtually every segment of the Dominican population. Some responsibility for that failure was Sullivan's; he was unfit for the job, distrusted by the Dominicans, and served his own interests and those of his New York backers rather than doing his job. In June and July 1914, for example, he sent home a number of totally false reports concealing how unpopular Valdés had become so that the administration would continue to back the dictator.

Reports of corruption began to filter back to the State Department within a few months after Sullivan's arrival. In December 1913, the *New York Times* charged that Sullivan was suspected of transferring money that Walter Vick had collected into the bank controlled by Sullivan's supporters. (The transfer was discovered, and the money moved to a different bank.) Bryan spoke up for Sullivan, but in March 1914 matters became more serious when Vick took his charges against Sullivan to both Wilson and Bryan. When they refused to investigate, Vick went to the *New York World,* which conducted its own probe and published the results between December 7 and December 13. The articles charged that Sullivan was profiting from corrupt connections to local banks and construction companies. Finally alarmed, Wilson appointed James D. Phelan, a California Democrat and an administration loyalist, to investigate. Phelan's May 9, 1915, report acquitted Sullivan of graft, but found that he was unfit for the job and had improper ties to New York financiers. The report uncovered enough for Wilson and Bryan to force Sullivan to resign on July 8, but the report was not made public until July 21 and then only under pressure from the *New York World.*

To this day, historians remain uncertain about how much Sullivan profited from his acts. Wilson continued to believe that he had been "very foolish rather than anything worse." Bryan was more cynical, noting that "we were deceived as to the interests which supported Mr. Sullivan's candidacy."

HENRY M. PINDELL,
AMBASSADOR TO RUSSIA

Henry Pindell, a loyal Democrat, had been offered lucrative rewards, including the ambassadorship to Russia, for his support of Wilson in the 1912 elections. Pindell was confirmed, but the Russian government refused to receive him.

As a newly elected president, Woodrow Wilson was determined to break the long-hallowed tradition of giving ambassadorships "to the merely rich who were clamoring for them." Unfortunately, his attempts to nominate worthy men had to run a gauntlet of opposition that included Secretary of State William Jennings Bryan, who wanted all such posts to go to "deserving Democrats." It also included politicians who had their favorites to nominate and the unfortunate fact that the position typically did not pay well enough to cover expenses.

Nevertheless, Wilson tried to find able men. He asked Harvard's Charles W. Eliot to be ambassador first to China and then Great Britain. Eliot refused both offers. Wilson offered John R. Mott, the missionary, and Dean Fine of Princeton the posts in China and Germany, respectively. Both turned him down. Those most qualified, it seemed, could not afford to take the jobs. In exasperation, on March 23, 1913, Wilson issued a public statement saying: "It is a great pity that the country has to ask such sacrifices of those who are invited to serve abroad—a service which every year becomes more exacting and more important."

One ambassadorship seems to have been regarded as not particularly exacting. On September 7, 1913, Henry M. Pindell, a well-to-do newspaper editor in Peoria, Illinois, received a letter from his U.S. senator, James H. Lewis. It was not the first letter Lewis had sent Pindell. In mid-August he had written to offer Pindell the job of federal income tax collector for his area. Pindell had ignored the offer.

Now, a new offer was on the table: "It is up to the Administration to appoint an Ambassador to St. Petersburg." Secretary Bryan wanted Pindell to accept it, "and all the honor that goes with the position." He need not worry because the demands of the Russian ambassadorship would not be great. He "could resign in a year—say October 1, 1914." Nor was any particular skill required. "There will be no treaties to adjudicate, and no political affairs to bother with." In fact, the whole affair could be regarded as an extended vacation. He "would not be tied to St. Petersburg, but would have trips to Berlin and Vienna and the other capitals of Europe, and also Stockholm, and perhaps Copenhagen, with all the attendant delights that go with such trips."

Despite word of Senator Lewis's offers leaking to the press, Pindell accepted the nomination and the Senate confirmed it. But problems developed on the other side of the Atlantic. Outraged by what had appeared in the papers, the Russian foreign minister informed the American Embassy in St. Petersburg that if Pindell were sent to their country, the imperial authorities would publicly refuse to accept him. Pindell then withdrew, and it took Wilson almost a year to find someone who was acceptable to the Russian government.

FRANKLIN K. LANE, SECRETARY OF THE INTERIOR

Lane was charged with validating claims by oil companies operating on government lands despite the fact that the oil reserves had been set aside for the navy by President Taft's executive order.

In August 1916 the chief forester of the Interior Department, Gifford Pinchot, published an "Open Letter to the Honorable Franklin K. Lane, Secretary of the Interior, Concerning the Navy's Oil Lands." Pinchot's language was blunt: "There is a widespread impression that you have made yourself the champion of the conservation of our natural resources for the general benefit. That impression is less justly founded than I could wish."

For much of the public, the spectacle of one noted conservationist attacking another was confusing. Coming on the heels of an attack a month earlier and from one of the leading Republican progressives, it was also intensely political, deliberately intended to pose a threat to President Woodrow Wilson's reelection chances. But Pinchot was not motivated by politics. He and Lane were on different sides of an intensely divisive question: What policy should the government take concerning the development of oil deposits that lay under federal lands in the West? The roots of the conflict reached back to September 27, 1909, when President Taft issued an executive order banning further oil development on federally owned lands. The order was bold, but implementing it would prove extremely messy.

The first problem was the legality of the order—did the president have the authority to do what he had done? With the Pickett Act of June 25, 1910, Congress backed up Taft's order by passing a law having the same effect. But Congress never declared the previous executive order legal. That determination had to wait until a February 23, 1915, Supreme Court decision upholding the order in the case of the Midwest Oil company. As a result, Taft's executive order remained legally ambiguous for more than five years. Those who defied it could argue that they had acted "in good faith," assured by their lawyers that Taft had made a mistake.

Second, the development of oil land is a complicated operation, and, no matter what day the ban went into effect, exploration, construction, drilling, and production would be at different stages on different sites. Taft's order had recognized the validity of existing claims, but just how much development created a valid claim was uncertain. In *The United States Oil Policy,* John Ise lists seven different classes of claimants with varying degrees of legitimacy. Wherever the line was drawn, it seemed that a single day's work might make the difference between owning an enormously productive claim or wasting thousands of dollars. Secretary Lane and other supporters of oil developers wanted to interpret the law generously for their benefit.

Many of the oil companies exaggerated the amount of development they had done at contested sites before the critical dates. Long after Taft's original order, Congress would debate various relief bills for firms caught by it. The bills that attracted industry support typically contained provisions directing the Interior Department not to look for fraud or, even more disturbing, allowing a fraudulent claim to become valid if the purchaser had acted "in good faith" when buying it. Such a provision would allow a bogus claim that could not be developed to be sold at full value to someone who then acquired full rights to develop it. That was the sort of behavior that led Pinchot and others to label all those with claims as no better than trespassers and thieves. As a result, they tended to be as harsh with claimants as Secretary Lane was lenient.

While these claims for relief were making their way through Congress, the legislature was working on bills to bring order to development on federal land. Older laws intended for solid minerals were extremely wasteful when applied to oil. The policy that allowed wells to be drilled on small plots of land in an effort to permit ordinary people to benefit was a disaster. The result was often hundreds of closely spaced wells in a single oil field, each drawing off the oil so rapidly that most of it would never be harvested. Unfortunately, two issues that should have been kept separate —relief bills and development bills—tended to get merged into one measure that stood no chance of passage. Typical was the behavior of the powerful California congressional delegation, whose members had close ties to oil men. If their relief bill failed, they would tack it on to a development bill. That was one reason why Lane complained that 6 million acres of land were being locked up by a debate over 5,000 acres.

As Lane indicated, most of the debate was not over vast tracts of land that may or may not have contained oil. It was over a single tract, Naval Reserve No. 2, in the Buena Vista Hills of California. Of the two reserves Taft had set aside to provide the U.S. Navy with oil in wartime, No. 2 was the only one known to contain vast quantities. In a mere two years the wells that Standard Oil controlled on a single square mile in the middle of the reserve had produced an astonishing 12 million barrels of oil. Nearly all the fighting during the Wilson administration was over the Buena Vista fields. Standard Oil and other large oil corporations argued that so much of

Franklin Lane

the land could now be developed that the field was useless as a naval reserve. With support from the attorney general, the secretary of the navy argued that if fraudulent claimants were tossed out, Buena Vista would be just what the navy needed. The conflict between those two men and Lane left many with the legitimate impression that the Wilson administration did not have a coherent oil policy.

Historians are uncertain how to assess Lane's motives. Was he under the control of oil developers as Pinchot and others alleged, or was he a sincere conservationist as his published writings and many of his other deeds suggest? Three factors probably played a role in Lane's behavior.

First, during this era, nothing predicted attitudes toward resource development better than where someone lived. Easterners wanted to conserve the natural resources for future generations. Much closer to those resources, westerners wanted to develop them rapidly. Lane was from California.

Second, Lane's reputation as a conservationist rests primarily on his talent as a writer. His much-praised writing style reflected the tastes of his generation and was more sentimental than logical. A great champion of the American pioneer, he seems to have equated the oil explorers with those who, a generation earlier, had braved the American plains. Logically, such thinking was nonsense; Buena Vista was so rich in oil, there was little risk for those drilling there.

Third, Lane was not only a lawyer, but also both he and his brother George had spent their early careers with the Independent Oil Producers Agency. He supported the oil industry, and Pinchot could say nothing to change his mind. That also explains why, when he resigned as secretary of interior, he seems to have had no qualms about taking a $50,000 job representing an oil company.

In 1918 an assistant attorney general, Francis J. Kearful, testified to the House Committee on Public Lands that Lane was permitting oil leases to go through in cases "where charges of fraud had been made and without investigation." These charges angered some Democrats, particularly in the West, but eastern Democrats who supported conservation were equally upset that the charges were ignored.

With the continuing existence of the Buena Vista reserves in doubt, in 1915 Wilson, with Lane's approval, created a third naval reserve, located in Wyoming and known as Teapot Dome. Nine years later it would become the focus of one of the worst political scandals in the nation's history. In *The Origins of Teapot Dome,* historian J. Leonard Bates traced its roots to the weak and ineffective handling of the Buena Vista frauds.

DOLLAR-A-YEAR MEN

Charges of widespread abuse were raised when the government used corporate executives on loan from their companies to aid in the war mobilization effort. These executives were still in the pay of their employers and often ruled on issues and on contracts that specifically involved their companies.

On March 25, 1918, Maj. Gen. Leonard Wood testified before the Senate Military Affairs Committee about what he had seen during his recent tour of the nation's military forces in Europe. What he said shocked both Congress and the nation. The Wilson administration and its Committee on Public Information had been telling the American public that the first waves of a vast air armada had begun to arrive in Europe. General Wood told the committee that was a lie. Although some $840 million had been spent on aircraft production, there were almost no aircraft in Europe to support U.S. troops. Later General Wood observed, "I never saw a Committee more wrought up or more excited. They were gesticulating and swearing and generally shaking things up."

There was a reason why Wood's testimony was so troubling. When the United States entered the war the previous spring, the public was given a grand vision of a near bloodless victory. Europeans might fight and die by the tens of thousands in the muddy trenches of France, but American warriors would fly above the carnage in an armada of 100,000 aircraft. German aircraft would be swept from the skies, and their ground fortifications blasted to rubble. One of the chief promoters of the idea was an automobile salesman named Howard E. Coffin, chairman of the Aircraft Production Board. Although the number of promised planes would later be cut to 22,000, the gap between what had been planned and what had been delivered caused many to seek answers.

On April 10 the Senate Military Affairs Committee blasted the aircraft program as a complete failure. The majority report was remarkably bipartisan, supported by four Democrats and five Republicans. On April 18, with no explanation from the White House, both Coffin and Maj. Gen. George O. Squier, the chief of the Army Signal Corps, were relieved of their duties. At best, the administration seemed guilty of gross incompetence. Executives in the nation's fledgling aircraft industry hinted at worse. They suggested that the administration was allowing the already large auto industry to use the war to make huge profits and to set itself up to dominate aircraft production after the war, when some thought the public would begin to purchase a Model T-like "flivver of the skies."

Wood was not the first to make charges against the aircraft program. In November 1917 Gutzon Borglum had personally warned Wilson that his aircraft program was in serious trouble and that the auto industry intended to use it to crush competition from aircraft manufacturers. A sculptor and engineering genius, who would later create the monument at Mount Rushmore, Borglum was also an aviation enthusiast with an insider's

knowledge of aviation developments. With Wilson's backing and the cooperation of Secretary of War Newton D. Baker, Borglum investigated and on
January 21, 1918, presented his report to Baker and the president. The
report was critical of several important industrialists; Wilson and Baker
suppressed it and did nothing about its conclusions. They apparently
thought time would solve all the production difficulties, but Borglum was
not that easily silenced. By April he had managed to interest the newspapers in reporting his allegations. Forced to act, Wilson set up another
investigation, this one headed by a loyal Democrat, H. Snowden Marshall.
His April 12 report backed up some of Borglum's charges. Lying or conveniently forgetting the full authority he had given Borglum, Wilson broke
off contact with him, telling him, "I merely gave you the right to look into
the matter of your own volition."

With pressure mounting in the Senate for a full investigation, Wilson
was again forced to act. On May 6 he attempted to block the Senate probe
by ordering the Department of Justice to inquire into the matter. But senators in both parties vetoed the idea of an administration investigating
itself. Finally, Wilson was forced to do as his friends were advising. On May
16 he added Charles Evans Hughes, his Republican opponent in 1916, to
the investigation and, for good measure, Borglum. With Hughes part of the
investigation, Senate Republicans were forced to back off. Borglum would
later charge, with some justification, that the Justice Department report
had failed to condemn Henry Ford, despite strong evidence against him.
That year Wilson would support Ford's strange, nonpartisan run at a Senate seat.

A letter written in summer 1917 to Treasury Secretary William G.
McAdoo suggests the roots of the billion-dollar aircraft scandal. At a lun-
cheon at Delmonico's, a famous New York restaurant, a group of industrialists and public officials came up with the idea of building vast quantities
of planes. Knowing nothing about the difficulty of constructing planes out
of wood and fabric, they nevertheless concluded that, if a large number of
planes was needed, the auto industry was better qualified to build them
than the aircraft industry. In fact, contracts were given to paper corporations with no factories.

The aircraft debacle was the most expensive of the scandals that troubled Wilson's conduct of the war. The one person who was actually condemned by the Justice investigation—Col. Edward A. Deeds, head of
United Motors Company and vice president of Dayton Metal Products
Company—is an example of what went wrong. Deeds was a so-called dollar-a-year man. When the war began in April 1917, several hundred businessmen were given important, decision-making positions in the war
effort. Some were not paid at all, others received a token $1 a year, but
they continued to receive full salaries from their companies. Proponents of
the idea believed it gave businesses an opportunity to express their patriotism. Critics pointed out the enormous potential for conflicts of interest:

as government officials, these businessmen would be making decisions about awarding contracts to the same companies that were paying their salaries. That is undoubtedly why automobile executives such as Coffin and Deeds were steering lucrative aircraft contracts into an industry that did not know how to handle them.

In Congress, the most vocal critics of the dollar-a-year scheme were an odd blend of southern Democrats and Republican progressives. Against intense lobbying by the Wilson administration, they were able to achieve some results. The Lever Act of August 10, 1917, made it illegal for a government agent or adviser to contract for supplies in which they might financially benefit. On the other hand, a January 1918 bill by Sen. Kenneth McKellar of Tennessee was blocked. It would have ended the dollar-a-year program altogether and substituted employees paid by the government. A War Industries Board resolution of June 1918 did, however, require that board members declare their business ties and financial interests.

The other cause for various scandals in the procurement of war materiel was Wilson's partisanship. Had he conducted the war by staffing agencies with people from both parties, he could have selected the most talented individuals for the jobs. Moreover, the presence of people from both parties would have helped to keep everyone honest and expose any corrupt bargains with business.

Congress understood the need for bipartisan cooperation and early in the war tried to create a joint committee to oversee wartime spending. Wilson did not see things the same way. Referring to the "ominous precedent" of the Civil War and envisioning himself as a second Lincoln harassed by "daily espionage" from Congress, the president managed to use party loyalists to block legislation of that kind every time it arose. Calling his critics "noisily thoughtless and troublesome," Wilson seemed incapable of believing that they were as committed to winning the war as he, which was odd because some of his more vocal foes had championed war with Germany earlier and with more zeal than he. When members of both parties began to call for a more efficient organization of the war effort, all Wilson could see was, as he told reporters, "nothing more or less than a renewal of the perpetual effort of the Republicans to force representation in the administration." His appointments typically reflected a desire to surround himself with people loyal to himself. When he took over the nation's railroads, for instance, he appointed his son-in-law, William McAdoo, to run them. Wilson simply could not grasp that an effective war effort required that Republicans be brought into his administration and treated with respect.

The brevity of the war and Wilson's delaying tactics meant that scandals such as aircraft procurement did not get the attention they may have deserved. As soon as the war ended, the focus shifted to the debate over U.S. membership in the League of Nations.

A. MITCHELL PALMER,
ALIEN PROPERTY CUSTODIAN

*A. Mitchell Palmer, head of the Office of the Alien Property Custodian—
an agency formed to dispose of German-owned property—secretly sold
assets to friends at below-market prices. He was also accused of benefiting
directly from some of the transactions.*

In April 1917 the United States entered the war against Germany. In
October Woodrow Wilson created the Office of the Alien Property Custodian and appointed a progressive Pennsylvania Democrat, A. Mitchell
Palmer, as its head. Palmer had served in the House of Representatives
from 1909 to 1915, and he had helped swing the Democratic convention
to Wilson in 1912. Under Palmer, the custodian's office grew rapidly, and
in just a year had 300 employees in Washington alone.

The purpose of the office was to take over and administer German-
owned businesses within the United States, so they could not be used to
advance enemy purposes. The amount of property seized was immense. In
December 1918—a month after the armistice was signed—Palmer told a
group of New York City lawyers that his office was administering 29,753
trusts worth more than $506 million. He estimated that another $300 million in properties had not yet been brought under his control. The fact that
he was still acquiring property after the fighting was over should have
alerted his audience that something was wrong. However, it was not until
the mid-1920s that Republican administrations would investigate what had
happened. By then it was too late. When he left the government—after
serving as Wilson's attorney general—Palmer took critical documents
with him, making it difficult to ferret out his role in his subordinates'
wrongdoing.

The first of the misdeeds centered on the sale of property. The Trading
with the Enemy Act allowed alien goods to be sold only in certain
cases—for example, items that would spoil. Initially, Palmer acted as custodian for the rest. But during 1918, with government agencies spreading
lurid tales of espionage and sabotage, suspicion and hatred for all things
German began to grow in the population. In his *Alien Property Custodian
Report for 1918*, Palmer described the "great industrial and commercial
army which Germany planted here with hostile intent." He called on Congress to "make the Trading with the Enemy Act a fighting force in the war"
by allowing the custodian to sell all German-owned factories. He convinced Wilson that the owners were from Germany's militaristic and
monopolistic Junker class, the landed aristocracy. It would be wrong,
Palmer said, to give the profits these corporations had made to such men
after the war.

Assured of Wilson's support, Palmer went to Congress where he got
the powers he wanted, with one exception. Sen. Joseph S. Frelinghuysen,
Republican of New Jersey, insisted on an amendment requiring public

bidding so that Palmer could not use private sales to enrich his friends. The senator later told Congress, "I distrusted Mr. Palmer from the very bottom of my heart from the time that his weasel words about the sinking of the *Lusitania* were published in the *New York Times*." Unfortunately, the rest of Congress was not that shrewd.

To his credit, Palmer had taken some steps to prevent corruption. For the more important positions, he usually chose people of ability and integrity. He created the Advisory Sales Committee to rule on all sales and staffed it with four respected bankers and an eminent jurist. Not content to be mere figureheads, the committee members blocked some of the more dubious sales.

For other positions Palmer chose people he thought would be useful to his future run for the presidency, which he attempted in 1920. One of these was Joseph Guffey, director of sales. By law, the money from sales was to be placed immediately in the U.S. Treasury. Instead, Guffey placed the money in bank accounts that he controlled, held it for several months, used it for personal purposes, and kept the interest it earned. (In March 1921, with the Republicans about to take power, Guffey's superior forced him to pay back $400,000 in interest he had retained.)

The second of the misdeeds concerned property belonging to Germans seized in the Philippines. Palmer placed a friend, Francis B. Harrison, in charge of the property, and, by giving bidders very short notice, Harrison managed to sell the property to other friends at good prices. Palmer, fearful of a scandal, demanded that the sales be canceled. When Harrison refused, Palmer replaced him with a New York attorney, Douglas M. Moffat. Palmer's instruction to Moffat—"keep the lid on"—suggests that he cared less about how the property was sold than about avoiding "partisan investigations." With one exception Moffat resold the properties to the same people who had bought them the first time.

The third misdeed involved Bosch Magneto, the largest manufacturer of magnetoelectric machines in the country. By advertising a low assessment of the company's worth, requiring high bonds, and holding the sale in an obscure Massachusetts town, Palmer ensured that the firm was sold to his friend Martin E. Kern, a businessman who was also a convicted jewel thief. When the Senate Judiciary Committee investigated the sale in 1919, Palmer lied about the transaction. He told the committee that, although some of the government's custodians had been rewarded after the sale, they had received just a small block of stock, perhaps twenty-five or thirty shares. What he did not tell them was that only 250 shares had been issued, making their "small block" worth roughly $900,000. In 1926 Palmer, Kern, and four others were charged with defrauding the government, but the case was dropped in 1930 due to insufficient evidence.

The fourth misdeed caused the most lasting damage. Before the war, Germany had dominated the world's drug and dye industries, holding thousands of important patents. Palmer wanted to destroy Germany's U.S.

market by selling all the German patents to American companies, even though the war was over. In late November 1918 Wilson, in an attempt to stop Palmer, told him "that it would not be wise to add just now to the list of alien names, in view of the virtual cessation of hostilities."

Nevertheless, the patents were sold to American buyers at prices far below market value. Two lower federal courts and the Supreme Court ruled the sales legitimate. Palmer's own justification for what he had done is far more disturbing. In a law journal article in early 1919, he rationalized his "great work" this way: "The war power is of necessity an inherent power in every sovereign nation. It is the power of self preservation and *that power has no limits* other than the extent of the emergency." Chilling words in light of what another "sovereign nation" would do in the next war.

The harm that resulted from Palmer's confiscation of German patents is incalculable. According to the peace treaty, the money from such sales was to pay part of Germany's war indemnities. The pittance that was paid for those patents increased the financial burden on Germany, helping to fuel the anger that put Hitler in power. In one vicious act, Palmer had robbed Germany of the well-deserved fruits of its creativity and deprived it of one of its most effective ways to recover from the war. Nazism would fester and breed in a nation ravaged by Palmer's foolish act of "Americanism."

In his biography, Stanley Coben reaches the conclusion that Palmer "seems to have walked successfully the fine line which separates the legal from the illegal," but noted that there is "reason to believe that Palmer closed his eyes to the manipulations and dishonesty of some of his friends." In all probability, Palmer permitted the corruption and profiteering to make the sorts of "friends" he felt he would need to run for president.

BIBLIOGRAPHY

Anderson, Robert L. *The Diggs-Caminetti Case 1913–1917.* Lewiston, N.Y.: E. Mellen Press, 1990.

Baker, Ray S. *Woodrow Wilson: Life and Letters.* Garden City, N.Y.: Doubleday, Page, 1927–1939.

Bates, J. Leonard. *The Origins of Teapot Dome.* Urbana: University of Illinois Press, 1963.

"The Bryan Scandal." *Nation,* September 18, 1913, 256–257.

"The Case of Brother Pindell." *North American Review* 198 (December 1913): 752–758.

Caufield, Leon. *The Presidency of Woodrow Wilson.* Lawrence: University Press of Kansas, 1966.

Coben, Stanley. *A. Mitchell Palmer, Politician.* New York: Columbia University Press, 1963.

Coletta, Paolo E. *William Jennings Bryan.* Lincoln: University of Nebraska Press, 1969.

Hagood, Wesley O. *Presidential Sex: From Founding Fathers to Bill Clinton.* Secaucus, N.J.: Carol Publishing Group, 1998.

Heckscher, August. *Woodrow Wilson.* New York: Scribner's, 1991.

Hulbert, Mary Allen. *The Story of Mrs. Peck.* New York: Minton, Balch, 1933.

Ise, John. *The United States Oil Policy.* New Haven: Yale University Press, 1926.

Link, Arthur S. *Woodrow Wilson and the Progressive Era, 1910–1917.* New York: Harper, 1954.

Livermore, Seward W. *Woodrow Wilson and the War Congress, 1916–1918.* Seattle: University of Washington Press, 1968.

Mitchell, Jack. *Executive Privilege: Two Centuries of White House Scandals.* New York: Hippocrene Books, 1992.

Olson, Keith W. *Biography of a Progressive: Franklin K. Lane.* Westport, Conn.: Greenwood Press, 1979.

"The Pindell Incident." *Outlook,* November 22, 1913, 607–608.

Reagan, Michael D. "Serving Two Masters: Problems in the Employment of Dollar-A-Year and without Compensation Personnel." Ph.D. dissertation, Princeton University, 1959.

Ross, Shelley. *Fall from Grace: Sex, Scandal, and Corruption in American Politics from 1702 to the Present.* New York: Ballantine Books, 1988.

"Secretary Bryan and the Chautauqua Lectures: A Poll of the Press." *Outlook,* August 2, 1913, 746–748.

Walworth, Arthur C. *Woodrow Wilson.* New York: Longman's Green, 1958.

Woodward, C. Vann. *Responses of the Presidents to Charges of Misconduct.* New York: Dell Publishing, 1974.

WARREN G. HARDING

Twenty-Ninth President
1921–1923

Born in Corsica (now Blooming Grove), Ohio, on November 2, 1865, Warren G. Harding was the eldest of Phoebe and George Harding's eight children. He grew up on the family farm and was educated at home by his mother and at local schools. Harding showed an early talent in rhetoric, memorizing passages and reciting them to his classmates and teachers. At fifteen, he enrolled at Ohio Central College, graduating in 1882.

After teaching at a country school for one term, he moved to Marion, Ohio, where his family had settled. He studied law at his father's insistence and briefly sold insurance. He took a job as a reporter for the *Marion Mirror,* and in 1884 he and two partners purchased the nearly defunct *Marion Star,* publishing their first edition on November 26. Harding eventually became the sole owner of the paper and turned it into a successful operation. On July 8, 1891, Harding married Florence Kling DeWolfe, a thirty-year-old divorcée with a son. "Duchess," as Harding called her, was the driving force behind his success at the *Marion Star* and his political ambitions.

A Republican, he lost his bid for county auditor in 1892 in the heavily Democratic Marion County. In 1899, while campaigning for the Ohio state senate, Harding met Harry M. Daugherty, a political power broker who in time would help him secure the presidency. Harding won the senate seat and served two terms including one as majority floor leader. In 1903 he was elected lieutenant governor of Ohio. In 1910 he lost his bid for governor to his Democratic opponent.

Harding was elected to the U.S. Senate in 1914 in a campaign marred by the ardent anti-Catholic bigotry of his supporters, who attacked the Democratic opponent, a Roman Catholic. In the Senate, Harding followed the party line, made many friends, and avoided controversy. His attendance was poor—he missed more than two-thirds of all roll call votes. He voted in favor of Prohibition and women's suffrage, but against the Treaty of Versailles.

When the Republicans gathered in Chicago in June 1920 to select their presidential candidate, Harding was a very dark horse indeed. The front-runners included Gen. Leonard Wood, Gov. Frank Lowden of Illinois, and Sen. Hiram Johnson of California. However, the delegates were dead-locked after the initial balloting and recessed for the night. At that point, Daugherty—Harding's kingmaker—went to work to lobby for Harding as a compromise candidate. In a smoke-filled room on the thirteenth floor of the Blackstone Hotel, the party bosses decided on Harding because he was from a crucial state, popular, and had voted for both women's suffrage and Prohibition. Called to the hotel suite at 2:00 a.m., Harding was asked if there were any skeletons in his closet. Harding thought for a few moments and said there were not. On the tenth ballot, Harding won the nomination.

His opponent in the general election was fellow Buckeye, Democratic governor James M. Cox. The election was largely a referendum on the Wilson administration, which Cox supported wholeheartedly. In the end, Harding trounced his opponent by more than 7 million votes and won thirty-seven of forty-eight states.

Because the Senate had rejected the Treaty of Versailles, the Harding administration was responsible for settling World War I. Harding also par-doned Eugene V. Debs, the Socialist antiwar protester who had served three years of a ten-year sentence. However, the Harding administration is best remembered for its scandals. The president was largely innocent of any personal wrongdoing, but his associates were among the most unethi-cal ever to serve in government. At the height of the Teapot Dome scan-dal, he undertook a national speaking tour in an attempt to repair the dam-age. During the trip, he suffered from a variety of ailments including food poisoning, pneumonia, an enlarged heart, and high blood pressure. On the evening of August 2, 1923, Harding died in San Francisco, while his wife was reading to him. She refused to permit an autopsy, which led to spec-ulation that he might have committed suicide or been poisoned.

EXTRAMARITAL AFFAIRS AND AN ILLEGITIMATE CHILD

Harding was known to have had at least two long-term extramarital affairs and to have fathered an illegitimate child.

Carrie Fulton Phillips

In 1905 Warren G. Harding began a fifteen-year affair with Carrie Phillips, the wife of James Phillips, a longtime friend from Marion, Ohio. The pre-vious year James and Carrie had lost their first child, and James went to a sanitarium in Battle Creek, Michigan, to recover from the loss. Harding had recommended the place—he suffered from depression and, as a young man, had been hospitalized there himself. While James was away, Harding visited Carrie to see how she was getting along, and the affair began.

Although their spouses remained unaware of the relationship for some time, rumors began to circulate in Marion about Carrie and Warren. Nevertheless, the two couples were often in each other's company and vacationed together at least twice, once on a cruise to Europe in 1909 and once to Bermuda in 1911.

The relationship began to sour when Carrie insisted that Warren divorce Florence and marry her. He refused because he feared Florence's anger and the impact that a divorce would have on his political career. Carrie, who did not think much of his political ambition, left the United States with her daughter, Isabella, for Germany. Had it not been for the impending outbreak of the First World War, she might have stayed in Europe. However, she returned to the United States in 1914, and the affair resumed. This time Florence found out. She threatened to divorce Harding and even consulted an attorney. Her anger made life difficult for Harding, bringing a brief break to the affair, but it was not over.

The end came with the presidential campaign of 1920. The Republican National Committee and Harding's political advisers were concerned about the affair becoming public. Campaign manager Albert Lasker offered the Phillipses $20,000, a trip around the world, and a $2,000 monthly stipend if they stayed out of the country until after the election. The monthly allowance would continue if they stayed away while Harding was in office. The deal was simply too good to pass up, and, with the Phillipses out of the country, Harding was elected.

Many years later, in 1963, the court-appointed attorney and former guardian of Carrie Phillips—who had died penniless and senile in an Ohio state facility—found a lockbox in the Phillipses' home, which contained 105 letters from Harding to Carrie. At one time, Harding had asked Carrie to return his love letters because he feared she would blackmail him. (He had already given her a Cadillac and $5,000 a year.) For some reason, he gave the letters back to Carrie and continued to write more. The letters—which range from love poems to erotic banter—confirm in explicit detail the existence of the long affair. They are on deposit at the Library of Congress, but are under court seal until July 29, 2014.

Nan Britton

Nan Britton was born in Marion in 1896. She developed a teenage crush on Harding, already an established businessman and politician, when he ran for governor in 1910. During the summer of 1914, Harding and Nan began to write to each other, and that was the extent of the relationship for several years. In his letters, he would speculate about what life would be like with her instead of Florence.

On May 7, 1917, Nan wrote to Harding, who was now a senator. She was in New York, where she had attended secretarial school, and wanted him to help her find a job in Washington, D.C. Harding responded three days later that he would be happy to help her. After a few more letters, he went to New York to see her. She met him at his hotel and accompanied him to his room under the pretext of having a private conversation. Nan later wrote that he "had scarcely closed the door ... when we shared our first kiss." Harding convinced Nan that it would be better for her to stay in New York, and he helped her get a job at a major steel company.

Nan Britton with her daughter, Elizabeth Ann

In June Nan received the first of the many love letters (a forty-page tome) from Harding. The two exchanged letters regularly, and whenever possible Harding would go to New York or have Nan meet him in other cities when he was on tour. On July 30 Nan and Harding had sexual intercourse for the first time at a New York hotel. As sometimes happened when an unmarried couple occupied a hotel room, the police raided. But the officers recognized his name and let them go. Harding continued to see Nan at hotels in New York and other cities. Occasionally, she would come to Washington, although for obvious reasons that was more dangerous.

Nan became pregnant and gave birth to a girl, Elizabeth Ann, on October 22, 1919. Harding sent Nan money every month for the child's support. In June 1921 Nan visited Harding in the White House and, according to her account, "He introduced me to the one place where, he said, he thought we might share kisses in safety. This was a small closet in the anteroom ... for we repaired there many times in the course of my visits to the White House." On one occasion in October, Florence Harding demanded that the Secret Service agent guarding the closet door move out of the way. It appears that someone had told her that the president was "entertaining" in the closet.

In January 1923 Nan made her last visit to the White House. Harding seemed to be more distraught over his relationship with her than with the political scandals breaking around him. "Nan, our matter worries me more than the combined worries of the whole administration ... our secret must not come out. Why, I would rather die than disappoint my party!" He broke off the relationship, but continued to support Nan and their daughter. However, his death some months later left them without any means of support. In 1927 Nan Britton wrote a book, *The President's Daughter,* to make some money. According to the preface, she wrote the book to obtain legal and social recognition and protection of all children born out of wedlock.

TEAPOT DOME

One of the worst political scandals in the nation's history involved the illegal leasing of oil reserves by Interior Secretary Albert B. Fall. The scandal reached far and wide into the Harding administration and might have led to Harding's impeachment had he not died in 1923.

Less than an hour's drive north of Casper, Wyoming, is an odd-looking rock formation about seventy feet high. It is called Teapot Rock because, until a 1962 tornado knocked off its spout, it looked like an old teapot. By a strange quirk of history, that rock formation gave its name to one of the worst political scandals in U.S. history. For decades afterward, the teapot was a visual symbol of corruption much as the suffix "gate" became a symbol after the Watergate scandal of the early 1970s.

The teapot was such a potent image that in 1924 Eleanor Roosevelt traveled around New York State campaigning against her cousin Theodore Roosevelt Jr. in a car rebuilt to look like a steam-spouting teapot. She wanted to make certain that the former president's (Republican) son did not become governor and take on the mystique of the Roosevelt name before her (Democratic) husband, Franklin Roosevelt, had a chance to recover from polio and reenter politics. TR Jr. had little ground for complaint. As assistant secretary of the navy, he had played a role in blocking an early investigation of the Teapot Dome scandal under the mistaken impression that the scandal's main figure, Interior Secretary Albert B. Fall, had been one of his father's Rough Riders. Fall holds the distinction of being the first U.S. cabinet secretary to be indicted and convicted for deeds committed while in office.

The story began in the decade before World War I and the start of the conservation movement. Conservationists wanted to ensure that the nation's natural resources, particularly forests, oil, and coal, were wisely used so they would be available for future generations. Their new ethic clashed violently with the old idea that the nation's resources were inexhaustible. Fall exemplified the old ethic. When a National Park Service official asked him what his behavior would leave his grandchildren, Fall replied:

> I'm surprised at you. You've had a good education. You know something about history. Every generation from Adam and Eve down has lived better than the generation before. I don't know how [succeeding generations will] do it—maybe they'll use the energy of the sun or the sea waves—but they will live better than we do. I stand for opening up every resource.

The differences in the two points of view can be explained in part by differences in background. In general, conservationists lived east of the Mississippi where most natural resources had been transferred to private hands and their value determined by the market. In the East the opportunities to get rich exploiting natural resources no longer existed. In addition, the new ethic almost perfectly mirrored the mindset of "old money." Security was more important than opportunity. Inherited wealth must be carefully husbanded and passed on to future generations. In the arid, undeveloped regions of the West the opposite was true. Exploiting natural resources was just about the only way a man could make a living, and the immediate opportunity was more important than what might happen in the future. It is no accident that the other two major figures in the Teapot Dome scandal, Edward L. Doheny and Henry F. Sinclair, had risen from poverty to great wealth by discovering oil.

Because most of the land in the West was still owned by the federal government, its land-use policies played a much greater role in people's lives than in the East. Resentment at seeing that policy dictated by outsiders led some to justify illegal deeds. Teapot Dome would have been a minor scandal but for one fact: Secretary Fall took the money he secretly acquired from Doheny and Sinclair and spent it visibly improving his Three Rivers ranch.

The conservationists' first major success had come in 1906, when President Roosevelt issued an executive order setting aside 66 million acres of public coal land. At that time, coal was the nation's main source of energy, but the growing importance of oil soon attracted the conservationists' attention. Recognizing that it made little sense for the government to sell oil land for a pittance when the market was already glutted with oil, in September 1909 President Taft issued an executive order banning the sale of federal oil land, at the time about one-eighth of the nation's known oil lands. In 1912 Taft took one more step: he designated two particularly productive oil fields in California, Elk Hills and Buena Vista Hills, as Naval Petroleum Reserves No. 1 and 2. In 1915 President Wilson made that policy bipartisan by designating Teapot Dome a third naval reserve.

The reason for creating the naval reserves was that in 1913 the navy had made a commitment to convert its fleet from coal to oil. In time of war, it was believed that these three oil fields might provide the difference between victory and defeat. Their importance as a strategic reserve was so great that they were left untouched during World War I and not fully exploited until the Arab oil embargo of the 1970s. Because these fields were seen as vital to the nation's defense, the public was outraged when the scandal broke. Opening the fields to commercial exploitation was seen as an act of treason. The actual situation was much more complex. Fall, Doheny, and Sinclair had acted in ways that allowed them to assert with some legitimacy that they were acting in the interests of national security. They could make that claim because Congress had failed to follow up on what the three previous presidents had done by executive orders. Only Congress could provide the detailed legislation and funding.

Although Congress had backed up Taft's ban on the sale of oil lands with a June 25, 1910, law saying much the same thing, the legislature never established that Taft's action was legal. The nine months between Taft's order and congressional action and the additional five years until the Supreme Court ruled the order constitutional created a legal vacuum that allowed oil companies to establish quasi-legal claims to oil leases and in some cases to establish new wells on federal land. Congress failed to put a quick end to the oil rush and bogus claims, and much of the responsibility rested on those members of Congress who were bought with oil money, just as Fall was later.

After a decade Congress finally acted, passing the Leasing Law of 1920. As expected with legislation that must win the approval of so many special interest groups, the original bill, introduced by Sen. Reed Smoot of Utah, started out complicated and became even more so, ending up with thirty-eight long sections dealing with a wide variety of minerals including oil. There was something in it for everyone. Conservationists got leasing (instead of outright sales) and regulations designed to prevent waste. Oil companies got an end to the bans and a chance to validate pending claims. Progressives got regulations intended to prevent the monopolization of an oil field by a single corporation. Both the federal government and the states got a share of the lease income, which was particularly important to cash-poor western states.

The new legislation had a major impact on the two naval reserves in California. Taft had chosen them because they were known to be highly productive. However, there were also commercial oil wells inside of and adjacent to the reserves, and Taft's executive order had not altered the existing leases. Even if all the new claims that had been pending when Taft issued his order were rejected, over time these legal wells could still drain the naval reserves almost dry. The Leasing Law of 1920 made matters worse. Not only could existing claims be transformed into producing wells, but also new claims were possible with the approval of the Interior Department. Many already believed that the Buena Vista Hills naval reserve was doomed, which was why Wilson had set aside Teapot Dome as a third naval reserve in 1915. (The dome refers to the geological formation in which the oil was stored.) Aggressive development around Elk Hills might destroy it, and geologists debated whether Teapot Dome could be drained from wells in the nearby Salt Creek fields.

There was some hope, however, that Elk Hills might be saved if the navy could wrest its management from the Interior Department. At the insistence of Secretary of the Navy Josephus Daniels, a June 4, 1920, naval appropriations bill contained an amendment transferring control of the reserves to the navy. In the last months of the Wilson administration, Daniels asked for bids on twenty-one offset oil wells to be placed on the western edge of the Elk Hills reserve. The idea was to trap oil being drained away by wells outside the reserve. Daniels reasoned that it was better for the government to get income from the oil rather than Standard Oil. Unfortunately, Congress banned the navy from refining its own oil and permitted very little of the income from the naval reserves to go to the navy—a mere $500,000. The rest had to go into the Treasury. To add insult to injury, according to a 1913 law, the navy could not even store this oil in tanks for later use. For many naval strategists, that policy seemed foolish: even then Japan was seen as a growing threat in the Pacific. When the Teapot Dome scandal broke, many, including Fall, pointed out that oil stored in tanks at Pearl Harbor could double the effectiveness of the U.S. Pacific fleet. If the oil had to be taken out of the ground anyway, why not store it where the navy could use it? Behind that argument lay the rationale for the schemes that became known as Teapot Dome.

Historians have debated why the Republican Party selected Harding as its 1920 presidential candidate. During the height of the Teapot Dome scandal, it was suggested that oil money had bought a Harding candidacy. Little evidence of that was uncovered—the large oil companies seemed to have given freely to both parties. But it was true that certain powerful senators wanted to make sure that the party's candidate was not a strong leader like Theodore Roosevelt. They wanted a weak president, and they got exactly that.

At first, conservationists seemed happy with Harding. They were permitted to write the conservation plank of the party platform, even if Harding seemed a bit vague on the topic. Gifford Pinchot, a leading conservationist, endorsed him. After the election Harding invited Pinchot to visit him in Marion and to suggest candidates to head the Interior Department. In February 1921, however, conservationists became concerned about rumors that Harding would choose a Senate poker-playing friend, Albert Fall of New Mexico. As a precaution, Pinchot began to examine Fall's record, telling a friend, "He has been with the exploitation gang, but not a leader." Shortly after Harding selected Fall, Pinchot noted in a letter, "On the record, it would have been possible to pick a worse man for Secretary of Interior, but not altogether easy."

Although their numbers were small, the conservationists were highly organized and well connected. Before anyone else took notice of what Fall was doing, they targeted him as someone to be watched and later to be exposed and destroyed. In particular, the credit for bringing Teapot Dome to the attention of the public lies with Harry A. Slattery, a Washington, D.C., lawyer and a hardworking conservationist. Slattery became worried when Edwin Denby, a foe of conservation, became secretary of the navy. Rumors began to circulate that Denby had secretly transferred authority over the naval oil reserves back to Interior, but, before anything could be done about that, conservationists shifted their attention to countering Fall's plans to transfer some of the authority over Alaskan forests to his

The Teapot Dome scandal involved many levels of Harding's administration.

department. Throughout the rest of 1921 conservationists were busy mounting a publicity campaign against the forest transfer, and in spring 1922 they addressed the oil problem.

The rumors proved correct. On May 31, 1921, Harding had issued an executive order transferring authority over the naval reserves from the secretary of the navy to the secretary of the interior. Six weeks later, on July 12, Fall gave drilling rights at Elk Hills to Edward Doheny's Pan-American Petroleum and Transport. At this point, everything was legal and in the open. The drilling had been authorized by the previous secretary of the navy to stop the oil from being drained from outside the reserves. Three companies had bid on the contract, and Fall had accepted the highest bid. The same could be said of Fall's reopening of old oil claims and altering them in favor of the oil companies. Right or wrong, Fall's actions were within his authority and hence legal.

In early March 1922, however, Slattery heard rumors that Fall had just leased Doheny large tracts within Elk Hills. On March 15, he wrote to a supporter, Sen. Robert M. La Follette, suggesting that the Senate ask the interior secretary to provide details about all oil leases on Naval Reserves No. 1 and 2. A little over a month later Slattery wrote a friend, "There has been a sudden change—we are fighting old Fall on the 'oil line'—particularly naval oil reserves." La Follette's own investigations were making him equally suspicious. Navy officers opposed to leasing the reserves were being transferred to distant locations.

Fall may have gotten wind of their investigations. On April 7 he issued an announcement blaming the Wilson administration for the loss of 22 million barrels of oil from the California reserves and claiming that the only way the government's oil could be saved was by taking it out of the ground. In general terms, he described how companies would pay for the oil they extracted by placing a portion of it in tanks for navy use. Fall failed to mention that on that same day he had leased all of Teapot Dome to Henry Sinclair of Mammoth Oil. Three days later, Slattery got wind of that, and on April 14 it became a front-page story in the *Wall Street Journal*. On April 18 Fall's assistant formally announced the leasing of Teapot Dome and three days later gave the Senate a copy of the contract. Most of the lease followed standard industry practices, but one portion was unusual. Royalties were not to be paid in cash or oil but in certificates the navy could redeem for oil products or oil storage tanks. Money would have simply gone into the federal Treasury, and oil would have done the navy little good without tanks in which it could be stored. This scheme cleverly gave the navy both the oil and tanks it needed. Only two parts of the deal were suspicious: all the business would go to Mammoth Oil, and the contract had been made without competitive bidding. A week later, a similar contract was announced on the California fields with Doheny's company and included the provision that the oil was to be exchanged for oil, storage tanks, and port facilities at Pearl Harbor.

At this point, the arrangements, strange as they seemed, attracted little public attention. Even the fervently Democratic *New York World* confined itself to criticizing the secretiveness under which the new policy had been developed, calling it "underground government." The conservationists, through La Follette, succeeded in getting a Senate resolution on April 21 to require Interior to supply information about the leases. A week later La Follette subjected the Senate to a scathing speech calling for an investigation into why Mammoth Oil was being favored "by the Government with a special privilege in value beyond the dreams of Croesus?" (Both Doheny and Sinclair initially estimated their leases were worth $100 million.) Properly shamed, the next day the Senate voted 58 to 0 to investigate. Of those 58 votes, 39 were Republicans. Later, when Democrats tried to pin the scandal on the GOP, the Republicans could point to their willingness to investigate their own administration.

La Follette had requested that the Public Lands Committee hear the bill to authorize the investigation rather than the Naval Affairs Committee, which was filled with die-hard supporters of the administration. Public Lands had enough mavericks that it just might make something of the investigation. In the end, Sen. Thomas J. Walsh of Montana, a Democrat whom La Follette persuaded to head the investigation, would prove a wise choice. Although he cared little about conservation, Walsh was a man of integrity and obsessed with honest government. When he sensed corruption, he was relentless in its pursuit.

Eighteen months went by between the authorization of the investigation and the day hearings began. The main reason for the delay was the huge quantity of material that Fall had supplied the Senate, and the fact that Walsh, who had to review it, was one of the busiest men in Congress. As a result, the hearings began after Fall had resigned. On January 2, 1923, he announced that he was leaving office on March 4 to take care of business in New Mexico. He left office with his reputation intact, as did President Harding, who died August 2, after a brief illness. (See Coolidge chapter for more on the Teapot Dome scandal.)

HARRY M. DAUGHERTY, ATTORNEY GENERAL

Harding's friend Harry M. Daugherty was a source of ongoing controversy and scandal in the Harding administration. Rep. Oscar E. Keller introduced a resolution calling for Daugherty's impeachment on fourteen separate charges, including failure to prosecute indicted criminals and for his handling of the 1922 railroad strike.

On September 10, 1922, Rep. Oscar Keller, Republican of Minnesota, introduced a resolution calling for the impeachment of Attorney General Harry M. Daugherty. Keller did not submit the fourteen charges he said supported his call for impeachment until December. Even then, he was able to provide evidence on only two charges, and that evidence was far from impressive. His claim that Daugherty was not enforcing the railway safety appliance law was so weak that Keller's own lawyer admitted it was inadequate. Only marginally better was his charge that Daugherty's appointee to head the Bureau of Investigations, William J. Burns, was unscrupulous. The Judiciary Committee voted 12 to 2 that Keller had not substantiated his charges.

The allegations made Daugherty fighting mad. Two years earlier both Democrats and Republicans had tried to keep Harding from naming him attorney general by claiming he was not up to the job, which made Daugherty all the more eager to prove them wrong. Once in office, however, his inadequacies at prosecuting antitrust and war fraud cases made him consider resigning. Charges of corruption and incompetence would again make him determined to prove his critics wrong. That December before the House Judiciary Committee he claimed, "Back of this so-called impeachment stand arrayed certain radical leaders of certain organizations seeking to serve notice upon every future Attorney General that if he dare enforce the laws of the United States against such organizations, he does so under the pain and penalty of being haled before the Senate of the United States, sitting as a high court of impeachment under the Constitution."

Radical and some not-so-radical leaders had good reason to want Daugherty removed from office. During the war, Wilson's attorney general, A. Mitchell Palmer, had responded to public anger and fear by arresting radicals who opposed the war effort. After the war, the Wilson administration had refused to release 197 political prisoners, among them Socialist Eugene Debs and revolutionaries who belonged to the Industrial Workers of the World (IWW). With the war over, public fear subsiding, and a different party in office, civil rights groups hoped these political prisoners would be released. Harding was opposed to a general amnesty, but he was quite willing to have records reviewed and men released on an individual basis. He saw a political benefit in releasing Debs.

Harry M. Daugherty

Daugherty prided himself on being a "law and order" attorney general and was not eager to release these prisoners. He had Debs brought from the Atlanta Penitentiary to "present his cause to the executive branch of the Government." Daugherty found Debs quite charming and persuasive and for that reason did not want to release him. "In the world he has undertaken," he said, "those qualities make him a very dangerous man." Daugherty clearly wanted to continue holding these prisoners, not for anything they had done, but for speaking up for what they believed. Such deeds, Daugherty claimed, "are crimes of far greater menace to society and to the government at large than ordinary crimes, for they go to the life and strength of the nation."

Conceding that Debs was elderly, in poor health, and that his continued imprisonment was making him into a martyr, Daugherty advised Harding to commute his sentence, and Debs was set free. Daugherty was more opposed to freeing the approximately 150 IWWs, but from time to time Harding would have some of them released. Those who attached great importance to getting these men freed no doubt believed that with Daugherty out of the way, all of them would be released.

Even more anger was directed at Daugherty for his response to the 1922 railroad strike. That year the railroad companies managed to persuade the National Railroad Labor Board (NRLB) that their economic difficulties were severe enough to call for a 13 percent wage cut among their employees. The American Federation of Labor regarded the NRLB as little more than a tool of management and sent their 400,000 members of shipment unions out on strike. The chairman of the NRLB called the strike illegal and called for men to come forward to replace the striking workers.

The rail strike came on the heels of a coal workers strike that had begun in the spring and was still unresolved, so the stage was set for confrontation. In an era when coal was the primary source of energy and rail the most common form of long distance transportation, the two strikes endangered the nation's economy. Rail workers did not help matters by turning to violence or by abandoning trains and their passengers. The unions were clearly in a mood for confrontation. As one of their officials said, "A strike ain't no pink tea."

Even at his best, Daugherty lacked a disciplined mind and was inclined to see conspiracies where none existed. In the legitimate demands of workers not to have their pay reduced, he began to see a vast communist conspiracy. In late August he managed to persuade Harding, who, as always, was all too willing to accept the advice of friends, that a stern injunction against the strikers was needed. To ensure that it was accepted, he filed the restraining order in the Northern Illinois District Court in Chicago. Its judge, James H. Wilkerson, had been appointed at Daugherty's recommendation only two weeks earlier. No other member of the cabinet was consulted about the injunction.

As a result, on September 1 the most restrictive injunction ever imposed on a labor strike was issued. It forbade peaceful picketing, newspaper interviews, speeches at meetings, or any other form of public communication by the workers or union officials. In addition, the use of union funds to support the workers was banned, and the strike was declared illegal on the flimsiest of grounds.

When they heard the news, several members of Harding's administration were furious. In his *Memoirs,* Interior Secretary Hubert Work noted, "The morning papers brought me the news. I was outraged by its obvious transgression of the most rudimentary rights of men. Walking over to the Cabinet meeting that morning I met Secretary [of State Charles Evans] Hughes. He said that it was outrageous in law as well as in morals." Both Work and Hughes protested to Harding, who insisted that the disputed sections of the injunction be withdrawn. In the weeks that followed, Daugherty extended the injunction twice, removing only a few of the offending passages and attempting to have it converted into a permanent injunction. In later years, he became convinced that it had been his most outstanding achievement.

Perhaps the worst aspect of the injunction was that it came just as the two strikes were coming to an end. For reasons unrelated to the injunction, the coal strike was settled the next day, and the rail strike was already collapsing as the unions ran out of money and faced increasingly hostile actions at the state level. Railroad workers were forced to enter into negotiations with their legal status greatly weakened. Many of them had to accept the loss of their seniority rights, and in some cases a company-controlled union was forced on them. As a result, almost 35 percent of the shopmen refused to go back to work. The events poisoned relations between unions and the Justice Department for years afterward.

Daugherty's viciousness did not stop there. He had William Burns use Bureau of Investigations agents to investigate Representative Keller and search his office for anything that might be used against him. Daugherty's critics responded by pointing out that Keller's inability, with his limited resources, to substantiate his charges did not release the House Committee on the Judiciary from its responsibility to investigate the charges for itself.

Daugherty's problems did not end when Calvin Coolidge replaced Harding in the White House. In the end, his critics would succeed. Reeling from a continuing series of accusations of incompetence and corruption, Daugherty resigned on February 18, 1924.

ENFORCEMENT OF PROHIBITION

The Harding administration was criticized not only for its lax enforcement of Prohibition but also because the White House used alcohol recovered in raids.

When the Wickersham Report was released in January 1930, it noted that both the Eighteenth Amendment and the Volstead Act came "at the time best suited for their adoption and at the worst time for their enforcement." The same can be said for the Harding administration, the first to take office after Prohibition began.

As a U.S. senator, Harding understood the political power of a determined minority of voters who had long fought against the undeniable evils of saloons, liquor, and alcoholism. He was also astute enough to see that wartime patriotism was driving an ordinarily uncommitted majority to feel a need for sterner morality. The times were clearly right for passage of Prohibition. Encouraged by his political manager, Harry Daugherty, Harding became one of Prohibition's staunchest congressional supporters. During Senate debate, an amendment was offered that would extend the ban on the manufacture, sale, and transportation of intoxicating liquor to its purchase and use. Harding was one of only four senators to support the amendment. Later, it was he who offered the amendment setting a six-year time limit on state ratification (extended to seven in the House). That amendment may have won over enough votes to provide the constitutional amendment with the two-thirds majority it needed for passage. Throughout the debate, his constant refrain was, "I want to see this question settled. I want to take it out of the halls of Congress and refer it to the people, who must make the ultimate decision." For members of Congress who were tired of the debate, it was a persuasive argument. However, Harding's public behavior did not reflect what he did in private.

Like many in the "Ohio gang" that formed the nucleus of his administration, Harding liked fine liquor, poker-playing, and beautiful women. As
a result, the very administration charged with keeping the nation "dry" was
one of the "wettest" on record. With a sneer, Theodore Roosevelt's daughter, Alice Longworth, described how the Harding White House practiced
two kinds of hospitality. Ordinary guests were kept downstairs and served
fruit juices. The more privileged guests went upstairs, where "trays with
bottles containing every imaginable brand of whiskey stood about." Harding, Longworth added, "was not a bad man. He was just a slob." Sloppiness
and an indifference to the corruption around him characterized his administration's enforcement of Prohibition much as it did its enforcement of
virtually every other law. Harding had been elected on the promise to
return the nation to "normalcy" after the wartime shortages and global
moralizing of the Wilson administration. Many went beyond that easy normalcy to a wild and reckless abandon that became known as the Roaring
Twenties. That attitude meant that Prohibition came just at the time when
enforcement was next to impossible.

Rumors suggested that much of the whiskey at the White House came
from raids lead by Prohibition Bureau agents. Congress had passed Prohibition, but showed little interest in seeing it properly enforced. (Like the
White House, Congress had its own hideaways for drinking.) The Prohibition Bureau was placed under the Treasury Department rather than the
more appropriate Justice Department. Because the wealthy Andrew Mellon, who was the secretary of the Treasury, had once owned stock in a distillery, Prohibitionists charged that he had a reason to be lax in enforcement. Mellon was honest and capable—rare traits in the Harding
administration—but other difficulties hampered the bureau's effective-
ness. The commissioner of Internal Revenue did not want the thankless
task of administering the bureaus. Because Congress exempted the
bureau's agents from the civil service, it was filled with political appointees
and incompetents. Even if they had been competent, they were too few in
number to be effective. Pay was low, training poor, turnover high, and
bribery as widespread as it was difficult to prove. On the rare occasions
when enforcement was vigorous, it often resulted from wiretapping,
which made Americans uneasy. At times, gun battles between agents and
bootleggers resulted in the deaths of innocent bystanders. Stanley Walker,
city editor of the New York *Herald Tribune,* spoke for many in the larger
cities when he pointed out that despite the presence of a few good agents,
"as a class ... they made themselves offensive beyond words, and their
multifarious doings made them the pariahs of New York."

Historians remain divided over whether Prohibition might have been
more successful if strict, early enforcement had prevented bootlegging
from developing into a lucrative business with the power to buy not only
ordinary Prohibition agents and police officers but also people high up in
government. After he was successfully prosecuted, George Remus, nick-

named the King of Bootleggers, lamented: "I tried to corner the graft market, only to find that there is not enough money in the world to buy up all the public officials who demand a share in the graft." Under oath, Remus claimed to have paid $250,000 to an assistant to the attorney general, in exchange for protection from prosecution.

E. MONT REILY, GOVERNOR OF PUERTO RICO

E. Mont Reily was criticized for his colonial mentality and for his attacks on pro-independence citizens of Puerto Rico. His governorship eventually led to a congressional investigation of his actions.

Before he became president, Warren Harding regarded Mont Reily, a newspaper editor and friend from Kansas City, as a "regular nut." Harding's attorney general, Harry Daugherty, called him a "queer duck" who was eager to convert his early support for a Harding presidency into a lucrative government position. To get rid of him, on May 6, 1921, Harding nominated Reily governor of Puerto Rico. It proved to be a disastrous choice.

An independence movement was growing in Puerto Rico. Arthur Yager, the governor who preceded Reily, warned that his replacement would need to display a great deal of tact or he would alienate the population. He also urged that the new governor arrive in June, when the new fiscal year began. Instead, Reily began by offending the Puerto Ricans. He took the oath of office in Kansas City on May 16 but delayed his departure for Puerto Rico until late July because of personal business. Even before he arrived, residents began to hear things about their new governor that they did not like. With a great deal of insight, *La Correspondencia* noted that Reily possessed "negligent ignorance" about the island and an even "greater incompetence in discretion and tact which a person in his position should have."

Harding had ample warning about Reily's intended style of governing. Among the Reily papers is a copy of his inaugural speech with handwritten corrections by the president himself. Where Reily referred to himself as "Governor or ruler," Harding altered the text to read "Governor or executive." When Reily referred to the territory "over which I may rule," Harding changed "rule" to "administer." The president did not alter passages in which Reily advocated the vote for women (regarded as a local matter), denounced those who wanted independence, demanded more education in English rather than the island's native Spanish, and called for Puerto Rican statehood.

At one point Harding wrote to Reily and suggested that he either become more tactful or develop a thick skin. Reily did neither. The more he was attacked, the more violently he fought back, refusing to cooperate with the Puerto Rican Senate and firing officials who disagreed with him.

In a show of shoddy superpatriotism, Reily became obsessed with the one-star Puerto Rican flag that some were promoting. He bluntly told one audience, "Neither, my friends, is there any room on this island for any flag other than … the Stars and Stripes, and there never will be." He was also quoted as referring to the island's flag as "a dirty rag." When he arrived, the flag was primarily a symbol of the Unionist Party. By the time he left, it was well on the way to becoming a well-recognized symbol of the entire island. Soon what little support Reily had came only from "continentals" (Americans who had moved to Puerto Rico) and the rich. With the growing contempt he acquired a nickname, *Moncho Reyes*—Monty the Superking—and opposition newspapers began to refer to him as an "Emperor" or their "Darling Caesar."

By early 1922 Reily was also clashing with his immediate superior, Brig. Gen. Frank B. McIntyre, head of the Bureau of Insular Affairs. Sensing that his political troubles in Puerto Rico could cause problems back home, he began to write directly to the president, bypassing McIntyre. Harding continued to support his appointee, but others in the administration began to express their doubts. In August Secretary of War John W. Weeks wrote to Harding, "I am somewhat disturbed to see that the Governor seems to be making a clean sweep of officers in Puerto Rico."

By spring 1922 Reily had acquired an urgent reason to make sure his men occupied all the positions of power. On April 7, after several months of investigation, a San Juan grand jury brought charges of misuse of public funds against Reily and two of his assistants. The judge, Charles E. Foote, was a Reily man and refused to accept the grand jury's report. To keep the district attorney from moving against him, Reily fired him, and, when he refused to leave, Reily had the police remove him physically from his office. Historians are divided as to whether Reily was actually guilty or, as he claimed, the victim of a political attack, but his zeal to block any attempt to try him strongly suggests his guilt.

Members of the U.S. Congress began to get involved in the controversy. Horace M. Towner of Iowa, chairman of the House Committee on Insular Affairs, described Reily's behavior as "most embarrassing." Harding defended Reily in an April 15 press release, but by May was admitting in private that Reily had shown "very poor discretion." At the end of August he wrote to Towner, saying that Reily was not handling the Puerto Rican situation with "all the tact and poise that conditions require." During the winter several calls for an investigation were voiced because, in addition to his other misdeeds, Reily seemed to be filling positions with people whose only qualifications were friendship with him. No congressional investigation took place, but in January 1923 Sen. Albert B. Cummins suggested that the president replace Reily with Representative Towner.

Perhaps sensing that his difficulties had reached a critical point, in mid-December 1922 Reily returned to the United States. At that point, fate provided him with a graceful exit. While in Kansas City he had an automobile accident in which he claimed to have broken six ribs. Returning to Puerto Rico in early February, he found the combination of the accident and sea voyage had brought on a nervous breakdown. On February 16 he cabled his resignation to Harding, effective April 1. Harding eagerly accepted it and on March 4 named Towner as Reily's replacement.

CHARLES R. FORBES, DIRECTOR OF THE VETERANS BUREAU

Charles Forbes was convicted for selling hospital supplies as surplus material and profiting personally from the transactions.

Few criminals have been bolder than Charles R. Forbes, head of the Veterans Bureau under Warren Harding. With 30,000 employees and a budget of almost half a billion dollars, Forbes had many opportunities to steal, and he took full advantage of them.

The army's Quartermaster General Office had been placed under Forbes's control, and following World War I there were vast quantities of surplus materials. Forbes created a list of "damaged" items and managed to get the coordinator of the budget to approve their sale. He then added other items to the approved list—tripling its size—and sold the merchandise to friends at deeply discounted prices. For example, more than 80,000 bedsheets, almost all of them new and bought for $1 each, were sold for 20 cents apiece; more than 1 million towels bought at 54 cents were sold for 3 cents. All told, some $6 million in readily marketable goods were sold for $600,000 and transported from federal warehouses in 155 freight cars. In some cases, a particular item would be going out the back door at a discounted price at almost the same time a similar item was coming in the front door at a grossly inflated price.

Congress had given the Veterans Bureau $17 million to build new hospitals across the country. Forbes saw that as another opportunity for scams. He paid inflated prices for the land on which the hospitals were to be built and got kickbacks in exchange. In Missouri he paid $90,000 for land worth $35,000. In California he paid $105,000 for land a friend had purchased for less than $20,000 and received a $25,000 kickback. Forbes also hoped to get rich on hospital construction. Friends would get an advance look at the site, so they could plan their bids more carefully. Sealed bids submitted by others would be opened so friends would know precisely what to bid in order to win.

Like many of Harding's foolish appointments, Forbes shared the president's taste for women, liquor, and poker-playing. The two had met in Hawaii in 1915, when Harding was on a senatorial junket and Forbes was a colonel overseeing the construction of the naval base at Pearl Harbor. Neither Attorney General Harry Daugherty nor Surgeon General Charles E. Sawyer liked the Forbes appointment, but Harding was convinced he had made a wise choice. "With his fine record as a soldier," Harding told Daugherty, "and his genius for making friends he'll do great work there."

Forbes's downfall began with Harding's sister, Carolyn Votaw. As was his habit, Forbes flirted with her, and she fell for him and joined his life of partying. When their romance waned, however, she decided to tell Sawyer about Forbes's schemes. In January 1923 Sawyer took his evidence to Daugherty, who then went to the president. According to one report, Harding was so enraged at the personal betrayal that the next time he met Forbes he shoved his friend against a wall and screamed, "You yellow rat! You double-crossing bastard!"

Harding was unable to keep the story from coming out. Newspapers began to carry it, and on February 12 the Senate passed a resolution calling for an investigation. Forbes's testimony was not particularly convincing. "I worked sixteen long hours a day," he told Congress, "and I have been charged with inefficiency." Despite his anger, Harding allowed Forbes to flee to Europe before accepting his resignation on February 15. Forbes's general counsel, Charles F. Cramer, took a more radical approach. He went into a bathroom and shot himself.

In the winter of 1924 and 1925 Forbes was tried, convicted, sentenced to two years in prison, and fined $10,000. Given the magnitude of his theft, the sentence was light. It was the first scandal of the Harding administration to become public.

HARDING'S DEATH

Harding's untimely death led to rumors that his wife had killed him.

In 1930 Gaston Means published a sensational book, *The Strange Death of President Harding,* in which he suggested that Florence Harding had poisoned her husband. Means, a former agent of the Bureau of Investigations, who had served time for bootlegging and fraud, offered two possible theories as to why she might have done it. The first was that she was angry about his marital infidelities and could no longer take it. The second theory was that she hoped to prevent him from being drawn further into the Teapot Dome scandal and possibly impeached. Means painted the events of the Hardings' cross-country trip in the worst possible light, including portraying the president's brief bout of food poisoning as a failed murder attempt. He also questioned Florence Harding's reasons for not having an autopsy done to determine an exact cause of Harding's death. Means's theories cannot be disproved, but historians have generally discounted them.

BIBLIOGRAPHY

Bates, J. Leonard. *The Origins of Teapot Dome: Progressives, Parties and Petroleum, 1909–1921.* Westport, Conn.: Greenwood Press, 1963.

Behr, Edward. *Prohibition.* New York: Arcade Publications, 1996.

Britton, Nan. *The President's Daughter.* New York: Elizabeth Ann Guild, 1927.

Clark, Truman R. *Puerto Rico and the United States, 1917–1933.* Pittsburgh: University of Pittsburgh Press, 1975.

Daugherty, Harry M. *The Inside Story of the Harding Tragedy.* New York: Churchill, 1932.

Ferrell, Robert H. *The Strange Death of President Harding.* Columbia: University of Missouri Press, 1996.

Giglio, James N. *H. M. Daugherty and the Politics of Expediency.* Kent: Kent State University Press, 1978.

Hagood, Wesley O. *Presidential Sex: From Founding Fathers to Bill Clinton.* Secaucus, N.J.: Carol Publishing, 1998.

Means, Gaston. *The Strange Death of President Harding, from the diaries of Gaston B. Means, as told to May Dixon Thacker.* New York: Guild Publishing, 1930.

Mee, Charles L. *The Ohio Gang: The World of Warren G. Harding.* New York: M. Evans, 1981.

Merz, Charles. *The Dry Decade.* Garden City, N.Y.: Doubleday, Doran, 1931.

Mitchell, Jack. *Executive Privilege: Two Centuries of White House Scandals.* New York: Hippocrene Books, 1992.

Murray, Robert K. *The Harding Era: Warren G. Harding and His Administration.* Minneapolis: University of Minnesota Press, 1969.

Noggle, Burl. *Teapot Dome: Oil and Politics in the 1920's.* Baton Rouge: Louisiana State University Press, 1962.

O'Connor, Harvey. *Mellon's Millions: The Biography of Fortune.* New York: John Day, 1933.

Ravage, M. E. *The Story of Teapot Dome.* New York: Republic Publishing, 1924.

Russell, Francis. *The Shadow of Blooming Grove: Warren G. Harding in His Times.* New York: McGraw-Hill, 1968.

Schmeckebier, Laurence F. *The Bureau of Prohibition.* Washington, D.C.: Brookings, 1929.

Sinclair, Andrew. *The Available Man: The Life Behind the Masks of Warren Gamaliel Harding.* Chicago: Quadrangle Books, 1965.

———. *Era of Excess.* New York: Harper and Row, 1962.

Stratton, David H. *Tempest over Teapot Dome: The Story of Albert B. Fall.* Norman: University of Oklahoma Press, 1998.

Weisner, Herman B. *The Politics of Justice: A. B. Fall and the Teapot Dome Scandal.* Albuquerque: Creative Designs, 1988.

Werner, M. R. *Teapot Dome.* New York: Viking Press, 1959.

Woodward, C. Vann. *Responses of the Presidents to Charges of Misconduct.* New York: Dell Publishing, 1974.

CALVIN COOLIDGE

Thirtieth President
1923–1929

Calvin Coolidge was born July 4, 1872, in Plymouth, Vermont, the elder of John and Victoria Coolidge's two children. John Coolidge was a farmer and owner of a general store, and Calvin's early ambition was to be a storekeeper like his father. An average student, he failed the admissions exam to Amherst College in 1891 and enrolled at St. Johnsbury Academy in Ludlow, Vermont. Earning a college entrance certificate, he was automatically enrolled at Amherst, where he continued to be an average student. He graduated in 1895 and, because of his wit, was selected by his classmates to deliver the Grove Oration, a traditionally irreverent, satirical address. After studying law for two years, he was admitted to the bar in July 1897.

Coolidge practiced law in Northampton, Massachusetts, where he became active in the Republican Party. He was elected to the city council in 1900 and served as city solicitor from 1900 to 1902. He suffered his only electoral defeat in 1905, when he lost the race for school board. That same year on October 4, he married Grace Anna Goodhue.

Coolidge was a champion of progressive ideas, including a six-day workweek and labor laws to protect women and children. In 1906 he was elected to the Massachusetts House of Representatives. After two terms he returned to Northampton and was elected mayor in 1910. He cut taxes while eliminating the city's debt and expanded police and fire services and road and sidewalk construction. A state senator from 1912 to 1915, he spent the last two years as senate president. Starting in 1916 he served three terms as lieutenant governor before being elected governor in a close election in 1918. As governor, he gained national attention when he used state militia to replace striking Boston policemen and when he supported the mayor's decision not to rehire the strikers.

At the 1920 Republican Party convention in Chicago, Coolidge was a favorite-son candidate, receiving thirty-four votes on the first ballot. The nomination went to Warren G. Harding, but when Sen. Irvine Lenroot of

Wisconsin was nominated for vice president, many in the hall started chanting Coolidge's name. The convention chose Coolidge as Harding's running mate on the first ballot. Harding died August 2, 1923. Coolidge was vacationing in Vermont when word of Harding's death reached him just after midnight on August 3. Coolidge's father, a notary public, administered the oath of office.

In the first national convention to be broadcast on radio, in June 1924 in Cleveland, the Republicans nominated Coolidge for a full term. Charles G. Dawes of Illinois was nominated on the third ballot as his running mate. Coolidge handily won a three-man race that included Democrat John W. Davis of West Virginia and the Progressive candidate Robert La Follette of Wisconsin.

During his administration, Coolidge pursued a conservative economic program, cutting taxes in 1924 and 1926. He repeatedly vetoed farm relief measures that he though imprudent. He backed the Kellogg-Briand Pact of 1928, which renounced war as a means of settling international disputes.

Coolidge declined to seek another term, but it is not clear that the Republican Party wanted him to run again anyway. Many speculated that he stepped aside because he saw the onset of an economic depression; others believed that he was in failing health. His wife said that he knew he was not suited for the increased federal spending that would be necessary in the coming years as he had always been a fiscal conservative. He retired to Northampton to write newspaper columns as well as his autobiography. He campaigned for Herbert Hoover in 1928 and 1932 and died January 5, 1933, of a coronary thrombosis.

TEAPOT DOME

Although the oil lease scandals started before Coolidge took office, the investigations and prosecutions took place during his administration. (See Harding chapter.)

One of the first items facing the new administration was the opening of the Teapot Dome hearings, which began on October 22, 1923. Congress was at last ready to investigate the leasing of naval oil reserves to private companies. The former attorney general, Albert B. Fall, testified for two full days. Clashing with Democratic senator Thomas B. Walsh of Montana, Fall justified his policy as necessary for the nation's defense. As the hearings progressed, from time to time tantalizing hints indicated that something was amiss, but neither the press nor most of the committee members seemed to think the hearings were worth the effort. In December, however, Walsh began to hear rumors about "some significant land deals in New Mexico." It seemed that in the fall of 1923, when other local ranchers were suffering from a drought and depressed cattle prices, Fall suddenly had enough money to enlarge and improve his ranch. In testimony before the committee, oilmen Edward L. Doheny and Henry F. Sinclair both denied giving Fall any money. In December Fall made what he later said was the biggest mistake of his life. He sent Walsh a letter in which he claimed that his sudden prosperity had come from a $100,000 loan from Edward B. McLean, publisher of the *Washington Post*. At the end of December one observer said, "The impression in Washington is that Senator Walsh is up against a stone wall." Another termed the whole thing a mere "tempest in a teapot."

Then Walsh received an invitation to visit McLean, who was in Palm Beach for his health. Earlier, McLean had confirmed the Fall loan in a telegram, but said he would be willing to talk to the committee members if they came to Florida. Although he was discouraged about the investigation and planned to end it, Walsh went to Florida. There, on January 12, he was "dumbfounded" to discover that McLean now denied lending money to Fall. Because Fall was also in Palm Beach, Walsh asked him for a statement. Fall admitted that the money he had used on his ranch had not come from McLean, but continued to claim that the source was "in no way connected with Mr. Sinclair." He was technically right: the $100,000 had come from Doheny. Sinclair had provided Fall with $233,000 in Liberty bonds and $36,000 in cash. Altogether, Fall had taken about $409,000 from the two men.

Overnight a dull debate over oil and defense policy was transformed into a tantalizing tale of bribery, perjury, and cover-up involving two of the wealthiest men in the country. From that moment Fall was doomed, although he fought the accusations for years. For the committee, the difficulty lay in tracing money from Doheny and Sinclair to Fall. At this point Archie Roosevelt, one of Theodore Roosevelt's sons, came forward. He had not been involved himself, but reported that Sinclair's private secretary had told him about $68,000 that had been given to Fall's ranch foreman. The secretary denied it, but Roosevelt's January 21 testimony was followed on January 24 by Doheny's confession to the committee that on November 30, 1921, he had loaned Fall $100,000 in cash, sending it to him "in a little black bag." The next day, one of Sinclair's lawyers admitted to giving Fall "$25,000 or $30,000 in bonds" after Fall resigned. Two days later President Coolidge announced that he would be appointing "special counsel of high rank drawn from both political parties" to prosecute those who had violated the law.

When the story first broke, the Democratic Party hoped it would help them in the 1924 elections. That did not happen. Doheny, it turned out, was a Democrat, and he had been quite generous both to the party and to members of Woodrow Wilson's cabinet. One of the recipients of his generosity was William G. McAdoo, Wilson's secretary of the Treasury, and the leading contender for the party's presidential nomination. Only five days after he confessed to giving $100,000 to Fall, Doheny told the Senate committee that after McAdoo had resigned from the Treasury, Doheny had hired him "to represent us in Washington in connection with Mexican matters." Doheny testified that he had paid McAdoo $250,000 but later amended the amount to $100,000, exactly what he had paid Fall. The news destroyed McAdoo's chance for the presidency, but did nothing to hurt Coolidge.

To its credit, the Coolidge administration worked hard to undo the mess that Fall had created. On May 28, 1925, a Los Angeles judge ruled that Doheny's $100,000 loan had been a bribe and therefore the Elk Hills oil field contract was invalid. Doheny appealed and lost. He then appealed to the Supreme Court and on February 28, 1927, lost again. The Court ruled that Doheny could not even ask the government to repay his expenses at Elk Hills and Pearl Harbor.

On June 19, 1925, another judge in Wyoming declared Sinclair's lease on Teapot Dome still valid. The government, he pointed out, had been unable to submit direct proof that Fall had received the $233,000 from Sinclair. The government appealed and won. Sinclair then appealed to the Supreme Court and lost on October 10, 1927.

With unflagging persistence, Walsh uncovered the trail of the $233,000. From the serial numbers, he traced the money back to a Canadian corporation called Continental Trading Company. It was a scam set up to enrich its investors (including Sinclair) by buying oil at $1.50 a barrel and selling it at $1.75 without ever touching the oil. In less than a year and a half, it made more than $2 million for a few people. The corporation was then liquidated and its records destroyed. All those who might have known what happened to the bonds were either out of the country or claimed to know nothing. The only possible source of information was M. T. Everhart, Fall's son-in-law, and he refused to testify on the grounds that doing so might incriminate him. Refusing to give up, Walsh eliminated that objection by getting Congress to change the statute of limitations, so that Everhart's testimony could not be used against him. Four years after his original hearings, he was able to force Everhart to be the first witness at new Teapot Dome hearings, which began on January 24, 1928. Under duress, Everhart admitted that in May 1922 Sinclair had given him $233,000 in Liberty bonds that he had passed on to Fall.

The criminal prosecutions of Fall, Doheny, and Sinclair produced mixed results. All were indicted in June 1924 and charged with conspiracy and bribery. In November 1926 Fall and Doheny were tried for conspiracy. The jury found them innocent. In March 1927 Sinclair was tried and found in contempt of the Senate for an earlier refusal to testify. Seven months later he and Fall went to trial for conspiracy. Sinclair attempted to tamper with the jury and was discovered. A mistrial was declared, and Sinclair received a sentence of six months. In April 1928 again Sinclair went on trial for conspiracy. His $233,000 payment to Fall was now proved, but a jury found him innocent. In October Fall, now in ill health, went on trial for bribery and was found guilty and sentenced to one year. In March 1930 Doheny faced the same judge in the same courtroom, charged with offering the bribe that Fall had been found guilty of accepting. A jury found him innocent. Despite the best efforts of prosecutors, only Fall served time in prison for Teapot Dome. Sen. George W. Norris of Nebraska was so disgusted that he remarked sarcastically, "We ought to pass a law that no man worth $100 million should be tried for a crime."

On July 18, 1931, his appeals exhausted, an almost penniless Fall was taken to prison. Because of his poor health, he was allowed to serve his time in the New Mexico state penitentiary rather than a federal prison. President Hoover refused to grant him a pardon, and the parole board denied his application for early release. He spent his time in the prison hospital, earning release for good behavior after nine months and nineteen days. Doheny's $100,000 allowed him to assume control over Fall's ranch, but he allowed Fall to live there. After Doheny's death, Fall was evicted. His only income was a small pension from the Spanish-American War. In 1942, with money rumored to have come from Doheny's widow, Fall was placed in Hotel Dieu, a Catholic hospital in El Paso. He died November 20, 1944.

HARRY M. DAUGHERTY, ATTORNEY GENERAL

Harry Daugherty, who had been investigated during the Harding administration, came under investigation during Coolidge's tenure for illegal liquor dealings and defrauding the government in connection with his administration of the Office of the Alien Property Custodian.

When Calvin Coolidge took over the presidency, he did as expected and retained Harding's cabinet. One member, Attorney General Harry M. Daugherty, proved to be particularly troublesome. Accusations of corruption would haunt his days in office. Daugherty came from Ohio at a time when the state had an enormous influence on the Republican Party. He was exceptionally loyal to the party and to Harding. Newly elected, Harding told one critic, "I would not want the country to think me so much an ingrate that I would ignore a man of Mr. Daugherty's devotion to the party and to me as an aspirant and a candidate."

Others were more critical. Some objections to Daugherty's appointment were based on his incompetence. When Daugherty asked an old friend, J. O. A. Preus, to assist his nomination, Preus replied: "You're not qualified, Harry, to be Attorney General. You ought to know it and I think I know it." Other objections were based on his background as a lobbyist: getting paid to represent one side of an issue is poor training for an office that requires balance and objectivity. Both shortcomings were evident when Harding discovered that, with a railroad strike threatening, Daugherty had appointed railroad officials to be U.S. marshals. Criticism only led Daugherty to complain that Harding "never took any advice from me about anything . . . and on the whole considers me of very little good."

Daugherty's critics warned that the country needed an exceptionally talented attorney general. A. Mitchell Palmer, Wilson's attorney general, had left the Justice Department in disarray. Obsessed with fears of a Bolshevik revolution, Palmer had neglected other responsibilities, and cases involving Prohibition and various other reforms were flooding the federal courts. Charges of widespread corruption were beginning to surface, particularly in cases involving the tens of millions of dollars of alien (mostly German) property seized during the war (see page 246.) Not only was Daugherty inadequate for the job, but also his belief in the spoils system led him to appoint people who were incompetent or crooked.

The case that got Daugherty into the most trouble involved the German-owned stock of the American Metal Company. The stock had been seized by the Office of the Alien Property Custodian in 1918 and auctioned off in 1919. After the war, Richard Merton, president of the German corporation that had owned the stock, came to the United States for compensation. He claimed that the seizure was illegal because the stock had been transferred to a Swiss holding company one month before the war began. In fact, the transfer had not taken place until 1919, but, in an effort to evade the law, a fictitious 1917 oral agreement was created.

To reinforce a weak case, Merton needed supporters. John T. King, a member of the Republican National Committee, became involved and introduced Merton to Jesse Smith. Smith was so close to Daugherty that, although he was not a Justice Department employee, he had a desk there, courtesy of Daugherty. That desk gave the impression (probably correct) that Smith had influence with the attorney general and enabled him to take bribes. Merton was also introduced to Thomas W. Miller, an alien property custodian. With their help, on September 26, 1921, Merton received $6.5 million in Treasury checks and Liberty bonds.

By spring 1922 enough evidence of Smith's shady dealings had been presented to Harding that he met with Daugherty and insisted that Smith must go. Claiming to be stunned at his friend's deeds, Daugherty agreed to get rid of him. On May 25 Smith moved out of the Justice Department building; four days later he retrieved his papers from the building and destroyed them. The next day he committed suicide. In June a disgruntled Justice Department employee gave Harding a list of doubtful claims, one of which was for the American Metal Company. Daugherty defended the compensations, but the president remained suspicious enough that he began to review all claims over $10,000.

When Coolidge entered the White House, Daugherty made an effort to convince him that he was doing a good job. Coolidge remained skeptical but hesitated to act, knowing Daugherty's political connections. In early 1924, however, Senate investigations into possible ties between Daugherty and the Teapot Dome scandal made Coolidge look for an excuse to replace him. When Daugherty refused to permit the committee to see some Justice files, Coolidge asked for his resignation. On March 28, Daugherty complied.

Senate investigations into the Justice Department led in turn to Jesse Smith, and Smith led back to the American Metal Company settlement. Twice the government tried to convict Daugherty. The first trial began on September 7, 1926, in New York City and ended when the jury voted 7–5 for conviction. The second trial began on February 7 and got closer to conviction with only one juror holding out. Although the prosecution could trace some of Merton's payoff back through the now-dead Smith to Daugherty, Daugherty claimed the money was a repayment for money owed since the 1920 elections. Because Daugherty had deliberately destroyed his bank records in an effort, he claimed, to conceal a scandal involving the late President Harding, the final chapter in the case could never be closed beyond a shadow of a doubt.

For the rest of his life, Daugherty denied that he was guilty of any wrongdoing. In 1932 he published a book, *The Inside Story of the Harding Tragedy,* that attempted to prove his innocence. But his success at avoiding a criminal conviction rests on other grounds: his refusal to cooperate with investigators, his aggressive destruction of any records that might incriminate him, and his willingness to shield himself behind claims that he was acting to protect Harding from scandal. It is ironic that a man who got into office as a reward for his loyalty would end up trying to protect his reputation by violating that loyalty.

FORD-COOLIDGE DEAL

President Coolidge was accused of making a deal with industrialist Henry Ford to secure Ford's political support and a guarantee that he would not challenge Coolidge for the Republican nomination in 1924.

During World War I, the difficulty of getting enough nitrates from Chile for munitions led the federal government to begin an expensive series of projects near Muscle Shoals in the Tennessee River Valley of northern Alabama. To power the project, more than $16 million was spent on Wilson Dam, which was still less than one-third complete. More than $67 million was spent on one nitrate plant, and $13 million on another. After the war neither plant was in production, and their maintenance was running $250,000 a year. Only a steam plant, built at a cost of $5 million, was in use, and it was leased to the Alabama Power Company.

The region's poverty provided an additional incentive to act quickly. About 4 million people lived in southern Appalachia, most of them farmers in dire straits. Because flooding stripped away the topsoil, the area around Muscle Shoals was particularly poor. Only 2 percent of the area's farmers had electricity, even though they lived only a few miles from a dam, which, if completed, would generate abundant power.

The government was disposing of wartime projects for a fraction of their cost, and it seemed reasonable to do the same with those around Muscle Shoals. Farm leaders, particularly those in the Farm Bureau Federation, wanted to help the region's poor population and develop its nitrate plants to produce inexpensive fertilizer. In their search for someone with the skill and resources to take over the projects, they approached Henry Ford, whose Model T car and Fordson tractor were transforming rural life.

After studying the projects, Ford said his main objective would be to provide fertilizer to farmers at low cost and to maintain the plants' ability to be converted back to military use should that become necessary. He visited Muscle Shoals with his friend Thomas Edison and submitted a bid to the War Department on January 25, 1922. Ford offered to form a corporation that would complete Wilson Dam and one other dam for the government at cost and lease them for a century. He would buy the nitrate plants for $5 million and guarantee to manufacture fertilizer for sale to farmers at a profit of 8 percent or less. In addition, he would ensure that the larger plant was always available to make explosives and promised it could be transferred back to the government on five days' notice. Depending on how the interest was calculated, over the next century Ford would be paying the government between $50 million and $70 million on its investment. That return was far better than the approximately $4 million the government had received for the $80 million it had put into the Old Hickory Powder Plant.

A number of groups quickly spoke out for the plan. Agricultural groups such as the National Grange joined the Farm Bureau in favor of it. Many southern organizations, newspapers, and members of Congress also backed it. At its 1922 convention, the American Federation of Labor voted its approval.

But the plan also had foes, including Secretary of War John Weeks. Ford believed Weeks intended to get more money for the War Department by selling the projects off piecemeal. The steam plant had already been sold, and Ford claimed that one by one the other projects would follow, spelling "the end of Muscle Shoals as a possible demonstration of the cheapness with which power and fertilizer can be produced."

Ford's vision for the Tennessee River Valley required that its assets be kept together. When the prominent conservationist Gifford Pinchot warned, "The Ford plan is seven parts waterpower, one part fertilizer," he was implying that there was something evil in the plan to build dams with power capacity many times greater than the fertilizer plants would need. Ford's plan may have been excessively idealistic, but it was not evil. He spoke of using inexpensive power to create a seventy-five-mile-long city with a wide variety of industries. The city would be so spread out that its workers could live in small semi-rural communities while working at well-paying factory jobs. Ford may have been trying to correct the mistakes of concentrated production that were already obvious in Detroit. His plan for

Calvin Coolidge and Henry Ford

Muscle Shoals was popular with the general public, but had powerful forces arrayed against it. Perhaps the best indication of Ford's good intentions was the opposition mounted by the National Fertilizer Association and public utility magazines.

In addition, the War Department's chief of ordnance and chief of engineers issued a memorandum that put the plan in an unfavorable light. It pointed out that the government would have to invest another $40 million to $50 million to complete the dams. It also said that, although the plants were worth $8 million as scrap, Ford was paying only $5 million for them. But the region's flooding and the need for power meant that the dams would eventually be built, and selling the plants for scrap, while slightly more profitable for the War Department, would leave the country with no ability to covert them to wartime use. As a businessman, Ford was expecting to get a good deal, but it was in no way the robbery his critics claimed.

At the heart of the opposition to the bill was disagreement over the role the government should play in the construction of large hydroelectric dams. The powerful senator, George Norris, believed that the federal government should control all such dams. Ford's plan allowed the government to continue to own Wilson Dam, but he wanted a 100-year lease. A 1920 law limited such leases to fifty years. Longer leases might lead to private ownership.

Complicating matters was another of Ford's ambitions—a desire to transform the popular belief that he could work wonders into a run for the White House. That ambition may have led to a much-discussed meeting between Ford and Coolidge in December 1923. Shortly afterward,

Coolidge sent a message to Congress offering a plan to sell Muscle Shoals. Later that month Ford announced that he would not be running for president and would instead support Coolidge. To critics of Ford's plan, it looked suspiciously like a deal had been made, something neither Ford nor Coolidge ever denied.

For a time, the sale seemed assured. On March 10, 1924, the House voted 227–142 to accept Ford's offer. Only the Senate stood in the way, and Senator Norris used all his skills to block action. When the Nebraska legislature passed a resolution calling for him to change his mind, he fought the bill all the more. The Senate adjourned without acting. Seeing that nothing would come of his scheme as long as Norris opposed it, Ford withdrew his offer on October 15.

On the one hand, given his support for business, Coolidge could back the sale. On the other hand, as one of his biographers has pointed out, as a New England Republican, he had no reason to fight for a plan that would benefit southern Democrats. Finally, in March 1925, at the urging of Sen. Oscar Underwood of Alabama, Coolidge appointed a committee of laymen and scientists to study the sale. In November their report came out, split between the laymen who wanted fertilizer production and scientists who wanted power generation. Ford's bold plan to use both as part of a much vaster scheme had been forgotten.

Coolidge delayed any action until his address to Congress in December 1927, and then he did little more than define the problem, emphasizing power over fertilizer. Because the electric companies were opposed to any scheme that put them in competition with the government, Congress did not act. That same month, Senator Norris, who wanted the Muscle Shoals dams built under federal control, offered legislation that completed the dams but little else. The dams would not be used to develop the region, and the plants would emphasize research rather than cheap fertilizer. Even that watered-down bill died when Coolidge, a foe of federal dam-building, pocket vetoed it. Norris's ideas reappeared during the 1930s when President Franklin D. Roosevelt created the Tennessee Valley Authority. The much-debated dams became the centerpiece of a New Deal scheme to develop the region.

ANDREW MELLON, SECRETARY OF THE TREASURY

Congress investigated whether Andrew Mellon had used his influence as secretary of the Treasury to secure large tax rebates for companies in which he held a personal financial stake.

A scandal can start in many ways, and this one began with an exchange of letters between two very wealthy men, Sen. James Couzens of Michigan and Secretary of the Treasury Andrew Mellon. The topic of discussion was income taxes. Mellon was of the opinion that high tax rates on the very

Andrew Mellon

rich encouraged them to put their money into tax-exempt government securities rather than into investments that stimulated industrial growth. That belief led Mellon to question the senator's large investment in securities and Couzens to reply by asking about Mellon's own investments.

On February 21, 1924, Couzens introduced a Senate resolution demanding an investigation of Mellon's Bureau of Internal Revenue. Because the furor over Teapot Dome was at its height and Congress was intent on asserting its superiority over the executive branch, the Senate easily approved the resolution. Coolidge, however, considered these investigations "nonsense" and a distraction from what he considered really important—revising the tax code and eliminating the national debt. Couzens claimed that Coolidge tried to distract him from his mission by offering to appoint him ambassador to Great Britain. Couzens loudly refused to be "kicked upstairs."

Another Republican then entered the party squabble. Pennsylvania governor Gifford Pinchot, who opposed Mellon and supported Prohibition, claimed that the Internal Revenue Bureau was lax in enforcing Prohibition. He wanted the Senate to investigate the matter and suggested his friend Francis J. Heney for the job. In an era of tight budgets, the Senate questioned where the money for an investigator would come from, so Couzens offered to pay Heney out of his own pocket.

Mellon was outraged at the idea of a privately hired investigator being able to use the authority of Congress to fish through his files looking for something incriminating. He told Coolidge that if the investigation was not halted, he would resign. Coolidge did not want to lose one of the most valuable members of his cabinet. (Later, he was uncharacteristically vocal in Mellon's defense.) One of Couzens's allegations was that Mellon had given huge tax refunds to major corporations, including some in which he was invested. Despite his anger, Mellon cooperated with the investigations and persuaded the corporations to waive their right to privacy so that their records could be made public. The result was less than spectacular. The refunds had run into the millions, but resulted either from clerical errors or from favorable Supreme Court decisions (for example, a decision making stock dividends nontaxable). Other allegations led nowhere, including the claim that Mellon money was invested in an industrial distillery whose alcohol ended up in bootleg whiskey.

Normally, Congress would have dropped an investigation that was yielding so little. But with Couzens picking up the costs, administration foes had no reason to stop. Mellon, justifiably angry, unleashed a counterattack, warning that if "private resources" were allowed to interfere with the executive branch, "the machinery of government will cease to function." Coolidge backed him, claiming that established procedures for investigation were being evaded and hinting that the Treasury Department might refuse to cooperate. Perhaps because the investigation was so difficult to defend, Congress reacted to this criticism with hostility, but in the end it was forced to drop Heney and pay another investigator out of its own funds. The investigations continued for years, but all they proved was that the Bureau of Internal Revenue had been quite liberal in its interpretation of tax laws. Later, FDR's New Deal gleefully used Couzens's data to attack the Republican presidencies of the 1920s, but it did little to alter those policies. However, Couzens's one-man campaign had two enduring results: it ended the legal secrecy that had surrounded corporate tax rebates, and it gave Congress a resident staff of tax experts.

Mellon was correct when he accused Couzens of venting "some personal grievance" with his investigation. At that time the government was suing several Ford executives including Couzens for some $30 million. It claimed that Couzens and the others had come up with a scheme to sell their stock back to Ford in a way that evaded the excess profits tax. The suit was complicated, but years later Couzens and the other executives won and received a refund of $3.6 million. By then, legal fees had devoured much of what they gained.

At this time, the concept of the federal government deriving a major portion of its revenue from income taxes was new. Important precedents were being set, which stimulated intense feelings among the very wealthy. Mellon had one point of view, while Couzens had another, but their squabble was far outside the experience of most Americans. The Coolidge administration was not only committed to reducing taxes and ending the national debt, but also it was systematically working to remove millions of ordinary Americans from the tax rolls. With a large exemption for married couples, in 1927 some 98 percent of the population paid no income tax; in fact, 94 percent of income tax revenue came from the nation's wealthiest 0.3 of 1 percent.

CHARLES BEECHER WARREN, ATTORNEY GENERAL NOMINEE

Charles Warren's nomination ran into opposition in the Senate because of his association with the American Sugar Trust and the Michigan Sugar Company, which was under investigation for price fixing.

On March 4, 1925, President Coolidge nominated Charles Beecher Warren as attorney general. A number of senators opposed the nomination because Warren had been president of the Michigan Sugar Company. While working for the American Sugar Refining Company between 1902 and

1906, Warren had bought the stock of a number of small refineries and organized the Michigan Sugar Company, which was largely owned by the American Sugar Refining Company, the so-called Sugar Trust.

The Federal Trade Commission had recently cited the Michigan Sugar Company for illegally contracting to control the marketing of sugar pulp in violation of the Sherman Antitrust Act. On March 7 the Senate failed to confirm Warren in a tie vote. President Coolidge immediately renominated Warren and stated that he would be given a recess appointment if the Senate again voted against him. On March 18 the Senate voted 46–39 against Warren, who refused to accept a recess appointment.

BIBLIOGRAPHY

Abels, Jules. *In the Time of Silent Cal.* New York: Putnam, 1969.

Giglio, James N. *H. M. Daugherty and the Politics of Expediency.* Kent, Ohio: Kent State University Press, 1978.

Ferrell, Robert H. *The Presidency of Calvin Coolidge.* Lawrence: University Press of Kansas, 1998.

McCoy, Donald R. *Calvin Coolidge: The Quiet President.* New York: Macmillan, 1967.

Mitchell, Jack. *Executive Privilege: Two Centuries of White House Scandals.* New York: Hippocrene Books, 1992.

Nevins, Allan. *Ford.* New York: Scribner's, 1954.

Noggle, Burl. *Teapot Dome: Oil and Politics in the 1920's.* Baton Rouge: Louisiana State University Press, 1962.

O'Connor, Harvey. *Mellon's Millions: The Biography of a Fortune.* New York: John Day, 1933.

Ravage, M. E. *The Story of Teapot Dome.* New York: Republic Publishing, 1924.

Stratton, David H. *Tempest over Teapot Dome: The Story of Albert B. Fall.* Norman: University of Oklahoma Press, 1998.

Weisner, Herman B. *The Politics of Justice: A. B. Fall and the Teapot Dome Scandal.* Albuquerque: Creative Designs, 1988.

Werner, M. R. *Teapot Dome.* New York: Viking Press, 1959.

White, William A. *A Puritan in Babylon: The Story of Calvin Coolidge.* New York: Macmillan, 1938.

Woodward, C. Vann. *Responses of the Presidents to Charges of Misconduct.* New York: Dell Publishing, 1974.

HERBERT HOOVER

Thirty-First President
1929–1933

Born August 10, 1874, in West Branch, Iowa, Herbert Clark Hoover was the second of the three children of Jesse and Huldah Hoover. Jesse Hoover was a blacksmith and farm implement merchant. He died of typhoid when Herbert was six years old. Two years later his mother died of pneumonia, and Herbert was sent to Salem, Oregon, to live with his aunt and uncle, who were Quakers like his parents. He received an uneven education at the local schools, but excelled in mathematics.

Except for math, he failed the exams to enter the first freshman class at Stanford University, a newly established engineering school, but gained admission at the age of seventeen after some remedial work. Hoover studied geology and worked summers with the U.S. Geological Survey in Arkansas, California, and Nevada. Graduating in 1895, he decided to become a mining engineer.

Hoover at first had trouble finding work in his chosen field. He worked in a California gold mine until 1896, when he was hired by a San Francisco company to serve as a mining engineer overseas. His first job was to inspect mines prior to their purchase in Australia. He spent most of the next twenty-four years abroad, building his reputation and a fortune. Hoover returned to the United States to marry Lou Henry, whom he had met while a senior at Stanford, on February 10, 1899. The couple sailed for China, where Hoover's next job was the head mining engineer in developing coal deposits. In 1902 he returned to Australia to work zinc mines. He also worked at the Baldwin silver mine in Burma. In 1908 he established his own engineering company and by 1914 was worth an estimated $4 million. With his fortune made, Hoover turned his interests to philanthropy and government.

After the outbreak of World War I in 1914, Hoover became involved in relief work. He headed efforts to rescue Americans stranded in Europe and organized and directed the Commission for Relief in Belgium. He was responsible for the distribution of more than 34 million tons of aid valued at more than $5 billion. He also served on a number of boards, including the War Trade Council, Sugar Equalization Board, and European Coal Council. He was the economic adviser to President Woodrow Wilson at the Versailles peace conference. In 1919 he founded the Hoover Institution on War, Revolution, and Peace at Stanford University.

President Warren G. Harding appointed Hoover secretary of commerce in 1921, a post he also held during the Coolidge administration. During his tenure he expanded the role of the Bureau of Standards, Census Bureau, and the Bureau of Fisheries. In 1927, with the passage of the Radio Act, the regulation of the air waves came under his jurisdiction. He served on a number of commissions, including those that recommended the construction of the St. Lawrence Seaway and the construction of Boulder Dam (renamed Hoover Dam).

When Calvin Coolidge announced that he would not seek reelection in 1928, Hoover aggressively pursued the Republican Party's nomination, which he easily won on the first ballot. Charles Curtis of Kansas was nominated as his running mate. His Democratic opponent was Alfred E. Smith, the first Roman Catholic to be nominated by a major party. The campaign centered on religion and Prohibition. Vicious anti-Catholic pamphlets were distributed throughout the country, and the Ku Klux Klan even campaigned in the South for Hoover. The Republicans promised to enforce Prohibition, which Smith opposed, and crack down on the illegal alcohol trade and associated crime. Hoover won the fall election (his only elective office) by a margin of 58 percent of the popular vote to 41 percent. The electoral college vote was 444–87. Smith won only eight of the forty-eight states, including six in the deep South.

In October 1929, just seven months after Hoover took office, the stock market crashed. Billions of dollars were lost, unemployment skyrocketed, and the Great Depression was under way. Hoover tried to secure passage of progressive spending packages to aid farmers and others, but it did little good. He signed the Smoot-Hawley Tariff Act, believing that the protectionist measure would help farmers. Despite his efforts, the depression grew worse.

The administration kept its promise to enforce Prohibition, and prosecutions reached record levels. Hoover also signed the London Naval Treaty of 1930, which limited the growth of Europe's navies. The move inadvertently allowed Japan to increase its fleet to the size of the U.S. and British fleets.

Renominated in 1932, Hoover was soundly defeated by Democrat Franklin D. Roosevelt in the general election. He retired to his home in Palo Alto, but spent most of his time in residence at the Waldorf-Astoria Hotel in New York. Hoover was a strong critic of Roosevelt's New Deal. He also criticized the president for his decision to go off the gold standard, to recognize the Soviet Union, and for his attempt to pack the Supreme Court.

During World War II, Hoover served as chairman of relief organizations helping Poland, Finland, and Belgium. He was coordinator of the Food Supply for World Famine in 1946 and 1947. President Harry S. Truman appointed Hoover to chair the Commission on Organization of the Executive Branch of Government from 1947 to 1949, known as the Hoover Commission. He also chaired the Commission on Government Operations from 1953 to 1955. The two commissions recommended nearly 600 specific changes in the way the government operated, and more than 400 of them were adopted.

Hoover continued to support Republican Party candidates throughout his retirement, including Sen. Barry Goldwater for president in 1964. Hoover died a few weeks before the election on October 20. His body lay in state for two days in the Capitol Rotunda before burial in West Branch.

HOOVER AND THE CUBAN SUGAR LOBBYIST

A series of letters implied that Hoover traded information about the sugar tariff to a Cuban sugar interest in return for contributions to his 1928 election campaign fund.

In December 1929 a subcommittee of the Senate Judiciary Committee held hearings into charges that Herbert C. Lakin, a lobbyist for Cuban sugar interests, had engaged in improper activities to keep down the duties on sugar imported from Cuba. With the Great Depression beginning to generate large surpluses in U.S.-grown agricultural products, Cuban growers were anxious that duties on their sugar not be raised. President Hoover and Sen. Reed Smoot of Utah, chairman of the Senate Finance Committee, were drawn into the case because of allegations that Lakin was exerting influence on them through a lawyer named Edwin P. Shattuck. After Hoover was elected president in 1928, Lakin had hired Shattuck because he thought he was a close friend of Hoover.

The charges were based on letters that Lakin had written to his employers in Cuba, particularly two dated March 15, 1929. In the first letter Lakin wrote, "I have not yet had a second interview with Senator Smoot. Both he and Shattuck have had conferences on this subject with President Hoover, who has instructed them to confer together." In the second letter he wrote, "President Hoover has taken a direct hand. He has already suggested a possible solution to Senator Smoot and to Mr. Shattuck."

Some might suspect that Lakin was exaggerating what was happening or even inventing events to justify the fees he was charging Cuban growers. His description of a president, in office for eleven days, giving instructions to the head of one of the Senate's most powerful committees does not ring true. The second letter also exaggerates—Shattuck, as a lobbyist's lawyer, would be the one with an agenda, not the president. The idea that through Lakin's efforts Hoover was now taking a direct hand in the matter seems to be a case of Lakin telling the Cubans what they wanted to hear.

The Senate investigation confirmed that suspicion. Under direct questioning before the subcommittee, Lakin could not verify that Shattuck and Hoover had ever discussed sugar duties. For his part, Shattuck denied what Lakin had claimed in his letters. "I have discussed [the sugar duty] with Senator Smoot and others," he testified, "but I have had no directions from Mr. Hoover about the sugar tariff, nor have I discussed the sugar tariff with Mr. Hoover."

After its investigation, the committee reported that it had discovered "no impropriety or anything open to censure or criticism." The results were hardly surprising. Hoover's career in mining had made him wealthy, and he had devoted much of his time to humanitarian projects without remuneration, even paying his own expenses. Hoover could not be bought.

Shattuck does not appear to have been as close to Hoover as Lakin told the Cubans. Few biographies of Hoover mention him. Hoover names Shattuck only once in his 1952 account of his years as commerce secretary and as president. That mention came in a list of nine men of "ability and scrupulous integrity" who had assisted him in his wartime European relief efforts. Hoover also describes the disaster that resulted when President Wilson failed to take his advice and that of the Sugar Equalization Board to retain controls on sugar for the 1919 crop, the first after the war was over. The result was a rapid rise in the price of sugar, profiteering, and then, as Hoover wrote, "The sugar boom collapsed with great losses to thousands of retailers, wholesalers, and other innocent distributors."

SUMMER CAMP ON THE RAPIDAN RIVER

Several newspapers reported incorrectly that the summer camp built for Hoover on the Rapidan River was financed with taxpayers' money.

In his 1952 *Memoirs* Hoover describes Washington's hot, exhausting summers. Looking for a way to escape the heat, Hoover asked his assistant, Lawrence Richey, and Col. Earl Long of the U.S. Marines to explore the Blue Ridge mountains of Virginia for a site to build a presidential retreat. One hundred miles from the capital, they found a delightfully cool location 1,500 feet up at the headwaters of the Rapidan River. Under the direction of Lou Hoover and with Marine Corps labor, in the summer of 1929 enough log cabins were built to house twelve to fifteen guests. Hoover, a fishing fanatic, made his own contribution, moving boulders into the stream to create pools for trout fishing. "I have discovered," he remarked, "that even the work of government can be improved by leisurely discussions out under the trees." Hoover also discovered that the isolated location could work magic on visiting dignitaries. In the fall of 1929 Hoover and British Prime Minister Ramsay MacDonald worked out the details of a naval disarmament agreement sitting on a log beside the Rapidan.

Hoover paid for all 164 acres of land and the camp himself, but his foes in the press attacked. Soon headlines proclaimed, "Marines Building Camp for Hoover." On July 19 the president's secretary announced, "Every nail and every board in the President's camp was paid for by Herbert Hoover out of his own pocket." On August 2 Hoover released a letter to the Virginia Conservation Commission in which he promised that the camp was to be deeded to the nearby Shenandoah National Park, so the park could "hold it for the use of my successor." After his term, Hoover turned the camp over to the state of Virginia, which passed it on to the National Park Service.

As with many of Hoover's ideas, Camp Rapidan proved to be a sensible solution to a chronic problem. The need for a presidential retreat in the mountains soon became accepted. His successor, Franklin D. Roosevelt, visited the camp once, but he found the trails too steep to negotiate on crutches and shifted to a location in the Catoctin Mountains of Maryland. FDR named his camp Shangri-La. President Dwight D. Eisenhower enjoyed FDR's camp but renamed it for his grandson, David Eisenhower. It has been called Camp David ever since.

COLORADO OIL SHALE LANDS

Mid-level civil servant Ralph S. Kelley resigned from the Interior Department, claiming that there was widespread corruption in the leasing of oil shale lands in western Colorado. Kelley predicted that the scandal would rival Teapot Dome.

On Monday, October 6, 1930, Joseph Pulitzer's *New York World* began a series of articles purporting to show, as a front page headline proclaimed, "How Favorites Got Oil Billions." To the casual reader, the source's credentials were impressive. Ralph S. Kelley, the article said, "resigned his post as chief of the field division of the General Land Office, Department of the Interior, on September 28." The articles ran until October 19.

The real story of Kelley's resignation was a bit more complicated. It was true that in his letter of resignation a week earlier, Kelley had charged that "the large oil interests are endeavoring to secure titles by fraud." But Interior Secretary Ray L. Wilbur had refused to accept Kelley's resignation; instead, he demanded that Kelley back up his charges with facts and suspended him from his post until the issue could be settled. The day after the allegations were made, Wilbur asked the attorney general to investigate the matter, and on October 2 Seth W. Richardson, an assistant attorney general, was put in charge of the inquiry. Richardson asked Kelley to present his evidence, but Kelley refused, claiming that "members of the President's cabinet are much too closely bound together to permit impartial investigations of each other." He added, "I have made arrangements whereby the principal facts supporting the allegations contained in my letter of resignation will at once be presented for the consideration of the public."

Those arrangements turned out to be a $12,000 contract that Kelley had signed with the *World* on September 11. In 1930 that was no small sum for a 22,000-word series, a substantial 55 cents a word. The *World* clearly intended to get a good return on its investment: in the week before the series ran, it had tried to syndicate the articles to other papers, claiming that Kelley had exposed a "theft of oil lands that rivals Teapot Dome."

Kelley's charges were more like a tempest in a teapot than the infamous Teapot Dome scandal. Kelley claimed that the Colorado oil shale lands being transferred to private hands were potentially worth $40 billion based on estimates that they contained more than 44 billion barrels of oil. The truth appeared five days later buried in a tiny, inner-page article in the *World*. Associated Press reporters had questioned Dr. George O. Smith about Kelley's allegations. Smith, who headed the government's geological survey of the oil shale lands, replied that the lands' worth for oil extraction purposes was nil. With the world oversupplied with oil, the high cost of extracting it from shale "postpones beyond present calculation the time when a new oil industry" would be interested in shale. As Hoover, a former mining engineer, later noted, at that time oil shale leases "can be bought from private owners for a few dollars an acre." That meant that all the Colorado oil shale leases granted under Hoover and contested by Kelley were worth perhaps $250,000, a far cry from Kelley's estimate of $40 billion.

In a 60,000-word report dated October 28 the Justice Department found Kelley's charges completely baseless. It noted "that at the onset of the administration executive orders were issued withdrawing all oil and gas lands from lease applications, and on April 15, 1930, a like order was issued against all oil shale lands." In his *Memoirs* Hoover added that three days after the first order he issued another, canceling "permits over hundreds of thousands of acres, and the rights were returned to the government." Those lands, Hoover noted, were illegally being held for speculation. Hoover's order was not consistent with an administration intent on transferring oil shale leases into private hands. It was one reason why the report concluded that there was more evidence the Interior Department had "been exceedingly strict and exacting in resisting claims for patents." The facts lay in the statistics. Only a small percentage of the oil shale lands had been transferred to private interests, and only one-fifth of those during the Hoover administration. In fact, more than half (23,000 of 43,000 acres) of the land had been approved by Kelley himself.

Kelley's allegations faced another difficulty. If politicians with pull had intended to give the land away using complaisant officials of the government, as Kelley claimed, then why had the interior secretary put Kelley in charge of all pending oil shale claims? "There is no merit or substance," the report said, in Kelley's charges. That same day Secretary Wilbur fired Kelley.

Responding in the *World,* Kelley termed the report a ridiculous whitewash and claimed that the department's relevant papers "require at least six months to one year to digest instead of three weeks." He did not explain why fraud on the massive scale he had described would be so difficult to discover or why the *World* was not being irresponsible for publishing his allegations with absolutely no investigation into those papers. Something of his state of mind came through in his remarks about "the report's emphasis upon the fact that oil shale lands are not commercially productive at this moment. Nobody pretends they are. But everybody who knows anything about them knows they will be, perhaps in the near future, of vast commercial value." However, Kelley was wrong—the oil shale lands remain virtually worthless.

Kelley's motives for making his allegations can only be surmised. One reason was probably a clash he had with his superiors over a technical matter. Many geologists believed that in a particular Colorado formation, oil in surface layers almost invariably indicated oil in layers 200 feet down. Interior Department policy was to accept that as fact and not require claimants to go through the expense of drilling down to sample the lower layer. Kelley disagreed with that policy, but, rather than recognize it as a matter about which well-meaning people could differ, he interpreted it as proof that his superiors were in the pay of oil companies. Politics may have also played a part. In his articles he went out of his way to link allegations of corruption to "the last six years" (the Coolidge and Hoover administrations) and made an obvious effort to link those he charged to the Republican Party. For example, he described former interior secretary Hubert Work as someone "who resigned to become chairman of the Republican National Committee and a director of President Hoover's campaign two years ago." Finally, Kelley may have assumed that with a quarter of a century of government service behind him, his resignation would mean a comfortable retirement sweetened by a check for his articles that was equivalent to almost four years' income.

The *World*'s coverage of the story is an example of the worst kind of yellow journalism. Kelley's assertion that he had been "driven to the conclusion that there is no other way in which I may make effective protest" was not balanced by any mention of the fact that he had contracted with the *World* two weeks before making his allegations known to the secretary of the interior or that a high-level Justice Department investigation was already under way when the paper went to press. In addition, while Kelley's unfounded allegations got prominent front page display, Smith's far more expert testimony was buried far inside the paper. The *World,* well known as a Democratic paper, clearly had a political axe to grind and did not care who it savaged in the process.

By October 27, when the Justice Department report first became available, the paper was on the defensive. The editorial page claimed that when the editors first published the articles they had "no intention of prejudging the case." But the paper had made no effort to determine the truth or falsity of Kelley's claims, even though many facts, such as the Hoover administration's ban on new oil shale leases, were public knowledge. The paper's claim that Kelley "has a record of more that a quarter of a century of honorable service in a government department" was meaningless because the integrity of those he accused was also well known. The *World*'s attempt to grasp at one last argument—"that the government lost every case" with the oil companies—demonstrates the very opposite of what they claimed. The Interior Department lost its cases because, just as the Justice report concluded, it was trying too hard to restrict the few remaining oil shale applications still in the system.

Hoover was quite right on October 28 when he denounced the "reckless, baseless, and infamous charges in the face of responsible denial, with no attempt at verification." He was also right when he noted that the only way to attract people of "integrity and ability" to public service was to protect them from "infamous transactions of this character."

CHARLES G. DAWES AND THE RFC LOAN

Charles Dawes, the former director of the Reconstruction Finance Corporation, was investigated when his bank received a $90 million loan from the RFC.

During the final days of the 1932 presidential campaign, the rhetoric grew extremely nasty as each party made harsh accusations against the other. Many of the Democratic attacks centered on Hoover's Reconstruction Finance Corporation (RFC), an organization created the previous February and funded with $500 million in capital and $1.5 billion in bonds. One of its missions was to assist banks on the verge of collapse. Strange as it sounds today, on the night of November 4, just four days before the election, former Democratic National chairman John J. Raskob told a nationwide radio audience that the Democrats would "bring back prosperity quickly" by *lowering* income taxes, *reducing* federal expenditures, and *balancing* the federal budget. It was the Republicans who were accused of wasting money.

Speaking the same day, Sen. Robert F. Wagner of New York described Hoover's RFC as a "sinister resort to pork barrel methods." According to Wagner, there was "evil" in Hoover's $150 million in loans to more than 400 West Coast banks. Speaking the same day in Chicago, California's Sen. Hiram Johnson did not dare denounce loans that rescued his own state's banks, so he took a different approach. He blasted Hoover because:

The whole theory of the administration has been of aiding railroads, banks and great corporations and then that some little relief may filter through to those who so sorely need it. The filtering process, unfortunately, is not in operation . . . what is being attempted is to save the tree by fertilizing its top leaves and upper branches, forgetful of its roots.

At the center of the Democratic Party's attacks lay a scandal that became known as the Dawes bank loan. Taking events at their face value, the Democrats had every reason to be suspicious. In February 1932, when Hoover created the RFC, he appointed Charles G. Dawes as its president. Dawes had served as vice president under Calvin Coolidge and as U.S. ambassador to Great Britain. But in early June, Dawes resigned from the RFC. On June 15, just minutes before he was to leave the capital, he announced that he was returning to Chicago to take charge of the Central Republic Bank. The Dawes family had a large investment in the bank, and Dawes had once played an active role in its management. For seven years, however, he had held the title "honorary chairman" with no major responsibilities. Twelve days after his resignation, on June 27, Dawes's bank received a $90 million RFC loan, which had been approved in the early hours of a Monday morning with no prior public announcement.

Various letters and diaries revealed what inspired Dawes's sudden return to Chicago. In May 1932 some members of the Hoover administration became convinced that a much more serious economic crash was imminent. On May 16 Hoover told Secretary of State Henry Stimson that he expected it to come within three weeks. On June 13, two days before he left the city, Dawes told a senator that the country would soon experience a final, climactic crash. In order not to create panic, Dawes seems to have told almost no one that his return to Chicago was a desperate bid to save his family's troubled bank.

The same day that Wagner and Johnson blasted the RFC, Hoover spoke in St. Louis and defended the Dawes loan. Dawes, the president said, had not asked for a loan. He had been given one because the circumstances more than warranted it. "The constant misrepresentation of the loan for political purposes," Hoover said, "was a slander upon men of their party as well as a cruel injustice to General Dawes." The loan, he noted, was given to preserve "122,000 depositors, of whom 105,000 were savings depositors; that the average of the savings deposits was only $140 each, many of them working women and children."

Hoover also pointed out that the loan was made at "the insistence of the two Democratic members of the reconstruction board, sitting in the Federal

Charles G. Dawes

Reserve Bank meeting in Chicago" as well as that of "the leading Democratic banker of Chicago" and an equally prominent Democratic banker in New York City. "These men acted," Hoover said, "not because they were Democrats or Republicans but because they were loyal citizens of the United States." Hoover knew what he was talking about: he had been part of the long-distance telephone negotiations that went on in the late hours of Sunday night and into the early hours of Monday morning.

In 1951 Jesse H. Jones, one of the three Democrats on the RFC board, published a book that devoted an entire chapter to the Dawes loan. *Fifty Billion Dollars: My Thirteen Years with the RFC* describes in great detail how the loan came about. According to his account, Jones, more than anyone else, was responsible for the loan and that it might not have been made had he not been in Chicago to attend the Democratic National Convention. The decision-making process was both bipartisan and responsible.

Jones called the Saturday he arrived in Chicago "ominous." Walking about the Loop, he could see "the tail-end of the week's terrible runs on the big downtown banks." Thousands of people stood outside bank entrances or crowded into bank lobbies. Many had lost savings in the preceding three weeks as twenty-five outlying banks had collapsed. Seven banks had failed to open on Thursday, and eight more on Friday. The city's larger banks were now in danger. In the past year the Dawes family bank had seen its deposits plummet from $240 million to $120 million.

Dawes decided that his bank could not open Monday morning. Knowing his decision would place enormous pressure on the remaining banks, on Sunday he invited some thirty to forty of the city's leading bankers and businessmen in to explain his reason. The smart money, he told them, was already being withdrawn from his bank at the rate of $2 million a day. He could not stand by and let the bank collapse knowing that the losers would be his most trusting depositors. Senator Johnson had accused the Hoover administration of acting to save giant corporations; Dawes was trying to save the poorest and least informed of his bank's clients.

Jones was also invited to the Sunday meeting. Dawes, he said, made it clear that he was not asking for assistance, but everyone present knew that if the bank runs continued, every bank in the Chicago area would be forced to close and from there the panic could spread across the country, bringing the crash that Hoover and Dawes feared. Every banker present asked Jones to telephone the president and recommend that the government save the Dawes bank.

Taking several hours to examine the bank's books that Sunday afternoon, Jones reached the conclusion that the bank had sufficient assets to justify a $90 million loan. When Hoover was informed, he told Jones to get as much participation as possible from other banks and then do whatever was necessary. Long hours of negotiations followed with other Chicago banks as well as some in New York City. Finally, at four in the morning everything was complete. Five hours later the bank opened for business, and within two days the government had provided it with $90 million. The loan came not a moment too soon. On Saturday, the bank's stock had been at $47. On Monday it opened at $1. Although the bank was forced into bankruptcy, its assets were enough that the entire principal was returned along with $10 million in interest. The Dawes family contributed its full liability of over $1 million.

Jones's close involvement in the Dawes bank loan made it an unusual scandal. In most cases, those making the accusations were not a part of what occurred. Rather, they are forced to rely on an elusive paper trail of documents or on the testimony of witnesses who may or may not be telling the truth. This distance is often enough to justify their actions if the accusations later prove false. But in the Dawes scandal, the prominent Democratic politicians who made the accusations on the eve of the election had known four months earlier that several loyal party members and experienced public servants had been privy to the entire process. If they had wanted the truth, they could have learned it from those people. They chose instead to engage in slander. It was, as Hoover noted just before he was voted out of office, "an insult to the American people to substitute this sort of political action for competent discussion of the grave issues which lie before the country." At times, the truly scandalous behavior is that of the accusers, not the accused.

WALTER F. BROWN AND THE AIR MAIL CONTRACTS

Postmaster General Walter F. Brown was investigated for collusion and other illegal acts in the granting of air mail contracts.

In *Memoirs* Hoover expressed his pride in the growth of passenger air service during his four years as Coolidge's secretary of commerce. The only problem, he said, lay in economic factors that were creating "a permanent muddle such as had resulted from our chaotic railway development with all its separation into short and long lines, duplication and waste." When he became president, Hoover's plan for bringing order to that chaos led to the most serious charge of scandal against his administration.

The roots of the aviation industry's unhealthy dynamics were not hard to discover. The most lucrative way to take advantage of mail contracts was to ignore passenger transport and carry mail in old, open-cockpit biplanes. Passenger flights, where they existed, were only marginally profitable, so the fledgling airlines tended to choose short, easy routes. Longer routes, particularly over mountains, were avoided even though the greatest potential for expansion and profit lay there. With paper-thin profit margins, the airlines lacked the money to invest in modern aircraft, even though in the long run, new planes would have reduced costs and improved safety. All these problems, Hoover felt, could be solved by using Post Office contracts for air mail. Pound for pound, it was eight times more profitable to transport mail than passengers. Higher profits would enable the industry to move in a healthier direction. Unfortunately, Coolidge's postmaster general "took the attitude that under the law he was interested in mail only."

After he was elected president, Hoover chose Walter F. Brown, an aggressive Ohio attorney, as his postmaster general. He instructed Brown to meet with air transport companies and propose a revision in their contracts that would do the following: (1) reduce the high payments made to transport air mail; (2) force carriers to transport mail in larger aircraft that could carry passengers and express packages; and (3) consolidate routes so passengers and mail would not have to change planes to travel long distances. The goal was to create the world's best air transportation system. To do that, contracts could not just be awarded to the lowest bidder; rather, contracts would have to go to larger and more established companies. When his actions later came under fire, Brown justified himself by stating, "There was no sense in taking this government's money and dishing it out . . . to every little fellow that was flying around the map and was not going to do anything . . . to develop aviation in the broad sense."

The administration sought legal authority in the McNary-Watres bill. Its major provision changed the way companies would be paid for transporting the mail. Instead of the old pound-per-mile rate, they would be paid according to the amount of space the aircraft had available for mail. As Henry L. Smith notes in *Airways,* the law was an open invitation to order large, modern planes and fill the added space with passengers. Within a few years, the administration hoped the added economy of scale would make subsidies unnecessary.

The administration got most of what it wanted from Congress. The space-mile rate was substituted for the pound-mile rate, and the postmaster general received the authority to extend or consolidate routes in the public interest. One additional authority was not granted: Brown could not award contracts without competitive bidding even if he thought it was in the public interest. To carry out his agenda, he would have to push his authority to the limit of the law and even, his critics would say, beyond that limit.

Given the critical role that air mail contracts played, Brown became the industry's czar. Companies that fit the administration's plans got contracts; companies that did not were left out in the cold. Because Brown could not directly exclude inexperienced low-bidders, he added additional requirements, such as a stipulation that bidders must have flown at night for at least six months over a distance of not less than 250 miles. Like it or not, aviation would be forced to develop the ability to fly long distances at night, and willing or not, companies would be forced to merge to create consolidated cross-country routes. Critics later charged that Brown "colluded" with major companies, but it is difficult to find anything he did that anyone in the industry wholeheartedly endorsed.

The foundations for many of the accusations that were later directed against Brown were laid between May 15 and June 4, 1930. Just after the McNary-Watres bill became law, Brown called a series of meetings with people from selected airlines to develop an agreement about how the new contracts would be distributed. When one participant, fearful of antitrust prosecution, questioned the legality of the meetings, another executive replied, "I quite agree with you; if we were holding this meeting across the street in the Raleigh Hotel, it would be an improper meeting; but because we are holding it in the office of the Post Office Department, it is perfectly all right."

Over time, the meetings acquired the name "Spoils Conferences," but their real purpose seems have been to provide Brown with a forum in which to impose his will upon the industry. He had already decided that American Airways was to get the southern transcontinental route and that a merger of Transcontinental Air Transport with Western Air Express was to get the central route. The merger (which created TWA) was forced on the two parties. In August, when the contracts were awarded, the three largest airlines got eighteen of the twenty contracts.

Brown's foes also claimed that the meetings were held in secret. That was not the case. The Post Office included the meetings in its daily press releases, and the press covered them. On May 20, for instance, the *New York Times* noted, "Mr. Brown is known to have in mind the consolidation of various routes so as to cover the country with an air service." Even Brown's controversial tactics did not escape notice. In July *Aviation* magazine reported that the purpose of the meetings was "to issue ten-year certificates" to selected companies while avoiding "as much as possible, competitive bidding."

In the closing days of the Hoover administration, some congressional Republicans began to worry about the appearance of illegality in Brown's methods. Chairman James M. Mead of the House Post Office Committee held hearings but in the end found Brown blameless. With the new Democratic administration, matters would go differently. The New Deal wanted to appear to be the champion of the little man, and in this case that meant the smaller independents who had made good money under the old air mail system but were now without contracts.

The Democratic investigation became known as the Black Committee after its chairman, Sen. Hugo L. Black of Alabama, a future Supreme Court justice. The hearings began on September 28, 1933. When attention turned to air mail the committee began to generate front page news by its bold actions, such as a sudden move to seize the internal memos and letters of aviation executives. However, Brown's foes had difficulty finding how he had personally benefited. They thought they had a smoking gun when they discovered that he owned 225 shares of Pennsylvania Railroad, which owned shares of Transcontinental Air Transport, which owned shares of TWA. Once the various links were worked out, Brown's "ownership" in TWA amounted to less than one-third of one share. Even his worst enemies did not think that was enough to corrupt him.

"Collusion" became their battle cry, but nothing could have been further from the truth. As historian Henry Smith put it:

> Actually, there was no collusion at all, if the word implied a concert of action, since the operators failed completely to reach any kind of agreement. Suspicious, jealous of each other, and only too willing to stab a rival, the conferees got exactly nowhere in working out their own problems.

Much of Brown's power lay in the fact that only he could impose order on all this chaos.

For a time, however, Brown and all that he had done was discredited. Between the bitter testimony of executives who had been refused contracts and the heavy-handed techniques Brown had used, it certainly looked as if something corrupt was taking place. On February 9, 1934, Franklin Roosevelt ordered all air mail contracts canceled. Declaring a national emergency, he ordered the army air corps to transport the mail. As political theater, it could not be better—a bold new president was sweeping clean the corruption of the old. The results proved far different.

The last commercial mail deliveries were to take place on February 19. On the evening of February 18, the aviation industry made its own political statement. A revolutionary new airplane, the DC-2, had been rushed through production. At precisely 10 o'clock that night it took off from Union Air Terminal in Los Angeles bound for Newark, 3,000 miles away. At its controls were Jack Frye, a TWA executive, and Eddie Rickenbacker of Eastern Air Transport. The last load of mail to be carried under private contract was in the hold. Racing to beat a blizzard sweeping down out of Canada, the plane crossed the country in an amazing thirteen hours and four minutes, setting a new transcontinental flying record and demonstrating the transformation that commercial aviation had undergone in just four years.

The next day, after canceling almost half the nation's air mail routes, the army took over the mail. At the end of the first week, five army pilots were dead and six had been critically injured. Even after the more dangerous night flights—the cause of most of the accidents—were abandoned, pilots continued to be killed. On March 10 FDR stopped all air mail service, and, for the first time in thirteen years, the nation was without air mail. Attempts to restrict flying to days of near-perfect weather failed to stop the accidents. In all, twelve pilots were killed. Public opinion now turned against the administration. Even the finances of the military interlude were depressing. The military pilots earned half as much as commercial pilots, but the costs still worked out to $2.21 per mile. The administration was forced back to private contractors. In an effort to save face, it banned all those involved in the "Spoils Conferences" from bidding on the new contracts and pretended not to notice when they entered the bidding with only minor name changes. (American Airways became American Airlines.)

Seven years later, on July 14, 1941, Brown was vindicated. The U.S. Court of Claims stated in a 115-page decision that he had not engaged in fraud or collusion. Brown had been given the authority to use air mail contracts to serve the public interest by improving air transportation, and he had done precisely that.

In *Memoirs,* Hoover gave the relevant statistics. In the last fiscal year before his administration made its changes, air mail was being transported at an average cost of $1.26 per mile. Four years later the cost was a mere 26 cents per mile, a phenomenal 80 percent decrease. Yet air mail volume had increased dramatically: the mileage flown had grown almost 300 percent, and the government subsidy had been reduced by $3.5 million. All this was done while modernizing aviation to make air travel safer, increasing the number of air passengers by more than 300 percent, and multiplying the number of people employed in aviation by more than 200 percent. Mail that had once taken forty-eight hours to cross the country by air now took twenty-one. Whatever one might think about Brown's methods, the results were clearly impressive.

BIBLIOGRAPHY

Burner, David. *Herbert Hoover: A Public Life.* New York: Knopf, 1978.

Green, Carol W. *Herbert Hoover: A Challenge for Today.* New York: Evans Publishing, 1968.

Hinshaw, David. *Herbert Hoover: American Quaker.* New York: Farrar, Straus, 1950.

Hoover, Herbert H. *The Memoirs of Herbert Hoover.* New York: Macmillan, 1952.

Jones, Jesse H. *Fifty Billion Dollars: My Thirteen Years with the RFC.* New York: Macmillan, 1951.

Lyons, Eugene. *Herbert Hoover: A Biography.* Garden City, N.Y.: Doubleday, 1964.

Meyers, William S. *The Hoover Administration.* St. Clair Shores, Mich.: Scholarly Press, 1971.

Mitchell, Jack. *Executive Privilege: Two Centuries of White House Scandals.* New York: Hippocrene Books, 1992.

Nash, George H. *The Life of Herbert Hoover.* New York: W. W. Norton, 1983– .

Smith, Henry L. *Airways: The History of Commercial Aviation in the United States.* New York: Knopf, 1942.

Smith, Richard N. *An Uncommon Man.* New York: Simon and Schuster, 1984.

Woodward, C. Vann. *Responses of the Presidents to Charges of Misconduct.* New York: Dell Publishing, 1974.

FRANKLIN D. ROOSEVELT

Thirty-Second President
1933–1945

Franklin Delano Roosevelt was born January 30, 1882, in Hyde Park, New York. He was the only son of James Roosevelt and Sara Delano Roosevelt. James Roosevelt, who also had one son from his first marriage, was a lawyer and railroad executive with an inherited fortune. Sara Roosevelt also came from a wealthy family.

Franklin was tutored at home in his early years and attended Groton Academy from 1896 to 1900. He was an above average, but not brilliant, student. He attended Harvard University, where he continued to be an average student. He remained at Harvard an extra year to stay on as editor of the *Harvard Crimson,* the school's paper. He attended Columbia Law School from 1904 to 1907, when he passed the bar. Although he considered himself a Democrat, he cast his first presidential vote for his cousin, Republican Theodore Roosevelt, in 1904. FDR married Anna Eleanor Roosevelt, a distant cousin, on March 17, 1905. Eleanor became the most active first lady in history up to her time. She was a powerful force in FDR's life and stayed engaged in public affairs after he died.

Roosevelt practiced law in New York City from 1907 until 1911, when he was elected to the New York state senate. He became a leader of the progressive Democrats who challenged the power of Tammany Hall. In 1913 President Woodrow Wilson appointed FDR as assistant secretary of the navy. He held that post until 1920, resigning to accept the vice-presidential nomination on the Democratic ticket headed by James M. Cox.

When Republicans Warren G. Harding and Calvin Coolidge won the election, Roosevelt returned to the practice of law in New York City. In 1921 he was stricken with poliomyelitis and left severely crippled. He spent the next three years convalescing and building strength in his upper body. He returned to the practice of law in 1924. In 1928 he narrowly (2.13 million to 2.10 million) defeated state attorney general Albert Ottinger for the governorship of New York. Reelected by a wider margin in 1930, Roosevelt established himself as a progressive governor; he sought aid for the growing number of unemployed and increased credit for farmers. He also began to deliver what later became his trademark, radio addresses known as fireside chats.

The front-runner for the Democratic Party presidential nomination in 1932, Roosevelt defeated Alfred E. Smith of New York and House Speaker John Nance Garner of Texas on the fourth ballot, when Garner threw his votes to FDR. Garner was selected as the vice-presidential nominee. In an unprecedented move, FDR flew to Chicago to personally deliver his acceptance speech. In the fall election, Roosevelt faced the incumbent, President Herbert Hoover, who had been weakened by the 1929 stock market crash and the beginning of the Great Depression. Winning by more than 7 million votes, FDR took the electoral college 472 to 59. In 1936 FDR faced Republican governor Alfred M. Landon of Kansas. Landon campaigned by criticizing Roosevelt's methods for enacting New Deal legislation. Landon argued that the programs were full of waste and ultimately undermined the American system of government. FDR won by more than 11 million votes and an electoral college vote of 523 to 8; Landon won only Maine and Vermont.

In July 1940, when Democrats gathered in Chicago, it was still unclear whether FDR would seek an unprecedented third term. Rather than pursue the nomination directly, he sought to be drafted by the convention. He was selected on the first ballot. Vice President Garner was replaced on the ticket with Agriculture Secretary Henry A. Wallace of Iowa. In the fall FDR faced Democrat-turned-Republican Wendell Willkie of Indiana. The campaign focused largely on two issues—the war in Europe and the wisdom of a third term for any person. In the end, the voters gave FDR a margin of victory of nearly 5 million votes and the electoral college by 449 to 82. Renominating FDR for a fourth term in 1944, the party dropped Vice President Wallace in favor of Sen. Harry S. Truman of Missouri. The Republicans nominated Gov. Thomas E. Dewey of New York, who, as a successful U.S. attorney, had prosecuted gangsters associated with organized crime. The Republican campaign focused on Roosevelt's health, which was in obvious decline. Nevertheless, FDR was reelected by more than 3.5 million votes and an electoral college count of 432 to 99.

Roosevelt's administration—the longest in U.S. history—oversaw the enactment of the many pieces of legislation known as the New Deal. The programs included unprecedented direct federal relief and economic regulation that established the modern welfare state. Among the agencies established were the Civilian Conservation Corps, the Tennessee Valley Authority, the Federal Emergency Relief Administration, the Securities and Exchange Commission, the Works Progress Administration, and the Social Security Administration. In foreign policy the Roosevelt administration recognized the Soviet Union and aided countries that were fighting Hitler's Germany. Roosevelt also guided the U.S. entrance into World War II after the bombing of Pearl Harbor on December 7, 1941.

While at the Little White House at Warm Springs, Georgia, on April 12, 1945, President Roosevelt suffered a cerebral hemorrhage and died. A train brought his body back to Washington, where it lay in state at the White House. The train then took the body to Hyde Park for burial.

EXTRAMARITAL AFFAIRS

Roosevelt was rumored to have had many extramarital affairs, including two that were long term. One of the long-term affairs was with Lucy Mercer, Eleanor Roosevelt's social secretary, and the other was with Missy LeHand, his secretary.

Lucy Page Mercer Rutherford

Lucy Page Mercer was Eleanor Roosevelt's social secretary from 1913 to 1914. Although Franklin probably met her during this time, it was not until the summer of 1916, when Roosevelt was an assistant secretary of the navy, that their almost thirty-year affair began. Eleanor was away at the family compound at Campobello in Canada with the children. Lucy began to accompany Roosevelt to social functions and on overnight trips.

The next year Eleanor became suspicious when Roosevelt once again remained in Washington's heat and humidity while the family went to Canada for the summer. He came up to Canada for ten days only. He continued to see Lucy, including a trip on the presidential yacht with two married couples. Washington social circles gossiped about them, but Eleanor seems to have been either overly trusting or blissfully ignorant. However, in September 1918, Eleanor learned of the affair when she discovered several love letters written by Lucy to Roosevelt.

An angry, tearful Eleanor confronted Franklin in the presence of his mother, who threatened to cut him off financially if he did not end the affair. Eleanor offered Roosevelt a divorce, a course he could not take and maintain his budding political career. Roosevelt promised to end the affair, but he did not. Eleanor grew more independent and pursued her own projects and emotional support from others. Their marriage changed from a traditional relationship into a partnership.

In 1920 Lucy Mercer married Winthrop Rutherford, a wealthy fifty-eight-year-old widower with six children. The demands of marriage and family prevented her from seeing Roosevelt as often as she had in the past, but they continued to write to each other and see each other on occasion. At his first inauguration, Roosevelt sent a presidential limousine to escort Lucy to the ceremony, which she watched from the privacy of the car. She attended each of his

Lucy Mercer

inaugurations that way. In 1940 Roosevelt began to call and see her more often. After her husband's death in 1944, Lucy was a frequent guest at the White House when Eleanor was away. Lucy was with Roosevelt at Warm Springs, Georgia, the day he died. She was quickly sent away in a futile effort to prevent Eleanor from finding out that she had been there.

Marguerite Alice "Missy" LeHand

In 1921 Roosevelt began a long-term relationship with Missy LeHand, who had worked on his failed vice-presidential bid in 1920. After his bout with polio, the two were inseparable. Missy accompanied Roosevelt to his rehabilitation sessions, as well as performing secretarial duties. In 1923 she officially became his personal secretary, a post she held for nearly twenty years.

When Roosevelt was elected governor in 1928, Missy moved into the governor's mansion and occupied the room adjoining Roosevelt's; Eleanor's room was down the hall. When he was elected president, Missy also moved into a three-room suite in the White House, but she spent many nights in Roosevelt's room.

The affair came to an end in 1940, when Missy suffered a cerebral hemorrhage and had to be moved out of the White House. She died three years later. Roosevelt left half of his estate—valued at nearly $2 million—to pay her medical bills.

Princess Martha of Norway

During World War II, Crown Princess Martha lived in the United States and had total access to both the White House and Hyde Park (Roosevelt's New York home). While the two engaged in public flirting, it is unclear whether they ever did anything more than flirt, but the rumors were rampant.

Dorothy Schiff

Dorothy Schiff, the publisher of the *New York Post,* claimed that she and Roosevelt had an affair that lasted from 1944 to 1945. There is no corroborating evidence that Roosevelt engaged in an affair with her.

LOUIS MCHENRY HOWE, FDR'S SECRETARY

Louis Howe—one of FDR's closest political friends—was accused of awarding contracts for Civilian Conservation Corps supplies without competitive bidding.

On the night of the 1932 election, with his victory over Hoover assured, Franklin Roosevelt told his assembled supporters, "There are two people in the United States more than anybody else who are responsible for this great victory. One is my old friend and associate, Colonel Louis McHenry Howe, and the other is that great American, Jim Farley." Roosevelt had met Howe, a chronically impoverished journalist, in 1911, when Roosevelt was serving his first term as a state senator. According to Howe's biographer, Alfred Rollins, by the next year, "it would be impossible to think of Roosevelt or Howe without the other. They operated as parts of one political personality." For most of their combined careers, FDR provided the charm and vision, while Howe worked behind the scenes, manipulating the press and organizing political support. Howe became a well-known figure when he became secretary to the president. Only Missy LeHand, FDR's personal secretary, had an office closer to the president. Howe took particular interest in three New Deal projects: the Civilian Conservation Corps (CCC), the Subsistence Home Experiment, and the battle against organized crime.

The CCC was FDR's special project. Seeing a contrast between the health-giving qualities of outdoor life and the wickedness of big cities, where so many men were unemployed, the new president dreamed of putting 250,000 young men to work on rural conservation projects. But he had been in office only three months, and rushing the project turned it into an administrative nightmare. The army was to take care of housing; the National Park Service and Corps of Engineers were to develop work projects; the Labor Department had the task of recruiting workers; and Robert Fechner, a union official, was to be its official administrator. To shield FDR from bureaucratic squabbles, Howe had the unenviable task of making the scheme work. For a man whose health was in rapid decline, it was an exhausting job. By midsummer of 1933, however, Howe had enrolled 300,000 men in the CCC.

But in his haste to get the job done, Howe made an embarrassing mistake. Early in 1934 a Senate committee looking into the CCC came across a contract for 200,000 toilet kits that had been awarded without the usual competitive bidding. The committee traced the contract to Howe. What the contractor told the committee was political dynamite: he had seen Howe at 3 p.m. and a mere three hours later he had the contract in his hand. As a biographer put it, Howe "managed to squirm out" of the controversy by shifting the blame to Fechner. (Fellow New Dealer Harold Ickes was equally blunt, saying the matter had been "hushed up.") On paper, Howe had merely referred the contractor to Fechner. In practice, a request from Howe was an order that could, if necessary, be backed up by FDR's own signature. The Senate committee told Howe that it had found no foundation for any criticism of him.

Far worse was the Subsistence Home Experiment disaster. Behind it lay an idealistic dream that the New Deal could create self-sufficient rural communities for the poor. Before a year had passed, some fifty-two such projects had been approved. Howe and Eleanor Roosevelt focused their attention on what they hoped would be a showcase project in West Virginia called Arthurdale. Its people were poor coal-mining whites—they had to be white to keep the segregationist wing of the Democratic Party satisfied.

Arthurdale was also close enough to the capital to allow Eleanor and Howe to meddle in its details and share in its coming glory. As Alfred Rollins notes, "Howe *was* the Electrification Committee all by himself. Eleanor *was* the Population Committee." Congressional critics accused it of being "the death knell of individual liberty in America." These critics of creeping socialism were needlessly alarmist.

Howe and Eleanor would have done better if they had hired a reasonably competent building contractor. On August 12, 1934, the *Washington Post* magazine described what had happened under the headline: "Flimsy Homesteads Cost Fancy Price, Blunders at Arthurdale Put Burden on Miner and Taxpayer." The project had been so badly managed that the prefabricated homes were only about one-third the size of their prepared foundations and their chimneys stood a full ten feet away from the closest wall. Howe did little to calm the storm when he took to the radio to announce that the homes, built at the then-astronomical cost of "four, five or even six thousand dollars" had been demolished and would be replaced by something more permanent. Eleanor tried to explain away the problems by calling Arthurdale "a human experiment station." Privately, Harold Ickes said that since the first lady had "taken the project under her protecting wing . . . they had been spending money like drunken sailors." In 1935 the Subsistence Home Experiment was merged with the Resettlement Administration and allowed to die a quiet death.

Although he had no training in law enforcement, Howe also developed a personal interest in fighting the crime wave that had come with the end of Prohibition. When bootlegging profits dried up, organized crime turned its attention to kidnapping, protection, drug smuggling, and other enterprises. In a July 29, 1933, article in the *Saturday Evening Post,* entitled "Uncle Sam Starts After Crime," Howe advanced the idea of a national police force. It was typical of the New Dealers to see greater centralization as the solution to every problem. Some of Howe's ideas, such as a national crime laboratory, made sense and were merged into the Federal Bureau of Investigation. Others, such as basing jury decisions on a majority vote, were rejected. His idea to have the federal government take over the role of training police officers was blasted by *Harper's* magazine as being a step toward creating a federal secret police. It was an apt analogy. Much of nazism's successful capture of power hinged on Germany's highly centralized police force. Howe also carefully steered clear of the one area where federal help was urgently needed—lynchings that went unpunished by state or local laws.

An indication that Howe's ill health was affecting his judgment came one month after the fuss over the CCC contract. In 1934 the Roosevelt administration was worried about how the early elections in Maine would go, and Howe was pulling every political string he could to help the Democrats. One of those strings could have led to a political scandal. Even though the Maine-based Bath Iron Works had not been the lowest bidder,

Howe tried to get the company a contract to build a Navy destroyer. Near the end of August, he wrote the president a letter ranting, "I am so tired of the [naval establishment] running the awards of the Navy Department that I get hot under the collar." Roosevelt retained his cool and a week later wrote back that it would be "indefensible" to give a contract to a high bidder. Roosevelt's calm proved justified. The Democrats did well in Maine and in the November elections that followed.

THE SECOND LOUISIANA PURCHASE

Sen. Huey P. Long of Louisiana and President Roosevelt had feuded for years over policy. Long used his position in the Senate to instigate investigations of the Post Office and the Works Progress Administration. Roosevelt sought to embarrass Long by having him investigated for tax evasion. After Long's death, more than two dozen people associated with his Share Our Wealth organization were indicted, but Roosevelt gained the support of the Long machine by settling for civil judgments rather than prosecuting.

Watching from his post in the Roosevelt administration, Rexford Tugwell concluded, "If 1934 was a year when the reactionaries made the most noise, 1935 was dominated, in the same sense, by thunder on the left." The most powerful among those noisemakers was "the Kingfish," Sen. Huey Long, the former governor of Louisiana. Tugwell was present when Roosevelt received a call from Long, a fellow Democrat. In his book *The Democratic Roosevelt,* Tugwell claims that immediately after hanging up, the president said, "It's all very well for us to laugh over Huey. But actually we have to remember all the time that he really is one of the two most dangerous men in the country." According to Tugwell, FDR went on to explain that the danger from the right lay in those who, in troubled times, looked for a strong leader such as Gen. Douglas MacArthur (the other of his two most dangerous men). According to FDR, that danger was only latent. The greater danger lay in what Tugwell described as "the leftist or presumed leftist, appeals, in which everything was promised that anyone had ever longed for without the slightest acceptance of responsibility or acknowledgment of cost."

FDR was referring to Share Our Wealth, an organization Long had started in January 1934. Financed primarily by money drawn from Louisiana's corrupt politics, membership was free to all who asked. By April Long claimed a nationwide membership of more than 7 million, a figure not disputed by his critics. Long's skill at manipulating the media was at least the equal of FDR's. To what was termed "probably the largest radio audience in the history of America," he blasted the New Deal in the harshest terms: "While millions have starved and gone naked; while babies have cried and died for milk, while people have begged for meat and bread, Mr. Roosevelt's administration sails merrily along, plowing under and destroying the things to eat and wear, with tear-dimmed eyes and hungry souls made to chant for this New Deal, so that even their starvation dole is not taken away."

Share Our Wealth's agenda went far beyond anything ever contemplated by the New Deal. Eventually, Long would call for the government to confiscate all wealth over $5 million and all annual income above $1.8 million. The resulting wealth was to be shared with the entire population, providing every household with a guaranteed annual income of $5,000. Long seemed unconcerned that his figures did not add up. According to one calculation, even if nothing else changed, the government could provide the guaranteed income only by confiscating all income above $7,000 a year. The idea was crazy, but millions of desperately cold and hungry people seemed to believe him.

Huey Long

Worried about the 1936 elections, the Democratic National Committee financed a secret poll. It concluded that if Long ran as a third party candidate, he would win between 3 million and 4 million votes across the nation. Most of those votes would come at the expense of the Democratic Party, and in some states, including critically important New York, the voters who went for Long could give the election to the Republicans. "We must tame these fellows," FDR told Tugwell, "and make them useful to us." How FDR tamed them became a source of controversy.

Some measures had been in place since the early days of the New Deal, when the administration had made sure that in Louisiana the power to assign jobs financed by federal money stayed in the hands of those who were either neutral or anti-Long. That policy reduced Long's power base, but his hold on the state's politics was so great, it would never destroy him. For that, the Roosevelt administration turned to the Bureau of Internal Revenue.

The Hoover administration had taken the first step. Long's opponents had been besieging the federal government with accusations that taxes were not being paid on much of the millions that Long and his cronies were looting from the state. In 1932 Elmer Irey, chief of intelligence for the Treasury Department, sent an agent to Louisiana, and his report was encouraging: "Chief, Louisiana is crawling. Long and his gang are stealing everything in the state . . . and they're not paying taxes on the loot." But powerful political influences squelched the probe until early 1934, when Treasury Secretary Henry Morganthau Jr. called Irey into his office and told him to resume the investigation. If they could get Al Capone for income tax evasion, maybe they could do the same with Long.

On September 8, 1935, however, Long was shot by Carl Weiss, who was himself gunned down by Long's bodyguards. Weiss, a young physician, had apparently heard rumors that Long was about to discredit his father-in-law, an anti-Long judge, by accusing him of having Negro blood. In those days, such an accusation would have left both his wife and son with tainted blood. Long died thirty hours later of infection and internal bleeding.

Writing fourteen years later, Irey was certain that if the assassination had not occurred, he would have gotten Long for tax evasion. Others are less certain. For all his demagoguery, Long was a shrewd man. While he was certainly evading taxes, he was also being careful to keep his paper trail clean. One federal prosecutor admitted in private: "We have no income tax case against Huey Long. We've traced the money coming in, but it all stops at one of his lieutenants."

Long's death ended the threat he posed to FDR's reelection bid. Legally and ethically, the IRS probe into Long's lieutenants should have continued unabated. The original investigation may have been tainted by a desire to get Long, but there was plenty of evidence that his underlings had been guilty of tax fraud on a massive scale. That is not what happened; instead, the administration made a deal.

When the income tax evasion cases came up, U.S. Attorney René Viosca moved to have most of them dismissed because "the changed atmosphere since the death of Long made convictions extremely improbable." Criminal charges were dropped, and the government concentrated on collecting back taxes and imposing small fines—typically $1,000—instead of years in prison. Long's gang got off light.

When the story got out, newspapers across the country, both Democratic and Republican, were outraged. The Bureau of Internal Revenue made it clear that it had no part in the decision not to prosecute. Irey stated: "We made careful investigations and accumulated a mass of evidence which we felt, and which we still feel, provided the basis for successful prosecution." A conservative columnist named Westbrook Pegler termed the deal "The Second Louisiana Purchase." The first had bought the Louisiana territory from France; the second, he said, had bought Long's political machine for Roosevelt.

Only one part of the deal could be said to be in the national interest. Some of Long's underlings were attempting to follow in his footsteps, and there was a possibility that one might turn out to have the same genius for demagoguery as Long. But it is unlikely that such a possibility played a major role in FDR's calculation. The president's reasons for making the deal were clearly political. He intended to buy the silence of a very powerful set of critics on his left and ensure that Louisiana's congressional delegation supported his agenda.

Most presidents would have found what happened next embarrassing. On June 12, 1936, the president was passing through Texas on his way to fish in the Gulf of Mexico. To show their appreciation for what he had done, the entire Louisiana state legislature did something unprecedented. Accompanied by several hundred followers, the legislators left their state and convened on the Texas Centennial grounds to meet the president and adopt a resolution "praising divine providence for providing a great leader, Franklin D. Roosevelt, who saved the nation from ruin and chaos." It is easy to conclude that it was their own salvation from legal ruin and chaos that many were praising.

WORKS PROGRESS ADMINISTRATION

The role of the Works Progress Administration was an ongoing source of political intrigue. The agency was used to build party strength, with senior managers being appointed to it through the recommendation of Jim Farley, chairman of the Democratic Party. Charges were made that the relief rolls were being manipulated for electoral purposes.

In spring 1937 FDR's growing frustration at seeing the aging, conservative Supreme Court overturn one economic recovery measure after another led him to suggest a plan to change the makeup of the Court. His scheme would allow a president to appoint a new justice for every sitting justice over the age of seventy who refused to retire. Roosevelt suggested that the Court could expand to as many as fifteen members. The plan met with almost universal disapproval from Congress, the press, and the man in the street.

To show their displeasure, some congressional Democrats chose to do something almost unprecedented. In alliance with Republicans, they cut the pay of Harry Hopkins, head of the Works Progress Administration (WPA), from $12,000 to $10,000. The *Baltimore Sun* had this to say about the calculated insult:

> No member voiced on the floor the real reason for this feeling toward Hopkins, but there is no mystery about it. They hate Hopkins because they are afraid of him; and they are afraid of him because they think he is capable of building up an organization in their individual districts to fight them, if they do not vote according to his orders.

As the Democratic primaries of 1938 approached, Thomas L. Stokes, a reporter for the Scripps-Howard newspaper chain, made a startling exposé of events in Kentucky. In one WPA district, relief funds were used to survey the 17,000 people receiving benefits to see whether they supported Gov. Albert "Happy" Chandler or Sen. Alben Barkley, who was the administration's candidate for the Senate. In another district, those on relief were asked to sign papers promising to support Barkley and to wear campaign buttons. Some of those who refused were thrown off WPA rolls. Republicans were told that there would be no WPA jobs for them if they did not register as Democrats and vote for Barkley. Letters were also sent out to those working for the WPA that said, "We know you will appreciate the opportunity of being given a chance to take an active part in reelecting Senator Barkley by making a liberal contribution toward his campaign expenses."

If the victims had been the small number of congressional Republicans who had survived the elections of 1934 and 1936, the Democratic majority would have done little or nothing. But because Governor Chandler was a loyal Democrat, the Senate Campaign Fund Investigating Committee sent an investigator to Kentucky. His report led Sen. Morris Sheppard of Texas to charge that what was happening there imperiled "the right of the people to a free and unpolluted ballot." Soon evidence was pouring in that similar tactics were being used in Pennsylvania, Tennessee, and Illinois. Enough evidence was accumulated to show a pattern: a politicized WPA was being used to target Democratic senators that FDR had been campaigning against because they had refused to support his plan to pack the Supreme Court the previous year.

In his 1940 book, *Chip Off My Shoulder,* Stokes gave the background to this "era of vengeance within the Democratic Party." It arose, he said, "from the rank and poisonous hatred generated as passions were aroused by the fight over the Supreme Court." Jim Farley, perhaps the most astute political observer within the administration, noted that FDR regarded that defeat as the worst since his loss in a 1920 election. "Presidential pride was sorely scorched," Farley wrote in 1948. "For weeks and months afterward I found him fuming against the members of his own party he blamed for this bucket of bitterness." In August of 1937, Roosevelt told Farley, "I've got them on the run, Jim. . . . They have no idea what's going to happen and are beginning to worry. They'll be sorry yet."

There was more to it than that. In 1937 the economy had taken a downward turn, and by 1938 it was clear that it was still in trouble. The president and his most loyal supporters (including Hopkins) wanted to redouble their efforts—starting more programs and spending more money to restart the economy. In Congress, however, a broad but still informal group was beginning to have doubts about the wisdom of placing more power in the hands of the executive. Roosevelt's attempt to pack the Court had worried many, as did his attempt in 1938 to get far-reaching authority to reorganize the executive branch without legislative approval. Congress's rebuff on that issue had brought FDR a defeat that, in its practical significance, was greater than his defeat over the Court. In the late 1930s, with the rise of Stalin, Hitler, and Mussolini, FDR's critics thought they had a right to be suspicious. Sensing that momentum was passing out of his hands, in March 1938 Roosevelt issued a statement from Warm Springs: "I have no inclination to be a dictator."

It is in this context that the WPA scandal should be considered. Most congressional Democrats had no problem with using the taxpayers' money to buy votes—many of them owed their elections to New Deal largess. But they were unhappy that what the WPA had been doing in Kentucky and at least three other states had become a matter of routine within the executive branch. The administration was probably right when it claimed that the WPA efforts to support Barkley probably did no more than nullify Chandler's use of state government machinery in his campaign. But at a national level all the little local and state corruptions tend to cancel one another out. Politicizing the WPA and similar programs would not be balanced by anything else. It would place an enormous amount of power in the hands of the president.

A few days before Stokes published his exposé of WPA abuses, a bill by Sen. Carl A. Hatch, Democrat of New Mexico, to ban any political use of the WPA suffered a narrow defeat. The Republicans and conservative Democrats did well in the election of 1938, and, when the Hatch bill came up again, it passed, primarily with the support of those Republicans and conservative Democrats.

Stokes, for all his loyalty to liberal causes, found his New Deal friends turning against him, treating him as "an outlaw, a pariah." With obvious regret, he wrote:

> I was unable to understand the attitude of those with whom I had worked, whose social and economic objectives I had shared. They sought refuge in the seductive philosophy that the end justifies the means and, under this philosophy, they condoned the political organization of relief workers. It was vain to point out that relief is likely to continue for a long time, and that it might become a force which could be regimented politically in threatening directions.

TENNESSEE VALLEY AUTHORITY

Congress investigated charges of corruption in the administration of the Tennessee Valley Authority when Arthur Morgan, one of the three directors, was removed from his office after a White House meeting with Roosevelt.

On March 22, 1938, a headline in the *New York Times* boldly proclaimed "Morgan Defies Roosevelt." Arthur E. Morgan, whom FDR had appointed to head the Tennessee Valley Authority (TVA), was refusing to resign or withdraw charges he had made against the other two members of the TVA board. New Deal foes went further, claiming that the Roosevelt administration was caught in a scandal as great as Teapot Dome. FDR's defenders took the opposite tack, attacking Morgan's sanity. Writing almost a quarter of a century later, Francis Biddle, counsel to the congressional investigation into Morgan's allegations, could hardly contain his spite. He described Morgan as "loose-minded and touched with mysticism" as well as an "American zealot" driven by "destructive egotism" and a "Messianic" temperament.

The story began in 1933, when FDR began to consider remaking the unfinished Muscle Shoals, Alabama, dam and fertilizer factory project from World War I into a comprehensive flood control and relief program for the Tennessee River Valley of Alabama and Tennessee (see page 276). He turned to Arthur Morgan, a well-respected flood control engineer and the president of Antioch College. As an engineer on the 1913 Miami (Ohio) River Valley Project, Morgan had demonstrated great skill at building dams under tight financial restraints. At Antioch College he had shown an equal talent for developing innovative educational programs. Those abilities, coupled with a well-deserved reputation for integrity and nonpartisanship, made him an ideal choice for TVA director.

Instead, the appointment became a disaster for both Roosevelt and Morgan. In retrospect, the warning signs were present from the start. One was the contrast between the president's public and private attitudes toward patronage. In his message to Congress, Roosevelt had called for TVA to be "a corporation clothed with the power of government but possessed of the flexibility and initiative of a private enterprise." To achieve that, the enabling legislation took a unusual approach. TVA was to be exempt from civil service laws, but patronage of any sort was absolutely forbidden. If patronage was discovered, the law held the president personally responsible for removing the guilty board member.

Privately, things were different. At the time Morgan was appointed, FDR asked him to meet with James Farley, who was both postmaster general and chairman of the Democratic National Committee. Neither of Farley's positions had anything to do with water projects, but both had quite a bit to do with providing work for loyal Democrats. When Morgan refused to do as Farley demanded, Morgan was told repeatedly, as he said, "that such a policy would get me into a great deal of trouble," a warning he noted in writing as soon as the meeting was over. Unwisely, Morgan trusted Roosevelt's words—"There is to be no politics in this!"—and did not pay enough attention to the president's attempt to coerce him through Farley. Roosevelt made a similar mistake. He was unprepared for someone who refused to be compromised.

The other mistake concerned the two men chosen to serve on the board. As director, Morgan was to concentrate on building the dams and planning community outreach programs, particularly in impoverished areas. For agricultural programs, FDR chose the president of the University of Tennessee, Harcourt A. Morgan (no relation to Arthur). Harcourt Morgan was not a corrupt man, but he was cautious and, in the infighting that developed, he saw which side was going to win and joined it.

Most of Arthur Morgan's difficulties centered on the third board member, David E. Lilienthal. In temperament, he and Lilienthal were almost polar opposites. One observer who saw their conflict at close range described them this way:

Morgan was an awkward fighter. . . . In discussion his scrupulous anxiety to be accurate and fair made him hesitant . . . tending to becoming inarticulate in man-to-man controversy. He was not skilled in the ways of politics and politicians.

In contrast, "Lilienthal had a controlled, driving, effective intensity, and was brilliantly skillful in the use of many weapons." If Morgan had been a bit less trusting, he would have blocked Lilienthal's appointment, as he had been warned that Lilienthal was ambitious and would probably try to "steal the show." Soon after he was appointed, Lilienthal turned his considerable political skills to destroying Morgan.

Both Arthur Morgan and Harcourt Morgan were chosen for their technical skills. To those who lobbied for Lilienthal's appointment, his chief virtue was an all-consuming hatred of private power companies. Francis Biddle's accusation against Arthur Morgan—that he was a destructive zealot—was not even remotely true. Morgan was a conciliator and so self-effacing that during his first two years as director he never voted against his two colleagues. Lilienthal was a different sort. At eighteen he had written, "I am not moderate in any of my activities." Later, as a crusading lawyer, he talked of his "taste for blood" and claimed that his foe was always "either a shouldering bully or a vulpine shyster." Morgan, the so-called loose-minded mystic, was quite practical when it came to public policy issues: decisions about the merits of private or public power were to depend on which served the public better. Lilienthal was part of a small but powerful group that viewed commercial power companies as evil. Another member of that group, Sen. George W. Norris of Nebraska, preferred to see the Muscle Shoals dam sit uncompleted for a decade and a half rather than put it in the hands of a power company. Toward the end of 1936, when the clash was becoming heated, Norris wrote to Roosevelt that Arthur Morgan's negotiations with power companies indicated he had "gone over to the enemy." Roosevelt did not share this zeal. Instead, he used his clash with power companies as a tool to manipulate voters, playing on the anger many felt each month when their electric bill came. Just before the 1936 election Roosevelt, speaking of the power companies, told a Madison Square Garden crowd, "They are unanimous in their hate for me—and I welcome their hatred." Morgan would have no part of such appeals.

Three issues dominated the conflict between Arthur Morgan and Lilienthal. The first arose in the summer of 1935, when Morgan received solid evidence that Lilienthal was passing over more qualified applicants to give jobs to relatives of two Tennessee politicians. The positions were minor, but the law was clear and unequivocal. Morgan was so outraged at Lilienthal's use of patronage that he abandoned his policy of never voting against other members of the board.

News about the second issue reached Morgan in 1936. It concerned George J. Berry, a Tennessee union official and New Deal activist. In the

Efforts to portray disagreements over TVA as a scandal in a league with Teapot Dome failed, as shown in this cartoon from September 7, 1938.

fall of 1934 TVA's head geologist discovered that Berry had bought the mineral rights to land that would soon be covered with water from Norris Dam. In 1935 TVA hired outside geologists who confirmed what had been suspected all along: the quarries would be worthless, even if they were not under water. There was every reason to believe that Berry had bought the quarries in order to be compensated for their loss. Rather than treat the matter as a scam, however, in June of 1936, Lilienthal and Harcourt Morgan worked out a payment for Berry. Arthur Morgan openly opposed it, and on March 1, 1938, Berry lost in court after documents came out revealing his plans.

The third issue was an idea for regional power pooling, meaning that all the electrical generating capacity of a region would be tied together into one large grid. Everyone's generators would contribute power, and everyone, public or private, would draw from the pool. Estimates of cost savings ranged from 15 percent to 25 percent. Morgan became a strong supporter of the idea both for its savings and because it offered the opportunity for public/private cooperation. The motivations of FDR, Norris, and Lilienthal were more complex, but they hoped the power companies would either reject the idea so they could be attacked or would be so overwhelmed by FDR's 1936 victory that they would be forced to negotiate from weakness.

They were unhappy when the power companies enthusiastically adopted the idea, and they became even more unhappy in December of 1936 when the power companies won a federal court injunction against TVA expansion. The decision (later overturned) meant that power companies would be negotiating from a position of strength. Under those conditions, Lilienthal and Harcourt Morgan began to oppose the pooling plan. Arthur Morgan's refusal to change his position enraged them and led to accusations that he was an enemy to administration policy, even though, as the *New York Times* pointed out, the pooling idea "is the president's, not the utilities'."

In deference to the president, Arthur Morgan and Lilienthal restrained their attacks on one another until after the 1936 elections, but then the debate became public and heated. Knowing that FDR was trying to drive him out of office, Morgan began to insist on a congressional investigation, which FDR wanted to avoid. Morgan's charges were substantial and true. Lilienthal had clearly engaged in behavior that required his dismissal, and both he and Harcourt Morgan had shown poor judgment in the Berry case.

At that point FDR tried a tactic that had served him well in 1932 when he was governor of New York. By repeatedly harassing New York City mayor Jimmy Walker with questions, he had forced him to resign without losing the support of Tammany Hall, the city's Democratic machine. He thought he could do the same to Arthur Morgan. He invited all three TVA board members to confer with him. After twice refusing, Morgan responded to a direct order to appear at the president's office on March 11, 1938. Afterward, Morgan wrote to his wife that, while all three board members were supposed to be treated equally, the other two had shown up with well-prepared answers that "seemed to fit as in a catechism" with FDR's questions. For six hours FDR and Morgan went back and forth, with Morgan insisting on making a statement and calling for a congressional investigation and FDR pretending that he wanted "facts, and only facts." FDR's behavior was sheer pretense. He had wanted a TVA director who would be seen as a man of integrity, but had appointed one who actually had integrity. FDR tried two more meetings, each briefer than the first, before he fired Morgan on March 23.

With Republicans crying foul, Morgan got his hearings. A joint committee of Congress held hearings between May and December of 1938. No one was surprised when the majority and minority reports came out along party lines. The majority report, written by Biddle, exonerated Lilienthal and Harcourt Morgan. The minority report blasted TVA as wasteful and unnecessary.

Far more impressive was Arthur Morgan's refusal to use his best evidence of wrongdoing—solid proof that Lilienthal had made illegal patronage appointments—contained in a report prepared by Gordon R. Clapp. In his book, *The Making of TVA*, Arthur Morgan explained that had that report been made public, "I think Mr. Clapp would have been immediately dismissed." Senator Norris had refused to look at the Clapp report, and Morgan, perhaps cured of his former naiveté, had little reason to believe that it would change the president's mind or that of the congressional majority. He could do nothing to save himself, but, by protecting Clapp, he ensured that someone who shared his integrity would remain behind. In 1939 Clapp became general manager of TVA, and later, chairman of the board.

ROOSEVELT FAMILY

The Roosevelt family spent many years in the national spotlight. Eleanor Roosevelt was especially controversial. Two sons, James and Elliott, also ran into various difficulties.

Eleanor Roosevelt

The strongly independent Eleanor Roosevelt was a focus of scrutiny because of the active role she took in a number of policy initiatives. Of particular notice were investigations of her earnings while she was first lady and her relationship with Lorena Hickok.

Rep. Hamilton Fish, a Republican from New York, raised serious questions about the first family's tax returns for 1933 through 1938. Fish was reacting to a critic of the Roosevelts who estimated that Eleanor had earned more than $3 million in fees for her work as a radio commentator, lecturer, and newspaper columnist. The House of Representatives investigated the tax returns and cleared the Roosevelts of any wrongdoing.

In 1932 Eleanor Roosevelt met an Associated Press reporter named Lorena Hickok, who had been assigned to cover the nominee's wife at the Democratic National Convention. Hickok, a lesbian, eventually quit her job and in January 1941 moved into the White House. For the next four years, she lived in the executive mansion.

Even though she had her own room, she often stayed in Eleanor's room, according to one of the maids. FDR did not like the arrangement and was once heard to shout, "I want that woman kept out of this house!" It is possible that the two women shared a physical relationship, but Elliott Roosevelt, one of Eleanor's sons, thought it unlikely. However, her feelings are well documented. Eleanor wrote more than 2,000 letters to Lorena in the thirty years they knew each other. In those letters—which are housed at the Roosevelt Presidential Library at Hyde Park—Eleanor often writes passages that are strongly affectionate. For example, on March 7, 1933, Lorena's fortieth birthday, Eleanor wrote:

> Hick darling, All day I've thought of you & another birthday I will be with you. . . . Oh! I want to put my arms around you. I ache to hold you close. Your ring is a great comfort. I look at it and think she does love me or I wouldn't be wearing it!

James Roosevelt

In *The Roosevelt Myth* John T. Flynn reprinted a charge leveled against James Roosevelt, a son of the president, that he had used his father's name and the influence of the White House to develop a lucrative insurance business. James estimated that in 1937, before joining his father's administration at the White House, his income was nearly $44,000. The amount raised questions from critics. James responded by having his tax returns reprinted in a national magazine and by granting interviews to several others. In the end, no proof could be found that James had used his father's name or power to attract corporate clients to his business.

Elliott Roosevelt

Elliott Roosevelt, a son of the president, was involved in a procurement controversy. Elliott was an army air force officer assigned to aid in the development of a photoreconnaissance plane in 1944. After being the guest of aircraft manufacturer Howard Hughes, Elliott recommended the purchase of the Hughes F-11 reconnaissance plane. There was active disagreement as to the merits of the plywood plane, which was not ready for delivery until after World War II was over. In fact, Hughes was seriously injured in a crash of the first test model. In 1947 the Senate's special defense investigating committee called Elliott Roosevelt as a witness. He denied that Hughes's hospitality had influenced his decision and criticized the committee's investigation as an attempt to smear his father's reputation. The committee report did not charge Elliott with any wrongdoing, but questioned his technical qualifications to recommend the purchase of aircraft.

DOLLAR-A-YEAR MEN

The Roosevelt administration reinstituted Woodrow Wilson's policy of having major corporations provide managers to handle increased war production needs. A Senate committee, originally headed by Harry S. Truman, found widespread kickbacks and graft.

The outbreak of World War II required the government to hire more staff and to spend large amounts of money quickly. To get the sort of management expertise it needed, the Roosevelt administration adopted the same technique that Woodrow Wilson had used during World War I. The administration borrowed corporate executives and other experts from the business world and paid them either a dollar a year or nothing. These employees were referred to as w.o.c.—without compensation—but they continued to draw their regular salaries from their former employers. Portrayed in the best possible light, the system was beneficial. The government got the skills of individuals who might not have accepted these jobs at government salaries, which were much lower than corporate pay. The corporations got an opportunity to demonstrate their patriotism, and the borrowed employees received some assurance that their companies would take them back after the war. The number of such employees was substantial. Just a few months after the attack on Pearl Harbor, the War Production Board (WPB) alone had almost 1,300 people on loan from industry. Other agencies—ranging from the War Manpower Commission to the Petroleum Administration—also had large numbers of such staff.

Skeptics pointed out that the system was filled with conflicts of interest. In an effort to prevent problems, the WPB adopted four rules. First, anyone who was appointed must have outstanding skill, great integrity, and be "especially qualified for the work for which he is chosen." Second, no dollar-a-year man could be appointed to a position if someone equally qualified could be found who would work for "a regular Government salary." Third, no one could be placed in a position where he would "make decisions affecting the affairs of his own company." Fourth, all applicants had to undergo a government investigation.

Perhaps the most effective constraint on abuse was a bipartisan Senate committee, which was established before the war and led by Harry Truman (until he became FDR's vice-presidential candidate in August 1944). The Truman Committee members were skeptical of the wisdom of using dollar-a-year men. In their first annual report, dated January 15, 1942, they noted:

> The committee is opposed to a policy of taking free services from persons with axes to grind, and the committee believes that the Government should not continue to accept the loan of dollar-a-year and w.o.c men by companies with so large a stake in the defense program. . . . No man can honestly serve two masters.

It chose, however, to bend to the administration and permit the program to continue under congressional scrutiny.

During the war, critics leveled a number of charges against the dollar-a-year program. The first came in the early days when the federal government was trying to get businesses to convert from consumer goods to wartime production. Dollar-a-year men were said to have shown undue leniency in allowing businesses to delay their conversion. Much of the problem centered on timing. Many businesses preferred to wait until they had government contracts in hand before converting. As businessmen, the dollar-a-year men had no difficulty understanding that point of view.

Second, only relatively large businesses could afford to pay dollar-a-year men while they worked in government. As a result, many small businesses, eager to get their share of the wartime contracts, accused the dollar-a-year men of showing a bias for large business. Again the dollar-a-year men were probably not openly biased. They simply thought larger businesses were better qualified.

The third charge was the most serious—that dollar-a-year men favored their own companies or industries in their decision making. Here the problem was much more complex than simply barring someone from awarding a contract to his former employer. The allocation of scarce raw materials and industrial machinery, as well as price controls, all had an impact on how well companies and industries would do. Even a slight shift in how resources were allocated or how price controls were set could have enormous implications. Again, charges of favoritism were difficult to prove. Unlike peacetime, government contracts were so plentiful there was no need for obvious misdeeds such as not awarding a contract to the lowest bidder. Favoritism would express itself subtly and perhaps unconsciously in the details of how a contract was written or placed out for bids.

The fourth charge went in tandem with the second. To the extent that larger companies had been able to capture a greater share of wartime contracts, they would be at a disadvantage when the time came to convert back to producing consumer goods. Critics claimed that the dollar-a-year men delayed the conversion back to peacetime production longer than necessary to give their companies time to prepare.

In practice, in the confusion of war, with rapidly changing and often fiercely debated priorities, all these charges were difficult to prove. Undoubtedly, efforts to make the dollar-a-year men program free of bias could not succeed completely. However, the administration's diligence meant that the war effort benefited more from the dollar-a-year men's expertise than it was harmed by biases they may have brought to their jobs.

Left unanswered are the sorts of questions that Truman and other members of his committee repeatedly asked officials in the Roosevelt administration. During World War II millions of young men were drafted into the military. They were placed in harm's way, denied the opportunity to work at more lucrative jobs in war factories, and paid as little as $252 a year. Yet the nation was told that it could not acquire the expertise it required from corporate executives and industry experts if they were paid the $5,000 to $10,000 a year that the government paid its higher officials. A brief prepared by the Truman Committee's staff stated: "These dollar-a-year and w.o.c men have consistently maintained that business cannot go on as usual, that we must all make sacrifices. The testimony should indicate that this does not apply in the case of these men who have enunciated this 'sacrifice is necessary policy.'" That was perhaps the real scandal of the dollar-a-year men.

BIBLIOGRAPHY

Anderson, Patrick. *The President's Men.* Garden City, N.Y.: Doubleday, 1968.

Biddle, Francis. *In Brief Authority.* Garden City, N.Y.: Doubleday, 1962.

Burns, James MacGregor. *Roosevelt: The Lion and the Fox.* New York: Harcourt, Brace, and World, 1956.

Collier, Peter, and David Horowitz. *The Roosevelts: An American Saga.* New York: Simon and Schuster, 1994.

Davenport, Walter. "I'm Glad You Asked Me." *Collier's,* August 20, 1938, 9–12.

Davis, Kenneth. *FDR: The New Deal Years.* New York: Random House, 1986.

Faber, Doris. *The Life of Lorena Hickok, E. R.'s Friend.* New York: Morrow, 1980.

Flynn, John T. *The Roosevelt Myth.* Garden City, N.Y.: Garden City Publishing, 1948.

Freidel, Frank. *Franklin D. Roosevelt.* Boston: Little, Brown, 1952–1973.

Goodwin, Doris Kearns. *No Ordinary Time: Franklin and Eleanor Roosevelt.* New York: Simon and Schuster, 1994.

Graham, George A. *Morality in American Politics.* New York: Random House, 1952.

Hagood, Wesley O. *Presidential Sex: From Founding Fathers to Bill Clinton.* Secaucus, N.J.: Carol Publishing, 1998.

Hair, William I. *The Kingfish and His Realm.* Baton Rouge: Louisiana State University Press, 1991.

Hickok, Lorena. *Eleanor Roosevelt: Reluctant First Lady.* New York: Dodd, Mead, 1961.

High, Stanley. "The WPA: Politician's Playground." *Current History* 50 (May 1939): 23–25.

Johnston, Alva. "Jimmy's Got It." *Saturday Evening Post,* July 2, 1938, 8–9.

Kane, Harnett T. *Louisiana Hayride.* New York: Morrow, 1941.

Lash, Joseph R. *Eleanor and Franklin.* New York: New American Library, 1973.

McCraw, Thomas K. *Morgan v. Lilienthal.* Chicago: Loyola University Press, 1970.

———. *TVA and the Power Fight, 1933–1939.* Philadelphia: Lippincott, 1971.

Miller, Nathan. *FDR: An Intimate History.* Garden City, N.Y.: Doubleday, 1983.

Mitchell, Jack. *Executive Privilege: Two Centuries of White House Scandals.* New York: Hippocrene Books, 1992.

Morgan, Arthur E. *The Making of the TVA.* Buffalo, N.Y.: Prometheus Books, 1974.

Parks, Lillian R. *The Roosevelts: A Family in Turmoil.* Englewood Cliffs, N.J.: Prentice Hall, 1981.

Patterson, James T. *Congressional Conservatism and the New Deal.* Lexington: University of Kentucky Press, 1967.

Ribble, Donald H. *The Truman Committee.* New Brunswick, N.J.: Rutgers University Press, 1964.

Rollins, Alfred B., Jr. *Roosevelt and Howe.* New York: Knopf, 1962.

Roosevelt, Elliott, and James Brough. *A Rendezvous with Destiny: The Roosevelts of the White House.* New York: Putnam, 1975.

Schlesinger, Arthur M., Jr. *The Age of Roosevelt: The Politics of Upheaval.* Boston: Houghton Mifflin, 1960.

Stokes, Thomas L. *Chip Off My Shoulder.* Princeton: Princeton University Press, 1940.

Woodward, C. Vann. *Responses of the Presidents to Charges of Misconduct.* New York: Dell Publishing, 1974.

HARRY S. TRUMAN

Thirty-Third President
1945–1953

Harry Truman was born May 8, 1884, in Lamar, Missouri. He was the eldest of three children born to Martha Truman and John Truman, a mule trader. Harry attended public school in Independence, Missouri, and wanted to attend West Point or Annapolis. His poor eyesight, although corrected with glasses, disqualified him for the military academies. He learned to play the piano and was a voracious reader. Truman held a number of odd jobs until 1906, when he returned to help run the family farm in Grandview, Missouri. At age sixteen, he had his first political experience, serving as a page at the 1900 Democratic National Convention.

From 1905 to 1911 he served in the Missouri National Guard and reenlisted in May 1917 to serve in World War I. He rose from the rank of lieutenant to major by May 1919 having seen action in France. On June 28, 1919, Truman married Elizabeth "Bess" Wallace, the daughter of a local politician.

After the war, Truman and an army friend opened a haberdashery in Kansas City, but the venture failed in 1922. A lifelong Democrat, he decided to enter politics. He studied law at the Kansas City Law School from 1923 to 1925. With the backing of the Thomas J. Pendergast political machine, Truman was elected judge of Jackson County, Missouri. Defeated for reelection in 1924, he was then elected as the presiding judge of the county in 1926, a post he held until 1934.

In 1934 he was elected to the U.S. Senate over the incumbent Republican and was reelected six years later. Often referred to as the "senator from Pendergast"—because he owed his political career to the Kansas City machine boss—Truman claimed that Pendergast never asked him to do anything dishonest in return for his support. In the Senate, Truman generally supported the New Deal measures of FDR and gained national attention when he chaired an investigation that exposed $15 billion in military waste.

At the Democratic National Convention in 1944, party leaders sought to remove Vice President Henry A. Wallace from the ticket. Roosevelt decided on Truman, and he was nominated on the second ballot. Roosevelt died April 12, 1945, and the presidential oath of office was administered by Chief Justice Harlan Fiske Stone to Truman at 7:09 p.m. that day.

Truman oversaw the end of World War II including the decision to drop atomic bombs on the Japanese cities of Hiroshima and Nagasaki. He was also a driving force in the creation of the United Nations. Truman was elected to a full term in 1948 by a slim 1.3 million votes in a field that included Republican Thomas E. Dewey, Dixiecrat Strom Thurmond, and Progressive Henry Wallace. During his second term, Truman issued the Truman Doctrine, which stated that the United States would seek to contain the spread of communism. He also continued to spearhead European recovery through the Marshall Plan and recognized Israel in 1948. Truman turned his policy of containment into action during the Korean War. He also authorized the development of the hydrogen bomb.

Truman's domestic policy consisted of a set of legislative initiatives known collectively as the Fair Deal. The measures included the Housing Act of 1949, an increase in the minimum wage, expansion of Social Security, and the desegregation of the armed forces.

Truman decided not to seek a second full term as president and retired to Independence, Missouri, after campaigning for the losing Democratic candidate, Adlai Stevenson of Illinois. Throughout his retirement, he remained active in politics. In 1956 he again campaigned for Stevenson. In 1960 he worked for the nomination of Sen. Stuart Symington of Missouri for president over Sen. John F. Kennedy of Massachusetts, whom he regarded as too inexperienced. In the general election, he supported the party's nominee. In failing health for a number of years, Truman died December 26, 1972.

KANSAS CITY ELECTION INQUIRY

Truman tried to use his political connections to Kansas City Democratic machines to prevent the reelection of a Democratic House member who had opposed his legislative agenda.

On July 18, 1946, Truman announced he was opposing the renomination of Democratic representative Roger C. Slaughter from the Fifth District of Missouri, which included Kansas City. Slaughter had offended Truman by his vote in the House Committee on Rules to bottle up the Fair Employment Practices bill, which Truman considered important to the upcoming congressional elections. Truman favored Slaughter's primary opponent, Enos Axtell, and encouraged the Pendergast political machine to work for his nomination.

Slaughter was the overwhelming favorite in the August 6 primary, but amazingly lost by 2,300 votes. The president had played an active role in the campaign. He even flew to Kansas City on the day of the primary to rally support for Axtell. The voting results were suspicious: Axtell carried the four Kansas City wards controlled by Pendergast by ratios of 5 to 1.

Rumors of fraud and gangsterism began to circulate almost immediately. The Slaughter campaign complained that almost all of the watchers and challengers that the Kansas City election board had certified were members of the Pendergast machine. The *Kansas City Star* cried foul and sent investigators who collected 1,400 affidavits that recounted threats and payoffs for votes.

In October the clamor forced Attorney General Tom C. Clark to permit an investigation by the FBI. Theron Lamar Caudle, the assistant attorney general in charge of the criminal division, gave the FBI its instructions. It was not until June 1947 that it was disclosed that Caudle had authorized FBI agents to make only a "preliminary investigation" and had instructed them to interview only two reporters from the *Star* and four election inspectors. Of its report, the FBI explained, "Its contents do not constitute the results of an investigation but pursuant to the specific instructions of the Attorney General are merely a summary of the data developed by the *Kansas City Star* and the Election Board." U.S. Attorney Sam Wear prepared a synopsis of the report and submitted it to three federal judges in Missouri who concluded there was no basis for a grand jury investigation. On January 6, 1947, the Justice Department issued a statement that also concluded there was no basis for grand jury action and declared the case closed.

However, the investigations did not end there. In spring 1947 Sen. James P. Kem, Republican of Missouri, began an inquiry. A grand jury in Jackson County, Missouri, which had been investigating the vote frauds, made its report in a courtroom in Independence on May 27. It declared that the evidence showed that "there had been a deliberate and calculated plan to miscount votes and otherwise steal the election." The grand jury concluded that Slaughter had been deprived of the nomination by fraud. This grand jury and another produced twenty-four indictments. All ballots and records used by the grand jury in its investigation were returned to the vaults of the Kansas City Board of Elections for safekeeping. However, the day before public hearings were to begin, all of the ballots and records from the primary disappeared. The vault had been blown open, and the records were gone. No doors in the building had been forced.

Without the documentary evidence, Senator Kem's investigation had little to go on. The committee heard testimony from witnesses concerning the FBI's investigation, and Attorney General Clark testified, "The FBI at my instance conducted a full investigation as to the charges of fraud in the primary—no evidence of a federal violation was established." The Kem investigation stalled before it ever got started, as did the prosecutions of those indicted by the grand jury. Without the ballots and records, there was no way to prove fraud.

Suspicion lingered concerning the role of the Justice Department. The 1947 committee narrowly rejected an investigation of the part played by Attorney General Clark, and the minority criticized him for inaccurately representing the nature of the original investigation. As Caudle conceded later, the FBI effort had been carefully limited and had received "top-level attention." A member of a House subcommittee investigating the Justice Department in 1952 charged further that Clark had removed reports on the primary from the FBI files for two years, until 1949. That same subcommittee noted that Justice Department officials who were involved in the case "fared unusually well in their subsequent careers." Most notably, Caudle was moved to a more desirable post in the tax division. It is almost impossible to determine, however, to what extent such advancement was a reward, or what role, if any, the White House played in either the investigation or the promotions.

HARRY H. VAUGHAN, STAFFER

Harry Vaughan, who served on Truman's Senate and White House staffs, engaged in numerous swaps of access for gifts and favors.

Brig. Gen. Harry H. Vaughan, a Missourian, had served on Truman's senatorial staff and continued to be a trusted adviser in the White House. But Vaughan was a wheeler-dealer who used his influence to aid political friends. On May 1, 1945, for example, he wrote a note on White House stationery to obtain a wartime travel priority for perfume manufacturer David Bennett. Vaughan managed to secure Air Transport Command space on a plane for Bennett and John F. Maragon of Kansas City. Bennett and Maragon were caught smuggling forty-one kilos of perfume raw materials worth more than $53,000 from Europe. Nonetheless, only months later, Vaughan successfully recommended Maragon for a position with an American mission to Greece.

Vaughan was also a major participant in a celebrated incident that made the deep freeze a symbol of corruption in the Truman administration. According to Vaughan, "In 1945 I had a talk with two old friends of mine— Mr. Harry Hoffman and Mr. David Bennett. The subject of deep-freeze units came up, and I said that I would like one for my house and that I would also like to send one to the Little White House [the Truman residence] in Independence." Hoffman, a Milwaukee manufacturer, sent not merely a freezer for Vaughan and for Mrs. Truman but four more for other members of the administration—John W. Snyder, federal loan administrator; Fred Vinson, secretary of the Treasury; and James K. Vardaman and Matthew Connelly of the White House staff. Only Vinson sent his back.

Another incident that earned Vaughan notoriety was his effort to assist Tanforan racetrack, a California enterprise controlled by gambling interests. By exerting heavy pressure on the housing expediter, Vaughan cleared the way for Tanforan to receive an allocation of $150,000 worth of scarce building materials.

Until mid-1949 Vaughan's activities had been carried on largely in secret, but a wave of revelations exposed one of the most corrupt practices and worst examples of influence peddling. Government procurement offices often hired freelance agents to act as intermediaries between corporations and government agencies. These agents were paid a commission of 5 percent on the value of the contract. A story surfaced in the *New York Herald Tribune* that a furniture manufacturer reported that he had bribed James V. Hunt, a paid consultant to the War Assets Administration. Hunt worked through Gen. Alden H. Waitt of the Army Chemical Corps, quartermaster general Herman Feldman, and Vaughan to secure a lucrative government contract.

Harry Vaughan

The story led to a congressional investigation of Vaughan, which was headed by Sen. Clyde R. Hoey, Democrat of North Carolina. Hearings began in August 1949, and a committee report was issued January 18, 1950. The investigation resulted in a perjury conviction for John Maragon, a 5 percenter who had used his contacts with Vaughan to enrich himself, and severe criticism of Vaughan for making Maragon's "fixing" operations possible. Yet in none of his activities, save that of the freezers, was Vaughan accused of accepting personal payment, although it was alleged that he collected political contributions.

President Truman remained loyal to his longtime aide. In a news conference August 18, 1949, he specifically declined to discuss the Hoey investigation and suggested to reporters that they "suspend judgment on General Vaughan until he has been heard by the committee." Even after the committee had chastised Vaughan, Truman did not publicly discipline him; in fact, the general remained in the White House to the end of the Truman administration. Nor did the administration undertake major reforms as a result of the 5-percenter investigation, beyond a hasty announcement by the Department of Defense that it had altered procurement procedures to permit business people to deal directly with the Pentagon without intermediaries.

GRAIN COMMODITY SPECULATION

At the same time President Truman was criticizing grain speculation, several members of the White House staff were engaging in speculation.

A pattern that persisted through the Truman administration was the president's refusal to disavow associates whose actions threatened to embarrass him. A striking instance occurred in October 1947, when the president criticized speculation in the grain market only to have the White

House physician, Dr. Wallace H. Graham, admit two days later that he was one of the speculators. (Dr. Graham also asserted falsely that he had pulled out of the market; he did not actually withdraw until December 18, a day before the names of speculators were revealed to Congress.) Another speculator, on a much larger scale, was Edwin Pauley, who had been named a special assistant to the secretary of the army. He was accused by Harold Stassen, a potential Republican presidential candidate, of having "profiteered" in grain to the tune of $1 million on the basis of inside information. Pauley denied obtaining such information but conceded that he had made profits of $932,703 in three years of speculation. He resigned from the Department of the Army January 11, 1948.

The commodity investigation spread well beyond the White House. The Senate Appropriations Committee, seeking further information on insider trading, asked the Commodity Exchange Authority for the names of speculators. It took a joint resolution of Congress to get the Agriculture Department to comply, but on December 29, 1947, it released the names of 100 federal, state, and municipal officials involved in commodity speculation. In 1948 a House select committee reported that 823 federal employees had made between $10 million and $20 million in the grain market during 1946 and 1947, but it did not charge that these employees had used inside information illegally or unethically.

RECONSTRUCTION FINANCE CORPORATION INVESTIGATION

The Senate investigation of the RFC uncovered favoritism in its dealings and forced President Truman to reorganize the agency.

On February 8, 1950, the Senate—voting only a few days after the Reconstruction Finance Corporation (RFC) had filed suit to foreclose on the Lustron Corporation, which had defaulted on $37.5 million in loans—ordered an investigation of the RFC and its handling of the Lustron loans and others. The subsequent inquiry revealed that RFC directors had been manipulated not only by influence peddlers but also by party officials and at least one member of the White House staff. Two directors in particular were found to be subject to influence: Walter L. Dunham, a token Republican who owed his appointment to the Michigan Democratic national committeeman, and William E. Willett, who had risen through the RFC ranks. The committee cited several specific instances of the two being controlled by others, including Joseph H. Rosenbaum, chief partner of a Washington law firm. Rosenbaum had boasted that he had Willett and Dunham in his "hip pocket."

The shenanigans within the RFC gradually emerged during the Senate investigation headed by Sen. J. William Fulbright, Democrat of Arkansas. An interim committee report issued on May 19, 1950, sought to prevent an RFC loan of $10.1 million to the Texmass Petroleum Company, which had used the services of two former administration officials, E. Merl Young, who had been an RFC examiner but had since taken a job with Lustron the day after one of its loans was approved, and William M. Boyle Jr., who had been on Truman's Senate staff and was currently Democratic Party chairman. Both the RFC's Dallas office and its review committee had opposed the Texmass loan, but the RFC directors approved it, 2–1. The Fulbright committee's criticism failed to stop it. A second interim report, on August 11, found fault with RFC supervision of a Lustron transportation contract that had permitted the milking of Lustron funds. In September the committee discovered that two potential purchasers of RFC properties were under indictment and forced the RFC to call off the sale.

Despite the growing investigation, President Truman remained loyal to Dunham and Willett and reappointed them in August 1950. The Senate rejected their nominations. Truman also nominated C. Edward Rowe to be the RFC vice chairman. His job, according to his later testimony, was to clean up the RFC. Rowe came to the post from the Harrington & Richardson Arms Company of Massachusetts, which had received a $300,000 RFC loan in April 1950.

The Fulbright committee's "Favoritism and Influence" report revealed the pressures on directors, most notably from Donald Dawson, the personnel adviser to the president. Dawson's wife was the chief custodian of RFC files, and he had been the RFC personnel officer and responsible, at least in part, for appointing Dunham and Willett. The report recommended that the agency be placed under a single administrator because of "deterioration of the top management structure . . . attributable to the equal division of the management responsibility among the members of the five-man Board of Directors." After discussing the situation with the president in private, the committee, dissatisfied with his response, made the report public on February 2, 1951. The president responded at a news conference that he had long since proposed such a change "and that reorganization plan was rejected at the behest of this committee that has written this asinine report."

Truman submitted a reorganization plan soon after, which Congress rejected. However, on April 30 the board of directors was abolished in favor of a single administrator. Four days later, Truman appointed Stuart Symington to fill that post.

But the president's action failed to resolve the controversy with Congress. Although RFC officials and outsiders such as Merl Young testified in public hearings, Truman declined to permit Dawson to appear for more than two months and apparently tried to pressure one of the committee members to cancel Dawson's subpoena. On May 10 Dawson testified. He denied that he had exerted influence in favor of specific loans, but admitted that he had accepted the hospitality of the Saxony Hotel in Miami Beach, which had received a loan of $1.5 million. Despite this and other damaging admissions, Dawson was retained on the White House staff.

The subsequent report on the RFC by the Senate Banking and Currency Committee did not discuss the role of the White House in creating the conditions that made the scandals possible. Even the hostile minority report conceded, "Other than the direct intervention in the ill-starred Lustron venture, there is no evidence that the Offices of the President were officially and responsibly used in influencing lending policies of the Corporation." Nor did that single "direct intervention" necessarily reflect on the president: when Lustron wanted to fire Young, Dawson called the matter to the president's attention, and Truman made the "very proper response" that Lustron should do what was best for the company. However, the fact that the employment of an influence peddler was checked with a president suggests an unhealthy relationship between the RFC and the White House.

BUREAU OF INTERNAL REVENUE

A House investigation into the bureau's records led to charges of graft and corruption and the removal of nine of the sixty-four district collectors.

The expansion of federal tax collections in the war and postwar years offered a fertile field for those seeking special favors from the government and those willing to dispense them. During the Truman administration, the Bureau of Internal Revenue was collecting taxes at eight times the prewar level, but its organization was antiquated and ill-equipped to handle such a load. Much of the responsibility fell to the sixty-four district collectors, who were political appointees. Flexible, complex tax laws administered by officials selected on bases other than expertise and the confidential nature of transactions between the bureau and the taxpayer resulted in the most widespread and serious official misconduct of the Truman years.

The scandal came to light in 1950 as a result of the efforts of Sen. John J. Williams, Republican of Delaware. An informant had told Williams of irregularities in the office of New York's third district. (Unknown to Williams, Commissioner George D. Schoeneman—former director of White House personnel—had already asked Treasury Secretary John Snyder to remove the district collector, James W. Johnson.) Williams asked for records of the New York office, but was refused. Undeterred, he reported his information to the Senate Finance Committee in executive session. Despite damning evidence against Johnson—including the bribery of eight of his subordinates by taxpayers—he clung to office for a year, defying both an informal presidential request and a resolution, introduced by Williams, calling for his removal.

In 1951 allegations of abuses in the Bureau of Internal Revenue brought about a full-blown congressional inquiry. Rep. Cecil R. King, Democrat of California, headed the House subcommittee, which throughout 1951 and 1952 uncovered illegal activity in collectors' offices and in the Washington headquarters. The investigation resulted in the removal of nine of the sixty-four district collectors. The King committee reported:

> Two of the nine Collectors separated from service had extorted large sums from delinquent taxpayers. Several evaded personal income taxes while in office and at least one Collector used his authority to prevent audit of his returns. The total confusion which reigned in the office of two Collectors demonstrated their incompetence as administrators. . . . Field investigations by this subcommittee disclosed that in a number of these offices conditions had been allowed to deteriorate as long as 16 years, because Bureau officials were unwilling to offend the politically appointed Collectors.

The most noted of these collectors was James P. Finnegan of the first Missouri (St. Louis) district, a friend of President Truman and Secretary Snyder. His name had also come up in the Fulbright subcommittee hearings on the RFC, not only because he had associated with the Dunham-Dawson-Young circle, but also because while he was a collector he had acted as attorney for American Lithofold Corporation, which had paid him $45,000 for his services.

Finnegan's abuses of taxpayers were revealed in 1950. Investigators in St. Louis found that Finnegan had taken part in a racket that involved referring tax delinquents to an insurance company that split its receipts with the collector, but this investigation produced no formal charges against him. In March 1951 a former employee complained to a federal judge in St. Louis that the district office had failed to act on tax fraud cases that involved clients defended by lawyers with political connections. Although a grand jury brought no immediate indictments, Finnegan resigned April 14, and the president accepted "with regret."

But that was not the end of his case. Senator Williams urged Secretary Snyder to take further action, and a grand jury was empaneled. Despite an apparent effort by the Justice Department to hamper the investigation, the grand jury handed up indictments. In October 1951, a week after he had admitted to congressional investigators that he had taken insurance proceeds and had accepted fees from a St. Louis law firm that owed back taxes, Finnegan was indicted on two counts of bribery and three counts of misconduct in office. He was found guilty in 1952 on the misconduct charges and served eighteen months in prison. President Lyndon B. Johnson pardoned Finnegan shortly before his death in 1967.

In 1951 alone 166 Internal Revenue officials were fired or forced to resign. The investigation also uncovered the fact that one former commissioner, John D. Nunan, had evaded taxes. He was convicted on related charges in 1954. His successor, Schoeneman, while not subject to charges of wrongdoing, nonetheless resigned July 31, 1951, after having failed to persuade Secretary Snyder to take sterner measures. Charles Oliphant resigned as the bureau's general counsel on December 4, 1951, a day after a disgruntled Chicago taxpayer had mentioned him as a member of a purported government ring attempting a half-million-dollar shakedown. Caudle, mentioned as another member of the ring, had been removed as head of the Justice Department's tax division less than three weeks before.

The Internal Revenue scandals came even closer to the president—in fact, producing the only criminal charge against a member of Truman's White House staff—when Matthew Connelly, Truman's appointments secretary, was shown to be involved. Connelly had worked for Truman on the Senate War Investigating Committee during World War II and had been on the White House staff since April 1945. In September 1952 Caudle, who had handled the Kansas City election fraud investigation, while testifying before the subcommittee investigating the Department of Justice, mentioned Connelly's name in connection with the tax case of Irving Sachs of St. Louis. According to later charges, Connelly had accepted gifts from Sachs's lawyer—a topcoat, two suits, and an oil royalty worth $7,000—for unspecified assistance. Connelly, moreover, had accepted these gratuities in 1951 and 1952 at the height of the tax investigation. Despite Connelly's purported aid, Sachs was convicted and fined. On December 1, 1955, the lawyer, Caudle, and Connelly were indicted for conspiracy. All three were convicted. Connelly served a term of less than a year in federal prison in 1960 and was pardoned by President John F. Kennedy in 1962.

The administration's countermeasures against this scandal resembled those taken in the RFC investigation—a willingness to make institutional changes combined with slowness to admit the fault of erring appointees. When John B. Dunlap succeeded Schoeneman as commissioner, he was given powers to investigate bureau employees, and one of his first steps was to order a check on employees' tax returns for the previous three years.

In the meantime, however, instances of misconduct surfaced in other tax offices. The administration was criticized and questioned about whether it had sought and ousted wrongdoers promptly. The president defended himself in a news conference on December 13, 1951:

> The collector in Boston was fired before anybody began to look into his situation, except the Treasury Department. The collector of revenue in St. Louis was dispensed with long before any committee went into it, and a grand jury right now in California has just indicted him. The necessary action in all these things had been taken by the executive branch of the Government whenever it was necessary.

Yet the chronology of the investigation shows that the sequence was more complicated than the president indicated. James Finnegan of the St. Louis office had indeed resigned early, but the administration had not looked into his misconduct, despite a damning Treasury agents' report. James G. Smyth of San Francisco was dismissed more than a month after—

not before—the subcommittee began its investigation of his office. Nor is the picture clear with respect to a number of other resignations or dismissals because they often just preceded or followed public testimony by the individual. Although the housecleaning was eventually widespread and thorough, the timing suggests that much of it was done in response to the heat of publicity.

On January 2, 1952, Truman announced a reorganization of the bureau. The plan set the following changes: (1) abolition of the sixty-four collectors' offices; (2) appointment of only one officer, the commissioner, by the president, with all other positions to be filled through civil service; and (3) establishment of an inspection service independent of the rest of the bureau. The House of Representatives approved the plan on January 30.

SPECIAL CORRUPTION INQUIRY

Charges of corruption were widespread in the Truman administration. The attorney general's roadblocks to an effective investigation led to his dismissal.

As 1951 was coming to a close, the White House was swamped with charges of corruption. In addition to the Reconstruction Finance Corporation and Bureau of Internal Revenue scandals, six other executive agencies were charged: the Office of Alien Property Custodian, the Federal Power Commission, the Antitrust Division of the Justice Department, the Maritime Commission, the Securities and Exchange Commission, and the Civil Aeronautics Board. To make matters worse, the touring congressional committee headed by Sen. Estes Kefauver of Tennessee had uncovered potentially damaging evidence of a link between the Democratic Party and organized crime, most notably at the local level in cities such as New York. The Agriculture Department was also under growing scrutiny as it was discovered that $10 million worth of government grain had been "converted" to private hands.

In his December 13, 1951, news conference, President Truman was repeatedly questioned about the plan of action he was going to take. Truman ignored questions about the appointment of a special prosecutor and/or the appointment of a commission to investigate all of the charges.

Eventually, however, he was forced to take action. After a federal judge declined to lead an investigation, Truman turned to Attorney General James Howard McGrath. This assignment was to be in effect only until the administration could find a suitable independent candidate. Truman then appointed Justin Miller, a former federal judge. When McGrath refused to step aside and let Miller take command of the investigation, Truman balked. He decided that there would be no special investigation and that the Justice Department would run any inquiry.

Republicans and the press were not satisfied with his decision and doubted whether McGrath would conduct a thorough and fair investigation, as he had shown no particular zeal for administering his department.

In addition, he was considered too political—he had served as Democratic National Committee chairman before joining the administration. In an attempt to quiet criticism, McGrath appointed Newbold Morris, a liberal New York Republican and former president of the New York City Council, as his special assistant in charge of the investigation. Congress was not happy with Morris for a number of reasons, including that, as part of the "5 percenters" investigation, Morris's law firm and a foundation he headed faced possible legal action because of its trading of government tankers. In addition, Morris antagonized some members by charging them with character assassination. Congress, for its part, refused to grant Morris subpoena power. While conflict with Congress might have been expected, the Justice Department also threw up roadblocks to the investigation. The financial questionnaire that Morris had designed to be submitted by all Justice Department employees earning more than $10,000 a year was not delivered by order of McGrath. The attorney general also refused to give Morris access to files that he requested.

On April 3, 1952, McGrath fired Morris, and Truman fired McGrath. Truman then named James P. McGranery, a federal judge and former Democratic representative from Pennsylvania, as the new attorney general. McGranery closed the special investigation.

DEPARTMENT OF JUSTICE INVESTIGATION

The House investigated the Justice Department, even though Attorney General McGrath had been fired. This probe focused on Theron Caudle, an assistant attorney general.

The investigation of the Justice Department did not end with James McGranery's appointment. The House had been in the early stages of its own inquiry even before the appointment of Newbold Morris as special assistant to the attorney general. Rep. Frank L. Chelf, a Democrat from Kentucky, chaired the investigation.

The administration resisted Chelf's request for files on specific cases under investigation, but Truman later agreed to release some of the information. On April 12, 1952, just days after Attorney General James McGrath had been removed from office, the president issued an executive memorandum that ordered cooperation with the investigating committee.

The committee focused largely on the activities of Assistant Attorney General Theron Caudle, who had been involved in a number of previous probes, including the Kansas City voting fraud case. A controversial figure, Caudle had been investigated by the FBI in 1945, when he was a federal attorney in North Carolina, for his handling of the Office of Price Administration prosecutions. Caudle had been appointed to the criminal division, but then transferred to the tax division, despite his lack of knowledge of tax law. What the committee found was a pattern of special treatment of tax cases including favors, delays, failures to prosecute, and dismissals for health reasons. The committee found that associates of Caudle's were representing clients, that Caudle dismissed a case against a Democratic National committeeman, and that he had dispensed special favors in exchange for campaign contributions.

Despite all the charges, Truman remained loyal to Caudle until it was revealed that he had accepted a $5,000 commission on the sale of a friend's airplane to a relative of a man against whom the tax division had a case. After the sale, Caudle recommended against prosecution. On November 16, 1951, Truman removed Caudle from office and replaced him with Ellis Slack (who was later named a co-conspirator in the St. Louis tax investigation). Caudle appeared before the Chelf committee but was not charged with any specific crimes. Chelf and ranking Republican Kenneth B. Keating issued a statement that declared, "We feel that he is an honest man who was indiscreet in his associations and a pliant conformer to the peculiar moral climate in Washington." Four years later, however, Caudle was indicted and convicted in the St. Louis tax case that also led to the conviction of presidential secretary Matthew Connelly. Caudle served a brief prison term and was pardoned by President Lyndon B. Johnson in 1965.

The committee's report was not issued until six months after Truman had left office. In it, however, the committee concluded that the misconduct so clear in the Department of Justice was also to be found in other departments of the Truman administration.

BIBLIOGRAPHY

Abel, Jules. *The Truman Scandals.* Chicago: Regnery, 1956.

Anderson, Patrick. *The President's Men.* Garden City, N.Y.: Doubleday, 1969.

Bolles, Blair. *How to Get Rich in Washington.* New York: Norton, 1952.

Cochran, Bert. *Harry Truman and the Crisis Presidency.* New York: Funk and Wagnalls, 1973.

Donovan, Robert J. *Tumultuous Years: The Presidency of Harry S. Truman.* New York: Norton, 1982.

Graham, George A. *Morality in American Politics.* New York: Random House, 1952.

Hamby, Alonzo L. *Beyond the New Deal: Harry S. Truman and American Liberalism.* New York: Columbia University Press, 1973.

Miller, Richard L. *Truman: The Rise to Power.* New York: McGraw Hill, 1986.

Mitchell, Jack. *Executive Privilege: Two Centuries of White House Scandals.* New York: Hippocrene Books, 1992.

Sternberg, Alfred. *The Man from Missouri: Life and Times of Harry S. Truman.* New York: Putnam, 1962.

Truman, Margaret. *Harry S. Truman.* New York: Morrow, 1973.

Woodward, C. Vann. *Responses of the Presidents to Charges of Misconduct.* New York: Dell Publishing, 1974.

DWIGHT D. EISENHOWER

Thirty-Fourth President
1953–1961

Dwight David Eisenhower was born in a rented room near the railroad tracks in Denison, Texas, on October 14, 1890. He was the third of David and Ida Eisenhower's seven sons. When Dwight was a baby the family moved to Abilene, Kansas, where his father got a job as a mechanic in a creamery. Dwight, nicknamed Ike, attended local schools and worked in the creamery after classes. He continued working after graduating from high school because he did not have the money to attend college.

He received an appointment to West Point in 1911 and graduated in 1915, ranking sixty-fifth in a class of 164. He was commissioned a second lieutenant and by May 1917 had risen to the rank of captain. On July 1, 1916, Eisenhower married Marie "Mamie" Doud, the daughter of a wealthy Denver businessman.

During World War I, Eisenhower requested overseas duty, but was assigned as a training instructor at Fort Oglethorpe, Georgia, as well as posts in Maryland and Pennsylvania. In June 1920 he was promoted to major, and for the next two years he served as a tank commander. He was assigned to a post in the Panama Canal Zone from 1922 to 1924. He attended Command and General Staff School from 1925 to 1926 at Fort Leavenworth, Kansas, graduating first in a class of 275. He attended the Army War College from 1928 to 1929 and served on the staff of the assistant secretary of war until 1932, when he was appointed an aide to Gen. Douglas MacArthur. He accompanied MacArthur to the Philippines in 1934 and while there received his pilot's license. Eisenhower returned to the United States as a lieutenant colonel and continued to rise in rank while serving on various generals' staffs.

Eisenhower's skill as a tactician and his ability to unify military leaders holding diverse views led to his promotion in March 1942 to major general and his appointment as commander of U.S. forces in Europe. The following month he was named Allied commander in chief for the invasions of North Africa and Italy. In February 1943 General Eisenhower was named supreme allied commander by President Franklin D. Roosevelt, who instructed him to develop a plan to invade France. Operation Overlord, as it was called, resulted in the D-Day invasion of June 6, 1944. He continued to press the war until the Germans surrendered on May 7, 1945, at Rheims. In November 1945 Eisenhower, a five-star general, was appointed army chief of staff to replace Gen. George C. Marshall.

In February 1948 he resigned from the army and became president of Columbia University, serving largely as a figurehead until 1950, when President Harry S. Truman appointed him supreme commander of the North Atlantic Treaty Organization forces in Europe. He resigned this post in May 1952 to pursue the Republican Party nomination for president.

Sen. Robert Taft of Ohio came to the July 1952 Chicago convention as the front-runner, but a draft Eisenhower movement, headed by two-time losing candidate Thomas E. Dewey, won the day, and Eisenhower was nominated on the first ballot. At Dewey's suggestion, Ike chose Sen. Richard Nixon of California as his running mate. In the fall election, Ike faced Adlai E. Stevenson of Illinois, the grandson (and namesake) of Grover Cleveland's second vice president. The campaign focused largely on "Communism, Corruption, and Korea," and it fell to vice-presidential nominee Nixon to carry the attack, while Ike remained above the fray. Eisenhower won by more than 6.5 million votes and an electoral college vote of 442 to 89. Four years later, he again faced Stevenson in the presidential election and, despite some health problems, won by more than 9.5 million votes and an electoral college vote of 457 to 73.

The Korean War was coming to a close as Eisenhower began his first term. The armistice signed at Panmunjom in July 1953 brought an end to open hostilities. Continuing Truman's policy of containing communist expansion, Eisenhower ordered the massive buildup of nuclear weapons as a deterrent.

In 1957 he reluctantly sent federal troops to Little Rock, Arkansas, to enforce the integration of black students into Central High School. The year before he signed into law a far-reaching interstate highway system act that called for the construction of more than 42,000 miles of roads.

Eisenhower retired in 1961 to his farm at Gettysburg, Pennsylvania. During his retirement, he wrote his memoirs and golfed regularly. He supported the Republican Party nominations of Richard Nixon in 1960, Barry Goldwater in 1964, and Nixon again in 1968. He died of a heart attack March 28, 1969.

EXTRAMARITAL AFFAIR

Ike carried on an extramarital affair with his wartime driver, Kay Summersby, and entertained thoughts of marrying her.

Eisenhower met Kay Summersby in May 1942, when he was sent on a ten-day fact-finding trip to London. Kay, a well-educated Irish woman of thirty-one, had been assigned to drive Ike and Gen. Mark Clark around war-torn London. In June Ike returned to London and requested that Kay be assigned as his personal driver.

Mamie Eisenhower was aware of the growing relationship between Ike and Kay. The press reported the general's activities daily, and Kay could be seen in photographs in the papers. Ike often reassured Mamie that although he "liked some—been intrigued by others," he had not strayed from his wife.

On a trip to Algiers, Ike invited Kay to join him, and the rumors continued to grow that they were involved in an intimate relationship. Kay dismissed the suggestion, reminding friends that she was happily engaged to a colonel. When Eisenhower received word that Kay's fiancé had been killed inspecting a minefield, he broke the news to her himself.

The first overture of love was made, according to Kay's 1976 book, when Eisenhower was ordering new uniforms and asked the tailor to make several for his driver. When she protested that he had already been too nice to her, he said, "You are someone very special to me."

Much of their relationship consisted of stolen kisses here and there because they were rarely alone. After a twelve-day stint in the United States in the fall of 1943, Ike and Kay became passionate the night he returned to London. The intimacies did not include sexual intercourse because, according to Kay's book, Ike was impotent.

It is clear that Eisenhower was deeply in love with Kay, and she with him. Ike wrote to General George Marshall telling him of his intentions to divorce Mamie and marry Kay. The letter was eventually placed in Eisenhower's personnel file at the Pentagon. President Truman, who saw the letter, had it destroyed, as he thought it should not be used against Ike. After V-E Day, Ike brought up the subject of children with Kay, a topic they had discussed on a previous occasion. Ike told Kay that he wanted to have a child by her and that he would "try my damnedest." On October 15 they again tried to have sexual intercourse, but Ike was unable to overcome his impotence.

When Eisenhower was recalled to Washington to serve as army chief of staff, Kay was not included in the staff that was recalled to the Pentagon. She was discharged from the army and moved to New York City, where Ike had become president of Columbia University. Meeting on campus one day, Ike told Kay, "It's impossible. There's nothing I can do." It was finally clear to her that there was no chance of the two of them being together again.

Kay wrote two books about her time with Ike. The first, entitled *Eisenhower Was My Boss*, made no mention of the intimate relationship they shared. The second, *Past Forgetting: My Love Affair with Dwight D. Eisenhower*, was published in 1976, a year after she died.

NIXON SLUSH FUND

During the 1952 presidential campaign, the press reported that vice-presidential nominee Richard Nixon had accepted large contributions from wealthy Californians as a "secret" slush fund with which to cover political costs.

On September 18, 1952, the *New York Post* ran a story charging that a number of California businessmen had created a slush fund in 1950 for Eisenhower's running mate, Sen. Richard Nixon of California. Neither Nixon nor the fund's executor, Dana C. Smith, a Pasadena attorney and investment banker, denied the existence of the fund. Rather, Nixon and Smith argued that it was used exclusively for public purposes such as stamps, phone calls, and the like. However, Nixon suffered from the political fallout. Leading newspapers such as the *Washington Post* and the *New York Herald Tribune,* which supported Republican causes, called on Nixon to resign from the ticket.

On September 23 Nixon addressed the nation in an emotional appeal to save his political future. The speech became known as the "Checkers" speech because in it Nixon admitted that he had accepted a personal gift of a cocker spaniel puppy named Checkers. He said his children loved the dog and that he would keep it no matter what anyone said about it. He also addressed the specific charges about the slush fund. He argued that the fund was not a secret, that it had saved taxpayers money by paying for things they would normally have paid for, and that he had not abused the franking privilege of his office. He challenged the Democratic presidential and vice-presidential candidates to publish their financial statements as he had done. He also offered a legal opinion from a prominent Los Angeles law firm that he had violated no laws by having a fund for expenses. Eisenhower, who had kept silent on the matter, gave his unqualified support to his running mate.

Dwight D. Eisenhower, left, and Richard Nixon at the Republican National Convention.

But several of Nixon's claims were dubious. He said the fund was not secret, but neither the general public nor the Republican National Committee had known about it. He also claimed that the fund saved public money, but he had already spent all of the federal funds allotted to his office for expenses. Finally, Nixon had used his congressional frank to send more than 23,000 surveys to California constituents prior to the Republican National Convention.

Despite these inconsistencies, the Checkers speech was a great success with the public. It undoubtedly saved Nixon's candidacy in 1952 as well as his political future.

SHERMAN ADAMS, ASSISTANT TO THE PRESIDENT

Sherman Adams was accused of accepting gifts from textile manufacturer Bernard Goldfine in exchange for favorable treatment by two government regulatory agencies.

Presidential aide Sherman Adams, a former governor of New Hampshire, had a reputation for being as "cold and clean as New Hampshire granite—a barrier against the corrupting influences of personal and political favoritism." But that was before the findings of the House Special Subcommittee on Legislative Oversight were revealed in February 1958. The committee learned that in 1953 Adams, at the request of attorney Murray Chotiner, had discussed a civil aeronautics case involving a client of Chotiner's with the acting chairman of the Civil Aeronautics Board (CAB). In one of the two letters addressed "Dear Murray," Adams relayed some advice on legal strategy that had been given to him by the CAB official.

When Eisenhower was asked about Adams's activities at a press conference on February 26, the president appeared uninformed, and the Washington press corps' long-held suspicions about Eisenhower—that he did not know what was going on—appeared to be confirmed. The *New Republic* wrote, "Eisenhower's ignorance shows the range of Adams's opportunity to operate."

On June 10 the House special subcommittee introduced further evidence of Adams's wrongdoing. A committee investigator, Francis X. McLaughlin, reported that New England industrialist Bernard Goldfine, a friend of Adams for more than fifteen years, had paid for Adams's hotel stays in Boston to the tune of $1,600 between November 1955 and May 1958. In return, the committee learned, Adams had secured favorable treatment by the Federal Trade Commission (FTC) and the Securities and Exchange Commission (SEC) for Goldfine, who was currently under investigation by the two agencies.

Adams, who was away on a fishing trip in Maine, quickly returned to Washington. In a June 12 letter to the subcommittee he claimed that its conclusions were "unwarranted and unfair." Adams admitted that Goldfine had paid the hotel bills, but that his own inquiries into the FTC and SEC investigations were not meant as repayment. Adams said he thought Goldfine maintained the hotel suite on an ongoing basis and did not realize that the charges incurred by Adams and his wife were not already covered.

Within twenty-four hours of his letter being read into the record, the press corps had further evidence that Adams had accepted expensive gifts from Goldfine, including a $700 vicuna coat and a $2,400 oriental rug. Less than seventy-two hours later, McLaughlin testified that Adams had accepted another stay at a hotel suite in May 1954 from Goldfine in the amount of $267 at New York's Waldorf-Astoria, thereby casting doubt on the explanation Adams had offered for his frequent stays at the Boston hotel—that Goldfine was paying for the suite on a continuing basis.

As damaging as this evidence was, the worst was yet to come. An attorney for the FTC testified that he had recommended that criminal proceedings be instituted against Goldfine, his son, and three of their mills for repeatedly violating the Wool Label Act. According to the attorney, Goldfine's textile mills were falsely labeling coats as containing 90 percent wool and 10 percent vicuna, when the 10 percent was actually nylon. The recommendations were rejected in favor of a "cease and desist order." FTC chairman Edward F. Howrey sent a memo to Adams that the entire matter could be handled on a "voluntary cooperative basis." During a meeting scheduled between Goldfine and Howrey in the spring of 1955, Goldfine let it be known that he was a close friend of Adams by calling Adams from Howrey's office.

Adams had refused to testify, claiming executive privilege due to his close working relationship with Eisenhower, but on June 16 he announced that he would voluntarily appear before the subcommittee. The following day, Adams testified that he had erred in making phone calls for Goldfine, but that he had not exerted any influence in his friend's behalf. He claimed that he did not report the coat because he thought it an inexpensive gift and that the rug was only on loan to him. Adams admitted that appointments between Goldfine and the agencies had been cleared through him

Sherman Adams

and that he had recommended Howrey's appointment to the FTC. With regard to the SEC, Adams claimed that all he did was ask that Goldfine's case be expedited.

The next day, Eisenhower reaffirmed his belief in Adams: "I believe that the presentation made by Governor Adams . . . truthfully represents the pertinent facts. I personally like Governor Adams. I admire his abilities. I respect him because of his personal and official integrity. I need him."

Although the subcommittee refused to take action against Adams, Republican Party leaders sought to oust him to keep the scandal from undermining their electoral chances in the fall. In general elections in Maine, which at that time were held before the rest of the country, incumbent Republican senator Frederick Payne lost his reelection bid, even though Eisenhower had endorsed him. It turned out that Payne had also accepted hotel stays and a vicuna coat from Goldfine. With pressure mounting, Eisenhower sent Vice President Nixon to get Adams to resign, but Adams insisted on a personal meeting with Ike. The two met September 22, and Adams resigned that night.

Adams was found in contempt by the House of Representatives and later received a prison sentence following conviction for violations on his tax returns. For the Republicans, the scandal was one of many reasons they did poorly in the November midterm elections.

DIXON-YATES CONTRACT

Conflict of interest charges were raised when the government used an outside consultant, who stood to profit from the deal, to negotiate a contract with a private power company.

The controversy surrounding the Dixon-Yates contract led to "one of the most celebrated, hard-fought, and bitter disputes of the whole Eisenhower administration." The city of Memphis, Tennessee, was in need of more electricity, and the issue was whether the federally funded Tennessee Valley Authority (TVA) or private providers would meet that need.

President Eisenhower thought the Roosevelt-created TVA was a prime example of creeping socialism, which he believed was undercutting the foundations of American life. In a cabinet meeting in the summer of 1953, Eisenhower said of TVA, "By God, if ever we could do it, before we leave here, I'd like to see us sell the whole thing, but I suppose we can't go that far." Therefore, it came as no surprise that Eisenhower rejected TVA's proposal to increase its generating capacity to supply the Memphis area and sought, instead, to have a private company do the job. Presidential assistant Sherman Adams stated that Eisenhower's "only motive in sponsoring the privately owned power plant was to check further growth of the TVA, which he regarded as a product of the 'whole-hog' theory of the previous Democratic administrations—the idea that the Federal Government must undertake great resource development projects alone, freezing out the energy and initiative of local government and local people engaged in private enterprise."

Once the decision was made, its implementation was left to Rowland Hughes, director of the Bureau of the Budget (BOB). In conjunction with Adm. Lewis Strauss, the chairman of the Atomic Energy Commission (AEC), administration representatives met with Edgar H. Dixon, president of Middle South Utilities, and Eugene A. Yates, chairman of the Southern Company, in the winter of 1954. In April 1955 Hughes recommended that the AEC be instructed to negotiate an agreement with Mississippi Valley Generating Company, a newly formed Dixon-Yates corporation. In June Eisenhower issued the order to the AEC to conclude a final agreement.

Almost immediately, there were cries of cronyism. Democratic National Committee chairman Stephen A. Mitchell charged that Eisenhower's decision to give the contract to Dixon-Yates was influenced by his golfing friend, Bobby Jones, who was on the board of directors of the Southern Company. Jones, a world-famous golfer, stated that the charges against him were "utterly ridiculous and without foundation." Ike admitted that he was "a little astonished that any kind of such innuendo should include a private citizen of the character and standing of Bob Jones."

The president, who was angered by the attacks stemming from the Dixon-Yates contract, ordered that the complete record of negotiations be made public. Expecting that opening the files would end the debate, Eisenhower was surprised when the chronologies prepared by BOB and the AEC only raised more questions. On February 18, 1955, Sen. Lister Hill, Democrat of Alabama, a strong proponent of TVA, announced in a Senate speech that Adolphe H. Wenzell, a vice president and director of First Boston Corporation, which specialized in underwriting utility issues, had advised BOB on the Dixon-Yates contract. Hill charged that the "facts have been deliberately concealed from the Congress and the American people." BOB director Hughes had acknowledged only a week before to Hill that Wenzell had served as an unpaid consultant on the project. But Wenzell was not a disinterested party. His company, First Boston, was in line to sell $120 million in securities for Dixon-Yates and to make a great deal of money.

Members of the Antitrust and Monopoly Subcommittee, which convened in the summer of 1955, were convinced that the administration had tried to conceal Wenzell's role in the Dixon-Yates contract. It concluded that the BOB and AEC chronologies "were false. Important names, documents, and many important meetings held and attended by government officials in regard to the matter were deleted, despite President Eisenhower's pledge of the 'complete record.' " The subcommittee also complained that it had been "completely blocked from getting to the bottom of the Dixon-Yates contract by the very men in the White House who were involved in the negotiations." Citing the frequent claims of executive privilege by administration officials, the panel concluded that the administration "has demonstrated contempt of Congress and its constitutional powers, as well as disregard of the democratic processes."

Eisenhower did not help matters when he appeared at press conferences unprepared to answer questions about Dixon-Yates. On June 29, four months after the public learned that Wenzell had been a party to the negotiations, Eisenhower told reporters, "Mr. Wenzell was never called in or asked a single thing about the Yates-Dixon contract. . . . My understanding is that quickly as the Dixon-Yates thing came up he resigned . . . because he was connected with a great Boston finance company." The trouble Eisenhower had in getting the facts straight continued to plague him. At a news conference in late July, he was asked whether he knew Wenzell's name had been deliberately excluded from the AEC chronology at the recommendation of BOB. The president, with noticeable irritation, asserted: "I don't intend to comment on it any more at all. I think I have given to this conference, time and again, the basic elements of the whole development, and everything that I could possibly be expected to know about it. . . . I don't know exactly such details as that. How could I be expected to know? I never heard of it." Richard Rovere, the Washington correspondent for *New Yorker* magazine, wrote in December 1955 that the president's "personal responsibility in Dixon-Yates is unclear, but his ignorance and innocence are quite evident."

In July the president ordered the Dixon-Yates contract canceled, not because of the controversy, but because the city of Memphis had decided on June 23 to build its own power plant. The AEC ruled that Wenzell's role in the Dixon-Yates contract voided all of the federal government's obligations to make payment to the Mississippi Valley Generating Company. The company sued the government. The court of claims ruled in its favor and ordered the government to pay damages of nearly $1.9 million. The Justice Department appealed the decision to the U.S. Supreme Court, and on January 9, 1961, the Court decided, 6–3, in favor of the government. The majority opinion argued that the records "disclose numerous instances in which Wenzell seemed to be more preoccupied with advancing the position of First Boston or the sponsors (Dixon-Yates) than with representing the best interests of the Government." Finding Wenzell's allegiance to the government "a fleeting one," the Court declared his activities in violation of the conflict of interest law.

PRESIDENTIAL GIFTS

The press reported on a number of occasions that Eisenhower had accepted numerous gifts valued at more than $300,000 for his farm in Gettysburg, Pennsylvania. When questioned about the propriety of accepting gifts, the president maintained that the conflict of interest law did not apply to him.

In December 1955 *Newsweek* magazine estimated that during the first three years of his administration, President Eisenhower had accepted gifts valued at more than $40,000, including livestock and equipment for his Gettysburg farm. The same month, *U.S. News & World Report* published an article about the president receiving a tractor and cultivator from three farm cooperatives. The article concluded that the White House had no clear policy on the acceptance of gifts. It seemed that the only limitation was that the president would not take cash. When questioned about the gifts, a White House aide responded, "The office of the President is too big to be influenced by any gift."

At a July 31, 1957, news conference, Eisenhower was asked about the numerous gifts he had received. He responded that because he was an elected official, "the conflict of interest law does not apply to me." This comment led Sen. Wayne Morse, Democrat of Oregon, to state two days later that the administration was following a "shocking code of political immorality." Morse continued, "Acceptance of a $4,000 tractor with a cigarette lighter attached, the acceptance of a $1,000 bull, or one of even greater value, the acceptance of a large part of the rest of the livestock and the machinery for the farm, along with thousands of dollars worth of other gifts for his farm cannot be regarded by the President as falling within the spirit and intent of the conflict of interest policy."

On August 7 Eisenhower responded to Senator Morse's comments by stating, "Most presents come to me from large organizations, voluntary organizations, and I make this stipulation: anything that is given me is right out on the record, and it is given for a particular purpose." He continued his defense by saying, "As far as I am concerned, I need no gifts and I never accept gifts that I believe have any personal motive whatsoever behind them, I mean any selfish motive of any kind." As proof of his policy, Ike cited the fact that he had never "accepted one from a corporation or business firm."

The matter would have ended there if syndicated columnist Drew Pearson had not continued to investigate and report on Eisenhower's gifts. In 1958 during the controversy surrounding Sherman Adams's acceptance of gifts from Bernard Goldfine, Pearson reported that Eisenhower had received vicuna material from Goldfine. Press secretary James Hagerty told the media that the president had received the material, but had given it to a friend. In May 1960 Pearson estimated that Eisenhower had received more than $300,000 worth of machinery, livestock, and horticultural products for the Gettysburg farm. In the winter of 1961, after Eisenhower had left office, Pearson reported that three wealthy oilmen—W. G. "Billy" Byars, W. Alton Jones, and George E. Allen—had leased the farm from Ike while he was president. The three never tried to run the farm profitably, and Allen took a large tax deduction on losses incurred on the farm.

BIBLIOGRAPHY

Adams, Sherman. *First-Hand Report.* London: Hutchinson, 1962.

Ambrose, Steven E. *Eisenhower.* New York: Simon and Schuster, 1983–1984.

Donovan, Robert J. *Eisenhower: The Inside Story.* New York: Harper, 1956.

Frier, David A. *Conflict of Interest in the Eisenhower Administration.* Baltimore: Penguin, 1969.

Greenstein, Fred I. *The Hidden-Hand Presidency: Eisenhower as Leader.* New York: Basic Books, 1982.

Larson, Arthur. *Eisenhower: The President Nobody Knew.* New York: Scribner, 1968.

Lyon, Peter. *Eisenhower: Portrait of the Hero.* Boston: Little, Brown, 1974.

Mitchell, Jack. *Executive Privilege: Two Centuries of White House Scandals.* New York: Hippocrene Books, 1992.

Mollenhoff, Clark. *Washington Cover-Up.* Garden City, N.Y.: Doubleday, 1962.

Morgan, Kay Summersby. *Past Forgetting: My Love Affair with Dwight D. Eisenhower.* New York: Simon and Schuster, 1976.

Neal, Steve. *The Eisenhowers: Reluctant Dynasty.* Garden City, N.Y.: Doubleday, 1978.

Rovere, Richard. *The Eisenhower Years: Affairs of State.* New York: Farrar, Straus, and Cudahy, 1956.

Waltzman, Sanford. *Conflict of Interest: Politics and the Money Game.* New York: Cowles, 1971.

Wildavsky, Aaron. *Dixon-Yates: A Study in Power Politics.* New Haven: Yale University Press, 1961.

Woodward, C. Vann. *Responses of the Presidents to Charges of Misconduct.* New York: Dell Publishing, 1974.

JOHN F. KENNEDY

Thirty-Fourth President
1961–1963

Born on May 29, 1917, in Brookline, Massachusetts, John F. Kennedy was the second of nine children born to Joseph P. Kennedy, a wealthy businessman, and Rose Fitzgerald Kennedy, daughter of a former mayor of Boston. Joseph Kennedy served as U.S. ambassador to Great Britain from 1937 to 1940.

John Kennedy graduated from Choate preparatory school in 1935 and studied at the London School of Economics that summer. He started college at Princeton, but an illness forced him to withdraw after two months. He entered Harvard University in 1936 and majored in political science and economics, graduating with honors in 1940. His senior thesis, an examination of British appeasement of fascism before World War II, was eventually published as *Why England Slept.* He studied briefly at Stanford Business School in 1940 and 1941.

Kennedy tried to enlist in the army in 1941, but was rejected because of a back injury, a condition that would plague him throughout his life. He strengthened his back through exercise and managed to pass the navy's physical later that year. He rose from the rank of ensign to lieutenant, and in April 1943 was given command of a PT (patrol torpedo) boat in the South Pacific. When his boat, PT-109, was rammed by a Japanese destroyer, Kennedy and his crew were forced overboard, and he swam for four hours while towing an injured sailor. Kennedy received the Purple Heart medal for his bravery, and the events were reported in newspapers nationwide. Discharged from the navy in December 1943, JFK worked as a journalist covering the United Nations Conference on International Organization for the *Chicago Herald-American* and the Potsdam Conference for the International News Service.

In 1946 Kennedy was elected to the U.S. House of Representatives from the working-class districts of Boston, Cambridge, and part of Somerville. He served in the House from 1947 until 1953, accumulating a record as a liberal. He supported much of the Truman administration's

Fair Deal programs, but criticized it for its policy on China. In 1952 Kennedy ran for the Senate and defeated the incumbent Republican, Henry Cabot Lodge, by 70,000 votes. Six years later, he was overwhelmingly reelected with 78 percent of the vote. He served on the Government Operations Committee, Foreign Relations Committee, and the Joint Economic Committee. Kennedy was in the hospital when the crucial vote to censure Sen. Joseph McCarthy came to the floor. He was criticized for ducking the vote because his brother, Robert F. Kennedy, had served on McCarthy's staff and McCarthy was a family friend. While recovering from back surgery, Kennedy wrote *Profiles in Courage,* which won a Pulitzer Prize. On September 12, 1953, he married Jacqueline L. Bouvier, daughter of a wealthy stockbroker.

At the Democratic convention in July 1960 in Los Angeles, Kennedy was the front-runner in a field that included Sen. Lyndon B. Johnson of Texas and two-time standard-bearer Adlai E. Stevenson II. Kennedy was nominated on the first ballot, in part because of the expert political organization that Robert Kennedy had built. Kennedy selected Johnson as his running mate to gain support in the South and to get the potentially obstructionist Johnson out of the Senate. In the fall, JFK faced Vice President Richard M. Nixon. Kennedy defeated Nixon by fewer than 125,000 votes out of more than 68 million cast. He won in the electoral college, 303–219 and became the youngest man ever to be elected president.

The Kennedy administration was marked by a number of international events. Just months after taking office, he carried out an action against Cuba that had been planned during the Eisenhower administration. The Bay of Pigs invasion took place April 17, 1961, and was a fiasco. Kennedy continued U.S. involvement in the Vietnam conflict, sending increased numbers of U.S. military there. In October 1962 he ordered a naval blockade of Cuba to force the Soviets to dismantle their missile bases there. In 1963 he concluded a nuclear test ban treaty with the Soviet Union. Kennedy also promoted the space program, urging the United States to be first to land a man on the moon. He started the Peace Corps and introduced the bill that led to the passage of the Civil Rights Act of 1964.

On November 22, 1963, while riding in a motorcade through the streets of Dallas, Texas, Kennedy was assassinated by Lee Harvey Oswald, an ex-marine who had once denounced his American citizenship and spent years in the Soviet Union. Two days later, while in police custody, Oswald was shot dead by Jack Ruby, a Dallas nightclub owner. Ever since, conspiracy theories have suggested that Kennedy's assassination was ordered by the Mafia, or by Fidel Castro, or even by various elements within the U.S. government. The Warren Commission, headed by Chief Justice Earl Warren, concluded that the president was shot by Oswald, the self-avowed Marxist, who was working alone.

SEXUAL ESCAPADES

John Kennedy had numerous sexual encounters before and after his marriage. His extramarital affairs continued after his election to the presidency.

Inga Arvad

From 1941 to 1944 Kennedy carried on an affair with Inga Arvad, a former Miss Denmark, whom he called "Inga Binga." Before coming to the United States, Arvad had been an actress in Germany. The FBI suspected her of being a spy, bugged her apartment, and secretly recorded her sexual encounters. Some have speculated that FBI Director J. Edgar Hoover used these recordings and other information about JFK's sexual activities as job security. In any case, Kennedy was informed that Arvad's apartment was bugged and began to meet her in hotels. Arvad gave birth to a son, Ronald McCoy, on August 12, 1947. She claimed Kennedy was the father.

Strippers and Prostitutes

In 1955 Kennedy had several sexual encounters with Tempest Storm, a six-foot tall stripper. In 1960 he had sex at a hotel with the stripper Blaze Starr, who was Louisiana governor Earl Long's fiancée, while Long was at a campaign party next door. In London in 1960 and 1961, JFK had sex with a number of call girls, including Suzy Chang and the nineteen-year-old Maria Novotny. During a joint FBI–Scotland Yard investigation, Novotny told agents that she had met Kennedy in December 1960 at a party hosted by singer Vic Damone and that JFK's brother-in-law Peter Lawford had asked Novotny to arrange "something a bit more interesting for the president." Novotny reported that she and two other prostitutes dressed like nurses and provided sexual services to their patient.

Joan Lundberg

Kennedy met Joan Lundberg, a divorcée with two children, at a California bar in 1956 while he was visiting his sister Pat and her husband, Peter Lawford. JFK commented that Joan resembled Pat. During their four-year affair, JFK and Joan could travel alone together because many people assumed they were related. JFK provided financial support for Joan, including the offer of $400 for an abortion. The affair ended amicably when he won the Democratic Party nomination for president.

Pamela Turnure

Kennedy began an affair with Pamela Turnure while he was a senator. She eventually became his receptionist, and, when he became president, she was hired as Jackie Kennedy's press secretary. Turnure's Georgetown landlords, the Katers, disapproved and collected proof of the affair. They sent their information to the FBI and also to the media, but nothing came of it. The Katers began attending political rallies carrying signs that charged JFK with adultery. Mrs. Kater even picketed the White House with a sign that read "Do You Want an Adulterer in the White House?" Jackie knew about the affair between JFK and Turnure, but may have thought it wise to have Turnure in the White House where she could keep an eye on her.

Florence Prichett Smith

Kennedy started an affair with Florence Prichett Smith, the fashion editor of the *New York Journal-American* and wife of E. T. Smith, U.S. ambassador to Cuba, in 1957. JFK visited Smith in Cuba and once he was president saw her in Miami and Palm Beach.

Priscilla Wier and Jill Cowan

Given the Secret Service code names Fiddle and Faddle, Priscilla Wier and Jill Cowan were among a number of secretaries with whom JFK (code name Lancer) had sex. These two, however, were often with the president together and help confirm the rumor that JFK enjoyed ménage à trois. Although they had no specific duties, the two women often traveled with the president to destinations like Nassau, Palm Beach, and Yosemite National Park.

Judith Campbell

Judy Campbell met Kennedy on February 7, 1960, when he stopped over at the Sands Hotel in Las Vegas to see Frank Sinatra's show during a campaign trip. Their sexual relationship began a month later, on the eve of the New Hampshire primary, at the Plaza Hotel in New York, and continued through the presidential primaries. On April 5 Judy met JFK at his Georgetown home while the pregnant Jackie was away in Florida. They made love in the master bedroom.

According to Campbell's published account in her 1977 book, *My Story,* they met a week later in her hotel room at the Fontainebleau in Miami. On that occasion they did not make love, but JFK told her that if he did not win the Democratic Party nomination for president, his personal life was going to change. He did not promise that he was going to divorce Jackie, but told Judy that his marriage was not happy and that things would change if he lost.

Judy claimed that on July 11, the first night of the Democratic National Convention in Los Angeles, JFK wanted her to participate in a ménage à trois. She refused and left the hotel. The next morning he asked her to forget about the previous night. They made up on August 3 in Judy's New York apartment. They made love several more times during the next two weeks. Then on August 19, she met him again at his Georgetown house.

Campbell continued to see JFK even after he became president. White House logs show that Campbell called at least seventy times during 1961 and 1962. The last phone call coincided with a meeting JFK had with J.

Edgar Hoover on March 22, 1962. Hoover warned the president to end his affair with Judy because she was also involved with Mafia boss Sam "Momo" Giancana. JFK was aware of this relationship and had asked Judy to arrange a meeting with Giancana to enlist his help in the primary campaign against Hubert Humphrey in 1960. A Giancana lieutenant met JFK and used mob money to help Kennedy win West Virginia.

The affair became public knowledge in December 1975, when Campbell was called to testify before the Senate Select Committee on Intelligence Operations. The committee wanted to know if the Central Intelligence Agency had been involved in a plot to assassinate Cuban leader Fidel Castro. Campbell claimed no knowledge of such a plot, but admitted to an intimate relationship with JFK. Her testimony was sealed and will not be made public until 2025. Her version of her affair with JFK first appeared in her 1977 book, but over time her account of events changed. She later admitted to lying to the Senate committee and in her book. She died September 24, 1999.

Mary Pinchot Meyer

Mary Pinchot Meyer had known Kennedy since he was a student at Choate. However, the two did not begin an affair until January 1962. Mary was the sister-in-law of *Washington Post* executive editor Benjamin Bradlee. She was an artist and lived a bohemian lifestyle after divorcing her husband of fourteen years in 1959. Mary and JFK carried on an affair until his death in November 1963. On several occasions, Mary brought drugs into the White House for Kennedy and herself. One week before a White House conference on drugs, Mary supplied the marijuana, and JFK joked that he would be unable to push the button if there were a nuclear attack. Mary also introduced JFK to LSD.

Mary was murdered in October 1964 on the towpath in Georgetown. A laborer was arrested, but not convicted, for the crime, which remains unsolved. According to Bradlee, Mary's diary was turned over to CIA agent James Angleton, who was a friend. Angleton claimed that he destroyed the diary to protect Mary's sons.

Jayne Mansfield

Actress Jayne Mansfield's publicist, Raymond Strait, reported that Mansfield and Kennedy had a brief affair that began at the Democratic National Convention in 1960. Strait claimed that Mansfield and JFK made love in Kennedy's West Hollywood apartment even though Mansfield was eight months pregnant at the time.

Angie Dickinson

Despite rumors, actress Angie Dickinson has never denied or confirmed an affair with Kennedy. She has said little except to express her admiration for him. If the two did have an affair, it was most likely during 1962 when

JFK was also having affairs with Jayne Mansfield, Marilyn Monroe, Mary Pinchot Meyer, and Judith Campbell.

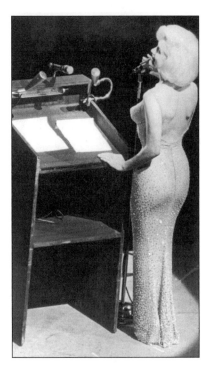

Marilyn Monroe singing "Happy Birthday, Mr. President" to John F. Kennedy in 1962.

Marilyn Monroe

Kennedy met Marilyn Monroe at a 1954 party given by Hollywood agent Charles Feldman. JFK's brother-in-law, actor Peter Lawford, had invited the Kennedys. Monroe and Kennedy flirted until she left with her husband, Joe DiMaggio. However, she managed to slip JFK a piece of paper with her phone number on it. Marilyn divorced DiMaggio in early 1955 and later married playwright Arthur Miller. With Lawford's help, Kennedy and Marilyn carried on a relationship well into his presidency. On one occasion, Marilyn, disguised as Lawford's secretary, was picked up in Los Angeles by *Air Force One*.

Marilyn told friends that making love with JFK was "less than inspired." She said that "he made love like an adolescent." However, she would also daydream about him divorcing Jackie and making her first lady. During his presidency, the affair became more obvious to those around him. Secret Service agents and White House personnel often found them in compromising situations.

In May 1962 several members of his cabinet protested when they learned that Marilyn would perform at the president's forty-fifth birthday party, which was also a party fundraiser. Jackie was so angered that she did not attend. Marilyn's rendition of "Happy Birthday" was as scandalous as the dress she wore. The two spent what was likely their last night together on that occasion. Soon afterwards, Kennedy stopped taking Marilyn's phone calls. She was angry and threatened to make their affair public. Kennedy sent brother Bobby to calm the waters, which he seemed to have accomplished. However, he may have started his own affair with her. On August 4, 1962, Marilyn was found dead of an overdose of sleeping pills.

STEWART UDALL, SECRETARY OF THE INTERIOR

Interior Secretary Stewart Udall was accused of asking oil executives to raise funds for the Democratic Party. His solicitations were seen as a conflict of interest because his department was responsible for regulating the oil industry.

For John Kennedy, the accusation could not have come at a worse time. Less that a week earlier, the president, who had been in office just over three months, had offered Congress a proposal that would tighten laws governing conflict of interest. It was the continuation of a campaign strategy that claimed that the past eight years of Republican rule had been rife with incompetence and corruption. Now his own administration was charged with influence peddling. The story broke in the *Washington Daily News* on May 3, 1961, and was picked up by newspapers across the country. The front page headline in the *New York Times* aptly summarized what had happened: "Udall Accused of Seeking Party Aid from Oil Man."

The oil man was J. K. Evans, a representative of Asiatic Petroleum Company, a subsidiary of Shell Oil. The "party aid" was $100 a seat tickets to the Jefferson-Jackson Day dinner to be held on May 27, two days before Kennedy's forty-fourth birthday, and Udall was apparently soliciting contributions from an industry his department regulated. In an April 5 letter sent to fifty-six Washington, D.C., area oil and gas company representatives and lobbyists, Evans had written, "Secretary Udall, who happens to be a friend of long standing, has asked me as a personal favor to him to solicit the Oil and Gas Industry in Washington in an effort to help the Secretary dispose of his 'very sizable quota of tickets for the Jefferson-Jackson Day Dinner.' " There was no mention of any favors Udall might render in return.

At a press conference Udall categorically denied asking Evans to solicit contributions, stating that he had done no more than tell his friend that he hoped "he and some of his friends would be at the dinner." Describing how he had attended the dinner in previous years and seen Evans with "sometimes four or six people or something of that order," Udall claimed that was all that he had intended by his conversation. The letter, he said, was the result of Evans "attempting to impress some people in the oil industry."

Udall's claims are difficult to reconcile with two passages in Evans's letter. The remark about a "very sizable quota of tickets" is in quotes, suggesting that Udall used those exact words in his conversation with Evans. If cabinet members were expected to fill ticket quotas, Udall would have been under pressure and, knowingly or not, could have communicated that pressure to Evans. It is difficult to imagine that Evans would not feel obligated, particularly because Udall had recently made a decision about oil residuals that embarrassed Evans and hurt Shell Oil. If Evans had brought four, five, or six people to a Democratic fundraiser under a Republican administration, then—it was implied—he should bring substantially more now that Democrats were in power.

The second remark was more direct: "The procedure that the Secretary has asked me to follow is to have all checks made payable to the Democratic National Committee, and if for some personal reason you do not wish to follow this suggestion, please contact me." Whatever Udall may have believed he said, it is clear that Evans got the impression that he would be very welcome if he showed up at Udall's office with a dozen or more checks from oil industry officials.

The letter was carbon copied "The Honorable Stewart L. Udall." Udall claimed he did not see a copy of the letter until one of its recipients contacted him a few days after it was mailed. He said he then called Evans, saying that "I was flabbergasted at what he had done and that I hoped that he would recall the letters." Evans apparently did so.

Udall seemed unwilling to take any blame for Evans's behavior. At the press conference, he quipped, "I will say I can take care of the Republicans, but who is protecting me from my friends." That placed the onus for the gaffe on Evans but did not explain why an experienced Washington operative could have misunderstood him so badly. A statement issued a few hours later shifted the blame yet again, claiming the story was "a political plant by the Republican national committee timed to coincide with the special election in Arizona today." In that election Udall's brother, Morris K. Udall, won a close race to fill Stewart's former congressional seat. But if the Republicans had planted the story, it was very clumsy of them to wait until election day to spring it. Udall mentioned that several reporters had known about the story for more than a week, giving the Republicans a good reason to suspect that the Democrats had been trying to suppress it until after the election.

At his next news conference, Kennedy displayed irritation when asked if his administration's "ethical standards have appeared to falter." He tried to shift the blame. He attacked campaign finance laws, called for government financing of campaigns, and warned that "no one should contribute to any campaign fund under the expectation that it will do them the slightest bit of good."

By the night of the Jefferson-Jackson Day dinner, the affair had faded. At the beginning of his speech, Kennedy drew laughs by including among those who were responsible for the dinner "Mr. Udall, who handled the publicity."

TFX FIGHTER-BOMBERS

A Senate investigation was initiated by Sen. Henry Jackson when a major contract for the construction of the TFX fighter-bomber was awarded to General Dynamics, even though Boeing had submitted a better proposal.

As secretary of defense under John F. Kennedy and Lyndon B. Johnson, Robert S. McNamara forced the navy and the air force—over their strong protests—to unite on a single aircraft design called the TFX. In addition, he chose General Dynamics rather than Boeing as the prime contractor, again against the services' unanimous recommendations. The result was an unmitigated disaster. A plane that was supposed to save $1 billion ended up with $1 billion in cost overruns. Equally disturbing was the circumstantial evidence that political favoritism played a major role in awarding the contract. Two Democrats loyal to the administration, John L. McClellan of

Arkansas and Henry Jackson of Washington, were disturbed enough to support congressional investigations into what had happened.

The story began in the late 1950s when both the air force and navy were looking for a new swept-wing aircraft. The air force wanted a plane that could fly subsonic to the borders of the Soviet Union with an 8,000-pound nuclear bomb and then streak through Soviet air defenses just above the ground at high speed. The navy wanted a supersonic plane that could be launched from a carrier, loiter in the air for hours, watch for incoming enemy aircraft with five-foot diameter nose to hold its radar antenna, and carry nothing heavier than air-to-air missiles. Any competent engineer could see that the air force's long, thin, heavy arrow-shaped plane could not be combined with the navy's short, fat-nosed, light plane.

McNamara was not an engineer, once admitting, "I am completely unmechanical." He was also arrogant and regarded himself as one of JFK's new generation of whiz kids. McNamara claimed that "advances in technology" would make the TFX a success, and he ignored the advice of experienced military personnel.

The first request for proposals went out on December 6, 1961, and six companies submitted plans. Some 225 experts looked at the plans and concluded that none met the nearly impossible requirements. Although the navy's five-foot diameter nose had been reduced to three feet, it was still large enough to increase drag and make sustained supersonic flight difficult. Even more ominous, the aircraft's weight was near the limit for carrier landings. Two companies, Boeing and General Dynamics, were chosen to resubmit bids. The second time Boeing's design was better than General Dynamics's, but neither was acceptable, and a third set of proposals was solicited. This time Boeing's proposal was clearly better. General Dynamics had become so confused that it presented six alternatives and told evaluators to choose among them.

At this point, the superiority of Boeing's design team was so obvious to military evaluators that rumors were beginning to circulate that the administration had a political agenda that required the Defense Department to award the contract to General Dynamics. Despite Boeing's superior design, Defense called for an unprecedented fourth round of proposals. Again, the Boeing design drew the support of all the military evaluation teams. But, on November 21, 1962, McNamara signed an internal memorandum awarding the contract to General Dynamics, and three days later, the news was released to the public.

Both Boeing and the military were shocked. Some Defense Department civilians were equally surprised. Albert W. Blackburn, a technical adviser on

Robert McNamara

the TFX, later told Congress that there was "no real, supportable case to be made for [McNamara's] choice on the ground of operational, technical, management, or cost considerations." Those who thought McNamara had brought to the department a sophisticated knowledge of systems analysis had another surprise coming. The only on-paper justification for the choice was a brief November 21 memo that was so badly done it contained several errors in arithmetic. When the Government Accounting Office was called in to evaluate the process, McNamara said he had the figures in his head. It was not an impressive performance.

At an estimated $6.5 billion, the TFX contract was expected to be the largest military aircraft contract of the 1960s. General Dynamics was located in Texas, and its contractor for the navy planes was the New York-based Grumman. Both were in states that had gone for Kennedy in 1960. Boeing, on the other hand, would have built the plane in Kansas and Washington State, two less-populous states that had voted for Richard Nixon. Other ties were even more direct. Kennedy's close win in Illinois owed something to Chicago's wealthy Crown family, one of General Dynamics's major shareholders. In his public statements, the president claimed to be above that sort of pork barrel politics, but the more knowledgeable had reason to be skeptical. That same year the president's brother Edward Kennedy was running for the Senate from Massachusetts, promising to bring more defense contracts to the state. No paper trail was found linking the president to the decision, and Kennedy claimed it "was completely the Defense Department." The Democratic Congress did not look deeply into any role the White House may have played in the decision and, in that pre-Watergate era, few journalists did their own probes. The most that can be said is that Kennedy seemed indifferent to just how disastrous the decision might become.

Congress joined the controversy when Senator Jackson became concerned that one of his state's most important businesses had lost a major contract. Knowing that many would question his motives, Jackson took his suspicions to Senator McClellan, the powerful chairman of the Permanent Subcommittee on Investigations. McClellan had a well-earned reputation for rooting out corruption. In a December 21 letter to McNamara he asked that the formal award of the TFX contract be delayed while his committee did an investigation. Instead, Assistant Secretary of Defense Roswell L. Gilpatric signed the contract that very afternoon, a move that aroused McClellan's suspicions.

McClellan discovered that two people who were closely involved in the decision also had close ties to General Dynamics. The first was Gilpatric. Before coming to Defense, he had worked for Cravath, Swaine, and Moore, a law firm that often represented General Dynamics. Gilpatric had told Congress that he had no plans to work at the law firm again, but, when the controversy forced him out of government in January 1964, he became a senior partner there.

The other official was Secretary of the Navy Fred Korth, a lawyer and bank president in Fort Worth, where General Dynamics had its main factory. Just before he came to Washington, Korth's bank had made a $400,000 loan to General Dynamics. In addition, while serving in government, Korth retained stock in the bank and solicited business for it. McClellan's investigation discovered a letter in which Korth promised on official stationery to take some of the bank's "very best customers" for a ride on the presidential yacht *Sequoia*. Korth was also forced to resign.

No dubious financial ties were found linking McNamara to General Dynamics. Already a wealthy man with relatively simple tastes, McNamara was more interested in acquiring power than money. Just after the Kennedy administration took office, the new secretary of the air force, Eugene M. Zuckert, got a critical insight into how McNamara functioned. Delays in construction of the Titan and Atlas missile sites had led to a conference among those involved, and the group asked the newly appointed McNamara for permission to be left alone to work out their difficulties. McNamara refused, telling them that he would look to Tom Morris, an assistant secretary who had yet to be sworn in, for answers. As the TFX decision later showed, McNamara attached little importance to knowledge and experience. He wanted people who were loyal to him and would do as he wanted. "And that," Zuckert said, "is the way it went from day to day."

If there was a technical reason for McNamara's choice of General Dynamics, it was the desire to create aircraft for the air force and navy that shared as many parts as possible. For the last round of bids, Gilpatric stressed that requirement to each company. As a result, the General Dynamics design had 84 percent of the parts in common versus 75 percent for Boeing's design. Boeing supporters were undoubtedly right when they pointed out that the differences lay in parts that rarely needed to be replaced. But from McNamara's perspective that was irrelevant. General Dynamics had shown a willingness to comply, and McNamara was counting on their engineers to overcome the problems and prove him right.

There was only one thing wrong with his idea. What if the basic design of the TFX was so flawed that the plane was a failure? That is exactly what happened. As the work on the plane progressed, it became clear that it was in trouble. The plane was too heavy to land on carrier decks, and a 1964 National Aeronautics and Space Administration study indicated that it would not perform as expected. All this was confirmed when the first planes took to the air.

BILLIE SOL ESTES

Billie Sol Estes was investigated for receiving favorable treatment from the Department of Agriculture and Secretary Orville Freeman. Estes used his position to build a paper financial empire based on crop and storage guarantees.

Billie Sol Estes grew up poor in depression-era West Texas. After World War II he made his first real money in what became his trademark: he learned how to exploit the federal government. He bought military housing at cut-rate prices, moved it off base, and sold it for a handsome profit. His illegal behavior came after 1951, when he settled in Pecos and began to exploit agricultural programs created during the New Deal.

The Great Depression had hit the nation's farmers particularly hard. Even in the best of times, many of them barely eked out a living. To assist farmers, the Roosevelt administration created a government-run cartel to control agricultural production and keep the cost of farm products high.

Arguably, these programs should have been phased out with the end of the depression. During the prosperous 1950s, the Eisenhower administration tried to cancel them, but ran into opposition in Congress. By 1962 federal aid provided 40 percent of farm income. As the Estes scandal would demonstrate, programs that had been set up to save small farmers became a lucrative source of income for large agribusinesses that were, in turn, generous with political contributions.

The problem was that the agricultural programs had not established a true cartel that could control farm production. The programs typically offered price supports on certain crops, such as grains and cotton, guaranteeing farmers that, whatever the market conditions, they would be able to sell at a price that ensured an ample profit. The farmers had an incentive to produce as much as possible, and the result was chronic overproduction. To stem the surpluses, the government began "soil banks" to pay farmers to take land out of production. Farmers responded by taking their least efficient fields out of production and using heavier doses of fertilizer to raise the productivity of the remaining fields. For certain crops, such as cotton, the government set up allotments and offered price supports, but only to those farmers who had been raising that product at the time the allotments were established. The government also tried to deal with surpluses by storing them in warehouses. Estes figured out ways to exploit each one of these programs.

The dry fields of West Texas needed only two things to become highly productive: water pumped from underground aquifers and fertilizer in the form of anhydrous ammonia. In the mid-1950s Estes went into the fertilizer business and, by undercutting his competitors, quickly became the largest supplier of that fertilizer in West Texas. In fall 1958 his supplier, Commercial Solvents, became concerned about his $550,000 debt, so Estes cut a deal. In exchange for more credit, he would give Commercial Solvents the income from a grain elevator he was about to purchase. Part of the motivation for this joint scheme was obvious: both parties wanted to crush the competition. Estes and Commercial Solvents were later prosecuted under Texas's antitrust laws.

The other part of Estes's scheme was more devious. Even if he had achieved a monopoly on fertilizer, Estes probably would have not raised his prices much—it would have been too easy for competitors to return to the market. Instead, he intended to develop a cooperative arrangement with farmers. They would buy cheap fertilizer from him and use it to raise their productivity. The resulting surpluses would then be stored in Estes's warehouses at government expense. Farmers would benefit from having their expenses indirectly subsidized by the government. Estes would absorb a small loss in the fertilizer business and get a large share of the more lucrative federally financed warehousing business. Estes already knew what a Senate subcommittee would discover in a 1960 probe—that warehousing grain was extremely profitable. (The subcommittee found profit margins ranging from 84 percent to 265 percent.) Even Commercial Solvents would benefit, getting a near monopoly on fertilizer sales and a share of his warehouse profits.

Estes did very well storing grain for the government. In less than three years he had moved past many other larger companies to become one of the largest such businesses in the country. There was only one difficulty: Commercial Solvents was taking such a large share of the profits from his silos that Estes was left with little money to build more. It was then that Estes turned to fraud. In concert with Superior Manufacturing of Amarillo, he began to borrow money on nonexistent fertilizer storage tanks. Under the impression that they were part of a legitimate business deal, farmers lent him their credit to buy what they thought were storage tanks that would be rented out to others. The rent, they were told, would meet the payments on the tanks and they would be given 10 percent for their participation. In reality, only a few of the alleged 33,500 tanks actually existed. Estes had a crew that raced ahead of finance company inspectors and changed the serial numbers of tanks to give the impression everything was legitimate. His scheme, exposed by the local newspaper *Independent and Enterprise*, resulted in a fifteen-year sentence for mail fraud and conspiracy.

Exposure and prosecution also brought an end to Estes's last scheme. Government price supports on cotton were set at a level that allowed farmers in the Southeast to stay in business despite their low productivity. Under those same supports, growing cotton in West Texas was extremely profitable. However, only those with an existing cotton allotment could benefit from the price supports, and Department of Agriculture regulations made it extremely difficult to move an allotment to West Texas. Estes managed to find loopholes in all the rules except one—a farmer with an existing allotment must farm at the new location. Estes tried to escape that provision by simply lying, but government officials caught him and levied a large fine. At the time he was exposed for his tank scam, Estes had managed to use bribes (expensive clothing and shoes) and political connections to get his case reconsidered. One of those bribed, Emery E. Jacobs, a deputy administrator in the Agriculture Department, told one of his investigators "to send me a report containing every justification that you can find to permit the retention of these allotments." In the ensuing controversy, Jacobs was forced to resign.

At the time the Estes story broke, there was widespread speculation about how high the scandal might reach, with some Republicans calling for Secretary of Agriculture Orville Freeman to resign. Estes was a liberal Democrat and a generous party supporter. He had avidly supported Adlai Stevenson in 1956 and paid for tickets so some of Lyndon Johnson's staff could attend the Kennedy inaugural ball. He believed his liberal Democratic friends could be trusted to protect the agricultural programs that were making him rich. Just before his schemes fell apart, he told a Dallas lawyer, "Now we've got the agricultural program wrapped up in a real ball." Warming to the topic, he said, "I want to tell you that we've got such control over this that if they elected so-called conservatives every election it would take eight years to get us out of control."

Although he may not be a trustworthy source, Bobby Baker, another political operative, probably got it right in his book *Wheeling and Dealing,* when he described a conversation with John Kennedy. Kennedy asked him, "How about this damned Texas tycoon—what's his name? Billie Sol Estes? Is he a pal of yours?" Baker replied, "Mr. President, I thought I knew every thief who'd ever crossed the Potomac with his hand out. But we got lucky on the Estes thing. He's in the political camp of Senator Ralph Yarborough of Texas, and you know, sir, that Lyndon [Johnson] and Ralph have always gotten along like cats and dogs. So I'm proud to say I've never had any association with Billie Sol. He was never an LBJ man."

Estes may have never been an "LBJ man," but he was someone that the vice president intended to please. Department of Agriculture memos indicated that, until the scandal broke, Johnson aides had been almost as busy as Yarborough's in attempting to smooth the way for Estes to get the cotton allotments he wanted.

BIBLIOGRAPHY

Art, Robert J. *The TFX Decision.* Boston: Little, Brown, 1968.

Blair, Joan, and Clay Blair Jr. *The Search for JFK.* New York: Putnam, 1976.

Burns, James MacGregor. *John F. Kennedy.* New York: Harcourt and Brace, 1960.

Duscha, Julius. *Taxpayer's Hayride.* Boston: Little, Brown, 1964.

Eddowes, Michael. *The Oswald File.* New York: Crown, 1977.

"Estes: Three-Sided Country Slicker." *Fortune,* July 1962, 166–170.

Exner, Judith. *Judith Exner: My Story.* New York: Grove Press, 1977.

Giglio, James N. *The Presidency of John F. Kennedy.* Lawrence: University Press of Kansas, 1991.

Goodwin, Doris Kearns. *The Fitzgeralds and the Kennedys: An American Saga.* New York: Simon and Schuster, 1987.

Hagood, Wesley O. *Presidential Sex: From the Founding Fathers to Bill Clinton.* Secaucus, N.J.: Carol Publishing Group, 1998.

Hersh, Seymour M. *The Dark Side of Camelot.* Boston: Little, Brown, 1997.

Lasky, Victor. *JFK: The Man and the Myth.* New York: Macmillan, 1963.

Mitchell, Jack. *Executive Privilege: Two Centuries of White House Scandals.* New York: Hippocrene Books, 1992.

Mollenhoff, Clark R. *The Pentagon.* New York: Putnam, 1967.

Reeves, Thomas C. *A Question of Character: A Life of John F. Kennedy.* New York: Free Press, 1991.

Schlesinger, Arthur M. *A Thousand Days: John F. Kennedy in the White House.* Boston: Houghton Mifflin, 1965.

Shapley, Deborah. *Promise and Power.* Boston: Little, Brown, 1993.

Wills, Garry. *The Kennedy Imprisonment: A Meditation on Power.* Boston: Little, Brown, 1982.

Woodward, C. Vann. *Responses of the Presidents to Charges of Misconduct.* New York: Dell Publishing, 1974.

LYNDON B. JOHNSON

Thirty-Fifth President
1963–1969

Lyndon Baines Johnson was born August 27, 1908, in Stonewall, Texas. His parents were schoolteachers. When he was five years old, the family moved to Johnson City, a small town named for his grandfather. Lyndon worked during most of his teen years and put himself through Southwest Texas State Teachers College. He graduated in 1930 and taught for a year.

Rep. Richard Kleberg invited Johnson to join his congressional staff in Washington. During his four years in Washington, Johnson learned the legislative process and became an ardent supporter of the New Deal. He enrolled in Georgetown Law School, but gave up his studies and the position with Kleberg when President Franklin Roosevelt appointed him the Texas director of the National Youth Administration.

Johnson married Claudia Alta "Lady Bird" Taylor, the daughter of a storekeeper and rancher, on November 17, 1934. In 1937 he campaigned successfully for the U.S. House of Representatives as a New Deal Democrat and served six terms. He saw active duty briefly during World War II as a lieutenant commander in the navy, winning a Silver Star in the South Pacific.

He was elected to the Senate in a controversial election in 1948. In 1953 he became the youngest minority leader in Senate history, and the following year, when the Democrats won control, majority leader. An effective politician, he was largely responsible for the legislative successes of the Eisenhower administration.

In the 1960 presidential election, Johnson was selected by John F. Kennedy as his running mate, largely to create a geographically viable ticket representing the Northeast and the Southwest. Johnson became president on November 22, 1963, when Kennedy was assassinated.

One of the first measures Johnson pursued as president was the Civil Rights Act of 1964, a measure that Kennedy had championed. The act protected black voting rights and established the Equal Employment Opportunity Commission. Johnson also urged the nation "to build a great society, a place where the meaning of man's life matches the marvels of man's labor." In 1964 Johnson won a landslide election over Arizona senator Barry Goldwater, taking 61 percent of the vote. Armed with this mandate, Johnson pressed his Great Society programs: government aid to education, medical care, urban renewal, conservation, and measures to reduce crime and delinquency.

Continuing Kennedy's efforts to protect South Vietnam from communist aggression, Johnson sent increasing numbers of U.S. troops. The war effort diverted attention and money from Johnson's domestic accomplishments, but failed to win the war. He announced that he would not seek a second full term so that he could put politics aside and work for peace. He also stated that he did not want to be the first president in U.S. history to lose a war.

Out of political office for the first time in more than thirty years, Johnson and his wife retired to their ranch in Texas. In 1971 he published a book about his years as president. He died of a heart attack January 22, 1973.

1948 SENATE ELECTION FRAUD

Johnson defeated his Democratic primary opponent, Coke Stevenson, by a mere eighty-seven votes. Johnson's campaign had bought the support of a number of local machines, including the one run by George Parr in southeastern Texas.

In 1948 Lyndon Johnson decided to challenge Gov. Coke Stevenson in the Democratic primary for U.S. Senate. Few seasoned politicians gave Johnson more than an outside chance of beating the popular Stevenson. In fact, polls conducted a week before the August 28 primary had Johnson trailing him 46 percent to 54 percent among voters most likely to vote.

Johnson's campaign decided to change tactics and go after blocs of voters to close the gap. Edward Clark—dubbed the secret boss of Texas—Alvin Wirtz, and the Brown brothers (Herman and George, prominent lawyers and businessmen) organized a series of trips to visit local political bosses whose support could be bought. Using private planes owned by the Browns, they went to the counties with large Mexican-American populations, including Webb County and San Antonio. They also wanted to make a deal with George Parr, who controlled the votes of six counties plus the Hispanic portions of Corpus Christi.

Alvin Wirtz took care of Parr, and the Johnson campaign got to the judge who controlled the county's elections. In San Antonio the campaign had three separate organizations. The first was headed by Dan Quill, who had run Johnson's first failed bid. The second was led by San Antonio sheriff Owen Kilday. John Connally, who served as governor of Texas (1963–1969) and U.S. secretary of the Treasury (1971–1972), once admitted that he would not be surprised if more than $50,000 in bribes

had not been given to the Kilday organization. The third group was headed by the black boss Valmo Bellinger.

On election night, the early returns had Stevenson ahead by some
20,000 votes, mostly from the cities of Austin, Houston, Dallas, and Fort
Worth. When the returns came in from San Antonio, where Stevenson had
defeated Johnson 2–1 in 1941, the results were shocking. Johnson had not
been beaten by a landslide; he had won the area by nearly 100 votes out of
31,000. Webb County reported a 5–1 margin for Johnson. By the time the
Texas Elections Bureau closed at 1:30 a.m., Stevenson's lead had been cut
to 854 votes.

Election fraud was common to Texas politics, and almost everyone
knew it. In 1941 Johnson had made the mistake of letting his opponent
know too early how many votes he controlled and could switch. So the
1948 election became a waiting game to see who would produce the votes
first. Johnson controlled more votes in this election because of his campaign's last-minute efforts to get at the Mexican-American vote. That
night, calls were made to political bosses to see if more votes could be
found. George Parr indicated that more votes would be on their way. On
Sunday night, after a day of changed votes from all over the state, Duvall
County called in with 427 previously uncounted votes. All but two went
to Johnson, who now overtook Stevenson for the first time.

The counting and recounting continued for days. By Monday night,
Stevenson led by 117 votes. By Tuesday night, Stevenson led by 349 votes
(494,555 to 494,206). Little change occurred on Thursday and Friday, but
almost all observers believed that Stevenson was going to win by the
slimmest of margins. On Thursday night, Stevenson's lead was 351 votes.

On Friday morning, George Parr's machine started churning out additional votes from the other counties that he controlled. By noon, Stevenson's lead had been cut to 157 votes. Jim Wells County ultimately played
the deciding role in the drama. As the county's Democratic executive committee met to review the vote tallies, it discovered a 200-vote error from
the 13th Precinct. Luis Salas, who was responsible for the counting in
Alice, admitted nearly forty years later that he had doctored the count to
favor Johnson. With these votes, Johnson won the election by 87 votes out
of the 988,295 cast.

Coke Stevenson immediately cried foul and tried to have the results
overturned. His campaign was especially suspicious of the results coming
out of the 13th Precinct in Jim Wells County. The Stevenson campaign
asked for a recount, which the Johnson campaign, using every method at
its disposal, managed to prevent.

Stevenson next tried to acquire voter lists and interview voters. When
that failed, he hired famed Texas ranger Frank Hamer to assist his attorneys
in getting the necessary information. The group obtained written statements from voters that showed the revised tallies were likely fraudulent.
Stevenson's lawyers sought to have the election overturned in both state

and local courts, while he tried to have the results voided by the state Democratic Party at its convention in Fort Worth on September 13. When these measures were blocked, Stevenson turned to federal courts to have the election results overturned by having the ballot boxes in Jim Wells County opened and recounted.

Johnson struck back. He took to the airwaves, giving speeches in which he claimed that it was Stevenson who had tried to steal the election with fraudulent votes coming out of the big cities. Johnson also had a battalion of attorneys who fought Stevenson's lawyers at every turn, including obtaining a state injunction against the Jim Wells Democratic Committee—the body responsible for certifying the results—from opening Box 13 for a recount. Finally, with Abe Fortas representing Johnson before Justice Hugo Black of the U.S. Supreme Court, Johnson's team won an injunction to prevent the federal district court in Texas from opening the ballot boxes. Fortas argued that it was a violation of the constitutional directive that states manage their own elections to allow the federal judiciary to supervise election results. Justice Black was convinced and issued a stay that was upheld by the full Court when it refused to hear Stevenson's appeal.

Once certified as his party's candidate for the November election, Johnson easily defeated the Republican challenger. Stevenson's calls for the Justice Department and the FBI to investigate the election fell on deaf ears. Even the Senate performed only a pro forma investigation. Although public speculation continued about the honesty of the 1948 senatorial election, Johnson had secured the next rung of the ladder that led eventually to the White House. Had he lost the 1948 election, LBJ's skyrocketing political career probably would have come to a halt.

ROBERT G. "BOBBY" BAKER

Bobby Baker, who served as Johnson's secretary when he was majority leader in the Senate, used his influence to secure lucrative vending machine contracts with the defense industry.

On September 9, 1963, a lawsuit was filed against Bobby Baker, who had served as secretary to Senate Majority Leader Lyndon Johnson. The suit charged that Baker had used his position of power to obtain Defense Department contracts for his vending machine firm. On October 7 Baker, who had stayed on at the Senate after LBJ became vice president, resigned rather than face questions from Senate leaders. However, three days later, the Senate authorized an investigation to be conducted in closed-door sessions by the Committee on Rules and Administration. Some speculated that President Kennedy would use the scandal to drop Johnson from the ticket in 1964.

The investigation, which began on October 29, was interrupted by Kennedy's assassination on November 22. When the investigation resumed, President Johnson made his tax records available to the committee. The investigation into Baker's business dealings and his connections with LBJ continued into 1964. In January Don B. Reynolds, a suburban Maryland insurance agent, claimed that he sold a $100,000 policy to Johnson in 1957 and was then pressured by Walter Jenkins, Johnson's administrative assistant, to purchase advertising time on KTBC, Lady Bird Johnson's Austin television station. Reynolds paid more than $1,200 for the spots, which he resold at a loss to people who could actually use the time. Reynolds also claimed that Baker, who had become a vice president in Reynolds's firm, convinced Reynolds to buy a $600 stereo for the Johnsons. In 1962 Johnson purchased another $100,000 policy from Reynolds.

The Johnson administration hoped to delay the public disclosure of Reynolds's testimony. Abe Fortas and Clark Clifford, trusted Johnson advisers, urged newspaper editors to hold off on publishing the story. They also advised Johnson that Walter Jenkins should not be allowed to testify before the committee. Jenkins limited his testimony to a written statement. The hearings were suspended on March 25, 1964. Nearly four months later, on July 8, the committee issued its report, which condemned Baker's actions. The report was also critical of Reynolds, whom the majority (Democrats) found to be a less than compelling witness. Republicans on the committee complained that the investigation had been a whitewash to protect the president and Jenkins.

This report, however, was not the end of the investigation. Sen. John Williams, Republican of Delaware, had been conducting his own investigation of Bobby Baker, and he alleged that Baker had been involved with arranging an illegal contribution to the 1960 Democratic campaign. President Johnson ordered the FBI to investigate the charges, and the Senate

Bobby Baker, right, and his attorney, Edward Bennett Williams, appear before the Senate Rules and Administration Committee, February 2, 1964.

reopened its probe into Baker's conduct. Republicans wanted to call Walter Jenkins as a witness, but committee Democrats refused to subpoena him because Jenkins's doctors said he was in no condition to testify (see below). In March 1965 the FBI issued its report, which stated that it found no evidence to support Williams's allegations. By a party-line vote of 6 to 3 the panel accepted the FBI's report as the final authoritative statement.

In a supplemental report issued in June, the committee praised the president for his cooperation with the investigation and formally cleared both him and Jenkins. Republicans continued to claim that the investigation had been short-circuited.

In 1966 Bobby Baker was indicted on nine counts of fraud, conspiracy to defraud the government, and income tax evasion. He was convicted on seven of the nine counts. Baker served three years in the federal prison at Lewisburg, Pennsylvania.

WALTER JENKINS, CHIEF OF STAFF

Walter Jenkins, Johnson's chief of staff, was arrested on a morals charge in the men's room of a downtown Washington YMCA.

On October 7, just a month before the 1964 elections, police arrested White House chief of staff Walter Jenkins in the men's room of a YMCA located a block from the White House. Jenkins, a Johnson aide for more than twenty-five years, was arrested on a morals charge—a polite way of saying that he had been caught in a compromising sexual encounter with another man. He was released and told no one at the White House about it. However, a reporter hot on the story telephoned Jenkins asking him to confirm it and another allegation that he had been arrested on similar charges in 1959. When Jenkins could no longer keep the matter private, he called Abe Fortas. Johnson and many of his top aides believed that Republicans had set a trap for Jenkins to embarrass the president just before the election.

With President Johnson in New York on a campaign trip, Fortas took charge of damage control. He advised Jenkins to check into a hospital. Fortas enlisted the aid of Clark Clifford to help him persuade newspaper editors not to publish the story right away. Fortas and Clifford argued that they needed time to inform Jenkins's family privately, that Jenkins was already seeking medical help, and that Jenkins would be asked to resign. The three Washington daily papers agreed to give Fortas and Clifford more time, but United Press International broke the story on the afternoon of October 14. Johnson showed no surprise; he had been told of the events a week earlier. Johnson's Republican opponent, Barry Goldwater, made no public comments about Jenkins during the campaign.

Columnists, including James Reston of the *New York Times,* called for an investigation into whether Jenkins's behavior had caused any national security risks. Johnson asked the FBI to investigate, and on October 22 the FBI concluded that no national security interests had been compromised. The FBI report took only a week to prepare—unusually swift. Many wondered why the FBI had failed to uncover Jenkins's 1959 arrest on morals charges during his routine background check. Johnson attacked the Republicans, who, he said, had been out to get his people at any cost. Johnson also claimed that President Dwight D. Eisenhower had similar problems with some of his aides, a charge Ike denied. Jenkins's hospitalization prevented him from testifying before a Senate committee investigating the activities of Bobby Baker. In the end, the scandal failed to have any real impact on the election.

JOHNSON FORTUNE

Reporters raised questions about the Johnsons' personal fortune, estimated at $14 million in 1964. Of specific concern was the radio/television monopoly that his wife held in the Austin, Texas, area.

In spring 1964 questions were raised about the sources of the Johnson family wealth. Johnson had been born into poverty, but, by the time he assumed the presidency, he was one of the wealthiest men ever to hold the office. Unlike John Kennedy, who had inherited his wealth, Johnson served in public office and amassed a fortune at the same time. The foundation of the Johnson wealth was KTBC, the lucrative radio-TV station in Austin, Texas. Lady Bird Johnson had acquired the radio station in 1943. Her husband's backroom dealings had been crucial in securing the option to buy the station and obtaining Federal Communications Commission (FCC) approval, which took only three weeks.

KTBC had a unique position—it was the only TV station in the Austin area, giving Lady Bird a total monopoly in a large television market. Some speculated that Lyndon Johnson had received favorable treatment from the FCC, the agency that regulates the broadcast media. For example, after twice postponing decisions, in December 1963 the FCC denied an application to grant a broadcast license for a community antenna television service. The approval of such an application would have adversely affected KTBC's worth.

Presidential aides had encouraged LBJ to sell the station when he took office, but he refused, saying that Lady Bird did not want to part with the business she had made so successful. Instead, the president placed the broadcast properties in a blind trust administered by an old family friend. LBJ's choice of a trustee also caused some concern as to how blind it really was. The trust had been set up by Abe Fortas and administered by Donald S. Thomas, an attorney, and Jesse Kellans, the executive director of the Johnsons' television and radio stations.

Johnson tried to stay out of the fray over his finances by discussing the subject as little as possible. In April Johnson stated at two press conferences that he did not own any interest in government-regulated industries. Johnson's plan was to rely on the technicality that he did not personally own the station because it was in his wife's and daughters' names. He could not maintain his silence for long. On August 21, 1964, *Life* magazine published an article that estimated the Johnson family's fortune to be a staggering $14 million. Several days later, the president released a professionally prepared audit that set the Johnson assets at $3.5 million. However, the figures used in the audit were based on the purchase price of assets acquired two decades earlier, not their true market value.

Although the audit was disingenuous, it quieted the storm. In the end, the story disappeared because none of the investigating reporters could prove that either the president or first lady had used political influence to generate the wealth they had amassed.

ABE FORTAS, SUPREME COURT JUSTICE

Abe Fortas's elevation from associate justice to chief justice was blocked because of outside income he earned for lecturing. He had been paid by individuals with business before the Court.

Abe Fortas had been Lyndon Johnson's trusted adviser and political ally since the 1948 senatorial election. Johnson appointed Fortas to the U.S. Supreme Court in 1965, after persuading Justice Arthur Goldberg to resign and become U.S. ambassador to the United Nations. Fortas was part of the Court's liberal wing, which included Chief Justice Earl Warren. In June 1968 Warren informed Johnson that he wanted to retire and that Johnson should select his replacement. Although he was still in good health, Warren was seventy-seven. He needed to retire before the next election to ensure that a Democratic president would be able to choose the next chief justice.

Johnson turned to his friend Abe Fortas as a way to solidify the Great Society within the judiciary. Fortas was not interested in being elevated to chief justice, but he accepted the nomination at Johnson's request. However, Fortas met with strong resistance to his appointment. The opposition was based on a number of factors, including his voting record. Johnson tried to appease the critics by nominating federal judge Homer Thornberry, a Texas crony, to Fortas's seat. Johnson believed that Thornberry's appointment would mollify southern senators who would then vote to confirm Fortas.

Abe Fortas gets a friendly version of the well-known "treatment" from Lyndon Johnson.

However, the opposition to Fortas grew stronger; he was seen as a Johnson political adviser despite his position on the Court. In fact, according to White House records, Fortas and Johnson had 145 meetings between November 25, 1963, and July 2, 1968. This number did not include telephone conversations. Johnson defended his relationship with Fortas as a practice that was common in earlier administrations. However, in 1966 Fortas crossed all ethical lines when he informed Johnson about an illegal wiretap of a Washington lobbyist, which had been authorized by Robert F. Kennedy. This sharing of information gleaned from a private discussion among the justices was a violation of judicial ethics.

Ultimately, Fortas's nomination failed not because of his close interaction with the executive branch, which was an open secret in Washington, but because of a course he taught at American University. The summer seminar at AU was paid for by Fortas's former clients and others who might have an interest in business coming before the Court. Fortas received $15,000 for the nine-week course. At the time his associate justice salary was $39,500. For senators looking for an excuse to abandon the Fortas nomination, this was it. Although the Judiciary Committee voted in favor of Fortas 11 to 6, the full Senate could not break a filibuster against the nomination. Fortas resigned from the Court May 14, 1969.

EXTRAMARITAL AFFAIRS AND ILLEGITIMATE CHILDREN

Johnson was proud of his womanizing. He carried on with secretaries, aides, and other women throughout his political life. He was quoted as saying that he had "more women by accident than Kennedy did on purpose." In addition, Johnson never tired of discussing his sexual appetites and prowess. Despite his promiscuity, Johnson had at least two long-lasting affairs.

Alice Glass

From 1938 until 1965 Lyndon Johnson carried on an affair with Alice Glass, the mistress and later the wife of Texas millionaire Charles E. Marsh, a publishing tycoon with newspaper interests across the nation. Johnson and Glass first met in 1937 at Longlea, Marsh's Culpeper, Virginia, estate. Glass, who was more than twenty years younger than Marsh, found Johnson irresistible.

At one time Glass believed that Johnson was ready to divorce his wife to marry her but then realized that he could not do so because a divorce would have destroyed his political career. Instead, the two became long-term lovers, sometimes meeting at the Mayflower Hotel in Washington and sometimes at Longlea. Undoubtedly, both Lady Bird Johnson and Charles Marsh knew of the affair and resigned themselves to it.

The affair ended around 1965, when the two began to have sharp disagreements about the war in Vietnam. Alice, an idealist, could not support the war and in symbolic protest burned the love letters Johnson had written to her.

Madeleine Brown

In 1948 Johnson began an affair with the twenty-three-year-old Madeleine Brown, who bought radio time for an advertising agency. She first met Johnson at a reception hosted by KTBC, the Johnson station, in Austin. They met again at another station event, after which, according to Brown, they made love at an Austin hotel. According to Brown, the relationship produced a son, Steven, in 1951.

The station manager acted as the intermediary for a number of future encounters between Johnson and Brown. The two would meet at various hotels in Texas when Johnson was there on business or campaigning. In 1950 Brown told Johnson that she was pregnant with his child. However, on the birth certificate, Brown listed her estranged husband as the father. In 1987 Steven Brown filed a $10.5 million lawsuit against Lady Bird Johnson, claiming he had been denied his inheritance and his name. The suit never went to trial as Steven, who many said resembled LBJ, died of lymphatic cancer.

The affair ended in 1969 at a meeting at the Shamrock Hotel in Houston. Brown claimed that in a two-hour conversation she tried to persuade LBJ to admit that Steven was his son. Shortly after Johnson's death in 1973, Brown received a letter from Texas attorney Jerome T. Ragsdale stating that provisions had been made to continue support for her and Steven. Ragsdale had been providing financial support, including a house, to Madeleine since Steven's birth. He also visited regularly to be sure they had everything they needed. He often was a surrogate father to young Steven.

In 1997 Brown published an account of the affair entitled *Texas in the Morning: The Love Story of Madeleine Brown and President Lyndon Baines Johnson.*

BIBLIOGRAPHY

Baker, Bobby. *Wheeling and Dealing: Confessions of a Capitol Hill Operator.* New York: Norton, 1968.

Brown, Madeleine Duncan. *Texas in the Morning: The Love Story of Madeleine Brown and President Lyndon Baines Johnson.* Baltimore: Conservatory Press, 1997.

Caro, Robert. *The Years of Lyndon Johnson.* 2 vols. New York: Knopf, 1982 and 1990.

Dallek, Robert. *Lone Star Rising: Lyndon Johnson and His Times, 1908–1960.* New York: Oxford University Press, 1975.

Hagood, Wesley O. *Presidential Sex: From the Founding Fathers to Bill Clinton.* Secaucus, N.J.: Carol Publishing, 1998.

Kahl, Mary. *Ballot Box Thirteen: How Lyndon Johnson Won His 1948 Senate Race by Eighty-Seven Contested Votes.* Jefferson, N.C.: McFarland, 1983.

Mitchell, Jack. *Executive Privilege: Two Centuries of White House Scandals.* New York: Hippocrene Books, 1992.

Mollenhoff, Clark. *Despoilers of Democracy.* Garden City, N.Y.: Doubleday, 1965.

Mooney, Booth. *LBJ: An Irreverent Chronicle.* New York: Crowell, 1976.

Murphy, Bruce Allen. *Fortas: The Rise and Ruin of a Supreme Court Justice.* New York: Morrow, 1988.

Roberts, Chalmers. *LBJ's Inner Circle.* New York: Delacorte, 1965.

Wheeler, Keith, and William Lambert. "The Man Who Is President, Part III: How LBJ's Family Amassed Its Fortune." *Life,* August 21, 1964, 62–74.

Winter-Berger, Robert. *The Washington Payoff.* New York: Dell Publishing, 1972.

Woodward, C. Vann. *Responses of the Presidents to Charges of Misconduct.* New York: Dell Publishing, 1974.

RICHARD M. NIXON

Thirty-Seventh President
1969–1974

Richard Nixon was born January 9, 1913, in Yorba Linda, California. He was the second of the five sons of Hannah and Francis Nixon, a lemon farmer. When Richard was nine, the family moved to Whittier, California, where Francis Nixon managed a combination gas station and general store.

A hardworking, serious student, Richard attended public school in Yorba Linda and Whittier. In 1930 he entered Whittier College and in his senior year was elected president of the student body. He majored in history and was the captain of the debate team. He graduated second in his class in 1934 and attended Duke Law School on a scholarship. Nixon finished third of twenty-five students in the class of 1937. Later that year, he was admitted to the bar in California. On June 21, 1940, Nixon married Thelma Catherine "Pat" Ryan in Riverside, California.

Nixon practiced law for several years in California before forming a business, Citra-Frost, which manufactured frozen orange juice. The company failed in 1941, and Nixon took a job with the Office of Price Administration in Washington, D.C. He enlisted in the navy, served from June 1942 to March 1946, and was discharged with the rank of lieutenant commander. He was cited for meritorious and efficient conduct while serving in the Pacific theater.

Returning to California, Nixon was elected to the U.S. House of Representatives in 1946, upsetting the five-term incumbent Democrat, Jerry Voorhis. Nixon was reelected in 1948. He became a national figure by leading a House Un-American Activities Committee investigation into charges made by Whittaker Chambers against Alger Hiss, a former State Department official. Although President Harry Truman and Hiss denied the charges, Chambers had convincing evidence of Hiss's espionage. Hiss was ultimately convicted of perjury in 1950 as the statute of limitations had expired on the espionage charge.

In 1950 Nixon defeated fellow representative Helen Gahagan Douglas for the U.S. Senate. During the campaign, Nixon's organization distributed pink sheets that attempted to link Douglas to the goals of the Communist Party. Nixon dubbed her the "Pink Lady," and one independent newspaper labeled Nixon "Tricky Dick"—a moniker that stuck. In the Senate he served on the Government Operations Committee and the Permanent Investigations Subcommittee chaired by Sen. Joseph McCarthy of Wisconsin. Nixon was critical of the Truman administration's handling of Korea and the firing of Gen. Douglas MacArthur.

At the Republican National Convention in 1952, Dwight D. Eisenhower selected Nixon to be his running mate because of his conservatism and because he represented a large western state. During the campaign, the press broke a story about a secret fund that Nixon had been using for political purposes (see page 000). Nixon defended the fund in his now-famous Checkers speech before the nation. Eisenhower decided to back his vice-presidential nominee, and the two were elected in a decisive victory in the fall. Nixon served as vice president from 1953 until 1961. He traveled abroad extensively. During a trade fair in Moscow he engaged in a spontaneous debate with Soviet Premier Nikita Khrushchev on the relative merits of communism and capitalism. Their talk became known as the kitchen debate because it took place in a model kitchen, part of the U.S. exhibit of a typical American house. The debate made Nixon familiar to millions around the world.

The Republican presidential nominee in 1960, Nixon lost a close election to Sen. John F. Kennedy of Massachusetts. During the campaign, he and Kennedy engaged in the first-ever televised presidential debates, which Kennedy won, at least according to those watching television. Nixon, who was ill, looked haggard and uncomfortable on television, in contrast to the handsome relaxed Kennedy. Two years later Nixon ran for governor of California against the incumbent, Edmund G. "Pat" Brown, and lost 52 percent to 47 percent. In his postelection press conference, Nixon announced his retirement from politics and lashed out at the press "You won't have Dick Nixon to kick around anymore!" Nixon practiced law in New York City from 1963 to 1968. In 1964 he supported and campaigned for the Republican Party nominee, Sen. Barry Goldwater of Arizona.

At the Republican convention in August 1968, Nixon was the front runner in a field that included Gov. Nelson Rockefeller of New York and Gov. Ronald Reagan of California. Nixon won the nomination on the first ballot. Gov. Spiro T. Agnew of Maryland was selected as his running mate. Nixon faced Democratic vice president Hubert H. Humphrey and a third party candidate, Gov. George Wallace of Alabama, running on the American Independent Party ticket. In the general election, Nixon garnered only 500,000 more votes than Humphrey, but won 32 states and 301 electoral votes to Humphrey's 13 states and 191 votes. Wallace won 5 states and 46 electoral votes.

Nixon was easily renominated in 1972 and faced Democratic senator George S. McGovern of South Dakota. The McGovern campaign suffered a setback when it was disclosed that the vice-presidential nominee, Sen. Thomas F. Eagleton of Missouri, had undergone electric shock therapy treatment for depression. Eagleton withdrew, and McGovern selected a new running mate—R. Sargent Shriver, former Peace Corps director and a brother-in-law of John F. Kennedy. The liberal McGovern went down to a crushing defeat. Nixon won 61 percent of the vote and carried forty-nine states. McGovern won only Massachusetts and the District of Columbia and 38 percent of the vote.

The Nixon administration faced a number of international and domestic crises. The Vietnam War was still raging in Southeast Asia. National Security Adviser Henry Kissinger engaged in protracted negotiations to end the conflict and signed a peace agreement in Paris in January 1973. In 1972 Nixon became the first president to visit Communist China. That same year, Nixon signed the first arms treaty with the Soviet Union to limit ballistic missiles (SALT I). On the domestic front, the administration was faced with a growing economic recession. In 1971 Nixon imposed wage and price controls to control inflation. Most of the restrictions were removed by the end of 1973. Nixon also took the lead on three major crime bills and several pieces of legislation that dealt with environmental protection. In 1971 the Twenty-sixth Amendment to the Constitution, which lowered the voting age from twenty-one to eighteen, was ratified.

However, the administration was also caught in a scandal that eventually resulted in Nixon's resignation from the presidency. Watergate began as a minor incident, but the attempts to cover it up cost Nixon his job. He resigned August 9, 1974, rather than be impeached (see page 374).

Nixon received a full pardon from his successor, Gerald R. Ford, in September 1974 (see page 387). Nixon moved to New York City and eventually to New Jersey. Still popular abroad, he traveled extensively. He wrote numerous books on his public life and foreign policy and acted as an unofficial adviser to the Reagan administration. In 1985 he mediated a settlement between major league baseball and the umpires' association. As time passed, Nixon gained a reputation as an elder statesman. He died April 22, 1994.

MARIANNA LIU

Nixon seemed to have a close friendship with a Hong Kong cocktail waitress named Marianna Liu, although the exact nature of their relationship was unclear. The FBI became interested because of the suspicion that Liu might have been a Chinese spy.

Vice President Nixon first met Marianna Liu, a part-time guide, in 1958 while on a tour at a Buddhist temple outside Hong Kong. The two met again in 1964 and 1965, when Nixon was in Hong Kong representing clients of his law firm. In 1966 Nixon visited the Hong Kong cocktail lounge where Marianna was working. Later that same evening, according to the Royal Hong Kong Police, who were monitoring the Nixon-Liu relationship, Marianna and another woman visited Nixon and his friend Bebe Rebozo in his hotel suite. Later, Marianna would claim that nothing sexual took place that evening, that the four simply shared drinks and conversation. On a return trip to Hong Kong a few months later, Nixon sent flowers and a bottle of her favorite perfume when he learned she was in the hospital.

The Special Branch, the British equivalent of the FBI, informed the FBI about the contacts, but the U.S. agency ignored them until Nixon became a presidential candidate in 1968. The FBI began to investigate the relationship because it feared that Liu might be setting up Nixon for a blackmail scheme. The FBI had several reasons for suspicion. Liu had no identification when she arrived in Hong Kong after the communist revolution in China. She had a close friend whose father was a general in the Chinese Red Army. She worked as a cocktail waitress but owned large quantities of real estate in Hong Kong. The FBI continued to investigate her as a possible communist spy until 1969 when President Nixon ordered that the investigation cease. By that time, the FBI had pretty much discounted the possibility that Liu was a spy.

Liu became a permanent resident of the United States in 1969. The following year she visited the White House on two occasions. Whatever her relationship with Nixon, it ended after her second visit because, according to some, Pat Nixon complained about her.

SPIRO AGNEW, VICE PRESIDENT

Vice President Spiro Agnew was forced to resign from office when a federal grand jury investigation discovered he had accepted kickbacks on construction contracts when he was a county executive and the governor of Maryland.

In August 1973 Vice President Spiro Agnew announced that he was the target of a federal grand jury investigation. The charges alleged that Agnew had received kickbacks from contractors, architects, and engineers during his terms as Baltimore County executive and governor of Maryland. Agnew faced indictment on charges that included bribery, conspiracy, extortion, and tax fraud stemming from the $1,000-per-week payment he received while in county and state office and the lump sum of $50,000 he received when he became vice president. Federal prosecutors claimed that Agnew continued to take money while he was vice president and promised his contributors that he could help them with federal contracts.

Agnew initially denied any wrongdoing, and President Nixon supported him. On October 10, however, Agnew pleaded *nolo contendere* (no contest) to the charges of income tax evasion and immediately resigned. The plea was part of a bargain that he would leave office and plead guilty to lesser charges in exchange for no jail time.

Attorney General Elliot Richardson, the chief prosecutor in the case, let Agnew escape jail even though similar charges against another person would have meant a prison sentence. Richardson agreed that Agnew would not have to admit to receiving illegal payoffs on the condition that he allow the full publication of all of the evidence amassed against him. Had the case gone to trial, the prosecution also faced the problem of whether newspaper reporters, who would have to be subpoenaed, would reveal their sources. Noting that it would not please every-

Spiro Agnew

one, the judge accepted Agnew's plea, fined him $10,000, and sentenced him to three-years probation.

Nixon selected Rep. Gerald R. Ford of Michigan, the House Republican minority leader, as the new vice president on October 12. In May 1974 a Maryland court of appeals disbarred Agnew for his crimes.

NIXON JEWELRY

The Nixons were accused of accepting $2 million in jewelry from wealthy Arab leaders, including the shah of Iran and Prince Fahd of Saudi Arabia, in violation of the federal law that prohibits accepting gifts valued at more than $50.

During the height of the Watergate investigation (see below), *Washington Post* reporter Maxine Cheshire wrote an article that accused the first family of secretly accepting jewelry valued at $2 million from Arab leaders. In the May 14, 1974, story, Cheshire reported that in 1970 Pat Nixon had received a $1 million gift of emerald and diamond jewelry from the Shah of Iran. However, when Cheshire checked with the gifts unit of the protocol office, there was no record of the jewelry

By law government officials and their families are not allowed to accept gifts over a certain value. In 1966 Congress amended the Foreign Gifts and Decorations Act of 1881 to make it illegal for "Every person who occupies an office or a position in the Government of the United States . . . or is a member of the family and household of such a person" to accept and keep any gift with a value of more than $50. However, the law failed to specify when such gifts had to be turned over to the gifts unit, or even what the penalties were for violating the act.

Cheshire discovered that Pat Nixon had been given emerald and diamond earrings by Prince Fahd of Saudi Arabia on October 14, 1969. The

First Lady wore them at her birthday celebration at the White House in 1973. The earrings were appraised for insurance purposes at more than $50,000. Records for the gifts unit indicated that a number of items of jewelry given to Pat Nixon and her daughters Julie and Tricia had not been turned over to the office. Evidently, the pieces were being held in a bedroom safe.

The White House claimed that the Nixons had no intention of keeping the pieces, but were merely using them while they occupied the executive mansion. Calling the jewelry "private gifts," J. Fred Buzhardt, the president's legal counsel, stated that the intention had always been to deliver the pieces to the gifts unit at the end of the president's tenure.

After Nixon resigned, the General Services Administration tried to recover the jewelry, and a legal battle ensued. In the end, neither Congress nor President Gerald Ford took strong action to recover the jewels from the Nixons.

WATERGATE

A botched break-in at the Democratic National Committee's headquarters at the Watergate and the ensuing cover-up of the deed led to President Nixon's resignation.

Named for the Washington hotel and office complex where it all began, the Watergate scandal eclipsed all other aspects of the Nixon presidency and culminated in his resignation. But the real scandal neither began nor ended with the botched break-in. Americans watched in disbelief as Watergate grew from an inconsequential burglary into what remains the most infamous political scandal in U.S. history. It resulted in a criminal investigation that reached the highest levels of government, including the office of the president. So deeply did it touch the country's political conscience that it spawned the custom of tagging other political scandals with the suffix "gate," as in Irangate, Filegate, and Monicagate.

It all started with Nixon's fierce determination to ensure his reelection in 1972. Ironically, he probably would have been reelected without any illicit activities, as the Democrats were badly divided. At a contentious convention, the Democrats nominated Sen. George McGovern of South Dakota, a highly controversial candidate. The Nixon campaign easily capitalized on McGovern's association with hippies and the antiwar movement, which alienated many traditional Democratic supporters. That November Nixon enjoyed a landslide victory, receiving more than 60 percent of the popular vote and losing only Massachusetts and the District of Columbia. The Republican win was not absolute, however, because the Democrats managed to hold on to decisive majorities in both houses of Congress.

But none of this was clear a year before the election, and Nixon chose not to leave anything to chance. Rather, he tacitly encouraged the aggressive and illegal campaign strategies of his loyalists on the White House staff and the Committee for the Re-election of the President (widely known as CREEP). Nixon's actions brought about a remarkable sequence of escalating scandal, starting with a pathetic break-in, that led directly to the start of impeachment proceedings and his resignation.

Late in his first term the Nixon administration was shaken by the *New York Times'* publication of what came to be called the Pentagon Papers. Daniel Ellsberg, a special assistant in the Pentagon's Office of International Security Affairs, had given portions of a Defense Department study to the *Times* and the *Washington Post*. The study was a history of the Vietnam War prepared by the Pentagon for the benefit of future scholars, and it contained a great deal of top secret information. Ellsberg, a critic of the war, hoped that the public would be so angered by what the documents revealed that it would demand an end to the war. Instead, he earned himself Nixon's personal ire.

By now the administration was fed up with leaks it perceived to be damaging to sensitive areas of national security, most particularly their efforts to bring a satisfactory end to the war in Vietnam. To address the problem, Nixon and his advisers created a special clandestine unit with the goal of putting an end to the security breaches. The unit, informally known as "the plumbers" for their work plugging leaks, was the result of a legally questionable partnership between the Nixon administration and its allies in the CIA Agency. On September 3 the plumbers broke into the Los Angeles offices of Dr. Lewis Fielding, a psychiatrist who had once treated Ellsberg. The administration defended the break-in on national security grounds, a nebulous defense that would be invoked time and again as criticism of the president grew.

Nixon aides later admitted that the L.A. break-in was precipitated more by a desire for vengeance than by security interests. They hoped to discover damaging personal information about Ellsberg, which they planned to use to disparage his character and discredit him before he was tried for espionage. They wanted to sway public opinion against him and increase the likelihood of his conviction.

The Ellsberg plot backfired. The Nixon administration's involvement in the break-in came to light more than two years later during the Watergate hearings. Three of the president's men, including his assistant for domestic affairs, John D. Ehrlichman, were eventually convicted of conspiring to deprive Ellsberg of his civil rights. In light of the government's misdeeds, all charges against Ellsberg were dismissed. More important, the Ellsberg incident was later shown to be just one link in a chain of illicit and clearly unconstitutional activities Nixon and his aides had sanctioned.

The most famous political scandal in modern American history began with an almost comical caper of cops and robbers. In the early hours of June 17, 1972, a private security guard discovered that a fire exit door leading to the parking garage at the luxurious Watergate complex was open. The door's lock had been taped to prevent it from closing. The guard did not call the police. He simply removed the tape and continued his rounds.

Later that night, he discovered that the lock had been taped again. His suspicions now aroused, the guard summoned the police, and three officers responded within minutes. As they climbed the stairs, they discovered that every exit door had been taped. On the 6th floor, they found that the fire exit door that opened directly into the suite of the Democratic National Committee had been jimmied. The offices were dark. In the office of the deputy party chairman, the police found five unarmed men dressed in business suits and surgical gloves.

The five men were charged with felonious burglary and possession of implements of crime—burglar tools. All five gave false names upon their arrest, but their true identities were soon discovered. Among them were three native-born Cubans, each with a history of clandestine involvement with the CIA, including the failed 1962 Bay of Pigs invasion. Another man was said to have fought alongside Castro in the Cuban revolution before switching sides and training Cuban exiles for guerrilla activities. The fifth man, James W. McCord, was an ex-CIA operative who was later revealed to be on the payrolls of both CREEP and the Democratic National Committee as a security consultant. Evidence soon also implicated White House operatives E. Howard Hunt Jr. and G. Gordon Liddy in the crime.

It seems likely that the so-called burglars were intent on leaving things as well as taking things. The drawers of a filing cabinet hung open, and panels had been removed from a secretary's office ceiling. The men had extensive photographic equipment, as well as sophisticated electronic eavesdropping devices capable of intercepting and transmitting conversations and telephone calls. Evidence suggests that the men planned to bug Democratic National Chairman Lawrence F. O'Brien's office, as well as repair a malfunctioning telephone bug that had been placed during a break-in three weeks earlier. The burglars had also photographed seemingly innocuous files.

In addition to the cameras and bugging equipment, the police found a walkie-talkie, forty rolls of unexposed film, lock-picking kits, door jimmies, and three pen-sized tear gas devices. In what would prove to be the most important discovery, the police found $2,300 in

Government evidence from the Watergate break-in

sequentially numbered $100 bills in the hotel room of one of the would-be burglars—the clue that set investigators on a trail that eventually led to the nation's highest office. The burglary suspects were arraigned the following day.

Two days later a story in the *Washington Post* announced that one of the Watergate burglars, James McCord, was the salaried security coordinator for President Nixon's reelection committee and that he also provided services for the Republican National Committee. Administration officials immediately terminated McCord's contracts, claiming to be "surprised and dismayed" by his arrest.

As the investigation deepened, the *Post* began uncovering new evidence of corruption and complicity on an almost daily basis. Two young *Post* reporters, Bob Woodward and Carl Bernstein, covered the initial break-in and had the persistence and determination to keep digging for the truth. Their stories won them the Pulitzer Prize. It has been alleged that Woodward and Bernstein had an inside source, the mysterious "Deep Throat," who confirmed or denied information and led to the heart of the matter. Deep Throat's identity is still unknown. Indeed, it is not certain he ever existed.

Fearing that the Watergate burglary would soon be traced to CREEP and then to the administration, White House aides began to cover up. Jeb Magruder, Nixon's deputy campaign director; John Dean III, White House counsel; and others began destroying evidence and lying to official investigators. Chief of Staff H. R. Haldeman devised a plan to derail the FBI's investigation by suggesting that it would interfere with what was really a sensitive CIA operation. Later, acting FBI director Patrick Gray stepped down after admitting he had given FBI files on the Watergate investigation to Dean.

Meanwhile, Watergate accomplice E. Howard Hunt had made it clear that the White House would have to pay dearly for his continued silence, leading John Dean to utter some now-famous lines to President Nixon: "We have a cancer within—close to the presidency—that's growing. It's growing daily. It's compounding. We're being blackmailed; people are going to start perjuring themselves very quickly." Dean indicated to the president that the price of Hunt's silence might be as high as a million dollars. Nixon replied, "You could get the money. You could get it in cash. I know where it could be gotten."

Attorneys at the Democratic National Committee were outraged by the break-in and eager to take advantage of what might very well be a political jackpot. They quickly filed suit in federal court against CREEP, seeking $1 million in damages for its alleged involvement in events at the Watergate.

John N. Mitchell, Nixon's first attorney general, became the first Watergate casualty. On July 1, 1972, he resigned his post as campaign manager, citing an ultimatum from his wife that he leave politics. The *Wash-*

ington Post reported that a $25,000 cashier's check, funds donated to the president's reelection campaign, had been deposited in the Florida bank account of one of the five Watergate burglars. Follow-up stories revealed that Mitchell had acted as comptroller of a secret intelligence fund that contained as much as $700,000 in undeclared cash donations. The funds were disbursed from the office safe of Nixon campaign finance chairman Maurice H. Stans. The one-page, hand-written record of where the funds went was destroyed, but investigators slowly pieced the facts together during the next two years. Mitchell denied the allegations, calling them "the most sickening thing I've ever heard."

Further developments were even more sickening. The *Post*'s next story described the activities of a one-time Treasury Department attorney, Donald H. Segretti, who had been hired by CREEP for "intelligence gathering activities" that included spying, disrupting Democratic political rallies, and making false accusations to discredit Democratic candidates. CREEP sought to sow discord among the hopefuls running in the upcoming Florida primary. Segretti cracked under questioning and revealed details of the "dirty tricks" campaign, indicating that the White House sanctioned his activities and naming Dwight L. Chapin, the president's appointments secretary, as one of his contacts.

In January 1973, almost six months after the Watergate break-in, the heavily publicized trial of the burglary came to an end. Of the seven men indicted by Judge John C. Sirica, five pleaded guilty to charges of illegal breaking and entering, conspiracy, and wiretapping. Only McCord and Liddy held out, choosing to stand trial. They were subsequently convicted of the same charges.

Throughout the proceedings, Judge Sirica publicly voiced his belief that the Watergate defendants were not being truthful and that the incident was part of a much larger conspiracy to commit political espionage. Sirica's performance is the subject of considerable controversy. From the beginning, he took an investigative approach, questioning witnesses and inspiring criticism that he overstepped the limits of judicial impartiality. When the jury returned a guilty verdict, Sirica meted out conditional sentences of twenty to forty years to each of the defendants, the maximum allowed by federal law, in a blatant attempt to make them reveal their secrets in exchange for favorable consideration during final sentencing.

James McCord was the first to take Sirica's bait. In a letter that Sirica later made public, McCord admitted that he and the other defendants had been put under tremendous pressure to plead guilty and remain silent. Specifically, he admitted that people "high up" were involved directly in the Watergate break-in. McCord charged that John Dean and John Mitchell had ordered him to commit perjury to conceal their participation in the break-in, and that he and his accomplices had been offered money for their silence. McCord was the first in a parade of witnesses that eventually offered to testify in the hope of protecting themselves from prosecution.

Thus, the seven convictions by no means marked the end of the scandal. Democratic outrage, together with the publicity generated by Sirica's proceedings, resulted in the Senate's unanimous decision to establish the Select Committee on Presidential Campaign Activities, chaired by North Carolina Democrat Sam Ervin, as well as the Justice Department's calling a grand jury. Sirica's courtroom remained an important locus for the continuing cover-up trial, particularly when a bitter battle developed over the release of presidential tape recordings, the existence of which had been inadvertently disclosed in congressional testimony by White House aide Alexander Butterfield.

The administration was in disarray. Nixon approached Dean, asking him to sign a statement naming himself as the principal author of the cover-up. Dean refused to become the administration's scapegoat and threatened to testify. On April 30, 1973, Nixon held a press conference to announce the resignations of Haldeman, Ehrlichman, and Attorney General Richard Kleindienst, a seemingly innocent victim of his close association with the others. He was replaced by Elliot Richardson. The president insisted that the resignations did not indicate guilt, but that the investigation had made it impossible for them to fulfill their duties. The same day Nixon issued a terse statement announcing Dean's dismissal.

Congressional Republicans breathed a cautious sigh of relief. Still believing the president's repeated denials that he had any involvement in the Watergate cover-up, they hoped that the administration's apparent housecleaning would be enough to dissuade further investigation and put the scandal to rest. Their wish, however, was not to be granted any time soon. Indeed, the departure of the president's principal aides increased the pressure on Richardson to appoint a special prosecutor. On May 25 Richardson appointed Archibald Cox, his former law professor at Harvard, as special prosecutor and turned over to him the Justice Department's investigation of the Watergate affair.

Hoping to stay out of jail and preserve his right to practice law, Dean offered to testify in exchange for immunity from prosecution. Dean claimed that he was only a loyal White House aide who was following orders from his superiors. He told investigators that the president had warned him "in the strongest terms" never to reveal the covert activities of the Nixon administration. He also testified that he had discussed the cover-up with the president on at least thirty-five separate occasions, most of which had occurred in Nixon's office.

Cox began his investigation by issuing a subpoena for the tapes that Nixon had secretly been making of his conversations in the Oval Office. The existence of these tapes proved to be one of the most shocking revelations of the investigation. Nixon had ordered the installation of voice-activated recording devices throughout the White House and in the Camp David retreat some time in 1971, and only a handful of his closest advisers knew about them. The tapes, which Nixon had ordered in an effort to preserve a record of his administration for posterity, proved to be the most damning record of the president's participation in the Watergate cover-up.

It was obvious that the tapes might be the key to understanding what had transpired in the White House before and after the Watergate break-in. Judge Sirica ordered Nixon to immediately give the tapes to the grand jury and the Senate Committee. Nixon refused the order, arguing that the doctrine of executive privilege gave the president the right to decide which of his communications he would disclose. The U.S. court of appeals upheld Sirica's order, directing Nixon to turn over the tapes. He again refused but offered a bargain: he would allow Democratic senator John Stennis listen to the tapes and then approve an edited version that would be distributed to investigators. Cox declined Nixon's offer and demanded the immediate release of the complete, unedited tapes. When Nixon refused to comply with a subpoena to surrender the tapes on July 26, 1973, the executive and judicial branches of the federal government arrived at a showdown.

In the meantime, the president went on national television and again said he would not release the tapes. At the same time, hoping to calm public outrage, the White House put out more than 1,000 pages of edited transcripts. Even in their edited form, the White House transcripts gave the nation an unsettling glimpse into the Nixon presidency. They revealed an embattled president who lived in a gangland-style atmosphere of foul language, populated by loyal sycophants plotting against perceived enemies. The presidential image was irreparably tarnished, forever marked by the endlessly repeated editorial note *expletive deleted.*

The demand for full disclosure continued, and tapes were released in a piecemeal fashion. In November 1973 it was revealed that one of the tapes had an unexplained silence lasting eighteen and a half minutes. Nixon's longtime personal secretary, Rose Mary Woods, testified before the congressional committee that she had accidentally caused the deletion while preparing the transcriptions. The next day she modified her testimony, saying that she was not responsible for more than five minutes of the eighteen-minute gap. A panel of experts in electronics then testified that the missing parts were the product of at least five separate erasures—the tapes had been purposely altered. The content of those eighteen minutes have fueled speculation ever since, but the culprit remains unknown.

Nixon insisted on his innocence. "I had no prior knowledge of the Watergate break-in," he told a rapt nation in a televised speech August 15, 1973. "I neither took part in nor knew about any of the subsequent cover-up activities; I neither authorized nor encouraged subordinates to engage in illegal or improper campaign tactics. That was and is the simple truth."

But many were convinced he was not telling the truth, and pressure mounted for the release of the tapes in their entirety. It had become obvious that the tapes were the missing link that would prove or disprove the president's innocence. Nixon continued to claim executive privilege and refused to comply with the demands of Judge Sirica and the special prosecutor. Nixon was blatantly trying to stonewall investigators. Executive privilege was being invoked by many of the White House witnesses who wished to avoid testifying before Senator Ervin's committee. The frustrated chairman threatened to bring contempt of Congress charges against any witness who refused to testify on the grounds of executive privilege.

In a final desperate attempt, Nixon ordered Cox to make no further efforts to obtain the tapes. Cox refused to obey. On October 20, in what became known as the "Saturday night massacre," Nixon ordered Attorney General Richardson to fire Cox for failing to comply with his order. Richardson immediately resigned rather than fire Cox. Nixon then ordered Deputy Attorney General William D. Ruckelshaus to dismiss Cox. Ruckelshaus also refused and was fired. Finally, Solicitor General Robert Bork, who had assumed the role of acting attorney general, carried out the president's wish.

For many, the Saturday night massacre was the last straw. Nixon had obviously engaged in an aggressive effort to impede the investigations, but now he was also threatening the independence of the judicial process. His actions all but confirmed his guilt in the eyes of most Americans. Editorial pages across the country decried what they saw to be an egregious abuse of executive power. Critics called for Nixon's resignation, and members of Congress began to talk about impeachment.

Sensing that the president was doomed, many of his strongest supporters began to distance themselves from him. On March 17, 1974, the grand jury investigating the Watergate affair indicted seven former Nixon administration officials for conspiracy to obstruct justice: H. R. Haldeman, John Ehrlichman, John Mitchell, Charles W. Colson, Gordon Strachan, Robert C. Mardian, and Kenneth W. Parkinson. John Dean and Jeb Magruder, as well as several others lesser figures, had already pleaded guilty. The grand jury's report also named Nixon as an unindicted co-conspirator. Unlike so many members of his administration, including some close personal friends, Nixon was never convicted and never served any prison time.

On June 3 Colson, a White House special counsel, pleaded guilty to charges related to his role in the Ellsberg case. Colson claimed that he was following directions from the president. Finally, the president's last-ditch attempt to protect some of the White House recordings was effectively ended by the Supreme Court. On July 24 the justices decided, 8–0, that Nixon had to surrender any of the tapes that could be used as evidence in the criminal trials of his former subordinates. Left with no other course, Nixon appointed a new special prosecutor, Texas attorney Leon Jaworski, and agreed to turn all of the tapes over to Judge Sirica and Congress. On July 12 Ehrlichman was convicted of conspiracy to obstruct justice and perjury in the Ellsberg case. The man who had directed "the plumbers" served eighteen months in prison. Convictions of other administration officials followed.

Nixon is caught in his web of lies about Watergate.

On July 24 the House Judiciary Committee opened formal debate on the impeachment of the president. Three days later the committee voted 27 to 11 to approve Article I of an impeachment resolution. Article I charged Nixon with obstruction of justice. On July 29 the committee approved Article II by a vote of 28 to 10. The charge was systematic abuse of power and violations of citizens' constitutional rights. The article made specific reference to the 1969–1971 wiretapping program. The next day Article III, accusing Nixon of contempt of Congress, was approved by a vote of 21 to 17. Two additional articles were rejected.

Meanwhile, prosecutors continued to press Nixon's aides in an attempt to ascertain his role in the scandal. They also aggressively pressed Nixon to stop delaying and immediately release of all remaining tapes, which were now only beginning to trickle out of the Oval Office. Nixon had played all of his cards; he could stonewall no longer. On August 5 he released the three tapes that collectively became known as the "smoking gun" because they were the final, irrefutable proof linking the president to the crime. The tapes demonstrated irrevocably that he had ordered a full-scale cover-up of his administration's involvement in the Watergate burglary on June 23, 1972, six days after the break-in. They also demonstrated that Nixon knew from the beginning of the involvement of White House officials and CREEP.

After listening to the "smoking gun" tapes, the eleven Republicans on the Judiciary Committee who had voted against the articles of impeachment said they would change their votes. It became clear that Nixon would be impeached by the House and convicted in the Senate.

The stage was set for the final act, a vote by the full House followed by the president's trial in the Senate. Rather than face the shame of being the first president in U.S. history to be removed from office, he choose to leave. On August 8, in an emotional speech to the nation, Nixon announced that he would resign the presidency at noon the following day. "By taking this action," he said in a televised speech from the Oval Office, "I hope that I will have hastened the start of the process of healing which is so desperately needed in America." Leaving office before his term was complete, stated the president, "is abhorrent to every instinct in my body." But, "as President, I must put the interests of America first," he said. And although Nixon conceded that some of his actions "were wrong," he made no mention of the charges that had been leveled against him during the impeachment proceedings.

At noon on August 9 more than two years of investigation, accusation, and cover-up came to an end. In a simple, one-line letter—"I hereby resign the Office of President of the United States"—directed to Secretary of State Henry Kissinger, Richard Nixon became the first president to resign from office.

Nixon insisted that if his officers and aides had committed any crimes, they did so while acting in what they believed to be the best interests of the nation. "No man or woman came into this administration and left it with more of this world's goods than when he came in," said Nixon before boarding the helicopter that would carry him away from the White House.

Gerald Ford, who had been sworn in as vice president on December 12, 1973, became the thirty-eighth president of the United States. He took the oath of office just after noon on August 9, 1974, and served the remainder of Nixon's term. On September 8, stating that the country had already suffered enough and that another trial was not in the national interest, Ford granted Nixon a "full, free and absolute pardon" for crimes he committed while in office.

BIBLIOGRAPHY

Agnew, Spiro T. *Go Quietly . . . Or Else.* New York: Morrow, 1980.

Ambrose, Stephen E. *Nixon: The Education of a Politician, 1913–1962.* New York: Simon and Schuster, 1987.

———-. *Nixon: The Triumph of a Politician, 1962–1972*. New York: Simon and Schuster, 1989.

Bernstein, Carl, and Bob Woodward. *The Final Days*. New York: Simon and Schuster, 1976.

Brodie, Fawn M. *Richard M. Nixon: The Shaping of His Character*. New York: Norton, 1981.

Cohen, Richard M, and Jules Witcover. *A Heartbeat Away: The Investigation and Resignation of Vice President Spiro T. Agnew*. New York: Viking, 1974.

Colson, Charles. *Born Again*. Old Tappen, N.J.: Chosen Books, 1976.

Dean, John. *Blind Ambition*. New York: Simon and Schuster, 1976.

Ehrlichman, John. *Witness to Power: The Nixon Years*. New York: Simon and Schuster, 1982.

Eisenhower, Julie Nixon. *Pat Nixon: The Untold Story*. New York: Simon and Schuster, 1986.

Knappman, Edward, ed. *Watergate and the White House*. New York: Facts on File, 1973.

Kornitzer, Bela. *The Real Nixon: An Intimate Biography*. New York: Rand McNally, 1960.

Kutler, Stanley I. *The Wars of Watergate*. New York: Knopf, 1990.

Liddy, G. Gordon. *Will: The Autobiography of G. Gordon Liddy*. New York: St. Martin's, 1980.

Mitchell, Jack. *Executive Privilege: Two Centuries of White House Scandals*. New York: Hippocrene Books, 1992.

Orman, John M. *Presidential Secrecy and Deception*. Westport, Conn.: Greenwood Press, 1980.

Ross, Shelley. *Fall from Grace: Sex, Scandal and Corruption in American Politics from 1702 to the Present*. New York: Ballantine Books, 1988.

Sirica, John. *To Set the Record Straight*. New York: Norton, 1979.

White, Theodore. *Breach of Faith: The Fall of Richard Nixon*. New York: Atheneum, 1975.

Wicker, Tom. *One of Us: Richard Nixon and the American Dream*. New York: Random House, 1991.

Wills, Garry. *Nixon Agonistes*. Boston: Houghton Mifflin, 1970.

Witcover, Jules. *White Knight: The Rise of Spiro Agnew*. New York: Random House, 1972.

Woodward, Bob, and Carl Bernstein. *All the President's Men*. New York: Simon and Schuster, 1974.

GERALD R. FORD

Thirty-Eighth President
1974–1977

Gerald Ford was born July 14, 1913, in Omaha, Nebraska. His birth name was Leslie Lynch King Jr., but his parents divorced when he was two. His mother moved to Grand Rapids, Michigan, where she married Gerald R. Ford, who adopted young Leslie and gave him his name. Gerald attended public school in Grand Rapids and became a star football player at South High School.

In 1931 Ford enrolled at the University of Michigan, where he had a partial football scholarship. An All-American center, he turned down professional contract offers from the Detroit Lions and Green Bay Packers. Instead Ford accepted an offer to be assistant football coach and head boxing coach at Yale University. In 1938 he was admitted to Yale Law School and continued to coach to support himself. He earned his degree in 1941 and was admitted to the bar.

Ford practiced law in Grand Rapids until the United States entered World War II. He served in the navy from April 1942 until February 1946, rising from the rank of ensign to lieutenant commander. Ford saw active duty in the South Pacific aboard the USS *Monterey,* a light aircraft carrier. After he left the service, he returned to Grand Rapids to practice law. On October 15, 1948, he married Elizabeth Anne "Betty" Bloomer.

He became involved in local politics and made a successful run for the U.S. House of Representatives. He was reelected twelve times, each time receiving more than 60 percent of the vote. During his tenure in Congress, Ford established himself as a moderate on foreign affairs and a conservative on domestic issues. In 1952 he supported Dwight D. Eisenhower for president and was a leading defender of his friend Richard Nixon when some sought to drop him from the 1952 presidential ticket.

In 1963 Ford was elected chairman of the House Republican Conference. He was one of the two House members selected to serve on the Warren Commission, which investigated the assassination of President John F. Kennedy. In January 1965 Ford successfully challenged Rep.

Charles A. Halleck of Indiana to become House minority leader, a post he held for nine years. In 1967 he criticized the Johnson administration's conduct of the Vietnam War, asking "Why are we pulling our best punches in Vietnam? Is there no end, no other answer except more men, more men, more men?" Ford sought either a policy that would mobilize enough force to win or a policy of withdrawal.

When Nixon was elected president in 1968, Ford became one of the administration's staunchest supporters. After the Senate rejected two of Nixon's nominees to the Supreme Court, Ford tried to impeach Justice William O. Douglas, the Court's most liberal member, for paid activities Douglas had performed for the Parvin Foundation. Ford was asked if Douglas's activities were impeachable. He responded:

> An impeachable offense is whatever the majority of the House of Representatives considers it to be at a given moment in history; conviction results from whatever offense or offenses two-thirds of the other body considers to be sufficiently serious to require removal of the accused from office.

Under the provisions of the Twenty-fifth Amendment, when the vice presidency becomes vacant, the president nominates a new vice president who must be confirmed by both houses of Congress. Spiro Agnew resigned in 1973, and President Nixon selected Ford to replace him (see page 372). Confirmed by the Senate, 92–3, and the House, 387–35, Ford took the oath of office on December 6, 1973. On August 9, 1974, President Nixon resigned in the wake of the Watergate scandal, and Ford was sworn in as president.

Ford selected New York governor Nelson A. Rockefeller to serve as his vice president and retained many members of Nixon's cabinet. During his administration, Ford dealt with the ongoing communist threat in Southeast Asia as well as a worsening economic situation in the United States. In addition to his pardon of President Nixon, he also offered clemency for Vietnam War draft dodgers and deserters.

In 1975 Ford was the target of two separate attempts on his life. On September 5 Lynette "Squeaky" Fromme, a disciple of mass murderer Charles Manson, pointed a loaded pistol at him as he moved through a crowd in Sacramento. A Secret Service agent disarmed her before she could fire. On September 22 political activist Sara Jane Moore fired a handgun at Ford as he was leaving a hotel in San Francisco. The bullet wounded a taxi driver. Both women were arrested and convicted.

Defeated in the 1976 election by Jimmy Carter, Ford retired to Rancho Mirage, California. He wrote his memoirs and engaged in an active speaking schedule. He served on a number of boards for major corporations. In 1980 he briefly considered joining the Reagan ticket as vice president, but declined.

NIXON PARDON

President Ford issued a "full, free, and absolute pardon" to former president Richard M. Nixon for any crimes he may have committed while in office. Many speculated that the pardon was part of a deal between Ford and Nixon.

When Jimmy Carter moved into the White House in January 1977, the first movie he watched was *All the President's Men,* a dramatization of the *Washington Post*'s investigation into the Watergate scandal. It was a not so subtle admission of the major role that the scandal played in his defeat of Gerald Ford. In his memoirs, *Keeping Faith,* Carter suggested that President Ford's pardon of Nixon had been a "largely unspoken though ever-present campaign issue."

Ford issued a "full, free, and absolute pardon" to Richard Nixon on September 8, 1974, knowing that he was taking a serious political risk. *Newsweek* magazine had just reported a Gallup poll showing that 58 percent of the American people opposed giving Nixon "some form of immunity from criminal charges." Only 33 percent supported a pardon. A similar poll done two days after Ford's announcement found that 62 percent of the American people disapproved of his action. In a week his general approval rating plummeted from 71 percent to less than 50 percent. The pardon spelled the end of Ford's honeymoon with a Democratic Congress and with a large portion of the public.

Why did Ford take such an unpopular step just one month into his administration? Some conspiracy theorists claim that Nixon and Ford had made a deal in which Ford got the presidency in exchange for a promise to pardon Nixon. No evidence for such an agreement has surfaced, and Ford denied it to a House committee. "There was no deal, period," he said.

There was, however, a source for the allegation. On August 1, 1974, just days before Nixon resigned, Ford met with Alexander Haig, Nixon's chief of staff. Robert T. Hartmann, a member of Ford's staff, was also present. After asserting that "the whole ball game might be over" for Nixon, Haig described six possible options for the president. The sixth option was: "Nixon could agree to leave in return for an agreement that the new president—Gerald Ford—would pardon him." Later, Hartmann told Ford that, by not openly rejecting the last option, Ford had implied assent. Ford denied that was the case, but the next day in Hartmann's presence he called Haig and told him that nothing they discussed the previous day "should be given any consideration" in Nixon's decision making. If that account is true, Nixon was able to learn that Ford was not unalterably opposed to a pardon.

A number of other factors may have worked to persuade Ford that, however unpopular, a pardon was necessary. On August 9, in his first speech as president, Ford expressed the belief that "our long national

At the steps of the helicopter that will fly them away from the White House, the Nixons say good-bye to the Fords.

nightmare" was over. He soon found that was not the case. With the investigations continuing, friends and colleagues began to suggest that something more needed to be done to put the matter behind the country. Senate Minority Leader Hugh Scott said, "For God's sake, enough is enough. [Nixon's] been hung, and it doesn't seem to me that in addition he should be drawn and quartered." On *Meet the Press* Vice President–designate Nelson Rockefeller agreed with Scott.

On the afternoon of August 28, his first press conference as president drove home that point. Like any president, he wanted the press to focus on what he was accomplishing, not on what his predecessor had or had not done. Instead, he found himself questioned about if and when he might issue a pardon. The next day he told his senior staff that he was considering pardoning Nixon. According to Hartmann, Ford now intended to issue a pardon "as soon as he was sure he had the legal authority to do so." Among the issues to be settled were whether a pardon could be issued before Nixon was charged and whether the pardon should include an admission of guilt.

In addition, the matter of Nixon's presidential papers and tapes remained to be decided. Nixon was on sound legal ground in his demand that the papers be transferred to his control. Other presidents had been able to take their personal papers with them as a matter of course. But Nixon's papers were different. They were the focus of an ongoing criminal investigation. What if Nixon took the papers and either destroyed them or refused to hand them over? Along with Ford's insistence that any pardon be accompanied by a statement of contrition from Nixon, the papers became a bargaining point as the two parties negotiated under what conditions the pardon would be issued.

In addition, Ford was concerned by reports that Nixon's health was deteriorating rapidly. Benton Becker, an attorney who was conducting some of the pardon negotiations, claimed the former president looked like someone in "an octogenarian nursing home." Meeting with Ford, Becker said, "I really have serious questions in my mind whether that man is going to be alive at the time of the elections." When Ford answered that 1976 was a long time away, Becker responded, "I don't mean 1976. I mean 1974." The elections were just around the corner.

The final factor may have come from negotiations between Ford's staff and Leon Jaworski, the Watergate special prosecutor. A presidential pardon would do little to heal the nation if the prosecutor insisted in continuing his investigation of Nixon. In later interviews, members of Jaworski's staff admitted that their boss must have at least hinted that a pardon would end the Nixon investigation.

Ford's decision to pardon the former president but not the other Watergate conspirators also drew criticism. How could justice be evenhanded if Nixon went free while his underlings faced months of trials, mounting legal bills, and the possibility of prison? It is true, as Ford noted, that as president Nixon had been the special focus of "ugly passions." But with Nixon beyond reach, it was reasonable to suspect that those hatreds would turn on others less well connected.

Ford paid a big price for his decision. Although historical what-ifs are impossible to settle, some have suggested that had he not pardoned Nixon or had he waited until public sentiment changed, Ford might have been elected in 1976.

BETTY FORD'S ADDICTIONS

Betty Ford kept hidden from the Washington press and outsiders that she was addicted to both alcohol and pain killers while she was first lady.

Betty Ford and her family had a secret that they went to great pains to hide. For more than a decade, Betty Ford had been abusing alcohol and drugs (mostly pain pills). Her addiction had started innocently enough with the traditional drink at the cocktail hour. However, the tradition turned to abuse when she started to drink by herself. The drugs began as a prescription for a pinched nerve but continued long after the physical pain had ended.

Throughout her family's time in the White House, Betty Ford struggled with her problem. Her children would try to ascertain her condition before bringing friends home out of fear of them discovering that their mother—the first lady—was a drunk. To add to her problems, Betty Ford was also treated for breast cancer. In 1978 her family confronted her about her alcohol and drug abuse and persuaded her to seek treatment. Her recovery led to the founding of the Betty Ford Center, the world-renowned addiction treatment center in California.

BIBLIOGRAPHY

Ford, Betty. *Betty: A Glad Awakening.* Garden City: Doubleday, 1987.

Ford, Gerald R. *A Time to Heal: The Autobiography of Gerald R. Ford.* New York: Harper and Row, 1979.

Greene, John R. *The Presidency of Gerald R. Ford.* Lawrence: University Press of Kansas, 1995.

Mitchell, Jack. *Executive Privilege: Two Centuries of White House Scandals.* New York: Hippocrene Books, 1992.

Mollenhoff, Clark R. *The Man Who Pardoned Nixon.* New York: St. Martin's, 1976.

Schapsmeier, Edward L. *Gerald R. Ford's Date With Destiny: A Political Biography.* New York: P. Lang, 1989.

Thompson, Kenneth W., ed. *The Ford Presidency: Twenty-two Intimate Perspectives of Gerald R. Ford.* Lanham, Md.: University Press of America, 1988.

JAMES E. CARTER

Thirty-Ninth President
1977–1981

James Earl Carter Jr. was born October 1, 1924, in Plains, Georgia, the eldest of four children of James and Lillian Carter. From earliest childhood he preferred to be called Jimmy. His father was a storekeeper, farmer, and insurance broker who also served as a public official. Jimmy Carter was educated in the public schools of Plains. After graduating from high school, he attended both Georgia Southwestern College and Georgia Institute of Technology before being admitted to the U.S. Naval Academy at Annapolis in 1943. He graduated fifty-ninth in his class of 820 in June 1946. A month later he married Rosalynn Smith, a lifelong friend of his sister, Ruth.

Carter decided to make the navy his career. He served aboard a number of vessels including the *Sea Wolf,* one of the first atomic submarines. However, when his father died in 1953, Carter ended his naval career and returned to Plains to manage the family peanut farm. He gradually increased his land holdings and started several businesses, including a peanut-shelling plant and a farm-supply company. He was a millionaire by 1979. During this time, Carter also became active in local politics. In 1962 he was elected to the Georgia state senate after proving voter fraud in his primary opponent's results. He was easily reelected in 1964.

In 1966 Carter ran unsuccessfully for the Democratic nomination for governor, finishing third behind Lester Maddox and Ellis Arnall. In 1970 Carter again ran for the nomination against former governor Carl E. Sanders, a political moderate. To distinguish himself from Sanders, Carter ran a conservative campaign that included opposition to busing for school integration. After his victory in the fall, however, Carter actively worked to increase opportunities for blacks and the poor. He equalized funding for all state school districts and appointed a large number of blacks to state agencies. He supported U.S. war efforts in Vietnam and worked for the nomination of Sen. Henry Jackson of Washington for president in 1972. In

1974 he served as the chairman of the Democratic National Campaign Committee.

A relative unknown going into the Democratic Party primaries in 1976, Carter was not considered a serious candidate. He stunned more seasoned politicians with early victories in Iowa and New Hampshire and came to the convention in New York in July with enough votes to secure the nomination. Sen. Walter F. Mondale of Minnesota was selected to be his running mate. His opponent in the general election was incumbent Republican Gerald Ford, who had fought off a challenge by the former governor of California, Ronald Reagan. Ford chose Sen. Robert Dole of Kansas as his running mate.

In the campaign Ford seemed to overcome the criticism that followed his pardon of Richard Nixon. However, in the second of three presidential debates, Ford made a blunder when he stated that Eastern Europe was not under the domination of the Soviet Union. Carter used the misstep and went on the offense. He won the election by fewer than 300,000 votes and an electoral college vote count of 297 to 240. (Reagan received one electoral vote from Washington State.)

On his first full day as president, Carter pardoned the estimated 10,000 draft dodgers of the Vietnam War. He faced a growing number of economic problems that seemed to overwhelm his administration. Rising unemployment, inflation, and interest rates strangled the economy. However, his administration was not without its successes. In 1978 Carter brokered the historic Camp David Accords, in which President Anwar Sadat of Egypt and Prime Minister Menachem Begin of Israel pledged peace between their two countries and ended the state of war that had persisted for thirty-one years. He also established diplomatic relations with China. However, it was also in the realm of foreign policy that Carter suffered his worst crisis. On November 4, 1979, Iranian militants seized the U.S. Embassy in Tehran and took sixty-three Americans hostage. The Iranians held fifty-two of the hostages for a total of 444 days, releasing them January 20, 1981, when Ronald Reagan was sworn in as president.

Carter returned to his home and business in Plains, Georgia. In his nearly two decades of retirement, he has been a high-profile volunteer for Habitat for Humanity, a project that builds homes for low-income families. He also established the Carter Presidential Center at Emory University in Atlanta, which works on a variety of national and international relief operations, including an effort to eradicate the Guinea worm parasite in Africa.

PLAYBOY INTERVIEW

In an interview with Playboy *magazine, candidate Jimmy Carter revealed he had committed adultery in his heart.*

Carter's 1976 campaign was momentarily thrown into disarray when the candidate made a surprising revelation in the pages of the November *Play-*

boy magazine. Carter had agreed to an interview with a reporter from the magazine, and, according to Carter, all went well. As the reporter thanked him and turned off his tape recorder, he said, apparently off the record, "Governor, there is still one thing that really concerns me. You are a farmer, living in a small town, who has pledged never to lie to the American people. You also claim to be a born-again Christian. The citizens of our country and other public officials are not perfect. How will you be able to relate to them, when you consider yourself to be so much better than they are?"

Carter's response was surprising. He said, "I try not to commit a deliberate sin. I recognize that I'm going to do it anyhow, because I'm human and I'm tempted. And Christ set some almost impossible standards for us. Christ said, 'I tell you that anyone who looks on a woman with lust has in his heart already committed adultery.' " He went on to admit that he had "looked on a lot of women with lust. I've committed adultery in my heart many times. This is something that God recognizes I will do—and I have done it—and God forgives me for it." For a time the interview was the subject of headlines as well as jokes on late-night talk shows.

BILLY CARTER AND THE LIBYAN CONNECTION

President Carter's brother, Billy, was investigated by the Senate and Justice Department for being an agent of the Libyan government.

During Jimmy Carter's 1976 election campaign the media usually portrayed the candidate's much younger brother as a beer-drinking good old boy. It is easy to understand why. The fun-loving Billy Carter provided an entertaining contrast to his intense and often moralizing brother. For a time after his brother was elected, Billy made a good income traveling around the country and giving speeches that poked fun at the nation's extended first family. He even marketed a beer made from peanuts.

In September 1978 Billy accompanied some Georgia legislators and businessmen to Libya as guests of the Libyan government, which was suspected of supporting international terrorism. In January 1979 the Libyans made a return visit to attend a lavish reception in Atlanta. Billy was not alone in extending a hearty welcome to oil wealth: Georgia's governor, the president of Georgia Tech, and other local notables attended the reception. But none of them made the sort of remarks that Billy made. Asked why he was there, he responded, "The only thing I can say is there is a lot more Arabians than there is Jews." If that had been the only thing he said, it would have been controversial enough, but he went on to claim that the "Jewish media [tore] up the Arab countries full time," and that a "heap of governments support terrorists and [Libya] at least admitted it." "The Libyans," he added, "are the best friends I've ever made in my life."

When those remarks hit the national news, President Carter was quick to distance himself from his brother, telling NBC News, "I don't have any control over what my brother says [and] he has no control over me." Billy also apologized, claiming that what he said "was not intended to be anti-Semitic." But some were wondering why the president was not doing more to restrain his brother.

Billy claimed that he had informed his brother about the upcoming reception when the president was in Plains for Christmas. In his memoirs, the president said that it was "early the next year" when he "learned from the news reports" that Billy had hosted the Libyans. Carter foe William Safire went further, asking in his *New York Times* column if Billy was holding something over his brother. Earlier, when the investigation of Bert Lance's bank finances had disclosed a large loan to the Carter family peanut business, Billy had taken the Fifth Amendment rather than incriminate himself (see page 398). Safire was suggesting that in a family business, arrangements that incriminated Billy probably would have incriminated his brother.

In July 1980 the president's troublesome brother was again in the news. The Senate and Justice Department were looking into reports that Billy was acting as an agent of the Libyan government. Billy needed money. His speaking engagements had dropped to almost zero because of his well-publicized ties to Libya. In addition, he had developed a severe drinking problem that required seven weeks of expensive hospitalization in California. To help with his finances, the Libyans had advanced him $20,000 in January 1979 and $200,000 in April. These payments were the first installments of a $500,000 advance on the money he was expecting for brokering the sale of Libyan crude oil to the Charter Oil Company of Florida.

Billy Carter, left, appeared with Libyan foreign minister Ahmed Shaejki, right, on "Good Morning America," on February 7, 1979.

Learning of Carter's Libyan contacts—but not of the money—in 1979 the State Department told him that under a 1933 law he needed to register as an agent of a foreign power. When he ignored the directive, the State Department began an investigation that led in May 1980 to the discovery of his $220,000 loan. Two weeks later he agreed to meet with the Justice Department and on July 14 belatedly registered as a foreign agent. Because it seemed clear that the only reason the Libyans employed Billy was his closeness to the president, a firestorm of criticism erupted. Some Republicans began calling the scandal Billygate.

White House attempts to calm the situation only made it worse. In a July 22 statement the administration revealed details about its ties to Libya through Billy in an effort to show that no harm had resulted. At the request of Zbigniew Brzezinski, the national security adviser, in November of the previous year, Billy, a Libyan official, and a representative of the National Security Council had met to discuss the possibility of Libyan help with U.S. hostages held in Iran. Over the rest of the summer, other revelations dribbled out just often enough to keep the fuss alive. Copies of diplomatic cables, none confidential, had been given to Billy when he visited Libya a second time in early 1980. First lady Rosalynn Carter had encouraged her husband to use Billy's Libyan connection to free the hostages. Billy had arranged a meeting between the president and the Libyan envoy to Washington. Although no evidence surfaced that the administration had done anything illegal, the story added to the impression that Jimmy Carter was not up to the office he held.

In an August 10, 1980, interview with Carter, CBS correspondent Dan Rather suggested that the president was "attempting to frame the issue incorrectly" when he "argued that Billy never influenced American policy on Libya." That, Rather said, was "not really in dispute." What was being discussed was whether the president "may have showed a lack of judgment in permitting Billy to lead the Libyans on when you should have and could have stopped him right away." Carter's evasive reply did nothing to clear away that impression.

HAMILTON JORDAN, PRESIDENTIAL AIDE

Hamilton Jordan was often criticized for his boorish behavior. He was also investigated by federal authorities for sniffing cocaine at a trendy New York disco, Studio 54.

As the nation prepared for the 1976 campaigns, *Harper's* magazine began to examine the presidential candidates. In March they turned to Jimmy Carter, and the article was far from flattering. Carter, the article concluded, was a man with "no philosophy and brilliantly packaged." Most disturbing was the description of Carter's successful 1970 bid to become governor of Georgia. Two of the people most responsible for packaging

Carter in that campaign were Gerald Rafshoon, his media director, and Hamilton Jordan, his campaign manager. (In the White House, Rafshoon became Carter's assistant for communications, and Jordan became the president's counsel and later his chief of staff.)

In his run for governor Carter faced two major opponents, Carl Sanders, a racial moderate, and C. B. King, a black lawyer. The only part of the political spectrum left for Carter was the segregationist right. During the campaign, anonymous leaflets were mailed to whites in small towns across the state. They showed Sanders being given a champagne shampoo by two black players on the Atlanta Hawks, a basketball team he and partners owned. The leaflets were intended to alarm those who abhorred whites socializing with blacks. Ray Abernathy, a public relations man who worked for Rafshoon, said, "We distributed that leaflet. It was prepared by Bill Pope, who was then Carter's press secretary. It was part of an operation we called the stink tank." He went on to note that Hamilton Jordan was "directly involved in the mailing. He and Rafshoon masterminded it." Pope confirmed Abernathy's claim that the Carter campaign was involved, but denied his role. Carter, Rafshoon, and Jordan denied their campaign was involved. Once elected and in the lights of the national media, Carter proclaimed himself an "enlightened" southerner. In 1972 Jordan developed a detailed plan to package Carter for a run at the presidency in 1976.

No allegations of a stink tank troubled Carter's time in the White House. The lessons of Watergate were too firmly fixed in everyone's mind. But on several occasions, Hamilton Jordan embarrassed the president with highly publicized events that suggested he could be as crude in his personal life as his Georgia campaigning had been.

The first occurred near the end of Carter's first year in office. In a *Washington Post* gossip column, Sally Quinn reported on a dinner hosted by Barbara Walters, at which Jordan was a guest. He was seated next to the wife of the Egyptian ambassador. According to Quinn, "fortified with an ample amount of the host's booze," Jordan "gazed at the ambassador's wife's well-endowed front, pulled at her elasticized bodice, and said, loudly enough for several others to hear, "I've always wanted to see the pyramids." The White House denied the story.

Early in 1978 Jordan and his wife announced that they were separating after four years of marriage. Less than three weeks later, on January 27, another incident occurred. According to the *Washington Post* magazine, Jordan was drinking at Sarfield's Bar, a favorite haunt of White House staff, when he began to exchange insults with a young woman. The clash concluded when Jordan allegedly spat his drink on the woman's blouse. Little would have come of the incident, but the White House, responding to the strong public criticism, launched a full investigation and produced a thirty-three-page report. Columnists had a field day, some poking fun at the entire incident, others questioning whether the bartender's testimony was accurate, given that the bar's owner had been active in the Carter campaign.

In his memoirs, Carter did not directly comment on the problems Jordan created, but one reported incident provides a tantalizing clue. On July 3, 1979, the president invited some advisers to Camp David to discuss a suggestion by Jordan that Carter needed to portray himself as a more forceful leader. They also discussed possible changes in administration staff. Starting with the cabinet, the group debated which members to fire. When attention turned to White House staff, Carter asked Jordon and Jody Powell to leave the room. Then, according to Carter:

Hamilton Jordan

> The group agreed that my White House team was competent, but thought that it was impossible for the press or public to acknowledge it because most of those around me had an air of immaturity about them. The strong advice of everyone present was that I bring in some more mature and substantive people to strengthen my personal staff.

Afterward, Carter did try to portray himself as a strong leader. Members of his cabinet were forced to resign, and Jordan was made chief of staff. But his seeming immaturity continued to put him in the news. That September the owners of New York's exclusive Studio 54 disco accused Jordan of using cocaine on their premises, a charge that triggered an automatic federal investigation. Jordan denied the charge as well as another that he had used cocaine at a Beverly Hills party in October 1977. No charges were ever filed.

To the very end of the Carter administration, Jordan remained obsessed with Carter's public image. Jordan's book *Crisis: The Last Year of the Carter Presidency* describes how Jordan spent the last minutes before Ronald Reagan was sworn into office huddled in the White House situation room. The American hostages were sitting in two planes on an Iranian airfield waiting to take off. Over and over, Carter called to ask if there was any news. Both knew what the retiring president had in mind:

> Reagan is taking the oath of office while a very conspicuous Carter aide rushes down the Inaugural platform to hand Carter a note. Carter smiles broadly, walks up to the Chief Justice who is about to administer the Presidential oath to Reagan and says, excuse me, Governor Reagan, I have an announcement to make.

However, the planes remained on the ground until Reagan began his inaugural speech. Jordan's last effort to repackage Carter had failed.

BERT LANCE, BUDGET DIRECTOR

Bert Lance, Jimmy Carter's longtime political friend, was investigated for illegal banking activities, including receiving preferential treatment on unsecured loans and large overdrafts at two banks he headed in Georgia.

The Lance affair began with a cover-up of campaign finance violations. In 1974 Bert Lance had made an unsuccessful run to become governor of Georgia. Two years later, the Justice Department investigated to determine whether the First National Bank of Calhoun—a bank headed by Lance—had illegally allowed his campaign to overdraw its account. On December 2 the U.S. attorney's office in Atlanta squashed the probe. The very next day President-elect Jimmy Carter announced that he was appointing Lance to be director of the Office of Management and Budget (OMB).

Carter and Lance had been close friends for many years, and Carter's peanut business had once been the largest borrower from the National Bank of Georgia, another bank that Lance headed. In his memoirs, Carter stressed the importance of the OMB appointment and the need to fill it with someone who was "honest and competent." Lance, Carter told a journalist, "was the first person that I thought about when I was finally sure that I would be elected President."

In an effort to distinguish his administration from the recent Republican administrations, Carter ordered all those he appointed to reveal their financial holdings and to sell anything that created a conflict of interest. Lance had to divest himself of $3.3 million worth of National Bank of Georgia stocks. With the approval of the president and Congress, Lance placed the stock in a "blind trust with the trustee under orders to sell all of it by the end of 1977." However, the trust was hardly blind: Lance knew what it held and that it would be sold during the coming year, which gave him every incentive to use his position to enhance the trust's value. It was later learned that Lance had met in his OMB office with NBG officials and had written Senate Banking chairman William Proxmire a letter criticizing anti-redlining legislation that might harm the bank.

Lance breezed through his Senate confirmation with little investigation. The first doubts about Lance surfaced on July 12, 1977, when Carter sent an innocent-appearing letter to Congress. Lance, the letter explained, was under an undue financial burden. Word had gotten out that the NBG was planning to write off bad loans and might not pay dividends that year. Lance's $3.3 million in stock was now worth $1.7 million, and he wanted an unlimited extension of the December 31 deadline to sell the stock. Things began to heat up when, in a July 21 article, William Safire charged that Lance had benefited from a sweetheart loan of $3.4 million from the First National Bank of Chicago. The only reason for the loan, Safire claimed, was Lance's close ties to the president. In Senate testimony, Lance convinced most members of the banking committee that he had done nothing wrong. Sen. Abraham Ribicoff, Democrat of Connecticut, even thought Lance had been the victim of a smear campaign—after all, Safire had been a speechwriter for Richard Nixon. Lance had survived his first crisis.

The next crisis was more damaging. Comptroller of the Currency John Heimann had launched his own investigation into allegations that swirled around Lance's relationship to the two national banks he had headed. On August 18 he issued a 400-page report. Attempting to put a positive spin on the investigation, Carter came in from Camp David that afternoon to hold a press conference with Lance in which he proclaimed, "Bert Lance enjoys my complete confidence and support." Hugging his friend, he said, "Bert, I'm proud of you." The next day, Vice President Mondale expressed his belief in Lance's honesty and integrity. "The difficulties are behind us," Mondale claimed.

The administration's difficulties, however, had only just begun. Although the report did not accuse Lance of any illegality, it charged him with unsafe and unsound banking practices. Among other things, he had allowed bank officers and their relatives to make large overdrafts. Reading the report, Senator Ribicoff now suspected that some of Lance's activities were questionable and that his days as budget director were numbered.

With attention now focused on Lance, other charges began to reach the public. The suppressed story about Lance's campaign overdrafts surfaced, as did reports that Carter had flown free on a NBG airplane while campaigning for governor. Denying he had broken the law, Carter nevertheless paid the bank $1,800 for the flights. On September 6 Heimann issued another report finding similar patterns of suspicious borrowing by Lance and noting that the aircraft use matter was being referred to the Justice Department and the Internal Revenue Service.

Until September 15 Carter continued to defend Lance, asking that judgment be deferred until his friend had appeared before the Senate Government Affairs Committee. Lance, charming as always, did well before the committee, but could not silence his critics. The next day, Carter noted in his diary that Lance had "won a great victory and now should step down." Lance resigned September 21, a day Carter later described as "one of the worst days I've ever spent."

The Lance affair probably would have damaged any presidency. Coming so early in an administration that had loudly proclaimed its integrity, it did irreparable harm. One of Carter's aides called it a critical turning point. He went on to lament that "Carter did not recognize and look at the evidence more carefully." Writing his memoirs five years later, Carter seemed to blame Lance's troubles on a willingness to help ordinary people get loans and the fact that he sent flowers to their sick wives. That was not even remotely close to what the well-substantiated accusations were about. Even more disturbing, in the memoirs, Carter transformed his unpaid campaign use of a bank aircraft into Lance's "use of the National Bank of Georgia's airplane to entertain customers."

BIBLIOGRAPHY

Blount, Roy. *Crackers.* Athens: University of Georgia Press, 1998.

Carter, James E. *Keeping Faith.* New York: Bantam, 1982.

Dumbrell, John. *The Carter Presidency: A Re-evaluation.* New York: St. Martin's, 1993.

Glad, Betty. *Jimmy Carter: In Search of the Great White House.* New York: Norton, 1980.

Jordan, Hamilton. *Crisis: The Last Year of the Carter Presidency.* New York: Putnam, 1982.

Kaufman, Burton I. *The Presidency of James Earl Carter, Jr.* Lawrence: University Press of Kansas, 1993.

Kucharsky, David. *The Man from Plains: The Mind and Spirit of Jimmy Carter.* New York: Harper and Row, 1976.

Lance, Bert. *The Truth of the Matter: My Life In and Out of Politics.* New York: Summit Books, 1991.

Mitchell, Jack. *Executive Privilege: Two Centuries of White House Scandals.* New York: Hippocrene Books, 1992.

Mollenhoff, Clark R. *The President Who Failed.* New York: Macmillan, 1980.

Stapleton, Ruth Carter. *Brother Billy.* New York: Harper and Row, 1978.

Stroud, Kandy. *How Jimmy Won: The Victory Campaign from Plains to the White House.* New York: Morrow, 1977.

Thompson, Kenneth W., ed. *The Carter Presidency: Fourteen Intimate Perspectives of Jimmy Carter.* Lanham, Md.: University Press of America, 1990.

Wooten, James. *Dasher: The Roots and Rising of Jimmy Carter.* New York: Summit Books, 1978.

RONALD REAGAN

Fortieth President
1981–1989

Born February 6, 1911, in a five-room apartment above a bakery in Tampico, Illinois, Ronald Wilson Reagan was the younger of Nelle and John Reagan's two sons. Ronald received the nickname "Dutch" when his father commented, "For such a little bit of a fat Dutchman, he makes a hell of a lot of noise, doesn't he." The Reagan family moved several times during Ronald's childhood, settling in Dixon, Illinois, when he was nine. As a youth, Ronald worked as a circus roustabout and a manual laborer. From 1926 to 1933 he spent his summers as a lifeguard and in that time saved seventy-seven people. He went to public school, graduated from Dixon High School in 1928, and then attended Eureka College on a partial football scholarship from 1928 to 1932. To make ends meet, Reagan washed dishes at his fraternity house and worked as a lifeguard and swim coach.

Reagan got a job as the weekend sportscaster at a Davenport, Iowa, radio station in 1932. By 1934 he had been promoted to staff announcer, but had decided by then that he wanted to try show business. He was transferred to the NBC station in Des Moines, Iowa, and was the voice of major league baseball and Big Ten football.

A friend arranged a screen test for Reagan at Warner Brothers, which resulted in seven-year contract starting in June 1937. Reagan quit radio and moved to California to pursue his dream. In his first year at the studio, Reagan played the lead in a number of B movies and supporting roles in others. In 1940 he starred in *Knute Rockne—All American,* playing the terminally ill George Gipp. In this film Reagan uttered the memorable line, "Go in there and win just one for the Gipper," which earned him another nickname. In his most critically acclaimed role, he played Drake McHugh in *Kings Row.* On January 26, 1940, Reagan married actress Jane Wyman. The couple had one child and adopted another. They divorced in 1948.

Reagan's career seemed to be on an upward spiral when World War II intervened. He served as a second lieutenant in the Army Reserves from

April 1942 until July 1945, rising to the rank of captain. Because of poor eyesight, he was exempted from combat, but served at Fort Mason in San Francisco loading convoys. He transferred to the Army Air Force First Motion Picture Unit, where he narrated preflight training films and appeared in Irving Berlin's *This Is the Army* in 1943.

After the war, Reagan returned to Warner Brothers and in 1946 signed another seven-year contract. He was again relegated to a number of forgettable movies, including *Bedtime for Bonzo* in 1951. On March 4, 1952, he married actress Nancy Davis, and they had two children. Reagan began a new career in television. He hosted the "General Electric Theatre" from 1954 until 1961. In 1962 he became the host of "Death Valley Days."

Reagan was elected president of the Screen Actors Guild from 1947 to 1952 and from 1959 to 1960. A lifelong Democrat, he was also slowly going through a political transformation and becoming more anticommunist. He had appeared as a friendly witness before the House Un-American Activities Committee. He supported creation of the Hollywood blacklist, which denied work to writers and actors suspected of having communist ties.

Reagan campaigned for Helen Gahagan Douglas against Richard Nixon in 1950, but supported Eisenhower in 1952 and 1956. In 1960 he actively campaigned for Republican presidential nominee Richard Nixon and formally changed his party affiliation to Republican. In 1964 he delivered a thirty-minute television address for Republican presidential nominee Barry Goldwater.

Reagan was elected governor of California in 1966 with 58 percent of the popular vote over Gov. Pat Brown, the Democratic incumbent. Reagan established a record as a fiscal conservative and was reelected in 1970 with 53 percent of the vote. In 1976 Reagan decided to challenge Gerald Ford for the Republican nomination and fell just sixty delegate votes short of winning the nomination at the convention.

In 1980, however, Reagan came to the convention with the nomination in hand. His strongest opponent, George Bush, had withdrawn from the race when it was clear that Reagan would win. Former president Gerald Ford declined the number two spot on the ticket, and Reagan chose Bush as his running mate. In the fall, Reagan faced the weakened incumbent, Jimmy Carter, and John Anderson, an independent candidate. The election turned not only on the economic recession that had marked the Carter administration but also on the continuing hostage crisis in Iran. Reagan won with 51 percent of the vote and an electoral college vote of 489 to 49. In the 1984 election Reagan and Bush faced a ticket headed by former vice president Walter F. Mondale and New York representative Geraldine Ferraro, the first woman nominated by a major party. Reagan won reelection with 59 percent of the popular vote and 525 electoral votes out of a possible 538. Mondale won only his home state of Minnesota and the District of Columbia.

During Reagan's eight years in office, the economy experienced a dramatic turnaround. With policies collectively dubbed "Reaganomics," the president pushed for a supply-side economy. Primary to his goals were tax cuts to spur growth and the cutting of federal spending. He succeeded in achieving the first of these goals, but the Democratic House was reluctant to cut spending.

Reagan oversaw a foreign policy based on military strength. He called for a space-based missile defense system, which Congress did not back. He deployed missiles in Western Europe to counter the Soviet Union's growing nuclear capabilities. In October 1983 U.S. forces invaded the tiny island of Grenada to prevent its takeover by leftists. Reagan also funded a resistance movement, the contras, in Nicaragua, which was seeking to overthrow the communist government of Nicaragua. These activities eventually led to the largest scandal to mark the administration, the Iran-contra affair (see page 415).

After seeing his vice president inaugurated, Reagan retired to his Santa Barbara ranch. For the first few years of his retirement, he maintained an active speaking schedule and wrote his memoirs. As time passed, however, he made fewer public appearances and finally announced that he had Alzheimer's disease, which causes progressive mental and physical deterioration. Nancy Reagan became a leading advocate for funding research into the disease as well as a protector of her husband and his image.

DEBATEGATE

President Jimmy Carter's debate briefing book mysteriously ended up in the hands of the Republican campaign and was used to prepare candidate Ronald Reagan for the presidential debates.

During the 1980 presidential campaign, a copy of President Jimmy Carter's presidential debate briefing book fell into the hands of the Republican campaign. Several theories were advanced as to how the book ended up in the Reagan camp. One was that the Carter campaign had a mole who supplied the book. Evidence for this theory comes from a number of memos written by a Reagan campaign volunteer named Daniel Jones to Reagan staffers Robert Gray, William Casey (future director of the Central Intelligence Agency), and Edwin H. Meese (future attorney general). In any event, the Reagan camp used the book to help prepare their candidate to debate President Carter. To that end, the contents were shared with a number of campaign advisers, including Howard Baker (future chief of staff) and David R. Gergen (future director of communications).

Carter's campaign staff insisted that the book had been stolen in a clandestine operation that was the equivalent of a Watergate-style break-in of the White House. Carter supporters labeled the event "Debategate" and "Briefingate," but Reagan's aides called it "Pseudogate," meaning it was a phony issue.

A Justice Department inquiry came to no final conclusions about the book's appearance in the Reagan camp. Its brief report, issued in February 1983, concluded that the eight-month investigation had "uncovered no credible evidence that the transfer [of campaign documents] violated any criminal law."

The House conducted its own investigation headed by Rep. Donald Albosta, Democrat of Michigan. Campaign officials and interns from both the Carter and Reagan camps were called to testify. After more than a year and hundreds of interviews, the committee issued a 2,314-page report. It concluded it was likely that the Reagan campaign had acquired two copies of the debate briefing book and that at least one of them had come through Casey. But even the exhaustive Albosta report did not know how the documents were obtained. It also could not identify any specific laws that were violated by the use of the book.

OCTOBER SURPRISE

The freeing of American hostages in Iran at the exact moment President Reagan was inaugurated gave rise to charges that the Reagan-Bush campaign had struck a deal with the Iranians.

As Ronald Reagan prepared to take the oath of office January 20, 1981, the news media were also following a breaking story. Fifty-two Americans, who had been held hostage in Tehran since November 4, 1979, were about to be flown out of Iran. The hostages were U.S. Embassy personnel seized when Islamic militants stormed the embassy. President Jimmy Carter managed to reach an agreement with Iran for their release, which he announced in a brief statement the night before Reagan's inauguration. But the hostages were not permitted to leave Iran while Carter was still president; instead, the planes carrying them to freedom took off after Reagan was sworn in.

Almost immediately rumors began to circulate that the Reagan-Bush campaign had made a deal with the Iranian government to delay releasing the hostages. According to those who supported the theory, then-candidate George Bush along with senior campaign officials, including William Casey—campaign chairman and future director of the CIA—flew to Paris on October 19, 1980, and conducted secret negotiations with Iranian officials. To help ensure a landslide Reagan-Bush victory over Carter, Bush allegedly promised a payment of $40 million and future arms shipments if the Iranians agreed not to release the hostages before the election, which might have enhanced Carter's reelection chances.

Abolhassan Bani-Sadr, ex-president of Iran, and several shady characters, including Ari Ben-Menashe, a convicted arms dealer, stated on several occasions that a deal was struck between the campaign and the Iranian government. In 1989 Barbara Honegger published a book, *October Surprise,* in which she claimed to have overheard a conversation in 1980 about such a deal. She also recounts others' stories, including that of a pilot, Richard Brenneke, who claimed to have firsthand knowledge of the plot.

However, many of the facts put forward by conspiracy proponents do not stand up to scrutiny. For example, Brenneke's story is problematic. His desk diary shows that he was traveling in Oregon and Washington State during the period in question. Further, Secret Service records from the period show that George Bush could not have left the United States in October 1980.

In the end, the investigation authorized by the U.S. Senate in November 1991 produced no clear evidence that there was a secret agreement between the Reagan-Bush campaign and the Iranians. Supporters of Presidents Reagan and Bush have asserted that the story was kept alive because of partisan politics.

SAMUEL PIERCE, HUD SECRETARY

A congressional investigation into the Department of Housing and Urban Development showed widespread corruption in the awarding of Section 8 contracts and led to the appointment of an independent counsel to investigate the department and Secretary Pierce's role.

The Department of Housing and Urban Development (HUD) had been a source of petty scandals and conflicts of interest since its inception in 1965. Whatever the department's reputation for problems, the magnitude of HUD improprieties under Secretary Samuel Pierce were unprecedented.

The revelations about mismanagement and possible criminal acts at HUD under Pierce did not come to light until Reagan was out of office. In April 1989 Paul Adams, HUD's inspector general, published a report that was highly critical of the Moderate Rehabilitation Program (MRP or Mod Rehab).

Congress created Mod Rehab as part of the Section 8 Existing Housing Program under the Housing and Community Development Act of 1978. The purpose of the MRP was to distribute federal funds to private development groups for the repair and renovation of substandard rental housing and to provide subsidies to low-income families to rent housing they otherwise could not afford. Tenants would pay 30 percent of their income in rent, and the government would pay the remaining portion to bring the payment up to fair market value. To encourage participation, landlords were guaranteed fifteen years of rental income on the properties. In addition, developers were given tax credits of up to 90 percent over ten years to encourage new construction.

Until 1984 MRP funds were distributed in a relatively equitable manner throughout the nation. However, Congress modified the rule requiring the equitable distribution to ensure that the money was spent where it might do the most good. Secretary Pierce interpreted this change in the law to mean that the distribution of MRP funds was now discretionary.

According to Adams's report, ten states were allocated more than 50 percent of MRP funds between 1984 and 1988, although these same states would have received only 16 percent had the funds been distributed equitably. Conversely, six states, including California and New York, declined from a 39 percent share to only 11 percent. Adams also reported the perception that former HUD employees were particularly successful in obtaining Section 8 funding. Others charged that decisions were based on politics, not housing needs.

Pierce was also criticized for the use of his discretionary fund to award two grants in May 1985 to the Center for Resource Development in East Orange, New Jersey. The center's president had served as Vice President George Bush's deputy chief of staff in the first Reagan administration. Others charged that Pierce made funding decisions based on his likes and dislikes of applicants and their political allies.

A congressional investigation led to a largely bipartisan condemnation of Pierce's administration of HUD in general and the MRP in particular. The majority report of the House Government Operations Subcommittee concluded, "During much of the eighties, HUD was enveloped by influence peddling, favoritism, abuse, greed, fraud, embezzlement, and theft." The report stated, "In many housing programs, objective criteria gave way to political preferences and cronyism, and favoritism supplanted fairness. 'Discretionary' became a buzzword for 'giveaway.' " In 1990 Attorney General Richard Thornburgh and the House Judiciary Committee requested the appointment of an independent counsel to investigate the various allegations against HUD.

The independent counsel, former federal judge Arlin Adams, uncovered a variety of improprieties, including widespread cronyism in the awarding of funds. In 1987, for example, the Winn group was successful in six of its seven applications for MRP funds, which represented one-sixth of all funds available that year. DuBois Gilliam, a senior official, left the department with a severance package that included 250 units of Section 8 funds that were worth approximately $1.5 million. Deborah Gore Dean, Pierce's assistant, was later indicted for accepting a bribe of $4,000.

What is clear from the various investigations is that HUD and its programs were a "swamp," as Jack Kemp, President Bush's HUD secretary, called it. By Kemp's estimates, mismanagement and corruption had cost the department $2 billion. Senate Majority Leader George Mitchell placed the price tag at $6 billion to $8 billion. In either case, the HUD scandal was one of the most expensive in U.S. history.

Arlin Adams's investigation resulted in the indictments and convictions of several senior members of the department. Pierce was indicted, but not convicted. By all accounts, Pierce never gained financially from any of the corruption. He had been widely praised during his confirmation hearings in 1981, but later commentators agreed that he proved unsuited to handle the vast bureaucracy with its technical regulations and procedures.

WEDTECH

President Ronald Reagan praised the success of Wedtech at a dinner at the Waldorf-Astoria. Little did he know that the company's success was largely illusionary and resulted from bribes and extortion by highly placed individuals. The company's bankruptcy in 1986 eventually led to federal prosecutions and the appointment of an independent counsel.

At first glance, Wedtech appeared to be an American success story. The company's president, John Mariotta, had been born in Spanish Harlem and was a dropout from vocational high school. In 1965 the mechanically inclined Mariotta was made a partner in the Welbilt Electronic Die Company, a small machine shop in the Bronx. In 1971 he bought out his retiring partner and brought in Fred Neuberger, who bought half the equity in the business.

Welbilt won its first defense contract in 1975 and, around the same time, applied to the Small Business Administration (SBA) for minority-owned status, which would make the company eligible for minority set-asides. To qualify, Neuberger had to exchange his half interest for one-third ownership, so that the business would be minority owned. Welbilt received minority status on September 25. The new status, along with its accompanying aid and loan guarantees, helped to propel Welbilt from a struggling enterprise to a business with contracts worth more than $4 million in 1979.

Welbilt was profiled in the *New York Tribune* in January 1978 as a "ray of hope" in the Bronx. Two New York Democrats, Rep. Mario Biaggi and Rep. Robert Garcia, assisted Welbilt in obtaining government contracts and loans in exchange for political contributions and other considerations.

However, the company had financial problems. On the verge of bankruptcy, Welbilt began to submit invoices for work it had not finished. The Defense Contract Audit Agency failed to notice the doctored invoices and paid them. Critical to the survival of the company was securing an Army engine contract that was designated a minority set-aside. However, Welbilt's bid of $19 million was well over the expected limit. Welbilt's bid was high because it did not have the necessary equipment or expertise to meet the army's criteria. The army sought to have the contract removed from minority set-aside, but that was not permitted.

Mariotta and Neuberger toyed with the idea of blackmailing the army procurement officer, but instead decided to pursue the contract through political channels. They approached E. Robert Wallach, a successful lawyer and friend of Ed Meese, who had just been appointed White House counsel. Wallach agreed to talk to Meese, who had an aide look into the contract. In addition, Mariotta and Neuberger formed the Latin American Manufacturers Association (LAMA) as a lobbying agency. LAMA wrote letters introducing Mariotta to Hispanic members of Congress as well as to Lyn Nofziger, Elizabeth Dole, Michael Deaver, and James Baker.

Biaggi helped secure the support of fellow Rep. Joseph P. Addabbo of New York, chairman of the Small Business Committee and a member of the military appropriations subcommittee. Sen. Alfonse D'Amato wrote to Secretary of the Army John Marsh on Welbilt's behalf. In the end, the army reviewed its decision, but a gap of $9 million existed that the SBA refused to bridge.

In January 1982 Welbilt, through LAMA, engaged the services of Lyn Nofziger, who had recently left the White House to form his own public relations firm. On April 5 Nofziger met with Meese about the contract. Eleven days later, however, the army once again decided against Welbilt. Jim Jenkins, Meese's aide, continued to make inquiries into the matter. On May 19 he had a meeting with Welbilt, the army, HUD, the SBA, and the Economic Development Administration (EDA). The parties agreed that Welbilt should be awarded the contract and that the necessary funds would come from several sources, including an SBA development grant. On September 28 the contract was declared final, and Jenkins informed Meese that his "personal go ahead . . . saved the project."

However, once again Welbilt was in need of a cash infusion. Commercial banks were unwilling to advance the company any additional funds, so Mariotta and Neuberger decided to take the company public. To do that, however, they had to doctor the books. The head of the audit team and the chief auditor were both made officers of the company and given 9 percent and 1.5 percent of the stock, respectively, for their help in the deception. The firm changed its name from Welbilt to Wedtech to avoid a suit with the Welbilt Corporation of New York. Between August and September 1983, more than 5 million shares in the company were sold.

The stock offering was lucrative, but it threatened the company's status as minority owned and a small business. Wedtech needed to maintain its status so that it could bid on an upcoming navy contract worth more than $100 million. Receiving a three-year extension of its minority status, Wedtech asked Nofziger and others to lobby the acting assistant secretary of the navy, Ev Pyatt, to place part of the contract in a minority set-aside. The navy's inspectors determined that Wedtech could not meet the production schedule, but discussions with the navy continued.

Wedtech was eventually awarded part of the contract, but it did not have the necessary expertise and fell behind schedule. Seeking an extension, Wedtech asked Biaggi to intercede, which he did for a price. When Wallach heard about the payoff, he also wanted to be paid. Wedtech's first product was rejected, but the navy was in so deep that it decided to pay more money to Wedtech to make it right. Through the efforts of Biaggi and others, Wedtech received an additional $51.5 million for the project.

To those unfamiliar with its dealings, Wedtech looked like a spectacular success story. President Reagan praised the company and its executives at a dinner at the Waldorf-Astoria on March 6, 1984. A Defense Department audit raised serious doubts about the company, but Wedtech demanded another audit and was declared solvent. The navy renewed its contracts.

In mid-1984 the veneer began to peel off. Other minority-owned businesses began to complain about Wedtech's practices, and several government agencies began to question the company's performance. In addition, the amount of money that Wedtech was paying to "consultants" was draining its resources. Wallach, who had demanded and received $150,000 in 1984, received an additional $300,000 for future consideration. Wallach was about to join the Reagan administration along with his friend Ed Meese, who had been nominated for attorney general. Wallach promised the company access to high-level officials. Others, including Jim Jenkins and SBA head Peter Neglia, were also demanding that Wedtech pay for their "services." Representative Garcia received campaign contributions plus a lucrative job for his wife.

Rep. Parren Mitchell, chairman of the House Small Business Committee, began an inquiry into Wedtech. On September 25 Mitchell sent a confidential letter to the SBA that asked very specific and embarrassing questions. Neglia did not respond to the questions until April 1985. In the meantime, LAMA protested that Mitchell's investigation amounted to persecution of a Hispanic-owned business. Biaggi and Garcia tried to persuade Mitchell to drop his inquiry.

In February 1986 Mariotta was removed as Wedtech's chairman. On March 27 the firm resigned its minority status, but the action was not made public until April 17, giving Mariotta, Neuberger, and another partner, Mario Moreno, time to sell their stock. With news reports growing that Wedtech was engaging in illegal practices, the company's lines of credit dried up, and the firm filed for bankruptcy in December.

Federal prosecutors began to investigate Wedtech's sudden demise, and, as it became clear that members of the administration may have been involved in illegal activity, the Justice Department called for the appointment of an independent counsel. James McKay was appointed to investigate the role that Nofziger and other White House officials had played in Wedtech's meteoric rise. Between the federal prosecutor and the independent counsel, several convictions were obtained.

Nofziger was convicted and sentenced to ninety days in jail and a $30,000 fine for violating the Ethics in Government Act. His conviction was overturned on appeal. Mariotta, Neuberger, and Moreno all pleaded guilty to a number of charges and testified against others involved. Biaggi resigned from the House and was convicted of extortion. His son Richard, who was on retainer for the firm, was also convicted. Garcia resigned from Congress, and he and his wife were convicted for extortion. Wallach was also convicted for his role. The Garcia and Wallach convictions were overturned on appeal. Meese, who had become the attorney general in February 1985, was criticized for his role in Wedtech's getting the original army contract but was not charged with any criminal wrongdoing. He stepped down August 12, 1988.

ANNE GORSUCH BURFORD, EPA DIRECTOR

The House investigated alleged conflicts of interest in the EPA's administration of superfund money as well as the awarding of sweetheart deals to certain corporations.

In 1976 Congress passed the Resource Conservation and Recovery Act, which authorized the Environmental Protection Agency (EPA) to regulate hazardous industrial waste from its creation to its disposal. The act also established regulations for landfills and set penalties for violation of those regulations. In 1982 the Reagan administration's EPA sought to discontinue parts of the act. The EPA argued that, with 60,000 large waste generators and 15,000 waste haulers filing yearly reports about the dissolution and burial of toxic wastes, it was impossible to enforce the regulations with its budget and staff.

In fall 1982 several congressional subcommittees began investigations into the EPA's $1.6 billion superfund, which had been created to clean up the country's worst toxic waste dump sites. Congress was interested in charges of mismanagement, conflict of interest, and sweetheart deals with corporate and industrial polluters. The EPA prevented a full investigation by blocking access to critical documents relating to the agency's superfund management. President Reagan ordered Anne Gorsuch Burford, the EPA administrator, not to turn over certain requested documents. Further, Reagan warned Congress that he would invoke executive privilege to prevent the release of those documents because—the administration argued—disclosure of the contents would jeopardize ongoing investigations by the agency. When Congress did not receive the documents it had requested, it voted, 259–105, to hold Burford in contempt of Congress.

The controversy continued to brew for the next six months with neither the administration nor Congress budging from its position. On March 9, 1983, Burford resigned as head of the EPA. "It was clear that my resignation is essential to termination of the controversy and confusion generated by the outstanding dispute over access to certain EPA materials," she said. After Burford's resignation, President Reagan sought the resignation of the superfund administrator, Rita Lavelle, who, prior to joining the EPA, had worked for Aerojet General Corporation, one of California's chief polluters. When Lavelle refused to resign, she was dismissed. Lavelle was indicted for perjury for the testimony she gave to two separate House committees investigating her for conflict of interest. She was sentenced to six months in prison, served four, and was released in September 1985.

In an effort to prevent further criticism of the administration, President Reagan eventually released the documents Congress had requested. He stated that he did not want to "foster suspicion in the public mind that, somehow, the important doctrine of executive privilege is being used to shield possible wrongdoing."

The political purges and release of documents did not end the affair. The House Judiciary Committee issued a 1,200-page report in which it detailed additional evidence that suggested misconduct was widespread. In April 1986 an independent counsel was named to investigate former assistant attorney general Theodore B. Olson on charges of perjury in connection with the withholding of subpoenaed documents. After nearly three years, independent counsel Alexia Morrison issued a report in early 1989 exonerating Olson. During her probe, however, the U.S. Circuit Court of Appeals for the District of Columbia ruled that the independent counsel provision of the 1978 Ethics in Government Act was unconstitutional. In *Morrison v. Olson* (1988) the Supreme Court overturned that decision.

JAMES WATT, SECRETARY OF THE INTERIOR

James Watt was forced to resign because of comments he made about the makeup of a newly formed federal commission.

Secretary of the Interior James Watt was a lightning rod for controversy. Watt, who was criticized by environmentalists as not caring much about nature, was a strong proponent of a more business-friendly attitude at the department. He once commented that the environmentalists were "pursuing a greater objective of central control in society, as the Nazis and Bolsheviks did." Comments such as that ultimately cost Watt his job. In describing a newly formed federal advisory commission on coal leasing, he stated that the group consisted of "Three Democrats, two Republicans, every kind of mix you can have. I have a black, a woman, two Jews, and a cripple. And we have talent." Undoubtedly, Watt meant the comment to be witty, but it outraged so many people that he was forced to tender his resignation on October 9, 1983.

RAYMOND DONOVAN, SECRETARY OF LABOR

Independent counsel Leon Silverman conducted a long investigation of Raymond Donovan's possible illegal activities while he was an executive of the Schiavone Construction Company.

President Reagan selected New Jersey construction executive Raymond Donovan to be the secretary of labor. Donovan, a political novice, had been a substantial fundraiser for the Reagan campaign and had the strong support of union heavyweights. However, when Donovan arrived at his confirmation hearings, he found the Senate Labor and Human

Resources Committee, chaired by Sen. Orrin Hatch of Utah, armed with serious allegations that Donovan's company, Schiavone Construction, was "mobbed up" and had engaged in unethical, if not illegal, activities. The FBI had interviewed numerous informants who said that Schiavone made pay-offs to union officials. Donovan denied any wrongdoing.

After Donovan's denial, FBI official Francis Mullen reported to the committee that the FBI was unable to confirm the allegations made against Donovan and Schiavone Construction. The ranking Democrat on the committee, Sen. Edward Kennedy of Massachusetts, demanded that the probe continue because of evidence that Schiavone's upper management was tied to the Vito Genovese crime family. Despite Kennedy's pleas, the committee voted out the nomination and recommended that Donovan be confirmed. The full Senate confirmed him, 80–17.

However, Donovan's troubles did not end there. Only four months into his term, Donovan was again the target of an FBI investigation. The Justice Department's Organized Crime Strike Force uncovered charges that in 1977 Schiavone officials had bribed the president of the New York City Blasters' Union, Local 29. The informant, Mario Montuoro, told investigators that he was present when a Schiavone executive paid $2,000 to the union president. The story made headlines in December 1981, and Attorney General William French Smith had no choice but to call for another FBI investigation.

Leon Silverman, a prominent New York attorney, was appointed independent counsel to conduct an investigation. While Silverman was empaneling a grand jury, Senator Hatch began an investigation into the FBI's background check. By spring 1982, both investigations were in full swing. Federal investigators became concerned when a former Mafia courier named Fred Furino, who had repeatedly failed lie detector tests on whether he knew Donovan, was found dead in the trunk of his car. Additionally, Frank Silbey, a Labor Committee staffer, received a threatening phone call. The anonymous caller told Silbey that he should "lay off" Donovan. "If you keep messing with [Donovan]," the caller said, "your wife and children [will] end up in pine boxes." The Schiavone Company, for its part, hired its own investigators.

The FBI had plenty of information that Donovan was friendly with, if not tied to, the Mafia. It had tapes of discussions in which another Mafia boss discussed laundering money through Schiavone, and it knew that Donovan was often in the company of Salvatore "Sally Buggs" Bruguglio.

Donovan testified before Silverman's grand jury for more than five hours and continued to insist on his innocence. On June 28, 1982, Silverman announced that he was ending the investigation because there was "insufficient credible evidence" to warrant prosecutions. Although he was still uneasy about the number of accusations against Donovan, Silverman issued an 111-page final report in September. The report found no corroborating evidence against Donovan. Appearing before the press, Donovan said he was angry that he "had to endure months of relentless press coverage of groundless charges made by shameless accusers."

But still his troubles were not over. Two years later, a federal grand jury indicted Donovan and six other Schiavone officials for participating in a scheme to defraud the New York Transit Authority of $7.4 million. Donovan resigned on March 15, 1985, several months after the indictment. After two years of pretrial motions and an eight-month trial, Donovan and his codefendants were acquitted on all charges on May 25, 1987.

LOBBYING VIOLATIONS

Two of President Reagan's longtime political associates, Michael Deaver and Lyn Nofziger, were investigated for violating the 1978 Ethics in Government Act when they each formed a lobbying firm after leaving the White House.

Michael Deaver, Deputy Chief of Staff

Longtime friend and political aide-de-camp, Michael Deaver was also an experienced public relations executive who understood the importance of managing the president's image in the media. Deaver was largely responsible for the casting and choreography of Ronald Reagan's television appearances and photo opportunities.

In the spring of 1985, Deaver made his only memorable public relations blunder. He arranged for President Reagan to be televised while placing a wreath in a cemetery in Bitberg, Germany, which also contained the graves of some Nazi soldiers. Many Jewish leaders took offense. Nancy Reagan openly criticized Deaver, even though he was a close friend. Deaver left the White House and set up his own public relations firm.

The PR firm had no shortage of clients willing to pay Deaver's six-figure retainer because it was understood that Deaver still had unparalleled ties to the president. In fact, Deaver was permitted to retain his White House pass and had access to the president's daily personal schedule. In late fall 1985, Deaver made the cover of *Time* magazine as one of the nation's top powerbrokers.

Deaver's high profile also made him a target of criticism and allegations of possible wrongdoing. Rep. John Dingell, Democrat of Michigan, ordered the General Accounting Office to investigate Deaver's $105,000 contract with the Canadian government to represent it on the acid rain problem. The investigation discovered that even before Deaver left the administration, he was actively lobbying for a special envoy to settle the U.S.-Canadian conflict.

In the end, the U.S. government agreed to pay $5 billion in cleanup costs. The GAO report suggested that Deaver's activities violated the 1978 Ethics in Government Act, which banned contacts with former executive branch employees for one year after leaving office.

The GAO report led to a referral to the Justice Department, which, bowing to political pressure, agreed to seek the appointment of an independent counsel. New York attorney Whitney North Seymour Jr. was appointed to investigate the matter.

The press and congressional Democrats continued to examine the details of Deaver's activities in behalf of other clients, such as Boeing and CBS. Deaver defended himself by saying, "I didn't use my influence with the president or the White House at any time." Reagan also defended his friend. "Mike has never put the arm on me, or sought any influence from me since he has been out of government," Reagan said.

Seymour's investigation ultimately led to Deaver's indictment, not for violating the Ethics in Government Act, but for perjury. Deaver, according to the indictment, had lied to both Rep. Dingell's committee and the grand jury. In a desperate attempt to save Deaver from conviction, his lawyers argued that his previously unrevealed alcoholism had prevented him from being able to recall details. However, in December 1987 Deaver was convicted on three of the five charges and sentenced to 1,500 hours of community service and a $100,000 fine.

Franklyn "Lyn" Nofziger, Presidential Adviser

The perpetually rumpled Lyn Nofziger was a former newspaper reporter who reveled in his street-fighter image. He and Reagan were old friends, and Nofziger often referred to the president as "Governor." Sensing that a lucrative opportunity was at hand, Nofziger left the administration in January 1982 and opened Nofziger and Bragg Communications with Mark Bragg, a well-heeled California businessman.

The new company had little difficulty in attracting high-paying clients. One was Comet Rice, which needed Nofziger's help in getting State Department approval to augment one year's rice harvest with another for a sale to the government of South Korea. Nofziger wrote a letter to National Security Adviser William Clark, pointing out "that once again the administration is on the wrong side of a political issue." He continued, "I wish you would take a look at this, because it seems to me that once again we're in a position of screwing our friends and rewarding our enemies." Nofziger wrote two additional letters to Clark, but Clark refused to get involved in what he saw as a largely domestic matter.

Nofziger's work in behalf of Comet Rice was just the first of a number of Nofziger and Bragg's controversial and perhaps illegal ventures. Fairchild Republic Corporation hired the firm to save the production of the A-10 plane, which both the air force and Congress wanted to stop funding. Nofziger sent a barrage of letters to save

Lyn Nofziger

the A-10 and even met with members of the National Security Council. Nofziger's own lawyer warned him that he might be violating ethics laws.

Another client, the Marine Engineers Beneficial Association, engaged Nofziger to lobby the White House to increase civilian crews on maritime ships. The plan, which Reagan approved of on principle, was expedited because of Nofziger's lobbying efforts. The Long Island Lighting Company (LILCO) paid the firm a retainer of $20,000 a month. LILCO wanted Nofziger's help in getting its Shoreham nuclear power plant on line over the objections of federal regulators. Sen. Daniel Patrick Moynihan, Democrat of New York, called for an investigation of Nofziger.

A separate investigation, headed by Rep. Ted Weiss, Democrat of New York, was looking into work Nofziger had done in behalf of International Medical Centers. The company paid $300,000 to have Nofziger lobby for the loosening of federal regulations of Medicare. According to the committee's investigation, Nofziger had played a major role in securing a waiver from the Health Care Financing Administration. Nofziger was also a central figure in the Wedtech scandal (see page 407).

An independent counsel, James McKay, was appointed to investigate Nofziger's activities in behalf of Wedtech, Fairchild, and the Marine Engineers. Indicted for violating the Ethics in Government Act, Nofziger was convicted on three counts and sentenced to ninety days in jail and a fine of $30,000. His conviction was overturned by a federal appeals court; two of the three judges ruled that McKay had failed to show that Nofziger knew that what he was doing was illegal.

DOUGLAS GINSBURG, SUPREME COURT NOMINEE

Douglas Ginsburg's nomination to the Supreme Court had to be withdrawn when it was learned he had smoked marijuana as a law professor.

When Justice Lewis Powell retired from the Supreme Court in 1987, President Reagan nominated Judge Robert H. Bork to succeed him. The Senate failed to approve Bork, and Reagan nominated Judge Douglas Ginsburg. However, the nomination was quickly withdrawn when Ginsburg admitted that he had smoked marijuana, not in his youth, but while he was a law professor. The episode was a political embarrassment to the White House and to first lady Nancy Reagan's "Just Say No" antidrug campaign. Reagan then nominated Anthony Kennedy, who was quickly confirmed without controversy.

IRAN-CONTRA AFFAIR

The Reagan administration's anticommunist policy led to the creation of a complex covert operation that sold arms to the Iranian government, the proceeds of which went to Nicaragua to fund the anti-Sandinista rebels known as the contras.

The Iran-contra affair, the biggest scandal of the Reagan White House, grew out of the administration's determination to prevent the spread of communism in Central America. Reagan came into office already believing that the 1978 overthrow of Nicaraguan leader Anastasio Somoza Garcia by the Sandinista revolutionaries posed a threat to the stability of the region. From the first, Reagan sought to support the anti-Sandinista rebels, known as the contras, a poorly organized armed resistance.

By December 1981 President Reagan had made the contras the highest priority foreign policy issue in the Western Hemisphere. He signed a national security decision directive that authorized the CIA, headed by former Reagan campaign chairman and World War II master spy William Casey, to conduct "political and paramilitary operations" against the Sandinistas. Reagan lied to Congress, saying that the funds he was requesting were to be used to keep arms out of Central America.

Congress became suspicious of the ever-increasing amounts of money being spent on arms interdiction. In December 1982 Congress enacted the first of two versions of the Boland Amendment, which was named for the chairman of the House Select Committee on Intelligence, Edward Boland, Democrat of Massachusetts. The measure specifically barred the CIA and the Defense Department from spending funds to overthrow the Sandinista government or to promote conflict between Nicaragua and Honduras, the site of contra bases. Reagan continued his media campaign against the Sandinistas, referring to the contras as "freedom fighters."

In the meantime, CIA-backed operatives mined the harbors of Nicaragua. By April 1984 the CIA-backed action caused a major strain between the administration and members of Congress, such as Sen. Barry Goldwater, who chaired the Senate Intelligence Committee. The committee invited Casey to explain the CIA's actions in a special closed-door session. The result was an agreement between Casey and the committee that there would be prior consultation for covert operations. This agreement, known as the Casey Accords, had no force other than the director's word.

In a further attempt to stem the flow of arms, Congress revised the Boland Amendment. Specifically, it forbade U.S. intelligence agencies from furnishing any lethal aid to the contras. With the CIA and the Department of Defense now barred from supplying weapons, the administration decided to use the National Security Council (NSC), an organization created in 1947 to help the president coordinate the actions of various agencies into a coherent foreign policy. The NSC staff, which is borrowed from other departments and agencies, is answerable only to the president; it has no statutory obligation to report to Congress. which puts it effectively beyond the reach of the legislative branch. The administration, believing that the Boland Amendment did not apply to the NSC staff, put Oliver North, a marine colonel, in charge of the contra operation. North was a decorated Vietnam veteran and had been on the team that coordinated the invasion of Grenada in 1983. Casey continued to oversee the operation, which was called the Enterprise.

With Casey's guidance, North established a number of complex operations that raised money for the contras, sold weapons to the Iranian government, sought the release of Americans held in the Middle East, and provided military strategy for the growing conflict in Nicaragua. To facilitate his activities, North recruited two civilians, Richard Secord and Albert Hakim. Secord, a retired air force general, had extensive contacts in the intelligence community and became a leading adviser to Casey and Project Democracy, as it was termed. The Iranian-born Hakim established a complex web of overseas bank accounts and front companies through which money could be laundered. These two men, along with North and Casey, formed the core of the operations.

This group recruited others including John Singlaub, a retired general who had openly criticized President Carter's decision to remove troops from Korea. Singlaub had deep contacts in Asia, especially Korea and Taiwan, that could be exploited. National Security Adviser Robert McFarlane was also used to obtain funds from Middle East sources, especially Saudi Arabia. Carl "Spitz" Channell was recruited to establish the National Endowment for the Preservation of Liberty (NEPL), which raised money from private donors, such as Nelson Bunker Hunt, who personally donated nearly $500,000 to help the contras. Channell associate and former Reagan administration staffer Richard Miller was engaged to coordinate a pro-contra public relations operation, which he did with his consulting business, International Business Communications.

The money-raising operations brought in nearly $48 million in two years. After expenses, nearly a quarter of that amount was available to buy weapons for the contras. The rebel organization became a well-armed, if largely unorganized, band. North had a contra airstrip built in Costa Rica, which helped the rebels to establish a southern front in the conflict. Former air force lieutenant Richard Gadd was hired to airlift supplies into Costa Rica. North manipulated the State Department's Nicaraguan Humanitarian Assistance Office by arranging for a contract to be given to former Senate staffer Robert Owen's Institute for Democracy, Education, and Assistance. The contract provided cover for Owen and his company to supply intelligence from within Nicaragua.

As the scope of the operations and the number of people involved continued to grow, word of the operation began to leak and stories began to appear in the press. Members of Congress asked McFarlane if the rumors were true; he lied to them repeatedly. Enterprise participants were encouraged by Reagan's 1984 landslide victory over former vice president Walter Mondale, and, with Reagan's popularity at an all-time high, the group escalated its operations.

In addition to the contras, President Reagan was concerned about a number of Americans who were being held hostage in Lebanon and in other Middle East countries. Their captors were Shiite Muslims with ties to the radical government in Iran. Relations between Iran and the United

States consisted of the Iranians calling the United States the "Great Satan" and Reagan referring to Iran as part of "a new, international version of Murder, Incorporated." The Enterprise entered the hostage fray by suggesting that it could broker a deal with the Iranians for the release of the hostages. David Kimche, an Israeli foreign ministry official and intelligence officer, met with McFarlane to discuss an arms-for-hostages deal.

Kimche engaged Iranian Manucher Ghobanifar as a middleman in the operation. Ghobanifar, who was known to the CIA as an untrustworthy schemer, used his connections with Casey's friend Roy Furmark to become part of the plot. In mid-September 1985 one of the hostages, Rev. Benjamin Weir, was released. At the time, the public did not know that his release had cost 500 TOW antitank missiles. Believing that it had found the way to free the hostages, the Enterprise sent more weapons—HAWK antiaircraft missiles—from Israel to Iran. However, this shipment was rejected by the Iranians, who claimed that the missiles were defective.

Both Secretary of State George Shultz and Secretary of Defense Caspar Weinberger heard rumors about the swap and urged Reagan to refrain from further tactics along this line. Reagan ignored their advice. Because the Iranians had rejected the last shipment from Israel, the decision was made to cut out the Israeli middlemen. The direct sale of weapons to Iran now came under North's direction. In making these transactions, North began to generate a profit, which he decided should be diverted into the contra accounts. Thus, the link between the contras and the Iranians half a world away was created. The sale of weapons generated more than $3.8 million for the contras.

McFarlane left the NSC in late 1985 and was replaced by his deputy, Adm. John Poindexter. In May 1986 McFarlane went to Tehran to negotiate the release of additional hostages. After several days of negotiating, McFarlane left Iran empty-handed. The Iranians had upped the ante by demanding the release of Shiite Muslims in Kuwait. Despite the Iranians' lack of cooperation, the shipment of weapons continued.

The entire operation began to unwind on October 5, 1986, when a C-123 cargo plane loaded with weapons and other supplies for the contras was shot down over Nicaragua. One of the four crew members, Eugene Hasenfus, survived and was captured. Documents found in the wreckage proved that the plane belonged to Southern Air Transport, a CIA front in Miami. This event triggered investigations by the FBI, the Customs Service, members of Congress, and the press. In addition, the Lebanese magazine *Al Shiraa* published a story about the McFarlane mission to Iran that was confirmed by the speaker of the Iranian parliament.

President Reagan took to the airwaves and made a statement that attempted to minimize the situation. However, it was too late. Attorney General Edwin Meese added to the mess by trying to hammer out a coherent story from the pile of lies and half-truths. Documents that did not fit with the story were ordered destroyed. Shredding parties were held at the

NSC, and North's loyal secretary, Fawn Hall, even smuggled some documents out of the Old Executive Office Building in her underwear.

Despite these efforts, on November 22 Justice Department officials discovered a memo in NSC files that indicated that funds from the sale of arms to the Iranians would be used to fund the contras. Meese met privately with the principal players to discuss the fallout.

Three days later, President Reagan announced the formation of a special review committee headed by former senator John Tower, Republican of Texas. The panel also included former secretary of state Edmund Muskie and National Security Adviser Brent Scowcroft. After three months of investigating, the Tower Commission issued a 300-page report that was highly critical of the president's leadership.

Oliver North testifying before Congress.

Although the Tower Commission was hard on the administration, it did not head off a congressional investigation or the appointment of an independent counsel, Lawrence Walsh. It was the congressional investigation and its nationally televised hearings that shed the most light on what had gone on in the offices of the NSC. In an effort to get the complete story—which the Democrats hoped to exploit politically—the committee granted limited immunity to North and Poindexter. Poindexter, for his part, shielded Reagan by claiming that he had not informed the White House of the Enterprise's activities. He stated more than 175 times that he could not remember specific details of the operation. McFarlane admitted to lying to Congress in the past. Casey never testified because he died May 6, 1987, while recuperating from surgery to remove a brain tumor.

The highlight of the hearings was Oliver North's testimony. Dressed in his military uniform, North recounted the many details of his operations and maintained that he had been authorized by the highest authorities to carry them out. To this day, it is unclear whether President Reagan ever connected the two halves of the story—the arms sales to Iran and funding of the contras.

Walsh's $32 million, five-and-a-half-year investigation led to North's being found guilty of obstructing Congress, destroying government documents, and accepting an illegal gratuity—a security fence for his home. However, his convictions were overturned by an appeals court, which ruled that Walsh had used North's immunized testimony to build the case. Poindexter was the only other principal convicted, and that was for lying to Congress. Other minor players were convicted of various charges ranging from lying to Congress to unlawfully withholding information. The end came when President Bush gave full and complete pardons to all involved, including Caspar Weinberger, who was shortly scheduled to go on trial.

INSIDER TRADING AND OTHER FINANCIAL IRREGULARITIES

Several members of the White House staff were investigated for insider trading and other financial irregularities.

Richard Allen, National Security Adviser

In November 1981 Japanese newspapers reported that National Security Adviser Richard Allen had been paid $1,000 to arrange an interview with Nancy Reagan with a Japanese women's magazine. The interview took place the day after President Reagan's inauguration. Allen claimed that the money was given to him to give to Nancy Reagan, as it is a common practice in some countries for magazines to offer honorariums for interviews with prominent people. Allen said that he gave the money to his secretary and she put it in the office safe. In the meantime, Allen changed offices and forgot about the money, which was found by career bureaucrat Jerry Jennings when he opened the safe.

Jennings, unsure about the origins of the money, took the matter to White House counsel Edwin Meese, who ordered an investigation. Most were willing to accept Allen's story until it was also revealed that he had accepted two watches worth about $135 each. While the Justice Department continued its investigation, the FBI conducted its own investigation into Allen's business, which he claimed he had sold in 1978, but in fact held until January 1981. In addition, questions were raised about whether the envelope originally contained $1,000 or $10,000, as noted on the outside.

Allen announced on November 29 that he was taking a leave of absence from his post until the Justice Department inquiry was concluded. In December the Justice Department cleared him of any wrongdoing. Despite this, the White House announced Allen's resignation effective January 1, 1982. He was replaced three days later by Judge William P. Clark Jr.

William French Smith, Attorney General

In 1982 William French Smith was investigated for an impermissible oil and gas tax shelter and for accepting a $50,000 severance check after he was nominated to head the Justice Department. The check came from a company on whose board he served. Although he was cleared of any wrongdoing by the Justice Department, Smith adjusted his returns to reflect the ruling about his tax shelter. He returned the severance check, which was more money than he had received for his service on the board for the previous six years.

William Casey, CIA Director

In 1983 William Casey was investigated for insider trading of companies that had contracts with the CIA. He was also investigated for the sale of oil stocks worth more than $600,000 during 1981. At the time Casey sold the stock, he was the only high-ranking government official with access to classified estimates of worldwide oil production. Casey had sold out of the market at a high point, avoiding the devastating losses that the oil sector experienced that year. Roundly criticized for his activities, Casey placed all of his holdings into a blind trust.

BIBLIOGRAPHY

Arnold, Ron. *At the Eye of the Storm: James Watt and the Environmentalists.* Chicago: Regnery Gateway, 1982.

Barrett, Laurence I. *Gambling with History.* Garden City, N.Y.: Doubleday, 1983.

DeLeon, Peter. *Thinking About Political Corruption.* Armonk, N.Y.: M. E. Sharpe, 1993.

Draper, Theodore. *A Very Thin Line: The Iran-contra Affairs.* New York: Hill and Wang, 1991.

Honegger, Barbara. *October Surprise.* New York: Tudor, 1989.

Johnson, Haynes B. *Sleepwalking Through History.* New York: W. W. Norton, 1991.

Kmiec, Douglas W. *The Attorney General's Lawyer: Inside the Meese Justice Department.* New York: Praeger, 1992.

Marshall, Jonathan, Peter Dale Scott, and Jane Hunter. *The Iran-Contra Connection: Secret Teams and Covert Operations in the Reagan Era.* Boston: South End Press, 1987.

Mitchell, Jack. *Executive Privilege: Two Centuries of White House Scandals.* New York: Hippocrene Books, 1992.

Persico, Joseph. *Casey: From the OSS to the CIA.* New York: Viking, 1990.

Smith, William French. *Law and Justice in the Reagan Administration: The Memoirs of an Attorney General.* Stanford: Hoover Institution Press, 1991.

Sternberg, William, and Matthew C. Harrison Jr. *Feeding Frenzy.* New York: Hold, 1989.

Tower, John. *Consequences: A Personal and Political Memoir.* Boston: Little, Brown, 1991.

Truab, James. *Too Good to Be True: The Outlandish Story of Wedtech.* New York: Doubleday, 1990.

Walsh, Lawrence E. *Firewall: The Iran-Contra Conspiracy and Cover-up.* New York: Norton, 1997.

Wills, Garry. *Reagan's America: Innocents at Home.* Garden City, N.Y.: Doubleday, 1987.

GEORGE H. BUSH

Forty-First President
1989–1993

B orn in Milton, Massachusetts, on June 12, 1924, George Herbert
Walker Bush was named for his maternal grandfather. His father,
Prescott Bush, was a wealthy Wall Street banker who served one
term as a U.S. senator from Connecticut. George Bush grew up in Greenwich, Connecticut, and attended a private elementary school before
enrolling in Phillips Academy in Andover, Massachusetts, at age thirteen.
At this exclusive prep school, Bush excelled in athletics as well as in his
studies. He was elected president of his senior class.

When Bush graduated in 1942, the United States was at war. He
deferred his admission to Yale University and on his eighteenth birthday
enlisted as a seaman second class in the navy. He served until September
1945, rising to the rank of lieutenant. Earning his wings in 1944, he
became the youngest pilot in the navy. During his service he flew fifty-
eight missions in the Pacific. He brought his last mission to a successful
conclusion, even though his plane had been hit and was on fire. Rescued at
sea by the submarine *Finback,* Bush spent a month on board while it completed its mission. He was awarded the Distinguished Flying Cross. Bush
was sent to Oceana Naval Air Station in Virginia to prepare for a final
assault on Japan. Only President Harry S. Truman's decision to drop the
atomic bomb prevented him from seeing further duty. On January 6,
1945, Bush married Barbara Pierce, the daughter of Marvin Pierce, the
publisher of *Redbook* and *McCall's* magazines.

After the war Bush went to Yale University, where he majored in economics and was captain of the baseball team. He graduated with honors in
1948. He turned down the offer of a lucrative job with an investment firm
and instead accepted a position with an oil company in West Texas. He started at the bottom, but soon was promoted to a job selling drilling equipment. After taking increasingly more responsible positions, Bush formed his
own oil development company in 1950 with John Overby. Bush-Overby
merged with Liedtke Brothers in 1953 to form Zapata Petroleum Corpo-

ration. Zapata struck it rich in the Jameson Field southwest of Abilene. The company ventured into off-shore drilling in 1954, and Bush bought out his partners to take full charge of the off-shore division in 1959. In February 1966 he sold Zapata Off-Shore to a Texas businessman for $1 million.

Bush had been active in Republican Party politics for a number of years and in 1964 decided to run for the U.S. Senate against Ralph Yarborough, the incumbent Democrat. He lost that election, 57 percent to 43 percent, but in 1966 was elected to the House of Representatives from the newly created Seventh District (Houston) by a margin of 57 percent to 42 percent. In 1968 he was unopposed in his reelection bid. In the House, Bush earned a reputation as a fiscal conservative and social moderate. He voted to approve the Civil Rights Act of 1968, which was highly unpopular in his district. Bush decided to try another Senate race. He had planned on facing Yarborough again, but Yarborough was defeated in the Democratic primary by Lloyd Bentsen. Bush lost, in part because he refused to wage a negative campaign.

President Richard Nixon appointed Bush ambassador to the United Nations in 1971, when his first choice, Daniel Patrick Moynihan, declined the appointment. As ambassador, Bush was a strong proponent of the two-China policy. In 1973 Nixon persuaded Bush to become chairman of the Republican National Committee. Bush spent most of his time shoring up party morale as the Watergate scandal grew more serious. On August 7, 1974, he sent a letter to the president asking him to resign. Bush called his twenty-month tenure at the RNC "a political nightmare." He was considered for the vice presidency when Gerald Ford assumed the presidency, but Ford chose Nelson Rockefeller of New York. Bush was then offered his pick of diplomatic assignments. Passing over plum posts in London and Paris, Bush chose to become chief U.S. liaison in China, a position he held from 1974 to 1975. Although he would have preferred to stay in China, Bush accepted an appointment to be CIA director in 1976. He was an able administrator and achieved recognition for improving the agency.

Out of office with the election of Jimmy Carter, Bush began to plan his own run for the White House. On May 1, 1979, he announced his candidacy and in January 1980 won a stunning upset over Ronald Reagan in the Iowa caucuses to become Reagan's chief challenger for the nomination. Reagan eventually captured the nomination and, after negotiations with former president Gerald Ford ended, Reagan selected Bush as his running mate. Bush served eight years as Reagan's vice president, and, like most in that position, took a largely supportive approach. He served on a number of commissions, attended state funerals (he coined the self-deprecating phrase, "You die, I fly"), and served as a general adviser to the president.

Bush was easily nominated to be the Republican Party standard-bearer in 1988. He shocked the convention with his selection of conservative senator Dan Quayle of Indiana as his running mate. In the fall election, the Bush-Quayle ticket faced the Democratic governor of Massachusetts,

Michael Dukakis, and Sen. Lloyd Bentsen of Texas. Bush handily won the election with 54 percent of the popular vote and an electoral college tally of 426 to 111; he took forty of the fifty states.

His administration was marked by a number of problems, including the saving and loan crisis and the continuing investigation of the Iran-contra affair. Bush oversaw the demise of the Soviet Union and continued to be a strong advocate for military strength as a pivotal component of diploma-cy. When Iraqi forces overran Kuwait, Bush orchestrated a worldwide effort to stop the aggression. His leadership and success in the Persian Gulf War gave him high approval ratings in the early part of 1991, and he looked unbeatable in the 1992 election. However, as the economy began to falter, so did his electoral chances. He was defeated by Democrat Bill Clinton of Arkansas.

Bush retired to homes in Houston and Kennebunkport, Maine. He has remained active in Republican Party politics and has written several books. Bush has generally shunned the spotlight during his retirement, preferring to spend the time with his family and close friends. Two of his sons are in politics: George W. Bush is the governor of Texas and a leading candidate for the Republican presidential nomination in 2000, and Jeb Bush is the governor of Florida.

JOHN TOWER, SECRETARY OF DEFENSE NOMINEE

John Tower was rejected for a cabinet post in the Bush administration because of his alleged drinking problems, womanizing, and defense consult-ing work.

President George Bush nominated John Tower, a former senator and fellow Texan, to be secretary of defense. Tower served twenty-four years in the Senate and held a number of positions in the Reagan administration; he headed the Iran-contra investigation. Few would have believed that he

would run into problems with his confirmation. However, on March 9, 1989, the Senate rejected the nomination by a vote of 53 to 47.

Three types of allegations were made concerning Tower. First, he was accused of inappropriate behav-ior with women on a number of occasions. The nom-inee had a reputation as a womanizer and not know-ing the bounds of decency. National headlines reported him dancing unclothed with a Russian bal-lerina on top of a piano. He also allegedly fondled a female member of the military in front of thousands of people—a charge made by a sergeant who was not present at the event in question.

The second charge was that he had a drinking problem. According to the FBI report done on Tower

John Tower

for the committee, Tower showed "a clear pattern of excessive drinking and alcohol abuse" during the 1970s. Those opposed to his nomination pointed out that a problem with alcohol as late as the 1970s would have disqualified Tower from holding many senior posts in the Defense Department because of the sensitive nature of the positions.

The final charge was the potential for conflict of interest because Tower had served as a defense industry consultant and lobbyist. Opponents claimed that Tower would have the power to award contracts to companies that had previously employed him. Further, they questioned the sums of money he had been paid as a consultant.

Tower was the first cabinet appointee rejected since 1959, when President Dwight D. Eisenhower nominated Lewis L. Strauss for secretary of commerce.

JOHN SUNUNU, CHIEF OF STAFF

John Sununu, former governor of New Hampshire, was forced to resign because of criticism of his use of military aircraft for personal trips, including visits to a stamp show and his dentist.

Vice President Bush fared so poorly in the 1988 Iowa caucuses that a win in the New Hampshire primary became absolutely necessary. New Hampshire governor John Sununu and his well-organized supporters played a pivotal role in handing Bush the much-needed victory. Bush rewarded the blunt, outspoken Sununu by appointing him White House chief of staff, a position of great power.

To some the match seemed ideal. Amiable and unintellectual, with almost no domestic agenda, Bush would be balanced by Sununu, a tough, highly intelligent governor who did have a domestic agenda. Bush, who had promised a kinder, gentler America, would have someone to say no for him. As in an old movie, Sununu would play bad cop to Bush's good cop.

Sununu's fellow White House staffers had varied opinions about him. Some emphasized his intolerance of opposition; others stressed that disagreement did not usually lead him to carry a grudge. All agreed that he had a hot temper, with one person noting, "He was a great screamer. He'd have these tantrums that were just ludicrous." Perhaps the best analysis of Sununu's personality came from his assistant, Ed Rogers, who remarked, "He felt no pain and you have to, to some degree, to be a good chief of staff." Sununu simply did not feel the hurt that his insults and belittling words inflicted on others, nor did he have the feedback to warn him that he was accumulating powerful opponents and needed to be careful.

Because the chief of staff controls who sees the president, complaints soon arose that Sununu was isolating Bush from differing points of view. Others countered that, given Bush's instinctively gregarious nature, Sununu's efforts had little impact. More telling was a criticism from Vin Weber, a conservative member of Congress from Minnesota. Weber noted that under Ronald Reagan different issues had to be taken up with different officials, such as James Baker, Edwin Meese, or Caspar Weinberger. "When you ask how to influence decision making in the Bush White House, it's always the same answer: Sununu."

Sununu's situation began to worsen in 1990, when Bush broke his "read my lips, no new taxes" pledge and raised taxes with the support of congressional Democrats. Although Sununu, a conservative New Englander, probably opposed the increase, he was too loyal to Bush to disagree. When congressional Republicans made it clear they would not support Bush, Sununu turned ugly, claiming that Bush would campaign against them in the 1990 election. It was an empty threat. Many Republicans were all too willing to distance themselves from Bush over taxes.

By 1991 Sununu had few friends. The White House staff was demoralized by his behavior, and conservative Republicans were angry over the tax deal. The Democrats, however, were delighted at anything that made the Republicans look bad. As *Newsweek* put it in May, "If you're going to make such armies of enemies inside the Beltway, you'd better be sure there are no chinks in your armor."

Some chinks in Sununu's armor had just appeared. Pressured by the *Washington Post* and *U.S. News & World Report,* the White House had been forced to release records of numerous flights Sununu had taken on military aircraft. In two years he had flown seventy-seven times, costing taxpayers more than $500,000. These accommodations were not canvas seats on a noisy military transport crowded with soldiers. Sununu and those he brought with him had the exclusive use of the military version of the Gulfstream III corporate jet. Although the aircraft cost almost $4,000 an hour to operate, for those trips that could not be called official business, Sununu paid only the coach fare plus $1. Skeptics also questioned whether some of

his trips—such as two taken to ski in Colorado—were really official business. Each cost about $30,000, but Sununu had paid only a little over $2,000 for his wife's travel. Technically, Sununu had broken no laws or ethical guidelines. In fact, he had done precisely what was expected of him under a 1987 policy that required a few high-level White House officials to fly on military planes so they could be reached at any time.

Sununu's real problem lay in who he was. A champion of big budgets and bloated bureaucracies might have escaped the scandal, but the tight-fisted Sununu had preached frugality while he appeared to be living lavishly. Moreover, the issue was easy for the average American, who has to wait in long lines to take commercial flights, to understand. Publicly, Sununu seemed unfazed, telling the audience at one speech, "Sorry I'm late. I couldn't find a place to land." As

John Sununu

expected, Bush stood up for his assistant, noting that "he has to comply with this policy." Privately, Bush was said to be upset enough to ask his counsel, C. Boyden Gray, to see if the travel policy could be changed.

During 1991, as the economy faltered and Bush's own popularity waned, Sununu's chance of retaining his job faded. His confrontational style had made enemies of those Bush would need for his reelection bid. Sununu's mishandling of a civil rights bill in November seems to have been the final straw. On December 2 a *Newsweek* article asked, "There he goes again—but this time, will Sununu be gone?" The next day he resigned, and Secretary of Transportation Samuel Skinner became Bush's chief of staff.

CLARENCE THOMAS, SUPREME COURT JUSTICE

The nomination of Clarence Thomas, a conservative black jurist, to the Supreme Court hit a roadblock when allegations surfaced that he had behaved inappropriately toward a female subordinate, Anita Hill, while serving as head of the EEOC.

In 1991 President Bush selected Clarence Thomas, a conservative black jurist, to replace retiring justice Thurgood Marshall on the Supreme Court. Shortly before the Senate Judiciary Committee was to vote on Thomas's nomination, an allegation of inappropriate sexual conduct came to light. Law professor Anita Hill, who had worked for Thomas at the Equal Employment Opportunity Commission and the Department of Education, had reported the alleged misbehavior to a committee staffer. The confirmation hearings turned into an investigation of the charges. Hill testified that Thomas had made crude sexual comments to her, repeatedly asked her out on dates, and often talked about pornographic materials. Thomas, in his response, called the allegations false. He likened the Senate's investigation to a "high tech lynching." Senators on both sides of the aisle seemed at a loss as to how to resolve the controversy. President Bush remained committed to Thomas's nomination.

The hearings were broadcast nationwide and proved to be very divisive, with liberals and feminists siding with Hill, and others with Thomas. There were no corroborating witnesses to Hill's testimony. Despite the efforts of feminist groups to block Thomas because of his stance on abortion and their fear he would vote to overturn *Roe v. Wade,* Thomas was confirmed to the post of associate justice.

JENNIFER FITZGERALD, WHITE HOUSE AIDE

President Bush was accused of having an extramarital affair with a former aide, Jennifer Fitzgerald.

In the midst of the 1992 presidential election, when the question of candidate Bill Clinton's fidelity to his wife was being called into question, rumors also surfaced about President Bush. The story was that Bush had carried on an affair with Jennifer Fitzgerald, a top aide on his vice-presidential staff, who had become the State Department's deputy chief of protocol.

In April 1992 Hillary Clinton said in an interview with *Vanity Fair* that the "establishment" had protected Bush's extramarital affair from becoming public while running stories about her husband and Gennifer Flowers (see page 433). Several news agencies took exception to this characterization. They stated that they had investigated the charges several years before and found no evidence of an affair. *Washington Post* reporter Ann Devroy spent two full months tracking down leads and investigating the allegations, finding no substantiation.

Bush refused to answer any questions regarding the allegations. "I'm not going to take any sleazy questions like that," he said. Barbara Bush called the story that eventually appeared in the *New York Post* "a lie in every way, shape or form." The original allegation appeared in the book *The Power House* by Susan Trento and was based on an interview with Louis Fields, a government official who died before the scandal broke.

ELIZABETH TAMPOSI AND THE PRIVACY ACT

Elizabeth Tamposi, a political appointee at the State Department, violated Freedom of Information Act guidelines by expediting a search into candidate Bill Clinton's passport file.

In October 1992, when the mudslinging of the presidential campaign was in high gear, the Bush administration responded to a Freedom of Information Act (FOIA) request filed by the media. The request had been made to see if there was any truth to the rumor that Bill Clinton had explored the possibility of changing his citizenship to avoid serving in Vietnam. Clinton denied that the rumor was true, but the administration allowed a search of his passport records.

Elizabeth Tamposi, a political appointee at the State Department, was one of several officials who expedited the search, even though there was no official need for haste. Under the law, an expedited response is appropriate in two situations: when "an individual's life or safety would be jeopardized by the failure to process a request immediately" or "whenever it is shown that substantial due process rights of the requester would be impaired by the failure to proceed immediately." The file of Clinton's mother, Virginia Kelley, was also searched, a clear violation of the Privacy Act because no FOIA request had been filed on her.

The Clinton campaign charged that the search was a serious violation of the law and that "not since the Nixon campaign of 1972 has there been such a pattern of misuse of government agencies to smear an opponent." Tamposi resigned her State Department post, and the scandal faded quickly.

IRAN-CONTRA PARDONS

In late December 1992 President George Bush issued full pardons to six people, including former defense secretary Caspar Weinberger, who were under investigation for their involvement in the Iran-contra affair. Critics said that Bush issued the pardons to protect himself from being more deeply implicated in the Reagan administration scandal.

On Christmas Eve 1992, when most Americans had something other than politics on their mind, George Bush issued presidential pardons for President Reagan's former defense secretary, Caspar Weinberger, and five others. Weinberger and Duane R. Clarridge, the former head of CIA operations in Latin America, were awaiting trial. The other four had been convicted of various offenses against Congress, typically of lying or withholding information about weapons shipments. None of their crimes had been serious enough to warrant punishment any harsher than parole, community service, and, in one case, a fine. None was charged with having profited from the Iran-contra deal. Bush carefully steered away from pardoning eight others whose motives were more questionable. Compared to a governor's pardon of a convicted criminal, Bush's act of pardon was small potatoes.

Lawrence Walsh, the independent counsel for the Iran-contra investigation, did not see it that way, but, by the time he issued his 2,507-page final report on August 4, 1993, the Iran-contra investigation was history.

BIBLIOGRAPHY

Brock, David. *The Real Anita Hill: The Untold Story.* New York: Free Press, 1993.

Bush, Barbara. *Barbara Bush: A Memoir.* New York: Scribner's Sons, 1994.

Bush, George. *Looking Forward: An Autobiography.* Garden City, N.Y.: Doubleday, 1987.

Campbell, Colin, and Bert A. Rockman, eds. *The Bush Presidency: First Appraisals.* Chatham, N.J.: Chatham House, 1991.

Ellis, Richard J. *Presidential Lightning Rods.* Lawrence: University Press of Kansas, 1994.

Kilian, Pamela. *Barbara Bush: A Biography.* New York: St. Martin's, 1992.

Matalin, Mary, and James Carville. *All's Fair: Love, War, and Running for President.* New York: Random House, Simon and Schuster, 1994.

Mayer, Jane, and Jill Abramson. *Strange Justice: The Selling of Clarence Thomas.* Boston: Houghton Mifflin, 1994.

Mervin, David. *George Bush and the Guardianship Presidency.* New York: St. Martin's, 1996.

Mitchell, Jack. *Executive Privilege: Two Centuries of White House Scandals.* New York: Hippocrene Books, 1992.

WILLIAM J. CLINTON

Forty-Second President
1993–

ill Clinton, whose original name was William Jefferson Blythe IV, was born August 19, 1946, in Hope, Arkansas. He was named for his father, who had died in a traffic accident three months before his son was born. When Bill was four years old, his mother married Roger Clinton of Hot Springs, Arkansas, and as a teenager, Bill adopted his stepfather's name. He attended public school and was an excellent student and interested in politics from an early age. While in high school, he traveled to Washington as a Boys Nation delegate and shook President John F. Kennedy's hand at a Rose Garden reception. Clinton credits this meeting with inspiring him to enter politics. Clinton attended Georgetown University from which he graduated in 1968. He then attended Oxford University for two years on a Rhodes Scholarship. He entered Yale Law School and earned his J.D. in 1973.

Clinton was teaching law at the University of Arkansas when he ran for the U.S. House of Representatives in 1974 and lost. In 1975 he married Hillary Rodham, whom he had met at Yale Law School. The politically ambitious Hillary Rodham Clinton became her husband's strong supporter and adviser.

In 1976 Clinton ran a successful campaign for attorney general of Arkansas and was elected governor two years later. He was defeated for reelection in 1982 in large part because of the increase in taxes he had approved. Learning the political lesson in that defeat, Clinton was reelected governor in 1986 and served until 1992. Announcing his presidential candidacy in 1991, Clinton—a relative unknown—joined a crowded field of Democrats that included Sen. Al Gore of Tennessee, former governor Jerry Brown of California, and Sen. Bob Kerrey of Nebraska, among others. On the campaign trail he was successful despite being dogged by a number of scandals over marital infidelity, the Vietnam draft, and marijuana use.

Successful in the primaries, Clinton came to the Democratic National Convention in New York City with his victory assured. He chose Gore as his running mate and in the fall defeated incumbent president George Bush, who only eight months earlier had looked invincible. Clinton was handily reelected in 1996 over the Republican candidate, former senator Bob Dole of Kansas.

Clinton's administration has benefited from and helped to further an exceptionally strong period of prosperity. The nation's strong economy enabled his administration to balance the budget through a mixture of spending cuts and moderate tax increases. But the administration got off to a rocky start. Clinton expended a vast amount of political capital on an ill-fated health care reform program championed by Hillary Clinton. His policy on gays in the military proved unpopular. Worst of all, over time his administration suffered from a huge number of scandals that at times crippled his ability to be an effective leader in either domestic or foreign affairs. No matter what his legacy, history will record that Clinton is just the second president in the history of the United States to be impeached.

In foreign policy Clinton's record has been mixed. Many credit him with helping to broker a peace agreement in Northern Ireland, while others say that he has stretched America's military commitments to the breaking point by getting involved in hot spots around the world, including Somalia, Haiti, Bosnia, and Kosovo.

DRAFT STATUS

Serious questions were raised during the 1992 campaign about what Clinton did to avoid being drafted during the Vietnam War.

When Bill Clinton graduated from Georgetown University in 1968, all graduate school draft deferments had been abolished by the Johnson administration. Clinton had received a Rhodes Scholarship and planned to attend Oxford University. His uncle Raymond Clinton convinced Lt. Cmdr. Trice Ellis Jr. to create a naval reserve position for Clinton in Hot Springs, Arkansas, even though none was available. Clinton, however, never reported to Hot Springs because he had pulled other strings. An aide to Sen. J. William Fulbright, for whom Clinton had worked, called the Hot Springs draft board and had Clinton's induction into the draft postponed for a year, enabling him to go to Oxford without fear of being drafted.

The following year Clinton received his draft notice. He applied to the air force and navy officer programs, but failed both physicals. He then arranged to join the ROTC program at the University of Arkansas Law School, and the commanding officer of the program, Col. Eugene Holmes, issued a 1-D deferment to Clinton's draft board. However, Clinton did not enroll at the University of Arkansas in the fall, nor did he inform Holmes of his plan to return to Oxford to finish a second year there. At the time he had already decided to go to Yale University Law School after finishing at Oxford. On December 3, 1969, two days after receiving notice that he was number 311 of 365 in the draft (and therefore unlikely to be drafted), he wrote to Holmes that he would not be accepting a post in the ROTC program. The letter also said that he had informed his draft board of that decision in a letter dated September 12. In fact, Clinton had not informed his draft board, violating a federal law that required him to do so within ten days of his change in status. It became clear that Clinton had used the ROTC program as a possible safety valve to avoid the draft.

In a 1992 affidavit, Holmes stated that Clinton had used him. Holmes said that he would not have given Clinton the 1-D deferment had he known that Clinton planned to return to England. Holmes, a highly decorated World War II veteran, was particularly angered by the "thank you" he received from Clinton in the December letter for "saving me from the draft." Holmes asserted that doing so had never been his intention as both of his sons served in Vietnam.

While in England, Clinton participated in two antiwar demonstrations outside the U.S. Embassy in London. The protests were organized by a British peace organization affiliated with the World Peace Council, a front for the KGB. Clinton's draft record and his antiwar activities in England became serious issues during both the Democratic Party primaries and during the general election. Clinton refused to address the concerns directly, claiming that he had never tried to dodge the draft.

MARIJUANA USE

For a number of years Bill Clinton provided hair-splitting answers to questions about whether he had ever used marijuana. In the end, he admitted that he had tried it, but had not inhaled.

The question of whether Clinton had used marijuana or other drugs dogged him for years. When he ran for governor in 1986, he was asked if he had ever used drugs and said he had not. By 1989 he had refined his answer to the statement that he had never used illegal drugs as an adult in Arkansas. During his 1990 gubernatorial campaign, he was asked again and said that he "had never violated the drug laws of the state." In 1991 *Arkansas Gazette* reporter Scott Morris asked a more narrowly drawn question— whether Clinton had ever tried marijuana in college. Clinton said no. In a 1991 speech at the National Press Club, Clinton stated that he had not violated any state or federal drug laws.

However, the press persisted and kept refining the way the question was phrased. During a 1992 primary debate, Clinton finally said, "When I was in England I experimented with marijuana a time or two, and I didn't like it. I didn't inhale it, and never tried it again." (Two women with whom Clinton had affairs contradicted this claim. Gennifer Flowers and Sally Perdue alleged that Clinton smoked marijuana in their presence.)

Most Clinton critics were not concerned that he had used marijuana— after all, in 1988 several other Democratic candidates, including Al Gore and Bruce Babbitt, had already admitted to experimenting. What concerned them was the lengths to which Clinton went to conceal the truth. They argued that it pointed to a character flaw that he could not just admit what he had done.

When asked in an MTV interview session with teenagers what he would have done differently concerning his marijuana use, Clinton replied flippantly that if he had to do it all over he would have inhaled.

SEXUAL AFFAIRS

Both before and after he married Hillary Rodham, Bill Clinton had numerous sexual partners. According to their testimony and that of others, some affairs were fleeting and others endured.

Dolly Kyle Browning

According to Dolly Browning, in 1964 she and Bill Clinton began a sexual relationship that lasted thirty-three years. She had originally met him in 1959 on a golf course in Hot Springs, Arkansas, when she was only eleven and he was thirteen. She was immediately smitten with Clinton. In 1997 she published a thinly veiled fictional account of their relationship entitled *Purposes of the Heart*. Literary agent Lucianne Goldberg secured a six-figure advance for Browning if she would rewrite the book as nonfiction. Browning refused, in part because the self-published book was written as a kind of therapy for the sexual addiction from which she was suffering. When the book was published, the White House refused to comment on it.

Browning alleges that she was approached during the 1992 presidential campaign by a tabloid newspaper reporter who was writing a story on Clinton's extramarital affairs. Unsure what to do, she sent word to Clinton, who asked her brother, Walter Kyle, a Clinton campaign worker, to tell her that if she cooperated with the reporter, she would be "destroyed." The two talked for the first time in years in 1994 at their high school reunion in Hot Springs. Browning asserts that Clinton invited her to move to Washington and rekindle their relationship. Browning, a successful attorney in Dallas, declined.

Subpoenaed by the lawyers for Paula Jones, Browning indicated that, under oath, she would confirm the "distinguishing characteristic" of Clinton's private parts. However, with the settlement of the sexual harassment suit, her testimony in open court was not needed (see page 439).

Women Named in Nichols Lawsuit

Larry Nichols was a former Arkansas state employee who was fired by Gov. Bill Clinton in 1990 because he had used state telephones to raise money for the Nicaraguan contras. Nichols denied the allegations and filed a lawsuit against Clinton for defamation of character and libel. In his court filings, he also charged that Clinton had been guilty of misconduct in office because he had kept a secret slush fund of taxpayer money that he used to entertain women. He named five women (see below); the sixth he declined to identify but said she had "become pregnant and had an abortion." The five women named in the suit were Deborah Mathias, Elizabeth Ward, Susie Whiteacre, Lencola Sullivan, and Gennifer Flowers.

Deborah Mathias was a reporter for the *Arkansas Gazette* who had previously worked with Gennifer Flowers at KARK-TV. Flowers said she was not certain if Clinton and Mathias had had an affair, but Clinton warned her about Mathias, saying that she "had a big mouth."

Elizabeth Ward was a beautiful young woman who had won both the Miss Arkansas crown and the Miss America crown in 1981. According to Nichols, shortly after Clinton met Ward, they began a torrid sexual relationship. Ward left Arkansas "because her affair with Clinton got too hot to handle." In 1992 Ward posed for *Playboy* magazine. At the time, the Clinton campaign issued a signed statement from Ward denying the affair.

Susie Whiteacre was Governor Clinton's press secretary. Nichols claimed that Clinton used state troopers to transport Whiteacre and the governor to various locations so that they could engage in sexual activity. Whiteacre denied that she had a sexual relationship with Clinton.

In September 1980 Clinton met Miss Arkansas, Lencola Sullivan, a lovely African American woman who had taken fourth place in the Miss America pageant. Nichols claimed that an affair between Clinton and Sullivan began that same month. Sullivan had taken a job with KARK-TV and would be working alongside Deborah Mathias and Gennifer Flowers. However, Sullivan did not stay in Little Rock long. She moved to New York City, even though she had no job or a place to live there. According to Nichols's lawsuit, Sullivan was rushed out of Arkansas to prevent the affair from becoming public. Nichols claimed that the affair did not end with Sullivan's move, but that Clinton went to New York on three occasions at taxpayer expense to continue his relationship with her.

The best known of the women named in Nichols's lawsuit was Gennifer Flowers. She claimed to have had a twelve-year affair with Clinton beginning in 1977 while he was attorney general. According to Flowers, the two met when she was a reporter for KARK-TV and assigned the story of interviewing Clinton at the airport. The relationship began shortly after that encounter.

Flowers and Clinton would meet at the Excelsior Hotel or at her apartment at the Quapaw Towers, where the manager has confirmed that Clinton was a frequent visitor. In December 1977 Flowers thought she was pregnant, and Clinton provided money for her to have an abortion. It was at this time that Flowers realized that she would never be more than a mistress to Clinton.

Flowers wrote in her 1995 book *Gennifer Flowers: Passion and Betrayal*, that she and Clinton would have sex as often as three or four times a week.

She also claims that he liked phone sex and introduced her to oral sex. According to Flowers, Clinton had researched the subject and believed that oral sex did not constitute adultery. Flowers said that as the relationship progressed, Clinton wanted to get even wilder sexually. He asked to tie her up and when she refused, he asked to be tied up. He also enjoyed being spanked and once asked that she use a vibrator on him. Clinton suggested a ménage à trois, but Flowers found that "repugnant" and just too "kinky." She said that marijuana was used on several occasions and that Clinton inhaled.

In 1989 Flowers ended the relationship because she had met someone she thought she might want to marry. A year later, when Nichols's lawsuit was filed, Flowers began to tape record her telephone conversations with Clinton to document her story should it became necessary. On three occasions in 1991 to 1992, she called Clinton and recorded their conversations.

Flowers claimed that she was approached by Arkansas Republican Ron Fuller to go public with her story for $50,000 in October 1991, shortly after Clinton announced his presidential candidacy. She refused. However, on January 13, 1992, the *Star* supermarket tabloid featured a story about Clinton's affairs with the five women named in Nichols's suit. A subsequent edition of the *Star* published a detailed account of the Flowers-Clinton relationship. Flowers had met with managing editor Dick Kaplan because he had told her that he was going to run a story whether she confirmed it or not. Flowers was paid between $100,000 and $150,000 for confirming her affair with Clinton.

Hillary Clinton fired back, claiming that Flowers had fabricated the story for the money. On Super Bowl Sunday 1992, the Clintons were interviewed on *60 Minutes.* The Clintons acknowledged "trouble in the marriage" in the past, but denied that Clinton had an affair with Flowers. Clinton asserted that Flowers was just "a friendly acquaintance." As part of his Paula Jones deposition in 1997, however, Clinton admitted to having a sexual relationship with Flowers, but he still denied it was twelve years in length.

The *Star* arranged a press conference the day after the *60 Minutes* interview at the Waldorf-Astoria in New York. There, Flowers read a prepared statement and played a portion of one of her taped conversations with Clinton. Flowers was also paid for an appearance on *A Current Affair.* Mimicking Marilyn Monroe's performance at John F. Kennedy's birthday celebration, Flowers sang "Happy Birthday, Mr. President" on Comedy Central. She also appeared in *Penthouse* in a photo layout and story of the affair.

Arkansas State Troopers' Statements

Flowers was attacked as a liar who had fabricated the affair to make money, but four Arkansas state troopers confirmed her story. The troopers said they had taken hundreds of calls for Clinton from her, that they had often driven Clinton to her apartment complex, and that Clinton had tried to find employment for her.

On December 20, 1993, the conservative publication *American Spectator* published the stories of four troopers, Larry Patterson, Roger Perry, Danny Ferguson, and Ronnie Anderson. They stated that part of their duties was helping to facilitate and cover up Governor Clinton's extramarital affairs. The troopers claimed that Clinton was juggling about six "steady girlfriends whom we saw two or three times a week." According to them, they would often run interference with Hillary Clinton and warn him of her whereabouts so that she could not catch him in the act.

Ferguson claimed that he had been offered a federal job as a regional director of the Federal Emergency Management Agency (FEMA) or as a U.S. marshal. Ferguson's boss, Raymond L. "Buddy" Young, who headed Clinton's security detail for two years, was made a regional director of FEMA. Perry and Patterson also claimed that they were offered jobs for their silence.

The April-May edition of *American Spectator* ran a story about another state trooper, L. D. Brown, who served on the Clinton detail from 1982 to 1985. Brown claimed he had solicited more than 100 women for Clinton.

Sally Perdue

In an interview with the *Sally Jesse Raphael Show* in July 1992, Sally Perdue said she and Bill Clinton had a three-month affair that began in August 1983. Perdue stated that she had met Clinton a decade earlier when she was a reporter for Little Rock's PBS station. A former Miss Arkansas, Perdue did not care that Clinton was married because she saw the relationship as a brief encounter. She claimed that Clinton often smoked marijuana and that he said it "enhanced his sexual pleasure."

The talk show, which had been recorded before a studio audience, was never broadcast. In a subsequent interview published in London's *Sunday Telegraph,* Perdue insisted that she had been offered a good paying job if she kept her mouth shut during the 1992 presidential campaign. Trooper Brown stated in the *American Spectator* that Clinton told him about the affair with Perdue.

Bobbie Ann Williams

Bobbie Ann Williams, an African American woman who used to be a prostitute on Little Rock's Hookers Row, claimed that she had been paid to have sex with Clinton on a number of occasions in 1984. According to her, she was paid $200 for performing oral sex during their first encounter and arranged for an orgy with two other prostitutes, each of whom was paid $400. Williams says that she would often meet Clinton late at night at the Holiday Inn. She also insists that her mixed-race son, Danny, who was born in 1985, is Clinton's child.

Monica Lewinsky

In May 1995 Monica Lewinsky moved to Washington, D.C., to begin an unpaid White House internship. Recently graduated from Lewis and Clark College in Portland, Oregon, she lived in a Watergate apartment with her mother, Marsha Lewis. Her internship was with Leon Panetta, Clinton's chief of staff, which brought her into contact with the president. When the government shut down in late 1995, President Clinton and Monica saw more of each other because many executive employees were not permitted to show up for work. According to Lewinsky, the affair began on November 15, 1995, and lasted, on and off, for two years. With her internship about to end, Lewinsky was given a full-time paid position on November 26, 1995.

The amount of time that Lewinsky spent in and around the Oval Office did not go unnoticed. Evelyn Lieberman, the deputy chief of staff, grew concerned that something was wrong with the way Lewinsky conducted herself. Although Lieberman denied that she thought an affair was taking place, she did successfully seek Lewinsky's transfer from the White House to the Pentagon in April 1996. The move, however, did not end the relationship; Lewinsky continued to visit the White House, usually under the pretext of visiting Betty Currie, Clinton's personal secretary.

At the Pentagon Lewinsky became friends with Linda Tripp, who had worked at the White House during the Bush and Clinton administrations. According to statements from Tripp, she was appalled at the way the Clinton White House was run.

The Clinton-Lewinsky relationship consisted mostly of her performing oral sex on him, with him doing little to reciprocate. The two also engaged in phone sex. Clinton tried several times to end the affair and ultimately did so, fearing discovery and perhaps feeling the heat from the Paula Jones lawsuit that was in full swing (see page 439).

Dissatisfied with her position at the Pentagon, Lewinsky began to pressure Clinton to allow her to return to the White House. The more unhappy she became, the more she confided in Tripp, who, without Lewinsky's knowledge, began to tape their telephone conversations. Tripp eventually took these tapes to independent counsel Kenneth Starr.

Lewinsky was offered a job in New York working for UN Ambassador Bill Richardson, but she declined, saying that she wanted to work in the private sector. Clinton friend and Washington power broker Vernon Jordan was asked to assist Lewinsky in her job search. He arranged interviews for her with American Express and Revlon, neither of which offered her a job.

A month later, on December 17, 1997, Lewinsky was subpoenaed to testify in the Paula Jones sexual harassment lawsuit. Jordan found her an attorney, and she prepared a false affidavit in which she denied having a physical relationship with Clinton. She signed it January 7, 1998, and the next day had a second interview with Revlon. She received a job offer on January 13.

Monica Lewinsky

However, the story of Monica Lewinsky and Clinton was about to go public. On January 21, 1998, the *Washington Post* ran a story alleging that Lewinsky had been conducting an affair with Clinton. Clinton repeatedly denied it. Cabinet members appeared outside of the White House supporting the president against what they termed as false allegations. On January 26 Clinton uttered a statement that would come back to haunt him numerous times throughout the ensuing investigation and impeachment (see page 453). Wagging his finger at the press, he said, "I want you to listen to me. I'm going to say this again: I did not have sexual relations with that woman—Miss Lewinsky." The next day, Hillary Clinton appeared on the *Today Show* and stated that the false allegations were part of a "vast right-wing conspiracy that had been conspiring against my husband since the day he announced for president."

Starr's investigation into whether the president had committed perjury in his civil deposition, encouraged the submission of a false deposition by Lewinsky, and obstructed justice ultimately led to Clinton's acknowledgement that he had had a sexual relationship with Lewinsky, a term he refused to use because he and Lewinsky had not had intercourse.

SEXUAL MISCONDUCT AND HARASSMENT

Clinton was accused by three women who claimed that he did everything from making unwanted advances to committing rape.

Juanita Broaddrick (Jane Doe Number 5)

The story concerning Juanita Broaddrick came to light as part of the Paula Jones sexual harassment case against Bill Clinton (see page 439). In their attempt to show a pattern of behavior by Clinton, Jones and her lawyers uncovered Broaddrick's story. Although she signed an affidavit to the contrary, Broaddrick announced that in 1978 Clinton, the attorney general of Arkansas, raped her.

According to Broaddrick, the attack took place at the now-defunct Camelot Inn in Little Rock on April 25. Broaddrick and a friend were attending a conference sponsored by the American College of Nursing Home Administrators. Broaddrick, then thirty-five, had met Clinton, who was running for governor, when he visited her nursing home facility in Van Buren a week or so earlier.

She called campaign headquarters and was patched through to Clinton who told her that he would not be in that day, but would like to stop by her hotel for a visit. When he arrived, he called her and asked if he could come to her room for coffee to avoid the reporters. Broaddrick recounted, "Stupid me, I ordered coffee to the room. I thought we were going to talk about the campaign."

Broaddrick says that the two spent only a short time chatting before he tried to kiss her. She attempted to resist, but he forced himself on her. According to her account, Clinton was biting her upper lip and raped her. She said that she did not scream because it happened all too fast and he was biting her lip. When he finished, he said, "You better get some ice for that," referring to the cut lip, and put on his sunglasses and left. Broaddrick also claims that Clinton told her not to worry about becoming pregnant as he was sterile from the effects of a childhood disease.

Although there were no witnesses to the alleged assault, Norma Rogers, who was attending the conference with Broaddrick, returned to the hotel to find her badly shaken and with a swollen lip. Broaddrick's husband, Dave Broaddrick, has also said that she told him of the events at the time. However, neither believed there was much they could do because at that time they were both married to other people and were themselves carrying on an adulterous relationship.

Juanita Broaddrick, right, with Bill Clinton and two residents of the nursing home she owned.

Broaddrick says Clinton called several times afterwards, but she always refused to take the calls. In 1991 while attending another nursing home conference in Little Rock, she was called out of a session to meet with him. According to Broaddrick, Clinton kept trying to hold her hand and said, "Can you ever forgive me? I'm not the same man I used to be." She replied that he could go to hell and walked away.

Questions arose as to why she had not told her story before. She says that she was embarrassed and blamed herself for the rape. She said, "It was twenty years ago, and I let a man in my room and I had to take my lumps." Asked why she had denied the allegations in her January 2, 1998, affidavit, she stated that she could not face retelling the story. She hoped that she could forget the events of that day and go on with her life. However, she finally came forward—she claimed—in the hopes of bringing the nightmarish memories to a close. Clinton's lawyer, David Kendall, denied the allegation.

Paula Corbin Jones

On May 6, 1994, Paula Corbin Jones filed a civil suit against President Clinton in U.S. district court in Little Rock, Arkansas, seeking $700,000 in damages for "willful, outrageous, and malicious conduct" at the Excelsior Hotel in Little Rock on May 8, 1991. The suit also named Arkansas state trooper Danny Ferguson as a co-defendant. Ferguson stated in court papers that Jones had offered to be Clinton's girlfriend. This sexual harassment suit ultimately led to Clinton's impeachment on charges of perjury and obstruction of justice.

Jones was a state employee working for the office of economic development, which was hosting a conference at the Excelsior. According to Jones, she was told that Governor Clinton wanted to see her for a moment in his hotel suite. Jones went to the room, where she claims Clinton propositioned her and exposed himself to her. She says she refused to comply with a request for oral sex and was told by Clinton that she had better keep the matter to herself. Jones claimed that she could prove that Clinton had exposed himself because his genitals had a "distinguishing characteristic."

On December 28, 1994, Judge Susan Webber Wright ruled that no trial could take place until after Clinton left office, but that fact-finding could begin immediately, including the taking of depositions. Jones's lawyers appealed the decision, and on January 9, 1996, a federal appeals court overturned Wright's decision. Clinton appealed to the Supreme Court, a move that postponed the final decision on a trial until after the November 1996 election. Before the Supreme Court decision was announced, attorneys for Jones and the president discussed a settlement, but no agreement was reached. On May 27, 1997, the Supreme Court ruled that the lawsuit could move ahead. On June 2, Clinton's team offered to settle the suit for a $700,000 payment to a charity with no apology or admission of guilt. Jones rejected the offer, insisting that any settlement must include an apology.

In an attempt to show a pattern of behavior, Jones's lawyers issued subpoenas to dozens of individuals, including Arkansas state troopers and women in Arkansas and Washington, D.C. One of these women was Mon-

ica Lewinsky, whose affair with Clinton had been revealed to Whitewater independent counsel Kenneth Starr. Thus, the link between Whitewater and Paula Jones's lawsuit was made. On September 9 Jones's attorneys withdrew from the case, citing differences with Jones over strategy. They were replaced by a team headed by John Whitehead, president of the conservative Rutherford Institute. Despite the change in Jones's legal representation, the judge ruled that the May 27, 1998, trial date could not be changed. Three months later, Jones reduced the amount of the damage award she was seeking to $525,000. She also dropped the charges against Clinton co-defendant Danny Ferguson.

Starr received formal approval to investigate whether Clinton had suborned perjury or obstructed justice in the Jones case on January 16, 1998. The next day Clinton was deposed by Jones's attorneys in

Paula Jones

the offices of his lawyer, Robert Bennett. Starr, who by now was focusing his investigation on Lewinsky, asked for and received from Judge Wright an order that prevented Jones's lawyers from using anything about Lewinsky and to prevent their continued trailing of his investigation. Wright issued the ruling to keep Jones's attorneys from having the "inevitable effect of disrupting" the investigation.

On February 17 Clinton's attorney filed a motion asking Wright to dismiss the suit because Jones had failed to prove that she suffered any harm to her career or any serious emotional anguish. In response, the Jones legal team filed 700 pages of documents showing a pattern of Clinton making advances against women, including an allegation that Clinton had raped a woman in the 1970s (see page 438). On April 1 Judge Wright dismissed the suit. Fifteen days later, Jones announced that she would appeal that decision.

While the Jones team prepared their appeal, Clinton was facing serious charges of perjury and obstruction of justice, and the stakes for settlement were raised by the likelihood that the president would be impeached. A wealthy Democratic supporter offered Jones $1 million to drop her suit. Jones's lawyers asked for $2 million, a proposal Clinton rejected. Clinton settled the Jones lawsuit for $850,000, but did not apologize or admit guilt.

The November 13, 1998, out-of-court settlement did not end all of Clinton's legal problems arising out of the Jones suit. Judge Wright cited Clinton for contempt of court in April 1999 for filing a false affidavit and for committing perjury in his own testimony. The possible consequences included the loss of his license to practice law and a fine that would cover some of Jones's legal costs.

Kathleen Willey

In an interview aired on *60 Minutes* on May 15, 1998, Kathleen Willey, an attractive fifty-one-year-old woman, recounted the events of a meeting on November 29, 1993, in which she claimed President Clinton groped and kissed her. Willey—like a number of women—had been drawn into the spotlight by the Paula Jones sexual harassment lawsuit. She came forward in 1998 because, she said, "Too many lies are being told, too many lives are being ruined."

Willey first met Clinton in Richmond, Virginia, in 1992, when Clinton was campaigning for the presidency. Seeing her on a rope line, Clinton obtained her phone number and called her at her home in Williamsburg. Hearing his voice, she said he sounded a little hoarse and could use some chicken soup. He asked her to bring it to him and that he would get rid of the Secret Service agents assigned to him. She said she did not go "because my instincts told me he wasn't interested in chicken soup."

Willey and her husband had contributed money to the Clinton campaign, and after the election she worked as a volunteer in the administra-

tion. Willey's husband began to have financial problems, and she requested the November 29 meeting to ask Clinton for a paying job. According to
Willey, Clinton feigned concern for her situation in order to take advantage of her sexually. Willey claims that he kissed her on the mouth, fondled
her breasts, and put her hand on his genitals. She pulled away and left. Willey learned later that day that her husband had committed suicide.

White House staffer Linda Tripp confirmed the general timing of events
and the general allegations made by Willey. Tripp claimed she saw Willey
as she left the Oval Office after the encounter and overheard it recounted
to a third party. Willey also claimed that a wealthy Democratic donor tried
to pay her not to tell the grand jury investigating Clinton about the
November incident. However, Julie Hiatt Steele, a onetime friend of Willey, testified that Willey asked her to corroborate her story about Clinton,
even though both women knew it to be false.

In a sworn deposition in the Paula Jones lawsuit, Clinton stated that he
had embraced Willey and kissed her on the forehead in an attempt to con-
sole her, a story that was repeated by presidential attorney Robert Bennett. The White House went on the offensive by supplying to news organizations notes and cards that Willey sent to Clinton after the alleged
incident that show her to have remained friendly with him. Willey claims
that she wrote the notes to keep open the possibility of obtaining a high-
paying federal job because she was now a widow.

ZOË BAIRD AND KIMBA WOOD, ATTORNEY GENERAL NOMINEES

*Clinton's first two nominations for attorney general, Zoë Baird and Kimba
Wood, were withdrawn by the White House when it was discovered that both
women had hired illegal immigrants as household help.*

The Clinton transition team promised to create a cabinet that looked
more like America and in which women would have a greater role. To fulfill that promise, Clinton nominated Zoë Baird, general counsel of the
Aetna Life and Casualty Company, to head the Justice Department. However, her nomination was ultimately withdrawn when it was disclosed that
she had hired an illegal immigrant couple to work in her home. Victor and
Lillian Cordero were employed in violation of federal law that prohibits
the employment of undocumented workers. In addition, Baird, who was
considered a conservative in the areas of criminal justice and tort reform
and who had the support of several Republicans, failed to pay the required
Social Security taxes on the couple's wages. Baird decided to withdraw
from the process and return to her job at Aetna, which paid more than
$500,000 annually.

In the wake of the failed Baird nomination, the Clinton White House
gave in to pressure from women's groups to nominate another woman to

be attorney general. The administration's second choice was a federal judge, Kimba Wood. However, the nomination was withdrawn when the White House discovered that Wood also had hired an illegal immigrant as a childcare provider.

Women's groups were outraged because the Baird and Wood cases were substantially different. When Wood hired the immigrant worker, doing so was not against the law. Further, Wood had paid the appropriate Social Security taxes on the wages she paid. The White House did not think that it could make that distinction stick politically and therefore abandoned its second choice for attorney general. The White House eventually nominated unmarried and childless Janet Reno, the Dade County district attorney for the post. Reno, a political unknown, was confirmed without any controversy.

WHITEWATER LAND DEAL

A land development partnership formed in the late 1970s led to serious charges of corruption, loan fraud, and other activities that led to the conviction of a number of Clinton friends and associates.

In 1978 Attorney General Bill Clinton of Arkansas and his wife, Hillary Rodham Clinton, formed a partnership with James McDougal, the owner of a savings and loan association, and his wife, Susan McDougal, to buy 220 acres of land on the Whitewater River. The partnership, Whitewater Development Corporation, planned to sell the lots for the construction of vacation homes. However, the partnership floundered from the outset and in 1992 it was dissolved with the Clintons reporting a net loss of more than $40,000. (McDougal's bank, Madison Guaranty Savings and Loan, eventually failed and cost taxpayers $65 million.)

Allegations of possible wrongdoing were made during the 1992 presidential campaign, and, after the election, the issue would not go away. An independent counsel was appointed to investigate whether the president had engaged in any financial improprieties. The first appointee, Robert Fiske, was criticized for the less than aggressive nature with which he pursued the charges. In 1994 Fiske was replaced by Kenneth Starr, a former federal judge and solicitor general in the Bush administration. The extended investigation led to several convictions, but the Clintons escaped unscathed.

A former municipal judge, David Hale, who had pleaded guilty to fraud, claimed that he had arranged a fraudulent $300,000 loan, backed by the Small Business Administration, for Susan McDougal. McDougal used part of the money to help shore up the struggling Whitewater partnership. Hale told investigators that Clinton had pressured him to approve the loan.

In pursuing Hale's charges, the Whitewater investigation entered into other areas. It discovered that Hillary Clinton's law partner, Webster

Hubbell, who had worked with her on Madison Guaranty legal matters at the Rose Law Firm, had embezzled from the firm. Hubbell pleaded guilty and agreed to cooperate with the investigation, but he provided little help.

In 1995 the independent counsel's office obtained the indictments of the McDougals and Gov. Jim Guy Tucker on charges of fraud. The following year all three were convicted. Jim McDougal, who was convicted on eighteen counts of fraud, offered to work with prosecutors in exchange for a lenient sentence. McDougal told investigators that Bill Clinton had lied when he testified on videotape that he had no knowledge of the fraudulent SBA-backed loan. McDougal also provided documents that showed that Clinton had received a loan from Madison. Even though McDougal implicated Clinton, some questioned his credibility. McDougal died of a heart attack in federal prison on March 8, 1998.

Susan McDougal decided to go to jail rather than cooperate with the Whitewater investigation. When subpoenaed before the grand jury, she refused to testify and was jailed on contempt charges, pending obstruction of justice charges. In April 1999 a jury cleared McDougal of some of the charges of obstruction for her refusal to testify before the grand jury, but was hung on other charges.

Governor Tucker, who resigned when he was indicted and who also faced a long jail term because of his convictions, decided to cooperate with the investigation. He was in poor health and wanted to avoid dying in jail. When Tucker appeared before the grand jury, he stated that he did not know much about the small business loan. He also denied that President Clinton had talked to him about a number of criminal referrals in October 1993.

Webster Hubbell, who never gave the prosecution the help it sought, was paid more than $700,000 as a consultant for jobs arranged by senior White House aides. Starr began to investigate whether this money went to Hubbell to buy his silence. Hubbell was indicted for tax evasion for failing to report most of the money. Initially, the indictment against Hubbell was dismissed when the judge ruled that Starr's office did not have the jurisdiction to pursue a tax evasion charge against him. However, on January 26, 1999, a federal appeals court reinstated the charges, stating that they had enough to do with Starr's Whitewater investigation that he had the authority to seek the indictments. Hubbell faced more than a dozen charges including lying to Congress, lying to federal banking regulators, and tax evasion.

Added to the long investigation was the thirteen-month committee investigation by a special Senate Whitewater Committee headed by Sen. Alfonse D'Amato, Republican of New York, which ended in 1996 having accomplished little. The committee's Republicans complained that the White House had stonewalled. Of particular interest were billing records from the Rose Law Firm on Madison Guaranty and another real estate development called Castle Grande for which Hillary Clinton had done legal work. Jim McDougal and Jim Guy Tucker said they could provide evidence of wrongdoing in this deal. Madison Guaranty lost $2 million on Castle Grande, and it was Hillary Clinton who, according to the FDIC, drafted a real estate option agreement used by Madison to deceive federal regulators in 1986. The subpoenaed billing records were missing for more than two years but suddenly turned up on a table in the residence section of the White House.

In February 1997, while the investigation was in progress, Starr announced he was resigning to become the dean of Pepperdine University School of Law, but he changed his mind a few days later because of a barrage of criticism. Starr's office was also investigating a number of unrelated events including Filegate, Travelgate, and the suicide of deputy White House attorney Vincent Foster. The Whitewater investigation ultimately led to Starr's looking into whether the president or his friend Vernon Jordan had encouraged Monica Lewinsky to lie about an affair she was having with the president in the Paula Jones sexual harassment lawsuit. Starr received that authority because he was already investigating Jordan in relation to a $60,000 retainer he had arranged for Webster Hubbell. This thread from the original Whitewater investigation would lead to impeachment proceedings against the president (see page 453).

FILEGATE

The White House requested and received hundreds of FBI files on Republicans, even though the files were protected by the Privacy Act and the White House had no legitimate purpose for requesting them. The controversy ignited charges that the files were being used for political purposes.

In 1993 and 1994 the Clinton White House requested more than 900 confidential FBI files. A background check on a job seeker is a legitimate use of an FBI file, but these files belonged mostly to Republicans who were not seeking appointments in the administration. Among the files were those of former White House spokesman Marlin Fitzwater and former secretary of state James A. Baker III. The revelation set off a storm of controversy that the Clinton administration was using FBI files to dig up political dirt. The administration tried to portray the events as just a mistake.

At the center of the controversy was Craig Livingstone, director of personnel security, whom many said was unqualified for the post he held. Described as a former bouncer, henchman, and political operative, Livingstone had no background in security, personnel, or any other field typically associated with his job. In fact, his employment record was less than stellar—he had been fired from a number of low-level jobs. Livingstone, who resigned in the wake of the controversy, testified during the House Government Reform and Oversight Committee's hearings that the files had been sent to his office because he had inadvertently used an outdated

Secret Service list. Livingstone denied intentional wrongdoing and apologized. He said, "At no point do I believe I betrayed anyone's confidence for any purpose whatsoever, and I have no reason to believe that anyone else in my office ever did so."

However, the committee was not concerned that Livingstone's office had been using the files, but that more politically active arms of the White House had done so. Former White House counsel Bernard Nussbaum, who had authorized the file transfers, was subpoenaed to testify. He claimed that the forms were preprinted with his name and that he did not know anything about the events. Nussbaum took exception to being labeled unethical by committee chair William F. Clinger Jr., Republican of Pennsylvania, but Clinger stuck to his charges that Nussbaum was not only aware but had authorized the file transfers.

As the investigation continued, the central question became who had hired Livingstone. Evidence pointed to Hillary Clinton—an FBI agent testified that Nussbaum had told him in 1993 that she had hired Livingstone. However, William H. Kennedy III, a former White House associate counsel, testified that he believed Vincent Foster, the deputy White House counsel, had hired Livingstone.

In its 205-page report issued in September 1996, the House committee charged that the matter needed further investigation because the White House had been less than fully cooperative. The report also questioned the wisdom of appointing Livingstone to such a sensitive post considering his checkered past.

TRAVELGATE

The administration called on the FBI to investigate the highest-ranking employees of the White House travel office on charges of corruption. The president had seven employees fired and passed the business on to his Hollywood friend and part owner of a travel business, Harry Thomason.

On May 19, 1993, the Clinton administration fired the entire team of longtime aides that coordinated White House travel arrangements. The administration then passed the lucrative travel business to a travel agency partly owned by Hollywood producer and Clinton supporter Harry Thomason.

According to documents uncovered during an FBI investigation and congressional hearings by the House Government Reform and Oversight Committee, Thomason and a partner outlined a plan to take over the travel office as early as February 1993. Other memos placed first lady Hillary Rodham Clinton at the center of the firings. In a memo dated May 14, 1993, White House aide David Watkins wrote that Hillary Clinton had told him to get rid of the travel staff. "Harry says his people can run things better, save money, etc. And besides, we need those people out—we need our people in. We need the slots." Chief of Staff Mack McLarty wrote on one memo "HRC pressure."

Defenders of the administration charged that there was widespread corruption in the office, especially by its director, Billy Dale. As the investigations into the charges continued, however, the administration appeared to backtrack from its original assertions. Five of the seven fired employees were given jobs in other agencies, and another was allowed to retire with full benefits. However, the White House pursued embezzlement charges against Billy Dale. He claimed he was innocent of any wrongdoing, and a jury believed him. He was acquitted of all charges in November 1995.

VINCENT FOSTER SUICIDE

Actions at the White House following Vincent Foster's suicide raised questions about the circumstances of his death.

On July 20, 1993, Vincent Foster, deputy White House counsel and Arkansas friend of the Clintons, committed suicide in a Virginia park located near Washington. The public might have quickly forgotten the death had it not been for the activities of the White House staff immediately after the body was discovered. The initial explanation from the White House did not match the facts. In the end, it was discovered that Hillary Clinton's press secretary, Maggie Williams, and White House counsel Bernard Nussbaum entered Foster's office and removed files that related to Whitewater and other tax issues. At the time, the Clintons were under investigation for the Arkansas land deal.

In addition, questions were raised as to whether Foster committed suicide where his body was found. The first police officers on the scene reported finding no gun. In addition, Foster had shot himself with a .38 caliber pistol in the mouth, but there was much less blood at the scene than would be expected. Conspiracy theorists have suggested that Foster was murdered because he knew too much about the Clintons' dealings in Arkansas and was starting to crack under the pressure of hiding the truth.

The Senate Special Whitewater Committee, chaired by Alfonse D'Amato, Republican of New York, conducted an investigation into Foster's death during its probe of Whitewater in July 1995. The committee issued a finding that Foster's death was not relevant to Whitewater. Independent counsels Robert Fiske and Kenneth Starr both found that Foster's death was a suicide and unrelated to the Whitewater investigation.

MIKE ESPY, SECRETARY OF AGRICULTURE

Mike Espy was indicted and eventually acquitted on charges of corruption stemming from gifts that he had received from companies over which his department had regulatory control.

Rep. Mike Espy of Mississippi, a young rising star in the Democratic Party, was tapped by Bill Clinton on January 5, 1993, to be secretary of agriculture. At the time of his appointment, Espy was the first African American and first person from the deep South to hold the post.

In September 1994 Donald Smaltz was appointed independent counsel to investigate reports that Espy had actively solicited and accepted gifts in excess of $35,000 from companies that his department regulated. The following month, Espy announced that he would resign his cabinet post at the end of the year to concentrate on clearing his name.

For two years, Smaltz conducted an intensive investigation of Espy and his close associates and family members. That investigation resulted in the conviction on September 25, 1996, of Sun-Diamond Growers, a major California food cooperative, for illegally giving Espy and his girlfriend gifts that included meals and an all-expense paid trip to New York for the U.S. Open tennis tournament.

On August 28, 1997, Espy was indicted on thirty-nine charges of corruption. The charges included mail and wire fraud and lying to the Agriculture Department's inspector general, the FBI, and the White House. He was also charged with tampering with a witness by ordering a subordinate to change an inspector's travel itinerary. The grand jury heard testimony that Espy accepted gifts and failed to report them on his federal disclosure form as required by law. The grand jury also heard evidence that Espy tried to cover up his activities by trying to repay donors.

In the time between Espy's indictment and the start of his trial on October 1, 1998, Smaltz obtained several guilty pleas and convictions. On December 10, 1997, Tyson Foods pleaded guilty to giving Espy $12,000 in gratuities and agreed to pay $6 million in fines and costs and to testify against Espy at his trial. On March 19, 1998, a top aide to Espy was sentenced to twenty-seven months in prison for lying about $22,000 he received from two Mississippians who later obtained large farming subsidies. On June 27 a Tyson executive was convicted of making illegal gifts to Espy, and the company's chief lobbyist was convicted of lying to the FBI and other investigators about the favors Tyson Foods received from the Agriculture Department.

Espy went to trial October 1, 1998, on thirty-eight of the original thirty-nine charges. The trial judge dismissed a number of the charges on November 25, saying that the prosecution had failed to show any criminal conduct on Espy's part for accepting Super Bowl tickets and a Waterford crystal bowl from two companies with business before his department. On December 3 Espy was acquitted of the remaining thirty charges of the indictment. Although the evidence was clear that Espy had accepted gifts, the jurors decided that the prosecution had failed to show that the donors had received anything in return.

After his acquittal, Espy had harsh words for the investigation that had cost more than $17 million and lasted for more than four years. Espy likened independent counsel Smaltz to a "schoolyard bully" against whom you have to take a stand and "let him know you're not going to back down." Smaltz offered no apologies for his investigation, which secured fifteen convictions and generated $11 million in fines.

HENRY CISNEROS, HUD SECRETARY

Henry Cisneros, the former secretary of the Department of Housing and Urban Development, was indicted on eighteen counts relating to his lying to the FBI about an extramarital affair he had while he was the mayor of San Antonio.

In December 1997 independent counsel David M. Barrett obtained an eighteen-count indictment against former Housing and Urban Development (HUD) secretary Henry Cisneros on charges that he had lied to the FBI. In the course of the background check on Cisneros, the FBI asked him about an adulterous relationship he had while serving as the mayor of San Antonio. Cisneros had paid his mistress $250,000 in hush money to keep her from revealing the secret relationship. Cisneros, who was forced to resign, was charged with conspiracy, obstruction of justice, and making false statements.

Two former Cisneros aides pleaded guilty to lesser charges stemming from their involvement to cover up the affair. The mistress was sentenced to three and a half years for lying about the purchase of a home with the money Cisneros allegedly paid her to keep quiet. On September 8, 1999, one day after his trial date was set, Cisneros pleaded guilty to a single misdemeanor count of lying to the FBI. He was fined $10,000 but given no jail time or probation.

RON BROWN, SECRETARY OF COMMERCE

The investigation of Secretary of Commerce Ron Brown for improper financial dealings came to an end when Brown was killed in a plane crash.

Ron Brown was a powerful man in Washington and Democratic Party circles long before he joined the Clinton administration as secretary of commerce. Brown was a partner at Patton, Boggs, and Blow, a prominent Washington law and lobbying firm, and chairman of the Democratic National Committee. He became controversial when allegations surfaced in May 1995 that seats on foreign trade missions were being sold to Democratic Party contributors.

A seat on a trade mission gave corporations access to millions—perhaps billions—of dollars in deals that they might not have been able to make on their own. Others used the trips to negotiate better tax situations in the foreign countries visited. In short, accompanying Brown on one of his numerous trade missions was a profitable enterprise.

In July 1995 independent counsel Daniel Pearson was appointed to investigate the charges against Brown. The investigation was expanded to include a $160,000 payment made by an Oklahoma gas company, Dynamic Energy Resources, to Brown's son, Michael, who only three months earlier had been placed on the company's board. The probe was under way when the secretary's plane crashed in Bosnia April 3, 1996, killing all aboard. Brown's death brought an end to the investigation.

1996 CAMPAIGN FUNDRAISING

The Justice Department and Congress began investigating alleged illegal campaign contributions and practices shortly after the November 1996 election. President Clinton, Vice President Gore, and several senior members of the Clinton staff were the focus of the investigation.

In the wake of charges of widespread illegal campaign fundraising by the Clinton-Gore reelection committee, two separate congressional investigations, one chaired by Rep. Dan Burton of Indiana, and the other by Sen. Fred Thompson of Tennessee, were begun. At the same time, the Justice Department was investigating the activities of White House officials, including the president and vice president.

The House investigation, which began in March 1997, focused entirely on the Democrats' fundraising activities, which brought cries of partisanship. The hearings were marked by frequent confrontations between Republican and Democratic committee members. The chairman of the Democratic National Committee (DNC) said that the investigations were an attempt to destroy the party financially and that the DNC would resist subpoenas. In an attempt to gather more information, the House Committee on Government Reform and Oversight sought to immunize several witnesses. However, that attempt failed. In addition, more than ninety potential witnesses had either left the country or invoked the Fifth Amendment, and the House investigation sputtered to an uneventful end.

Hearings in the Senate were less partisan than those in the House. The Senate looked into Republican Party fundraising practices as well as the Democratic Party's. However, the main focus of the Senate investigation was the charge that the Chinese government had conspired to influence the elections through campaign contributions. The hearings revealed that U.S. intelligence agencies had warned the administration that the Chinese might try to influence the elections. It also explored how Buddhist nuns, sworn to a life of poverty, had money to donate to the Clinton-Gore campaign when the vice president visited their temple in California. The committee concluded that Gore knew the April 1996 event was "designed to raise money for his party." On March 6, 1998, the Senate Governmental Affairs Committee issued its report that found widespread abuses in the 1996 campaign.

On April 15, 1997, Attorney General Janet Reno turned down a Republican request to appoint an independent counsel to investigate charges of illegal fundraising. Instead, Reno expanded the Justice Department task force that was conducting its own investigation. On September 21, Reno initiated a preliminary probe into whether illegal fundraising telephone calls were made from the White House. However, the department's investigation was hampered by internal disputes and organizational problems.

On January 28, 1998, the Justice Department indicted Yah Lin "Charlie" Trie, an Arkansas friend of Clinton, on charges that he funneled illegal foreign money into Democratic coffers. Trie was indicted on a straw donor scheme, in which he allegedly collected money from foreign businessmen, who are barred by law from donating to U.S. political campaigns, and passed it onto the DNC. Trie also donated more than $450,000 to the Clinton legal defense fund. All of that money was returned.

On February 19 a grand jury indicted Maria Hsia for laundering illegal contributions from a California Buddhist temple. The six-count indictment against Hsia and unnamed temple employees charged that they had solicited $55,000 for the DNC the day Vice President Gore was at the International Buddhist Progress Society in Hacienda Heights, California. Hsia also worked closely with John Huang who fronted for illegal contributions from Indonesian businessman James Riady. However, on September 11 a federal judge threw out most of the case the Justice Department had compiled against Hsia.

One of the central figures in the investigation was Democratic fundraiser Johnny Chung, whom the FBI had labeled a hustler trying to capitalize on his relationship with Clinton. Chung, who arranged a number of visits to the White House by donors, including a group of Chinese businessmen, agreed to cooperate with the Justice Department. Chung reported that a Chinese military officer, who was also an executive in a state-owned aerospace company, gave him $300,000 to be donated to the president's reelection. Chung also told the Justice Department that top DNC officials knew that the contributions he was generating were illegal but continued to solicit them. On one visit to the White House, Chung handed a check for $50,000 to Hillary Rodham Clinton's chief of staff, Maggie Williams, who later passed the check onto the DNC. Williams took the check, even though federal law prohibits the acceptance of campaign contributions on government property. In addition, the Justice Department task force began to probe whether the administration's decision to sell satellite and computer technology to the Chinese was in return for funds for the campaign.

On July 14, 1998, Pauline Kanchanalak and her sister-in-law, Duangnet Kronenberg, were indicted on charges of funneling foreign contributions to the DNC and other political committees. Kanchanalak, a friend of John Huang, arranged a White House coffee with Clinton at which time more than $135,000 was donated to the DNC. Also invited were three top officials of the Sino-Thai conglomerate Charoen Pokphand Group. In their indictments, the two women were charged with funneling more than $675,000 in illegal contributions to the DNC.

Despite the growing call for the appointment of an independent counsel, Reno held fast to her decision, even in the face of intense questioning by Republicans on the Senate Judiciary Committee on July 16. On August 7 a House committee voted to hold Reno in contempt of Congress for refusing to turn over several Justice Department memos from chief task force investigator Charles LaBella and FBI Director Louis Freeh. The memos urged Reno to appoint an independent counsel.

On August 27 Reno ordered a preliminary investigation into whether Gore had lied to investigators about phone calls he had made from his office in the White House. According to the many investigations, Gore played a central role in raising millions of dollars for the Democratic Party. When solicitation of the funds from his office was questioned, Gore declared that he had broken no laws and that there was "no controlling legal authority" that would indicate he had. Between November 1995 and May 1996, Gore spoke with at least forty-six people and each time sought contributions of between $25,000 and $100,000 of soft money, which is money donated to a party and not to a particular campaign. There are no limits on the amount of soft money a party can raise. It was later learned, however, that more than $120,000 that had been solicited as soft money was not used as soft money. Despite notations on memos that indicated Gore was aware that he was soliciting hard money illegally and other evidence of wrongdoing, Reno announced on November 25 that there were "no reasonable grounds" to pursue a case against Gore on charges that he lied to Justice Department officials during their investigation.

The Justice Department continued to investigate the fundraising practices of the 1996 Clinton-Gore reelection campaign. However, the department's piecemeal approach—investigating each charge independently rather than as a part of a wider attempt to violate campaign laws—made it difficult to unravel the various events and players. At the least, the Clinton-Gore fundraising activities often gave the appearance of impropriety. Although it is not illegal for the president to invite a generous donor to spend a night in the Lincoln bedroom, for many the practice proved that the wealthy can buy access to the corridors of power, even if those corridors are upstairs in the White House.

SPYING AT LOS ALAMOS LABORATORY

After learning that nuclear secrets were being stolen from Los Alamos National Laboratory, and by whom, the Clinton administration allowed the alleged spy to remain in his job with access to sensitive nuclear secrets for several years.

On March 8, 1999, Energy Secretary Bill Richardson fired a Los Alamos National Laboratory weapons designer, Wen Ho Lee, who had failed an FBI polygraph. Lee also refused to cooperate with an FBI investigation into whether he had stolen nuclear secrets and passed them to the Chinese government. The administration was criticized for its slow response in dealing with the allegations of spying.

According to reports, the Clinton administration had been aware of the nuclear thefts for several years and had been investigating Lee as the chief suspect since late 1997. The FBI was also investigating a Taiwan-born scientist, Peter Lee, for espionage. In December 1997 Peter Lee confessed to turning over laser technology to the Chinese during a trip to China in 1985. He was sentenced to twelve months in a halfway house.

Many members of Congress and the media criticized the Clinton administration's laxness in addressing such security breaches. In fact, some on Capitol Hill called for Richardson's resignation. The allegations of espionage by the Chinese was especially controversial because of suspicions that the Chinese government had illegally funneled money into the Clinton 1996 reelection campaign.

IMPEACHMENT

President Clinton was the second president in the history of the United States to be impeached, but the Senate trial acquitted him of charges arising out of the Paula Jones sexual harassment suit.

Independent counsel Kenneth Starr's investigation of President Clinton, which began with the Whitewater matter, came to a head when he delivered his report to the House of Representatives September 9, 1998. In an effort to prove that Clinton had lied in his deposition in the Jones case and had induced Monica Lewinsky to submit a false affidavit in which she denied the affair, Starr included every lurid detail. Starr said he had found "substantial and credible information . . . that may constitute grounds for impeachment."

The independent counsel had learned of the president's affair with Lewinsky when Linda Tripp, a former White House staffer, turned over tape recordings she had secretly made of her phone conversations with Lewinsky. The tapes revealed many intimate details, including the existence of a semen-stained dress.

No advance copy of the Starr report was given to the White House. Two days after the report was delivered to the House, the members voted, 363–63, to make it public, even though most of them had not read it. Within hours the entire report was available on the Internet, and much of it appeared in newspapers the next day. With the midterm elections approaching, some saw the release of the report as a partisan attempt to sway public opinion. However, polls showed the president's approval ratings remained high. Also released was the four-hour videotape of Clinton's August 17 grand jury testimony.

The House voted 259–176 on October 8 to begin an impeachment inquiry. House Judiciary Committee chairman Henry Hyde of Illinois announced six days later that the inquiry would focus on perjury, witness tampering, and obstruction of justice.

If the Republicans expected the impeachment issue to influence the midterm elections, they were correct, but not the way they hoped. Instead of gaining seats in the House—and the opposition party traditionally gains seats in the midterm elections—the Republicans lost five seats; and the Senate remained almost unchanged. Faced with the unhappy results, Speaker of the House Newt Gingrich of Georgia, who had predicted a thirty-seat gain for the Republicans, resigned not only the speakership but also his seat.

On November 13 Clinton reached a settlement with Paula Jones. Six days later Starr appeared before the House committee in a twelve-hour session to answer questions about his referral. In written answers to committee questions, Clinton maintained that his testimony before the grand jury was "not false and misleading." Largely along party lines, the Judiciary Committee approved four articles of impeachment to be sent to the floor of the House: two alleged that Clinton lied in the Jones sexual harassment case and in his testimony before Starr's grand jury, and others alleged that he abused the powers of his office and obstructed justice in the Lewinsky affair. Formal hearings began November 19 and proved contentious, with Democrats asserting that the president's actions were private and did not rise to the level of an impeachable offense. While mud was being

Kenneth Starr

thrown, a story surfaced about a past affair that Hyde had with a married woman. It broke up her marriage. Hyde did not deny the story, but said it was a youthful indiscretion—he was about forty at the time.

On December 19, William Jefferson Clinton became only the second president—Andrew Johnson was the first—to be impeached. The House of Representatives, largely along party lines, approved two articles of impeachment that charged Clinton with perjury before a federal grand jury and obstruction of justice in his attempts to conceal his affair with Lewinsky. The House vote came just hours after Louisiana Republican Robert Livingston, who was expected to be elected the next Speaker of the House, announced that he would resign his seat because his own adulterous affairs had been revealed.

The Senate trial began January 7, 1999, with Chief Justice William Rehnquist presiding. More somber and more dignified than the House hearings, the trial lasted a little more than a month. No witnesses were called. After the lawyers for both sides had presented their case, the senators deliberated behind closed doors for three days. On February 12 they said they were ready to vote. As Chief Justice Rehnquist called each name, the senator rose and announced his or her vote. The Senate acquitted Clinton on the perjury charge by a vote of 55 to 45. The vote on the obstruction of justice charge was 50–50. Neither article came close to achieving the two-thirds vote necessary to convict.

Rep. Christopher Cannon, Republican of Utah, may have been speaking for the nation when he said February 8, 1999: "I hope that history will judge that we have done our duty well. We have been congratulated and condemned, but we are done."

BRUCE BABBITT, SECRETARY OF THE INTERIOR

An independent counsel was appointed in March 1998 to investigate whether Interior Secretary Bruce Babbitt had lied to Congress about his department's 1995 rejection of the license of an Indian casino in Hudson, Wisconsin, and whether the decision had been improperly influenced by the White House and the Democratic National Committee (DNC).

Economic growth is the most important issue for many Indian tribes, and to create jobs and wealth, some tribes have opened gambling casinos. Such operations are exempt from state regulation, but still must be approved by the Department of the Interior. The owner of a money-losing dog track in Hudson, Wisconsin, and three poor Chippewa bands of Indians decided to apply to the Interior Department for permission to install an off-reservation casino at the track. The regional office of the Bureau of Indian Affairs approved the proposal. Those opposing the casino contacted, among others, presidential adviser Bruce Lindsey, deputy chief of staff Harold Ickes, and Democratic National Committee chairman Donald Fowler. Among the casino's opponents were wealthy Minnesota tribes that had their own casinos and wished to prevent competition.

Each side hired lobbyists. The Chippewas secured the services of Secretary Bruce Babbitt's friend Paul Eckstein. Babbitt and Eckstein met July 14, 1995, the day the application was rejected, and Babbitt indicated that the casino was not going to be approved. Babbitt told Eckstein that the decision came from Ickes. The opposition had out-lobbied the Chippewas by engaging Patrick O'Connor, a Democratic Party operative, who had direct contact with President Clinton and Ickes.

After the Chippewa casino deal was rejected, the Minnesota tribes donated $270,000 to the 1996 Democratic presidential campaign, bringing their total contributions to more than $350,000. As part of the Senate investigation into campaign finances chaired by Fred Thompson, Republican of Tennessee, Babbitt testified on October 30, 1997, that he had mentioned Ickes to Eckstein, but that the decision was not influenced by political pressures from Ickes. Senators were unconvinced that Babbitt had lied to an old friend just to end an awkward meeting. Instead, they suspected that improper White House and Democratic National Committee influence had resulted in the rejection of the Chippewa application.

On February 12, 1998, Attorney General Janet Reno announced that the Justice Department was seeking the appointment of an independent counsel to investigate whether Babbitt had lied to Congress. Carol Elder Bruce was appointed by a special three-judge panel. In the charge given to Bruce, Reno authorized the investigation of Babbitt on possible charges of perjury or violation of the false statement law. Reno also authorized Bruce to investigate the role of the White House and the DNC in making the decision on the casino.

ALEXIS M. HERMAN, SECRETARY OF LABOR

An independent counsel was appointed to investigate whether Alexis Herman used her position to secure lucrative contracts for a company that she had formerly owned.

On May 11, 1998, Attorney General Janet Reno announced that she had requested an independent counsel to investigate allegations of influence peddling against Secretary of Labor Alexis Herman. Reno sought the appointment after her own department's 150-day investigation could neither conclusively clear nor find fault with Herman's actions.

According to the allegations, Herman—while head of the White House Office of Public Liaison—accepted a payoff from African businessman Laurent Yene and Vanessa Weaver. According to Yene, he gave Herman an envelope full of cash, which represented her share of consulting fees that Yene and Weaver's company, International Investments and Business Development (IIBD), had received from a client for whom they had helped secure a federal license for a satellite telephone system. Herman was one of the original owners of IIBD before she joined the administration in 1993.

Justice Department officials were split as to whether an independent counsel should have been appointed in Herman's case. Some pointed to Yene's credibility problem as a major reason not to pursue the matter. A special three-judge panel appointed Ralph I. Lancaster Jr. of Portland, Maine, who had no previous prosecutorial experience. This appointment was the seventh time Reno sought an independent counsel to investigate a high-ranking member of the Clinton administration.

BIBLIOGRAPHY

Allen, Charles F. and Jonathan Portis. *The Comeback Kid: The Life and Career of Bill Clinton.* New York: Carol Publishing Group, 1992.

Bennett, William J. *The Death of Outrage: Bill Clinton and the Assault on American Ideals.* New York: Free Press, 1998.

Brown, Floyd G. *Slick Willie: Why America Cannot Trust Bill Clinton.* Annapolis-Washington Book Publishers, 1992.

Bugliosi, Vincent. *No Island of Sanity.* New York: Ballantine, 1998.

Carpozi, George, Jr. *Clinton Confidential.* Del Mar, Calif.: Emery Dalton Books, 1995.

Flowers, Gennifer. *Gennifer Flowers: Passion and Betrayal.* Del Mar, Calif.: Emery Dalton Books, 1995.

Hagood, Wesley O. *Presidential Sex: From the Founding Fathers to Bill Clinton.* Secaucus, N.J.: Carol Publishing, 1998.

Levin, Jerome D. *The Clinton Syndrome: The President and the Self-Destructive Nature of Sexual Addiction.* Rocklin, Calif.: Forum, 1998.

Morton, Andrew. *Monica's Story.* New York: St. Martin's, 1999.

Maraniss, David. *First in His Class.* New York: Simon and Schuster, 1995.

McDougal, James, and Curtis Wilkie. *Arkansas Mischief.* New York: Henry Holt, 1998.

McSorley, Richard. *Peace Eyes.* Washington, D.C.: Georgetown University, 1978.

Stephanopoulos, George. *All Too Human.* Boston: Little, Brown, 1999.

Walden, Gregory. *On Best Behavior.* Indianapolis: Hudson Institute, 1996.

INDEX

ILLUSTRATION CREDITS

ANDREW JOHNSON • 122, 126/ Library of Congress; 132/ Collection of the Supreme Court of the United States.

ULYSSES S. GRANT • 135, 137/ Library of Congress; 138/ Naval Historical Center; 140/ State Historical Society of Iowa.

RUTHERFORD B. HAYES • 155, 158, 160/ Library of Congress; 163/ Naval Historical Center.

JAMES GARFIELD • 167/ Library of Congress.

CHESTER A. ARTHUR • 174/ Library of Congress; 177/ Naval Historical Center.

GROVER CLEVELAND • 179, 181/ Library of Congress; 183/ National Portrait Gallery, Smithsonian Institution.

BENJAMIN HARRISON • 188/ Library of Congress; 198/ The Historical Society of Pennsylvania.

WILLIAM MCKINLEY • 200, 204/ Library of Congress.

THEODORE ROOSEVELT • 206, 212/ Library of Congress; 209/ National Portrait Gallery, Smithsonian Institution.

WILLIAM HOWARD TAFT • 223/ Library of Congress; 228/ National Portrait Gallery, Smithsonian Institution.

WOODROW WILSON • 231/Library of Congress; 236, 241/ National Portrait Gallery, Smithsonian Institution.

WARREN G. HARDING • 250, 258, 261/ Library of Congress; 253/ AP/Wide World.

CALVIN COOLIDGE • 270/ Library of Congress; 278/ From the Collection of Henry Ford Museum and Greenfield Village; 280/ National Portrait Gallery, Smithsonian Institution.

HERBERT HOOVER • 283, 291/ Library of Congress.

FRANKLIN D. ROOSEVELT • 298, 312/ Library of Congress; 300/ AP/Wide World; 305/ file photo.

HARRY S. TRUMAN • 319/ Library of Congress; 323 / Harry S. Truman Library.

DWIGHT D. EISENHOWER • 332, 335, 337/ Library of Congress.

JOHN F. KENNEDY • 343/ Library of Congress; 348/ Archive Photos; 351/ AP.

LYNDON B. JOHNSON • 358, 365/ LBJ Library Collection; 362/ Corbis-Bettmann.

RICHARD M. NIXON • 369/ White House; 373/ Library of Congress; 376/ National Archives; 382/ Library of Congress, Courtesy of the Swann Collection of Caricature and Cartoon.

GERALD R. FORD • 385/ Library of Congress; 388/ Nixon Project, National Archives.

JAMES E. CARTER • 391/ Jimmy Carter Library; 394/ AP; 397/ file photo.

RONALD REAGAN • 401/ White House; 414/ AP; 419/ AP/Wide World Photos.

GEORGE H. BUSH • 422/ Courtesy of Bush Presidential Materials Project; 424/ Paul Conklin; 426/ White House.

WILLIAM J. CLINTON • 430/ White House; 438, 454/ Reuters; 439, 440/ AP.